中国特色经济地理学探索

李小建　著

科学出版社
北　京

内 容 简 介

本书基于作者近30年的研究，对国际背景下中国特色的经济地理学进行了多视角的探索。全书分为经济地理学理论探索、农户地理研究、公司地理研究、经济地理学的小尺度研究、区域研究，共5篇48章。近一半的内容曾在《地理学报》和国际著名英文期刊上发表，被广泛引用。

本书集合了作者在理论和实践上对中国特色经济地理学的重要研究成果，可作为政府决策人员，以及地理学、经济学、管理学、规划学等学科的教学、科研人员和研究生、高年级本科生的重要参考书。

图书在版编目（CIP）数据

中国特色经济地理学探索/李小建著. --北京：科学出版社，2016.1

ISBN 978-7-03-046138-4

Ⅰ.①中… Ⅱ.①李… Ⅲ.①经济地理学-研究-中国 Ⅳ.①F129.9

中国版本图书馆CIP数据核字（2016）第255828号

责任编辑：张　欣/责任校对：李　影　何艳萍

责任印制：徐晓晨/封面设计：北京图阅盛世文化传媒有限公司

科学出版社出版

北京东黄城根北街16号

邮政编码：100717

http://www.sciencep.com

北京建宏印刷有限公司印刷

科学出版社发行　各地新华书店经销

*

2016年1月第　一　版　开本：787×1092　1/16

2020年9月第五次印刷　印张：36 1/4

字数：860 000

定价：258.00元

（如有印装质量问题，我社负责调换）

New Approaches to Economic Geography: A Chinese Perspective

Li Xiaojian

Science Press
Beijing

序

从1982年初在河南大学工作算起，我从事地理学教学与研究已有34个年头。如果算上读大学地理专业的4年，算上在海军部队从事测绘工作的4年零5个月，与地理学的结交有40多年了。这期间，从学习地理学、认识地理学，逐渐到从一个方面（经济地理学）进入地理学并做了一些探索研究，发表了一些文章、出版了几本著作。在有些研究问题上，积累了些许研究体会。为交流学术思想，求教于同行，我基于几十年在经济地理学研究探索上的一些文章，重新梳理编纂成书，供大家参考讨论。

（一）

经济地理学从1893年大学开设课程算起，不过一百多年的历史。20世纪中期以来，随着社会经济的发展，这个学科在世界范围内取得了较快发展。60年代的数量革命促使经济地理学研究由描述走向解释。沿着这一脉络发展，区域科学应运而生。与此同时，一些地理学家沿着对经济地理现象解释的方向，追根溯源，从各个不同角度探索其影响动力及影响因素。诸如，20世纪70年代产生的政治经济学派强调政治和社会力量对空间经济形成的影响，认为经济景观不是区位理论中的理性选择结果，而是不同社会力量介入并长期较量的结果。相应地，在经济地理学研究上出现了制度转向、文化转向、关系转向、尺度转向等。同时，在研究方法上，也从数量模型和统计检验转向包括定性案例分析的多元研究方法。90年代的后结构主义、后现代主义、女性主义学派强调地理研究中对人、文化制度和女性的关注，等等。继演化经济学的出现，也有些学者从演化视角看待经济地理现象的发展变化。从而形成经济地理学研究中多元化共存的局面。

回到国内，经济地理学是长期以来最受社会持续关注的人文地理学科。20世纪前半期，经济地理学以引介西方理论和结合中国实际的经济地域考察分析为主，中期一段时间，在学习原苏联经济地理学的基础上，围绕中国经济建设的需要进行考察和规划工作。改革开放以后，西方相关理论和方法引入和拓展，特别是中国的迅速发展为经济地理学兴盛带来了难得的机遇。新的研究主题不断出现，研究区域类型、研究内容、研究视角、研究尺度、研究方法迅速多元化。但与西方相比，中国经济地理学研究多元化有一些不同。除了研究主题、研究方法多元化之外，中国学者还注重自然地理要素对经济现象的影响，同时，中国政治体制也对经济地理学研究提出不同的决策需求。

经济地理学研究的多元化给人以云雾缭绕的感觉，不少人在这些林林总总的术语面前，难以厘清前进的方向。我自己就曾这样徘徊，在困惑中不断思考，试着理一理思路。在30多年的研究思考基础上，大致梳理出这样的逻辑思维脉络。

第一个问题，经济地理学中的“经济”和“地理”是什么关系？经济地理学一开始出现，就融入地理学家和经济学家从两个学科角度的持续探索。虽然两个群体不断学习、取长补短，但不同的学科背景有各自不同的出发点和观察问题的视角，其研究成果及其积累形成的学科框架明显带有各自的特点。尤其是，20 世纪上半叶的区位论、中期的区域科学、后期的新经济地理学的研究范式在经济地理学领域产生了重要的理论影响。特别是经济学家 P·克鲁格曼获得诺贝尔经济学奖，在更大程度上促使社会，甚至学术界，从偏重经济学角度认识经济地理学。

但探求源头，"经济地理学"这个术语，首先是由地理学家提出的；经济地理学课程也是首先在大学的地理学院系开设的；最早的 *Economic Geography* 学术期刊也是地理学家主办的。从科学术语的角度，经济地理学首先是地理学的一个分支，它应该带有地理学的一般属性。其次，依上述逻辑，经济地理学应该是从地理角度研究经济现象，注重地理圈层（包括人居圈、大气圈、水圈、地貌、土壤圈等）对经济活动产生的作用和影响。最后，经济学家的经济地理学所注重的空间分布、空间差异等，只是经济现象的地理性的一部分，人类经济活动与地理环境的关系和人类其他活动的经济后果等也是很重要的经济地理学研究内容。

从这个角度看，西方经济地理学新近出现的研究主题与研究方法的多元化，以"多元转向"（见本书第 1 章）为标志的地理学科的"新经济地理学"，以数学与计量模型为代表的经济学科范畴的"新经济地理学"是经济地理学研究的主要内容，并对该学科发展具有重要的促进作用，但这绝不是完整的经济地理学，尤其不是地理学科的经济地理学。

第二个问题，经济现象怎么认识？经济现象包罗万象。从经济活动主体的角度，有全球公司、跨国公司，有中小企业、农户；从经济景观角度，有基于大城市、特大城市形成的体量巨大的经济集聚体，也有村落、工厂等较小的经济空间；从与行政关联角度，有与国际经济组织相关联的跨国经济合作体，也有一个国家内部不同层级政府相关的区域经济体系；从外在显示角度，有的经济现象可以明晰从外部看出，有些从外部无法判断（如互联网经济）……在这些众多的经济现象中，如何把握经济地理学的研究重点，研究者多仁者见仁、智者见智。

本人觉得，这些经济现象都很重要，都值得研究。但在力量有限情况下，应有轻重缓急之分。如果从由浅入深角度，第一，不妨先研究国家以内的区域经济现象，再逐渐扩大视野，研究国家或全球经济地理主题。除了国际经济问题比较复杂之外，其很多研究中的问题离不开区域尺度的分析，如全球经济中心转移，是个全球性的经济地理研究主题，但经济中心本身又离不开区域，甚至城市的基础研究。此外，其他一些学科，如经济学同样关注各个国家的经济发展，国际经济学、国际贸易学同样关注全球经济变化。如果不具有很好的区域经济研究功底，很难突出经济地理学在这方面的研究特色。第二，不妨先关注具良好可视化的经济地理景观研究，再逐步转向外部难以判断的经济地理现象研究。尤其运用现代遥感技术、大数据挖掘和分析技术，可能很有利于取得令人信服的成果，占领为社会经济服务的重要阵地。第三，不妨先关注微观经济活动主题的研究，再逐渐向其他影响经济活动的相关机构延伸。这些经济主体是地球表面经济现象差异形成的最直接决定者，其他机构和相关制度只是间接作用于这些主体。

第三个问题，什么是经济地理学中的“地理”？换句话说，什么是经济活动的地理角度？广义上说，经济活动都离不开一定的环境，经济增长和经济发展不是在各个地方同时出现和以同样的速度进行，经济现象都或多或少带有一定的空间性。空间分布、空间差异、空间联系等空间性属于“地理”，但并不等于“地理”。“地理”在空间性之外有更多的内涵。例如，经济现象的空间性与其他地理圈层（大气圈、水圈、地貌、土壤圈、人居圈等）的关系，一般的经济空间分析很少涉及，但它却是重要的经济地理学中“地理”所包含的内容。

以上个人对经济地理学的认识，虽然不断有所变化，但对自己的经济地理学研究具有重要影响。

（二）

本人1986年考入南开大学经济研究所从事博士研究生阶段的学习和研究。当时，中国改革开放虽有7个年头，但整个经济仍然带有非常浓厚的计划色彩。虽然外资企业已经进入，但整体上企业在经济活动中的自主作用非常有限。中国经济地理学研究，多从政府需求的视角出发。南开大学成立有大洋洲研究室，我当时的论文设想主要围绕澳大利亚经济地理。在查看英文文献的过程中，接触了 *Progress in Human Geography* 期刊，对于其中公司地理的文章，感到非常新颖，做了一些读书笔记。

1988年年初，经当时的国家教育委员会推荐和澳大利亚大使馆考试，我获得了中澳交换留学生计划的资助，以博士生联合培养名义到澳大利亚国立大学地理系学习研究。澳大利亚国立大学有一个太平洋研究学院，集聚了一批有国际影响力的学者。其中，做过较多公司地理研究的麦克·泰勒（M Taylor）教授就是队伍成员之一。虽然，他刚去澳大利亚联邦交通部任职，但仍与大学保持密切的学术联系。在这种氛围下，我原来对公司地理的兴趣有了继续发展的条件。在博士论文的选题中，逐渐考虑形成一个思路：集中于常规区域分析与公司地理分析的结合部位，对澳大利亚东南部的工业区域变化与公司活动进行研究，审视澳大利亚联邦政府为解决工业过度集中而选择远离都市区的增长中心分散发展举措，揭示其为什么最终不成功的原因。论文完成后在澳大利亚国立大学举行的报告会上，得到了与会专家的充分肯定。

1990年4月回国后，我继续沿着这一方向，在国家自然科学基金、国家教委优秀年轻教师基金和留学人员基金、教育部人文社会科学和自然科学基金的资助下，先后从事了具有中国特色的农村工业企业、具有中外交合特征的外资企业和具有计划经济特点的国有企业的研究。研究内容除了企业与区域关系之外，还涉及企业空间扩张、环境与企业发展的相互关系、不同类型企业的空间结构等问题。在实际研究的基础上，1999年初步理出公司地理的研究框架，出版了系统阐述公司地理的专著《公司地理论》，并于2002年修订再版。所主编的《经济地理学》教材（1999年第1版，2006年第2版）也是围绕企业作为经济地理现象的主题来组织其框架结构的。

公司地理，尤其是大型公司研究中，接触公司案例对研究非常重要。我对外资大型企业的研究，主要调查位于上海的公司。这对于工作地在河南的研究者，有诸多不便。

沿着聚焦经济活动主体的思路，我开始考虑具有河南特色的农区经济地理研究。由于中原地区以传统农业为主，农业联产承包责任制又加强了农户在生产中的核心作用。21世纪开始，我从不同角度研究农户作为主要生产单元下的农区经济问题。包括，农户对发展的期望和途径与环境的关系、农户生产的投入产出与人地关系、农户居住行为、农户生产区位、农户外出务工区位、农户自主发展能力、农户群体的经济地理行为等。尤其是2005年在国家自然科学基金重点项目资助下，进行了较大规模的农区、农户调研，为后续的多角度研究奠定了很好的基础。由于该研究方向具有突出的地域优势，我的同事、博士生们相继开展了围绕农户的研究，形成了有初步影响的研究群体。

在关注经济活动主体的同时，我也开始考虑在地理单元上，经济地理学如何从微观角度入手。传统的农村聚落是长期人地相互作用的产物，同一聚落的居民经济活动具有一定的同质性。可否从聚落入手探索农村地区经济地理学的基本微观单元？沿这个思路，21世纪开始，引导博士研究生选题围绕村域进行。例如，通过详细的地块调查，研究村域内人地系统投入产出特征与地理环境的关系，研究村落地理环境与专业村形成的关系，研究村庄之间外出务工的差异等。博士生乔家君（河南省特聘教授）还沿着这个方向，出版了《典型农区村域人地系统定量研究》（科学出版社，2005）和《中国乡村地域经济论》（科学出版社，2008）。博士生李二玲（河南省特聘教授）进行了村域农户经济社会网络的研究，出版了《中部农区产业集群与中小企业网络》（科学出版社，2011）。博士生高更和（河南财经政法大学特聘教授）进行了村域农户经济活动区位的研究，出版了《中国中部农区农户经济活动区位研究——以河南省南阳市6个村为例》（经济科学出版社，2013）。在进行村落地理研究中，也借助遥感与地理信息系统方法，进行更小尺度的人地关系探索。在区域可持续发展评估中，根据研究区各点位（如用TM影像数据的30m×30m）的生境条件和一段时间内人类利用情况，建立相关判断基准，来评估各点位变化是否更趋于可持续发展。

经济地理学微观单元的研究，背后关联着经济地理学中科学研究哲学的变化。经济地理学在相当长的一段时间内，强调综合论，着重应用归纳法。这些哲学思想和方法论对促进经济地理学研究起着重要作用。微观单元的研究，可用“还原论”哲学思维来解释。一些人认为，科学发展历史的核心特征是还原论和可重复性。还原论强调对研究对象简化，对研究对象挑选；可以用低层次的规律解释高层次现象；可以把复杂现象打碎，逐个元素进行分析。例如，物质世界那么复杂多样，但都离不开到目前为止发现的118种化学元素，这些元素是物质世界最简单、最基本的组成部分。这些元素的状况、它们的组合状况，影响各种物质的性质。沿着这一思路，找出基本单元、基本单元的特征、基本单元的组合特征、基本单元组合体的特征，不失为经济地理学研究的另一探索方向。只是经济地理现象有很多人文因素的参与，研究对象比自然现象更复杂多变，机理具有不可重复性，找出其中的基本单元更难。但艰难中的探索，更具有挑战意义。所取得的进步和发展，对学科更具有引领影响。

由于有一段在澳大利亚学习和在美国做客座教授的经历，又有几次在香港进行合作学术研究，我在一段时间内，研究选题以追随西方经济地理学相关理论或研究趋势、进行中国相关研究为重点。公司地理、跨国公司与中国区域发展等选题主要是这种影响的结果。相关研究在国际期刊连续发表，在一段时间内成为在国际期刊发表文章较多的国内经济地理学者。在研究中，我也不断反思着所进行的工作，尤其是对欧美主流经济地理学受社会思潮影响所产生的各种“转向”，以及经济学家从事的经济空间现象研究形成的“新经济地理学”，逐渐形成一些看法。感到西方发达国家的研究角度与思路，以及它们对经济地理学中的逻辑定位，与中国均存在一些错位。中国与欧美发达国家所处的不同发展阶段遇到的不同经济问题，中国与欧美国家的不同自然环境、自然资源禀赋，不同的政治社会经济制度和文化价值，对经济地理现象产生不同的影响，使我们从独特国情角度考虑发展中国特色的经济地理学。尤其从逻辑角度，经济地理学不能脱离地理学，必须加强其与地理学其他分支学科的联系。但西方经济地理学近期发展，不能清楚看到这一发展趋势。为此，我在经济地理学结合中国实际的研究中，结合自己的体会写了一些文章，和同行一起讨论。

（三）

本书作为过去一段时间研究的总结，多数成果的主要观点包含在过去发表的文章中。全书共分 5 篇 48 章。每篇集中一个研究侧面，分别论述经济地理学的理论探索、农户地理研究、公司地理研究、经济地理学的小尺度研究和区域研究。

第一篇对经济地理学的理论探索包括 8 章。前 4 章集中对西方经济地理学的发展评述，其中，有 2 章对经济学家的经济地理学（区域经济学）思想专门做一讨论。第 1 章分析了西方经济地理学在 20 世纪 80 年代以来所发生的“多维转向”和经济学家“新经济地理学”的发展背景及其特点，提出这些新近发展对中国经济地理学的启示。第 2 章评述了诺贝尔经济学获奖者在区域差异、区域经济发展、区域竞争与合作等方面的区域经济思想，大致归纳出这些经济学家由忽略空间到关注空间、由宏观研究分析到宏微观兼顾、由一般定量分析到精细模型分析的演变。在一般分析的基础上，第 3 章专门对唯一由经济区位研究获得诺贝尔经济学奖的克鲁格曼的经济地理学思想进行深入分析。在介绍了克鲁格曼学术生涯和主要贡献之后，专门阐述了其创新研究对经济地理学发展的重大意义。主张科学吸收其理论思维和方法论的精华，在中国经济地理学中重视规范分析和计量方法。第 4 章把国际经济地理学发展作为背景来看待如何建立中国特色的经济地理学。本章反思过去较为普遍的“引入国外理论—结合中国实际验证—相关理论总结”的研究模式，提出“中国实际研究—相关理论归纳—国际比较—理论创新”的新模式。

第 5 章至第 8 章为中国经济地理学一些理论方面的思考。第 5 章探索了经济地理学与区域经济学的区分，从学科渊源组成、研究内容层次和研究思维三个侧面分析了两个学科的差异，强调两学科的研究侧重、研究视野具有明显区别。第 6 章沿公司地理、农户地理和小尺度研究三个层面分析了经济地理学的微观研究，提出微观研究有利于探索经济地理现象形成的基本单元，揭示经济地理现象的形成机理。第 7 章在第 4 章分析的基础上，提出基于中国特殊的地理环境、特殊的人口与资源环境关系、特殊的政府与社会关系、特殊的文化、特殊的学科联系建立中国特色的经济地理学。中国特色的经济地理学应侧重经济社会发展、侧重人地和谐、侧重政府的特殊作用、侧重区域间关系与全球化的影响、侧重与自然地理学的关系等。第 8 章基于《地理学报》创刊 80 年来刊登的经济地理文章，梳理了中国经济地理学的发展特点。中国经济地理学在形成紧密服务国家需求、侧重宏观研究、侧重经济发展、侧重应用研究等特点的同时，在微观研究、综合研究、理论凝练等方面有待加强。

第二篇集中于农户地理研究，分 6 章。第 9 章首先讨论了科学哲学中的还原论与农户地理研究的出发点，接着用数理证明了农户与农区发展的关系，分析了农户地理研究的基本框架与主要内容，强调农户区位、农户空间结构、农户自主发展能力、农户活动与环境的关系在理论和实践上都具有重要研究意义。第 10 章用作者团队对河南西部山地丘陵区 10 县（市）332 家农户调查数据，分析了欠发达农区制约经济发展的农户行为，为农户参与下的农区发展提供参考。同时，通过对这些数据的量化分析，揭示了农户收入与环境的关系。第 11 章利用河南省 16 个村 1000 家农户数据，分析了 20 世纪 80 年代以来农户兼业化的三个发展阶段，并对兼业的影响因素进行了量化研究。第 12 章利用作者团队调查的河南 11 个村 1251 家农户数据，对农户收入的环境影响进行了量化研究。发现不同收入阶段的农户，影响农户收入的地理环境因素在发生变化，自然环境因素的影响逐步下降、社会经济环境因素逐步上升。第 13 章引入农户自主发展能力概念，研究不同农户对环境的利用能力差异。用和第 12 章同样来源的农户数据，发现农户自主发展能力对农户收入具有显著影响，不同发展阶段这种影响有显著差异；随着经济发展水平的提高和环境变化，农户自主发展能力的作用会进一步显现出来。第 14 章利用作者团队对 3 个样本村的 288 家农户调查数据，分析了农户外出务工区位的选择，发现务工者本人特征（年龄、性别等）、家庭特征（人口、代数等）和社区特征（发展水平、区位等）对务工区位选择具有重要影响，但务工距离、务工所在地带、务工空间类型的影响因素又有差别。

第三篇公司地理研究分 16 章。其中，总体研究 2 章，跨国公司研究 9 章，国有企业 1 章，农村工业企业 2 章，金融地理及银行业企业 2 章。第 15 章论述了公司地理的主要特征和主要内容，并结合中国国情讨论了开展适应中国国情的公司地理研究的主要意义。第 16 章在工业区域研究中，引入企业分析法，通过区域数据的定量分析，理清工业区域变化的基本状况；再用企业调查数据分析这种变化的深层原因。使用这种方法对澳大利亚东南部的工业变化分析结果，在后来的发展实践中得以证实。第 17 章在对国际相关文献评述的基础上，对跨国公司的区域经济影响做一理论探讨。指出，跨国公司的生产链、组织链和所有权关系三个关联系统和接受投资地区域等级系统，是决定跨国公司与区域关系的主要基点。由此决定的两者关系影响着区域从跨国公司投资中的获益情况。第 18 章针对国际学术界就跨国公司对区域差异影响的不同研究结论，以中国实证数据，得出与他人不同的结果。认为跨国公司对中国区域经济差异的影响处于变化之中，从缩小到扩大差异，随着经济发展和跨国公司投资区域变化，还会发生其他变化。第 19 章以上海为例，分析了本地合资方的强势地位，通过在产业链和相关行业的广阔关系网络，加强着跨国公司的本地嵌入，这种根植性对促进当地经济发展具有重要作用。第 20 章从新的角度切入，研究跨国公司与投资地所在区域（而不是合资企业）

之间的讨价还价（bargaining）关系。通过建立讨价还价的度量指标，用实地调查的数据，证明在发展中国家有一些特殊区域在与跨国公司的博弈中，具有比其他区域较强的优势，从而为该区域争取较大利益。该研究结果的论文发表后，曾得到国际上一些学者的积极反应。

第21章以中国案例，具体分析了跨国公司进入中国的区域变化，指出这种变化符合一般规律，也有与其不相符合的表现。中国特殊的人际关系、政治制度以及中国合资方的路径依赖，影响着跨国公司的投资区位选择。第22章研究跨国公司与区域关系中被人忽视的非投资地所受到的影响。该章以上海大众为例，通过调研其产业联系对贵州的区域经济带动，证明仅仅关注投资地所受到的跨国公司影响是有明显缺陷的。第23章研究了大型劳动密集型公司——富士康的快速空间扩张的区位选择，发现除了劳动力、地价、交通、开放程度之外，政府强有力的游说和支持起着重要作用；中国特殊的强政府体制使世界上十分罕见的企业在短期内迅速扩张（1～3年内由建厂到20万人以上的规模）、快速生产得以实现。第24章调查分析了香港对大陆投资的区位变化及其原因。发现前店（香港）后厂（大陆）的运行模式和人际关系作为重要区位选择影响因素，决定着相当长的一段时间内港资高度集中于中国南部；随着内地市场的进一步开放和交通条件的改善，其投资会逐渐“北上”和“西进”。第25章通过定量模型分析表明，外商投资对中国沿海地区的经济增长具有显著影响，其中，广东、福建、上海、江苏的外商带动弹性系数较高（1.27～3.45）；对大型国有外资企业的调查表明，外商投资在技术、管理水平提高等方面的带动也很明显。

第26章以中国一拖集团为例，研究了改革开放后大型国有企业空间网络变化，发现其供货商数量在增加，但平均距离在大幅度减小；销售联系的平均距离也有所缩短，反映了企业由执行计划到适应市场经济的逐渐运行结果。第27章根据河南虞城县南庄村钢卷尺（该村生产的钢卷尺占全国市场的70%）企业的调查，分析了规模经济、分工经济和网络联系的机理作用，以及模仿创新、中原文化背景、制度扶持、较低的劳动力成本和土地成本的区域环境的影响，造就了中部农区中小企业集群中的竞争优势。第28章根据20世纪90年代早期对河南5个不同发展水平县域118家农村工业企业的调查，分析了当时这些企业的产业类型、产业联系与企业发展，归纳出3种发展模式。由于90年代是中部地区农村工业企业大发展时期，该研究具一定的历史意义。第29章评述了国际金融地理学理论研究文献，从金融机构的空间结构、空间发展过程，以及金融机构与环境关系等方面分析了金融地理学的主要研究内容，进而阐述了金融地理学的主要理论问题和中国金融地理学研究的主要切入点。第30章以河南四大国有银行为例，研究了发展中地区金融业的空间系统变化，发现与发达国家相同，中国研究区的银行业逐步向中心城市集中，但中心城市银行业区位在不断扩散，人均收入对银行布局起着重要影响。

第四篇为经济地理学的小尺度研究，内容包括8章，在一般尺度分析之后，沿着县、乡镇、村、点位等不同尺度的逻辑关系展开。第31章探讨了经济地理学中的尺度问题，包括尺度的概念、经济地理学中尺度的意义、经济地理学研究中的尺度变化和经济地理学中的微观研究等，认为中国经济地理学具有明显的宏观特点，但微观经济地理学研究相当薄弱，应该从多个角度加强相关研究。第 32 章基于县域空间数据，分析了 20 世纪末 10 年的中国区域经济变化，认为研究时段内全国县域经济发展水平相对差异明显变小，但沿海省份与内陆省份的县域差别在变大；经济增长较快的县域自一些增长中心向外扩散，形成沿海地带、沿京广线、沿长江带三大增长轴；经济不发达的县域主要集中于中西部，但沿海也存在一些不发达县域。第 33 章同样从县域尺度分析了河南省经济空间结构变化及其效应，发现河南作为欠发达区，经济空间呈现集聚变化趋势，总体呈现明显的中心-外围模式，县域经济增长的空间相关性不显著。第 34 章从乡镇尺度定量分析了河南省的农区经济差异，认为地理因素对农区经济发展具有重要影响，但随着经济水平的提高，传统地理因素（如地形、农业资源等）的影响逐渐被与经济集聚明显相关的地理临近性、基础设施条件等因素所取代。第 35 章集中研究村庄周围的农业生产区位变化，发现人口密度高的平原地区，存在以村庄为中心带状作物区位变化，其原因不是交通费用影响，而是作物劳动密集度和地块肥力的差异。第 36 章基于相关经济学和地理学理论，建立了揭示专业村形成机理和形成类型的理论框架，用数理方法推理了村庄产业结构变化和专业村的形成，并用河南省的专业村数据，实证研究了村环境条件对专业化率的影响。第 37 章根据实地调查，从农田地块尺度分析了农业生产中的物质、能量传递和转换，发现地形因子对山区农田人地系统投入产出具有重要影响，探索了人地关系的微观量化研究。第 38 章从更小尺度（30m×30m 的遥感解析尺度）探索了区域可持续发展的评估。在研究中提出评估区域可持续发展的相对原则，即区域可持续发展应通过评估相关指标的变化方向来判定，而判定的准则应倾向于这种变化是否适应当地环境条件；并通过一个小区研究，证明这种方法的可行性。

第五篇包括 10 章内容，为中国区域研究的一些探索。第 39 章揭示人文（经济）地理学研究中对社会不公平问题的忽视，如区域发展中的不公平、城市内部不同区域的不公平、农民与农区问题，以及一些特殊社会问题的地理研究等。第 40 章聚焦中部地区，讨论经济发展与社会福利水平的关系，从县域尺度的定量分析表明，人均 GDP 指标的伸缩性明显大于社会福利指数的伸缩性，经济水平较低的地区，福利水平呈现较高水平。在此基础上，第 41 章提出经济地理研究中要注意区域关怀。该章分析了经济地理学研究中的“重富”传统，提出从区域关怀角度，应关注区域发展阶段的差异、关注区域优势的发挥、关注落后地区的发展、关注特殊问题地区的发展。第 42 章对增长极理论进行了科学分析，尤其区分皮鲁式增长极与修改式增长极，指出修改式增长极理论的不足，提出从宏观到微观、从推进式产业到推进式企业以及相关发展环境的增长极选择方法，并设定具体指标，进行实例研究。第 43 章从强调地理环境影响的基础出发，分析了黄河文明的起源、扩散与地理环境的关系，在此基础上，重新审视黄河流域特殊地理要素和社会文化优势，提出发挥黄河沿岸的上下、左右互动，综合谋划黄河沿岸地区的发展。第 44 章评述了国际农区地理学的研究进展，分析了一些具有重要意义的研究方向，梳理了在中国开展农区地理学研究的思路。

第五篇最后 4 章是关于新型城镇化的研究。第 45 章对中国政府提出的新型城镇化从历史、中国国情和未来发展方向角度给予审视，认为这个概念既包含对中国过去城镇化道路的反思，也包含对西方城镇化过程中出现问题的思考和规避，更包含对世界未来新型城镇化前景的新设想。第46章从“人地协调”理论出发，强调在城镇化及新农村建设中，注重全面整合城乡聚落体系，使大小不同、功能差别、环境各异的各类聚落形成统一和谐的整体；还要注重土地城镇化与人口城镇化相协调，注重政府推动与市场力量相协调，注重顶层设计和基层具体操作相协调。第47章探讨了新型城村镇的人口规模问题，提出了一些可供选择的方案。第48章以河南巩义市为例，研究了近百年农村居民点空间格局的演变，发现聚落等级规模、空间格局在20世纪90年代后发生较大变化，但总体上县域中小聚落较多，大聚落发育不突出，从城镇化发展角度，未来聚落空间格局将会发生大的变化。

由于该书基于过去发表的论文，尽管作者在编排上尽量努力加强篇章之间的联系，但还没有完全避免前后内容有逻辑不甚严谨的情况发生，还望读者谅解、批评指正。

(四)

全书的内容多数为本人的研究成果，有些是与他人合作完成的。特别要提出的是，第19、20、21、23章是基于与香港中文大学杨汝万教授的合作成果，第1、42章是基于与河南大学苗长虹教授的合作研究成果，其他某些章内容的研究中，我过去的博士研究生、硕士研究生（包括乔家君、李二玲、高更和、樊新生、罗庆、时慧娜、许家伟、海贝贝、陈寿江）参与做了不少工作，河南财经政法大学周雄飞教授在第13、29、34、36章研究中作出了贡献。在编写过程中，高更和、樊新生、罗庆、许家伟、海贝贝、孟德友、杨慧敏付出了辛勤劳动。本书有些内容是以英文论文发表的，彭宝玉、吴娜琳、朱纪广、史焱文、杨慧敏参与了初译工作，为以后的修改提供了很好的基础。对于以上提到的以及没有提到的而从不同方面对本书研究支持的人们，表示诚挚的谢意！

编完这部近80多万字的书稿，回想起三四十年与经济地理学的结缘。十分荣幸在偶然中遇到地理学，并终身从事经济地理学的教学与研究。尽管有十多年接触大学的管理工作，但钟爱的地理学术事业始终是永远放不下的情结。习惯渐渐成瘾，周末和节假日总要进入这片天地，或重温旧情（原有研究领域），或结识新友（学习新的知识）。这部书稿的文字背后，或根植着澳大利亚新南威尔士州与维多利亚州交界处小城调研的记忆，或隐含着河南乡村企业、农户访谈的点点滴滴；或渊源于大师们指点下的灵感顿开，或受惠于同行或学生们的研讨辩论之中……在学术研究期间，本人借助财经类大学的管理机会，较多地接触了经济学、管理学及计算机、数学等学科的专家，在不同学科的切换中，学到了不少东西。从事管理工作，会较多考虑管理或决策者的需求，也引导我逐渐由纯学术研究转向社会经济的需求。结合经济地理学的应用特点，在研究中我不断反问自己，研究中的某些发现（或某种观点）究竟有什么实际应用意义？

研究工作的进行也受益于多次访学机会。在南开大学读博士研究期间，我以博士生联合培养的名义在澳大利亚国立大学学习研究两年多，开启了问题导向的研究思维。1995～1997年，在美国匹兹堡州立大学客座教授期间的教学经历，又加深了解了美国学生对地理问题的理解逻辑。其后，在香港大学、香港中文大学、澳大利亚莫纳什大学的短期研究，可以较深入地分析相关研究主题的国际文献，进入一定深度的探索之中。

而牛津大学、斯坦福大学、堪萨斯大学、纽卡斯尔大学的短期访问研究，得以在过去一定实证研究的基础上，暂时忘却身边琐事，静静地从国别比较角度思考经济地理学的一些发展问题。这种慢踱步、冷思考对于学术研究至关重要。从与本书关联角度，我要专门感谢纽卡斯尔大学城市与区域发展研究中心（Centre for Urban and Regional Development Studies）申请该校研究委员会资助，邀请我以客座教授（Visiting Professor）身份进行两个月的访问研究。利用这段时间，我集中精力完成该书关键问题的梳理编写工作。感谢该中心提供的研究便利，感谢中心主任派克（Andy Pike）教授和中心研究员王学峰博士的支持！还要感谢河南大学环境与规划学院的良好教学、研究环境，感谢河南财经政法大学同事们的理解和支持，感谢国家自然科学基金委员会对相关研究的持续资助（项目 49271027，49671035，49971024，40271038，40671048，41071082，41471117，40535025），感谢中原经济区“三化”协调发展河南省协同创新中心和河南大学地理学科的出版资助！

最后，借到纽卡斯尔两周后的一篇观感结尾，希望经济地理学汲取中国沃土中的丰富营养，长成在世界有重大影响的学术大树！

> 一方水土养一方人，一方水土更养一方树木。在纽卡斯尔大学附近的公园、在美丽的杜伦（Durham）小镇、在这个周末去的比美西露天博物馆（Beamish Open Air Museum），都见一种高大的树木，非常出类拔萃。今天刚好遇到一位喜欢植物的英国女士，说这种树木叫 Sycamore，查字典中文叫西克莫槭树。仔细观察，这种树年轻时树冠很像国内的法国梧桐，外形呈纺锤状。再成长时树冠变大，圆圆的很标准，远远看去像上尖的心型。长成大树后，像强壮的男子汉。树干粗大，树枝有力，从树底下向上看，很像结构合理的建筑骨架。骨架上的嫩绿硕大树叶，更增添了生命体的活力。大树的树冠层次感很强，一层一层叠加，给大地覆盖了厚厚绿色。如果天空靠大地支撑的话，这里的西克莫槭树最先触碰着北英格兰蓝色的天空，刻画着地平线的轮廓。

李小建
2015 年 8 月 12 日

Prelude: On the road towards new approaches to economic geography: A Chinese perspective

I have been teaching geography as a profession for 34 years since 1982 when I started my first academic job in Henan University, and, if taking the 4 years student life and 4 years and 5 months work experience of survey and mapping in the navy, it is over 40 years altogether. During this period, I gradually moved, from the initial cognition of geography, into a sub-discipline — economic geography, doing some researches and having a certain amount of articles and a few books published, and therefore have accumulated some ideological inspirations. In order to have a scholarly exchange and communication with colleagues and experts in the same field, I hereby compile those works into a single volume, and wish it may provide referential values for my readers.

I

Economic geography as a sub-discipline in geography has such a short history of a hundred years only, starting from the date when it was set as a university teaching course. It had a rapid development in the middle part of the last century, worldwide and with the growth of socio-economy. In the 1960s it started to go toward interpretation from description, owing to the quantitative revolution. Along this line came into being the regional science. At the same time, geographers moved in the direction of interpretive geography, trying to trace the sources, in order to carry out a comprehensive survey, from all perspectives, of its driving force and all relevant factors. For instance, in the 1970s of the last century, the school of politico-economy highlighted the influence from politics and the social forces, holding that the economic panorama was not a result from the rational choice in terms of the location theory, but the outcome of the long term interactions and interventions from various social forces.

Accordingly, then there appeared many new terms such as the institutional turn, the cultural turn, relational turn and scale turn, and so forth. Similar things happened as well in methodologies, which transformed itself from quantitative models and statistic verification to specific case studies and a diversity of approaches. And, in the 1990s, post-structuralism, post-modernism, feminism and so on emphasized the concerns with the human factors and cultural institutions, such and such. And, following the evolutionary economics, scholars began to look closely into the variation and development of the economic geography from the viewpoints of evolution, and therefore and so far, there is a situation of co-existing approaches in diversity.

Economic geography has been gaining most attention in human geography for a long time in China. In the first half of the last century, there was a trend for introducing the Western theories for the practice of regional investigations in China, and, then in the middle period, the focus was on geographical studies using the frameworks from the Soviet Union, getting involved with China's economic development and constructional planning. Since the reform and opening up, Western ideas have been further introduced and Western methodologies widely applied, as the rapidly developing China has brought out the best opportunities for economic geographers throughout the discipline's history. New subjects, research fields and types, the themes, the angles, the scales and methods, the new approaches, and so on, appeared in a great diversity. However, when compared with the West there are such differences as, for example, the emphasis on the elements of physical geography over economy activities and the researches covering governmental policies at all levels, and so forth.

This diversity of approach is confusing and perplexing, and manymay feel lost in the ocean of jargon and struggle to find a way through. I myself used to wonder and wander like this, meditating in puzzles and trying to sort out the logical lines. More than thirty years have passed, and now my thinking has been crystallized into logical thoughts as the following.

The first concern is about the relationship between economy and geography. Since its appearance, both approaches have co-existed from the viewpoints of either geographers or economists. Although they are complementary and mutually supportive, still, they remain distinctive because of the different starting points and observing viewpoints, as seen in their frameworks and academic achievements. Typical examples include the location theory in the first half of the last century, the regional sciences in the middle, and the new economic geography, its models and impacts and so on, at the end. It should be noted that P. Krugman won the Noble Prize in economics in 2008, which encouraged and stimulated the society, even the academic circle, to adopt somewhat economical viewpoints toward the understating of economic geography.

Etymologically, as a technical term Economic Geography was firstly put forward by geographers, and in parallel, the course was taught initially in the department of geography. Later on, *Economic Geography*, the first academic journal was founded by geographers accordingly. And second, methodologically, it is a branch or subdivision of Geography anyway, having lots in common as its properties, and logically, its scope covers both economy and geography, focusing on the interactive relations between the sphere of economic geography and the other geographical ones. Additionally, in the eye of economists, economic geography focuses on the spatial distributions and spatial differences. Giving significance of the geographical nature, so, the economic activities and its relations to the geographical environments, and the economic consequences caused by other human activities and the like are all substantial topics.

Therefore, the economic geography in its full sense and especially as a subject of geography, should be more than the recent progress of diverse methods and themes in the West, the new economic geography marked with the so-called "diverse trends" (Refer to Chapter One), and the one with the same title typified with mathematic and statistic models and so on, despite its significant devotion to and important promotion for this discipline.

The second query would be how to comprehensively understand the economic phenomena? As a big umbrella, it covers a wide range from, for instance, in terms of the economic agents, the global corporations, the transnational companies, to small and median-sized enterprises and rural households, and, in terms of the economic landscape, from the huge economic groups based in gigantic metropolises, big cities and to the small economic space like villages and industrial clusters. In terms of administrative liaisons, coverage ranges from the international economic organizations to the different regional economic systems at various local governmental levels. In terms of its visualization, subjects include from those with clear identifications from outside to those without any external features visible, e. g. , the internet trade. So complicated with such a complex, we are faced with a complex landscape. How do we reach the point of this economic geography? No definite solutions yet but many different views instead.

In my view, all are of importance and deserve attention, but owing to some limits, it is better to do the first thing first. Firstly, it may be wise to examine theregional or local economic phenomena, and expand the field afterward into both national and international economic geographies. The international issues are complicated but sometimes based on their analyses of regional scale, for example, the centre-shifting of the global economy is a topic of economic geography, while the research on the economic centre involves regional studies or even urban studies at the primary level. Apart from that, other disciplines like international economics and international trading pay equal attention to the changes of the global economy. It becomes impossible to do it well without a good foundation of regional researches. Secondly, it is better to care about the researches on the visible economic landscape in regional geographical studies, and later on turn to the economic geographical phenomena which are not easy to be judged from the outside. The evidence is convincing, especially when capitalizing on technologies of remote sensing and big-data processing. Thirdly, better to pay attention to the topics about the micro-economic actors, and later extend it over to the related institutions. These economic agents directly determine the differences and diversities on the globe's surface, and the rest institutions and systems only exert indirect influences.

Now, the third question: what is the Geography as in economic geography? Or, how to define the geographical perspective of economic activities? Generally speaking, economic activities cannot be separated from a certain environment, or context, e. g. the economy grows at different spaces in different paces which are more or less regional in a way. Such concepts as the spatial distribution, the spatial diversity and the spatial interrelations all belong with Geography, but they are the Geography per se. The concept of Geography has deeper and more connotations than that of the spatiality. For example, we rarely consider the relations between the economic spatiality and other geographic atmospheres (such as atmosphere, hydrosphere, geomorphology, pedosphere, human inhabitation sphere……), though it is an important geographical topic in the Geography of economic geography.

The aforementioned challenges continue to influence me, though my views have been undergoing many changes at the same time.

II

I was admitted into Nankai University as a PhD student in the Institute of Economics in 1986. That was the seventh year of China's reforming and opening up, but still, the tint of the planned economy remained very strong. Despite foreign investments, the market-oriented functions of enterprises were fairly limited. The research in economic geography satisfied the demand of the government. There was an Center for Australian Studies in the University, and my thesis was intended to focus on Australian Economic Geography. In literature review I came across the *Progress in Human Geography*, and was fascinated in the articles on corporation geography and took notes of them.

At the beginning of 1988, I passed the test set by Chinese Educational Commission and Australian Embassy, and was awarded a Sino-Australian Student-Exchanging Scholarship and began the study in Department of Geography of the Australian National University in the joint-supervision program for doctorial students. There was a Research School of Pacific Studies where assembled a group of world-wide influential scholars, among those was Prof. Michael Taylor who had researched on corporation geography. He just left for a position in the Department of Transportation of Australian Commonwealth Government but remained in close touch with scholarship in his university. That was a favorable climate in which my interest in the corporation geography developed. Choosing my PhD topic, my idea became crystallized: to concentrate on the joint-approaches between regular regional studies and corporation geography, specialized in the economic activities in the south-east of Australia, to examine the governmental measures for and solutions to the issue of the overwhelming concentration on manufacturing industries and population in two large cities and the difficulties of decentralization, and unveil its eventual failure. On completing the thesis and at a seminar held for me in the Australian National University, my thesis findings were positively acclaimed by the participating experts.

I came back to China in April, 1990. With the sponsorship from the National Natural Science Foundation of China, the funds of Excellent Young Teachers' and Overseas Returning Scholars from the Educational Commission, and the funds for Social Sciences and Natural Sciences of the Ministry of Education, I undertook several research projects focused on the rural industrial enterprises with Chinese features, the foreign and domestic joint ventures combining both domestic and exotic characteristics, and also the state-owned enterprises characteristic of planned economy. Besides, I covered topics including the spatial expansion of industrial enterprises, environment and its relations to the enterprise growth, the spatial systems of different types of business corporations, and enterprise growth and regional development. This provided the foundation of the publication of a book in 1999 (revised and reprinted in 2002), which proposes a research framework and a comprehensive narration of the study areas in corporation geography.

Case studies are important for the corporation geography, especially when large corporations are involved. My research of this type is based on the large scale business in Shanghai. This was inconvenient because I was based in Henan. So I later thought of concentrating on economic activities of the rural economy in my local province of Henan. Ours is a central part of China in some senses where the traditional farming leads the economy in general, and the Household Responsibility System commenced in 1980 highlighted the key function of the individual farming families. By the onset of the 21 century I had begun to examine the rural economy which was based on the farming unit of the household from various perspectives, including the developmental expectations and possible solutions of the farming households in various environments, households' input and output in production and the man-land relations, the location change of rural settlements, the farming zones around a village, the locations of households' migrant work, the ability and autonomy of self-developing, the economic behaviors of villagers as a group, and so forth. Especially in 2005, I was sponsored by a Key-Project from National Natural Science Foundation of China and undertook large scale surveys on villages and farming households, which paved the way to the later and further research investigations from multi-perspectives. Owing to the prominent local and regional advantages in this research area, my colleagues and PhD students carried on with it and formed a good team that exerted initial influences.

As well as dealing with the topic of economic actors, I began to explore the economic geography from the micro-geographical point of view. The traditional settlements resulted from the interactions between the human and the land, and households in a certain village display certain similarities in economic activities. Could I do the rural economic geography by exploring this basic micro-unit? Along this line, I encourage my

PhD students to select this kind of topics over the past decade. For example, by the detailed surveys on the divided land plots, we studies the relations of output and input features between geographical environments within village domains. We also examined the relations between the geographical environments and the formation of the specialized villages, and the difference among different villages in location selection of migrant work. Consequently, Prof Qiao Jiajun, then a PhD candidate, published in this regard *The Quantity Studies on Human-Land System in the Typical Rural Villages* (Science Press, 2005), and *Regional Economic Systems in China's Countryside* (Science Press, 2008). Prof. Li Erling and a PhD Candidate investigated the social networks of rural households and their impact on economic development, and published *The Industrial Clusters and Networks of Small and Middle Sized Business in Central China* (Science Press, 2011). The method of remote sensing technology and the geographical information systems was also employed for the more detailed researches on the relations between the human and the land. In the assessment of regional sustainability, we established a relative judgment standard and identified changes in each site-specific location (e. g, by the landsat data of TM 30m×30m), assessing whether such changes of each location improved the sustainable development.

Behind the geographical research on these micro-units is the mutations of the philosophy of economic-geographical science. For long, it is well known that the economic geography tends towards complexity and inductive reasoning, which has greatly promoted the discipline of economic geography. However, the research in economic geography may also be illustrated by the philosophical theory of reductionism. In this regard, belief is that the key to the scientific outlook of the historical development is the theory of reductionism and the repeatability. Reductionism theory means the simplification and selection of an object, and then the regulation at the lower level may explain the higher one, and, the complications may be broken asunder into elements for analyses.

For example, however complex the material world is, it may be reduced into the 118 chemical elements as cognized so far. Their conditions and structures determine the properties and natures of materials composed, and all the features as such may point to a different direction for the economic geography. However, human intervention in economic geography makes the research object more complicated and dynamic than that found amongst natural phenomena, with more impossibility of repeatability, and more difficulties in finding the basic unit. The more difficult this is, the better to take the challenge, and the more significant in leading this discipline.

My study and research experiences in Australia, USA, UK and Hong Kong, had allowed me to follow the Western trend of scholarship. By adopting the Western theories in economic geography, I had undertaken researches on China-related subjects. That resulted in such topics as the small and medium-sized industrial clusters, transnational corporations, state owned enterprises, the regional development in China, and so on. Such results were published on international refereed journals, and so much so that among economic geographers from mainland China, I became the one who was most prolific in the international publications in the early 21th century.

I often had reflections on what I had been doing, pondering much on the trend of economics-oriented development and the trend of multiple turns influenced by the Euro-American new economic geography, thus gradually formed my own ideology. I then felt that Western theories had been blithely applied to China, which did not meet domestic social and economic needs. China and those developed countries were not in the same phase and therefore encountered with different economic problems, differing in natural environments and natural resources, in socio-political regimes and cultural values, in geographical phenomena and their impacts, so that we needed to think of building up an economic geography with Chinese particularities. Logically speaking in particular, the economic geography cannot move too far from geography in general, instead, what was vital was the interrelations to all other sub-disciplines of geography. Where this was concerned, the recent behaviors of the Western Geography has blurred such a tendency, and this is exactly why I hereby offer my articles which take into account China's national practical matters, as referential material.

III

This book summarizes the results of my researches, most of which ideas has been publicized in my past publications. It has 48 chapters in 5 parts, each part focusing on a certain aspect, on the theoretical approaches, investigations of therural households, corporation geography, small-scale geographic researches and regional investigations as well.

Part One consists of 8 chapters. The first 4 chapters are concerned with the developments in the Western economic geography, a couple of which are specially devoted to the theories of economic geography (regional economics) from economists. Chapter 1 analyzes such matters as "multi-dimensional turns" which started from 1980s onward, and the New Economic Geography, its backdrop and features, and its inspirations to Chinese economic geography. Chapter 2 focuses on Nobel Prize winners, their theories on the regional differences, regional economic development, regional competition and cooperation. The general conclusion being that those economists are moving from the negligence of space to an emphasis on space, from macroscopic to macroscopic-and-microscopic analysis, and from general quantitative to sophisticated model analysis. And, on the foundations of general analyses, chapter 3 discusses indepth Paul Krugman's new geographical views, and following the introduction of his scholarship and contributions is another one of his creative research and its significance to the future of geography. It is held that sciences need to draw on the essence of critical thinking and methodology, and analytical standards and quantity measurements deserve more attentions in Chinese economic geography.

Chapter 4 deals with the way to build up Chinese economic geography with national features, against the background of the international economic geography. This is also a reflection over thepattern of Introducing Foreign Theories—Empirical Studies with China's Cases—Confirmation or revision—Theoretical Conclusions, and puts forward a new one of China's Particularities—Relevant Theoretical Analysis—International Comparison—Theoretical Grounding.

Chapters 5～8 are theoretically reflective on Chinese economic geography. Chapter 5 is about the distinction between economic geography and regional economics, in three aspects of the formation of disciplinary foundation, the levels of research objects and critical thinking. Chapter 6 is on micro-researches on three levels of corporation geography, geography of rural households and small-scale investigations, arguing that micro-research helps to understand the basic unit of geographical phenomena and exhibiting the anatomy of geographical phenomena.

Chapter 7 follows Chapter 4 and advocates Chines eeconomic geography with national features in the interrelations of the special geographical environments, population and resources, government and society, cultural particularity and disciplinary specialty. This special Chinese economic geography promotes the economy growth, the harmony between the human and the land, the special role of the state, the interrelations between regions, the global influences, and the close links with physical geography. Chapter 8 intends to trace the developing line of Chinese economic geography, categorize its characteristics, which is based on the articles published on Acta Geographica Sinica in the last 80 years. It is argued that Chinese economic geography came into being at the call of the state, which promotes macro-researches and economic growth, and in turn calls for would-be researches, though it leaves room for the further improvements in micro-researches, complex researches, theoretical condensation, and so on.

Part two focuses on geography of rural households, consisting of 6 chapters. Chapter 9 first talks about reduction theory as a scientific philosophical concept, showing the relation between households and the regional development of rural areas quantitatively, as well as the location, the spatial structure, the self-developing ability, of rural households, and the relation between household activities and the environments. This chapter is of importance in both theory and practice. Chapter 10 is based on the data from surveys of the author's team on 10 counties of the west hill-regions of Henan Province covering 332 households. It analyses their farming behaviors in the under-developed areas, with somewhat referential meanings for the rural development interacted with farmers, and reveals the relation between the farmers' income and the geographical condition. Chapter 11 is about the three stages of farmers' non-farming development, and conducts a quantitative study of influencing factors, using the data of the survey over 1000 families of 16 villages. Chapter 12 concerns farmers' income under a quantitative survey over 1251 families of 11 villages, noting the changes which governs their incomes: natural factors become less important and social ones more vital. Chapter 13 introduces the concept of farmers' self-developing ability, and examines difference in their abilities of capitalizing the natural resources. This shares the same data as used in Chapter 12, to highlight the impact of self-developing ability on household income and the differences in different developing stages. Chapter 14 details the choices of migrant working locations, which shows the influence of personal conditions (age, gender), family features (number of population, generation) and community features (development level, location); however, it should be pointed out that the distance of working, location and space types vary.

Part three composes 16 chapters, of which, 2 chapters are generalizations, 9 chapters ontransnational corporations, 1 on state-owned enterprises, 2 on rural industry, 2 on financial geography and banking commerce. Chapter 15 is on the features of corporation geography, its significances in China and its practical values for the nation. Chapter 16 introduces the analytical method of industrial organizations in regional research. Through quantitative study of regional data, the mutations of industrial zones are shown, and later on so is the deep reasons for the change in industrial organization. The result of the analysis on the development of Australian industry in the south-east is corroborated in reality. Chapter 17 is the theorization of the influences of the multinational corporations, and points out three interrelated schemes of the production chain, organization chain and ownership chain, which, together with positions of the invested region in regional hierarchies, are of essence, and determine their relations and profits. Chapter 18 uses Chinese empirical data to draw unique conclusions, which hold that the impacts of transnational corporations on regional imbalance in China are changing, from decreasing to increasing, along with the changes of the invested areas and the development of regional economy. Chapter 19 sets Shanghai as an example, and notes the advantage of local joint ventures.

With the industrial chain and broad network of related professions, transnational corporations roots more deeply in local communications, this kind of "thorough cure" improves the local economy. Chapter 20 deals, from a new perspective, with the bargaining relations between foreign invested companies and the invested regions (rather than the business organizations of joint venture): with the measuring criteria and filed data, it is shown that some specific areas in developing countries are more advantageous than other areas, in terms of bargain with foreign companies and thus can gain more benefits for the region. This conclusion is contained in my published articles and receives acclaims from scholars.

Chapter 21 illustrates Chinese case studies. It analyses the locational change for the investment of transnational corporations in China. This change is in accordance with, and also out of, the findings in previous literature. What affects how the transnational corporations to choose the location includes the special interpersonal connections, the political regimes, and the power of local companies as joint-venture partners. Chapter 22 is about the impact of foreign investment on the un-invested areas. Shanghai Volkswagen is set as an example, which shows it is obviously a flaw only to note the areas where are invested by the multinational corporations. Chapter 23 studies on the large scale labor-intensive corporations, and Foxconn Technology Group is set as the example, which was rapidly developed with its wise choice of the region, through which is noted that the governmental persuasion and supports are of consequences, and also it mentions that there has been rare industrial expansions in the world owing to Chinese governmental institutions (within one or two years the staff number increased up to 200000 which brought about the rapid speed of production) . Chapter 24 is about the survey of locations invested by Hong Kong in mainland China. It notes the operational model of Hong Kong and the Mainland, and the important factor of interpersonal relations which affect the choice of locations, which determined for a long, subsequent period that the south China be the densely invested region, and with the further market-opening and the improvement of transportation, the investment would move up north and westward.

Chapter 25 shows through a model of quantitative study that foreign investment has significantly affected economic growth in the coastal areas, among which is Guangdong, Fujian, Shanghai and Jiangsu, all of which have higher multiplier effects of the foreign investment (with elasticity ratios 1.27～3.45), and it is also obvious that the foreign investments have positively impacted on technology, management, and improvement of market system.

Chapter 26 sets China's First Tractor Group Co. Ltd as the example and studies on the changes of the spatial networks in business operations in reform-era: the number of suppliers are more but the average distance less, and the average distance of sale is shortened as well, which is a result of the smooth transition from planned economy to the market economy. Chapter 27 is about a small and medium-sized enterprise cluster manufacturing metal measuring tapes in Nanzhuang Village, Yucheng, Henan Province (its output takes 70% of the market of the nation) . The analysis investigates the economies of scale, the economies of the division of labor, and the network linkage, as well as the local culture, the imitative innovation, the institutional support, and the lower production costs which exert influence on the region and its environments, and contributes to the competitive advantage of this kind of clusters in the central China.

Chapter 28 investigates 118 rural industrial enterprises from 5 counties at different levels of development in the 1990s, and analyses their types, connections and growth, and summarizes 3 models of development. This is historically significant as the 90's was a period of rapid progress. Chapter 29 reviews the bibliographical references to international financial geography, ranging from the spatial structure of financial institutions, the process of spatial development, and the relations between financial institutions and the environments, and therefore analyses the major topics of financial geography in China. Chapter 30 sets China's four national banks as the example, and studies the changes of spatial system of the national banks in central part of China, and notes that compared with developed countries, China's banks in the researched areas are gradually centralized in central cities, and the locations in the central cities are spreading, and the average of individual income in a local area affects the locations of the banks.

Part Four contains the small scale studies of economic geography over 8 chapters. After a general analysis on scales, the logical relations are spread along different scales, from counties, towns, to villages and site-specific points. Chapter 31 touches the scales of economic geography, such as the concept, its significance, the change of scale and micro-perspective studies. It is noted that Chinese economic geography bears apparent macro-features but weak micro ones, the latter to be improved. Chapter 32 is based on county spatial data, analyzing the regional economic changes of the last decade of the 20th century in China. It is noted that national diversity in economic development at county level is narrowing, but that within coastal areas stands opposite. Owing to the expansion of rapidly growing counties, three major growth axes are apparent in national map, which are along the coastal line, along the rail-line between Beijing and Guangzhou and along the Yangtze River. The underdeveloped counties are mainly located in central and western regions, with a small number of those in the coastal areas as well.

Chapter 33 analyses the change in the spatial structures of economic development and its effects in Henan Province, noting that Henan is underdeveloped, with a process of spatial centralization in economic growth. it is basically a model of Centre-periphery, and less apparent in spatial correlation. Chapter 34 deals with the differences in Henan rural economy by using township data, noting the important influence from the geographical factors over the rural economy, but also pointing that along economic development, the traditional influence, like from landscape and resources, are gradually replaced by the geographical proximity and infrastructures. Chapter 35 examines the change of production zones, noting the crop-changes around villages owing to the differences in fertilization and the density of labouring. Chapter 36 is based on general theories, forming a framework to reveal the systematic organization of specialized villages, and uses mathematical models to predict the change in village industrial structure and formation, and with the data of the specialized villages in Henan Province, the influence rate of specialization from the village environment is proved. Chapter 37 is a field investigation: It analyses the transmission and transformation of energies in agricultural productions, and finds out that the factors of slop gradient and aspect are vital to farming input-output efficiency in the mountain areas, this being a micro quantitative study on the man-land relations. Chapter 38 is an even smaller scale study (30m×30m), assessing the sustainable development, of which is such a principle that the achievement of sustainability in a region should be judged by the changing direction on whether the changes suit the local environment in a time period concerned. The study then uses a hybrid model to develop typical suitable site conditions as benchmarks in determining the suitability of a specific land use type, and uses a multivariate technique for measuring the difference between benchmarks and the actual situation.

Part Five consists of 10 chapters on some critical consideration of China's regional issues. Chapter 39 exposes the issue of inequality and injustice in the researches from an economic geography perspective, such as the inequalities in regional development, inside the city and town, and about farmers and rural areas. Chapter 40 focuses on the relationship between economic development and social welfare, by quantitative analysis on county-level data in Central China, indicating the difference in two aspects of development measurement and higher social welfare coming with lower economic development in some areas. And upon the aforementioned conditions, Chapter 41 advocates more cares of, and attentions to, all different regions. It talks about the tradition of "favouring the rich" in regional studies, and calls for more assistance to the backward and disadvantaged areas. Chapter 42 expounds in a scientific manner the growth pole theory. Chapter 43 focuses on geographical environments, and analyses the origination and expansion of the Yellow River civilization. This includes its relations to the environment and re-examination of the geographical elements and the socio-cultural advantages of the Yellow River Reaches. Calls are made for the all-round-interactions between the upper and lower reaches and a better understanding of the comprehensive development of such region. Chapter 44 reviews the furtherance of international researches on rural geography, on the trends and directions, and sorting out the thinking thread on this type of research in this country of China.

Part Five, the final of 4 chapters, concentrates on New Urbanization. Chapter 45 goes over the past, present and future in so far as New Urbanization is put forward by the Chinese government, and argues that this concept, is a reflection on the history of Chinese Urbanization and Western Urbanization. It provides a vision of the world in the future. Chapter 46, adopting the theory of Man-Land Harmony, argues for a complex and compressive harmonious unity of settlement system including cities, towns and villages, which consists of all types of settlements varying in sizes, functions, surroundings. It is also noted that the urbanization of land must be coordinated with the urbanization of the population, which needs the governmental measures and also a harmony between the design in top ranks and operations at lower levels. Chapter 47 takes into account the issue of population size in new towns, and offers scenarios and suggestions for new town development. Chapter 48 is a case study of Gongyi City of Henan Province, about the evolutionary history of a hundred years during which rural habitants have been altering their residential formats, and notes the huge difference in scales and spatial formats in the 90's of the last century, and also points out that there are more small settlements rather than large ones, the development of the latter is significant, and expects an even greater change in near future.

My book herewith is a compilation of the published articles. I have tried my best to make all chapters logically connected to and communicated with one another, but I still have not managed to miss the accidents of illogicality and inaccuracy and so, for this, I expect criticism and corrections for the readership, and would like hereby to beg for their pardon.

IV

Chapters of this book are from my own research investigation and contribution of coauthors. It is worth pointing out that chapters 19, 20, 21 and 23 are based on the joint researches with Professor Yue-man Yeung, The Chinese University of Hong Kong, and Professor Miao Changhong from Henan University for his joint research partly adopted and rewritten in Chapters 1 and 42. Some of my postgraduate students have made substantial contributions to several chapters through their participation in my research project during their study. Among them are Qiao Jiajun, Li Erling, Gao Genghe, Fan Xinsheng, Luo Qin, Shi Huina, Xu Jiawei, Hai Beibei, and Chen Shoujiang. Professor Zhou Xongfei from Henan University of Economics and Law dedicated his computing analyses to Chapters 13, 29, 34 and 36. During the editing process, Gao Genghe, Fan Xinsheng, Luo Qin, Xu Jiawei, Hai Beibei, Meng Deyou, and Yang Huimin devoted their valuable time and efforts. Some of the chapters were originally published in English. Peng Baoyu, Wu Nalin, Zhu Jiguang, Shi Yanwen, and Yang Huimin translated them into Chinese, which provided a good basis for further modification. Besides the cooperators mentioned above, I would like to extend my sincere thanks to those who are not mentioned, for their contributions to the book and their support for my prior research from different perspectives.

On completing this book of over 800 000 Chinese characters, I recall my personal union with Economic Geography over the past 30 years, and my devotions to it with teaching and research. Although I have been involved in university administration for the past 14 years, yet I always love geography as the academic cause for life. Year in and year out I have been gradually addicted, and always step upon this horizon either at weekends or on holidays, when warming up the nostalgia (for the older learnings) or making fresh acquaintances (to renew my scholarship) . Between the lines of this manuscript lies the memory of doing research at a small town along the joint border of New South Wales and Victoria in Australia, or of the scenes and episodes of my visiting the farmers and rural industrial enterprises in Henan Province, China, or the instance I was inspired by some famed experts, or benefited from colleagues and students in discussion or at seminars. Owing to the opportunity of presiding administration, I was in close contacts with experts of economics, management, mathematics, and therefore learning much at the shifts of academic disciplines. When I was administrating, I naturally gave more consideration to the aspirations of the policy makers and enterprise managers, which led me away from pure academic activities to the socio-economic demands, and taking account of the application of geography, I often asked myself if there had been somewhat signification of the application and any meaning of practicality in this or that statement.

As mentioned above, my research benefits from so many opportunities of scholarly visiting. When reading my PhD in Nankai University, I had the benefit of a joint supervision program with Australian National University, offering an opportunity to exercise my ability of critical thinking. From 1995～1997 I was teaching as a visiting professor in Pittsburgh State University (USA), an experience which deepened my understanding of American students, and their logical theorization. I later went to the University of Hong Kong, the Chinese University of Hong Kong, and the Monash University (Australia) for short term visits and deeper researches. I also was in the University of Oxford, Stanford University, the University of Kansas, and Newcastle University upon Tyne, which enabled me to forget all trivialities but adopt an exotic view-angle and mediate over the development of economic geography. This kind of slow pace and pensive pondering are vital. As far as this book is concerned, I hereby express my gratitude to the Centre for Urban and Regional Development Studies (CURDS) at Newcastle University for their sponsorship for the two months' visiting professorship, during which time I concentrated on this book, and in speaking of this I would also like to thank Prof. Andy Pike, the director, and Dr. Xuefeng Wang, the research associate in the Centre. Many thanks are also given to the Henan University and National Natural Science Foundation of China for their support.

Finally, I borrow herewith the ending of aparagraph of my dairy written after my stay at Newcastle for two weeks, in order to express my wish that economic geography draw the nutrition from the Chinese soil, and grows into a huge bough in the land of international scholarship.

There is a saying in China, *A side water and soil raise a party people*. It is also true that a side water and soil create the environment for particular trees. A type of tree which is tall and preeminent came into view when I visited Leazes Park near the Newcastle University, and I met with the same view when visiting the pretty Durham Town and the vast Beamish Open Air Museum. Today I happened to know that the tree is called Sycamore from a lady who is a plant hobbyist. By scrutinization, this tree at its youth is very similar to the so-called French plane tree, shaped like a spindle. Growing, the top is bigger, fairly circular, like a heart upside down. And growing up, it is like a brawny pine tree, with powerful arms of the bough. Looked from ground, it resembles a reasonably constructed framework of a building. On the branches are verdant leaves of exuberant extension which add the tint of vitality. The treetop is multi-layered, layer upon layer, carpeting the land with exuberant verdure. If Heaven was really supported by the Earth, the Sycamore, right here with me, would be the first to touch the azure sky of Northern England, tracing the outline of the horizon.

Li Xiaojian

August 26, 2015

目　　录

序

第一篇　经济地理学理论探索

第 1 章　西方经济地理学进展 …… 3
1.1　地理学家的“多维转向” …… 3
1.2　经济学家的“新经济地理学” …… 6
1.3　西方经济地理学新进展的启示 …… 8
参考文献 …… 12
第 2 章　诺贝尔经济学奖中的区域经济思想 …… 14
2.1　诺贝尔经济学获奖者的区域经济学观点 …… 14
2.2　诺贝尔经济学获奖者的区域经济思想演变 …… 18
2.3　诺贝尔经济学获奖者的区域经济学思想对现实的解释 …… 18
2.4　结论及讨论 …… 20
参考文献 …… 22
第 3 章　克鲁格曼与经济地理学 …… 24
3.1　克鲁格曼学术生涯简介 …… 24
3.2　克鲁格曼对经济地理学的主要贡献 …… 25
3.3　克鲁格曼创新研究对经济地理学的启迪 …… 28
3.4　克鲁格曼获诺贝尔奖对经济地理学发展的影响 …… 30
3.5　结语 …… 32
参考文献 …… 32
第 4 章　国际背景与中国特色的经济地理学 …… 33
4.1　国际主流经济地理学近期发展特点 …… 33
4.2　中国经济地理学的研究背景 …… 36
4.3　中国经济地理学的研究特点 …… 37
4.4　发展中国特色的经济地理学 …… 39
参考文献 …… 40
第 5 章　经济地理学与区域经济学的区分 …… 41
5.1　研究现状评述 …… 41
5.2　经济地理学与区域经济学差异分析的新视角 …… 42
5.3　结论及讨论 …… 45
参考文献 …… 46

第 6 章　经济地理学的微观研究 …… 47
6.1　公司地理研究 …… 47
6.2　农户地理研究 …… 50
6.3　经济地理学的小尺度研究 …… 50
6.4　结论及讨论 …… 51
参考文献 …… 52
第 7 章　经济地理学发展的构思 …… 54
7.1　研究背景与问题 …… 54
7.2　经济发展阶段与经济地理学 …… 55
7.3　地理背景与经济地理学 …… 58
7.4　学科背景与经济地理学 …… 60
7.5　中国独特的经济地理学 …… 63
参考文献 …… 66
第 8 章　《地理学报》中的经济地理学发展 …… 68
8.1　经济地理学论文数量分析 …… 69
8.2　经济地理学发展脉络 …… 70
8.3　经济地理学研究范式的转变 …… 72
8.4　满足国家需要的研究主题变化 …… 75
8.5　经济地理学各学科研究的发展 …… 76
8.6　结论及讨论 …… 78
参考文献 …… 79

第二篇　农户地理研究

第 9 章　还原论与农户地理研究 …… 87
9.1　还原论与农户概念 …… 87
9.2　农户与农区关系的证明 …… 88
9.3　农户地理研究的基本框架 …… 92
9.4　农户地理主要研究内容 …… 93
9.5　结论与讨论 …… 96
参考文献 …… 97
第 10 章　欠发达农区发展中的农户行为 …… 99
10.1　理论背景与研究问题 …… 99
10.2　区域选择及数据分析 …… 100
10.3　经济发展中的农户行为特征 …… 102
10.4　农户行为对区域经济发展的影响 …… 107
10.5　结论及讨论 …… 108
参考文献 …… 109

第 11 章　欠发达区农户兼业演变 …… 110
11.1　研究问题…… 110
11.2　数据来源及处理…… 111
11.3　农户兼业化演变…… 112
11.4　兼业化对农户经济的贡献…… 113
11.5　进一步讨论…… 114
参考文献…… 116
第 12 章　农户收入的地理环境影响 …… 117
12.1　研究问题…… 118
12.2　数据来源…… 119
12.3　农户收入的差异分析…… 121
12.4　变量选择与模型建立…… 123
12.5　模型分析结果…… 124
12.6　结论与政策建议…… 126
参考文献…… 127
第 13 章　农户自主发展能力 …… 129
13.1　农户自主发展能力…… 130
13.2　空间增长与增长因素的贡献度…… 131
13.3　数据调查及数据处理…… 132
13.4　农户农业发展模型…… 133
13.5　农户非农发展模型…… 136
13.6　农户非农报酬率模型…… 138
13.7　结论及讨论…… 140
参考文献…… 141
第 14 章　农户务工区位选择 …… 143
14.1　数据来源与研究区域选择…… 143
14.2　理论分析与研究假设…… 145
14.3　变量设计与说明…… 146
14.4　模型与讨论…… 147
14.5　结论与政策建议…… 151
参考文献…… 152

第三篇　公司地理研究

第 15 章　公司地理的理论问题 …… 155
15.1　工业地理学的发展与公司地理…… 155
15.2　公司地理的主要特点…… 156
15.3　公司地理的主要研究内容…… 158

15.4 开展适应中国国情的公司地理研究…… 161
参考文献…… 163
第 16 章 工业区域变化的综合研究 …… 164
16.1 研究方法讨论…… 164
16.2 澳大利亚制造业结构变化分析…… 165
16.3 制造业区域变化分析…… 168
16.4 结论与讨论…… 171
参考文献…… 172
第 17 章 跨国公司对区域经济发展的影响 …… 174
17.1 跨国公司与区域发展研究的理论背景…… 174
17.2 跨国投资公司与区域发展的关系…… 178
17.3 结论与讨论…… 183
参考文献…… 183
第 18 章 跨国公司对区域经济差异的影响 …… 187
18.1 分析框架和研究方法…… 187
18.2 外国直接投资与中国区域经济发展差异…… 189
18.3 跨国公司投资的企业分析…… 199
18.4 结论与讨论…… 203
参考文献…… 204
第 19 章 跨国公司投资的地方根植性 …… 207
19.1 研究背景…… 207
19.2 案例区和跨国公司访谈…… 209
19.3 企业管理的本地化程度…… 210
19.4 产品生产的本地化程度…… 211
19.5 技术转让中本地参与程度…… 213
19.6 企业案例分析…… 214
19.7 结论与讨论…… 217
参考文献…… 218
第 20 章 跨国公司与投资地关系 …… 220
20.1 研究背景…… 220
20.2 影响讨价还价关系因素…… 221
20.3 讨价还价度量…… 222
20.4 上海讨价还价力量的来源…… 223
20.5 跨国公司的上海直接投资增长…… 224
20.6 上海与跨国公司的讨价还价分析…… 227
20.7 结论与讨论…… 234
参考文献…… 236

第 21 章　大公司空间扩张区位变化 …… 239
21.1　公司空间扩张规律…… 239
21.2　外国跨国公司在中国投资区位扩张规律…… 240
21.3　进一步讨论…… 243
参考文献…… 243
第 22 章　企业联系与跨国公司的区域影响 …… 245
22.1　跨国公司的影响和企业联系…… 246
22.2　公司选择和访谈…… 246
22.3　上海大众…… 247
22.4　上海贝尔…… 253
22.5　结论与讨论…… 256
参考文献…… 257
第 23 章　大型劳动密集型企业快速扩张区位选择 …… 260
23.1　研究问题…… 260
23.2　理论基础…… 261
23.3　富士康概况…… 263
23.4　空间扩张特征…… 264
23.5　空间扩张影响因素分析…… 266
23.6　结论与讨论…… 270
参考文献…… 270
第 24 章　香港大陆投资的区位变化 …… 272
24.1　文献评述、研究方法与数据…… 272
24.2　香港在大陆投资空间变化的统计分析…… 273
24.3　香港在大陆投资区位变化的企业分析…… 275
24.4　香港公司对大陆投资的空间行为分析…… 276
24.5　香港公司对投资环境的感知分析…… 278
24.6　创造吸引港资环境建议…… 280
参考文献…… 281
第 25 章　外商直接投资对中国沿海地区经济的影响 …… 282
25.1　外商直接投资与区域经济发展的理论简评…… 282
25.2　研究思路及数据…… 283
25.3　外商直接投资的区域分布及变化…… 284
25.4　外商投资与沿海地区经济增长的定量分析…… 286
25.5　外商直接投资影响的企业分析…… 287
25.6　结论与讨论…… 290
参考文献…… 291
第 26 章　大型国有企业空间网络变化 …… 293
26.1　研究背景…… 293

26.2　国有企业空间网络…… 294
26.3　管理网络…… 296
26.4　供应商网络…… 297
26.5　销售网络…… 300
26.6　技术网络…… 302
26.7　结论与讨论…… 303
参考文献…… 304
第 27 章　中部中小企业集群竞争优势 …… 307
27.1　中部农区企业集群的竞争优势来源…… 307
27.2　南庄村钢卷尺企业集群案例分析…… 309
27.3　结论与讨论…… 318
参考文献…… 318
第 28 章　产业联系与农村工业化 …… 319
28.1　理论思路及企业选择…… 319
28.2　产业联系类型…… 320
28.3　产业联系与农村工业发展…… 322
28.4　典型案例分析…… 323
28.5　区域模式…… 324
28.6　结语…… 326
参考文献…… 326
第 29 章　金融地理学理论探索 …… 327
29.1　金融地理学主要研究内容…… 327
29.2　金融地理学主要理论问题…… 331
29.3　中国金融地理研究…… 333
参考文献…… 335
第 30 章　发展中地区银行业空间系统变化 …… 337
30.1　研究背景…… 337
30.2　研究区域与数据来源…… 339
30.3　银行业空间系统的变化…… 340
30.4　银行业空间系统变化的宏观影响因素…… 345
30.5　银行区位选择的微观因素…… 347
30.6　结论与讨论…… 349
参考文献…… 350

第四篇　经济地理学的小尺度研究

第 31 章　经济地理学研究中的尺度 …… 353
31.1　尺度的概念…… 353

31.2　尺度在经济地理学研究中的意义 …… 354
31.3　经济地理学研究中的尺度变化 …… 357
31.4　经济地理学中的微观研究 …… 358
参考文献 …… 359
第 32 章　20 世纪 90 年代中国县域经济空间差异 …… 361
32.1　理论背景及数据分析 …… 361
32.2　1998 年中国县域经济空间格局 …… 362
32.3　20 世纪 90 年代中国县域经济空间变化特点 …… 365
32.4　中国县域经济增长类型简析 …… 367
32.5　结论与讨论 …… 369
参考文献 …… 370
第 33 章　20 世纪 90 年代河南经济空间结构变化及其效应 …… 371
33.1　河南省经济空间结构演变过程 …… 371
33.2　河南省经济空间集聚格局及其经济效应 …… 372
33.3　结语 …… 378
参考文献 …… 378
第 34 章　农区经济发展差异的乡镇尺度分析 …… 380
34.1　农民收入影响因素的一般性分析 …… 380
34.2　数据来源及其处理 …… 382
34.3　农区经济发展空间差异 …… 382
34.4　指标分析与模型建立 …… 384
34.5　模型分析结果 …… 385
34.6　结论与讨论 …… 388
参考文献 …… 389
第 35 章　中部平原村农业生产区位 …… 390
35.1　文献评述与理论分析 …… 390
35.2　研究村庄选择与数据获取 …… 392
35.3　农户农业区位的选择 …… 393
35.4　影响农户农业区位选择的主要因素 …… 398
35.5　结论与讨论 …… 399
参考文献 …… 400
第 36 章　欠发达区专业村空间分析 …… 402
36.1　理论基础 …… 402
36.2　专业村与环境关系的数理分析 …… 404
36.3　数据讨论 …… 406
36.4　专业村与环境关系的经验分析 …… 409
36.5　专业村类型与环境关系模拟 …… 411
36.6　结论与讨论 …… 413

参考文献 …… 415
第 37 章　山区农田系统投入产出分析 …… 416
37.1　分析模型 …… 416
37.2　研究区概况与数据处理 …… 417
37.3　地形对农田投入产出的影响 …… 420
37.4　结论与讨论 …… 424
参考文献 …… 425
第 38 章　中尺度流域土地利用/土地覆盖变化评估 …… 426
38.1　研究思路与方法 …… 426
38.2　研究区概况 …… 428
38.3　数据来源与数据库开发 …… 429
38.4　土地利用/土地覆盖变化：1996～1999 年 …… 430
38.5　结果讨论 …… 432
38.6　结论与讨论 …… 434
参考文献 …… 435

第五篇　区 域 研 究

第 39 章　社会不公平问题的地理研究 …… 439
39.1　区域发展中的不公平 …… 439
39.2　城市内部的不公平 …… 440
39.3　农民与农区问题 …… 441
39.4　特殊社会问题的地理研究 …… 442
39.5　结语 …… 443
参考文献 …… 443
第 40 章　中部地区经济发展与社会福利分析 …… 444
40.1　指标及数据来源 …… 444
40.2　中部地区经济与福利水平空间差异 …… 446
40.3　经济与福利水平之间关系分析 …… 449
40.4　结论与讨论 …… 451
参考文献 …… 451
第 41 章　经济地理学研究中的区域关怀 …… 453
41.1　区域经济研究的“重富”传统 …… 454
41.2　区域关怀研究的内容 …… 456
41.3　区域关怀研究中的思维转换 …… 458
41.4　结语 …… 459
参考文献 …… 460
第 42 章　增长极理论分析及选择研究 …… 461

42.1 增长极理论及实践…… 461
42.2 增长极选择的指标与方法…… 463
42.3 增长极选择案例…… 467
42.4 结论与讨论…… 469
参考文献…… 470
第 43 章 黄河沿岸人地关系与发展 …… 471
43.1 黄河文明起源与扩散…… 471
43.2 历史经济发展与黄河…… 473
43.3 黄河沿岸现代发展…… 474
43.4 结论与讨论…… 476
参考文献…… 477
第 44 章 农区地理学研究进展与发展思路 …… 479
44.1 农区地理学发展特点…… 479
44.2 农区范围界定…… 480
44.3 农区地理学的新近研究方向…… 481
44.4 中国农区地理学的研究思考…… 484
参考文献…… 486
第 45 章 新型城镇化概念分析 …… 488
45.1 新型城镇化是对中国过去城镇化的反思…… 488
45.2 新型城镇化是对发达国家“城市问题”的规避…… 489
45.3 新型城镇化是对中国理想城镇化模式的新构思…… 490
第 46 章 新型城镇化中的协调思想 …… 492
46.1 新型城镇化本质是城乡协调…… 493
46.2 新型城镇化核心是内部协调…… 493
46.3 新型城镇化机制强调市场协调…… 494
46.4 新型城镇化实施强调上下协调…… 495
46.5 结论与讨论…… 498
参考文献…… 499
第 47 章 新农村建设中新村镇规模探讨 …… 501
47.1 建设新型村镇的意义…… 502
47.2 研究区概况…… 502
47.3 数据标准与方法…… 504
47.4 不同人口规模下新型村镇的指标对比…… 504
47.5 结论与讨论…… 507
参考文献…… 508
第 48 章 近百年农村聚落空间格局演变 …… 510
48.1 文献评述…… 510
48.2 研究区及数据处理…… 511

48.3　聚落规模变化…… 513
48.4　聚落的空间格局演变与机制分析…… 518
48.5　结论与讨论…… 524
参考文献…… 525

Contents

Prelude: On the road towards new approaches to economic geography: A Chinese perspective

Part I Is there an economic geography with Chinese characteristics

Chapter 1 Recent progress of economic geography in Western World …… 3
1.1 "Multi-dimensional turn" from perspective of economic geography …… 3
1.2 "New economic geography" from economics …… 6
1.3 How will economic geography in China go? …… 8
References …… 12
Chapter 2 Spatial perspective from Nobel Prize winners in economics …… 14
2.1 The views on regional economics of Nobel prize-winning economist …… 14
2.2 Evolution of spatial ideas from Nobel Prize economist …… 18
2.3 Explanation on realities from Nobel Prize economist's theories …… 18
2.4 Conclusions and discussion …… 20
References …… 22
Chapter 3 Krugman and new economic geography …… 24
3.1 The academic career of Paul Krugman …… 24
3.2 Krugman's main contribution to the economic geography …… 25
3.3 Krugman's perspectives and research of economic geography …… 28
3.4 Impact of Krugman's Nobel Prize on development of economic geography …… 30
3.5 Conclusions …… 32
References …… 32
Chapter 4 International background and economic geography with Chinese characteristics …… 33
4.1 Recent developments of economic geography in the international mainstream …… 33
4.2 Background of economic geography in China …… 36
4.3 Different features of China's economic geography …… 37
4.4 Development of economic geography with Chinese characteristics …… 39
References …… 40
Chapter 5 Differences between economic geography and regional economics …… 41
5.1 Research problems and literature review …… 41

5.2 Comparison between economic geography and regional economics ········ 42
5.3 Conclusions and discussion ········ 45
References ········ 46
Chapter 6 A micro-perspective in economic geography studies ········ 47
6.1 Firm geography ········ 47
6.2 Geography of rural households ········ 50
6.3 Small-scale study in economic geography ········ 50
6.4 conclusions and discussion ········ 51
References ········ 52
Chapter 7 Development framework of economic geography ········ 54
7.1 Research background ········ 54
7.2 The stages of economic development and economic geography ········ 55
7.3 Geographical background and economic geography ········ 58
7.4 Academic background and economic geography ········ 60
7.5 Economic geography in China ········ 63
References ········ 66
Chapter 8 Development of economic geography from 80 years of Acta Geographica Sinica ········ 68
8.1 Analysis of papers published on economic geography ········ 69
8.2 Development course of economic geography ········ 70
8.3 Paradigm shift in economic geography research ········ 72
8.4 Topic changes and social needs ········ 75
8.5 Main sub-disciplines of economic geography ········ 76
8.6 Conclusions and discussion ········ 78
References ········ 79

Part II Geography of rural households

Chapter 9 Reductionism and geography of rural households ········ 87
9.1 Reductionism and rural households ········ 87
9.2 Rural households and rural areas ········ 88
9.3 Framework of geography of rural households ········ 92
9.4 Contents of rural household geography ········ 93
9.5 Conclusions and discussion ········ 96
References ········ 97
Chapter 10 Behavior of rural households in the underdeveloped rural area ········ 99
10.1 Background and research problems ········ 99
10.2 Regional selection and data analysis ········ 100

10.3 Characteristics of rural household behavior ······ 102
10.4 Impact of rural household behavior on regional economic development ······ 107
10.5 Conclusions ······ 108
References ······ 109
Chapter 11 Change of employment structure in rural households ······ 110
11.1 Research problem ······ 110
11.2 Data sources and processing ······ 111
11.3 Structural change of rural household employment ······ 112
11.4 Contribution of non-agricultural employment to rural household income ······ 113
11.5 Further discussion ······ 114
References ······ 116
Chapter 12 Impact of geographical environment on rural household income ······ 117
12.1 Research problems ······ 118
12.2 Data source ······ 119
12.3 Differences in rural household incomes ······ 121
12.4 Variables and model ······ 123
12.5 Analysis of empirical results ······ 124
12.6 Conclusions and policy suggestions ······ 126
References ······ 127
Chapter 13 Self-development capacity of rural households ······ 129
13.1 Concept explanation ······ 130
13.2 Spatial growth and growth factors ······ 131
13.3 Data collection and processing ······ 132
13.4 Agricultural development model based on rural households ······ 133
13.5 Non-agricultural development model based on rural households ······ 136
13.6 Non-agricultural return model based on rural households ······ 138
13.7 Conclusions and discussion ······ 140
References ······ 141
Chapter 14 Location choice of migrant workers from rural areas ······ 143
14.1 Study area and data collection ······ 143
14.2 Theories and hypotheses ······ 145
14.3 Variable selection ······ 146
14.4 Model and empirical research ······ 147
14.5 Conclusions and policy suggestions ······ 151
References ······ 152

Part III Geography of firms

Chapter 15 Review of firm geography ········ 155
15.1 Development of industrial geography and firm geography ········ 155
15.2 Main characteristics of firm geography ········ 156
15.3 Areas of firm geography ········ 158
15.4 Firm geography in the Chinese situation ········ 161
References ········ 163
Chapter 16 A combination approach to regional industrial change study ········ 164
16.1 Research methods ········ 164
16.2 Structure change of Australian manufacturing industry ········ 165
16.3 Regional change of Australian manufacturing industry ········ 168
16.4 Conclusions and discussion ········ 171
References ········ 172
Chapter 17 Review on transnational corporations and regional economic development ········ 174
17.1 Theoretical background ········ 174
17.2 Relationship between transnational corporations and regional development ··· 178
17.3 Conclusions and discussion ········ 183
References ········ 183
Chapter 18 Transnational corporations and their impact on regional imbalance ······ 187
18.1 Analytical framework and research approach ········ 187
18.2 Regional analysis of FDI and economic development in China ········ 189
18.3 Cases of the invested TNCs in China ········ 199
18.4 Conclusions and discussion ········ 203
References ········ 204
Chapter 19 Transnational corporations and local embeddedness ········ 207
19.1 Research background ········ 207
19.2 Shanghai and company interviews ········ 209
19.3 Levelof management localization ········ 210
19.4 Levelof production localization ········ 211
19.5 Extent of local involvement in R & D ········ 213
19.6 Evidence from company cases ········ 214
19.7 Conclusions and discussion ········ 217
References ········ 218
Chapter 20 Bargaining with transnational corporations: the case of Shanghai ······ 220
20.1 Research background ········ 220

20.2 Determinations of the bargaining relationship ········ 221
20.3 Measurements of bargaining outcome ········ 222
20.4 Sources of Shanghai's bargaining power ········ 223
20.5 Rapid expansion of TNC's direct investment in Shanghai ········ 224
20.6 Bargaining analysis between Shanghai and TNCs ········ 227
20.7 Conclusion and discussion ········ 234
References ········ 236
Chapter 21 Spatial expansion of transnational corporations ········ 239
21.1 The laws of spatial expansion ········ 239
21.2 Empirical investigation of TNC's location change in China ········ 240
21.3 Further discussion ········ 243
References ········ 243
Chapter 22 Inter-firm linkage and regional impact of transnational corporations ········ 245
22.1 TNCs and inter-firm linkages ········ 246
22.2 Company selection and interviews ········ 246
22.3 Shanghai Volkswagen ········ 247
22.4 Shanghai Bell ········ 253
22.5 Conclusions and discussion ········ 256
References ········ 257
Chapter 23 Location choice in the rapid expansion of large labor-intensive firm ··· 260
23.1 Research background ········ 260
23.2 Literature reviews and research framework ········ 261
23.3 Foxconn Technology Group ········ 263
23.4 Location change in the spatial expansion in China ········ 264
23.5 Mechanism behind the spatial expansion ········ 266
23.6 Conclusions and discussion ········ 270
References ········ 270
Chapter 24 Hong Kong investment in China's mainland ········ 272
24.1 Literature review, research methods and data ········ 272
24.2 Statistical analysis on spatial change of Hong Kong investment in China's mainland ········ 273
24.3 Company studies on spatial change of Hong Kong investment in China's mainland ········ 275
24.4 Spatial behavior of Hong Kong invested companies ········ 276
24.5 Perception of Hong Kong companies for investment environment ········ 278
24.6 Conclusions and policy suggestions ········ 280
References ········ 281
Chapter 25 Economic impact of foreign direct investment on China's coastal area

…… 282
25.1 Literature review …… 282
25.2 Research approach and data …… 283
25.3 Regional distribution and transformation of FDI …… 284
25.4 Quantitative analysis of FDI on economic growth in coastal areas …… 286
25.5 Company case studies …… 287
25.6 Conclusions and discussion …… 290
References …… 291
Chapter 26 Spatial networks of large state-owned enterprises in reform-era China …… 293
26.1 Research background …… 293
26.2 Business networks and SOEs in China …… 294
26.3 Managerial networks …… 296
26.4 Suppliers' networks …… 297
26.5 Sales networks …… 300
26.6 Technology networks …… 302
26.7 Conclusions and discussion …… 303
References …… 304
Chapter 27 Competitive advantages of SME cluster in central China …… 307
27.1 Sources of competitive advantages for SME clusters in rural areas …… 307
27.2 Steel tape cluster of Nanzhuang village …… 309
27.3 Conclusions and discussion …… 318
References …… 318
Chapter 28 Industrial linkages and rural industrialization …… 319
28.1 theoretical discussion and enterprises interview …… 319
28.2 Types of industry linkages …… 320
28.3 Industrial linkage and industrial development in rural areas …… 322
28.4 Case studies …… 323
28.5 Regional model …… 324
28.6 Conclusions …… 326
References …… 326
Chapter 29 Review on financial geography …… 327
29.1 Major research areas of financial geography …… 327
29.2 Major theoretical issues of financial geography …… 331
29.3 Development of Chinese financial geography …… 333
References …… 335
Chapter 30 Spatial change of the banking systems in Henan, China …… 337
30.1 Theoretical frameworks …… 337

30. 2 Study area and data ········ 339
30. 3 Spatial change of banking systems in Henan ········ 340
30. 4 Quantitative analysis on the determination factors ········ 345
30. 5 Evidence from the interviews ········ 347
30. 6 Conclusions and discussion ········ 349
References ········ 350

Part IV Small-scale study of economic geography

Chapter 31 Scale in the economic geography research ········ 353
31. 1 Discussion on scale ········ 353
31. 2 Significance of scale in the economic geography research ········ 354
31. 3 Evolution of scale in teconomic geography ········ 357
31. 4 A micro-approach to economic geography research ········ 358
References ········ 359
Chapter 32 County-level economic disparities of China on the 1990s ········ 361
32. 1 Research background and data ········ 361
32. 2 Spatial pattern of economic development by county in 1998 ········ 362
32. 3 Spatial change of county economy in the 1990s ········ 365
32. 4 Types of county in economic development ········ 367
32. 5 Conclusions and discussion ········ 369
References ········ 370
Chapter 33 Change of spatial structure in economic development in Henan ········ 371
33. 1 Evolution process of spatial structure in economic development ········ 371
33. 2 Patterns of spatial agglomeration and its economic effect ········ 372
33. 3 Conclusions ········ 378
References ········ 378
Chapter 34 Geography and economic development in rural China: A township level study in Henan Province ········ 380
34. 1 General analysis on the factors of farmers' income ········ 380
34. 2 Data collection and processing ········ 382
34. 3 Spatial analysis on economic development in rural area ········ 382
34. 4 Variables and models ········ 384
34. 5 Analysis of model results ········ 385
34. 6 Conclusions and discussion ········ 388
References ········ 389
Chapter 35 Location of agricultural production around village in central China ········ 390
35. 1 Literature review and research problems ········ 390

35.2 Village selection and data surveys ······ 392
35.3 Location choice of villager's farming ······ 393
35.4 Factors related to farming location ······ 398
35.5 Conclusions and discussion ······ 399
References ······ 400
Chapter 36 Spatial analysis of specialized village in the undeveloped area ······ 402
36.1 Theoretical frameworks ······ 402
36.2 Mathematical analysis on specialized villages and their environment ··· 404
36.3 Data process ······ 406
36.4 Empirical analysis on specialized villages and their environment ······ 409
36.5 Simulation on specialized villages and their environment ······ 411
36.6 Conclusion and discussion ······ 413
References ······ 415
Chapter 37 Input-output analysis on farmland systems in the mountainous area ··· 416
37.1 Analytical model ······ 416
37.2 Study area and data collection ······ 417
37.3 Input and output analysis by farmland plots ······ 420
37.4 Conclusions and discussion ······ 424
References ······ 425
Chapter 38 Assessing regional sustainability: the case of land use/land cover change in the middle Yiluo River catchment ······ 426
38.1 Research methods ······ 426
38.2 Study area: middle Yiluo basin ······ 428
38.3 Data source and database ······ 429
38.4 Land use/cover change from 1996 to 1999 ······ 430
38.5 Analysis of the change ······ 432
38.6 Conclusions and discussion ······ 434
References ······ 435

Part V Regional studies

Chapter 39 Geographical research on social inequality in China ······ 439
39.1 Regional inequality ······ 439
39.2 Urban inequality ······ 440
39.3 Rural inequality ······ 441
39.4 Geographical research on special social problems ······ 442
39.5 Conclusions ······ 443
References ······ 443

Chapter 40 Economic Development and Social Welfare in central China ······ 444
40.1 Indicators and data ······ 444
40.2 Spatial differences in economic development and welfare ······ 446
40.3 Relationship between economic levels and welfare ······ 449
40.4 Conclusions and discussion ······ 451
References ······ 451
Chapter 41 Regional concern in the economic geography research ······ 453
41.1 Tradition in favor of "the rich" in economic geography ······ 454
41.2 Issues emerging from regional concern perspective ······ 456
41.3 Ideological transform in the regional concern research ······ 458
41.4 Conclusions ······ 459
References ······ 460
Chapter 42 Growth pole theory and application in regional development ······ 461
42.1 Growth pole theory and practices ······ 461
42.2 Methods of growth pole selection ······ 463
42.3 Empirical case of growth pole selection ······ 467
42.4 Conclusions and discussion ······ 469
References ······ 470
Chapter 43 Human-land relations and development in the areas upon Yellow River ······ 471
43.1 Origin and spread of the Yellow River civilization ······ 471
43.2 History of economic development and the Yellow River ······ 473
43.3 New development strategies for the areas upon Yellow River ······ 474
43.4 Conclusions and discussion ······ 476
References ······ 477
Chapter 44 Recent progress and development of rural geography ······ 479
44.1 Development trends of rural geography ······ 479
44.2 Definition change of rural areas ······ 480
44.3 New directions of rural geography research ······ 481
44.4 Thinking of Chinese rural geography ······ 484
References ······ 486
Chapter 45 New urbanization: what is the *New*? ······ 488
45.1 Difference from China's past urbanization ······ 488
45.2 Avoid suffering the "urban problems" of developed countries ······ 489
45.3 New proposal for the ideal model of urbanization in China ······ 490
Chapter 46 Coordination ideas in new urbanization ······ 492
46.1 Urban-rural integration ······ 493
46.2 Coherence among different aspects of urbanization ······ 493

46.3 Coordination between marketing mechanism and government promotion …… 494
46.4 Up-down and bottom-up combination …… 495
46.5 Conclusions and discussion …… 498
References …… 499
Chapter 47 Sizes of new villages and towns in planning new countryside …… 501
47.1 The value of constructing new villages and towns …… 502
47.2 Study area …… 502
47.3 Data process and methods …… 504
47.4 Scenarios of the new villages and towns with different sizes …… 504
47.5 Conclusions and discussion …… 507
References …… 508
Chapter 48 Changes in rural settlements between 1927 and 2015 …… 510
48.1 Literature review …… 510
48.2 Data processing in the study area …… 511
48.3 Size change in rural settlements …… 513
48.4 Evolution of spatial patterns and its mechanism …… 518
48.5 Conclusions and discussion …… 524
References …… 525

第一篇　经济地理学理论探索

第 1 章　西方经济地理学进展

20 世纪 80 年代以来，伴随着新技术革命的飞速发展、“新自由主义”思潮的全面兴起、资本主义市场经济的全球扩张、经济全球化的深入推进等资本主义社会经济所出现的系列新特征，西方经济地理学家相继对经济活动的空间组织与空间差异进行新的理论阐释。同时，由于经济理论的发展和不完全竞争模型分析的深入，一些主流经济学家也重新发现了“经济地理”的重要性，发表了一些重要成果。改革开放以来，我国经济地理学也在学习和借鉴西方经济地理学的基本理论和研究方法的基础上，结合转型时期经济和社会发展的新形势和新需要，在中国特色经济地理学理论建构方面取得了一定的成绩（吴传钧，1998；陆大道，2001）。但是，由于种种因素的影响，我国经济地理学在理论构建方面，还相对较为薄弱。本章拟在评述 20 世纪 80 年代以来，西方经济地理学新进展的基础上，对我国该学科的理论研究方向进行初步的探讨，以期促进中国特色的经济地理学理论体系的建立和相关研究工作的深入开展。

1.1　地理学家的“多维转向”

20 世纪 80 年代以来，西方经济地理学理论建构的一个显著特征，就是其理论视角的多元化，与此相应，一些学者用“复数”的“新经济地理学”（new economic geographies）取代过去作为“单数”的经济地理学（economic geography）（Barnes，2001；Yeung，2003）。该阶段的多元化可概括为“多维转向”，包括制度转向、文化转向、关系转向和尺度转向（苗长虹，2004）。

1.1.1　制度转向

在 20 世纪 50 年代以来西方经济地理学的发展中，“计量与理论”革命时期的经济地理学将其理论大厦建立在实证主义的基础上，其中心是空间科学与系统分析，这种地理学把经济主体的行为看做是理性的，并追求自身效用最大化，社会政治情景被忽视；而之后的激进地理学，则将其理论大厦建立在结构主义，特别是结构马克思主义的基础上，其中心是空间不平等发展理论，这种地理学将社会政治和文化结构看做完全是由经济过程所决定的，其对经济行为的影响要么被完全忽视，要么被置于被动和次要地位。也许，20 世纪 80 年代初，英国著名经济地理学家马西（Massey）所引领的“劳动地域分工”和“地方性”（locality）研究率先将资本主义空间不平等发展的现实同历史上所继承的社会政治与文化结构有机联系在一起（Massey，1984）。但制度主义或制度转向的经济地理学的真正发端，是一些学者对 70 年代末期以来在新技术革命和市场自由化体制推动下资本主义经济所出现的新时空变化，特别是区域经济复兴的研究。例如，皮埃尔（Piore）和赛布尔（Sable）对弹性专业化和新产业区的研究（Piore and Sable，

1984），加利福尼亚学派对新产业空间的研究（Scott，1988；Storper and Walker，1989），欧洲GREMI小组对创新环境的研究（Aydalot et al.，1988），库克（Cooke）等对区域创新系统和学习型区域的研究（Cooke et al.，1988；Morgan，1997）等。所有这些研究有一个共同的观点，就是如果不对经济活动赖以运行并受其改变的多种多样的社会制度给以应有的关注，就无法对资本主义经济景观的形成与演变进行充分的理解。这种“制度转向”大体有4方面的来源（Martin，2000）：①法国管制学派对“社会管制模式”的强调；②经济地理学对社会文化重要性日益增长的认识；③经济学、社会学、政治学等社会科学对“制度主义”的研究；④资本主义制度在过去20多年中所发生的实际巨变。实际上，对经济地理学制度转向影响最为深远的理论来源为经济社会学、制度经济学和演化经济学（苗长虹等，2002）。制度主义经济地理学的出现和发展是“制度主义”在西方社会科学中快速复兴的产物。它虽然继承了马克思主义政治经济学寻求资本主义积累的“内在逻辑”的传统，但在分析视角上，却以更加宽广的胸怀从多种政治经济学和新古典经济学的传统和最新发展中寻求思想源泉，它不仅致力于研究特定的制度及其在塑造和管制资本主义空间动态中的作用，而且逐步发展成为一种独特的思考空间经济及其演化的方法。2002年布伦纳（Brenner）等对“实际存在的新自由主义”及其空间动态的研究（Brenner and Theodore，2002），其理论视角就深深扎根于制度主义的理论方法中。

1.1.2 文化转向

在20世纪90年代中期以前，经济地理学、文化地理学、社会地理学等研究是可以明显加以区分的。但从90年代中期开始，伴随着经济地理学制度转向，一些经济地理学家和文化地理学家开始思考，经济生活在多大程度上是纯粹经济的？社会文化等非经济因素在经济生活中发挥什么作用？经济和非经济因素之间是如何相互关联的？二者之间有什么样的辩证法？对这些问题的思考和研究，引出了西方经济地理学远较制度转向意义更为宽广和深远的关于“文化转向”的讨论。倡导“文化转向”的经济地理学家认为，经济生活不仅是经济的，更是社会和文化的，经济过程也是一个社会文化过程（苗长虹和王兵，2003），“与其削弱经济，还不如通过将其置于其获得意义和方向的文化、社会和政治关系中而将其情景化”（Lee and Wills，1997）。因此，重视非经济因素，特别是文化因素在经济活动空间格局的形成和演变中的作用，着重从历史和文化的角度把握世界、国家和区域的时空变化，强调在社会文化与政治经济相互作用的动态过程中来认识一个具体区域的基本特征，真正把握区域发展的本质，更准确、全面地认识地方多样性和地理差异，进而希望用地方性文化来抗衡市场经济和全球化的负面影响（庞效民，2000），就成为西方经济地理学发展的一个重要方向。

在后现代社会，人们在关注生产与经济的同时，消费与文化也已成为西方社会科学研讨的核心（Featherstone，1991）。西方经济地理学“文化转向”的发生虽然源于多种因素，但最根本的是后现代主义思潮对西方经济地理学研究的侵入和经济地理学者的积极回应。由于文化概念内涵的包容性和多样性，后现代主义文化研究视角的多元性，决定了西方经济地理学的文化转向视角的多元性。

文化转向对西方经济地理学的影响是巨大而深远的，它促成了西方经济地理研究的创新和变革。在研究对象上，文化转向促使经济地理学重视对与区域发展密切相关的社会问题的研究，并关注空间结构与权力结构的关系，以及全球化与地方化的关系；在研究方法上，文化转向不再寻求决定性的因果规律，而是探索支持如果 A 成立则 B 成立的机制。同时，文化转向还对相关的区域研究和规划理论产生了重要影响（苗长虹和王兵，2003）。但另外，文化转向也使原本内涵明确的一些常用概念定义模糊化，同时也提出了许多内涵模糊的新概念，并严重削弱了经济地理学与政策实践的相关性，从而引致了一些学者的批评（Markusen，1999）。

1.1.3　关系转向

20 世纪 70 年代和 80 年代，伴随着公司地理研究的兴起和区域研究的深化，产业联系和区域联系成为经济地理学研究的一个核心内容，但这些研究大多局限于生产联系。与此同时，结构马克思主义虽然关注生产关系背后的社会关系和决定机制的研究，但由于其忽视经济行为者的能动作用，因而其对“关系”理论的建构具有明显的局限性。伴随着经济地理学的“制度转向”与“文化转向”，80 年代和 90 年代早期有关劳动空间分工、地方性和弹性专业化的争论，促使经济地理学研究不断从“生产的社会关系”向“空间与社会的关系”转变，从而使交织于多种地理尺度上的经济变化过程中的行为者的“社会-空间”关系日益成为理论分析和经验研究的焦点和核心。在此背景下，一些学者开始倡导经济地理学的“关系思考”（relational thinking）、“关系视角”或“关系经济地理学”（Amin，1998；Dicken and Malmberg，2001），杨伟聪认为，经济地理学这种“关系转向”的分析框架主要有 3 个方面（Yeung，2002）：①地方与区域发展中“关系资产”（relational assets）。涉及新产业空间、产业区、集群、学习型区域、全球城市中的马歇尔节点等热点领域。②社会行为者、企业和组织网络的关系根植性（relational embeddedness）。这种框架围绕着“网络”及其内部的权力关系这一核心，涉及全球-地方关系、组织空间的差别化生产、路径依赖、社会网络的关系杂合性与片段化（relational hybridity and fragmentation）、空间行动的多元逻辑与多重轨迹（multiple logics and trajectories）等研究领域。③关系的尺度（relational scales）。这种框架涉及长期困扰地理学研究的尺度地理问题，也涉及作为当前研究热点的全球化、城市与区域治理、地方劳动市场的社会管制等问题。

西方经济地理学的“关系转向”表明，“关系”、“网络”已经成为经济地理学理论建构的核心之一。由于行为者关系网络的多中心性和杂合性，“关系转向”为“后现代主义”经济地理学提供了理解资本主义新时空最为基本、最为通用的分析工具。它使经济地理学能够通过对各种行为者及其之间关系网络的分析，透视资本主义空间经济的建构过程、各种行为者（包括人类的和非人类的）在建构过程中的作用、网络机制的演化，以及空间经济的管制和治理模式。

1.1.4　尺度转向

尺度是地理学领域一个无法回避并具有本体性质的关键问题。美国国家研究院重新发现地理学委员会在其出版的《重新发现地理学》(*Rediscovering Geography Committee*, 1997)的报告中强调,"尺度间的相互依赖性"是地理学观察世界的独特的方法,是地理学对科学认识的重要贡献。在地理学观察世界的三个"透镜"(地方的综合、地方间的相互依存性和尺度间的相互依存性)中,对尺度的认识构成了地理认识论的基础,因为"谈论空间而不谈论尺度是不可能的"。但长期以来,作为空间科学的地理学一直用欧氏距离定义"空间尺度",并将"空间"看做是地理过程的平台;而早期一些结构马克思主义者,则将"空间"看做被动接纳社会经济活动的"容器"。直到21世纪初,一些政治经济地理学家在对经济地理学制度转向、文化转向和关系转向的争论中,才明确提出"尺度的地理学"(geographies of scales)和"尺度转向"问题(Brenner,2001)。这些学者从政治学、社会学、制度分析等学术思想中吸取营养,提出了"地理尺度是一种关系建构"、"社会关系是一种尺度建构"、"尺度重组"(rescaling)和尺度的"相对化"(relativization)等理论视角,并将尺度的社会政治建构看做是理解当代资本主义的全球化及其地域结果、城市与区域的管制和治理的关键。这些学者强调尺度的过程、演化、动态和社会政治竞争等性质,认为地理尺度是社会建构的,它本身也是参与社会建构的基本力量,地理尺度的重组过程和一定的尺度构造是激烈的社会政治斗争的产物,"空间"不仅是不变的、有界的、自我封闭的、事先给定的社会经济活动的"容器",更是社会空间实践的竞技场(arena)、脚手架(scaffolding)和层级组织(hierarchy)。因此,西方经济地理学的"尺度转向",实质上是一场关于"尺度"的"本体论"革命,它使经济地理学从关于尺度的"空间科学"而转向尺度的政治学(politics of scale)。进而,有关尺度的层级、关系、过程和动力的研究,便构成了当代西方经济地理学和整个人文地理学的核心论题之一。

1.2 经济学家的"新经济地理学"

与地理学研究方法的多元性相比,主流经济学则一直以其简洁、有力的理论预设及一贯的、几乎被所有经济学家公认的首尾逻辑一致的分析方法著称。由于地理学的区域性和综合性,其自身严谨规范的理论建构向来较为薄弱,因而在地理学特别是经济地理学的发展中,往往从其他社会科学,特别是经济学,"借用"有关的理论和方法。但20世纪90年代以来,西方一些主流经济学家对"经济地理"重要性的重新发现,使主流经济学长期忽视"空间"的研究取向得到明显改变,空间经济学和区域科学在经历了一段沉寂之后,出现了新的复兴。虽然与上述地理学研究的"多维转向"相比,这种趋向在研究方法上存在着本质上的差别和激烈的争论(Martin and Sunley,1996;顾朝林等,2002),但其所关注的主要社会经济问题,或者说其研究对象,大体是相同的,其核心就是解释地理空间中的经济集聚与区域增长。

1.2.1 地理经济学的新发展

虽然以克鲁格曼(Krugman)为代表的主流经济学家将其对"经济地理"的研究称作"新经济地理学"(Krugman,1991,1998),但是,一方面,20世纪80年代以来西方地理学研究的“多维转向”本身已经成功孕育了地理学意义上的“新经济地理学”；另一方面，一些主流经济学的工作乃是艾萨德（W. Isard）的“区域科学”传统的继续，其核心是“地理的经济学”（economics of geography）而非“经济问题的地理学”（geography of economics）。因此，主流经济学家所谓的“新经济地理学”并非真正地理学意义上的“新经济地理学”，而是“新地理经济学”或“新空间经济学”。

我们知道，艾萨德区域科学基于德国的“区位论”和新古典经济学的“均衡经济学”，力图回答：空间为什么对经济行为重要？空间如何对经济行为重要？为回答这两个基本问题，区域科学围绕着经济活动的空间集聚、运输成本的作用和区域经济的动态三个论题展开研究。但是，传统区域科学对这些论题的研究面临着许多困难，如新古典经济学的一般均衡是建立在完全竞争的基础上，而经济活动的空间集聚所导致的收益递增和不完全市场结构与完全竞争的一般均衡是不兼容的；对于运输成本，一方面，其重要性在迅速下降；另一方面，传统新古典经济学并没有看到其与其他类型成本的重要差别；对于区域经济动态，虽然也建构了投入产出、产业综合体、社会核算矩阵等一些分析模型，但这些模型既缺乏微观经济基础，同时也不能真正对区域经济动态提供科学的解释，并且与国家干预主义经济理论与政策的紧密联结，也同20世纪80年代以来流行于西方国家的“新自由主义”理论思潮背道而驰。与传统区域科学相比，90年代以来，以克鲁格曼为代表的“新经济地理学”一方面仍遵循新古典经济学“理性选择与实证方法”的方法论传统，并将其理论建立在牢固的微观经济决策的基础上；但另一方面却充分吸收了20世纪70年代以来主流经济学在收益递增与外部经济、内生增长理论、新贸易理论等诸多方面的理论成果，以一个多部门或多区域的世界为基本出发点，以收益递增与外部经济为核心，以一个空间经济系统的一般均衡模拟为平台，将Dixit-Stigliz的垄断竞争一般均衡模型、萨缪尔森（P. A. Samuelson）有关运输成本的“冰山”理论，以及强调历史与偶然性作用的演化观念有机结合，通过核心-边缘模型、演化城市系统模型和产业集中与贸易模型的建造，来构建和逐步拓展其内生的空间集聚与分散理论（如区域核心-边缘结构的形成、城市的发生与成长、产业的联系与集聚、交易成本与集聚、溢出与集聚、增长与集聚等），提出了一个新的、规范的分析框架（苗长虹和崔利华，2003），并得出了与地理学多维转向研究非常相似但更为精细的研究结论，这就是城市与区域经济的增长源于在性质上是地方化的某些因素，如地方的外部性与收益递增、不完全竞争、历史和偶然事件、路径依赖等（Fujita and Krugman，2004）。经济学家的“新经济地理学”的主要贡献，乃在于其建构的清晰、严谨、精致的模型打破了传统国际贸易理论中生产要素不能流动而商品贸易又无成本的不实际假设，使经济集聚与区域增长在一定程度上成为了主流经济学关注的中心，并从微观经济机制上解释了经济集聚与分散的向心力与离散力，在经济地理模型建造、经济集聚与区域增长机理分析，以及与之相关的政策实践等方面，均取得了令人瞩目的进展（李小建，2002）。

1.2.2　地理经济学与经济地理学

主流经济学有关地理经济学的研究及其对“新经济地理学”名称的占用，对倡导多维转向的地理学家产生了极大的刺激。在西方地理学界，虽然也有越来越多的学者倡导二者之间的相互学习和交流（李小建，2002；Clark et al.，2000），并为此出版了由地理学家和经济学家共同编写的《牛津经济地理学手册》和创办了供经济地理学家和地理经济学家相互交流的刊物《经济地理学杂志》，但地理学和经济学的学科传统和研究方法存在着根本性的差别。一些倡导经济地理“多维转向”的学者认为，地理经济学应用不完全竞争、收益递增和多重均衡的模型分析方法，只不过是区位理论和区域科学的重新数学化的版本而已（Martin，1999）；地理经济学用同一个模型来解释现实中决定因素差别很大的、空间尺度不同的集聚现象，是不适合解决地理问题的（Olsen，2002）；更有学者认为，由于经济学势力强大，经济地理学应远离地理经济学，应从对新古典经济学进行批判的各种异端的、社会的、文化的“经济知识”中汲取营养（Amin and Thrift，2000）。当然，也有一些学者认识到，当前西方经济地理学的制度转向、文化转向、关系转向和尺度转向还是很肤浅的，除了研究论题和认识论、本体论方面的转向外，其方法论和理论建构上还存在许多问题，许多概念和理论建构缺乏严谨性，其与正统经济学疏离而与非正统经济研究亲和的走向，以及在政策实践上的软弱性急需深刻的反思，有的学者甚至提出“过分的文化转向会杀死经济地理学”（Rodriguez-Pose，2001）。我们认为，来自地理学和经济学的两种经济地理学新近进展，均有可取之处，但同时也有一定的限制。分析这些新进展对我国经济地理学的发展启迪，并结合中国国情，提出中国特色的经济地理学发展思路，具有重要意义。

1.3　西方经济地理学新进展的启示

西方发达国家的经济地理学新进展在国际学术界具有较大影响。一方面，我们应当承认，这些进展推动着经济地理学的发展，进展中的许多理论观点和观点背后的思维创新，对其他国家的地理学家具有重要启迪。另一方面，我们也应该清醒地认识到，不能盲目跟着主流观点走，发展中国家经济地理学家对待西方学者的研究更应如此。这主要是因为，发展中国家与发达国家处于不同的发展阶段，其研究对象及研究中的重要问题均会有所不同。此外，一些发展中国家支配社会科学研究的哲学方法与西方发达国家不同，也不宜完全照搬西方经济地理学研究模式（李小建，2004）。根据以上对西方学术进展的分析，针对中国经济地理学的发展背景特点，本章着重从以下 3 方面论及中国特色的经济地理学构建。

1.3.1　科学借鉴西方理论

在西方经济地理学的近期进展中，可以对中国经济地理学发展以启迪之处很多。从理论和方法论角度，以下 4 点更为重要。

1. 科学分析与提炼理论问题

西方学者在经济地理学研究中，十分注重对与研究课题相关的理论进行科学分析，从中提炼科学问题，作为研究的切入点。其中，尤为重要的是，他们具有挑战权威理论的勇气，以不断地否定之否定，促进学科的健康发展。其次，他们在研究中不断磨炼对问题的敏锐（sharp）观察力。考虑问题不一定面面俱到，但一定要以尖锐的目光发现问题，提出解决问题的独特切入点。

2. 注重引入相关学科理论

近 20 年来西方经济地理学的理论进展，与整个社会科学和哲学的发展大背景具有十分密切的关联。来自地理学研究中的文化、制度和关系转向，均是借助了人文社会科学中其他相关学科的研究观点，如经济学家和管理学家在此之前已关注文化、制度和关系等因素。“新经济地理学”中的不完全竞争、收益递增和多重均衡等模型分析，也得益于诸多经济学家的贡献。

3. 合理使用模型与计量方法

近期西方主流经济地理学研究似乎变得更加侧重定性分析问题，认为这样更易于解释经济地理现象的发生原因（Barnes，2001）。但西方主流经济学家的研究仍强调精细的模型分析。我们认为，在中国特色的经济地理学构建中，在注重定性和定量两者相结合的同时，应该考虑中国经济地理学的地理学科性质，更加强调在合适的场合使用科学方法和计量方法。复杂的地理事物难以概括出定律、公理，但通过模型的重建，可以凝练出相对共性的观点（白光润，1995），促进地理理论的不断完善。

4. 加强微观视角研究和政治经济分析

西方经济地理学研究中，长期侧重微观视角和政治经济分析。正是从厂商角度的分析，带来了区位论和公司地理学的建立，从而促进经济地理学的科学化和理论化；也正是由于重视政治经济分析，带来了结构主义地理学的产生及近年来的多维转向。中国经济地理学半个多世纪来的研究，总体上表现为重宏观轻微观，重整体轻分解，重形态轻机制。尽管在经济地理学的研究中，各种视角的研究均很重要，但就目前中国经济地理学的研究来说，微观视角的研究和政治经济分析更应得到加强。20 世纪生物学通过微观化而取得巨大进展，也许可给地理学以启发。

1.3.2　突出中国国情特点

与经济地理学发展相关，这些特点主要包括以下 3 点。

1. 重视中国经济地理学的发展背景

中国经济地理学发展中有一些独特的背景。例如，中国为世界上最大的发展中国家，人均收入处于较低水平。但近 20 余年来，经济增长十分迅速，成为世界经济奇迹，在增长中区域差异十分显著。此外，中国的人口与资源环境的关系在世界各国中具有独特性。一方面，中国是人口大国，人均资源处于较低水平；另一方面，资源区域分布很不均衡，造成区域性人口与资源环境矛盾十分突出。近期中国政府提出的科学发展观和统筹城乡发展、统筹区域发展、统筹人与自然和谐发展等“五个”统筹思想，以及实行新型工业化的发展思路，在发展中国家具有一定的独特性。

2. 科学看待已有研究特点

与中国国情背景相关联，中国经济地理学逐渐形成了一些特点。例如，①侧重于与促进经济发展相关的诸多应用课题的研究：如流域规划、资源调查、土地利用、区域规划、地区工业布局、旅游规划、开发区战略等，与欧美发达国家侧重于对发展中所出现的问题的研究形成对比。②研究侧重宏观尺度和宏观视野：半个多世纪以来，中国经济地理学以政府关注的问题为导向，以政府委托课题为支撑，在全国或大区域层面作了诸多有影响的工作，这也与西方国家侧重于微观（企业）尺度的研究形成对比。③研究模式深受自然地理学影响：在中国，地理学被定位于自然科学，地理学中自然地理学又占据主导地位，经济地理学家多数受到良好的自然地理训练；与此相关联，在科研项目、论文、成果等学术研究的认定中，经济地理学的自然科学倾向也很明显。而欧美经济地理学研究的人文社会科学特征突出，近年盛行的新经济地理学更侧重于向经济学和社会学延伸。中国经济地理学研究的以上特点，作为构建中国特色经济地理学的重要背景，应该予以足够的重视。

3. 发掘特殊的思维方式

儒家思想在中国科学研究中仍潜移默化地产生着影响（潘家铮，2002）。例如，儒家思想强调社会和谐，主张全面辩证地分析问题。天人合一观念是中华传统文化的理论核心。由此演变而来的人与自然和谐的观点，必然影响以人地关系为研究对象的地理学研究。受此影响，学者们在研究中会强调综合性和各种观点的共处。在地理学研究中，一元地理观易于被接受。这对经济地理学发展有一定的积极意义。但是，儒家反对竞争、冒险思想不利于学术创新，所以对中国传统思维方式的合理扬弃，是有益于经济地理学研究的一项工作。

1.3.3 抓住重点研究问题

在特殊的背景下，中国经济地理学中存在许多独特的研究问题。科学借鉴西方理论和继承中国传统，集中研究这些特色突出的研究主题，十分有利于中国经济地理学的创新。以下选其要者，介绍 4 个重点问题。

1. 经济发展空间格局的理论研究

经济活动的空间格局差异，是经济地理学的重要研究内容。迄今为止，经济地理学中的重要理论建树，也主要是来自这些方面的研究。由于中国发展历史悠久，但各地经济发展地理背景具有巨大差异；20 余年来，虽然经济体制逐步由计划经济向市场经济转型，但政治体制对经济发展仍有重大影响；全国平均经济增长十分迅速，但各地差异又十分明显；所有这些共同作用，带来了特殊的经济发展空间格局。基于中国实例的该方面理论研究，曾经取得了创造性的成果（陆大道，2001），进一步的研究，还有许多问题有待澄清。例如，区域经济协调发展问题、快速增长区的演进问题、经济增长中区域之间的关联与层次划分问题、区域中的多极增长现象等。对这些问题的深入研究不仅对我国区域政策制定具重要参考意义，而且也会对国际上相关理论构建有重要贡献。

2. 区域文化与经济关系研究

与国际学术界的“文化转向”和“制度转向”相对应，中国各地的多元文化与其经济发展的关系，为相关研究提供了一个很有特点的对象。以目前国际学术界十分热衷的产业集群研究为例，欧美国家学者成果很多，但这些成果之外，中国特殊政治文化背景下产业集群形成机制具有很多特殊性。例如，基于家庭、亲缘等的信任关系在农区中小企业集群中起重要作用，模仿创新在传统产业集群中扮演着重要角色，政治制度改革带来农村工业经历由“村村点火，处处冒烟”到集群的演变等，这些相关研究，均有望取得新的理论突破。

3. 城市与区域发展的关系研究

根据世界上一些国家的工业化进程，学者们总结出了城市化与工业化的一般规律。但由于各国国情不同，也会出现不同的发展道路。中国作为发展中大国，工业化进程开始较晚，但近20余年来发展十分迅速。伴随着农村经济改革及农村工业蓬勃发展，出现了城市化滞后于工业化的现象。与这种现象相关联，中国城市与区域发展的关系中有许多理论问题值得研究，如：①城市化与工业化的关系一般规律的悖论问题。可以通过对中国城市化和工业化进程与国际上一般规律不一致原因的探索，分析其存在的客观性，并在此基础上，对国际相关理论提出反思。②城市与区域发展的互动分析。在承认社会经济发展带动城市化、城市化又反过来促进社会经济发展的同时，要客观分析城市化的代价或城市化的弊端。这种辩证的观点，对中国这一正在快速城市化的发展中大国，具有重要意义。③适宜城市化模式研究。城市化进程并非越快越好，城市并非越大越好，城市化水平也并非一概越高越好；城市化进程和城市规模要与区域的社会经济发展水平相适应。④城市化中的空间进程与社会进程关系研究。城市化不仅是人口、生产方式和生活方式的转变过程，也表现为空间上的人文景观形态变化。同样的城市化进程，可以通过不同的空间进程表现出来。科学地研究两者关系，对全面协调的城市化十分重要。

4. 区域人口、资源、环境与经济协调发展研究

中国作为世界上第一人口大国，尽管资源总量丰富，但人均资源量却很低，尤其是中国的人口集中地区与资源富集地区在空间上不一致，再加上20余年经济的高速增长带给环境巨大压力，致使中国的人口、资源、环境与经济发展之间的矛盾十分突出。资源、生态环境在很大程度上制约着经济和社会的发展。如何实现区域经济的可持续发展，有一系列理论问题亟待研究。例如：①人口、资源、环境与经济协调发展研究中指标体系选定问题。如何科学地选择相关指标、如何确定这些指标的权重并没有相对公认的意见。②区域发展质量的科学认定。包括区域经济增长与社会发展的关系度量问题，绿色GDP的量化计算问题等。尽管资源环境定价涉及多个学科，但经济地理学家在其中的贡献不可缺少。③微观尺度的可持续发展问题。资源环境问题，可以在细微尺度上

（如每一个点位上）表现出差异；资源环境的变化也必须从细微尺度上才能确切度量。所以在研究中应该借用地理信息和遥感方法，探讨运用大比例尺地图和高分辨率遥感影像进行精细分析的理论和实现途径。④区域生态型经济和循环经济系统的建立问题。包括用生态学的思想构建经济结构，构建企业之间的关系和“生态工业园”，以及工业生产中的“绿色制造”和农业生产中的“绿色农业”等问题，可以通过对这些问题的单项研究，逐步构建生态型区域发展系统。

参考文献

白光润. 1995. 地理学的哲学贫困. 地理学报，50（3）：279～287

顾朝林，王恩儒，石爱华. 2002.“新经济地理学”与经济地理学的分异与对立. 地理学报，57（4）：497～504

李小建. 2002. 经济地理学近期研究的一个新方向分析. 经济地理，22（2）：129～133

李小建. 2004. 国际背景与中国特色的经济地理学. 人文地理，19（1）：27～31

陆大道. 2001. 论区域的最佳结构与最佳发展——提出“点-轴系统”和“T”型结构以来的回顾与再分析. 地理学报，56（2）：127～135

苗长虹，崔利华. 2003. 产业集聚：地理学与经济学主流观点的对比. 人文地理，18（3）：42～46

苗长虹，樊杰，张文忠. 2002. 西方经济地理学区域研究的新视角. 经济地理，22（6）：644～650

苗长虹，王兵. 2003. 文化转向：经济地理学研究的一个新方向. 经济地理，23（5）：577～581

苗长虹. 2004. 变革中的西方经济地理学：制度、文化、关系与尺度转向. 人文地理，19（4）：68～75

潘家铮. 2002. 正视儒家思想对科技发展的负作用. 光明日报. 5～17，B1（科技周刊）

庞效民. 2000. 90年代西方经济地理学的文化研究趋向评述. 经济地理，20（3）：5～8

吴传钧. 1998. 人地关系与经济布局. 北京：学苑出版社

Amin A，Thrift N. 2000. What kind of economic theory for what kind of economic geography? Antipode，32（1）：4～9

Amin A. 1998. Globalization and regional development：A relational perspective. Competition and Change，1（3）：145～165

Aydalot P，Keeble D，et al. 1988. High technology industry and innovative environments：The European experience. London：Routledge

Barnes T J. 2001. Retheorizing economic geography：From the quantitative revolution to the “culture turn”. Annals of the Association of American Geographers，71（3）：546～565

Brenner N，Theodore N. 2002. Cities and the geographies of “actually existing neoliberalism”. Antipode，34（3）：349～379

Brenner N. 2001. The limits to scale? Methodological reflections on scalar structuration. Progress of Human Geography，25（4）：591～614

Clark G L，Feldman M P，Gertler M S，et al. 2000. The Oxford Handbook of Economic Geography. Oxford：Oxford University Press

Cooke P，Uranga M G，Etxebarria G. 1998. Regional systems of innovation：An evolutionary perspective. Environment and Planning A，(30)：1563～1584

Dicken P，Malmberg A. 2001. Firms in territories：A relational perspective. Economic Geography，77（4）：345～363

Featherstone M. 1991. Consumer culture and postmodernism. London：Sage Publications

Fujita M, Krugman P, Venables A J. 1999. The Spatial Economy: Cities, Regions, and International Trade. Cambridge: MIT Press

Fujita M, Krugman P. 2004. The new economic geography: Past, present and the future. Papers of Regional Science, 83: 139～164

Krugman P. 1991. Geography and Trade. Cambridge: The MIT Press

Krugman P. 1998. What's new about the new economic geography? Oxford Review of Economic Policy, 14 (2): 7～17

Lee R, Wills J. 1997. Geographies of Economies. London: Arnold

Markusen A. 1999. Fuzzy concepts, scanty evidence, policy distance: The case for rigour and policy relevance in critical regional studies. Regional Studies, (33): 869～884

Martin R L. 1999. The 'new economic geography': Challenge or irrelevance? Transactions of the Institute of British Geographer, 24 (4): 387～391

Martin R L. 2000. Institutional approaches in economic geography. In: Sheppard E, Barnes T J. A companion to economic geography. Oxford: Blackwell, 77～94

Martin R, Sunley P. 1996. Paul Krugman's geographical economics and its implications for regional development theory: A critical assessment. Economic Geography, 72 (3): 259～292

Massey D. 1984. Spatial Divisions of Labour. London: Macmillan

Morgan K. 1997. The learning region: Institutions, innovation and regional renewal. Regional Studies, 31 (5): 491～503

Olsen J. 2002. On the units of geographical economics. Geoforum, 33 (2): 153～164

Piore M, Sable C. 1984. The second industrial divide. New York: Basic Brooks

Rediscovering Geography Committee. 1997. Rediscovering Geography. Washington: National Academy Press

Rodriguez-Pose A. 2001. Killing economic geography with a "cultural turn" overdose. Antipode, 33 (2): 176～182

Scott A J. 1988. New Industrial Spaces: Flexible Production Organization and Regional Development in North American and Western Europe. London: Pion

Storper M, Walker R. 1989. The Capitalist Imperative: Territory, Technology and Industrial Growth. Oxford: Blackwell

Yeung H W C. 2002. Towards a relational economic geography: Old wine in new bottles? Paper presented at the 98th Annual Meeting of the Association of American Geographers, Los Angeles

Yeung H W C. 2003. Practicing new economic geographies: A methodological examination. Annual of the Association of American Geographers, 92 (2): 442～462

第 2 章　诺贝尔经济学奖中的区域经济思想

自 1969 年第一届诺贝尔经济学奖颁发以来，截至 2014 年，已有 74 人获得该奖项，其中不少获奖者的学术观点涉及区域经济学。例如，1971 年的获奖者库兹涅茨（S. Kuznets）关于经济增长与收入分布的观点，1974 年的获奖者缪尔达尔（G. Myrdal）关于区域发展循环积累因果效应的观点，1979 年刘易斯（W. A. Lewis）的发展经济学中关于后发地区的发展思想等。尤其是 2008 年的克鲁格曼（P. Krugman）因其对贸易模式和经济活动区位的研究而获得诺贝尔经济学奖。虽然诺贝尔经济学奖获得者的区域经济学思想涉及区域差异与贸易、区域经济发展、区域竞争与合作等各个领域，但这些思想之间具有一定的关联。总的来看，诺贝尔奖得主的学术观点反映出经济学研究逐渐关注区域（空间）问题，区域经济研究逐渐转向宏微观兼顾，研究方法更加精细化。受诺贝尔经济学获奖者区域经济学思想的启发，中国经济现象研究应更加关注空间因素，注重对具有中国特色的事物及现象的研究，使区域经济研究向规范和精细化方向发展，同时关注制度创新研究，培育中国特色的经济地理学。

2.1　诺贝尔经济学获奖者的区域经济学观点

对历届诺贝尔经济学奖获得者的学术思想进行系统分析，发现涉及区域经济学方面的内容和观点主要集中在区域差异与贸易、区域经济发展和社会发展、区域竞争与合作等的分析和解释上。具体来讲，有 30 余位获奖者的学术思想涉及这些内容。

2.1.1　区域差异与贸易

截至 2014 年，有四位诺贝尔经济学奖获得者的研究涉及区际贸易和区域差异（表 2.1）。这些学者的思想已经成为区域经济或经济地理学科内容体系的一部分（孙久文和叶裕民，2010；李小建，2010；安虎森等，2008；魏后凯，2006），并成为相关领域学者研究的基础和进一步验证、挖掘的参照。

表 2.1　涉及区域经济思想的诺贝尔经济学奖获得者及其主要思想领域

区域经济思想涉及领域	获奖者（获奖年份）
区域差异与贸易	库兹涅茨（1971）、缪尔达尔（1974）、俄林（1977）、克鲁格曼（2008）
区域经济发展	刘易斯（1979）、舒尔茨（1979）、索洛（1987）、卢卡斯（1995）
区域竞争与合作	科斯（1991）、诺斯（1993）、纳什（1994）、海萨尼（1994）、泽尔腾（1994）、谢林（2005）、奥曼（2005）

俄裔美籍经济学家库兹涅茨于 1955 年在“*Economic Growth and Income Inequality*”（Kuznets，1955）一文中提出的“倒 U 型曲线”假说对区域经济差异理论有重要启迪。库氏通过分析经济增长早期阶段的普鲁士（1854～1857 年），经济发展后期阶段的美国、英国和德国萨克森地区（1880～1950 年）人均收入差距的统计数据，总结并提出了收入不均与经济发展水平之间关系的演化规律，即“倒 U 型曲线”假说。该假说认为，在经济发展的早期阶段，人们之间的收入差距处于较低水平，随着经济不断增长，收入差距逐渐扩大并趋于稳定，当经济进一步增长时，收入差距又逐渐缩小。库氏的研究并非基于某一地区的时序数据，而是不同发展阶段的多个地区数据，但已经暗含了收入的区域差异思想。美国经济学家威廉姆森则进一步发展了这一思想，他将时序问题引入区域空间结构变动分析，提出了解释区域经济差异的倒“U”理论，并提出均衡与增长之间的替代关系依时间的推移而呈非线性变化的。

1974 年诺贝尔经济学奖得主缪尔达尔的“循环累积因果理论”是区域经济学中解释区域差异及趋同的最重要理论之一。缪氏认为，在初始偶然性因素的作用下，由于循环因果和累积效应，市场力量促进资本、劳动力、技术等要素由外围向中心的流动，即“回流效应”（backwash effects）。“回流效应”倾向于使得富裕区域更加富裕，贫穷区域更加贫穷，造成中心与外围地区的差距扩大。到一定阶段后，该效应转化为“扩散效应”（spread effects）。“扩散效应”表现为上述要素由中心向外围流动，在外围区产生一系列的循环累积增长，从而使得外围区摆脱贫穷，并逐渐趋于繁荣。据此，缪氏提出一个区域发展的大概过程，即初始时期区域之间分异加大，伴随着经济的增长将产生趋同（Myrdal，1957），这一观点已被大多数发展经济学家所接受。

由于区域差异和区域之间的非同质性，产生了区际贸易。瑞典经济学家俄林和美国经济学家克鲁格曼在区际贸易领域的贡献使他们分别于 1977 年和 2008 年获得了诺贝尔经济学奖。受其老师赫克歇尔关于生产要素比例的国际贸易理论的影响，俄林提出了要素禀赋学说，即著名的赫克歇尔-俄林理论（简称 H-O 定理），认为区域之间或国家之间生产要素的禀赋差异是它们之间出现分工和贸易的主要原因（李小建等，2000）。这一学说表明了区域之间贸易分工的形式，指出了生产要素对区域分工及贸易交换的影响，为区域利用贸易交换发挥自身优势、合理利用资源、促进经济发展提供了理论指导。

“新贸易理论”是克鲁格曼的主要思想之一。克氏认为，经济活动的空间分布并不遵从主流经济学所假设的规模报酬不变和完全竞争。他在规模报酬递增和不完全竞争的前提下，借用迪克西特-斯蒂格利茨模型（D-S 模型），第一次系统地将产业组织理论和市场结构理论应用到国际贸易问题研究中，分析国际贸易的起因和利益来源，揭示了传统贸易理论无法解释的诸如技术创新、产业内贸易等新的贸易现象。同时，克氏将研究从国际层面延伸到国内区域产业集聚层面（李小建和李二玲，2009），通过规模报酬递增、冰山成本和历史偶然及预期等研究工具，解释了特定产业在某一区域而非其他区域集聚的现象，为区域经济中有关产业集聚的研究提供了新的分析思路。

2.1.2 区域经济发展

将主流经济学的经济增长理论应用到区域经济发展中来，是应用性较强的区域经济学科历来较为重视的研究范式。细数下来，诺贝尔经济学奖已颁发给多位对经济增长理论有所贡献的经济学家，其中，刘易斯、舒尔茨、索洛、卢卡斯的经济增长理论均蕴含着一些区域经济发展思想。

刘易斯和舒尔茨于1979年同时获得了诺贝尔经济学奖，两位学者的思想和观点均对区域经济学开拓新的研究领域具有重要影响。刘易斯的劳动力迁移理论重在解释城乡二元结构下，大量农村劳动力向城市迁移，人口由农业部门向二、三产业等非农业部门集中，城市人口不断增加这一宏观经济现象。刘易斯将发展中国家的经济划分为城市现代工业部门和农村传统农业部门。在传统农业部门，存在大量低收入、可无限供给的劳动力；而工业部门只需支付稍高于传统农业维持生存相应的工资便可获取无限的劳动力供给。城市工业部门与农村农业部门收入的差异，劳动力转移的无障碍，以及资本积累的欲望诱发剩余劳动力源源不断地从农村流向城市，直到农村剩余劳动力被城市完全吸收，农村工资和城市工资趋向一致为止（刘易斯，1989）。二元经济模型的提出，为人口乡城迁移和城市化研究提供了重要理论基础。

舒尔茨对发展中国家的经济发展做出了开创性的研究。舒尔茨认为，农业也可以成为发展中国家促进经济增长的源泉，多数国家需要对传统农业进行改造，并进一步提出了三条可供考虑的途径。一是要建立一套适于农业改造的制度；二是要从供给和需求两方面为引进现代生产要素创造条件；三是对农民进行人力资本投资。其中，舒尔茨强调了人力资本的作用，认为教育和人力资本投资对一国或地区经济发展具有重要作用。经济发展主要取决于人的质量的提高，而不是自然资源的丰瘠或资本的多寡（舒尔茨，1990）。他强调穷国要想改造传统农业，必须向农民投资，对农民进行农业技术培训、提供教育资源等（舒尔茨，2006）。

1987年诺贝尔奖得主索洛（R. M. Solow）重新审视了经济增长的动力来源，由传统强调资源、资本、劳动力等要素转向技术进步，强调知识和创新的重要性，认为知识将取代物质资本成为最重要的生产要素。索洛的研究为区域经济增长理论范式的转变提供了基础，使区域创新能力和技术进步纳入到区域发展分析框架中来。1995年诺贝尔奖获得者卢卡斯（R. Lucas）将人力资本引入索洛增长模型中，说明了经济长期增长的动力来源。卢卡斯借鉴了舒尔茨等对人力资本研究的成果，将人力资本纳入经济增长模型中，强调人力资本因素对经济增长的作用，认为人力资本积累是经济得以持续增长的决定性因素和产业发展的真正源泉。

2.1.3 区域竞争与合作

诺贝尔经济学奖中关于博弈论的研究为区域竞争与合作的分析提供了新的视角。1994年诺贝尔经济学奖得主纳什、海萨尼、泽尔腾在非合作博弈方面的贡献进一步增强了博弈论的适用范围和预测能力。其中，纳什均衡具有重要意义。所谓纳什均衡，是指给定其他人的选择，每个参与者都作出了最优的选择，从而使自己的利益最大化。在纳什均衡中，由于每一个参与者都选择针对其他参与者策略的最佳策略，因而每一个参与人都没有改变其最初策略的激励，因而纳什均衡是稳定的。纳什均衡揭示了博弈均衡与经济均衡的内在联系，为区域合作、区域贸易、污染治理等区域经济领域的研究奠定了基础。

2005 年度诺贝尔经济学奖获得者谢林和奥曼进一步发展了博弈理论，他们试图解释冲突与合作的最根本动因，进行一般性的理论概括。通过对人类社会交互作用的深入分析，奥曼建立了重复博弈理论体系，研究多次合作关系中个体之间的决策选择。谢林将博弈论研究从数学语言和公理性手段拓展到诸如传统的沿袭、声誉创造、建立自信、显示大度等非数学因素的分析上，使博弈论的研究更接近于现实状况。目前，已有研究将博弈论及纳什均衡应用到区域分析中来，分析区域合作及地方政府在区域竞争与合作中的作用（马丽和庞效民，2001；梁艺桦和杨新军，2005；Grilo et al.，2011；Li，2011），对于地区协调发展具有显著的现实意义。

除博弈论之外，新制度经济学派代表人物科斯和道格拉斯·诺斯的思想也对区域竞争与合作的研究产生了一定影响。科斯揭示了经济制度结构中交易费用和产权的重要性，从而为区域之间资源竞争、责任与义务的界定和推诿的研究提供了新视角。斯蒂格勒（G. J. Stigler）将科斯有关产权与交易费用的研究总结为科斯定理，即“只要产权是明确的，并且交易成本为零，那么，无论在开始时将产权赋予谁，市场均衡的最终结果都是有效率的，都将实现资源配置的帕雷托最优”（斯蒂格勒，1992）。据此，从区域竞争与合作的角度来讲，只要对资源的使用权、对流域污染权在区域之间界定清晰，那么，区域政府之间就可以通过讨价还价进行权力的再分配。但是，现实情况是，产权的清晰界定是需要成本的，或者说并无统一的价值观去认定清晰的产权归属，这也往往成为区域之间博弈的基础。

诺斯（D. C. North）恰当地吸收了科斯、斯蒂格勒等的研究成果，发展出一套包括所有权理论、国家理论和意识形态理论在内的“制度变迁理论”，从而为构建区域竞争和合作过程中的有效组织和制度环境提供了重要启迪。诺斯认为：“制度是一系列被制定出来的规则、守法程序和行为的道德伦理规范，它旨在约束追求主体福利或效用最大化利益的个人行为”（诺思，1999）。据此，可以将诺斯的“制度”定义为“博弈规则”。按戴维斯和诺斯（1996）的理解，制度环境“是一系列用来建立生产、交换与分配基础的政治、社会和法律基础规则”。制度概念包括组织的含义，一个组织一般被看做是一个决策单位，对资源的控制由组织实施（拉坦，1996）。“有效的组织是制度变迁的关键”（诺思，1999）。从区域合作来看，区域经济合作机制的实现不但要有良好的制度环境，更要有实施合作的组织载体，即区域合作是通过区域合作组织进行的，它使区域利益主体的获利空间得以扩大或延伸，将原来对立的利益转化为一致利益，而且这种组织的安排方式处于动态调整过程中，它既可能是正式的，也可能是非正式的；既可能是强制性的，也可能是诱致性的。

2.2 诺贝尔经济学获奖者的区域经济思想演变

诺贝尔经济学获奖者有关区域经济的思想反映出其研究大致存在由忽略空间到关注空间、由宏观研究到宏微观兼顾、由一般定量分析到精细模型研究的演变。

第一，逐渐关注区域（或空间）问题。早期的研究者库兹涅茨在经济发展水平与收入差距方面的研究实质上并未足够重视空间因素，只是采用区域的数据验证了一个规律，而这一规律也并非是针对区域的。在他的启迪下，美国经济学家威廉姆森将库兹涅茨刻画收入分布的倒“U”型曲线应用到区域分析中来，提出了解释区域经济差异的倒“U”理论。随后的获奖者缪尔达尔的循环累积因果理论则直接考虑了区域特征。作为颇有成就的主流经济学家，在思考经济现象时直接考虑区域特征，一定程度上引导了经济学研究关注空间现象。克鲁格曼正是由于对经济活动空间现象的解释获得了诺贝尔奖。这使得经济活动的空间区位对经济发展的重要作用得以进一步强调，并赋予了空间经济学、区域经济学、经济地理学新的生命力。

第二，研究视角逐渐转向宏观微观兼顾。俄林致力于国际贸易的研究，缪尔达尔从中观区域尺度解释发达地区与欠发达地区之间的差距及其演化，2008 年获奖者克鲁格曼则把微观的区位理论和宏观的产业集聚及区域发展有机融合，从产品和企业角度进行分析，重新审视了产业向特定地区集中这一宏观现象的微观机制。同时，诺贝尔奖颁发给多位博弈论领域的研究者，引导区域经济逐渐从以假设为出发点的理想化向更贴近于现实的状态演变。并且，新近博弈论领域获奖者考虑经济因素之外的诸如道德、特殊的个人需求等更加细致的因素对个体决策的影响，增强了从微观个体行为出发解释宏观区域及国家之间发展趋势的说服力。

第三，区域（空间）研究更加精细化。无论在研究方法上，还是在对问题的讨论上，诺贝尔奖获得者的研究都向精细化方向发展。例如，早期俄林的要素禀赋理论建立模型时假定生产的规模报酬不变和完全竞争市场，这些假设条件同现实差距较大。缪尔达尔的循环累积因果理论未提及市场结构，也未进行严谨的模型分析。近期克鲁格曼根据所研究的问题，进行分析条件的简化假设。基于这些假设，进行十分严谨的分析，因此，多数观点伴以严格的数学证明。在对区域经济增长理论的探讨过程中，早期的研究者刘易斯的模型虽然开拓了发展经济学新的研究领域，但模型和论证都过于粗糙。随后，索洛增长模型已经考虑到技术进步的重要性，但并未将技术内生化于增长函数中。卢卡斯则进一步细化了模型，将经济分为人力资本生产部门、物质资本和最终消费品生产部门，将人力资本内生化于增长模型中。

2.3 诺贝尔经济学获奖者的区域经济学思想对现实的解释

2.3.1 新贸易理论与经济区位

克鲁格曼的新贸易及经济区位理论可以很好地解释区际贸易的现状及地区产业集中现象。首先，新贸易理论可以很好地解释当前国际和地区间贸易现象。克氏将原本关系并不大的国际贸易和经济地理区位的研究结合为一体，从而解释了当前国际贸易被出口和进口同类商品的国家所主导，以及为何相同的制造行业在某一国家或地区集中，形成全球性的专业化分工格局现象。例如，美国每年要出口大量的汽车，但同时又从日本、德国等地大量进口汽车，美国同日本、德国之间的差异程度要远远低于其与中国、印度等发展中国家的差异程度。这是俄林的要素禀赋理论不能解释的。而根据克氏的思想，贸易并不一定发生在技术或要素禀赋有差异的国家，在不完全竞争的市场结构下，即使两国间没有技术和要素禀赋差异，产品水平差异性和规模经济也可推动国际贸易，并且，这种行业内的贸易也是扩大市场及促进规模经济的一种途径（Krugman，1979）。

其次，目前我国产业结构的调整及升级亦可用克氏的观点来解释。一直以来，我国经济的快速增长主要得益于出口拉动，根据传统贸易理论（即要素禀赋差异理论），我国人口众多，具有明显的劳动力比较优势，我们一直出口劳动密集型产品，沿海地区也发展起来一大批代工企业。而依靠劳动力的大量投入是不可持续的，也是不稳定的，2008 年发生的金融危机致使大量工厂倒闭也印证了这一点。根据克氏的观点，贸易并非绝对来自比较优势，由于集聚带来的规模报酬递增也是发生贸易的重要原因。传统劳动力资源丰富的比较优势有可能被规模经济优势所取代，目前我国一些资本密集型的工业制成品（如机电产品）出口迅速上升也印证了这一点。机电产品有着较强的规模经济效应，中国国内市场规模的扩大促成了这类产业在中国形成了集聚，具有一定的规模经济优势（林发勤和崔凡，2008）。

2.3.2　库兹涅茨曲线的验证

库兹涅茨曲线提出后，诸多学者对多地区多阶段发展进行了验证，其中不乏肯定的研究（Chenery and Syrquin，1975；Ahluwalia，1976a，1976b；Papanek and Kyn，1986；Angle et al.，2009），也有部分认为现实情况并不符合倒 U 曲线（Barro，2000；Tridico，2010；Angeles，2009），原因可能在于所使用的数据及处理方法不同。实质上，库兹涅茨曲线总结的演化趋势基于多个发展阶段的国家，需要长期的时间序列数据进行验证。而目前中国仍处于中等收入水平，发展历程不足以提供长期数据来验证这一变化规律，即使个别省、市、县的收入水平略高，多数可归为行政区划的结果，而不可简单类比为处于不同发展阶段的国家（陈宗胜，2002）。但是我们依然可从当前发展趋势预见到我国收入差距演化符合库兹涅茨曲线规律。一方面，按照刘易斯的二元结构理论和法国学者皮鲁的增长极理论（李小建和苗长虹，1993），在工业化的初始发展阶段，区域之间、城乡之间由于资源禀赋、发展环境的不同，有些区域会优先发展，“极化”的过程会带来区域收入差距扩大；当发展到一定阶段后，由于生产成本差异，各种要素逐渐流向有更大发展空间的欠发达地区，区域收入差距会随“扩散”效应而逐渐趋于缩小。另一方面，到一定程度，政府会十分关注区域之间的差别问题，出台政策给予干预。尤其我国作为社会主义国家，实现共同富裕是本质要求，国家已提出以人为本的理念，更加关注低收入阶层。虽然改革开放 30 年来，收入差距整体上不断扩大，但是东北振兴、中部崛起、西部大开发等战略的实施，以及城乡统筹发展中对“三农”问题的关注和扶植，会对今后地区差距的减小有一定影响。实际上，我们的相关验证，近几年有些指标已有这种征兆。

2.3.3 缪尔达尔循环累积因果效应理论

研究表明，该理论适用于目前我国区域经济，尤其是相对发达的东部地区和较为落后的中西部地区之间差距的演化。改革开放以来，由于区位优势及国家的发展战略，东部地区经济快速增长（表 2.2），尤其是 1991～1998 年，其地区生产总值的增长率分别高于中、西部地区 2.7 个百分点和 4.3 个百分点。根据缪尔达尔的理论，由于回波效应，在这一时期，中西部地区的劳动力、资本等生产要素流向东部地区，使得东部和中西部增长差距拉大。而 2007 年呈现拐点特征，中部地区与东部地区增长率持平，西部地区则超过东部地区（表 2.2）。近年来，随着产业链条的全球化重组，加之东部地区生产成本提升，经济密集区域过于拥堵等原因，引致部分产业由东部向中西部地区转移，大量劳动力、资本等生产要素也向中西部地区扩散，我国区域经济迎来“缪尔达尔转折点”（王红和杨国才，2006），即中西部地区向东部地区的“回波效应”逐渐弱化，东部地区对中西部地区的“扩散效应”逐渐加强。

表 2.2 中国各地区 GDP 增长率

年份	增长率/%				
	地区合计	东部地区	东北地区	中部地区	西部地区
1980～1990	9.4	10.2	8.1	8.8	8.8
1991～1998	12.7	14.7	9.5	12.0	10.4
1999～2006	11.3	12.2	10.5	10.6	10.7
2007	14.2	14.2	14.1	14.2	14.5
2008	11.9	11.2	13.5	12.4	13.1
2009	11.6	10.8	12.7	11.7	13.4
2010	13.0	12.3	13.5	13.8	14.1

资料来源：2008～2009 年数据根据《中国统计年鉴 2009》和《中国统计年鉴 2010》相应省份数据计算得来；2010 年数据根据《中国统计摘要 2011》数据计算；1980～2007 年数据来自于魏后凯：“中国区域经济发展现状与前景”，载王振中主编的《展望 21 世纪中国经济》，宁夏人民出版社，2001；魏后凯：中国 GDP 与 GDP 增长率差异分析，《中州学刊》2009 年第 2 期。

2.4 结论及讨论

本章主要分析了诺贝尔经济学获奖者关于区域差异与贸易、区域经济发展、区域竞争与合作的思想。除此之外，诺贝尔经济学获奖者还有其他不属于区域经济学但对区域经济研究有一定启迪的思想，如 1982 年获奖者斯蒂格勒首次利用经济学理论分析利益集团对政府政策的影响，并开创性地提出国家俘获（state capture）理论；1986 年获奖者布坎南的公共选择理论，将政治决策的分析同经济理论结合起来，使经济分析扩大和应用到社会政治规则的选择领域；1998 年诺贝尔奖得主阿马蒂亚·森（A. Sen）通过阐明人们的生活质量应该不是根据其财富而是根据其自由来衡量，认为“发展可以看做是扩展人们享有真实自由的一个过程”（阿马蒂亚·森，2002）。这些观点对于区域经济学研究都有一定的影响。中国经济的高速增长与区域经济密切相关（魏后凯，2011），我国经济学研究具有更为独特的意义。评述诺贝尔经济学获奖者的区域经济学思想对我国区域经济学研究有以下启迪。

2.4.1　经济学家要关注空间现象

众所周知，无论何种经济现象总是要落实到具体的空间上。早期西方主流经济学的发展多为抽象一般性的理论，如供求关系理论、价格理论等，很少考虑空间因素。然而，随着经济活动的全球化和区域化，一些主流经济学家已开始关注空间现象，并试图将空间因素纳入到主流经济学分析框架中去。2008 年诺贝尔奖得主克鲁格曼对国际贸易和集聚的研究成果就是很好的例证。

然而，我国主流经济学家仍未很好地重视空间因素，即使在当前区域经济是国家经济繁荣的重要支撑这一客观现实下，国内主流经济学家们的主要理论成果依然很少涉及空间因素。当然，他们的研究成果对我国特殊国情下的经济运行、国企改革、金融市场、农村发展等的观点很有见地，但是很多理论是全国性的，有些是在东部沿海地区经济发展的基础上提炼而来的，未必完全适用于同东部地区差异较大的中西部地区。因此，学习和借鉴西方经济学，我国经济学家应当关注经济现象的区域性，在研究中注重空间因素。

2.4.2　区域经济研究中注重规范方法和制度创新

诺贝尔经济学获奖者的研究成果表明西方主流经济学研究在不断走向精细化，尤其是新近获奖者克鲁格曼的研究风格更是强调严谨而精细的工作。中国区域经济学也随着经济学的数理化，逐渐变得更加科学。很多观点可以证明，形成定理和定律。我们在学科研究中，应注重理论观点的提炼，注重严谨、细致的规范化分析，强调在合适的场合使用科学方法和计量方法（李小建，2002）。当然，经济活动的空间现象较为复杂，很难概括为统一的公理和定律，但规范化的、细致的、严谨的分析能够凝练出相对共性的观点，揭示事物的规律性，从而带动区域经济研究理论水平的提高，促进区域经济学的发展和完善。此外，区域合作机制的建立以及有效运转直接取决于良好的制度环境、合理的组织安排和完善的区域合作规则。其中，制度环境是基础保障，组织安排是结构保障，行为规则是具体的激励与约束保障。因此，经济学者在努力使区域经济学研究走向规范化、精细化的基础上，应关注制度创新研究，为中央政府与地方政府在各自范围内进行有效的制度创新并建立健全跨区的组织协调机制提供合理有效的指导。

2.4.3　强调中国区域经济的特殊性

紧紧追随不断出现的社会经济问题，提出各种可以解释现实的学说，并建立在严谨分析之上，是近些年经济学不断进步、发展的主要动力。中国特殊的国情提供了独特的区域经济研究对象。①中国为世界上最大的发展中国家，近 30 年来增长十分迅速，成为世界经济奇迹。在增长中区域差异十分显著，形成了非常复杂的区域发展格局。例如，2013年人均GDP最高的上海市是最低的贵州省的4.35倍；2013年中部和西部的人均GDP仅是东部的60%。②中国人口与资源的关系在世界各国中具有独特性。一方面，中国是人口大国，人均资源处于较低地位（李小建和苗长虹，2004）；另一方面，资源区域分布很不均衡，大量的人口和经济活动集中在相对发达的沿海地区，而资源则主要分布在中西部地区，人口、经济与资源的区域分布很不协调。③文化与区域经济关系的特殊性。中国地域文化差异显著。一方面，诸如中部地区的中原文化和西部地区的少数民族文化，有着深厚的小农思想情节、家族观念根基；另一方面，沿海地区的重商文化，具冒险精神和开拓意识。西方国家内部少有如此大的文化差异。地域文化对区域经济的影响，形成中国区域经济研究的另一特性。④中国农村的特殊性。中国是一个农业大国，约有1/2的人口生活在农村，与西方发达国家的后工业化社会有很大不同。农区地域广阔，农村工业发展迅速。同时，城市化快速推进，且在区域间不均衡，形成大规模大范围的农村务工人员地域流动现象。这些都构成我国区域经济研究十分独特的方向和领域。对这些特殊对象的深入研究，有望得出一些特殊的结论。

参考文献

阿马蒂亚·森. 2002. 以自由看待发展. 任赜等译. 北京：人民大学出版社

安虎森等. 2008. 新区域经济学. 大连：东北财经大学出版社

陈宗胜. 2002. 关于收入差别倒U曲线及两极分化研究中的几个方法问题. 中国社会科学，(5)：78～82

戴维斯，诺斯. 1996. 制度变迁的理论：概念与原因. 载《财产权利与制度变迁——产权学派与新制度学派译文集》. 上海：上海三联书店，上海人民出版社

道格拉斯·C·诺思. 1999. 经济史中的结构与变迁. 陈郁，罗华平译. 上海：上海三联书店，上海人民出版社

胡家勇. 1996. 政府干预经济研究. 大连：东北财经大学出版社

拉坦. 1996. 诱致性制度变迁理论. 载《财产权利与制度变迁——产权学派与新制度学派译文集》. 上海：上海三联书店，上海人民出版社

李小建，李二玲. 2009. 克鲁格曼、诺贝尔经济学奖与经济地理学发展. 经济地理，29 (3)：363～369

李小建，苗长虹. 1993. 增长极理论分析及选择研究. 地理研究，12 (3)：45～55

李小建，苗长虹. 2004. 西方经济地理学新进展及其启示. 地理学报，59 (增刊)：153～161

李小建，张晓平，彭宝玉. 2000. 经济活动全球化对中国区域经济发展的影响. 地理研究，(3)：225～233

李小建. 2002. 经济地理学近期研究的一个新方向分析. 经济地理，22 (2)：129～133

李小建. 2010. 经济地理学（第二版）. 北京：高等教育出版社

梁琦. 2008. 2008年度诺奖得主克鲁格曼学术成就评述. 国际经济评论，(6)：54～59

梁艺桦，杨新军. 2005. 区域旅游竞合博弈分析. 地理与地理信息科学，21 (2)：94～97

林发勤，崔凡. 2008. 克鲁格曼新贸易理论及其发展评析. 经济学动态，(12)：79～83

刘易斯. 1989. 二元经济论. 施伟等译. 北京：北京经济学院出版社

马丽，庞效民. 2001. 区域经济政策的博弈解析. 地理研究，20 (4)：498～505

舒尔茨. 1990. 人力资本投资：教育和研究的作用. 蒋斌等译. 北京：商务印书馆

舒尔茨. 2006. 改造传统农业. 梁小民译. 北京：商务印书馆

斯蒂格勒. 1992. 价格理论. 李青原等译. 北京：商务印书馆
孙久文，叶裕民. 2010. 区域经济学教程. 北京：中国人民大学出版社
王红，杨国才. 2006. 中国区域经济发展的"缪尔达尔转折点"及其跨越. 特区经济，(12)：225～226
魏后凯. 2006. 现代区域经济学. 北京：经济管理出版社
魏后凯. 2009. 中国 GDP 与 GDP 增长率差异分析. 中州学刊，(2)：29～34
魏后凯. 2011. 以战略思维谋划中国区域经济的发展. 中国经贸，(1)：64～66
Ahluwalia M. 1976b. Inequality, poverty and development. Journal of Development Economics, 3 (4): 307～342
Ahluwalia M. 1976a. Income distribution and development: Some stylized facts. American Economic Review, 66 (5): 128～135
Angeles L. 2009. An alternative test of Kuznets' hypothesis. Journal of Economic Inequality, 8 (4): 463～473
Angle J, Nielsen F, Scalas E. 2009. The Kuznets curve and the inequality process. MPRA Paper No. 16058
Barro R J. 2000. Inequality and growth in a panel of countries. Journal of Economic Growth, 5 (1): 5～32
Chenery H B, Syrquin M. 1975. Patterns of development. 1950 ～ 1970. New York: Oxford University Press
Grilo F, Mota I, Silva S. 2011. The use of game theory in regional economics: A quantitative retrospective. FEP Working Papers 419
Krugman P. 1979. Increasing returns, monopolistic competition, and international trade. Journal of International Economics, 9 (4): 469～479
Kuznets S. 1955. Economic growth and income inequality. The American Economic Review, 45 (1): 1～28
Li S. 2011. Regional competition and sustainable development: A game theory model for tourism destinations. European Planning Studies, 19 (4): 669～681
Myrdal G. 1957. Economic theory and under-developed regions. London: Duckworth
Papanek G, Kyn O. 1986. The effect on income distribution of development, the growth rate and economic strategy. Journal of Development Economics, 23 (1): 55～65
Tam H. 2008. An economic or political Kuznets curve. Public Choice, 134 (3): 367～389
Tridico P. 2010. Growth, inequality and poverty in emerging and transition economies. Transit Stud Review, 16: 979～1001
Williamson J G. 1965. Regional inequality and the process of national development: A description of the patterns. Economic Development and Cultural Change, 13 (4): 3～45

第3章　克鲁格曼与经济地理学

2008年10月13日，瑞典皇家科学院诺贝尔奖委员会在斯德哥尔摩宣布，将2008年诺贝尔经济学奖授予美国普林斯顿大学经济学家保罗·克鲁格曼，以表彰他在分析"国际贸易模式和经济活动区位"等方面所做的贡献。经济活动区位的研究，能够第一次作为重要贡献之一获得诺贝尔经济学奖，对经济地理学科以及经济地理学家都是一大盛事。然而，经济地理学家们对此的反应并不十分热烈。为此，本章对克鲁格曼经济地理学思想从贸易理论与区位理论相融合，从规模收益递增、要素流动和运输成本揭示空间集聚，从历史、预期和路径依赖揭示区域发展路径，区际关系量化分析四方面进行分析，从研究视角、研究范式和研究方法三方面分析克鲁格曼对经济地理学的启迪，从学科社会地位、研究范式和发展方向三方面分析克鲁格曼获得诺贝尔经济学奖对经济地理学的影响。在此基础上，对中国经济地理学发展提出了一些思考，以期对中国经济地理学发展有所帮助。

3.1　克鲁格曼学术生涯简介

保罗·克鲁格曼，1953年出生于纽约，1977年在麻省理工学院获得博士学位，先后在耶鲁、麻省理工、斯坦福大学任教，2000年开始在普林斯顿大学任经济与国际事务教授。1982～1983年，在白宫担任经济顾问。从1999年起，克鲁格曼开始给《纽约时报》撰写专栏文章。他撰写过大量的经济学专著和论文，撰写和编辑的经济类书籍有20多本，经济类论文超过200篇。他文笔清晰流畅，深入浅出，能用简明易懂的语言讲述严肃的经济学问题，是一位不可多得的大众经济学家。

克鲁格曼是主流经济学派的追随者和代表者，是萨缪尔森和索罗的好友。但同时，克鲁格曼又是一位创新者，敢于向任何传统理论开战。他所创建的新贸易理论，能够揭示除消费者对种类的偏好之外，生产中的规模经济如何在技术和生产要素禀赋相似的国家之间产生贸易，同时，还能够解释现实经济中发生的产业内贸易。这些成就使他于1991年获得了约翰·贝茨·克拉克奖。他还创建了新经济地理学帮助我们理解农村的衰退和城市的增长。据此，2008年他获得了诺贝尔经济学奖。瑞典皇家科学院在其获奖声明及授奖评语中说，贸易模式和区位一直是经济争论中的关键问题。自由贸易与全球化会带来什么影响？世界范围内城市化背后的驱动力是什么？保罗·克鲁格曼构建了一套全新理论来回答这些问题。他也因此整合了经济研究中先前完全互不关联的国际贸易和经济地理这两个研究领域，在自由贸易、全球化和推动世界范围内城市化进程的动因方面形成了一套新理论[①]。

事实上，克鲁格曼的经济思想并不局限于国际贸易和经济地理学，他在国际金融、货币危机、汇率变化与萧条经济学领域也有着突出的贡献。他的理论思想富于原创性，对经济生活中出现的具体现实问题具有敏锐的观察力。他的货币危机理论（克鲁格曼曾先后提出了第一代、第二代、第四代货币危机模型和著名的“三元悖论”）成功预言了1997年的亚洲金融危机，并对危机的形成以及本质上的制度缺陷给予了解释。数年后他断言美国总统乔治·W·布什政府的经济和外交政策终将引发严重经济危机，2008年由华尔街金融风暴引发的大规模、世界性的金融危机，对此断言又是一次有力的佐证。正是克鲁格曼重视解释现实问题，且其模型研究和现实拟合度较好，使得他成为知名度极高的“通俗”经济学家。他目前担任着许多国家和地区的经济政策咨询顾问，对这些国家如何利用公共政策手段应对世界经济波动给予指导。例如，他的汇率变化理论研究了汇率在目标区内变动的特征，当汇率在中心汇率上下一定幅度内波动时，政府不予干预，当汇率接近浮动上下限时，政府才出面干预（陈如，2008）。他的萧条经济学理论（1996年出版专著《萧条经济学的回归》）在否定东亚奇迹的经济成就后，指出当前经济的普遍问题是需求不足，并强调重视克服需求不足问题。而治理萧条的办法，对于富国而言应利用利率杠杆，对于穷国而言应放弃固定汇率，要改善对银行的监管，而且在出现危机时政府必须果断地实施紧急管制。

克鲁格曼对学术研究执著、大胆。成名后，他要在世界各地发表演说、参加研讨会、会见各式各样的人。但是面对荣誉和金钱，他仍保持着清醒的头脑，潜心于学术研究。克鲁格曼性格刚直，不附和权贵，敢于直言社会不公，有着一个学者的社会良知。在其2007年新作《美国怎么了？一个自由主义者的良知》（克鲁格曼，2008），阐述了20世纪70年代以后美国不断加剧的两极分化和社会不公，并警醒世人不要冷漠对待社会经济不平等议题，以免错失改革良机。

3.2 克鲁格曼对经济地理学的主要贡献

3.2.1 贸易理论与区位理论结合

1. 从贸易角度阐述了地理区位的作用

早在1933年，瑞典经济学家伯尔蒂尔·俄林（B. G. Ohlin）在其名著《区际与国际贸易》（*Interregional and International Trade*）》一书中就明确提出需要更好地理解地理区位在经济生活中所起的作用。他强烈倡导区域经济学和国际经济学之间进行更密切的合作。在1966年该书的修订版中他又提出贸易理论和区位理论交叉融合的观点，认为国际贸易理论是接近于区位理论的，区位理论比国际贸易理论更为广泛，贸易理论的一大部分可以看做是区位理论的一小部分（梁琦，2005）。但直到20世纪80年代，

① The Official Web Site of the Nobel Foundation. 2008. http://nobelprize.org/nobel_prizes/economics/laureates/2008/ presentation-speech.html. 2008-10-16。

随着计算机批处理复杂系统能力的发展及经济理论的进步（尤其是收益递增和不完全竞争理论的进步），克鲁格曼才将以上观点进一步延伸拓展，以此来解释经济活动跨空间分布的现象。

2. 从贸易视角构建了经济地理区位演化模型

克鲁格曼的新经济地理模型是在其新贸易理论的基础上引入与区位有关的运输成本，发现了经济活动的空间格局演化特点，从而弥补了传统经济地理学对空间集聚难以数理模型化的不足，“重新发现了地理学”（藤田昌久等，2005）。其“中心-外围”模型阐述了在规模收益递增（increasing returns to scale）、运输成本和劳动流动的相互作用下，基本条件原本相同的两个区域是如何最终演变成工业区的中心和农业区的外围的，揭示了不同贸易成本下引致的不同的区位格局和演化动态（即当运输成本很低或很高时，集聚不会产生或不可持续；只有当运输成本足够低、制造业差异化产品种类足够多、制造业份额足够大时，互为投入-产出联系的厂商之间的前后向联系效应最强，集聚才可以发生并持续下去），进一步从贸易视角打开了“经济活动空间分布”这个黑箱。

3.2.2 从规模收益递增、要素流动和运输成本分析空间集聚

收益递增机制是经济地理尤其是空间集聚中最重要的机制。克鲁格曼认为，收益递增在许多层次上影响经济地理。在最低层次上，一些特定行业的区位（如汽车在底特律、芯片在硅谷），很明显反映的是被“锁定”的转瞬即逝的优势。在中等层次上，城市本身的存在就明显是一种收益递增现象。在最高层次上，整个地区的不均衡发展可以是由累积过程驱动的，这些过程又是根植于收益递增的（克鲁格曼，2000）。低层次的收益递增带来产业地方化，高层次的收益递增带来不同地区的发展差异。

集聚是经济地理学经典的研究领域，是经济活动最突出的地理特征。为什么会产生集聚？传统经济地理学理论从许多影响因素出发对此问题进行了定性或定量论述，但大多有“集聚源于集聚经济的获得”这类循环解释的嫌疑。事实上，集聚经济是经济活动因集聚在一起而获得了平均成本下降的好处，无论是经济活动在同一个企业内部集聚而获得的内部规模经济，还是不同企业集聚而获得的技术外部经济和金融外部经济，都是一种规模收益递增，也就是说集聚相当于空间上的规模报酬递增。

运输成本和要素流动是引起经济地理差异的关键因素。运输成本的存在引起商品价格差异，进而造成工人名义上和实际上的工资差异，引起要素在空间上的流动，规模收益递增（包括市场的规模经济）使这种差异和流动持续下去，进而决定贸易在哪里发生。克鲁格曼在规模收益递增模型的基础上加入运输成本和要素流动，就抓住了引起经济地理差异的关键点。

基于以上三个关键因素的分析，克鲁格曼建立了空间集聚模型。在模型中，克鲁格曼克服了长期以来困扰主流经济学空间集聚模型化的技术难题，以规模收益递增为前提假设，以萨缪尔森的“冰山”形式简化运输成本，以动态模型考虑要素流动问题，巧妙地实现了将空间收益递增等要素的计量分析。克鲁格曼对空间经济问题的理论分析，具有十分重大意义。

3.2.3　从历史、预期和路径依赖解释区域发展路径

1. 区域发展具循环累积与路径依赖

克鲁格曼在解释空间集聚时发现产业的集聚具有自增强机制，是一种动态的累积过程。初始的微小优势经过累积和路径依赖被放大，打破原有的均衡形成地方产业，地方产业的形成又增强了本地的集聚力，这种循环的关系使已形成的产业模式锁定。因此，区域发展具有路径依赖性。例如，当一国或一个地区不论何种原因取得了外部规模经济后，即使已不再拥有比较优势，该国或该地区仍然能够维持其先期获得的竞争优势地位。

2. 历史与偶然事件对区域产业的最初区位产生深远影响

既然区域发展具有路径依赖与自增强机制，那么最初的集聚和累积是从哪里开始的呢？对此，克鲁格曼特别强调历史和偶然事件对区域发展的作用，认为，在许多层次上，从最小的集聚层次到最大的层次（如从大部分美国的管乐器生产集中在印第安纳州的埃尔克哈特小镇，到1/3的美国人口仍然生活在最初的13个殖民地），历史和偶然事件都对生产的区位产生了长远的影响，一个小小的历史偶然事件，可使一个地区成为工业中心的一部分，另一个地区成为初级产品为主的外围区；某些并无什么特色的区位，却成为千万人以上的特大城市，这些都是对历史依赖的有力证据（克鲁格曼，2000）。

3. 预期在区域发展演变中具特殊作用

克鲁格曼在强调历史偶然性的同时，认为区域发展路径在一定程度上还是一个“自我完成的预期”。在区域经济变迁的过程中，路径依赖和锁定会使一个区域生产的地理结构长期没有变化，但潜在条件的累积变化可能导致突变。突变的方向是不确定的，不仅会受到客观条件的影响，还会受到预期的作用。如果某种原因使得每个人都认为某个地区会发展为中心，并根据这个信念采取行动搬迁到那里，并且这种搬迁迅速发生，预期就会成为自我完成的预言（克鲁格曼，2000）。相反，如果由于某种原因，商人和工人对一个地区的前景变得非常悲观，这种悲观的预期也会影响相关区域的发展。

3.2.4　以量化模拟研究区际关系

1. 揭示了城市之间等级体系形成的自组织原理

无论是地区层面还是国家层面，克鲁格曼认为各层次的收益递增、要素流动、消费者多样化的偏好相互作用会自发产生多中心的城市等级关系。他在《自组织经济》一书中，运用自组织理论对城市等级体系进行了量化模拟。高人口区域具有吸引力，因为它们具有丰富的差异化商品选择机会。企业有移向高人口区域的激励，因为他们也能减少运输成本，同时从规模经济中获益。一个自增强过程就产生了，人口往城市迁移产生更大的规模经济，从而更增强了城市的吸引力。“集聚产生集聚”，引发了持续“选择”；而微观群组的选择，在经济体系规模收益递增的内在规定性作用下，“自下而上”地从

“不稳定”最终演化出宏观上新的“有序”的多中心城市空间结构（黄泽民，2005）。随着时间的推移，包含许多不同等级行业的经济体的增长，会自发形成城市等级体系。在这个层级体系中，与较低级别的城市相比，较高级别的城市包含更多的行业种类（藤田昌久等，2005）。新城市诞生、厂商重新定位、现有城市合并等过程使城市体系的演化在空间和行业结构上具有自组织性。

2. 对区域之间不平等发展进行模型解释

在中心-外围模型的基础上，克鲁格曼创建的国际专业化模型还解释了区域间差异化发展问题（藤田昌久等，2005）。在国家层面，商品可以在国家间贸易，但由于国界的存在，人口不能流动，因此，人口意义上的集聚不会发生，然而，产业部门之间的关联效应会导致特定产业向几个国家集聚，导致制造业在国家间的非均衡分布，随之就会出现工资率和生活水平不平等的可能性。由此可见，区域经济一体化趋势可以通过降低商品和人口的流动壁垒来缩小区域间的收入差距。

3. 对区域之间产业扩散进行模型解释

克鲁格曼创建的多国多产业模型阐述了工业化进程中不同的产业在国家间的扩散过程（藤田昌久等，2005）。模型发现，各国专业化发展的典型模式都是先生产某些产品，然后再把这些产业让渡给紧随其后的国家而向“高级产业（upscale）”转移。例如，对于劳动密集度不同的产业来说，假设最初国家 1 集聚了所有的产业，高工资导致产业重新选址，劳动密集度最高的产业最先离开国家 1 到国家 2 或国家 3 扎根，后转移的产业（即劳动密集度较低的产业）比先转移的产业能够更迅速地进入别国，这是因为先转移的产业形成了前向和后向关联，从而便于其他产业厂商的进入。这也解释了工业化进程的加速现象。

3.3 克鲁格曼创新研究对经济地理学的启迪

诺贝尔经济学奖和其他诺贝尔奖一样，对研究成果的原创性有很高的要求，即要求有革命性的发现。这种发现能够革命性地改变我们的思路，对人类有重大贡献。克鲁格曼的经济活动区位理论的成果作为获奖的两个重要发现之一，已经证明其具有重大原创意义。他的这种革命性贡献背后，是其与传统经济地理学不同的研究思路、范式和方法。

3.3.1 研究视角：宏观微观兼顾

前已述及，克鲁格曼的经济地理学思想与国际贸易理论有着密切的联系，甚至被认为是其国际贸易理论的拓展（吴意云和朱希伟，2008）。在解释为什么经济活动会在空间上集聚时，克鲁格曼没有满足于人们关于集聚带来企业之间技术上相互溢出从而使相关企业受益的观点，而是借用并发挥了俄林联系区位理论和国际贸易理论的研究思路（梁琦，2005），建立了国际贸易与产业集聚的数学模型。克氏认为，国家之间的贸易，尤其是相似国家同类产品的贸易，代表了这些国家根据规模收益递增原理而发展专业化的结果，与国家生产要素禀赋差异关系不大。假设市场环境为不完全竞争，在规模经济和收益递增的驱动下，产出规模扩大带来生产成本下降。各国通过发展专业化和贸易，提高其收益（李小建和李庆春，1999）。将这种国际贸易新理论拓展到区域层面，克氏引入了“金钱外部性”（pecuniary externalities）概念（供给与需求联系概念）。认为，以前向关联和后向关联为纽带的“金钱外部性”带来的集聚力量可以使初始状态完全相同的地区，由于某种“扰动”，而最终实现集聚的“差异”状态（吴意云和朱希伟，2008）。

从以上简要分析可以看出，克鲁格曼的研究视角从两方面融合着不同的尺度。一是沿着规模经济和收益递增的研究脉络，从国际层面对国家专业化的研究推延到国内区域层面的产业集聚研究；二是在以上两类研究中，他均关注了单个企业的经营偏好与企业群体效应。这也许可以启示我们，立足宏观视野的经济地理研究，可以使我们远观森林；而在微观层面的精细研究，又使我们近察树木。两者结合，优势互补，弱势互避，更有利于进行深层次的理论构建。

3.3.2　研究范式：规范分析

20 世纪的经济地理学理论化，伴随着不同研究范式的更替。杜能的农业区位论包括了个体动机与地理区位的关系。在构建理论时基于理性人假设，十分重视微观均衡分析。而韦伯的工业区位论，具有以问题为导向的实用主义特点（解决企业选址问题），故把经济活动的空间特征描述作为观察重点。这种研究范式一直延续到之后的区位论和区域科学研究之中。60 年代的数量革命，强调用统计和数学模拟方法探索经济活动空间结构。克鲁格曼的研究，则承继杜能及主流经济学的规范研究范式，重视理论的演绎，强调以精练的模型来揭示经济现象背后的个体理性动机，强调在理论演绎的基础上进行计量分析，即计量分析是对理论假设的检验，但理论假设并不直接来自计量研究（颜飞和罗永刚，2008）。基于该研究范式，他将不完全竞争、规模收益递增和运输成本纳入空间分析之中，将产业集聚的个体理性动机归结为规模收益递增，设计出了解释集聚形成的区域模型（中心-外围模型）、城市模型（城市层级体系演化模型）和国际模型（产业集聚与国际贸易模型）。

与克鲁格曼等相对应，地理学家在经济地理学研究中，受政治经济学和结构主义的影响，强调从社会、政治和文化角度解释经济地理现象（李小建，2004）。这种思想及其研究成果成为地理学家中研究的主流，在解释特殊背景下的经济地理现象时发挥着特殊的作用。尽管 21 世纪以来地理学家与经济学家分庭抗礼一段时间后，开始了互相借鉴和交流，但目前国内外地理学家中，还是很少人接受主流经济学家的研究范式。我们有必要冷静思考，在特殊经济地理现象的背后是否存在一般性的解释？如果承认这一点，我们就应该承认，我们长期远离了能够产生一般性解释的规范范式的经济地理学研究。真正科学的研究，应该在关注结构主义和“多维转向”的同时（李小建和苗长虹，2004），同样关注主流经济学家的经济地理学研究结论。

3.3.3 研究方法：重视计量

克鲁格曼在经济地理学研究中，十分注重建构清晰、严谨、精致的模型。首先，他根据所研究的问题，在对相关前提条件进行简化之后提出假设。接着，基于这些假设，他按照经济学原理，对研究对象的经济行为进行十分严谨的分析。因此，多数观点伴以严格的数学证明。如果简化假设基础上的抽象分析与实际有出入，将对这些假设条件进行修改。例如，在研究工商业、城市集聚时，为了建立向心力和离心力相互作用下的一般均衡模型，克鲁格曼利用了四种技巧：用于解释报酬递增和不完全竞争的“D-S模型”、用于衡量运输成本的“冰山模型”、用于描述历史和偶然事件带来的地理空间结构“特定动态演化（*ad hoc* dynamics）”方法，以及研究空间自组织形成的“计算机模拟”方法。

有人分析了近30年的诺贝尔经济学奖情况，认为经济学研究在不断走向深入和精细。西方现代经济学已被人称作是硬科学，它具有所有被称为科学的一个根本的共同特征：一个命题及其证明可被重复试验，可以证伪。这也正是克鲁格曼及其新经济地理学的基本研究风格。它之所以十分注意模型分析，就是要用数学语言来严谨地说明分析对象的因果关系。它将许多过去地理学所熟悉的经济活动空间格局思想（如集聚/分散、吸引/排斥、向心力/离心力相互作用等）以实在和精细的形式表达出来。这些应该是地理学，尤其是一些还没有经过数量革命和严格科学训练的中国地理学家所值得认真学习的。当然，这不是要我们非要在研究中搬用数学公式或数学符号，而是养成严谨的分析方法，争取使一些分析结果具有同等条件下的可重复性（李小建，2002）。

3.4 克鲁格曼获诺贝尔奖对经济地理学发展的影响

3.4.1 对经济地理学社会地位的影响

尽管克鲁格曼对经济活动空间集聚进行了富有说服力的理论阐述，但是他的研究并没有得到地理学家的很好认同。地理学家批评他的模型分析过于简单，很难具体应用于实证研究；分析中对社会政治因素考虑不够；重视市场规模经济同时忽视了技术的影响等。甚至地理学家对其使用“新经济地理学”名词也颇有争议。但是争论本身必然引起学界关注，从而也助于其学科地位的提高。正如克鲁格曼与藤田昌久对话中谈到的那样，经济学家使用“新经济地理学”并开展相关研究是很有建树性的，至少它吸引了传统地理学家的关注，使人们发现经济学家和地理学家在理解和对待经济空间上是如此不同（Fujita and Krugman，2004）。不仅如此，地理学家在与经济学家的交流对话中，开始认识经济学家从独特视角对经济地理学的贡献，逐渐认可其经济活动空间格局一般性解释的科学意义，认可其在经济空间预测的特殊作用。

从另一个侧面看，克鲁格曼等经济学家关于经济空间的研究贡献，逐渐得到主流经济学家的认可。从而有助于逐渐改变经济学忽视空间的传统，有助于把经济活动空间研究拉入经济学的主战场。尤其是2008年克鲁格曼以其在经济活动区位和国际贸易上的贡献获得诺贝尔经济学奖，不仅进一步在学术上承认了克氏在经济活动区位上的研究具有重要开拓意义，而且，在世界学术界第一次宣告经济活动的空间性或经济地理学在经济学中占据十分重要的地位。同时，通过诺贝尔奖本身及其相关的媒体宣传，也使社会大众进一步认识了经济地理学学科及其在社会发展中的重要作用。

这当然不等于说经济地理学家，尤其是地理学背景的经济地理学家可以自我陶醉其中。十分清楚，来自地理学家的经济地理研究与经济学家还有一定的不同。相关研究如何真正得到社会认可，还需要众多学者的共同努力。我们要使经济地理学实实在在地为经济社会提供多维度的服务，其中重要一项是对经济地理现象作出科学、精细的解释。

3.4.2 对经济地理学研究范式的影响

克鲁格曼经济地理学创新研究对我国经济地理学研究范式产生了重要影响。第一，它使我们进一步认识到本土化的研究范式的局限：这些研究在推动地方经济社会发展中起一定作用，但由于缺乏“科学”的表达，很难登上国际学术交流的主流平台（刘云刚和许学强，2008）。第二，它使我们进一步明确我们所了解的来自于西方地理学家的所谓的主流经济地理学，仅仅是世界范围内地理学研究的一部分。在它之外，还存在着同样十分有生机的经济学家的经济地理学。在西方发达国家之外，还存在其他不同的研究范式。

在具体研究方法上，克鲁格曼经济地理学研究具有以下影响。第一，促使引入相关学科理论。近 20 年来西方经济地理学的理论进展，与整个社会科学和哲学的发展大背景具有十分密切的关联。克鲁格曼经济地理学中不完全竞争、收益递增和多重均衡等模型分析，得益于诸多经济学家的贡献。第二，促使合理使用模型与计量方法。在中国特色的经济地理学构建中，在注重定性和定量两者相结合的同时，应该考虑中国经济地理学的地理学科性质，更加强调在合适的场合使用科学方法和计量方法。复杂的地理事物难以概括出定律、公理，但通过模型的重建，可以凝练出相对共性的观点，促进地理理论的不断完善（李小建和苗长虹，2004）。

3.4.3 对经济地理学发展方向的影响

随着克鲁格曼获得诺贝尔奖，是否会把经济地理学发展拉向主流经济学方向？目前西方学术界的反应似乎并不支持这种判断。地理学家对经济活动区位作为经济学诺贝尔奖授予的主要贡献之一的反响并不十分热烈。当然，这并不意味着地理学家会一意孤行，死死固守现行的研究思路，坚持现行的发展方向。由此带来的是，不同观点交融会进一步加强。20 世纪经济地理学的发展中，曾有不少不同观点的交流融合。21 世纪伊始所开始的经济学与地理学在经济地理学研究上的实质性交流（李小建，2002），将会不断为该学科注入新的研究观点和方法。从事经济地理学的学者们，不管来自于地理学还是来自于经济学，均会有更开阔的思路，掌握更多的相关知识和研究技能。人们不会过分强调哪一种研究方法是正确的，哪一种是错误的，而会发现多种方法均有其正确性，均有其适用的范围。然后根据具体实际情况，选择恰当的方法。

与此相关联，经济地理学前瞻性研究成果有望逐渐增多。过去经济地理学研究中，多侧重于对已有地理现象（事实）的描述和解释。预测性或前瞻性成果不多，尤其是缺少像经济学那样在解决现实重大问题上的大型政策指导性研究成果。与此相比较，克鲁格曼新经济地理学的一些结果，则表现出预测性特点。与新经济地理学的观点交流或进一步地与主流经济学的交流，会带动经济地理学向此方向努力。

综合多种观点的经济地理学，或称统一经济地理学，将可望成为经济地理学的重要发展方向之一。这种统一经济地理学，能够融合规范研究、实证研究和结构主义研究方法，融合计量和定性描述、解释的优点，能够将经济地理研究与自然地理、地理信息和遥感相结合，在研究经济、社会的空间格局时密切关注与资源环境的协调。它应该摈弃狭隘的学科偏向，以开放的思维，海纳地理学、经济学及其他相关学科中可以为其所用的精华。

3.5 结　　语

经济活动区位的创新成果作为重要依据之一使克鲁格曼获得诺贝尔经济学奖，为经济地理学发展带来了机会。但同时，来自地理学的经济地理学，也面临着一些挑战。如何发展才能使我们的经济地理学确实承担起解决现实重大实际问题的重任？如何才能推出得到学界普遍承认的革命性成果，并对人类社会做出更大贡献？这是我们必须正视的问题。以上分析表明，带有普遍意义的革命性成果，必须基于相应的创新思维、范式和方法。而我们现在的经济地理学研究，与此还有较大的差距。为此，我们要在科学定位的基础上，明确发展方向。既重视中国经济地理学的特殊发展背景，又善于科学引入他人观点。学习利用规范方法，合理使用模型与计量技术，深入解释经济地理现象的发生原因。在对复杂的地理事物的研究中，通过简化假设，演绎出定律、公理，凝练出相对共性的观点。中国经济地理现象具有世界其他国家所不具备的一些独特之处，基于中国的实例研究和理论构建，可望为世界经济地理学的理论创新做出特殊贡献。

参 考 文 献

保罗·克鲁格曼. 2000. 地理和贸易. 张兆杰译. 北京：北京大学出版社，中国人民大学出版社

保罗·克鲁格曼. 2008. 美国怎么了？一个自由主义的良知. 刘波译. 北京：中信出版社

陈如. 2008. 克鲁格曼经济思想综述. http://jenas9774. spaces. live. com/ [2008-10-14]

黄泽民. 2005. 我国多中心城市空间自组织过程分析——克鲁格曼模型借鉴与泉州地区城市演化例证. 经济研究，(1)：85～94

李小建，李庆春. 1999. 克鲁格曼的主要经济地理学观点分析. 地理科学进展，(2)：97～102

李小建，苗长虹. 2004. 西方经济地理学新进展及其启示. 地理学报，59 (s)：153～161

李小建. 2002. 经济地理学近期研究的一个新方向分析. 经济地理，22 (2)：129～133

李小建. 2004. 国际背景与中国特色经济地理学. 人文地理，19 (1)：27～31

梁琦. 2005. 空间经济学：过去、现在与未来. 经济学（季刊），4 (4)：1067～1086

刘云刚，许学强. 2008. 中国地理学的二元结构. 地理科学，28 (5)：587～593

藤田昌久，保罗·克鲁格曼，安东尼·J·维纳布尔斯. 2005. 空间经济学：城市、区域与国际贸易. 梁琦主译. 北京：中国人民大学出版社

吴意云，朱希伟. 2008. 从无差异到差异：2008 年诺贝尔经济学奖得主理论评价. 浙江社会科学，(11)：33～35

颜飞，罗永刚. 2008. 区域经济学理论范式演进与应用拓展. 财经问题研究，(8)：24～30

Fujita M，Krugman P. 2004. The new economic geography：Past，present and the future. Papers in Regional Science，83：139～164

第4章 国际背景与中国特色的经济地理学

20世纪80年代以来，以英美地理学家为主导的国际经济地理学界开始注重制度和社会文化因素对经济空间现象的影响。柔性专业化、网络与根植性、集聚与集群、区域管制等概念，频繁出现于国际主导地理刊物和国际会议讨论之中。国内也有一些学者引进这些相关理论并结合中国实例做了一些可喜的探索。这种引进理论—中国实际研究—理论总结的研究模式，推动着20世纪中国经济地理学发展。但是，从中国特色的经济地理学角度考虑，还应该探索其他研究思路。中国经济地理学发展背景，有一些在世界十分独特，如最大的且近20多年经济增长最快的发展中国家，工业化与城市化不相一致，体制变革、文化传统的特殊影响，人口与资源的尖锐矛盾，区域差异巨大，经济地理学在地理学中地位的特殊性等。根据这些背景，中国经济地理学需要冷静地审视国际学术动向和中国特色。立足中国实际，加强国际交流，凝练解释中国特殊经济地理现象的理论观点，逐渐培育国际经济地理学界中的中国流派。

4.1 国际主流经济地理学近期发展特点

在国际经济地理学的新近发展中，有来自主流经济学家和来自地理学家的研究成果。经济学家侧重于空间分布和均衡的经济学研究，强调收益递增、运输成本和其他贸易互相依赖等概念，地理学家则侧重于从社会、政治和文化角度研究经济地理现象。以下分析主要依据地理学家的成果。

4.1.1 理论进展及主要观点

20世纪80年代到21世纪初的国际经济地理学的主要理论进展，可以概括为以下7个方面（表4.1）。

表4.1 近20年来国际经济地理学主要理论观点

主要理论	兴盛期	主要贡献者	研究地理区域
1. 劳动地域分工	20世纪80年代	Doreen Massey	英国
		Gordon Clark	美国
2. 柔性专业化和新产业空间	20世纪80年代	Allen Scott，Michael Storper	美国
		David Harvey，Richard Florida	意大利
		Meric Gerler，Andrew Sayer	德国
3. 网络与根植性	20世纪90年代	Nigel Thrift，Peter Dicken	英国
		Gernol Grabher，Philip Cooke，Ash Amin	欧洲

续表

主要理论	兴盛期	主要贡献者	研究地理区域
4. 区域集聚和集群	20 世纪 90 年代中期	Michael Storper，Allen Scott Philip Cooke，Kevin Maskell Ray Hudson，John Lovering	美国 英国 欧洲
5. 干预（调节）论和管制	20 世纪 90 年代中期	Jamie Peck，Adam Tickell Erik Schoenberger	法国 英国、欧洲
6. 文化经济	20 世纪 90 年代中期	Linda McDowell，Trevor Barnes Julie Graham，Katherine Gibson Roger Lee，Jane Wills	英国 美国 加拿大
7. 关系论/关系转折	21 世纪初	Jeffrey Boggs 等 Harald Bathelt 等	美国 德国

资料来源：据 Yeung 和 Lin，2003 并修改补充（Yeung and Lin，2003；Boggs and Rantisi，2003）。

1. 劳动地域分工理论

该理论为 20 世纪 80 年代，一些激进地理学家在批判区位论基础上，用马克思主义观点对英国和美国区域工业化过程研究之后提出的。主要观点包括：资本主义生产的社会过程与产业、就业和阶级的空间结构和分布之间存在相互依赖关系。在政治经济学观点指导下，该理论主张对社会关系和生产关系进行空间化研究（Massey，1995）。

2. 柔性专业化和新产业空间

侧重于从生产技术变化入手，研究其对产业空间组织的影响。从福特主义大宗生产转向后福特的精益生产、柔性专业化、产品顾客化，出现了新的产业空间（Scott，1988）。转包、中小企业快速发展，以及由此带来的新的企业集聚，成为该学派的主要研究议题。受制度经济学的影响，该学派研究中，十分关注交易成本对产业空间格局的影响。

3. 网络与根植性

20 世纪 90 年代中期以来，企业根植的网络关系对企业空间的影响成为经济地理学家重要研究领域之一。该学派力图通过研究邻近性、根植性、隐含知识和学习、合作网络，来解释经济地理中的空间集聚现象。在研究中，侧重于组织理论和社会学方法（李小建，2002b）。

4. 区域集聚和集群

伴随着技术的发展，产业组织方式的变化，在全球化背景下的经济空间格局中新的集聚和集群现象，引起了经济地理学家的关注（王缉慈，2001）。这种集聚和集群的特殊企业组成、鲜明的专业化、特殊的区位特点，以及内部复杂的关联性，促使经济地理学家在研究中借鉴管理学、演化经济学、制度经济学、社会学等学科的方法。

5. 干预（调节）理论和管制

干预（调节）理论源于法国政治经济学派，管制是 20 世纪 90 年代英语国家社会科学中最关键的术语之一（Johnston et al.，2000）。干预（调节）主要指政府对市场的干预，管制则不仅限于政府（在组织上管制包括政府之外其他在政策形成过程起作用的组织，如非政府组织、半官方机构、私营公司、压力群体等；在组织间关系上，管制指相关组织的合作形式，而不是上下控制关系）（Johnston et al.，2000）。经济地理学家借用相关理论，在研究中强调干预和管制的空间意义。认为干预和管制的过程与一国之内（或一区之内）的空间经济和社会差异之间具有十分密切的关联。任何一种干预（调节）方式或管制措施均会对某些区域更为有利，对另一些区域更为不利。

6. 文化经济

以上观点有一些已经涉及从文化角度进行经济地理学研究。20 世纪 90 年代末国际经济地理学中的"文化转向"，更进一步强调经济与文化的关系（Crang，1997）。一些学者认为，经济空间只有放置于文化、社会和政治关系之中，才能很好地加以理解。其中，"文化经济"得到不少地理学家的关注。其研究视野非常宽泛，包括公司文化（公司的规范、习俗及非正式规则特征）、企业知识（公司自己拥有的知识）、组织学习、创新型产业、学习型区域等。

7. 关系论或关系转折

关注经济主体之间的关系对经济地理的影响。认为经济活动的各种参与者和它们相关作用关系所引起的经济地理发展和变化过程，应该成为研究的中心。例如，2003 年第 2 期"*Journal of Economic Geography*"专集讨论关系经济地理学。一些学者认为，经济地理学的研究范式正在向着关系经济地理学转变。这是由于：①从结构主义角度，社会和制度关系形成经济主体运营的重要背景；②从发展变化角度，经济过程具有路径依赖特征，与历史关系密切；③经济发展过程具有权变特征，经济主体的战略和行动是开放的，随环境条件而变化（Bathelt and Gluckler，2003）。

4.1.2 主要特点

1. 解释学理论构建

据巴恩斯（T. J. Barnes）研究，20 世纪早期、中期的区位论，以及 50、60 年代的数量革命，均以"认识论（epistemology）理论构建"为主，所强调的是对研究对象的精确反映。近 20 年的理论性成果，以"解释学（hermeneutics）理论构建"为主，强调更加灵活、开放和自由的探索方式。与"认识论理论构建"相比，它具有如下不同：①反对依据固定的和决定性的原则（而认识论则使用这些原则）；②激励实验活动和使用不确定术语；③培育对社会和历史区位的判断意识，承认其对知识的影响；④保持对话，以商讨性的态度处理理论与实践的关系（Barnes，2001）。

2. 非规范性和非精细性

20 世纪中期以前的经济地理学研究，注重物理模拟和数量分析，如用整齐线条和精确的几何图形，表达地理学家的理论构想。用数学模型描述复杂的现实世界。与此相比，近 20 年来，经济地理学侧重非正式理论构建。在图形表达中，认为世界太杂乱无章，太破碎，充满着方方面面的竞争，根本不能给予简洁的展示。

需要说明，新近由一些主流经济学家推进的经济地理研究，十分注重数量模型分析，用数学语言来严谨地说明分析对象的因果关系。这与地理学家的新近研究形成了对比（李小建，2002a）。

3. 社会科学特性

国际主流经济地理学在 20 世纪前末期的研究中，侧重于利用自然科学的方法论，强调数学理性推理。近 20 年来的新经济地理学，主要借助人文社会科学的方法论，强调经济的社会和文化特点。并引用相关人文社会学科的理论，来分析其对经济空间问题的影响。例如，劳动地域分工中借用马克思主义生产关系理论，新产业空间中借助经济学中的柔性生产概念，网络研究中借助社会学家的社会根植性概念，等等。

4.1.3 存在问题

1. 主要来自英美地理学家

所有近 20 年来的主流经济地理学理论观点主要为英美学者和少数其他发达国家学者的研究贡献（见表 4.1）。除此之外的其他国家（尤其是发展中国家）的学者的成果很少。

2. 主要依据发达国家实际

近 20 年来的主流经济地理学的理论主要依据对主要发达国家实际的研究，绝大多数国家（广大发展中国家）的实际没有在理论上反映出来。基于少数发达国家实际的理论抽象，是否可以应用到其他国家，值得分析。近年来，旅居海外的华人学者基于中国实例在国际上发表了不少成果，但理论贡献并未引起很大关注。

3. 发展中国家急需的经济地理学理论十分薄弱

发展中国家的发展环境、经济发展特点与发达国家均有不同，支配经济地理学研究的思维方式也会有所不同。因此，应该产生相关的理论。但目前状态十分不佳，相关理论构建十分薄弱。

4.2 中国经济地理学的研究背景

4.2.1 经济快速发展但仍处较低水平

1979～2013 年，中国人均 GDP 年均增长 8.49%，为世界经济奇迹。但是 2013 年人均 GDP 仅为 43320 元（国家统计局，2014），处于较低水平（据世界银行 WDI 数据库：2011 年中国人均 GNI 为 4940 美元，在所列举的 214 个国家和地区经济中居第 114 位）。

4.2.2 独特的经济发展特点

包括：①农村工业迅速发展，带来工业化与城市化关系与世界一般规律的不一致。例如，2000 年中国 GDP 达到 1 万亿美元，城市化率仅为 36%；而 20 世纪 60 年代美国 GDP 达到 1 万亿美元时，城市化率超过 80%，日本 20 世纪 80 年代 GDP 达到 1 万亿美元时，城市化率超过 65%（中国市长协会，2003）。②政治、经济体制的特殊方式变革，对经济发展产生了重要影响。由计划经济向市场经济分阶段逐步过渡，政治体制的缓慢变革，在转型国家中形成了一个特殊案例。相应地受其影响的区域经济发展格局特色明显。③发展中国家的外资引入大国。改革开放以来，中国外资引入数量增长十分迅速，现居全世界第一、二位，为发展中国家引入外资最多的国家。外资成为影响区域经济发展的重要变量之一。

4.2.3 人口、资源、环境关系独特

中国的人口与资源环境的关系在世界各国中具有独特性。一方面，作为世界第一人口大国，人均资源量处于较低地位；另一方面，这种资源的区域分布很不均衡，造成区域性人口与资源环境的矛盾十分突出。这为经济地理学的研究提供了特殊的背景。

4.2.4 思维方式

马克思主义、毛泽东思想和邓小平理论，主导着中国社会科学的研究方向。毛泽东关于实践与认识的关系论述，邓小平基于中国国情对发展理论的独到凝练方式，对经济地理学家的研究思路和思维方式均会产生重要启迪。

同时，儒家思想在中国科学研究中仍潜移默化地产生着影响（潘家铮，2002）。例如，儒家思想强调社会和谐，主张全面、辩证地分析问题。天人合一观念是包括儒家思想在内的中华传统文化的理论核心。由此演变而来的人与自然和谐的观点，必然影响以人地关系为研究对象的地理学研究。

此外，也应该注意在中国传统文化中，儒教的宇宙、天地、社会、世道停滞不变观点（天不变道亦不变），反对竞争、反对探索和冒险观点（天地亲师），以及几十年来相关的思想体系、教育模式的熏陶和约束，限制了人们的创新能力。这同样也会在经济地理学研究中反映出来。

4.3 中国经济地理学的研究特点

4.3.1 研究内容：侧重经济发展

作为发展中国家，中国经济发展问题是政府和民众最为关注的议题。与此相应，中国经济地理学家十分重视从地理角度对经济发展相关侧面的研究。诸如流域规划、资源

调查、土地利用；区域规划、地区工业布局、旅游规划、国土整治、开发区战略、可持续发展、企业集群等。这与欧美经济地理学家侧重于在经济发展中所出现的问题（如贫困问题、不平等问题等）的研究形成了明显的比较。

4.3.2 学科定位：自然科学倾向

20世纪中国地理学发展中，自然地理学占据着控制地位。自然地理学家队伍庞大，学科带头人在地理学界的影响也十分突出。近年来，地理基础学科迅速发展，进一步加强了地理学的自然科学倾向。国家学科定位中，地理学属于自然科学，经济地理学当然也不例外。经济地理学家多数均受到系统的地理学训练，自然科学知识比较坚实（但与欧美经济地理学家相比，经济学和社会学的知识则较薄弱）。与此相关联，在科研项目、论文、成果等的学术研究的认定中，自然科学倾向也十分明显。

4.3.3 研究模式：引入理论

中国经济地理学在半个多世纪以来，主要奉行引进理论—中国实际研究—理论总结的研究模式［图4.1a］。20世纪50～70年代，主要引进原苏联学者的经济地理学观点，并结合中国实践，在产业布局、区域规划、资源利用等方面为国民经济建设做了大量的工作。80年代以来，引进欧美学者的经济地理学理论，在区位理论、经济空间结构、外资影响、企业集群等方面进行了系列理论和实践研究。不可否认，以上研究模式对推动中国经济地理学的发展起着重要作用。但是，遵守这种模式的结果，到目前为止，国际经济地理学界来自中国地理学家的声音并不强大，尤其是相关的理论贡献仍很微小。

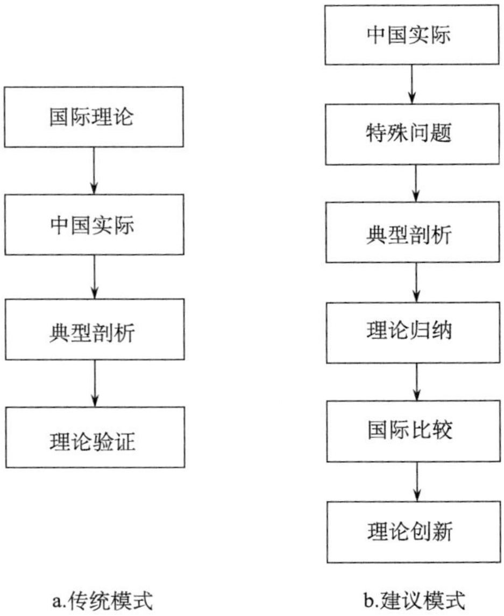

图4.1 研究模式比较

4.4　发展中国特色的经济地理学

4.4.1　深入挖掘中国经济地理学的独特性

在特殊的背景下，中国经济地理学中有许多独特的研究问题，诸如经济高速发展与区域经济格局，城市化与工业化关系（农村男性外出务工，女性在家种地），体制变革与区域发展，外资的区域影响，人口与资源环境关系的区域演化、中国特色的企业集聚（如传统文化与企业集群）等。经济地理学家应当深入挖掘这类具有特殊意义的研究方向，在与国际相关理论比较中，提炼创新观点。

中国经济地理学研究中的特殊思维方式，有不利于经济地理学研究创新的一面，但也有可以促成特殊理论成果的另一面。例如，马克思主义观点、中国传统文化和自然科学方法的共同影响，应该产生不同于欧美的研究范式。

4.4.2　探索新的研究模式

引入理论的研究模式的作用不容否定。但是，以下两个因素应该引起我们的注意：①由于发展阶段和国情不同，在人文社会科学领域，发达国家的经济地理学理论不一定适用于中国；②近 50 年的经验证明，采用引入理论的研究模式，中国并未推出在国际上有影响的理论成果。因此，我们也应该探索其他可能模式。例如，邓小平关于中国发展的系列思想，在世界上所有经济转型国家中具有重大创新意义。这些思想受到马克思主义基本原理的启迪，但是更为重要的是它根植于中国特殊国情，精辟透彻地反映了这一特殊国度的经济发展规律。受此启发，建议的新模式为：从实际出发，不带任何框框，锁定在世界有独特意义的中国经济地理学研究专题，在深入剖析的基础上，提出解释这种地理现象的特有理论，然后与国际相关理论比较，凝练理论创新，逐步构建中国特色的经济地理学（见图 4.1）。

4.4.3　国际接轨与中国特色

在科学文化国际交流日趋扩大的 21 世纪，学术研究的国际接轨对中国经济地理学的发展十分重要。这方面，我们还有许多工作要做。但是，国际接轨并不等于一味尾随。由于发展中国家的特性，发达国家所关注的热点问题，中国经济地理学家并不一定给予同样的关注。我们应该把重心放在促进我国经济发展的相关地理研究上来。

同样，对于英美国家经济地理学研究的社会科学化特点，我们也应给予科学分析。在肯定其积极影响的同时，不能忽视自然科学研究方法对中国经济地理学的发展仍具有重要意义。来自主流经济学家的数量方法、地理经济分析，仍有可借鉴之处。遥感和地理信息系统技术，是经济地理学研究的新的重要手段。

4.4.4　扶植队伍，选准方向，集中攻坚

学术研究需要科学的精神和长期不懈的努力。我国经济地理学研究中，存在一些不利于理论创新的倾向。例如，忙于应付应用性研究，项目成果雷同现象较为普遍；区域

性或专题性研究中，不注意科学问题的提炼和追踪探求；由于教学和研究计划的不断变更，导致学者们研究方向常常变化，等等。为此，建议相关院校，从学科理论创新的高度着手，着力扶植一批经济地理学的基础理论研究队伍。这批队伍能够在对国际学术前沿和中国实际认真分析的基础上，选准优势方向，在相关资金资助下，集中攻坚，持之以恒，一步一步地取得原创性成果。

参 考 文 献

国家统计局. 2014. 中国统计年鉴 2014. 北京：中国统计出版社

李小建. 2002a. 经济地理学近期研究的一个新方向分析. 经济地理，22（2）：129～133

李小建. 2002b. 经济地理学中的企业网络研究. 经济地理，22（5）：516～520

潘家铮. 2002. 正视儒家思想对科技发展的负作用. 光明日报，2002-05-17（B1）

王缉慈. 2001. 创新空间：企业集群与区域发展. 北京：北京大学出版社

中国市长协会. 2003. 2001～2002 中国城市发展报告. 北京：西苑出版社

Barnes T J. 2001. Retheorizing economic geography：From the quantitative revolution to the "cultural turn". AAAG，91（3）：546～565

Bathelt H，Gluckler J. 2003. Toward a relational geography. Journal of Economic Geography，3（2）：117～144

Boggs J S，Rantisi N M. 2003. The 'relational turn' in economic geography. Journal of Economic Geography，3（2）：109～116

Crang P. 1997. Cultural turns and the（re）constitution of economic geography. In：R Lee，J Wills，et al. Geographies of Economics. London：Arnold. 3～15

Johnston R J，et al. 2000. The dictionary of human geography. Oxford：Blackwell. 691

Massey D. 1995. Spatial Division of Labor：Social structures and the geography of production. New York：Routledge

Scott A J. 1988. New industrial space：Flexible production，organization and regional development in north America and western Europe. London：Pion

Yeung H W-chung，Lin G. 2003. Theorizing economic geographies of Asia. Economic Geography，79（3）：107～128

第 5 章　经济地理学与区域经济学的区分

经济地理学和区域经济学都强调空间的概念，考虑经济过程与空间的联系。两学科均与地理学和经济学关系密切（杨吾扬和梁进社，1997），具有综合性、区域性和应用性的特点（魏后凯，2006；杨万钟，1999），研究内容有一定相同（陆大道，2007a），在实践和理论渊源上具有一定的相似性。同时，两学科理论基础均相对薄弱（安虎森，2004；焦连成和陈才，2007）。长期以来，人们对经济地理学与区域经济学分界不甚清晰，有时将两学科互相替代。这种模糊性在一定程度上促进了两学科的交融和发展，但同时也带来了学术界和学生们的困惑。曾有不少人试图分析两学科的差别，研究成果对后人有一定的启发意义，但仍有不少地方难以厘清。鉴于此，本章试图在总结现有研究成果基础上，从学科渊源和继承发展出发，以新的视角（研究组分分解、研究对象层次分析和哲学思维等）对两学科的区分作一分析，以期有助于理清经济地理学和区域经济学的实质差异，促进两学科在相互学习中共同发展。本章中的经济地理学，是指地理学学科中的经济地理学，与经济学家所认为的经济地理学有所不同。

5.1　研究现状评述

近年来，经济地理学和区域经济学之间的联系及差别问题已引起关注。一些学者从学科属性、核心概念、理论基础、学科范式、研究方法等方面进行了对比，认为两学科存在明显区别。①在学科属性方面，一些学者认为经济地理学是自然、技术、经济三者之间的边缘学科。中国经济地理学具有自然科学倾向（李小建等，2004），国际经济地理学研究正发生制度、文化、关系等“多维转向”，其社会科学特性明显（李小建等，2006）。而区域经济学研究区域经济系统（陈秀山和张可云，2003），作为经济学的分支学科，属于社会科学。②在核心概念方面，由于两学科研究角度不同，同样的名词在两学科中拥有不同的内涵。例如，“区域”在经济地理学中是有界的、实体的地域，具有特定的资源、环境与人口特征（王铮等，2002），是一个具体的地表空间。而在区域经济学中区域则是一个客观上存在、但又抽象的空间概念，往往没有严格的边界以及确切的方位（安虎森，2004），其规模大小主要取决于所研究问题的范围和类型。再如，“区位”在经济地理学中主要指事物占有的场所，含有位置、布局、分布、位置关系等方面的意义（李小建等，2006；吴传钧，1998）；而在区域经济学中则是一种“经济区位”，它更多地强调由空间位置所标识的经济利益差别，往往被描述为距离某一个或几个特惠地点的不同位置所反映的市场、供求、（运输）成本等方面的差异问题（郝寿义和安虎森，1999）。③在理论基础方面，经济地理学强调人地关系地域系统理论（樊杰，2008）。区域经济学则侧重区位论和贸易理论，尤其是微观政策的假设推理范式对其影响很大（郝寿义，2007）。随着学科的发展，区域经济学初步形成了包含区域经济发展、区际经济关系和区域经济政策三大部分的理论体系（陈栋生，1993）。④在学科范式方面，经济地理学源自地理学，采用地理学范式，侧重综合思维方式（姚士谋等，2001）。由于地理要素的复杂性和多样性，这种综合性适应其学科研究特色，但也影响其对规律的发现。区域经济学源自经济学，遵循经济学范式（颜飞和罗永刚，2008），注重理论证明。⑤在方法论上，经济地理学受人文地理学方法论的重要影响，侧重于系统分析和区域个性的发挥，在发展过程中主要有经验主义、实证主义、结构主义和人本主义等方法论（贺灿飞，2009；刘卫东等，2009）。与之相比，区域经济学主要采用实证主义方法论，观察区域经济发展、提出假设、建模、检验，强调从一般到具体的演绎和定量分析，解释和建立模型是其中心任务（杨开忠，1999）。因此，它不像经济地理学拥有多元化的研究视角。⑥在具体研究方法上，经济地理学研究采用实地考察法、统计图表法、经济地图法和技术经济论证等传统方法（杨万钟，1999），以及遥感、GIS空间分析等现代方法。区域经济学则常用数学模型的抽象归纳与演绎，并且不同发展阶段侧重的方法不同（陆大道，2007b）。相关研究对理清两学科差异有重大帮助，但两学科的根本区别还要从新角度进一步探索。

5.2　经济地理学与区域经济学差异分析的新视角

5.2.1　学科渊源的组分分析

经济地理学和区域经济学之所以存在差别，在于两学科的研究对象中都有“经济”和“空间”要素。尽管两学科出自不同的角度，但目标对象的相似性及理论观点互相借鉴，和一些边缘学科一样，被学者和实践者拉到一起。两学科在许多方面相互杂交并互取其长，其特殊性渐渐模糊起来。按此发展逻辑，反向思维，我们从溯源的角度，对两学科进行组分分析，对于厘清两学科差别有着特殊意义。

经济学和地理学的交叉研究可以分为A、B和C三个组分（图5.1）。其中，A表示区域经济学所独有的组分，C表示经济地理学所独有的组分，B表示区域经济学和经济地理学所共有的组分。具体而言，组分A是把经济学理论应用于区域经济发展中的

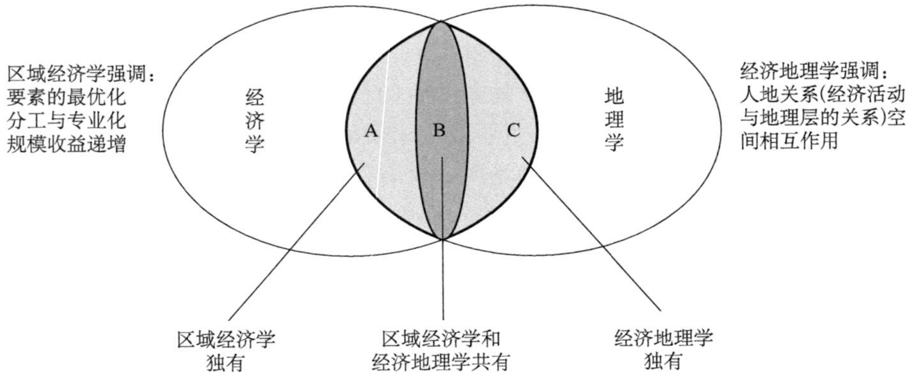

图5.1　区域经济学和经济地理学的组分分析

机理和政策之中，如贸易与区域专业化、产业集聚、区域差异等，主要理论是要素配置的最优化、分工与专业化，以及规模收益递增；组分 C 是把地理学理论落实在经济活动研究中，把经济活动作为人的社会活动的一种，考察自然地理对经济地理圈层的影响（圈层间的关系），如经济活动的地理基础、区域可持续发展、主体功能区（樊杰，2007）等。主要理论是社会经济活动与地理环境相互协调；组分 B 是经济地理学和区域经济学共有的内容，包括工业区位论、农业区位论、中心地理论、经济体的空间相互作用理论等。区域经济学研究 A 和 B 的综合，经济地理学则研究 B 和 C 两部分。

5.2.2 研究内容的层次分析

作为地理学的分支之一，经济地理学研究地球表层的经济圈层与其他地理圈层的关系，经济圈层内各亚圈层（工业、农业、运输业、城市等）关系及经济圈层内各经济活动主体之间的关系（图 5.2）。每个地理圈层不仅提供各种相关要素的质和量，还提供了各要素的空间区位。例如，工厂的建立，应该与自然资源圈层、地形圈层等密切相关。一个地方的经济发展又与其他圈层所提供的各种要素及其空间对应性具有密切关

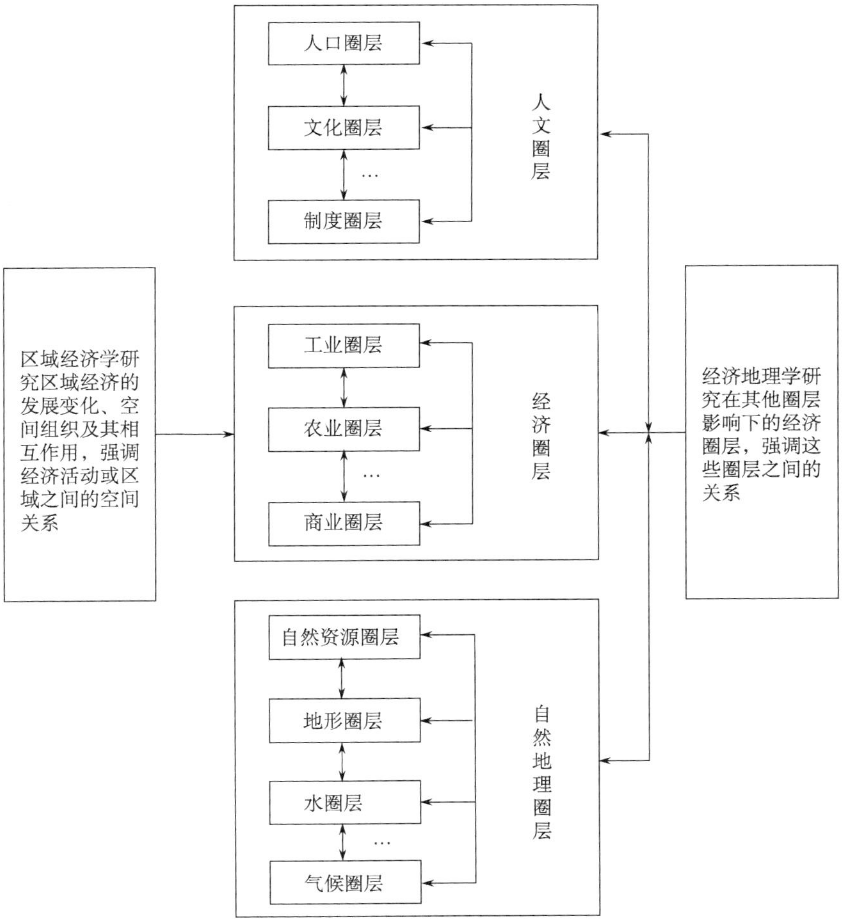

图 5.2 经济地理学与区域经济学研究对象比较

联。通过研究这些圈层的关系，并把经济活动圈层作为研究重点，可以凸显经济活动的地理特征。区域经济学集中于经济圈层内部各种不同区域之间的关系或者不同经济活动空间之间的关系。例如，经济体中增长极的极化和扩散，外围区对中心区的依赖，点轴、网络状空间结构等；区域之间的经济关系，区域经济差异变动趋势等。与经济地理学不同，区域经济学不要求把经济活动放在更广阔的自然背景中考察，也不要求考虑经济活动与自然地理各个圈层的关系。

经济地理学研究人类经济活动和地球表层各层面的关系，即研究人地关系圈层的一个亚层——经济地理层。此外，还研究人类其他活动与地理环境相互作用的经济效果。例如，人类探险并非经济活动，但可以产生经济效果。人类活动与地理环境相互作用效果有积极的一面，也有消极的一面。由于地理环境是一个开放的、复杂的巨系统，涉及自然、社会、文化、生态等各个方面，经济地理学必须用系统的、整体的观点，才能解释各种经济地理现象。

区域经济学强调以经济效果最佳为目标，其出发点要么在资源一定情况下，如何进行选择才能优化目的；要么是通过制度的设计减少资源稀缺程度。两种出发点都对区域经济的优化有积极作用，但多数人侧重于研究区域内各个生产要素如何组合才能达到最优效果。这种最优效果可以通过产出最大或成本最小或综合效益最大来衡量。最初区域经济学就是研究区域内生产要素在空间上如何组合，如工业区位论就是根据原料地、燃料地等，确定生产力如何布局。以后再发展为，区域内经济活动如何布局才能使区域内稀缺资源按照经济学的理论配置达到最优。再进一步引申到区域间的关系。值得注意的是，新近区域经济学也考虑制度、政策和其他上层建筑的作用。

5.2.3　研究思维的哲学分析

在价值判断上，经济地理学以人与自然的和谐为判断标准。它注重每一个区域根据各种自然环境的组合，实现人与自然的和谐相处，不一定达到经济效果最大化。这里的和谐是指一个地方在一定的条件下人们对社会经济感到满意，使用现有生产方式不会带来不可持续的后果，并能够很好地感受自然的给予。例如，西藏的一些地区，可能外界人认为很落后，而当地的人可能感到很满足，自然赐予人们清晰的环境，天然的食物，无虑的生活，这很难用经济收入标准来衡量。区域经济学则不同，它遵循经济学的思维，以人们所普遍认为的经济价值来判断区域经济活动的方向。它运用供求均衡分析、边际替代分析和成本收益分析等方法，追求把稀缺的资源配置到能产生最大利润的地方去，以提高经济效益。

在问题解决的思维上，经济地理学从描述经济活动的空间分布开始，归纳总结理论，强调更加灵活、开放和自由的探索方式（李小建，2004）。由于归纳的理论往往针对具体的研究对象，缺少普适性（梁进社，2008），但都对特殊研究对象具有很强的针对性。区域经济学往往是在一定的假设前提下，如理性人、完全市场结构的假设等，把众多影响区域经济发展的因素抽象为可测量要素（安虎森，2004）。在此基础上，运用演绎方法，尤其是用数学语言来严谨地说明分析对象的因果关系，由于将经济活动的复杂性简化为纯粹的经济因素分析、缺少明确的分析空间单元，以至于很多成果很难用于具体的区域（李小建，2002），但对于科学理论的发展都具有十分重要的意义。

5.3　结论及讨论

总体来看，经济地理学和区域经济学研究内容有重叠，但仍在许多方面存在差别。尤其在学科属性、核心概念、理论基础、学科模式、方法论及具体研究方法上存在一定差别。前人在此方面的努力对区分两学科差别，并互相借鉴具有十分积极意义。在此基础上，本人就学科渊源的组分、研究内容的层次及研究思维的哲学等方面进一步做了探索。

首先，两学科的研究侧重点不同。经济地理学关注经济活动与地理环境的关系，根据区域的自然禀赋，探求人地和谐的区域可持续发展；而区域经济学是把区域经济视为一种经济形态，研究一个区域经济体的增长、结构特征、变迁，以及区域经济体之间的关系，探求区域经济体的形成与发展规律，用经济学的理论和方法解释区域经济体的发展及区际经济关系变化。或者说，区域经济学是将区域内的资源当做生产要素，考虑如何促进稀缺资源有效空间配置的问题。其次，就研究视野而言，经济地理学研究范围大于区域经济学。经济地理学要研究区域经济与地理环境的关系，研究经济要素形成的地理渊源。从考虑区域发展问题看，经济地理学相比区域经济学，可能更长远、更综合。然而，从解释现实问题上看，区域经济学的解释广度、深度和系统性要强于经济地理学①。如果可以将两学科类比成中西医的话，那么经济地理学更像是中医，而区域经济学可能更像是西医。中医将人体看做一个系统，综合诊断，辩证分析所开药方可以治好病，然而可能说不清原理。西医善于运用各种技术诊断病因，然后针对具体病况开药，见效快，能够说清楚治疗的原理，然而可能带有副作用。经济地理学针对特定区域的具体情况，综合研究可对经济活动中人地关系的和谐发展提供好的建议。区域经济学通过分析区域经济问题，提出发展经济建议，但不探求与地理环境的协调发展。

可见，两个学科各有特点，在不同条件下都可以发挥作用。经济地理学在中国国情下有更好的发展空间，尤其是在强调可持续发展、科学发展观的背景下，经济地理学更具有价值，如主体功能区规划（樊杰，2007；中国科学院区域发展领域战略研究组，2009）。强调经济地理学并非轻视区域经济学，经济地理学应该向区域经济学学习，吸纳区域经济学的有益成分，如某些区域在经济发展的阶段，应注重经济效果，结合经济地理学强调环境的特点，考虑可持续发展的同时，进一步增加对经济产出的重视。

两学科过去在互相学习和交融中发展，今后还会在发展中加强合作借鉴。21 世纪以来，地理学家和经济学家共同认识到互相借鉴的重要性，在合作中做了一些实质性工作（李小建，2002）。一是两学科的著名学者合作编著《牛津经济地理学手册》，有 40 位来自欧美的著名地理学家和经济学家就经济空间问题研究的前沿动态和研究方法及今后一段时期经济地理学的研究论题进行论述，互相合作为经济地理学的发展开创了一个很好的先例。二是牛津大学出版社 2001 年新发行了期刊《经济地理学杂志》，由地理学家和经济学家共同担任主编，编委会也由两类学者基本平分。每期刊登大约相同数量的

① 受覃成林教授讨论的启发，特此感谢。

来自经济学家和地理学家的论文。这种交流在地理学和经济学界产生了良好反响，2005年该期刊位列地理学类国际期刊影响因子第一名，经济学类国际期刊影响因子第三名（Puga and Wrigley，2006）。三是地理学家和经济学家所关心的问题共同研讨。例如，2010年美国著名经济学家、诺贝尔经济学奖获得者克鲁格曼在美国地理学年会上发表报告，阐述了新经济地理学与传统经济地理学在学术模式上的差异（潘峰华和贺灿飞，2010），指出传统经济地理学的研究更加贴近实际，更能揭示现实世界的事实性和复杂性，从而为经济学家的新经济地理学的抽象研究在理论上和实践上提供思路；同时，经济学家的新经济地理研究在模型构建、理论演绎方面很值得经济地理学借鉴。双方的交流合作必将有助于经济地理学和区域经济学研究的深入。

参考文献

安虎森. 2004. 区域经济学通论. 北京：经济科学出版社
陈栋生. 1993. 区域经济学. 郑州：河南人民出版社
陈秀山，张可云. 2003. 区域经济理论. 北京：商务印书馆
樊杰. 2007. 我国主体功能区划的科学基础. 地理学报，62（4）：339～350
樊杰. 2008. 人地关系地域系统学术思想与经济地理学. 经济地理，28（2）：177～183
郝寿义，安虎森. 1999. 区域经济学. 北京：经济科学出版社
郝寿义. 2007. 区域经济学原理. 上海：上海人民出版社
贺灿飞. 2009. 关于经济地理研究方法的一些思考//刘卫东，柴彦威，周尚意. 2009. 地理学评论——第四届人文地理学沙龙纪实. 北京：商务印书馆. 65～69
焦连成，陈才. 2007. 中国经济地理学发展困境与对策刍议. 地理科学，27（5）：624～627
李小建，李国平，曾刚，等. 2006. 经济地理学（第二版）. 北京：高等教育出版社
李小建. 2002. 经济地理学近期研究的一个新方向分析. 经济地理，22（2）：129～133
李小建. 2004. 国际背景与中国特色的经济地理学. 人文地理，19（1）：27～31
梁进社. 2008. 经济地理学的九大原理. 地理研究，27（1）：75～84
刘卫东，柴彦威，周尚意. 2009. 地理学评论（第1辑）. 北京：商务印书馆. 1～81
陆大道. 2007a. 区域经济学原理（序一）. 郝守义. 2007. 上海：上海人民出版社
陆大道. 2007b. 中国经济地理学的发展历程. 世界地理研究，16（4）：1～4
潘峰华，贺灿飞. 2010. 新经济地理学和经济地理学的对话——回顾和展望. 地理科学进展，29（12）：1518～1524
王铮，邓悦，葛昭攀，等. 2002. 理论经济地理学. 北京：科学出版社
魏后凯. 2006. 现代区域经济学. 北京：经济管理出版社
吴传钧. 1998. 中国经济地理. 北京：科学出版社
颜飞，罗永刚. 2008. 区域经济学理论范式演进与应用拓展. 财经问题研究，(8)：24～30
杨开忠. 1999. 区域科学学科地位、体系和前沿. 地理科学，19（4）：358～363
杨万钟. 1999. 经济地理学导论.（修订四版）上海：华东师范大学出版社
杨吾扬，梁进社. 1997. 高等经济地理学. 北京：北京大学出版社
姚士谋，管驰明，范宇. 2001. 经济地理学新的思维范畴. 地球科学进展，16（4）：473～477
中国科学院区域发展领域战略研究组. 2009. 中国至2050年区域科技发展路线图. 北京：科学出版社
Puga D，Wrigley N. 2006. Editorial：Two years at the top. Journal of Economic Geography，6（5）：567～569

第 6 章　经济地理学的微观研究

本章沿公司地理、农户地理和小尺度研究三个层面探索了中国经济地理学的微观研究。公司地理主要研究内容包括公司增长空间轨迹、公司空间结构、公司与环境关系等；农户地理研究的主要内容包括农户自主发展能力、农户经济活动区位、农户发展环境、农户与地理环境相互关系等；小尺度研究的主要内容包括从地块角度研究人地系统、专业村与环境关系，以及从点位角度构建区域可持续发展模型等。经济地理学的微观研究有利于抓住经济地理现象形成的基本单元和组成结构，探索地理过程，以及揭示地理现象的形成机理。

经济地理学是从地理角度研究人类经济活动的学科，或者是研究人地关系经济影响的学科，包括人类经济活动对人地关系的影响，以及人地关系相互作用的经济效果。相关研究可以从多个角度进行。相当一段时期内，我国经济地理学侧重于重宏观层面的研究，如 20 世纪 50～80 年代以来，中国经济地理学家在流域规划、资源调查、区域规划、地区工业布局、国土整治、农业区划系统进行了卓有成效的研究（李小建，2005）。在这些研究的基础上，具有中国特色的宏观经济地理学发展起来（王铮，2002）。在研究中，综合性、区域性和应用性特点得以强调（杨万钟，1999）。

与综合性不同，一些学者坚持科学研究的还原论（reductionism）方法(Checkland，1999)。该方法认为，科学在某种意义上是还原的。第一，世界复杂多样，要进行研究必须予以简化、挑选，确定一研究就是为了实现某一目的而对世界某个部分的还原；第二，可以利用奥卡姆剃刀原则（Occam's Razor）进行解释上的还原，如用低层次的规律解释高层次的现象；第三，把现象的整体分解，逐个元素进行分析，这也是科学思维的核心。借鉴还原论原理进行经济地理学研究，可以把复杂的经济地理现象还原为经济活动的基本单元及其组合。就组织单元而论，在工商业为主的区域，企业是一个基本组织单元，区域经济活动的发展、规模、结构、质量等都与企业及其之间的结构有关。在工商业不发达的农村地区，生产组织的最基本的生产单元是农户。

沿着这一思路，与多年形成的中国经济地理学重宏观轻微观不同，本人从 20 世纪 80 年代后期开始着力于微观视角的经济地理研究，持续探索，试图找到经济地理的基本单元。通过研究基本单元的性质、相互结合来研究经济地理现象的形成机理，逐渐形成了公司地理和农户地理的研究方向。此外，人地关系研究可以从更小的空间单元切入，对此也进行了村落及点位角度的探索。

6.1　公司地理研究

对于公司地理，20 世纪后期西方学术界有阶段性研究，结合经验性成果，少数学者进行了理论性总结（McDermott and Taylor，1982）。在分析国外文献的基础上，结合中国实际，我们相继进行了农村工业企业、外资企业和国有企业的研究，重点研究公司增长空间轨迹、公司空间结构、公司与环境关系（李小建，2002），出版了《公司地理论》（1999 年首版，2002 年修订版），同时按照企业区位—区域内企业关系—跨区域企业发展的框架，出版《经济地理学》（1999 年第一版，2006 年第二版），重印 20 余次，被多数高校采用。在公司地理研究上，在以下方面提出一些新的观点。

6.1.1 公司空间扩张的“通道”观点

国际上有关公司空间扩张存在“近邻扩张”和“等级扩张”两种观点。然而，中国的特殊环境，影响公司按以上两种规律的扩张。例如，中国传统文化注重人际关系；在公司新区位选择或兼并其他公司时，熟悉的人际关系（如亲属关系、朋友关系等）易带来这些活动在相应区位发生。还有，计划经济时期的国有企业常隶属于中央某一部门，尽管改革开放以后，企业权力有所扩大，但其扩张中行政体制的影响仍然存在。从而使隶属关系在企业空间扩张中具有重要影响（李小建，2002）。对中国“一拖”（Li，2002）、上海大众（Li and Yeung，1999）等公司的研究表明，在两种扩张之外，中国公司还存在着“通道扩张”，即沿着产业联系、人际关系、体制根植形成空间扩张“通道”。这些通道并不符合“近邻”“等级”原则。这一研究发现为区域发展中借助区外公司的力量找到理论支持。

6.1.2 区域—公司地理研究的综合分析法

关于公司与区域发展的关系研究，地理学家的观点可概括为区域方法和公司地理两大类。前者侧重于区域单元上的统计数据的定量分析（包括结构分析），并不追究与这一变化相关联（或引起这一变化发生）的公司组织变化；后者侧重于公司组织（单个或多个组织）的变化、组织间联系、组织内部结构及其区域影响，并不考虑（或不重视）公司所影响的区域内的整体情况。换言之，前一方法侧重于区域经济变化的结果，另一方法侧重于区域经济变化的过程。

正如图 6.1 所示，企业组织有其自身的系统，一个公司可以仅拥有一个工厂（如公司 A），也可有多个工厂（如公司 B）；这些工厂可以集中于一个区域，也可以分散在多个区域、多个国家。区域也有其自身的系统，从小区到大区到全国到国家间；与工业组织联系起来考虑，区域可以仅有一个公司在此生产（如区域 1），也可以有多个公司在此生产（如区域 2）。从而形成了一个区域有一个（多个）公司进行生产，一个公司可在一个（多个）地区进行生产的排列组合。这种区域与公司组织间的不重合性意味着区域发展与公司发展的目标不一致，尤其是多区位公司与相关区域之间。区域-公司综合分析法将两者结合，从区域角度用多种定量模型分析经济发展的结果，从公司角度分析发展变化的过程（李小建，1991）。运用此种方法很好地解释了为什么一些西方国家（如澳大利亚）政府资助的增长中心不成功的原因，进一步强调了区域经济发展中人为干预与自身增长潜力的关系。进一步推理，区域规划者在澳大利亚区域发展时应该充分考虑公司的发展诉求；在处理公司与区域协调关系时，应充分考察公司的正负外部性。

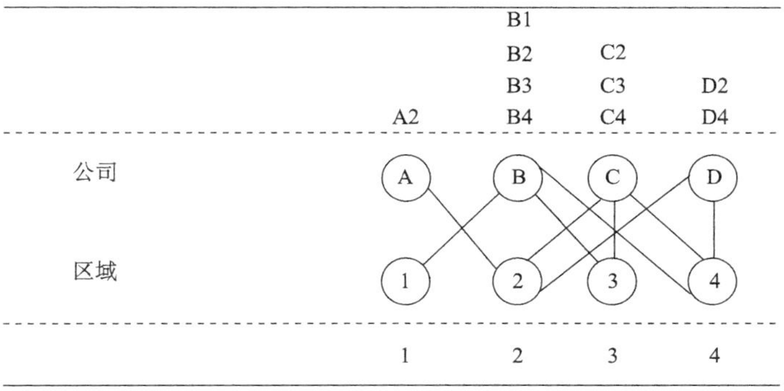

图 6.1　企业组织系统和区域组织系统

注：A、B、C、D 为公司；1、2、3、4 为区域

6.1.3　跨国公司（TNCS）与区域的关系研究

跨国公司对区域差异的影响在国际上存在扩大和缩小之争。不同的国家案例证明了截然不同的结果（李小建，2002）。然而，中国的研究表明，20 世纪 80 年代，海外直接投资主要注入经济不发达的广东和福建。在外资和其他相关因素影响下，这些省份经济迅速增长。反之，经济发展水平较高的上海、天津、辽宁外资投入较低，其经济增长速度也居全国最低之列。与之相应，中国区域差异呈现区域缩小趋势。90 年代，大型跨国公司较多投入沿海发展水平较高的省、市。接受较多跨国公司投资的上海、北京、天津、广东、江苏已属中国经济相对发达区，在外资的带动下，经济增长速度远高于全国平均水平。同时，中国的经济发展省际差异有所扩大。中国的案例证明，进入中国的区位与原有区域经济水平的关系，与国际上一些国家不同，外资对区域差异的影响存在先缩小、后扩大的特点（Li and Yeung，1998）。进一步推理，吸引外资对区域差异的影响，与区域自身条件和跨国公司影响的扩散度有关。

跨国公司与投资地之间的关系具有互补性、竞争性和变化性等特征。跨国公司与区域的讨价状况与各自在本领域内的地位关系密切。发展中国家接受跨国公司投资地区，并不全处于弱势地位，某些特殊地区具有较强讨价力量，从而为该地区带来较大收益。通过对上海市与跨国公司的相互作用研究表明，两者之间的交易关系具有如下特征：中方的交易实力不断提高、大致等同的互相选择以及股权变更上的交易，中方让步十分有限（Yeung and Li，1999）。上海在没有比其他省份对跨国公司作出更多让步（实际上比其他省份对跨国公司进入条件要求更为苛刻）的条件下，吸引了更多的外国直接投资，美国哥伦比亚大学马尔库塞（P. Marcuse）教授将该研究成果称为路径突破性(path-breaking)[①]。

中国外国直接投资的分布格局，综合反映了其他国家的研究结论。跨国投资企业的

① 来自 Peter Marase 1999 年 11 月 1 日 11 时 23 分的电子邮件。

集中区位，既包括了经济发展中心区（如上海、北京、天津等），又具有边界邻近地区的特征（如山东、辽宁与韩国和日本的邻近关系）。不过，由于历史上的联系和地理位置邻近性，以及经济基础条件的影响，不同国别的企业又有相对集中的省、市。尤其值得注意的是，港台投资区位与外资区位不同。他们更侧重人际关系，外资大公司侧重于经济基础和信息（李小建，1996）。

6.2 农户地理研究

农户地理主要研究农户区位、经济活动空间结构及其与地理环境的关系（李小建等，2009）。农户个体活动之外，农户之间通过正式和非正式联系，形成各种各样的群体。这些群体在从事经济活动时，具有一定的内部性。各相关农户行为的相似性和相互利用的正外部性，形成农户群体的空间行为。农户个体和群体行为受地理环境的影响。地理环境对农户的影响又因农户特征差异而不同，这种农户特征表现在利用外部环境谋取发展上，可用农户自主发展能力来度量。农户自主发展能力受地理环境的影响，又反过来影响着农户对环境的利用行为。同样的地理环境，不同的农户由于自主发展能力的差异，形成了不同的发展取向和结果。农户个体、农户群体的居住区位、各种经济活动的区位，这些区位与环境的关系，形成了不同的农户地理研究主题。但其核心是农户与地理环境的相互作用关系（见本书第 9 章）。

6.3 经济地理学的小尺度研究

从空间角度来看，什么是经济地理学研究的基本单元？传统的农村聚落对农村居民人地关系活动的空间具有较大影响。同一聚落居民的经济活动具有一定同质性，对环境的利用也表现出一定的相似性。尽管同一聚落居民的经济活动有差异，农户的经济活动也有差异，但还是可从聚落入手探索农村经济地理学研究的基本空间单元。

6.3.1 从地块角度研究聚落人地系统

在人地关系量化研究中，微观尺度的精细解剖，对于深入认识和解释其内部机理，具有十分重要的作用。基于对河南省巩义市吴沟村 482 块农田的调查实例分析表明，地形因子对山区农村的人地关系相互作用具有重要影响。研究表明：地形因子对山区农田人地系统投入产出特征具有重要影响。其中，高程的影响最为明显，具有随地块的高程增加而逐渐降低的特征；农田地块的坡位与其能量转换效率呈反比例关系；坡型也是影响农田投入产出效率的重要因素，凹坡、平坡产投比明显大于凸坡（李小建和乔家君，2004）。现有人地关系研究多停留在哲学层面，以上成果对人地关系研究从哲学层面进入到科学和操作层面进行了重要的探索。

6.3.2　村域单元研究专业村与环境关系

在农区发展中，专业村具有重要作用。到2010年年初，全国专业村已达45650个，专业村农民人均纯收入高出全国19.4%（孙鲁威，2010）。在分析中部欠发达农区专业村分布及其形成影响因素的基础上，建立了专业村形成和演化机理的分析框架，提出具有企业家精神的农户是专业村形成的核心因素，村庄的地理区位、资源禀赋、传统习惯和经济基础决定着专业村的发展方向，政府推进、市场、技术和宏观经济环境决定专业村的数量和规模。在此基础上，初步归纳出专业村形成发展的三定理：①农户的企业家精神有无决定着专业村的有无。正是那些具有企业家精神的核心农户，通过对传统农业活动的创新，促生新型经济活动的出现，才带来了专业村形成的先导农户。②村庄的区位、资源禀赋、历史传统等决定着专业村的类型。专业村的形成和发展中，村域环境直接或间接受地理因素影响，而企业家精神也是地理因素长期作用的相关联。③区域的政策、市场等环境决定着专业村的数量和规模（李小建等，2009）。

6.3.3　从点位角度构建区域可持续发展模型

在人地关系的研究中，借助遥感和地理信息方法，可以进行更小尺度的空间研究。以区域可持续发展为例，可将大比例尺的地形高程模型以及基于此的地理信息系统，与遥感数据结合使用，评估点位（site）尺度的人地关系协调程度。根据研究区域内各点位（如用TEM数据的30m×30m）的生境条件和一段时间内的人类利用情况，建立各类利用类型的判断基准，以此来评估各点位变化的方向是否更趋于可持续发展（Li et al.，2001）等。如果这种变化向可持续发展基准逼近，则认为该点位上的发展变化的可持续性增强；反之，则可持续性减弱。

6.4　结论及讨论

经济地理学研究涉及社会经济因素，不同尺度之间存在密切联系，探索其研究的基本单元非常复杂。本人沿着这一思路进行试探，有如下体会。首先，企业、农户是经济活动的基本组织单元，但是两者在不同的区域、不同的发展阶段，发挥的作用不一样。在以农业为主的欠发达区域，农户起着重要作用；在以较为发达的工商业为主的区域，公司作为更为明显。其次，与公司地理相比，农户地理有不同特点：①公司的初始区位与原料、劳动力和市场有关，农户的初始区位则与农户生存和生活条件有关。②公司随着规模增大，在空间上不断扩张，分化为不同层级；农户的空间扩张则为短期行为，跨区域空间结构只存在于亲缘农户群之中。③公司空间扩张遵循接触扩张、等级扩张和通道扩张；而农户的空间迁移则与空间效应有关，农户成员的外出务工不严格受空间距离约束。④公司与区域发展形成互相交错的关系；农户与区域发展目标函数则比较一致。这种差异加强了农户地理研究的特殊意义。

经济地理学空间基本单元的探索是一项艰难的工作，也是经济地理研究中最具挑战性的方向之一。不同空间单元存在各种联系，使得基本单元的选择存在种种迷雾。但是农村聚落是人类居住的固定场所，在长期的人地关系中，同一聚落的居民在利用环境进行经济活动中具有一定的同质性。同时，聚落也是人类群体差异性活动的最小空间单元。本章从农村聚落及其活动所涉及的周围地域的角度进行基本单元的探索。期盼相关证明及后续研究。

经济地理学的微观研究具有许多优点。首先，有利于抓住经济地理现象形成的基本单元和组成结构。譬如，农户不仅是一个家庭组织单位，也是欠发达农区重要的生产单元。从农户行为角度研究区域发展，对区域发展现状分析、区域发展目标制定，以及区域政策实施等，均具有特殊意义，其次，有利于地理过程的探索。宏观尺度的研究，离不开对微观尺度地理事实的了解。宏观尺度的研究成果，也不是微观尺度成果的简单综合。最后，有利于揭示地理现象的形成机理。从可持续发展角度，区域并非均质体。把区域作为一个整体忽视了区域内各细微尺度的差异。其研究成果并不能很好地反映所研究对象的实际情况，应用性成果在付诸实践时也会有一定困难。如果对不同的区域均从微观视角入手，借助地理信息系统和遥感技术，利用高速计算机，从点位角度研究区域可持续发展问题，便可收到较好的效果。

除具有上述优点之外，微观研究也具有某些局限。仅从农户（或企业）角度研究，缺乏对全局的把握，容易限制研究的视野，忽视区域背景、国家政策、科技教育对区域整体发展的影响。只有“远观森林，近窥树木”相结合，突出微观的同时又不忽视宏观，才能更好地进行经济地理的微观研究。同时，微观单元的行为和组织方式随着中国的制度变迁，在逐步发生变化。譬如，一些农户随着城镇化的进程，正在变成非农户；新的土地流转政策、新农村建设、农民工新一代的居住和务工行为变化都会在较大程度上影响农户的居住和经济空间行为。这对于经济地理的微观研究既是挑战又是机遇。

参考文献

李小建，高更和. 2008. 中国中部平原村庄农业生产区位研究——以河南南阳黄庄为例. 地理科学，28（5）：616～623

李小建，罗庆，樊新生. 2009. 农区专业村的形成与演化机理研究. 中国软科学，（3）：71～80

李小建，乔家君. 2004. 地形对山区农田人地系统投入产出影响的微观分析——河南省巩义市吴沟村的实证研究. 地理研究，23（6）：717～726

李小建. 1991. 论工业变化的综合研究：以澳大利亚制造业为例. 地理学报，46（3）：289～299

李小建. 1996. 香港对大陆投资的区位变化与公司空间行为. 地理学报，51（3）：213～223

李小建. 2002. 公司地理论（修订版）. 北京：科学出版社

李小建. 2005. 经济地理学研究中的尺度问题. 经济地理，25（4）：433～436

李小建等. 2009. 农户地理论. 北京：科学出版社

孙鲁威. 2010. 专业村成为农民增收就业新阵地. 农民日报，2010-02-26. P1

王铮. 2002. 理论经济地理学. 北京：科学出版社

杨万钟. 1999. 经济地理学导论（修订四版）. 上海：华东师范大学出版社

Checkland P. 1999. Systems，thinking，systems practice：Includes a 30-year retrospective. London：John Wiley & Sons Ltd

Li X J，Peterson J，Liu G，et al. 2001. Assessing regional sustainability：the case of land use land cover change in the Middle Yiluo catchment of the Yellow River basin, China. Applied Geography, 21 (1): 87～106

Li X J, Yeung Y M. 1998. Transnational corporations and their impact on regional economic imbalance: Evidence from China. Third World Planning Review, 20 (4): 351～374

Li X J, Yeung Y M. 1999. Inter-firm linkages and regional impact of transnational corporations: Company case studies from Shanghai, China. Geografiska Annaler B, 81 (2): 61～72

Li X J. 2002. The changing spatial networks of large state-owned enterprises in reform-era China: A company study. Tijdschrift voor Economische en Sociale Geografie, 93 (4): 383～396

McDermott P J, Taylor M J. 1982. Industrial organization and location. Cambridge: Cambridge University Press

Yeung Y M, Li X J. 1999. Bargaining with transnational corporations: the case of Shanghai. International Journal of Urban and Regional Research, 23 (3): 513～533

第 7 章　经济地理学发展的构思

本章指出现今国际经济地理学主流存在着基于少数发达国家的经济发展、基于少数国家的地理背景、基于经济学原理的偏颇，提出基于中国特殊的地理环境、特殊的人口、资源、环境关系、特殊的政府与社会关系、特殊文化、特殊的学科背景建立中国特色的经济地理学。中国特色的经济地理学应侧重经济社会发展，侧重人地和谐，侧重政府的特殊作用，侧重国内区域间关系与全球的影响、侧重与自然地理的关系，在研究中注重自然科学方法与社会科学方法兼顾。中国持续高速增长的经济地理研究、中等收入陷阱的国家与地区跨越、政府特殊作用下的区域发展、城镇化、信息化、工业化与农业现代化关系、人地和谐与区域发展、农村聚落格局的演变趋势等，可作为重要研究问题。

7.1　研究背景与问题

经济地理学的诞生，从 1826 年约翰·冯·杜能的《孤立国》（杜能，1997），1882 年德国地理学家葛茨（W. Götz）的《经济地理学的任务》（杨吾扬和梁进社，1997），1893 年康奈尔大学和宾夕法尼亚州立大学开设经济地理学课程，到 1925 年，*Economic Geography* 杂志出版，学科一直处于地理学和经济学的边缘地位，其发展不断融入了两学科学者的努力（谢泼德和巴恩斯，2003）。不同的学科背景，使地理学家和经济学家的经济地理学研究带有各自的特点。尤其是 20 世纪以后，经济学家在经济地理学领域所做的理论建树具有较大的影响力。20 世纪上半叶的区位论和区域科学以及后期的新经济地理学研究都产生了具有科学价值的理论框架。与此相应，经济地理学逐渐被拉向经济学。

同时，各国学者的研究多基于各自的社会文化背景和熟悉的国家、地区实践，并主要通过英语在国际经济地理学平台（学术会议、期刊、著作等）上交流，这一情况再加上发达国家在国际文化中的强势传统，使得国际经济地理学一定程度上代表着少数发达国家实践和发达国家学者的成果。

如此状况，有什么问题？如果经济学倾向的经济地理学能够解释或解决人们所面临、将面临的问题，如果地理学家接受经济学理论和方法，如果发展中国家会重复发达国家过去走过的路径，上述状况也许没有什么问题。但是，事实是：经济学倾向的经济地理学不能很好地解决人们遇到的问题，尤其是经济和资源环境的矛盾问题，发展中国家也并不完全走过去发达国家的路子。地理学家对逐渐失去地理本意的经济地理学感到担忧。所以，很有必要审视经济地理学的发展现状，对未来的经济地理学发展提出思考。尤其是，世界经济格局正在发生重大变化。诺贝尔经济学奖得主斯宾斯（2012）指出，1750 年开始的工业革命带来的经济快速增长仅限于少数发达国家，影响的只是全球大约 15%的人口。第二次世界大战之后，经济增长在发展中国家出现、蔓延并加速，可能到 21 世纪中叶，使全球 75%或更多的人口居住在发达国家。显然，新的增长所影响的

60%人口的国家的经济地理学成果在国际经济地理学中并无充分反映，这些国家在世界的独特性，使其不可能重复过去15%发达国家走过的路子。同时，占世界人口20%的中国崛起正带来世界经济地理格局的变化；快速增长大国内部经济地理格局的变化带来新的问题，以及经济发展与资源、环境关系的特殊关系带来新的问题。因此，很有必要分析中国特色的经济地理学发展背景，并努力建立重视发展中国家实践的经济地理学。这对于改变现在国际主流经济地理学的偏颇、扩大中国地理学的世界影响具有重要意义。

7.2 经济发展阶段与经济地理学

7.2.1 不同经济发展阶段的经济地理学

是否有不同阶段的经济地理学？也许有人认为，经济地理学主要研究经济地理现象的原因，不应该根据不同经济发展阶段进行划分。但是，一个国家在不同的发展阶段面临的发展环境不同，遇到的经济问题不同，发展的目标不同，经济地理现象发生的机制会不同。同时，随着经济社会的发展，还会出现新的因素，影响经济活动的机理。

1. 关注焦点不同

经济发展的早期阶段关注增长，即如何通过区位和区域空间格局为企业发展和国家经济的快速发展做贡献。例如，杜能、韦伯、克里斯泰勒及廖什的古典区位理论就是探讨如何形成合理的企业或市场区位以追求企业的成本最小或效益最大；佩鲁的增长极理论关注如何将有限的资源投资在具有空间集聚特点和创新能力的推动性行业中，以使经济的增长先发生在少数增长极上（李小建，2006）。后工业化阶段，经济增长的许多外部性显现出来，如区域贫富差距问题、衰退地区问题、环境污染问题、资源枯竭问题等，经济地理学更关注区域之间的协调，以及经济发展与人口、资源、环境的协调。例如，可持续发展理论、区域经济协调发展理论分别强调人口、资源与环境的协调和区域之间发展的协调。

2. 考虑因素不同

早期阶段，经济地理学所研究的影响因素比较简单。随着经济发展，解释经济地理现象发生的影响因素逐步增多，并且由硬到软、由单纯的地理或经济因素到社会、文化、制度因素。以产业集聚研究为例，早期的经济地理学重视产业分布的资源分布或硬设施影响。在工业化发展阶段，马歇尔从劳动力供需市场、中间产品部门的兴起和技术的溢出等几个方面强调了产业区形成的经济因素。而在后工业化时期，经济地理学者分别从产业联系、交易成本、地方根植性、学习环境和创新氛围等方面解释产业集聚的形成机制，出现了许多新的经济地理理论，如新产业区理论、集群理论和区域创新系统理论。这些理论更加强调行为主体之间的互动，以及本地社会文化和制度因素对经济空间系统的影响。在基础设施上从强调本地的交通通信等硬件设施转向强调信息、知识和创新的软环境的构建（王缉慈，2001）。

3. 思维方式不同

不同经济发展阶段，企业的经营行为、管理方式及市场组织方式会发生变化，与此相关，经济地理学研究方法、观察手段、分析技术、思维方式等也发生着变化。例如，在工业化的早期阶段，为追求生产率提高，标准化大批量的福特制生产组织方式占主导，相应地，企业逐渐变大；而在后工业化阶段，为满足消费者个性化的消费需求，使得弹性专业化、后福特制生产模式更有竞争力。由此带来大企业垂直分离，中小企业繁衍，催生了许多中小企业集群的产生。再如，全球经济、政治、社会、科学领域大规模的转型改变了经济地理学者的研究方式，如在经济发展的早期阶段，经济发展的封闭性使得经济地理研究者仅研究本区域内的经济地理现象，重视运输成本和距离成本，而在后工业化阶段，随着互联网和通信技术的爆炸性变革，人们对经济空间现象的关注方式发生改变，经济全球化研究兴起。跨国公司可以在全球范围内组织生产流程及销售渠道，更加重视交易成本、管理成本和创新成本。发展中国家以其特殊的方式融入全球生产网络。全球价值链理论及地方专业化理论成为经济地理学研究的重要理论。以上生产方式和技术手段的变化不仅改变着经济空间格局，也使经济地理学理论不断发生革命。

因此，不同的发展阶段有不同的经济地理学。工业化时代和工业化后期的国家由于关注焦点、考虑国情等的不同，可以出现不同的经济地理学理论和实践。发展中国家不应一味追随发达国家的经济地理学。不同的发展阶段应有与之相适应的经济地理学思想和理论。

7.2.2　经济发展阶段与经济地理学的通用理论

地理学的特点是研究复杂现象的统一（哈特向，1996）。其中，自然状况变化较慢，而人文因素比自然因素变化要快得多。人文现象分析中，包含的要素数目较多，种类也很复杂，并以不同的速度变化着。经济地理学就具有这种特点。但地理研究还是努力寻求其普遍性。从不同的经济发展阶段来看，经济地理学存在一些具有普遍意义的核心理论。

1．理性推理原则

经济地理理论研究中相当一部分是基于理性推理。例如，早期区位理论和当前新经济地理学中的基本逻辑就是这样。只是不同阶段针对不同的研究问题，会在理性推理基础上得出不同的结果，形成不同的经济地理理论。

2．区位分析原理

区位论的核心原理，即寻求对经济活动的空间位置作出解释的一般原理。其主要框架是考虑相关的条件，按照逻辑推理的方法，来寻找合理的区位；成本最小、收益最大或使决策者获得最大满意的区位就是经济活动发生的位置。

3．区域分析观点

有些区域分析的观点可用于解释不同阶段的经济地理现象。例如，增长极理论所揭示的区域增长的观点：经济增长通常是从一个或数个“增长中心”逐渐向其他地区传导。集聚与分散原理也是在任何经济发展阶段都通用的。另外，区域发展模型的建立原理、区域内部结构演变的规律、空间相互作用原理、重力模型等，在不同发展阶段也基本不变。

4．区际关系演化理论

区域间关系的演化存在着一定规律。例如，区域差异理论强调在经济发展中，区域之间应该存在一些差异，有差异才有发展的活力，但差异扩大到一定的程度必须进行干预来缩小差异。均衡发展理论就是在区域差异存在的基础上，为了干预差异扩大而采取的一种策略。在对不同发展时期的一定数量的国别差异分析基础上，威廉姆森等经济学家提出区域收入差异的倒“U”型假说（Williamson，1965）。从经济发展的理论推理和一些实证研究来看，这种区际经济关系的趋势是存在的。

7.2.3　相同经济发展阶段的不同经济地理学

与历史时期同一阶段的国家相比，当前处于该阶段国家的经济地理学，会有一些不同的条件，并影响其发展机理。例如，中国处于工业化中期阶段经济地理学和美国处于工业化中期阶段当时经济地理学就存在一些差别。

1. 后发优势的影响

与发达国家的相同发展阶段相比，后发展国家具有后发优势，这种后发优势作用于经济地理现象，影响区域经济发展机理。发展中国家在经过发达国家已经走过的相同工业化阶段时，就拥有了一些特殊有利的条件，即后发优势。该概念是由美国学者提出的，主要包括：①对现代化的认识更丰富；②可大量采用和借鉴先发国家成熟的计划、技术、设备，以及与其相适应的组织结构；③可以跳越先发国家的一些必经发展阶段；④可对自身现代化前景有一定的预测；⑤可以在资本和技术上获得帮助（格申克龙，2009；列维，1990）。之后，有人又提出了“赶追假说”（Abramjoritz，1989），并进而基于后发优势的技术发展建立了“蛙跳”（Leap-flogging）模型（Brezi et al.，1993），通过计量经济学方法，验证了经济欠发达国家可以通过技术的模仿、引进或创新，最终实现技术和经济水平的赶超（Barro and Sala-I-Martia，1995）。后发优势理论为后发地区的加速发展提供了理论依据和现实途径。

2. 资源环境条件的影响

发达国家在先期工业化的过程中追求经济增长带来了很多外部性问题，如能源消耗、环境污染等。后发展国家在发展中面临发达国家在相同发展阶段很少考虑的资源环境问题，这一方面增加了发展的困难，另一方面也迫使其考虑新的技术和新的发展理念。例如，目前中国在经济增长的过程中，可持续发展的理念已融入生产、社会的各个环节，绿色生产、低碳农业和循环经济等理念的考虑带来了相关经济地理空间的新变化，也引起经济活动与地理环境关系的新格局。同时，能源危机、资源短缺、环境保护等条件约束对后发展国家经济地理学研究具有很大的影响。

3. 世界格局变化的影响

后发展国家与发达国家在世界上的地位不同，可利用的资源、市场等也有很大不同。例如，英美工业化时，在世界上处于领先格局，可充分利用各地廉价的资源和广阔的市场，获取超额利润。然而，中国在进入工业化阶段时，经济发展水平，尤其是人均水平处在世界较低地位，同时许多发展中国家也处于工业化大发展阶段，市场竞争更加激烈。在全球产业整合的过程中，发达国家凭借其技术优势和资金优势占据价值链的高端，发展服务经济，而发展中国家只能以价值链的低端环节进入全球生产网络，沦为“世界工厂”。因此，世界地位的不同影响着国家发展，同时也影响到后发展国家的经济地理学。

7.3　地理背景与经济地理学

7.3.1　经济地理学的地理背景性

地理背景指当地影响经济发展的各种资源环境要素（包括自然、人文等方面）和制度设计。不同的地理因素组合会产生不同的经济地理现象。经济地理学理论多为基于不同的地理背景下的经济地理现象的总结、提升。

1. 经济地理学地理背景性的哲学解释

学科的分类主要基于研究对象抽象程度的层次降低。经济地理活动作为一种地理现象，虽然会遵循地理学规律，但也会有一些例外，也会有些解释的过渡地带。人文因素具有与自然因素不同的性质，从而使学者们将经济地理现象归类，产生了经济地理学。经济地理学是地理学中的一个组合层次，解决这个层次的特定的、自然与人文结合的科学问题。但是，由于经济地理现象的复杂性和影响原因的复杂性，有一些只在一些特定区域出现的特殊经济地理现象，或在特定地区表现突出的地理现象，它们具有特定的答案，特定的因果关系，组成特定的科学问题。因而，这就使得经济地理学进一步分化，产生针对特定问题的独特经济地理学(图 7.1)。

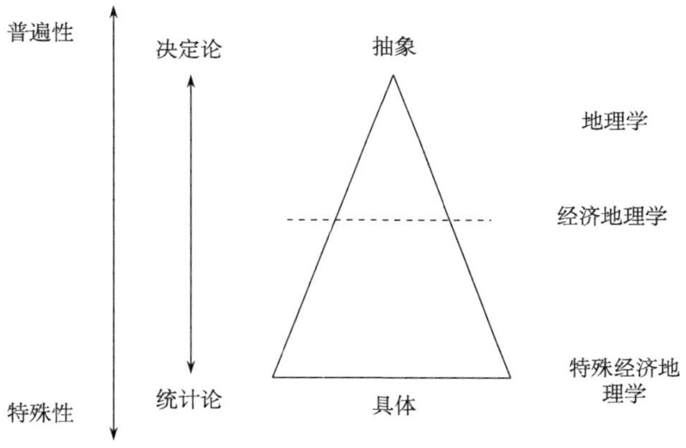

图 7.1　经济地理学地理背景性的哲学思维

2. 经济地理学地理背景性的实践证实

特定的地理背景会产生相应的经济地理学理论。例如，严谨缜密逻辑推理的影响，形成了德国经济地理学的理论演绎分析的传统。例如，杜能的农业区位论、韦伯的工业区位论、克里斯泰勒的中心地理论，都基于对地理事实抽象化，在一定的假设条件下，进行严密的逻辑推导，得出具有一定普适性的结论。区域学派产生于法国，法国地理学家强调区域综合分析，形成区域主义经济地理学（regionalism economic geography）（陆大道等，2003）。经济地域综合体理论产生于原苏联，根据专业化部门与综合发展部门的关系，以专业化部门的企业布局为中心，结合区域的资源、人口、城镇等的分布情况，合理布局综合发展而形成。该理论与原苏联计划经济体制密切关联，具有很强的地理根植性。人地和谐理论源于中国，根据这种文化思维，形成了强调人与地的和谐统一的理论倾向。

7.3.2　不同地理背景的经济地理学共性

在不同的地理背景下，经济地理学具有共性。经济地理学是关注经济活动区位、空间组织及其与地理环境关系的学科。无论是发达国家，还是发展中国家，农业区位论均关注农业经济活动的空间异质性问题，工业区位论、商业服务业区位论主要是资源空间配置的效益最大化。区位论所形成的基本思维逻辑基本一致，即把研究的问题进行简化假设，从而推出基本理论。再逐渐放宽假设，逐步接近现实世界。得出较好解释客观世界的理论。

1. 经济地理现象与地理环境的相互作用关系

自然环境对早期的经济地理现象有着较大影响。例如，英国中部曼彻斯特等工业城市，德国鲁尔工业区、美国东北部工业区都是世界上著名的工业发达区，其早期的发展与当地的资源条件具有密切关系。经济地理现象发展又有一定惯性。受路径依赖的影响，经济地理学发展到一定程度，常常保持着一定的既有态势继续向前发展。例如，区域产业发展的路径依赖（英国伦敦金融业，瑞士的钟表业等）。

2. 经济地理学研究的基本逻辑

经济地理学理论体系中包括的观点很多，但不同地理环境与其经济社会活动的关系有一个基本点，经济发展对自然环境的影响，与自然环境对经济发展的约束应该有一个均衡空间。超过这个空间，就会为两者带来冲突，与此相关，在经济活动中市场自由发展、社会力量推动、政府干预有一个结合点：经济活动的地理分布与资源环境的合理配置相协调。

7.3.3　特殊地理背景下的经济地理学

经济地理学理论含有普适性的规律，也有例外情况，前者是制约经济地理学的内生力量，后者影响经济地理学具有偶然性和特殊性。经济地理学并非在所有国家、区域同等地出现与发展，而是受相应的地理背景影响。特殊的地理背景对经济地理学发展起着重要作用，可以促进特殊的经济地理学。以下结合中国地理背景的特殊性，对其中三方面作以分析。

1. 国家政治制度的影响

世界各国采用不同的政治制度。不同的政府由于经济干预对国内区域的影响不同，形成不同的经济地理学发展背景。

中国是一个强大政府的国家，国家制度影响区域经济发展。国家在区域发展中的特殊作用使中国区域发展明显显现国家干预的特色。20 世纪中期到改革开放初期，中国政府主要加强东北老工业基地的发展、加大内地建设发展步伐。1979 年以后，陆续实施沿海发展、西部大开发、中部崛起、东北老工业基地振兴等战略（陆大道等，2003）。

在国家主导发展的基础上，陆大道（2001）以增长极理论和生长轴理论为基础，根据中国实际提出“点-轴系统”理论模型和国土开发与经济布局的“T”字形战略，后又对理论模型的科学基础及模式、形成机制进行推导和深入阐述，形成了系统的“点-轴”渐进扩散理论。

基于中国实际，中国经济地理学家提出了主体功能区规划。根据不同区域的资源环境承载能力、现有开发密度和发展潜力，统筹谋划未来人口分布、经济布局、国土利用和城镇化格局，将国土空间划分为优化开发、重点开发、限制开发和禁止开发四类，确定主体功能定位，明确开发方向，逐步形成人口、经济、资源环境相协调的空间开发格局（樊杰，2007）。

2. 国家规模的影响

国家规模及其资源组合情况影响经济地理学的发展特色。具有较大疆土的国家要比面积很小的国家区域问题更为突出。中国的沿海发达区，基本进入现代化，但中西部一些贫困区，仍然停留在较为落后的欠发达阶段，几十年来变化很小。与此比较，新加坡就没有什么区域差异。

如果一个大国又面临着区域差异巨大状况，而这种差异又伴随着国家的快速持续增长而发生巨大变化（如中国原有区域差异叠加上快速发展带来的新的区域差异），可为经济地理学带来独特的研究问题。

3. 特殊环境条件的影响

自然环境的特殊性会影响经济活动空间格局。例如，叶大年通过对自然地理与经济活动的关系研究，提出全新的观点：①地质的对称决定自然地理的对称；②自然地理的对称决定经济地理的对称；③气候条件，特别是雨量和年平均气温会改变自然地理的对称性，也对某些经济现象施以影响；④人们的重大政治经济活动会影响经济地理的对称性；⑤平衡发展是社会稳定的因素，区域发展不平衡的原因之一是区域地质地理条件的差异性，若一个地区经济地理格局不对称或反对称，则该地区经济就不能持续发展（叶大年等，2001）。

7.4 学科背景与经济地理学

7.4.1 学科背景与经济地理学差异

经济地理学的研究与经济学和地理学关系十分密切。由于学科背景不同，基于两个学科的经济地理学在学科属性、思维范式、具体方法和成果性质等方面都存在明显差异。

1. 学科属性的差异

在一些国家，经济地理学受社会科学的影响较大，经济地理学的发展更具有社会科学的属性，而另一些国家的经济地理学坚持自然科学属性。例如，在欧美一些国家，地理学系设在人文或社会科学学院，经济地理学中的"多维转向"很大程度上受人文社会科学研究的"多维转向"思潮影响；主要地理类期刊，如美国地理学家协会会刊 *AAAG*、*Professional Geographer* 和英国地理学家协会会刊 *Transaction of the Institute of British Geographer* 均为 SSCI 源期刊；经济地理学家可评选为中国社会科学院院士。中国的经济地理学研究具有自然科学倾向。大多数经济地理学家都受到过良好的自然地理学训练，在科研项目、学术论文及其他成果多归属自然科学（李小建，2004），经济地理学家可评选为中国科学院院士。

2. 哲学思维的差异

经济地理学有来自地理学和经济学的哲学思维，两学科的哲学思维方式存在着一些差异。来自地理学的经济地理学家侧重实证主义和统计论，强调综合思维（李小建，2002）。由于地理要素的复杂性和多样性，这种综合性适应其学科特色，但也限制其对规律的发现。来自经济学的经济地理学家侧重规范分析和决定论，强调理论证明。由于将经济活动的复杂性简化为纯粹的经济因素分析、缺少明确的分析的空间单元，以至于很多成果很难用于具体的区域（李小建，2002）。在价值判断方面，来自地理学的经济地理学家以人与自然的和谐为判断标准。它注重每一个区域根据各种自然环境的组合，实现人与自然的和谐相处，而不一定达到经济效果最大化；来自经济学的经济地理家则遵循经济学的思维，以人们所普遍认为的经济价值来判断区域经济活动的方向，强调运用供求均衡分析、边际替代分析和成本收益分析等方法，追求把稀缺的资源配置到能产生最大利润的地方，以提高经济效益。

3. 技术方法的差异

来自地理学的经济地理学家多采用实地考察法、案例分析法、遥感技术、GIS 空间分析、计量分析等技术和方法，对经济地理问题进行类型分析和机理分析。对于机理分析往往通过两种途径考察不同地理要素分布间的关系：一种是通过不同地图叠加；另一种是计量模型。例如，利用实地调查方法和计量模型对典型产业集群的形成和演化、社会网络与知识创新的关系等问题进行研究；借助地理信息系统和遥感技术，利用高速计算机，从点位角度研究区域可持续发展问题。来自经济学的经济地理家通过提出假设、建立模型、检验模型，强调一般性的因果关系的演绎和定量分析，与此相关，从一般规律到具体应用存在着许多需要解决的问题。

4. 成果性质的差异

地理学的经济地理学成果往往从描述经济活动的空间分布开始，归纳总结理论，强调更加灵活、开放和自由的探索方式（李小建，2004）。由于归纳的理论往往针对具体的研究对象，缺少普适性（李小建，2006），但对特殊研究问题具有很强的针对性，其成果倾向于解释过去事实和解决现在的问题（樊杰，2007；叶大年等，2001；李小建，2002）。经济学的经济地理学成果则在一定的假设前提下，如理性人、完全市场结构的假设等，把众多影响区域经济发展的因素抽象为可测量要素（李小建，2002）。在此基础上，运用演绎方法，尤其是用数学语言来严谨地分析对象的因果关系，其成果倾向于解决现有的问题和对未来的预测。例如，克鲁格曼通过假定从事制造业的劳动者可以自由移动，并且他们主要向高工资的地区移动，运用演绎方法得出结论：当运费和其他贸易费用较低，制造业部门将在一个地区不断集中；当运费和其他贸易费用超出由于集中生产所带来的收入递增的效果，那么，集中的趋势将会减弱，可能会出现分散布局的趋势（段学军等，2010）。

7.4.2 不同学科背景下经济地理学共性

1. 研究内容的共性

两个学科都强调空间的概念，考虑经济过程与空间的联系，核心都力图解释地理空间的经济集聚与经济增长。它们所共有的研究内容包括工业区位论、农业区位论、中心地理论、经济体的空间相互作用理论等。两个学科都强调经济空间关系，并且解释经济空间的形成时，都涉及其他的相关要素。

2. 理论渊源的共性

从农业区位论的产生到艾萨德的区域科学出现期间，两个学科在科学理论上注入了共同的东西。一方面，这一时期的学科分野不甚清楚，学者们从不同方面共同研究经济空间现象。譬如，杜能在构建农业区位理论的过程中，出色地应用了边际分析方法，并用这种方法分析了分配问题，最先把边际理论扩大到包括地租、利润和工资理论在内的全部分配理论，并把这些理论应用于空间分析（姚士谋等，2001；梁进社，2008）。另一方面，区位论是区域增长的总体分析和区域间关系分析的基础。尤其是20世纪80年代末以来，无论地理学家开展的新产业区、区域创新系统研究，还是经济学家所开展的经济活动空间聚集研究，也都是微观经济主体区位研究的拓展。譬如，克鲁格曼的新经济地理学着手微观的经济区位过程机制，并采用规模经济、报酬递增等作为宏观与微观衔接的线索，把微观的区位理论和宏观的区域发展和产业集聚融合，较为全面地论述了从区位到经济区域演化的路径（段学军等，2010）。

3. 研究动因的共性

两者都强调解决实际问题。长期以来，无论是地理学家所开展居民点的空间和等级秩序、制造和零售活动的最佳区位研究，还是经济学家所关注的贸易和交通通信的地理结构研究，其目的都是为经济主体的区位选择和区域发展提供理论基础和政策指导。例如，地理学家通过从制度经济学、经济社会学甚至文化经济学中寻求灵感，将原来单纯的经济要素分析转向社会、文化和制度要素与经济要素的综合研究，为新产业区的发展和区域创新系统的构建提供了理论支持。经济学家提出的工业区位理论主要围绕在原料、燃料和市场地给定的情况下，工业企业布局的最优区位而展开。区域科学围绕着经济活动的空间集聚、运输成本的作用，以及区域经济的动态演化三个论题展开研究（艾萨德，2009）。

7.4.3　地理学科中的经济地理学

地理学中的经济地理学，不仅研究经济活动区位、经济活动的空间组织，还要研究经济圈层与其他人文圈层、自然圈层的关系。第一，研究经济圈层与其他地理圈层的关系。一方面，自然地理圈层为经济圈层提供物质基础和活动场所。例如，微观层面上工厂的选址与矿产资源、水、地形等圈层等密切相关，宏观层面上某个地方的经济发展也与其他圈层所提供的各种要素及其空间组合具有密切关联。另一方面，经济圈层和人文圈层间的关系也十分密切。微观层面上，企业选址会受到当地的社会、文化、习俗和制度等的影响，宏观层面上地方的产业类型和经济绩效也与人文圈层密切相关。因此，通过研究这些圈层的关系，并把经济活动圈层作为研究重点，可以凸显经济活动的地理特征。尤其是在人口、资源、环境和发展相互协调不断得以关注的情况下，这种圈层关系研究更具有重要意义。第二，研究经济圈层内部各种不同区域之间的关系或者不同经济活动空间之间的关系。例如，区域中各种经济体的空间关系，经济体中增长极的极化和扩散，外围区对中心区的依赖，点轴、网络状空间结构等；区域之间的经济关系，区域经济差异变动趋势等。第三，研究经济圈层内各经济活动主体之间的关系。各经济主体（如农户、企业等）的区位及其空间关系是经济活动圈层内经济格局的微观基础，对经济地理学其他层面的研究具有重要意义。例如，传统工业区位论考虑根据原料地、燃料地和市场地的企业布局，公司地理考虑公司总体空间格局。中国农区主要经济活动主体是农户，农户居住区位、生产区位、务工区位形成各自的活动空间，各农户活动空间之间的关系形成特定的农区发展基础。

7.5　中国独特的经济地理学

7.5.1　构建的特殊视角

国际上主流的经济地理学，侧重于发达国家经济地理现象的理论总结，侧重于少数欧美国家地理背景的现象和机理的归纳，侧重于人文社会科学，尤其是经济学原理的应用。这种状况，对于推动经济地理学有一定积极意义的同时，也存在一些偏颇（图7.2）。

建立中国特色的经济地理学，要考虑众多中国特色环境因素，其中以下三方面值得特别关注：①考虑发展中国家，尤其是全球化快速推进、各种发展阶段并存背景下的发展中国家，尤其是占世界人口重要比重、其发展对世界有重要影响的发展中国家的实践。②考虑特殊国家的地理背景。尤其是人口、资源背景、政治背景、文化背景均十分特殊、在世界有重要影响的大国的地理背景与发展的关系具有重要意义。③考虑特殊的学科背景，尤其是经济地理学的自然学科属性、经济地理学与自然地理学的关系，尤其是在人们需求日益增长下经济发展与资源、环境协调的情况下的这种关系。中国特色的

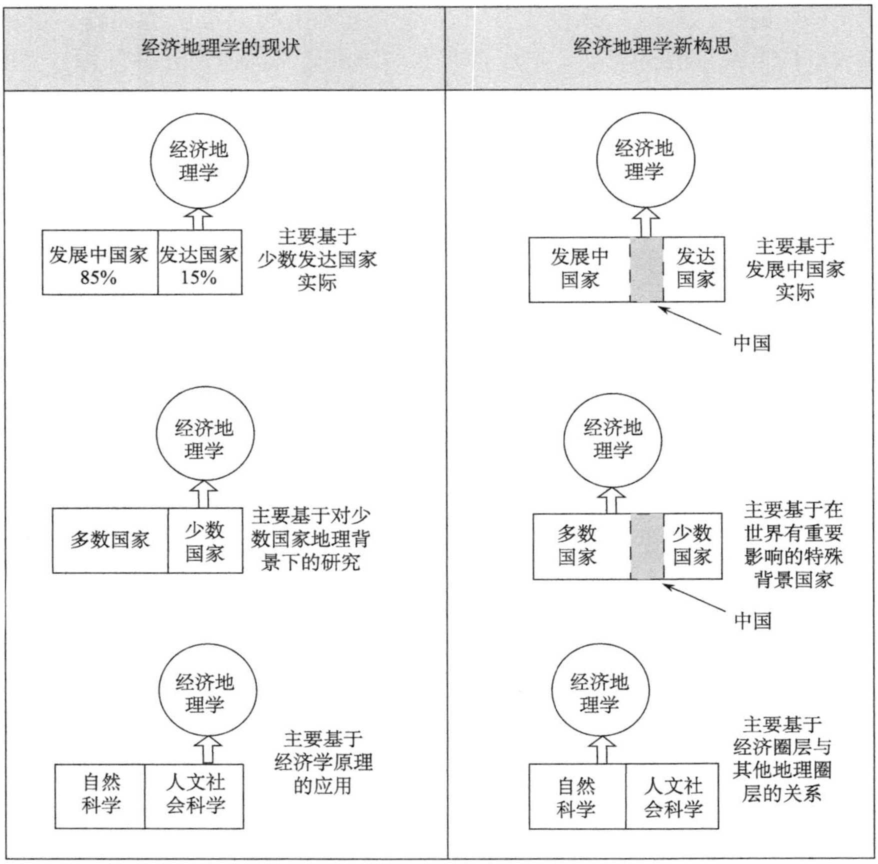

图 7.2　经济地理学的新构思

经济地理学就是对世界有重要影响的，具有特殊地理背景且快速增长的发展中大国，强调经济地理现象与人口、资源、环境协调关系的经济地理学。

7.5.2　发展中国特色的经济地理学的新考虑

在中国特殊的地理环境（大国、地理差异明显、经济差异明显等）、特殊的人口、资源、环境（人均资源贫乏、人口与资源分布错位明显等）、特殊的政府与社会关系和政治体制下，中国特色的经济地理学应该侧重经济社会发展、侧重人地和谐，侧重政府在发展中的特殊作用、侧重国内区域间关系与全球的影响、侧重经济地理与自然地理的关系，兼顾自然科学方法与社会科学方法（图 7.3）。

7.5.3　重要的研究问题

中国特殊环境下的经济地理学研究中，有许多研究问题在世界上具有重要意义。

1. 中国持续高速增长的经济地理研究

中国 1979 年以来连续 33 年的高速增长为国内各区带来机遇挑战，同时，中国高速

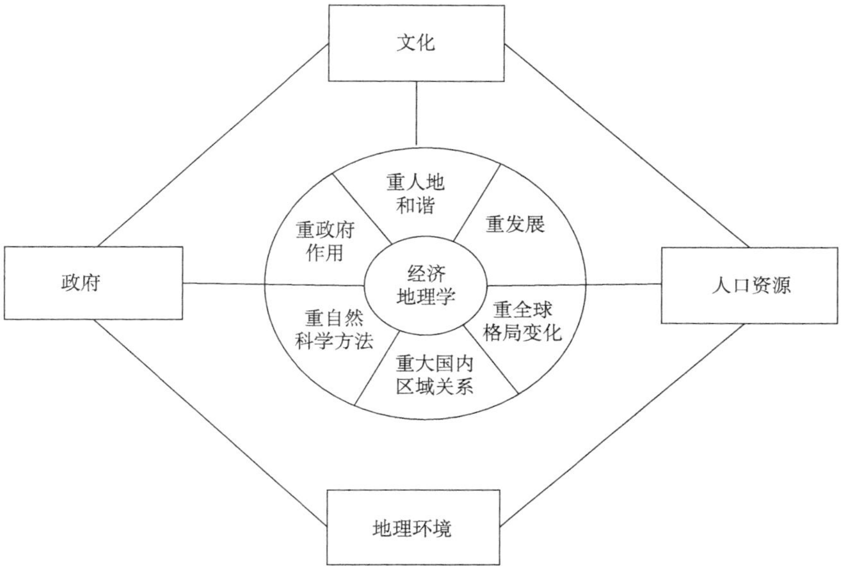

图 7.3　中国特色的经济地理学框架

增长带来了新的区域经济不平衡。后发展地区要发展，先发地区出现一些新的发展问题。中国持续高速增长对区域经济不平衡的影响，对资源环境的挑战，长期高速增长后的发展问题、典型区区域发展问题等都可能带来经济地理研究的新发展（中国科学院区域发展领域战略研究组，2009）。

2. 中等收入陷阱的国家与地区跨越

2011 年中国人均国内生产总值已超过 5000 美元，已处于“中等收入陷阱”阶段。与其他同阶段的国家一样，中国也出现城乡收入差别变大、“中等收入阶层”弱小等制约其跨越发展的瓶颈（蔡昉，2011）。但中国的经济增长速度仍然保持在较高水平，按现在的增长趋势，2022 年左右中国可能达到人均国内生产总值 1 万美元以上（胡锦涛，2012），实现“中等收入陷阱”的跨越，现在一些省、市、区（北京、天津、上海、浙江、江苏、内蒙古、广东、福建等）已达到该水平。中国的成功跨越将为世界发展中国家跨越树立典范。在跨越中各区域之间增长特殊问题、城乡协调问题、产业结构问题等都是经济地理学研究的重要课题。

3. 政府特殊作用下的区域发展

政府强大可以有效地促进经济发展，也有出现灾难的风险。中国政府的组织形式及影响力对中国经济发展具有特殊作用。与西方选举制度相比，中国政府不被利益集团所左右，决策可以符合区域总体利益；官员考核与经济发展挂钩，可以激励政府更多关注经济状况；中央集权也可以进行先试点再推广的改革模式，便于总结的区域政策在更大范围推广。当然政府的强大及集权决策，也可能带来“政绩”效应；缺乏科学论证，使决策人的短期利益造成长期的负面影响。但不管如何，中国政府与企业经济活动区位、区域经济的关系为经济地理学研究提供了独特的案例（陆大道等，2003）。

4. 城市化与工业化

中国的城市化明显滞后于工业化，城市化也表现出显著的区域差异（陈明星等，2010）。大量的农民工作为工业化的主力军；农村地区的工业仍然在工业化中占据一定份额。这种情况明显有别于发达工业化国家。由此形成的人口流动、工业化与城市化的空间格局有其一定的独特性，它是中国特殊的地理环境和社会环境的产物。同时，政府又通过多种方式加快城镇化。即使在快速城市化中的城市化与工业化关系也存在着与西方发达国家不同的路径。中国工业化空间差异明显（刘伟等，2008）。与此相关形成中国独特的空间价值链、空间生产链、空间消费链。这种链条影响着区域经济的差异，又表征着空间劳动分工。随着中国经济的发展，这种空间关系很值得关注。

5. 农村聚落格局的演变趋势

中国的农村聚落空间格局有长时间的演变历史。现在的聚落空间是长期的人地相互作用的产物（许家伟，2013）。随着城市化、工业化和农业现代化进程的加快（何传启，2012），聚落的格局正在发生重大变化。中国特殊情况下农村聚落演变有可能形成独特的空间结构模型。例如，农村聚落的最优规模问题、空间格局问题等，不同区域不同人地关系下规模结构会有不同，但支配其不同的基本理论是什么？德国地理学家对聚落等级中支配的中心地理论，在不同环境下会发生变形。但这种变形有没有异质性，同样的人地关系背景下有没有共同性，都非常值得研究。

6. 人地和谐与区域发展

“天人合一”是中华传统文化的主题。天，就是大自然；人，就是人类；合，就是互相理解，结成友谊。“天人合一”可以解读为，人类只是天地万物中的一部分，人与自然是息息相通的一体，要和平共处，不要讲征服与被征服（季羡林，2008）。地理学研究的核心是人地关系（吴传钧，1998）。经济地理学要研究经济活动与地理环境的关系及人地关系的经济效果。“天人合一”思想在经济地理学中的具体体现应该是人类经济活动的人地和谐。正像德国社会学家韦伯认为：中国文化的自然价值，与当代的环境保护与社会发展是相适应的（韦伯，2010）。坚持用中国传统文化基础上的经济地理学研究，对世界的经济地理学发展将会作出新贡献。

参考文献

埃里克·谢泼德，特雷弗·J·巴恩斯. 2003. 经济地理学指南. 北京：商务印书馆
蔡昉. 2011. “中等收入陷阱”的理论、经验与针对性. 经济学动态，(12)：4～9
陈明星，陆大道，刘慧. 2010. 中国城市化与经济水平关系的省际格局. 地理学报，65 (2)：1443～1453
段学军，虞孝感，陆大道，等. 2010. 克鲁格曼的新经济地理研究及其意义. 地理学报，65 (2)：131～138

樊杰. 2007. 我国主体功能区划的科学基础. 地理学报，62（4）：339～350
何传启. 2012. 中国现代化报告 2012：农业现代化研究. 北京：北京大学出版社
胡锦涛. 2012. 坚定不移沿着中国特色社会主义道路前进　为全面建成小康社会而奋斗. 人民日报，（11）：8，1
季羡林. 2008. 谈国学. 北京：华艺出版社
李小建. 2002. 经济地理学近期研究的一个新方向分析. 经济地理，22（2）：129～133
李小建. 2004. 国际背景与中国特色的经济地理学. 人文地理，19（1）：27～31
李小建. 2006. 经济地理学（第二版）. 北京：高等教育出版社
理查德·哈特向. 1996. 地理学的性质. 叶光庭译. 北京：商务印书馆
梁进社. 2008. 经济地理学的九大原理. 地理研究，27（1）：75～84
刘伟，张辉，黄泽华. 2008. 中国产业结构高度与工业化进程和地区差异的考察. 经济学动态，（11）：4～8
陆大道. 2001. 论区域的最佳结构与最佳发展——提出“点-轴系统”和“T”型结构以来的回顾与再分析. 地理学报，56（2）：127～135
陆大道等. 2003. 中国区域发展的理论与实践. 北京：科学出版社
马克思·韦伯. 2010. 中国的宗教：儒教与道教. 康乐. 简惠美译. 桂林：广西师范大学出版社
迈克尔·斯宾塞. 2012. 下一次大趋同：多速世界经济增长的未来. 王青，刘其岩译. 北京：机械工业出版社
麦里安·J·列维. 1990. 现代化的后来者与幸存者. 吴荫译. 北京：北京知识出版社
王缉慈. 2001. 创新的空间. 北京：北京大学出版社
沃尔特·艾萨德. 2009. 区域与空间分析. 杨开忠，沈提燕，方森等译. 北京：北京大学出版社
吴传钧. 1998. 人地关系与经济布局. 北京：学苑出版社
许家伟. 2013. 乡村聚落空间结构的演变与驱动机理——基于长时段视角对河南省巩义市的考察. 开封：河南大学环境与规划学院博士学位论文
亚历山大·格申克龙. 2009. 经济落后的历史透视. 张凤林译. 北京：商务印书馆
杨吾扬，梁进社. 1997. 高等经济地理学. 北京：北京大学出版社
姚士谋，管驰明，范宇. 2001. 经济地理学新的思维范畴. 地球科学进展，16（4）：473～477
叶大年，赫伟，徐文东，等. 2001. 中国城市的对称分布. 中国科学（D 辑），31（7）：608～616
约翰·冯·杜能. 1997. 孤立国同农业和国民经济的关系. 吴衡康译. 北京：商务印书馆
中国科学院区域发展领域战略研究组. 2009. 中国至 2050 年区域科技发展路线图. 北京：科学出版社
Abramjoritz M. 1989. Thinking about growth. Cambridge：Cambridge University Press
Barro R J，Sala-I-Martia X. 1995. Technological Diffusion，Convergence，and Growth，National Bureau of Economic Research，Working paper series No. 51
Brezi E S，Krugman P R，Tsiddon D. 1993. Leap-frogging in international competition：A theory of cycles in national technological leadership. American Economic Review，83（5）：1211～1219
Williamson J G. 1965. Regional inequality and the process of national development：A description of the patterns. Economic Development and Cultural Change，13（4）：3～45

第 8 章 《地理学报》中的经济地理学发展

总结一时期内的研究成果，对于梳理和展望学科发展具有重要意义。21 世纪以来，已有不少文章对经济地理学的发展进行回顾、反思和展望（陆大道，2000；樊杰，2008；刘卫东等，2011）。这些文章多纵览了地理学多种刊物及其他相关刊物发表的成果及学术专著，比较全面地总结了经济地理学的发展，梳理相关研究成果的思想脉络，对于扩大学科的影响及前瞻未来发展趋向起了重要作用。

《地理学报》作为中国地理学的最权威期刊，经济地理学作为重要的地理学科之一，80 年来《地理学报》刊登了一批具有各时代代表意义的经济地理学论文。除了极少数特定背景下引介国外学术思想的文章外，绝大多数论文反映了地理学家结合中国实际的高水平研究成果。评述 80 年来这些文章所反映出的中国经济地理学发展变化，可以从另一个侧面观察中国特色的经济地理学变化历程。如果说各种成果的综合评述描绘的是经济地理学这个"人"的全貌的话，那么，评述《地理学报》的经济地理学论文则可更加简洁地勾勒出"人"的骨骼。"骨骼"发育状况标志着"人"的健康成长，支撑着"人"呈现不同的外形。

由于地理学的论文存在一定的学科交叉，在以下研究中，我们主要依据论文主题是否研究经济活动来判断该论文是否属于经济地理学论文。具体包括经济活动区位、空间格局与演变，以及经济活动与地理环境的关系。对于一些跨学科的人文地理学论文，如果研究内容涉及经济活动、经济行为，如城市经济功能区、城市间经济网络，以及城市内部经济活动空间结构、旅游业发展等论文，也列在本章的分析之中。而城镇体系、城市化、城市功能空间结构、旅游行为方面的论文不再列为经济地理研究。书评和会议报道也未被纳入。按照以上标准，从 1934～2013 年，《地理学报》共发表经济地理论文 421 篇。

本章基于 80 年来《地理学报》发表的经济地理论文，从论文数量、发展脉络、研究范式、面向国家需求、学科发展变化等方面梳理了中国经济地理学发展，总结了相关研究特点。论文统计表明，经济地理学研究不断发展，各学科发展很不均衡。呈现密切联系经济发展中的新问题、从经济增长研究转向可持续发展研究、从与自然关系密切的要素研究转向人文要素的研究、研究领域从注重物质生产转向非物质领域等特征。分支学科发展侧重于区域、工业和农业，但交通、商业服务业、城市等也呈增长趋势。学术思想来源多元化、研究尺度多样化、研究方法定量化。总的来看，中国经济地理学呈现出紧密服务国家需求、侧重宏观研究、侧重经济增长、侧重应用型研究的研究特点，但在微观研究、综合研究、理论凝炼方面存在不足，同时也正在逐步加强。

8.1 经济地理学论文数量分析

8.1.1 经济地理论文数量的变化

相对于自然地理学，80 年来《地理学报》刊登的经济地理学类论文数量并不是很多。从绝对数量上看，80 年代中期之前每年在 5 篇之下，21 世纪随着地理学报变为月刊，总刊登数量增加，经济地理论文上升到 20 篇以上（图 8.1）。

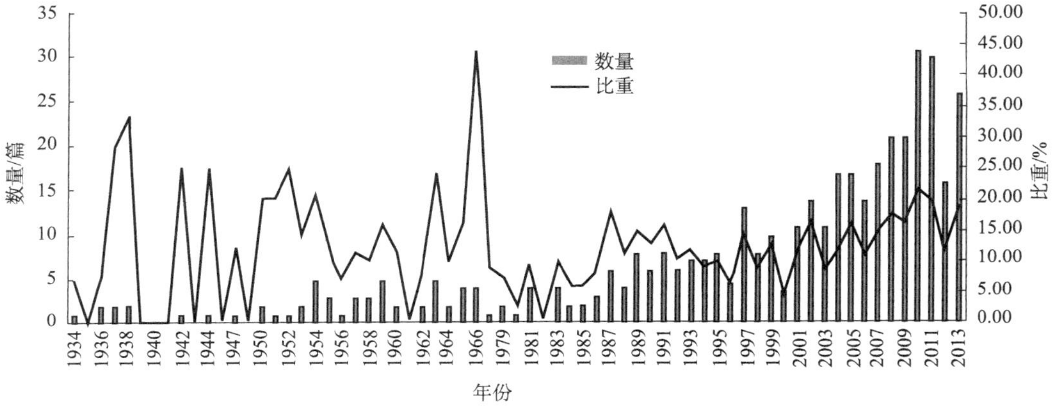

图 8.1 历年地理学报刊载经济地理类论文数量和论文比重图

如果把 80 年分为 1934～1949，1950～1979，1979 年以后三个阶段的话，发现阶段之间存在以下差异。1934～1949 年我国经济地理学发展非常缓慢。只是在农业区划、边疆考察等方面有小规模研究。这一时期，《地理学报》刊登经济地理类论文 10 篇，年均发表量不到 1 篇。其原因一是经济地理人才较少，经费缺乏。二是国内政局不稳定，经济发展缓慢，经济地理学的研究缺乏激励与需求。

1950～1979 年，在“以任务带学科”指引下，经济地理学科研和生产结合，学者们通过参加各种大规模综合考察和专题调查研究、农业区划，发表了大量密切结合国家经济建设需要的论文。同时也发表介绍苏联经济地理学家和经济地理理论的译文。期间，《地理学报》刊登的经济地理类论文 48 篇，年均发表量 4 篇（不包括 1967～1977 年停刊期）。其内容主要与经济地理调查任务有关（赵松乔，1953）。在实际研究的基础上，学者们对区域自然特性及其经济价值进行了一些理论总结（杨吾扬，1964）。

改革开放以后，西方理论大量引入，中西方交汇，促进了理论的深入与发展。同时我国经济迅速增长，新的主题不断出现，研究区域、研究内容、研究视角开始多元化，经济地理研究进入百花齐放的时期。《地理学报》刊登经济地理类论文增长的势头开始表现出来。1980～2013 年，总数量达到 365 篇，年均刊登量近 11 篇。

经济地理论文占总论文的比例，各年份虽然有些波动，但大致维持在 10%～15%（图 8.1）。20 世纪 80 年代之前，由于地理学报刊登的论文总数量相对较少，加上经济地理研究不稳定，所以所占比例波动大一些。80 年代之后，波动变小，稳定中微有所上升。在地理学学科不断分化、分支有所增加的情况下，经济地理学论文比例仍然能一直保持这一比例，表明经济地理学研究的持续发展。

8.1.2 论文的学科分布

根据 80 年所发表的经济地理论文的学科相近性，可以将其分为 10 个类别。从中可以看出，各学科发展很不均衡（表 8.1）。1979 年以前，《地理学报》刊登的经济地理论文中，农业地理居于首位，多数是农业区划、规划方面的成果。论文学科分布反映了经济地理学为农业服务这一特点。此外，该阶段理论经济地理学和区域经济地理学也有一定的发展。

表 8.1 《地理学报》1934～2013 年刊载的经济地理论文学科分布 （单位：篇）

年份	理论	区域	工业与企业	农业	商业与服务业	交通	旅游	能源	城市	其他	总计
1934～1949	0	2	1	4	1	2	0		0	0	10
1950～1979	20	5	3	16	0	4	0		0	0	48
1980～1989	8	9	5	3	2	1	1	1	4	0	34
1990～1999	16	26	15	5	2	6	2	0	6	1	79
2000～2013	13	55	44	23	32	28	14	5	30	6	250
总计	57	97	68	51	37	41	17	6	40	7	421

1979 年以后，经济地理学的其他分支学科论文发表数量有较快增加。其中，区域经济地理和工业地理呈现较快的发展势头。值得注意的是，农业地理学研究在 1979～1999 年一度减弱。2000 年以来，商业与服务业、城市、旅游、交通、区域等经济地理学分支学科研究发展旺盛，论文发表的数量也较多，少则 10 多篇，多则 50 多篇。受到我国新的经济发展阶段影响，消费、能源、碳排放、技术和海洋开始进入经济地理学的研究视野。

8.2 经济地理学发展脉络

《地理学报》作为国内高水平的地理学综合期刊，发表的论文代表着中国经济地理学的主要方向和水平。虽然这些论文研究的具体科学问题多种多样，但都没有偏离“区位、空间组织及其与地理环境的关系”这一经济地理学研究经济活动的视角。只是随着社会经济的变迁，经济活动空间的因素、条件、机制发生了变化，学者们不断从新的角度探索经济活动空间规律。分析《地理学报》80 年发表的经济地理论文，可大致梳理中国经济地理研究发展的脉络。

8.2.1 从与自然关系密切的要素研究转向人文要素的研究

20 世纪 80 年代以前，基于中国当时所处的发展阶段、产业结构特征及学科体系背景，经济地理研究主要面向国民经济紧迫需求，针对与自然资源开发（李文彦，1957）、自然地理环境密切相关的物质生产部门（李文彦，1978），解决发展中涉及生产力布局的一些重大问题。其中，农业地理和资源型工业部门地理是研究的重点领域。

改革开放以来，信息化、全球化、科技发展和创新能力等客观上成为影响中国区域发展的新因素、新产业空间形成的主导因素（苗长虹，2006）。区域竞争力等的核心构成要素，与传统的自然资源条件、交通地理位置等的关系逐渐疏远，而以科技创新为主体的区域创新能力、体制优势、文化和价值观的包容性等的影响作用越来越大，对其作用机制的研究加强了经济地理学对多种人文要素的分析，同时导致了学科在微观研究层面的进一步分化，科学问题具体化、多样化。

8.2.2 研究领域从注重物质生产转向非物质领域

20 世纪 80 年代以前，我国经济地理研究偏重于农业、工业、资源等物质生产领域，并进行了农业、工业布局理论与方法的总结（李文彦，1957）。80 年代以后，对非物质生产领域的研究逐渐加强，开拓了许多新的研究领域，如商业服务业、旅游、消费等，改变了农业地理、工业地理为主导的学科架构。从城市商业中心区位（宁越敏，1984）、零售业空间（杨吾扬，1994）探讨，到 21 世纪初的 CBD（阎小培等，2000），以及近年来对金融（李小建等，2006；贺灿飞和傅蓉，2009）、物流（孙峰华等，2010）、会展（方忠权，2013）、生产性服务业（申玉铭等，2007）的研究，体现了中国学者不断从新的视角、用新的理论来研究中国现实问题。其中，旅游业虽然起步较晚，但发展迅速，迄今为止，已在旅游区位、旅游发展影响因素、旅游客源市场与游客行为、旅游外部影响等方面取得了丰硕的研究成果。受一些国家后工业化研究影响，创意（朱华晟等，2010）、技术流（许学强等，2002）也开始成为经济地理学的研究对象。

我国经济地理学研究领域的这一变化一方面是和国际研究接轨有关，更重要的是和我国经济发展阶段变化有关。随着我国经济的发展，诸如旅游、物流、会展、金融等生产性服务业对于经济增长质量和效率、区域软环境的改善和竞争力的提高越来越重要，需要对这些产业的发展条件、区位、空间组织开展地理学研究。

8.2.3 在区域发展研究中，从经济增长转向可持续发展

在较长时间内，经济地理学论文集中于经济增长相关方面的研究。随着持续高速的经济增长对资源环境的压力增加，生态环境逐步恶化；同时，区域发展差距扩大，区域发展失衡；区域创新体系建设严重滞后，缺乏全球竞争力。在这一背景下，学者们研究了区域经济差异（李小建和乔家君，2001）、区域发展战略（陆大道，1987）、可持续发展问题（陆大道，1994）。以区域为主要研究对象，开展综合研究，实现资源、人口、环境、社会、经济的持续发展，克服了以往拼盘式或形式综合的缺点，体现了当今地理学走向统一的趋势。21 世纪以来，我国学者从区域承载力（毛汉英和余丹林，2001）、碳排放（张雷，2003）方面深入研究可持续发展问题。主体功能区研究使得我国经济地理学研究成果应用再次上升到国家战略层面（樊杰，2007）。

8.3 经济地理学研究范式的转变

8.3.1 学术思想来源变化

我国现代经济地理学发展受到国外一些学术思想的影响。《地理学报》发表的论文，直接介绍国外学术思想的不多，国外影响主要通过实际研究反映出来。1949 年以前，地理学家侧重于对中国农业地理的实际研究，唯见任美锷介绍西方工业区位理论（任美锷，1944）。德国学者韦伯 1909 年出版《工业区位论》，但其英文版则在 20 年之后。任美锷先生的文章对中国早期经济地理学发展具有重要影响。1950 年以后的一段时间内，我国经济地理学界主要学习原苏联。包括介绍原苏联著名经济地理学家（李文彦，1954），介绍原苏联经济地理课本的编写经验（巴朗斯基和王正，1954）。1955 年更有刊载的译文介绍经济地理学研究各国各地区社会生产配置的规律性，及其生产发展的条件和特点（瓦秀金和郭振淮，1955）。一段时间内，学界的理论讨论主要围绕这一问题，实际研究的指导思想也深受其影响。直到改革开放，陈才（1962）深受巴朗斯基区域学派的影响，同时又考虑中国传统的“人地关系”思想，发表文章提出经济地理学除了研究人地关系、生产配置外，还应研究经济区划与区域。

20 世纪 80 年代以后，我国经济地理学学术思想来源更为多元化。受计划经济的影响，在继续研究经济区划、产业布局问题时，陆大道以西方新老古典区位等理论为依据，并根据生产力空间发育的“点-轴”扩散原理提出我国未来工业空间发展的“T”形结构系统（陆大道，2001）。90 年代以来，受传统人地和谐思想的影响，学者们进行了区域可持续发展（毛汉英，1991）、主体功能区（樊杰，2007）的研究。同时，受西方经济地理学的制度转向、文化转向、关系转向、尺度转向和演化转向等思想的影响，有些学者运用新的视角、新的理论来研究中国现实问题。例如，在实地调查基础上对集聚与集群（王承云等，2013）、知识溢出与创新（王铮等，2003）、企业空间组织网络（王成金，2008）、全球化与地方化（苗长虹，2006）等问题进行理论分析；受微观研究思想的影响，对城市商业中心区位（宁越敏，1984）、农户行为（李小建，2002）等进行研究。与过去传统思想相比，这些融入新思想的研究颇显新意。

8.3.2 研究尺度与视角变化

尺度方面，经济地理学研究经历了小尺度到大尺度，再到多尺度相结合的变化过程。改革开放前，经济地理学以小尺度区域研究为主。期间《地理学报》所刊载的论文除少数介绍国外经济地理学研究和教学经验外，大多以省域或省域内某一区域为研究对象。1949 年之前，由于受经费限制和战争影响，资料收集不易，地理学者往往结合以前的资料，以及小规模的区域考察，开展经济地理学的研究；新中国成立后，经济地理学对农业区划、工业布局等问题进行理论探讨的同时，一些论文对县域农业区划的经验（萧俊城，1965）、人民公社的建设经验（张同铸等，1959）进行理论总结。此外，还有一些论文对河流流域（杨吾扬和蔡清泉，1959）、盆地（梁溥等，1956）等地理单元的经济地理现象和经济条件进行描述。改革开放以后，结合国家经济建设需要，经济地理学在较大尺度上围绕国土整治、流域开发、交通运输布局等进行研究，虽有少数学者结合特定区域实际，围绕工业区位（李为，1986）、城市内部商业区位（宁越敏，1984）、工业区（沈小平，1987）开展小区域尺度研究，但总体而言以大尺度研究为主，相对忽略区域内部差异的分析。20 世纪 90 年代以后，随着数据来源的多样化，GIS 技术和遥感技术的应用，经济地理学研究多尺度相结合，研究更加精细。例如，基于多尺度对中国区域经济差异（陈培阳和朱喜钢，2012）、以村镇为尺度对专业村发展（李小建等，2012）、村域经济转型发展（李裕瑞等，2013）等问题进行研究。即使是同样的研究地区，其研究也更加精细化。例如，以县域数据为基础研究全国的经济差异（李小建和乔家君，2001）、耕地利用和劳动力变化（刘彦随和李裕瑞，2010）、地域多功能性评价（刘彦随等，2011）；以乡镇数据为基础研究省域经济发展差异（李小建等，2008）。

视角方面，经济地理学研究由为政府管理服务的单一视角向政府、企业和农户相结合的多元视角转变。改革开放前，由于农业区划、人民公社建设等均以政府为主导，该时期所刊载的论文主要服务政府需求。改革开放后，大多学者继续从政府管理的角度对工业布局、流域开发等进行研究，但也有少数学者从企业的视角对特定经济地理问题（如工业区企业的布局、城市商业中心区位等）进行研究。尤其是 20 世纪 90 年代以后，学者们除继续重视从政府调控视角对区域经济差异（李小建和乔家君，2001）、主体功能区（樊杰，2007）、产业空间集聚（贺灿飞等，2007）等的研究外，越来越多的研究强调企业、农户等微观经济主体在经济地理格局塑造、变化中的作用。他们以农户为研究视角，对旅游决策行为（杨兴柱等，2005）、区域旅游开发（许振晓等，2009）等问题进行研究；以企业为研究视角，对跨国公司功能区位（贺灿飞和肖晓俊，2011）、外资银行区位（贺灿飞和傅蓉，2009）、信息通信企业区位（袁丰等，2010）、城市内部软件企业区位（毕秀晶等，2011）、会展企业集聚（方忠权，2013）等问题进行研究。

8.3.3 研究方法的转变

80 年期间，经济地理论文的研究方法大致呈现以定性为主，到定性和定量并重，再到以定量为主的变化过程（图 8.2）。20 世纪 80 年代中期以前，经济地理论文的研究以定性为主。其中，50 年代中期以前，文字描述和地图描述是经济地理学研究的基本方法。期间刊载的 10 篇经济地理论文，基本都是这种方法对农业生产分布（胡焕庸，1934）、工业区域（任美锷，1944）和交通运输（孙宕越，1937）等进行分析。50 年代中期以后，开始采用案例解剖、示意图、统计图表和不同类型地图对区域农作物生产力（任美锷，1950）、农业生产规划（程潞等，1959）、工业企业布局（陆大道，1979）等进行研究，同时，以归纳总结的方式对农业区划、工业布局、经济区划（李文彦和陈航，1983）的实践进行理论总结。此外，受原苏联经济地理学研究方法的影响，个别学者也尝试应用数理方法（杨吾扬，1963）。

80 年代中期以后，出于类型划分和机理分析的需要，以数理统计为基础的定量方法开始得到应用。一些学者继续运用案例研究、示意图等定性分析方法对工业区位模式（李为，1986）、地域结构的演变（蔡渝平，1987）、区域开发的宏观格局（陆大道，1987）、高新技术企业的集聚与扩散（王缉慈等，1996）等进行研究。同时，另一些学

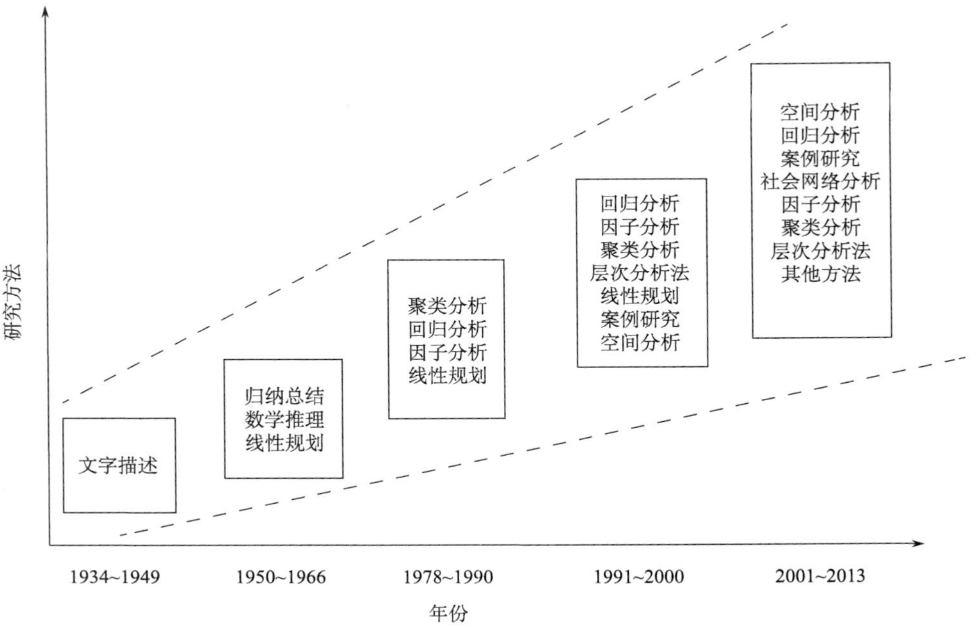

图 8.2　80 年来《地理学报》经济地理学论文研究方法变化示意图

者尝试构建衡量指标，使用聚类分析方法、回归分析方法、因子分析方法、投入产出表等定量方法研究工业布局变化（胡兆量，1986）、商业中心区位（宁越敏，1984）、城市与腹地的经济实力（顾朝林，1991）、城镇工业职能分类（周一星和布雷德肖，1988）、客流产生和分布的影响因素（张文尝，1988），以及工业综合体的结构（樊杰，1989）。值得注意的是，该阶段所采用的数据主要是横截面数据。

90 年代中期以来，随着 GIS 和遥感技术的广泛应用、计量技术的发展和学科间交流的增多，经济地理学研究方法呈现出更加定量化、多元化和综合化的特征。表现在：①用地理信息系统软件对城市软件企业分布（毕秀晶等，2011）、产业空间组织（刘鹤等，2011）、交通建设的经济贡献（王伯礼和张小雷，2010）等经济地理现象和过程进行更为深入的定量分析。②新的计量方法和模型的引入助推了各类经济地理过程的运行机理分析。例如，离散选择模型的运用有助于对各类型企业区位（贺灿飞和傅蓉，2009；毕秀晶等，2011）的影响因素分析；空间计量模型引入有助于区域间贸易流量（刘卫东等，2012）、信息技术对服务业创新影响（方远平等，2013），以及区域经济发展收敛（洪国志等，2010）等研究，可克服传统参数估计方法的偏误；向量自回归模型、脉冲函数和方差分解函数有助于揭示能源效率对产业结构、能源消费结构演变的响应机理（王强等，2011）。③模拟分析通过简化、概括所研究的经济地理现象和过程[如高铁经济区内城市通达基准点的时间（陆军等，2013）、商业空间结构（薛领和翁瑾，2010）]，可深入探明其本质和活动规律。④社会学、物理学和生态学等学科研究方法越来越多被引入经济地理研究中。例如，将社会网络分析方法引入旅游流空间网络结构（陈超等，2013）、城市经济网络（汤放华等，2013）、企业迁移（毕秀晶等，

2011)、供应货物网络(潘裕娟和曹小曙,2012)等研究中,生态学时空等价模型运用于区域经济发展机理研究中(陈国阶和王青,2004),引力模型、场强模型等用于对城市腹地范围(蒋海兵等,2010)、风景名胜区市场范围(王铮等,2001)等的研究;熵值法运用对城市投资环境的状态进行分析(程连生,1995),系统动力学模型用于对多种区域政策进行模拟仿真(刘小金等,1991)。

8.4 满足国家需要的研究主题变化

我国经济地理学研究十分注意与国家需求的紧密结合(陆大道,2000)。《地理学报》发表的论文很好地反映了对国家有重大影响的研究关注。

1. 20世纪50年代农业区划研究

新中国成立初期,为了指导农业生产,研究了全国农业分区问题,积极开展农业区划理论探讨,包括农业区域形成、农业区划的原则、农业区划体系(周起业,1957;周立三,1964)。一些农业区划实践工作也在《地理学报》上发表(宋家泰等,1959)。

2. 20世纪60年代的工业布局和区域规划

20世纪60年代,与国家经济建设需要相结合,经济地理学者开展了以重点项目布局和联合选厂为中心的区域规划、区域工业生产综合体、城市工业开发区和科技工业园区的发展论证等各项工作。一些学者对区域规划的主要任务以及经济地理学在区域规划工作的作用等给予了论述(张之和张学芹,1960)。对工业布局实际工作进行了理论与方法的总结(张文尝,1981)。

3. 20世纪80年代初的国土规划

我国政府提出开展国土规划,实施国土整治的战略任务。经济地理学者参加了全国和各地的国土规划工作,并开展了理论研究和总结(杨树珍,1983;魏心镇和林亚真,1989)。

4. 20世纪80年代以来的特定区域发展研究

一方面,随着地区经济实力的增强,区域性经济开发已经成为我国社会主义经济建设中具有战略意义和长远意义的问题之一,与此相对应,区域发展战略、发展政策、中心城市与区域开发方面的研究增多(陆大道,1987)。另一方面,许多地区发展与环境之间的矛盾更加突出,地区之间的发展差距明显扩大。经济地理学者也发表区域可持续发展(陆大道,1994;毛汉英,1991)和区域差异研究成果(李小建和乔家君,2001)。进入21世纪以来,为了实现国家区域之间,人口、资源与环境之间的相互协调,我国经济地理学家提出并开展了主体功能区理论研究和主体功能区规划实践工作(樊杰,2007)。

8.5　经济地理学各学科研究的发展

虽然经济地理类论文在《地理学报》比例不大，但各个时期发展的论文都代表了当时研究的最高水平，引领和反映了经济地理学各分支学科发展。

8.5.1　理论经济地理

由于经济地理学研究多是通过区域和产业研究开展的，经济地理理论研究论文不多，有 57 篇。主要探讨以下问题。一是对经济地理学研究对象和作用的讨论，这样的论文有 16 篇。包括经济地理学研究对象是生产配置还是生产力配置的讨论（曹廷藩，1958），主张人地关系、生产与部门配置、区域与规划是经济地理学研究的三个侧面。认为经济地理学在不同时期分别侧重于人与环境、地域分异和空间区位三个方面，有相互谐和的趋势（杨吾扬，1992），此外，也有论文讨论了在经济建设中，经济地理学如何为经济发展服务。例如，经济地理与区域规划的关系（张之和张学芹，1960），经济地理学如何评价自然条件（邓静中，1963），经济地理与持续发展研究（陆大道，1994）。2000 年以来，有一些讨论新经济地理学理论问题的论文，从制度、文化、关系重新理解区位和空间（李小建和苗长虹，2004），认为空间、区位是人类活动构建出来的。空间观与传统经济地理学物质空间、几何空间的空间观有较大的差别，但实证研究成果很少见到。

二是对实践的理论与方法的总结。包括地域结构理论及其相关的工业布局、农业区划理论与方法、国土规划理论（杨树珍，1983；胡序威和胡听主，1965；邓静中，1963）；空间运输联系规律和工业基地交通运输布局（张文尝，1981）等。也有学者提出区际联系研究，认为在过去从特定区域的个性或独特性，转向地域差异或分异，又转向区际联系（李春芬，1995），这是学科发展和客观形势的要求。

三是探讨信息化等技术变化对经济活动区位、空间组织的影响（刘卫东和甄峰，2004）。认为信息技术可以从企业、城市、区域多个层级变更社会经济空间组织，由于过程的复杂性，信息技术会导致经济活动集聚（集中）或者分散，还无法确定。

8.5.2　区域经济地理

20 世纪 50 年代以前，区域经济地理研究主要是开展一些经济地理调查。80 年代以来区域主要围绕区域发展理论和应用研究。理论研究集中于地域结构演变（蔡渝平，1987），区域经济增长因素（杨晓光等，2002），区域经济格局、差异及其演变（李小建和乔家君，2001），区域可持续发展（毛汉英，1991），区域经济增长阶段与转型（齐元静，2013）等。应用性研究包括区域发展战略与政策（陆大道，1999），区域经济布局与规划（魏心镇和林亚真，1989），区域开发与合作（林初升，1997）等。

这些论文发表时间和数量反映了我国区域经济地理研究的一些特点：一是从区域分异研究转向区域联系方向，如区域合作、一体化研究明显增多。二是从单纯的经济增长转向区域可持续发展综合研究。三是加强区域发展过程研究。总的来看，这些论文通过区域发展实践，实证了一些区域发展的理论观点，同时也从不同侧面对中国区域发展的过程进行了理论阐释，对区域发展的方向提出了有益建议。

8.5.3 工业与企业地理

80 年来，《地理学报》发表的工业地理论文有 73 篇，主要集中在 1990 年以后。20 世纪前半叶只有少数地理学家偶尔涉猎工矿调查或介绍国外工业区位理论（任美锷，1994）。新中国成立后，经济地理学家在学习和引进国外理论的同时，结合实际，对我国工业布局的基本规律进行了讨论和总结，如工业企业成组布局、地域工业综合体、自然与技术经济因素对工业布局的作用。这种理论总结工作一直持续到 20 世纪 80 年代末。

20 世纪 90 年代以来，工业与企业地理发展较快。一是研究领域有较大扩展，主要集中在高新技术产业（王缉慈，1996）；中国农村工业（苗长虹，1998）；外资（许学强和李胜学，1995）；产业集群（苗长虹，2006）；研发、创意产业（许学强和李胜学，1995）。二是从研究的视角看，更加重视微观经济主体，公司地理学发展较快。强调市场因素对工业区位的影响，计划经济时期的"布局"研究味道减弱。三是从知识、集聚等因素探讨工业区位的论文越来越多，资源、交通等传统因素的探讨逐渐减少。

8.5.4 农业与农区地理

20 世纪 30 年代，地理学家在农业区域划分及其影响因素上进行了研究。胡焕庸关于农业分区、人口密度与农产区域（胡焕庸，1934）、全国农业区划（胡焕庸，1936）的研究在农业地理研究方面具有一定开拓意义。周淑贞（1938）也发表了农业区划研究成果。

20 世纪 50 年代到 80 年代，农业地理处于一个相对稳定发展时期。一是农业区划理论研究深入。周起业（1957）提出了我国农业区划的基本原则。指出农业区划应该以乡、县为基本单元，划分全国一级农业区、省内二级农业区和县内三级农业区的农业区划体系。其他学者在农业区域的形成演变、内部结构及其区划体系（周立三，1964）、县级农业区划的任务、内容和方法方面进行了研究。二是对农业区划实践指导方面，研究了全国农业分区问题，形成农业区划的相关成果（宋家泰，1959）。在这一时期，郭焕成等进行了全国农业类型研究，建立了中国农业类型体系（郭焕成，1992）。

20 世纪 90 年代以来，以"三农问题"为主题，研究的问题较为综合。①农业地理研究由以前的农业区划向农业可持续发展转变。例如，通过农业结构的内涵，农业现代化过程引起的农业结构变化分析，提出发展农业地理学的若干思考（曾尊固，1994）。从区域比较优势发挥角度分析了中国农业产业结构调整的基本态势（刘彦随，2003）。②农区研究论文增多。包括从人口与资源、生态环境等因素探讨了农村经济发展的趋向、农村经济发展的制约因素和持续稳定协调发展的途径（周立三，1990）。从小尺度研究了地理环境对农区发展差异、专业村发展的影响，认为地理因素对农区发展的影响仍然存在，并没有变小（李小建等，2008，2012）。从不同类型农区发展的动力机制和发展模式，研究转型期的农区类型问题（张富刚和刘彦随，2008）。③关注农户行为研究。进入21世纪，地理学家根据对大量农户的调查，分析了制约欠发达农区的农户行为（李小建，2002）、农户自主发展能力（李小建等，2009）、农户收入的地理影响因素（李兴绪等，2010）等。

8.5.5 商业与服务业地理

20世纪80年代以来，商业、服务业、旅游业和消费等领域的研究迅速增多。该领域的研究早期集中于传统商业区位和布局研究。21世纪初，金融、生产性服务业、物流、会展业、写字楼（吴一洲，2010）、网络店铺（路紫等，2011）等新型服务业成为研究的主题。主要研究这些服务业的区位、空间格局与演变、影响因素、演变机制等。90年代以来，旅游经济地理研究兴旺，研究领域集中在旅游供给与需求（牛亚菲，1996）、客源市场空间结构（保继刚，2002）、旅游业区位（王瑛和王铮，2000）、地方参与旅游发展（许振晓等，2009）等方面。

8.5.6 交通地理

20世纪90年代以来，《地理学报》发表的交通地理论文逐渐增多，研究领域主要集中在以下几方面：空间运输联系理论及其基本规律的总结。在客货流研究的基础上（张文尝，1988），进一步探讨地域之间的运输联系规律（张文尝等，1994）；各种交通运输方式的布局规律包括铁路网络（金凤君和王姣娥，2004）、港口体系、集装箱运输网络（韩增林等，2002）、航空网（王姣娥等，2006）、公路网络（曹小曙等，2005）等设施网络的形成过程、机理、模式和空间格局等，以及运输方式之间的竞争问题（王姣娥和胡浩，2013）；区域通达性分析包括基于各种运输方式的区域通达性（张莉和陆玉麒，2006），以及区域交通优势的甄别（金凤君等，2008）；交通设施对区域经济影响（刘海隆等，2008）。从研究趋势看，高铁、航空、高速公路等新的交通运输方式研究较多。同时，基于交通网络与区域发展研究相结合的角度，研究区域总体的通达性及其对区域经济发展的影响。

8.6 结论及讨论

基于多种成果对经济地理学发展的评述，对经济地理学的发展具有很好的促进作用（陆大道，2000；樊杰，2008；刘卫东等，2011）。《地理学报》对文章的选择标准较高和更加突出实证研究基础上的发现，使所发表的文章具有“精、高、特、实”特点。经济地理文章在《地理学报》发文总量中所占比例不大，但这些文章总体上可以说是经济地理研究中的“精品”，代表着各个领域的研究方向，代表着各个时期的研究主题变化；《地理学报》的论文审稿时非常注重其原创发现，所刊登的经济地理论文在一定程度上标志着中国该领域的最高研究水平；与上述“精”、“高”相关联，《地理学报》论文注重中国特色的研究，注重中国特殊经济活动实践的研究，注重中国特殊问题的研究，已逐渐成为世界上中国地理研究的特殊平台；《地理学报》很少刊登纯理论的研究成果，多数论文在基于实证分析之上有独到创见，由此带来《地理学报》上的经济地理论文具有很强的实践基础，很扎实的数据支持。基于《地理学报》所发表的经济地理文章的梳理，可对 80 年来中国经济地理学的研究特点作以下概括。

(1) 我国经济地理学者一直以"为国民经济建设服务"为主旨，根据国家各个时期的要求开展了大量的研究工作，为相关决策提供了科学依据。这种面向国家需求的经济地理学研究特点在世界其他国家是不突出的。随着市场经济发展，我国经济地理学会逐渐增加面向企业、地方需求的研究。

(2) 我国经济地理学研究多是在不同区域尺度上进行的。把区域作为一个研究平台，剖析区域内部结构和区域间关系。这一研究特点与我国政府主导的经济体制有关。不过随着市场经济的发展，企业、农户个体的研究逐渐增多，有利于更好地揭示经济空间演变的机理、过程。

(3) 经济地理学研究多以经济增长为主要目标，并且注重从物质的角度研究。例如，工业布局、农业区划、区域规划、企业集群等各个方面研究的宗旨都是如何促进经济规模持续扩大。而西方发达国家的经济地理学研究则比较关注贫困问题、贫富差距、不平等问题、金融排斥、增长陷阱等经济问题。这样的中西方经济地理研究差异，与各自的经济发展阶段有关。随着我国向高收入国家跨越，可持续发展、社会经济问题的相关研究日益增多。

(4) 虽然《地理学报》发表文章强调学术意义，但理论文章明显少于应用文章。在 421 篇论文中，理论文章有 57 篇，更多的文章是结合特定区域问题、经济地理现象开展的实证分析。我国经济地理学发展主要是靠实践带动的，新的研究多来自实际问题的需要，很少来自学科发展的思考。面向实际问题的应用研究丰富了我国经济地理学研究，具体的科学问题多样化。但也有学者考虑综合研究和核心理论凝练（樊杰，2007）。

以上基于《地理学报》论文所概括的经济地理学研究特点是中国经济地理学家依据中国实际，把国际相关学科思想与中国历史传统相结合的长期研究结果，是学者服务于国家、社会和人民的体现，也是构建中国特色经济地理学的基础。但是我们也要看到，虽然我国的经济地理研究，理论不断凝练，方法越来越先进，在服务国家社会实际中发挥了重要作用，但能够主导国际学科发展的理论观点不够，经济地理学研究问题的独到性、科学性、前瞻性还需要进一步培育、完善和提高。同时期盼《地理学报》更好地发挥引领经济地理学发展的作用，推出更多更高水平的研究成果。

参考文献

巴朗斯基 H H，王正. 1954. 编写苏联经济地理课本的经验. 地理学报，20 (2)：239～243

保继刚，郑海燕，戴光全. 2002. 桂林国内客源市场的空间结构演变. 地理学报，57 (1)：96～106

毕秀晶，汪明峰，李健，等. 2011. 上海大都市区软件产业空间集聚与郊区化. 地理学报，66 (12)：1682～1694

蔡渝平. 1987. 地域结构的演变和预测. 地理学报，42 (1)：69～81

曹廷藩. 1957. 关于经济地理学当前争论问题的一些初步意见. 地理学报，24 (2)：189～210

曹小曙，薛德升，阎小培. 2005. 中国干线公路网络联结的城市通达性. 地理学报，60 (6)：25～32

陈才. 1962. 试论经济地理学的发展趋向. 地理学报，28 (4)：306～319

陈超，刘家明，马海涛，等. 2013. 中国农民跨省旅游网络空间结构研究. 地理学报，68 (4)：547～558

陈国阶，王青. 2004. 中国山区经济发展阶段的理论模型与预测. 地理学报，59（2）：303～310
陈培阳，朱喜钢. 2012. 基于不同尺度的中国区域经济差异. 地理学报，67（8）：1085～1097
程连生. 1995. 中国城市投资环境分析. 地理学报，50（3）：240～247
程潞，杨万钟，金家相，等. 1959. 江苏省苏锡地区农业区划. 地理学报，25（3）：180～200
邓静中. 1963. 经济地理学对自然条件的评价——中国地理学会经济地理专业委员会 1962 年学术会议讨论初步总结. 地理学报，29（1）：25～35
邓静中. 1963. 全国农业现状区划的初步探讨. 地理学报，29（4）：265～280
凡杰. 1989. 长治—焦作地域工业综合体的组织. 地理学报，44（2）：174～184
樊杰. 2007. 我国主体功能区划的科学基础. 地理学报. 62（4）：339～350.
樊杰. 2008."人地关系地域系统"学术思想与经济地理学. 经济地理，28（2）：177～183
方远平，谢蔓，林彰平. 2013. 信息技术对服务业创新影响的空间计量分析. 地理学报，68（8）：1119～1130
方忠权. 2013. 广州会展企业空间集聚特征与影响因素. 地理学报，68（4）：464～476
顾朝林. 1991. 中国城市经济区划分的初步研究. 地理学报，46（2）：129～141
郭焕成，姚建衢，任国柱. 1992. 中国农业类型划分的初步研究. 地理学报，47（6）：507～515
韩增林，安筱鹏，王利，等. 2002. 中国国际集装箱运输网络的布局与优化. 地理学报，57（4）：479～488
贺灿飞，傅蓉. 2009. 外资银行在中国的区位选择. 地理学报，64（6）：701～712
贺灿飞，潘峰华，孙蕾. 2007. 中国制造业的地理集聚与形成机制. 地理学报，62（12）：1253～1264
贺灿飞，肖晓俊. 2011. 跨国公司功能区位实证研究. 地理学报，66（12）：1669～1681
洪国志，胡华颖，李郇. 2010. 中国区域经济发展收敛的空间计量分析. 地理学报，65（12）：1548～1558
胡焕庸. 1934. 江苏省之农产区域. 地理学报，1（1）：93～106
胡焕庸. 1936. 中国之农业区域. 地理学报，3（1）：1～17
胡序威，胡听主. 1965. 工业布局的技术经济论证. 地理学报，31（3）：179～193
胡兆量. 1986. 我国工业布局的变化趋势. 地理学报. 41（3）：193～201
蒋海兵，徐建刚，祁毅. 2010. 京沪高铁对区域中心城市陆路可达性影响. 地理学报，65（10）：1287～1298
金凤君，王成金，李秀伟. 2008. 中国区域交通优势的甄别方法及应用分析. 地理学报，63（8）：787～798
金凤君，王姣娥. 2004. 20 世纪中国铁路网扩展及其空间通达性. 地理学报，59（2）：293～302
李春芬. 1995. 区际联系——区域地理学的近期前沿. 地理学报，50（6）：491～496
李为. 1986. 我国乳品工业区位分析. 地理学报，41（3）：224～232
李文彦，陈航. 1983. 中国能源经济区划的初步研究. 地理学报，38（4）：327～340
李文彦. 1954. 苏联经济地理学家 H. H. 巴朗斯基. 地理学报，20（2）：233～238
李文彦. 1957. 自然因素与技术经济因素在工业配置中的作用. 地理学报，23（4）：399～417
李文彦. 1978. 煤矿城市的工业发展与城市规划问题. 地理学报，33（1）：63～77
李小建，苗长虹. 2004. 西方经济地理学新进展及其启示. 地理学报，59（S1）：153～161
李小建，乔家君. 2001. 20 世纪 90 年代中国县际经济差异的空间分析. 地理学报，56（2）：136～145
李小建，周雄飞，郑纯辉，等. 2012. 欠发达区地理环境对专业村发展的影响研究. 地理学报，67（6）：783～792
李小建，周雄飞，乔家君，等. 2009. 不同环境下农户自主发展能力对收入增长的影响. 地理学报，64

(6)：643～653
李小建，周雄飞，卫春江，等. 2006. 发展中地区银行业空间系统变化——以河南省为例. 地理学报，61(4)：414～424
李小建，周雄飞，郑纯辉. 2008. 河南农区经济发展差异地理影响的小尺度分析. 地理学报，63(2)：147～155
李小建. 2002. 欠发达农区经济发展中的农户行为——以豫西山地丘陵区为例. 地理学报，57(4)：459～468
李兴绪，刘曼莉，葛珺沂. 2010. 西南边疆民族地区农户收入的地理影响因素分析. 地理学报，65(2)：235～243
李裕瑞，刘彦随，龙花楼，等. 2013. 大城市郊区村域转型发展的资源环境效应与优化调控研究——以北京市顺义区北村为例. 地理学报，68(6)：825～838
梁溥，曹廷藩，杨克毅，等. 1956. 南雄盆地经济地理. 地理学报，22(4)：353～372
林初升. 1997. 港粤整合与珠江三角洲的空间转型——以东莞为例. 地理学报，52(S1)：71～79
刘海隆，包安明，陈曦，等. 2008. 新疆交通可达性对区域经济的影响分析. 地理学报，63(4)：428～436
刘鹤，金凤君，刘毅，等. 2011. 中国石化产业空间组织的评价与优化. 地理学报，66(10)：1332～1342
刘卫东，金凤君，张文忠，等. 2011. 中国经济地理学研究进展与展望. 地理科学进展，30(12)：1479～1487
刘卫东，刘红光，范晓梅，等. 2012. 地区间贸易流量的产业——空间模型构建与应用. 地理学报，67(2)：147～156
刘卫东，甄峰. 2004. 信息化对社会经济空间组织的影响研究. 地理学报，59(S1)：67～76
刘小金，毛汉英，陈为民，等. 1991. 系统动力学在区域发展规划中的应用——以山东省莱州市为例. 地理学报，46(2)：233～241
刘彦随，李裕瑞. 2010. 中国县域耕地与农业劳动力变化的时空耦合关系. 地理学报，65(12)：1602～1612
刘彦随，刘玉，陈玉福. 2011. 中国地域多功能性评价及其决策机制. 地理学报，66(10)：1379～1389
刘彦随，陆大道. 2003. 中国农业结构调整基本态势与区域效应. 地理学报，58(3)：381～389
陆大道，刘毅，樊杰. 1999. 我国区域政策实施效果与区域发展的基本态势. 地理学报，54(6)：496～508
陆大道. 1979. 工业区的工业企业成组布局类型及其技术经济效果. 地理学报，34(3)：248～264
陆大道. 1987. 我国区域开发的宏观战略. 地理学报，42(2)：97～105
陆大道. 1994. 经济地理学与持续发展研究. 地理学报，49(S1)：723～728
陆大道. 2000. 50 年来我国经济地理学的发展. 经济地理，20(1)：2～6
陆大道. 2001. 论区域的最佳结构与最佳发展——提出“点-轴系统”和“T”型结构以来的回顾与再分析. 地理学报，56(2)：127～135
陆军，宋吉涛，梁宇生，等. 2013. 基于二维时空地图的中国高铁经济区格局模拟. 地理学报，68(2)：147～158
路紫，李晓楠，杨丽花，等. 2011. 基于邻域设施的中国大城市网络店铺的区位取向——以上海、深圳、天津、北京四城市为例. 地理学报，66(6)：813～820
毛汉英，余丹林. 2001. 环渤海地区区域承载力研究. 地理学报，56(3)：363～371
毛汉英. 1991. 县域经济和社会同人口、资源、环境协调发展研究. 地理学报，46(4)：385～395
苗长虹. 1998. 我国农村工业发展型式研究. 地理学报，53(3)：80～88

苗长虹. 2006. 全球-地方联结与产业集群的技术学习——以河南许昌发制品产业为例. 地理学报, 61 (4): 425～434
宁越敏. 1984. 上海市区商业中心区位的探讨. 地理学报, 39 (2): 163～172
牛亚菲. 1996. 旅游供给与需求的空间关系研究. 地理学报, 51 (1): 80～87
潘裕娟, 曹小曙. 2012. 广州批发市场的供应物流空间格局及其形成机制. 地理学报, 67 (2): 179～188
齐元静, 杨宇, 金凤君. 2013. 中国经济发展阶段及其时空格局演变特征. 地理学报, 68 (4): 517～531
任美锷. 1944. 工业区位的理论与中国工业区域. 地理学报, 11 (1): 15～24
任美锷. 1950. 四川省农作物生产力的地理分布. 地理学报, 16 (1): 1～22
申玉铭, 邱灵, 王茂军, 等. 2007. 中国生产性服务业产业关联效应分析. 地理学报, 62 (8): 821～830
沈小平. 1987. 试论工业区工业企业成组布局的经济效果和最佳规模的确定. 地理学报, 42 (1): 51～61
宋家泰, 张同铸, 苏永煊, 等. 1959. 江苏省淮阴专区农业区划. 地理学报, 25 (2): 120～134, 170～184
孙峰华, 陆大道, 柳新华, 等. 2010. 中国物流发展对渤海海峡跨海通道建设的影响. 地理学报, 65 (12): 1507～1521
孙宕越. 1937. 粤北与赣南湘南之交通与运输. 地理学报, 4 (1): 867～887
汤放华, 汤慧, 孙倩, 等. 2013. 长江中游城市集群经济网络结构分析. 地理学报, 68 (10): 1357～1366
瓦秀金 B Φ, 郭振淮. 1955. 社会主义生产配置的基本原理与经济地理学的任务. 地理学报, 21 (4): 349～358
王伯礼, 张小雷. 2010. 新疆公路交通基础设施建设对经济增长的贡献分析. 地理学报, 65 (12): 1522～1533
王成金. 2008. 中国物流企业的空间组织网络. 地理学报, 63 (2): 135～146
王承云, 秦健, 杨随. 2013. 京津沪渝创新型城区研发产业集群研究. 地理学报, 68 (8): 1097～1109
王承云. 2010. 日本研发产业的空间集聚与影响因素分析. 地理学报, 65 (4): 387～396
王缉慈, 宋向辉, 李光宇. 1996. 北京中关村高新技术企业的集聚与扩散. 地理学报, 51 (6): 481～488
王姣娥, 胡浩. 2013. 中国高铁与民航的空间服务市场竞合分析与模拟. 地理学报, 68 (2): 175～185
王姣娥, 金凤君, 孙炜, 等. 2006. 中国机场体系的空间格局及其服务水平. 地理学报, 61 (8): 829～838
王强, 郑颖, 伍世代, 等. 2011. 能源效率对产业结构及能源消费结构演变的响应. 地理学报, 66 (6): 741～749
王瑛, 王铮. 2000. 旅游业区位分析——以云南为例. 地理学报, 55 (3): 346～353
王铮, 马翠芳, 王莹, 等. 2003. 区域间知识溢出的空间认识. 地理学报, 58 (5): 773～780
王铮, 周嵬, 李山, 等. 2001. 基于铁路廊道的中国国家级风景名胜区市场域分析. 地理学报, 56 (2): 206～213
魏心镇, 林亚真. 1989. 国土规划的理论开拓——关于地域结构的研究. 地理学报, 44 (3): 262～271
吴一洲, 吴次芳, 贝涵璐. 2010. 转型期杭州城市写字楼空间分布特征及其机制. 地理学报, 65 (8): 973～982
萧俊城. 1965. 广东省东莞县综合农业区划工作方法. 地理学报, 31 (4): 277～286
许学强, 李胜学. 1995. 改革开放以来广东省利用外资的时空差异特征. 地理学报, 50 (2): 128～137
许学强, 王欣, 阎小培. 2002. 技术流的动力机制、渠道与模式——以珠江三角洲为例. 地理学报, 57 (4): 489～496
许振晓, 张捷, Geoffrey W, 等. 2009. 居民地方感对区域旅游发展支持度影响——以九寨沟旅游核心

社区为例. 地理学报，64 (6)：736～744
薛领，翁瑾. 2010. 基于垄断竞争的大都市商业空间结构动态模拟. 地理学报，65 (8)：938～948
阎小培，周春山，冷勇，等. 2000. 广州 CBD 的功能特征与空间结构. 地理学报，55 (4)：475～486
杨树珍. 1983. 国土整治与经济区划. 地理学报，38 (2)：105～112
杨吾扬，蔡清泉. 1959. 论新疆玛纳斯河流域棉花基地的经济条件. 地理学报，25 (4)：258～270
杨吾扬. 1963. 关于产销区划的一些原理、方法的介绍和体会. 地理学报，29 (1)：63～77
杨吾扬. 1964. 中国陆路交通自然条件评价和区划概要. 地理学报，30 (4)：301～319
杨吾扬. 1992. 经济地理学、空间经济学与区域科学. 地理学报，47 (6)：561～569
杨吾扬. 1994. 北京市零售商业与服务业中心和网点的过去、现在和未来. 地理学报，49 (1)：9～17
杨晓光，樊杰，赵燕霞. 2002. 20 世纪 90 年代中国区域经济增长的要素分析. 地理学报，57 (6)：701～708
杨兴柱，陆林，王群. 2005. 农户参与旅游决策行为结构模型及应用. 地理学报，60 (6)：50～62
袁丰，魏也华，陈雯，等. 2010. 苏州市区信息通讯企业空间集聚与新企业选址. 地理学报，65 (2)：153～163
曾尊固，熊先根. 1994. 论农业结构变化及其地理学研究. 地理学报. 49 (1)：84～91
张富刚，刘彦随. 2008. 中国区域农村发展动力机制及其发展模式. 地理学报，63 (2)：115～122
张雷. 2003. 经济发展对碳排放的影响. 地理学报，58 (4)：629～637
张莉，陆玉麒. 2006. 基于陆路交通网的区域可达性评价——以长江三角洲为例. 地理学报，61 (12)：1235～1246
张同铸，宋家泰，苏永煊，等. 1959. 农村人民公社经济规划的初步经验. 地理学报，25 (2)：107～119
张文尝，金凤君，唐秀芳. 1994. 空间运输联系的分布与交流规律研究. 地理学报，49 (6)：490～499
张文尝. 1981. 工业基地交通运输布局问题. 地理学报，36 (2)：157～170
张文尝. 1988. 我国客流的影响因素及其地区差异的研究. 地理学报，43 (3)：191～200
张之，张学芹. 1960. 经济地理学与区域规划. 地理学报，26 (2)：129～134
赵松乔. 1953. 察北、察盟及锡盟——一个农牧过渡地区的经济地理调查. 地理学报，19 (1)：43～60
周立三. 1964. 试论农业区域的形成演变、内部结构及其区划体系. 地理学报，30 (1)：14～24
周立三. 1990. 从人口资源与生态环境的观点分析我国国情与农村经济发展. 地理学报，45 (3)：257～263
周起业. 1957. 我国农业区划基本问题的探讨. 地理学报，23 (2)：127～144
周淑贞. 1938. 山西之农业区域. 地理学报，5 (1)：55～72
周一星，R. 布雷德肖. 1988. 中国城市（包括辖县）的工业职能分类——理论、方法和结果. 地理学报，43 (4)：287～298
朱华晟，吴骏毅，魏佳丽，等. 2010. 发达地区创意产业网络的驱动机理与创新影响——以上海创意设计业为例. 地理学报，65 (10)：1241～1252

第二篇　农户地理研究

第9章　还原论与农户地理研究

地理学发展中，相当一段时间内强调综合发展的道路。作为地理学重要特征之一（詹姆斯和马丁，1989），综合论一直在促进地理学的繁荣和发展。但是，在地理学的发展中，也有来自其他思想方法的积极贡献。20世纪的数量革命和空间科学发展阶段，曾有一些学者应用还原论的思想进行人文地理学研究，把复杂的地理景观还原为诸如几何设定、经济人等基本个体（Johnston et al.，2000）。沿着这一思路，本人在一个时期内着力于企业地理的研究，试图从微观组织视角探索以工商业为主的区域经济发展的机理。但在以农业为主的中国欠发达区域，企业并不发达，农户成为经济活动的基本组织单元。所以，有必要从农区的微观组织视角对农户地理做一研究。本章依据科学研究的还原论方法和数学逻辑，分析了农区经济活动的最基本组织单元——农户。从地理学、经济学、组织学相关原理中，建立了农户地理研究的基本框架。农户地理研究的主要内容包括农户自主发展能力研究、农户经济活动区位研究、农户发展环境研究、农户与地理环境相互关系研究。除了单一农户研究之外，农户地理还包括通过正式联系或非正式联系所形成的农户群研究。中国的特殊国情决定了农户在农区经济中的重要地位，农户与地理环境的长期相互作用轨迹及其相互印记又决定了农户地理研究在地理学中的特殊意义。

9.1　还原论与农户概念

9.1.1　还原论

还原论（reductionism）是与科学研究相关的重要科学哲学方法。相关的讨论有多种观点。一种认为“一个领域研究结果——无论是概念、研究方法、规律，抑或理论，可以用另一个更基本的领域概念资源予以理解和解释（Wimsatt and Sarkar，2006）。”例如，化学可还原为物理学，在物理学中，热力学可还原为分子动力学，孟德尔遗传学可还原为分子遗传学等。还原论一方面可以作为科学研究的策略和指导方法，另一方面可以通过研究结果来阐明某领域能还原为另一领域的主张。

在更广泛的意义上，Checkland（1999）认为科学发展历史的核心特征是还原论、可重复性和反驳。科学在三种意义上是还原论：第一，世界的多样性太过丰富，要进行融贯的研究，必须予以简化、对现象有所挑选，确定一研究就是为了某个目的确定的世界某个部分的还原；第二，利用奥卡姆剃刀原则（Occam's Razor）进行解释上的还原，如用低层次的规律解释高层次的现象；第三，把复杂现象打碎，逐个元素进行分析，这也是科学思维的核心。根据还原论的这些观点，尤其是第三个观点，我们可以把高层次的现象都可看作是更低级、更基本的现象的组合物，把高级运动形式还原为低级运动形式。

在相当长的一段时期内，科学方法本质上就是还原论方法。还原方法被称为科学研究的“标准操作”（王克迪，2006）。整个近代科学中，许多科学分支都用还原论方法研究各自的对象，如化学分子学说、生物细胞学说等，都深深打上了还原方法的烙印。尽管随着科学的发展，这种还原方法也遭到了一些质疑（黄欣荣，2008），认为低水平运动与高水平运动之间毕竟有所区别，不能完全用低水平运动规律代替高水平运动规律。但是，还原论方法作为一种主要科学研究方法，并不能被任何新的研究方法所取代。

借鉴还原论原理进行经济地理学研究，我们可以把复杂的经济地理现象还原为低层次的经济活动。在我国工商业不发达的农村地区，在现行的联产承包责任制下，生产组织的最低层次的基本单元是农户。

9.1.2 农户的概念

农户是一个多义的混合概念。结合农户的社会、经济特点，可把农户概括为以家庭为单位，以家庭成员为劳动力，完全或主要从事农业生产活动的经济组织。农户不仅是一个经济组织，还是一个发挥一定社会功能的组织。它既是主要从事个体农业经营和农业生产的经济组织，又是人们建立在姻缘和血缘基础上的社会生活组织。但农户与一般的经济、社会组织相比，又有自己的特点。例如，与企业相比，农户目标往往具有多重性，不仅仅是追求利润最大化。在劳动力使用上，以家庭成员劳动为主，不雇佣或很少雇佣劳动力（尤小文，2005）。

在中国，随着经济、社会结构的转型，农户的一些行为也在不断发生变化，如参与市场的程度在加深、非农兼业增多，甚至有的农户移民到城市。所以生活在农村从事农业生产的纯农户逐渐减少，农户的异质化程度在加深。这为我们很好地概括农户特征，准确定义农户带来了困难。鉴于此，为简单起见，我们这里按照中国的户籍管理制度来定义农户，认为农户是户口在农村的居民以家庭契约关系为基础组织起来的社会经济组织。

9.2 农户与农区关系的证明

9.2.1 农户与农区

中国农村地区的居民主要以农户为单元。但由于农业地位和农业组织不同，农户与农区之间关系亦有所不同。例如，在欠发达纯农业地区，由于目前农业生产型企业并不发育，农业生产以农户为经营单位。在非农业经济有所发展但农业仍占主要地位的农业地区，尽管基于农村的企业也作为经济活动的主体出现，但农户仍然为农区主要经营单位。随着经济的发展，一些农区的非农业经济活动逐步在经济中占重要地位。这时，农户的地位仍然很重要。一方面，他们仍然在农业经营中扮演重要角色；另一方面，非农业（如手工业、商业、服务业）经营中，也有一些以家庭为基础。

由于农户是农区经济组织中重要的基本单元，农户的状况与农区经济增长关系十分密切。就单一农户而论，不同的决策能力和家庭人员素质，影响着农户对自然资源和环境条件的利用（李小建等，2009b）。农户经济活动的不同区位选择，影响农户所在地区及其相关地区的经济发展。在农区现代化的发展途径中，无论是农村工业化、城市化，还是农业产业化，均离不开农户的参与。在一定程度上，农区发展方向是农户组织演化和农区产业演化共同决定的。随着经济发展和技术水平的提高，农户间职业分化和产业间分工会越来越明显，伴随着农户和产业的发展，有些农区会逐步向大农场企业、专业化产业区和半城市区域演变（李小建等，2010）。

9.2.2　农户与农区的目标函数

在对农户行为进行研究时，有人认为农户相当于资本主义市场经济中的企业（舒尔茨，1964），小农无论在市场领域还是政治社会生活中，都更倾向于按投资者的原则行事（Popkin，1979），即“舒尔茨-波普金的理性小农”命题。又有一些人认为小农坚守“安全第一”原则，提出“道义小农”命题，即小农宁可选择避免经济灾难，而不会冒险追求收益最大化（斯科特，2001）。这可称为“生存理性”，前者也称为“经济理性”。改革开放以来，由于农民基本生存得以满足以及农民义利观的变化，中国农户经济行为呈现出由生存理性向经济理性转变（李红涛和付少平，2002）。据此可以抽象掉不确定性，将农户的效用最大化行为还原为利润最大化。与此相一致，农区的目标函数假定为农区收入最大化。

9.2.3　农户选择和农区一般均衡

1. 农户选择

假定一个欠发达农区以农业生产为主，部分农户有劳动力出外打工；农户独立决策，具有相关信息；农户具有经济人特征。若全区有 I 个农户生产 J 种产品，由于农户之间的重复博弈，农户之间的长期共处和政府的干预，生产中的负外部性基本可以抑制；销售环节的外部性主要是农户之间的价格竞争，我们假定农户只是价格的接受者而非价格的制定者，据此暂时可忽略农户生产和销售过程中的负外部性。

假定农区劳动者的数量丰富，农民可在当地务农，也可以出外打工，打工的工资为 W，农民是市场既定工资的接受者。假定农户的耕地可以自己耕种，也可以出租给本农区其他农户耕种，甚至可以租用本区其他农户的耕地。对单个农户来说，土地的使用价格，即单位土地面积的租金 R 是既定的，租金由农区一般均衡决定，农户只是农区土地租金的接受者。由于在一区域的单位面积资本投入变动不大，为了简化问题，在模型中不考虑资本。

假定农户 i 生产任一产品 j 的生产函数为 $Y_{ij}=Y_j\ (A_{ij},\ L_{ij})$，其中，$Y_{ij}$ 是 i 农户生产的 j 产品的产量，A_{ij} 和 L_{ij} 是农户 i 生产 j 产品所使用的土地和劳动的数量。假定生产函数是递增的凹的一次齐次函数，即产量递增、边际产量递减和规模报酬不变。前两种假定是一般性的，规模报酬不变的假定来自我们探讨的农区是不发达农区，使用传统生产技术。使用现代技术生产导致规模报酬递增，形成大规模生产，而不是以农户为单位生产。

根据上述假定，农户 i 的最优化行为表现为选择土地和劳动投入而使家庭利润最大

化，即

$$\Pi_i(P, R, W) = \max_{A_{ij}, L_{ij}} \sum_j^J P_j Y_j(A_{ij}, L_{ij}) - R\sum_j^J A_{ij} - W\sum_j^J L_{ij} \tag{9.1}$$

式（9.1）右端是农户 i 的利润函数，即目标函数，第一项是农户收入，第二项是土地租金成本，第三项是工资成本。式（9.1）左端是优化后的农户的间接利润函数，它取决于农户的生存环境：既定的产品价格 P（J 种产品价格向量）、既定的租金 R 和既定的工资 W。式（9.1）的一阶条件为

$$P_j \frac{\partial Y_j(A_{ij}, L_{ij})}{\partial A_{ij}} = R \tag{9.2}$$

$$P_j = \frac{\partial Y_j(A_{ij}, L_{ij})}{\partial L_{ij}} = W \tag{9.3}$$

式（9.2）表明，土地的边际产值等于土地的使用价格，且隐含土地资源分配原则，生产各种产品的边际产值相等，式（9.3）与此类似。式（9.2）和式（9.3）各包含 J 个方程，由此联立可以求解出农户的 $2J$ 个决策变量：J 种产品中的土地投入 A_{ij}（P，W，R）和劳动投入 L_{ij}（P，W，R），$j=1$，2，…，J。如果农户的耕地多于他的耕地需求（J 种产品生产中所需的土地投入之和），那么他将有剩余耕地租给其他农户，否则租种其他农户的耕地；如果他的土地供给与需求相等，那么他将使用自己的土地耕种。如果农户的劳动力供给大于需求，那么他将有时间出外打工或从事其他职业，否则他将雇用他人生产。

2. 农区一般均衡

对于一农户而言，土地租金是既定的参数。但对于一农区而言，土地租金由农区的一般均衡决定，即由土地租赁市场的市场出清条件（供求相等）决定。由于我们假定土地租赁行为只在本农区内进行，所以农区土地供给是既定的数量 A。农区土地需求由各农户各产品的土地投入需求决定。定义农区土地的需求函数为各农户各产品投入需求之和，即

$$A^D(P, W, R) \equiv \sum_i^I \sum_j^J A_{ij}(P, W, R) \tag{9.4}$$

市场均衡要求需求等于供给，所以

$$A^D(P, W, R) = A \tag{9.5}$$

式（9.5）决定了土地租金函数 R（P，W，A），土地租金取决于产品价格、劳动工资和土地资源。

9.2.4 农区集中选择

农区集中决策时不存在土地使用权交易，不存在土地的租赁价格，农区的最优化问题是在农区既定土地资源的约束下最大化农区纯收入，即

$$M(P, A, W) = \max_{A_j, L_j} \sum_j^J P_j Y_j(A_j, L_j) - W\sum_j^J L_j, \text{ s.t. } \sum^j A_j = A \tag{9.6}$$

式中，目标函数的第一项是农区生产各种产品的市场价值之和，即农区总收入，第二项是生产各种产品的工资成本，约束条件是生产各种产品的土地投入之和等于既定的土地资源。产值函数是农区间接纯收入函数，它由农区环境决定。为求解式（9.6），建立拉格朗日函数：

$$\zeta = \sum_{j}^{J} P_j Y_j(A_j,\ L_j) - W\sum_{j}^{J} L_j + \lambda\left(A - \sum_{j}^{J} A_j\right)$$

由此得到一阶条件

$$P_j \frac{\partial Y_j(A_j,\ L_j)}{\partial A_j} = \lambda \tag{9.7}$$

$$P_j = \frac{\partial Y_j(A_j,\ L_j)}{\partial L_j} = W \tag{9.8}$$

式（9.7）和式（9.8）各包含 J 个方程，由此联立可以求解出农区的 $2J$ 个决策变量：J 种产品中的土地投入 A_j（P，W，A）和 J 种产品生产中的劳动投入 L_{ij}（P，W，A），$j=1$，2，…，J。式（9.8）表明，用来生产各种产品的劳动的边际产品价值等于劳动的使用价格，它与式（9.3）的含义类似。式（9.7）表明用来生产各种产品的土地的边际产值都相等，而且利用包络定理可以证明，式（9.7）中的乘子 λ 就是农区既定土地资源的影子价格，即

$$\lambda = \frac{\partial M(P,\ A,\ W)}{\partial A} \tag{9.9}$$

9.2.5　农户分散决策和农区集中选择的比较

福利经济学第一定理指出，在分散经济中，如果不存在外部性，那么任何竞争均衡都是帕累托有效。据此可以认为，农户分散决策与农区集中决策的结果是一致的。为了说明这种一致性，下面在生产要素的利用和配置上进行比较。

第一，分散经济和集中经济同样实现了土地资源的充分利用。分散经济的市场出清条件保证了土地供给与土地需求一致，集中经济中土地充分利用是作为约束条件出现的。第二，分散经济和集中经济同样实现了生产要素在各产品生产之间的最优配置。两种经济都是按照等边际产值原则把生产要素分配在各种产品的生产之中，式（9.2）和式（9.3）是分散经济分配土地和劳动的原则；式（9.7）和式（9.8）是集中经济分配土地和劳动的原则。第三，分散经济和集中经济都实现了生产要素的最优组合，式（9.2）和式（9.3）变形可以得到生产同一产品的两种要素的边际产值之比等于两种要素的使用价格之比，式（9.7）和式（9.8）与此类似。第四，在两种经济中，生产要素的配合比例是相同的。根据规模报酬不变的假定，生产函数可以变成密集形式。定义 $y_j \equiv Y_j$（A_{ij}，L_{ij}）$/A_{ij}$，$l_{ij} \equiv L_{ij}/A_{ij}$，所以 ∂Y_j（A_{ij}，L_{ij}）$/\partial_{ij} = y_j'(l_{ij})$，代入式（9.3）得

$$P_j y_j'(l_{ij}) = W \tag{9.10}$$

类似地，利用式（9.8）可以得到

$$P_j y_j'(l_j) = W \tag{9.11}$$

比较以上两式得到 $l_{ij}=l_j$，即生产同一产品时，分散经济实现的劳动与土地配合比例等于集中经济实现的劳动与土地配合比例。第五，分散经济和集中经济实现的出外打工的劳动数量相同，且实现了劳动力务农和打工之间的最优配置。前者是因为两种经济都实现了土地的充分利用，两种经济实现的劳地配合比例相同；后者是因为务农和打工是按等边际分配原则决定的。在家务农得到边际产品价值，出外打工同样得到边际产值，式（9.3）和式（9.8）确保了二者相等。出外打工的边际产值就是工资，工资对于务农来说是机会成本，对于打工而言是工资收入。以上分析证明，农户分散决策可以实现农区集中决策对生产要素的最优配置。所以，在一定条件下，农户最优与农区最优是一致的。

9.3　农户地理研究的基本框架

农户地理以农户作为研究客体，把农区（内外部）环境作为研究背景，主要研究农户区位、经济活动空间结构及其与地理环境的关系（图 9.1）。农户区位包括农户居住区位、农业区位、工商业区位、务工区位等。农户居住区位包括初始区位、迁移和目前区位特征。农业区位主要研究在农户联产责任制下，农作物种类围绕居民点的分布格局及其支配因素。由于改革开放以来中国农村工商业增长迅速，一些地区出现了从事工商业的农户。其区位既具有城市工商业的特点，也具有农村工商业特殊性。由于城市工商业及沿海地区经济的快速发展，吸引大量农村地区富余劳动力离开居住地来此务工，形成了新的经济活动空间类型。除此之外，还有农户从事文化、旅游等其他类型的经济活动，具有相应的空间行为特征。

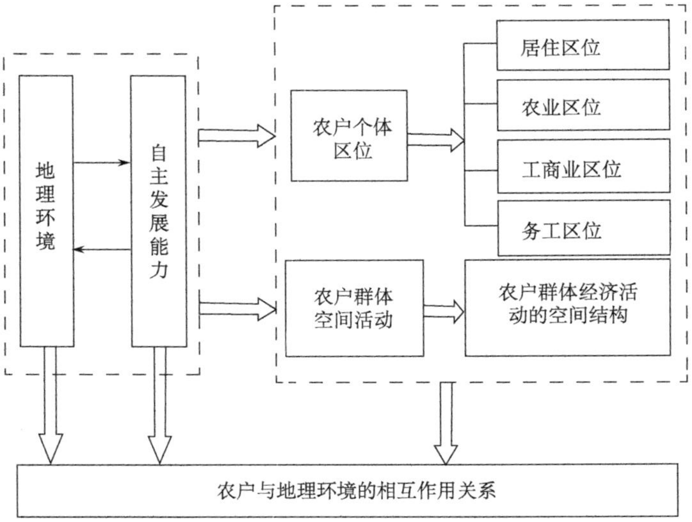

图 9.1　农户地理的研究框架

除农户个体活动之外，农户之间通过正式和非正式联系，形成各种各样的群体。其中一部分基于法律、政策、规定设立，如村委会、村民组、农村合作社等；一部分基于非正式联系形成，如亲缘群体、业缘群体、邻里群体等。这些群体在某些情况下从事经济活动时，具有一定的内部性。各相关农户行为的相似性和相互利用的正外部性，形成了群体空间行为特征。

农户个体和群体行为受地理环境的影响。地理环境对农户的影响又因农户特征差异而不同，这种农户特征表现在利用外部环境谋取发展上，可用农户自主发展能力来度量。农户自主发展能力受地理环境的影响，而自主发展能力又反过来影响着农户对环境的利用行为。同样的地理环境，不同的农户由于自主发展能力的差异，形成不同的发展取向和结果。

9.4　农户地理主要研究内容

9.4.1　农户区位研究

农户的居住区位是一定社会经济条件下农户的需求与环境综合供给的均衡结果。农户初始居住区位表现为较强的对自然环境和农业资源依赖性。随着经济水平的提高，农户居住需求增加，同时对环境的利用程度也在不断提高，农户逐渐向居住效用较大的区位迁移。这种区位迁移在理论上可以用区位效用变化来解释（图 9.2）。在农业生产为主的条件下，农户选择农业生产条件较好且距水源较近的区位，这时的效用水平 N_1 与当时的农户需求相一致。随着经济水平提高，农户空间需求逐渐超过区位所提供的效用水平（如交通不畅、空间狭小等），即通过区位迁移，实现向着居住区位效用水平与需求的新的均衡 N_2。依此类推，只要农户居住区位在原居住区位没得到满足，就存在向

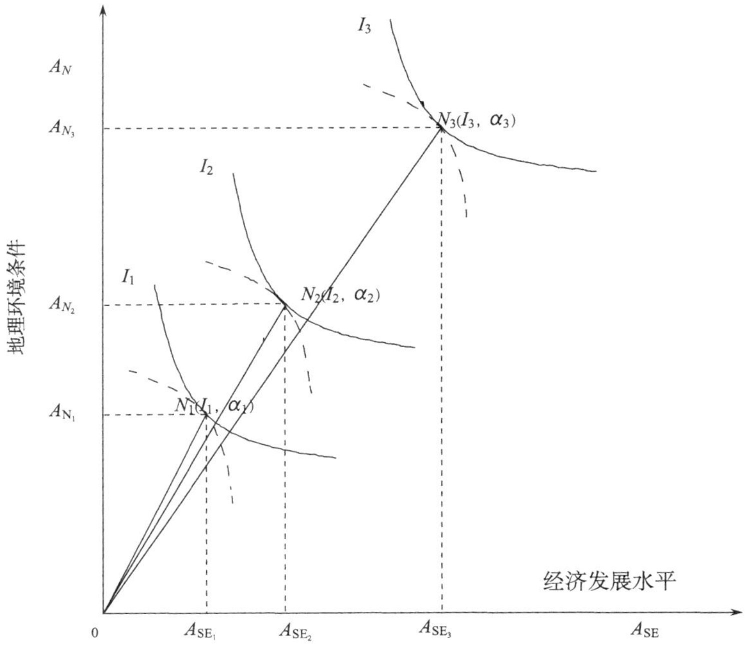

图 9.2　农户居民点区位迁移与区位效用水平变化

新的区位 [N_3 (l_3, a_3)] 迁移的动力（李小建等，2009c）。在居民点区位的迁移过程中，经济水平对效用水平的影响逐渐加大，地理环境的影响逐渐变小，表现为效用线与横轴经济发展水平的夹角逐渐变小。

西方经典农业区位论为基于城市周围地区的大农场经验数据得出的。中国农村情况特殊：人口密度较高，村庄密集，在经营上实行农户联产承包责任制。基于河南农村的调查，发现存在以村庄为中心的带状农业区位。从村庄向外，作物的劳动密集度逐渐降低，单位面积的投入和收益逐渐减少。但影响因素并不像杜能所指出的是由于距离和运费的增加，而是作物劳动密集度和地块肥力的变化（李小建和高更和，2008）。此外，中国欠发达农区的环状尺度很小，且为村中居住的所有农户单独决策所形成的综合结果。

农户工业生产活动的区位，具有和城市工业活动不同的特征，主要表现为分散布局。在早期阶段，工业活动多以家庭为单位，相当一部分工厂车间与居住混合，工业活动与农业活动混合。到一定阶段，则在村子周围集中建立一些工厂，形成工业集聚区（Li and Li，2007）。但总的来看，农户工业活动还是以分散布局为主。

农民出外务工是农户成员主要就业和收入渠道之一。农民工的出现改善着农户的经济空间行为和家庭的空间结构。农民的打工区位是经济收益和社会联系的共同作用结果。对河南农民工的分析表明，空间距离对务工区位具有一定影响，但就业机会和收入水平影响更为重要。样本农户有一半以上选择在距离较远的沿海省份务工，而在周围邻近省份务工人数较少（高更和和李小建，2008）。此外，地缘关系和血缘关系对务工区位选择具有十分重要的影响。样本农户中外出务工者集中在少数区位，形成特有的“簇状”分布现象（高更和等，2008）。

9.4.2 农户空间结构

农户经济的空间结构主要指农户群体活动所表现出的空间特征，也指从较大的尺度看各单一农户活动所形成的综合经济空间结构。农户群体行为的机理源于农户之间的互动，农户互动效应存在于正式组织和非正式组织之中。在非正式组织之内，亲缘、邻里与地块邻近农户之间的互动较为普遍。通过对河南省杞县孟寨村（大蒜专业村）第8小组42家农户的问卷，发现亲缘群体对技术扩散有更明显的效果；邻里群组和地邻群组中，农户个体特征对生产率的影响更为明显（罗庆和李小建，2010）。这种农户群体特征可有效解释农区专业化的演进。

在较大尺度上，通过对中国第一农业大省河南的乡镇数据分析，人均收入的空间差别具有一定的区域特征。中原城市群之内，形成高收入乡镇集中区。全省高人均收入的乡镇70%位于该区域之内。低经济发展水平的乡镇，主要集中在两类地区。一类是河南东部和南部平原地区。在商丘、周口、驻马店和南阳4个地级市的平原地区，共有乡镇606个，其中有351个乡镇的农民人均收入在2500元以下。第二类是河南西部山区。该地区的栾川、嵩县、洛宁、卢氏、西峡、淅川、南召、汝阳八个县共有山区乡镇84个，其中有62个乡镇的农民人均收入在2500元以下。模型分析表明，地形显著影响乡镇的人均收入，而且随着收入的增加，其影响程度递减。人均土地面积显著影响非农产业发展水平较低的乡镇的人均收入。地理位置影响着相关农区经济的发展，尤其是对收入较高的农区的影响十分明显。就单个乡镇而论，离县城的距离显著影响高收入乡镇的人均收入（李小建等，2008）。

9.4.3　农户自主发展能力

农户自主发展能力是指农户在经济利益驱动下，利用现有发展空间和发展机会追求目标时展示的一系列行为决策能力。通过选取 5 项 36 个相关指标，采用改进的信息熵值法和多元线性回归法对河南 11 个村 1251 农户调研数据进行处理，对不同地理环境条件下农户自主发展能力与农户持续增收的内在关系研究，发现：①农户的自主发展能力影响农户农业收入，但耕地和地形等地理因素的影响更为突出，且耕地增长的贡献度在山区最大，丘陵次之，平原最小，能力增长的贡献度恰好相反。②农户自主发展能力和家庭劳动投入显著影响农户非农收入，地理因素对家庭非农收入没有直接影响，地域通达性通过影响家庭自主发展能力间接影响家庭非农收入。③不同阶段农户自主发展能力对农户非农发展的贡献度不同。初级阶段，农户非农发展几乎完全依赖劳动投入的增长，能力增长几乎没有起作用；中级阶段，能力增长和劳动增长的贡献各半；高级阶段，能力的贡献度又跌至 15%。④农民非农收入报酬率的增长依赖农户能力增长和地域通达性提高。在低报酬阶段，能力的贡献度约占 2/3，但进入中下报酬阶段后，报酬的增长完全依赖地域通达性的增强，进入中上报酬阶段后，地域通达性的作用开始下降，到达高报酬阶段后下降到零，这时报酬的增长完全依赖能力的增长（李小建等，2009b）。

9.4.4　农户活动与环境关系

农户地理十分关注农户活动与地理环境的关系。这种关系在农户个体层面，表现在通过影响农户经营观念和资本投入进一步影响农户收入（李小建，2002a）。利用 1251 个农户的调查资料，从农户资本要素禀赋、农户经营结构和地理因素三个层面的分位数回归模型分析发现，各因素对不同收入水平农户的影响强度存在差异。在资本要素层面上，物质资本和人力资本对农户收入都具有显著的增加效应，但对高收入农户的收入增加效应更强。在经营结构层面上，通过兼业、务工等非农活动获得的工资性收入是农户收入的主要来源。而以上社会经济因素对农户收入的影响由于地理因素的影响而在村庄之间存在差异。具体表现在以下两个方面：①由于经济区位、地理邻近性等地理因素，农户兼业、务工等非农业活动在村庄之间存在差异，从而间接导致农户收入在村庄之间也存在差异；②地形、耕地资源等传统地理因素对农户收入的直接影响处于下降的趋势。因此，随着农村经济的发展，地理因素仍然对农户收入产生显著的影响，但地理因素对农户收入的重要程度和影响方式发生了变化（Li and Fan，2010）。

在村庄层面，地理环境直接影响人地相互作用。对河南一山区村 81 户 482 块农田的调查分析结果表明，山地农田系统人工能量的转换效率随地块高程的增加而呈降低态势，但农田的轮作特点和潜力的挖掘程度，又影响这种变化趋势；坡度与农田系统能量产投比显著负相关，坡向、坡度、坡位对农田能量的投入产出也有一定影响。以农田人工能量投入产出关系衡量山区农民对自然条件利用的过程，表现出明显的经验型利用特征。条件适宜区农田的过度利用，使得人工能源的投入产出效率明显下降；而其他高程和坡度的一些农田，仍有较大的利用空间。农田系统属半人工生态系统，具有很强的自然、人工特征，有助于我们在微观层面上研究人与地的关系（李小建和乔家君，2004）。

在农区发展中，专业村具有重要作用。到 2010 年年初，全国专业村已达到 45650 个，专业村农民人均纯收入高出全国 19.4%（孙鲁威，2010）。在专业村形成中，企业家精神是专业村形成与发展的核心动力，在传统农业文化占主导地位的农区，企业家精神决定着专业村的有无，对专业村的形成起着关键作用；正是那些具有企业家精神的核心农户，通过对传统农业活动的创新，促生新型经济活动的出现，才带来了专业村形成的先导农户。村庄所在地的资源禀赋、地理区位、经济基础和传统习惯，决定着专业村的类型。即村域环境决定着专业村发展的方向。同样具有企业家精神的先导农户，在不同类型的村域环境中，可以形成不同类型的专业村（李小建等，2009a）。专业村的形成和发展中，村域环境直接或间接受地理因素影响，而企业家精神也与地理因素的长期作用相关联。

9.5　结论与讨论

从农区的基本组织单元，本章证明了农户对农区发展的重要意义。建立了农户地理研究的基本框架，总结了农户地理研究的主要内容。中国特色的农户，为中国地理学家提供了独特的研究对象。农户区位、农户经济活动的空间结构、农户与地理环境的关系均有其不同于其他国家的特性。农户居住区位的迁移，逐渐实现较大的空间效应水平，也逐渐克服地理环境的约束。由于人口密度与地理环境格局的影响，中国中部地区村庄密集分布，农业生产区位具有环状特征，但形成原因与杜能环有所不同。农村工业企业分散布局、农民外出务工区位主要受就业机会和收入水平影响，空间距离影响退居次要地位。农户资本禀赋、经营结构和地理因素，影响不同收入水平的农户发展，且资本要素和经营结构因地理因素而出现影响程度差异。农户各种组织影响农户经济活动空间结构，在非正式组织中亲缘群体影响更为明显。在农区发展中，农户的企业家精神是专业村形成和发展的核心动力，而企业家精神是人与地理因素长期作用的结果。同时，村庄所在地的资源禀赋、地理区位、经济基础和传统习惯等又决定着专业村的发展方向。相关研究已经表明，农户地理研究具有独特的理论意义，同时对农户自主发展能力提高、农村聚落的改善及农区的持续发展也有重要的实践意义。

尽管农户地理也是从微观组织角度对区域的研究，但与公司地理相比，又有一些不同。公司的初始区位与原料地、劳动力和市场有关，农户的初始区位则与农户生存条件有关而不一定考虑市场因素。公司随着规模增大而在空间上不断扩张，同时又分化为不同层级；农户的空间分化则为短期行为，从长期发展来看，跨区域空间结构只有在亲缘农户群之中。公司空间扩张遵循接触扩张、等级扩散和通道扩张（李小建，2002b）；而农户的空间迁移则与空间效应有关，农户成员的外出务工不严格受空间距离约束。公司地理可研究单个公司的空间结构；农户地理则以农户组合所形成的空间结构为主。公司与区域发展形成互相交错的关系（李小建，1991）。农户与农区发展目标函数则比较一致。这种差异加强了农户地理研究的特殊意义，它为从微观视角进行基本单元的地理研究提供一个新的客体类型。

当然，农户地理研究又有一定的局限性。中国的农业和乡村发展是一个复杂的问题，涉及许多方面的研究（中国科学院区域发展领域战略研究组，2009）。仅从农户角度的研究，容易限制研究的视野，忽视区域背景、国家政策、科技教育对农业整体和农区整体发展的影响。只有“远观森林，近窥树木”相结合，把农区、农业和农村整体等宏观问题结合起来考虑，才能更好地进行农户地理研究。同时，农户行为和组织方式随着中国的制度变迁，在逐步发生变化。一些农户随着城镇化的进程，正在变成非农户；新的土地流转政策、新农村建设、农民工新一代的居住和务工行为变化都会在较大程度上影响农户的居住和经济空间行为。这对于农户地理研究既是挑战又是机遇。

参考文献

高更和，陈淑兰，李小建. 2008. 中部农区农户打工簇研究——以河南省三个样本村为例. 经济地理，28（2）：313～317

高更和，李小建. 2008. 中部农区农户打工距离研究——以河南三个样本村为例. 人文地理，23（6）：66～70

黄欣荣. 2008. 科学还原论及其历史功过. 江西财经大学学报，（4）：74～78

李红涛，付少平. 2002. 理性小农抑或道义小农，重读农民学经典论题. 读书，（2）：104～111

李小建，高更和. 2008. 中国中部平原村庄农业生产区位研究——以河南南阳黄庄为例. 地理科学，28（5）：616～623

李小建，罗庆，樊新生. 2009a. 农区专业村的形成与演化机理研究. 中国软科学，（2）：71～80

李小建，乔家君. 2004. 地形对山区农田系统投入产出影响的微观分析. 地理研究，24（4）：717～726

李小建，周雄飞，乔家君，等. 2009b. 不同环境下农户自主发展能力对收入增长的影响. 地理学报，64（6）：643～653

李小建，周雄飞，郑纯辉. 2008. 河南农区经济发展差异地理影响的小尺度分析. 地理学报，63（2）：147～155

李小建. 1991. 论工业变化的综合研究. 地理学报，46（3）：289～299

李小建. 2002a. 欠发达农区经济发展中的农户行为研究：以豫西山地丘陵区为例. 地理学报，57（4）：459～468

李小建. 2002b. 公司地理论（修订版）. 北京：科学出版社

李小建等. 2009c. 农户地理论. 北京：科学出版社

李小建等. 2010. 中部农区发展研究. 北京：科学出版社

罗庆，李小建. 2010. 农村社区农户互动效应的定量评估. 地理研究，29（10）：1757～1766

普雷斯顿·詹姆斯，杰弗里·马丁. 1989. 地理学思想史. 李旭旦译. 北京：商务印书馆

舒尔茨. 1987. 改造传统农业. 梁小民译. 北京：商务印书馆

孙鲁威. 2010. 专业村成为农民增收就业新阵地. 农民日报，2010-02-26. P1

王克迪. 2006. 科学研究方法的还原论本质. 学习时报，08（14）：7

尤小文. 2005. 农户经济组织研究. 长沙：湖南人民出版社

詹姆斯·斯科特. 2001. 农民的道义经济学：东南亚的反叛与生存. 程立显，刘建等译. 南京：译林出

版社

中国科学院区域发展领域战略研究组. 2009. 中国至 2050 年区域科技发展路线图. 北京：科学出版社

Checkland P. 1999. Systems, Thinking, Systems Practice: Includes a 30-year Retrospective. London: John Wiley & Sons Ltd

Johnston R J, Gregory D, Pratt G, et al. 2000. The Dictionary of Human Geography. Oxford: Balckwell

Li X J, Fan X S. 2010. Geography and rural household income: A village level study in Henan Province, China. Chinese Geographical Science, 20 (1): 1～8

Li X J, Li E L. 2007. Competitive advantages and rural industrial clustering: The case of steel measuring tape production in a Chinese village. China Review, 7 (1): 27～52

Popkin S L. 1979. The Rational Peasant: The Political Economy of Rural Society in Vietnam. Berkeley: University of California Press

Wimsatt W C, Sarkar S . 2006. Reductionism. In: Sarkar S, Pfeifer J, eds. The Philosophy of Science: An Encyclopedia. New York: Routledge. 696

第10章　欠发达农区发展中的农户行为

经济学研究的深入和精细，使其增强了对个体行为的关注（王丹红，2000；贺立平，2001）。企业（厂商）和家庭是个体经济行为研究的最基本单元，它们在经济运行中起着十分重要的作用。区域发展研究中，对企业作用已给予一定的重视（李小建，1999；王辑慈等，2001；费洪平，1994）。但家庭作为生产组织单位，其行为对区域发展的影响，现有文献较少涉及。而在欠发达农区，由于工商业十分薄弱，农业又主要以农户为生产单位。农户行为对区域发展起着十分重要的作用。2002年作者对河南西部山地丘陵区10个县（市）332家农户进行了调查分析。研究发现，欠发达农区制约区域发展的农户行为包括：①农户生产经营信息来源具有很大局限性；②农户收入严重依赖自然条件；③农村剩余劳动力转移存在着意识障碍，农民对非农业参与意识不强；④农户贷款积极性不高，且贷款多为维持日常生活需要；⑤农户更加期望用新增加的收入改变家庭生活状况，而不是发展生产。进一步的量化模型分析，揭示了农户收入在山区、丘陵和平原环境下受相关变量影响程度的差异，以及自给性与商品性生产不同比例农户在区域发展中的作用。

10.1　理论背景与研究问题

区域经济发展理论，在20世纪后半叶获得了大发展（陆大道，1995；谭崇台，1999；Peet，1999；Scott，2000）。早期的区域发展理论多将区域整体作为其研究对象，观察诸如区域结构、区域增长模型、区域制度、区域政策等问题。在微观层次上，区位论关注企业区位与环境的关系，为以后企业对区域发展影响的研究做了铺垫。70年代以来的新区域研究中，意大利学派追随马歇尔的产业区思想，研究该国东北部和中部手工业兴起与小区发展；加利福尼亚学派侧重于垂直分化、产业间交易网络对南加州工业企业集聚的影响；巴黎学派强调当地经济和文化背景下形成的创新力对区域经济增长的作用；柔性专业化学派侧重于手工业小区中新型技术组织范式的研究（Scott，2000）。学者们通过分析非正式文化、惯例和非贸易性互相依赖在当地生产系统的作用，能动学习和创新过程对区域经济变化的影响，来重新审视区域竞争优势的来源（Scott，2000；Feldman，2000；Antonelli，2000）。中小企业在区域发展中的作用也得到了国内学者关注（李小建，1999；王辑慈，2001；李小建，1998；仇保兴，1999）。

然而，纵观国内外文献，很少涉及家庭在区域发展中的作用。在发达国家中，经济学家主要从消费角度来关注家庭经济行为。新兴产业区中，中小企业并不完全依托于家庭单元。尽管为了充分就业，这些国家也鼓励家庭实业，但其在区域经济发展中的作用十分有限。与此相比，发展中国家的欠发达地区，家庭经济在区域发展中起着重要作用。尤其在我国的中西部农区，工商业十分薄弱，生产组织以家庭为单位，农户成为区内最重要、最基本的生产单元。因此，农户行为研究应成为该类区域发展研究中的重要课题。

农户行为在区域发展中的作用涉及很多方面。本章集中讨论在中国传统文化底蕴深厚的环境背景下，农户与区域发展相关的行为有什么特征？这些特征对经济发展影响如何？制约其发展的不利行为形成原因是什么？农户对未来发展的期望与决策者有何差异？如何发挥农户潜力促进农区发展？

10.2　区域选择及数据分析

10.2.1　豫西山地丘陵区概况

本章中豫西山地丘陵区指河南省的济源—新郑—鲁山—镇平以西地区（包括 30 个县和县级市；3 个地级市即洛阳、平顶山、三门峡所在市区）（图 10.1），总面积为

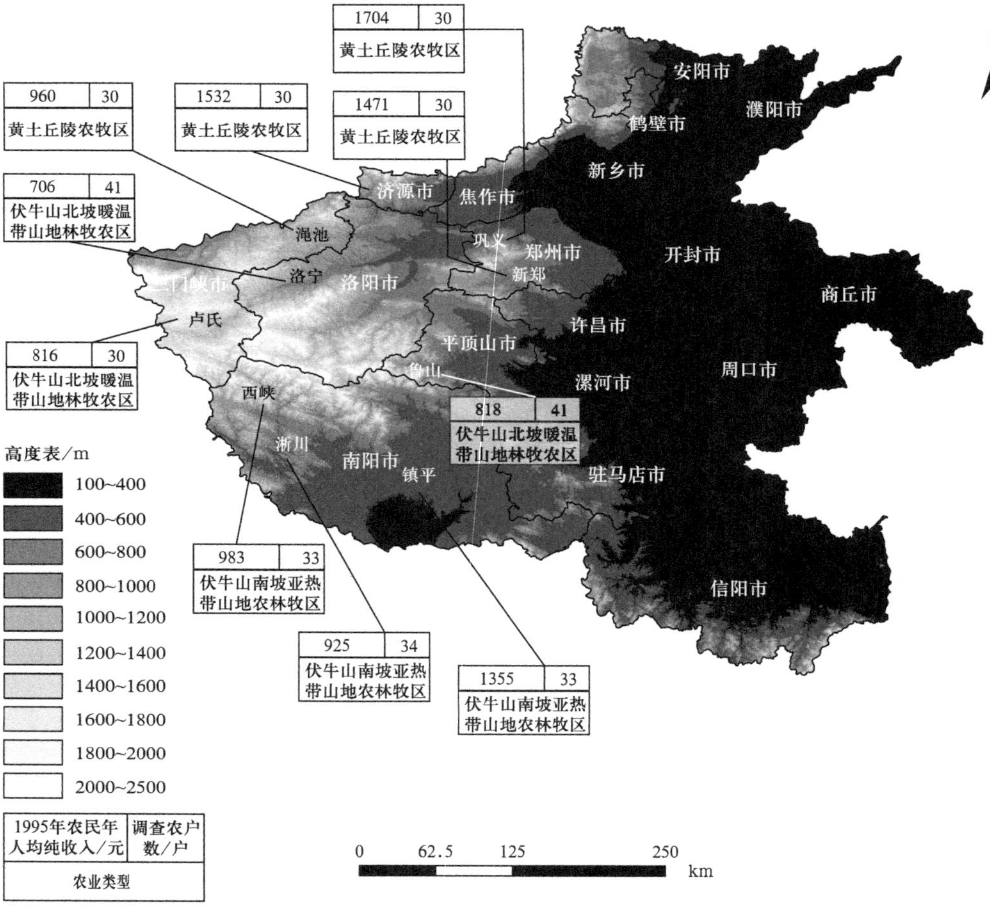

图 10.1　研究区地理位置及调查县域情况

注：调查农户涉及的县（县级市）均标有名称和其他相关数据。

52327km²，总人口为 1818.83 万（2000 年末）。在自然地理上，其位于我国西部山地和东部平原、亚热带和暖温带的过渡带。地貌复杂多样，以山地丘陵为主（河南大学地理系，1983）。1999 年全区 30 个县、市人均国内生产总值为 5628 元，农民年人均收入 2023 元，分别是河南省平均值的 115%、104%和全国平均值的 86%、91%。区内产业结构中（以增加值计），以农业为主的第一产业占 17.3%（其中，除郑州市所辖巩义、新郑、登封、荥阳外，第一产业占 22%）。相比较而言，北部沿陇海线和东部靠近京广线的县（市），经济发展水平相对较高；西部山区则交通不便、信息不畅，严重制约着经济发展。

10.2.2　调查区选择

选择调查县（市）时主要考虑以下原则：①兼顾不同收入水平；②兼顾河南西部农业类型，各类型均有一定代表性；③适当兼顾该区地、市级行政单元划分。依据这些原则，采取统计数据和专家经验相结合的方法，初选调查区。再由 15 名长期研究该区的各方面专家对选点结果进行论证。最后确定了 10 个县（市）为调查区（图 10.1）。

10.2.3　农户调查及数据分析

调查工作受到亚洲开发银行“河南西部项目”支持，在作者组织下于 1995 年 5～6 月进行。我们在每县（市）选择 3～4 个收入水平不同、地形各异（分别位于山区和丘陵区）的村庄，再在每个村庄按总户数多少选择 3～9 家农户作为调查对象。调查采用访谈式，依据事先印制好的问卷（该问卷曾在 30 家农户的调查试验基础上做了修改），请农户户主逐一回答有关问题。调查农户共计 332 家，占 10 县（市）总农户的 0.54‰。为了弥补数据年代过早的不足，2000 年 6～8 月和 2001 年 6 月作者又走访或通过电话调查了其中的 9 个县（市）中 1/3 的原调查村，发现除农户收入有普遍提高外，其他情况变化不大。所选 10 县（市）的收入水平代表性，除淅川县由 1995 年的中等收入水平变为 2000 年的低收入水平外，其余均保持不变（图 10.2）。

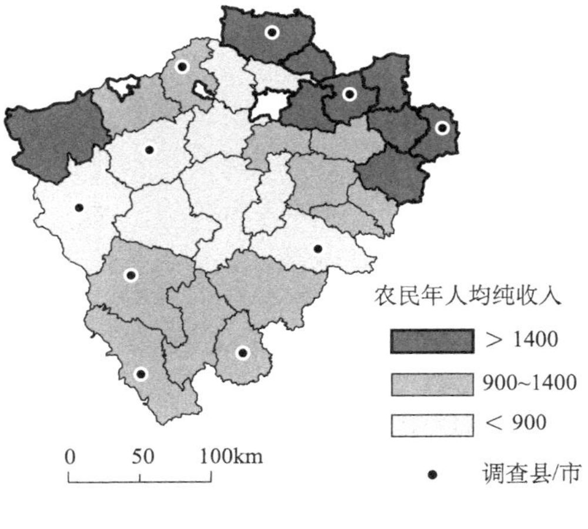

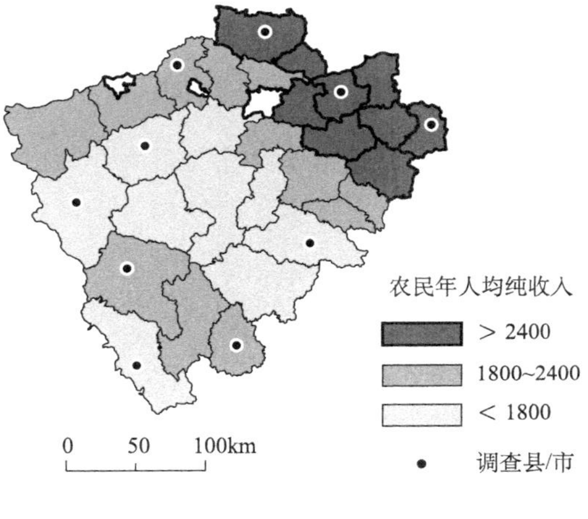

图 10.2　1995 年、2000 年豫西山地丘陵区农民年人均收入分布

调查问卷经过编码处理，在 SPSS 系统环境中，形成了 332 家农户，每个农户 652 个数据的数据库。该数据经过内部协调性检验，个别地方作了核实修改，成为本研究的依据。

10.3　经济发展中的农户行为特征

10.3.1　农户基本情况

332 户农户的基本状况反映了其欠发达经济社会特征（表 10.1）。标志其富裕程度的家庭电话和交通工具均处于很低水平。最高拥有度的为自行车和手表，平均每户 1.23 辆和 1.49 只，而每户平均人口达 5.11 人。这些物品多为户主拥有或全家共用。卡车和拖拉机作为现代农业生产工具，其家庭拥有度仅分别为 1%和 6%。与此相应，年人均毛收入仅为 1771 元。户主中 45%为初中以下文化程度，其中文盲占 9.34%。

表 10.1　豫西山地丘陵区 10 县（市）调研农户基本情况：1995 年（$N=332$）

序号	基本情况		序号	基本情况
1	家庭平均人口	5.11 人	10	户均洗衣机：0.10 台
2	户均自行车	1.23 辆	11	户均手表：1.49 只
3	户均摩托车	0.01 辆	12	户主文化程度：文盲 9.34%；小学 35.54%；
4	户均机动三轮	0.03 辆		初中 39.46%；高中 14.76%；中专 0.90%
5	户均人力三轮	0.006 辆	13	户主劳力状况：全劳力 93.4%；
6	户均卡车	0.01 辆		半劳力 5.1%；无劳动能力 1.5%
7	户均黑白电视机	0.57 台	14	户主非农工作月份：2.44 月
8	户均彩电	0.18 台	15	户均毛收入：9050 元
9	户均收录机	0.48 台		

10.3.2　农业发展中的农户行为

农业生产是所调查农户的主要经济活动。调查区域的经济发展状况又与农业生产密切相关。根据对调查结果的分析，农户在农业生产中的行为具有如下特征。

1. 信息获取行为特征

(1) 信息来源渠道具有很大局限性

由于户主文化程度普遍不高，加之研究地区均为山地丘陵区，交通和通信不畅，限制了信息来源渠道。在粮食种植技术信息，林果业价格信息和技术信息，畜牧养殖业价格信息和技术信息获取时农户所依赖的信息渠道多在两个以下，其中，相当一部分农户仅使用一种信息渠道（表 10.2）。

表 10.2　豫西山地丘陵区 10 县（市）调查农户的农业生产信息来源渠道：1995 年（$N=332$）

生产类型		1 个来源/%	2 个来源/%	平均数/个
粮食生产	技术	35.2	29.2	2.2
林果业	价格	59.9	27.8	1.5
	技术	25.6	27.2	2.1
畜牧业	价格	58.4	31.0	1.5
	技术	38.3	29.1	1.9

（2）信息获取具一定被动性

所调查农户中，超过一半以上（分别为 68.6%、55.2%和 54.9%）在粮食种植、林果业种植和畜牧业养殖中，将地方政府出面组织的农业技术员访问和技术推广站作为主要技术信息获取渠道。此外，24.2%和 11.7%的农户分别认为“其他农户”是畜牧业生产和粮食生产的技术来源。就林果、畜牧产品的价格而论，一半以上农户（55.7%和 56.4%）主要从买主处了解信息，占第二位的信息渠道为“从其他农民了解”（分别占农户的 29.5%和 26.3%）。价格信息对买主的依赖增加了交易的被动性。主要从身边了解价格信息，很难把握价格的变化趋势，很难主动地在农业生产中做出前瞻性决策。

2. 农业生产中存在的问题及解决方法

（1）调查农户对农业生产存在问题的反映具有 3 个明显特点。第一，豫西山地丘陵区的农业生产面临着诸多困难，但相当一部分农户找不到所存在的问题。在粮食种植、林果业和畜牧养殖业中，这样的农户分别占 17.8%、25.8%和 33.6%。第二，自然灾害是农户反映最多的问题。36.7%的农户认为种植业中最大的困难是缺水；18.6%和 13.3%的农户分别认为林果业生产的最大困难是虫灾和旱灾；22.4%的农户在畜牧养殖存在问题中提及疫病问题。第三，市场、信息和技术等问题并没有引起农户的关注。没有一家农户认为信息不畅影响农业生产；只有 3.6%的农户提及市场对林果业生产的影响；认为技术是农业生产的主要问题的农户，在粮食作物、畜牧养殖业和林果业中分别占 0.3%、2.2%和 12.5%。

（2）如何解决农业生产中存在的问题，农户的考虑具有与以上类似的特征。第一，更多的农户难以给出解决问题的方法。这类农户的比例在粮食种植业、林果业和畜牧养殖业中分别达 26.8%、30.0%和 46.3%，均明显高于找不到存在问题的农户比例。第二，农户所提到的解决问题的方法十分侧重于面向眼前的问题。例如，40.0%的农户提出通过修水渠、打井解决粮食生产中的问题，27.0%和 16.5%的农户提出改良品种和打药解决林果业生产中的问题，28.1%的农户提出打预防针、喂药解决畜牧业生产问题。第三，很少有农户提及农业生产中的体制和技术问题。尤其在粮食生产中，提及两个问题的仅有 1%；相比之下，林果业生产中，有 5.2%的农户关心管理体制的改革；畜牧养殖业中，有 4.1%的农户关注技术培训。

农户对解决农业问题的看法，与其文化背景有一定关联。文化程度较高的被访者，所提及解决问题方法的视野较宽广。在粮食生产中，初中以上毕业者，提及解决问题的方法达14种，小学毕业8种，文盲仅4种。畜牧业生产中，文盲中有50%没有提及任何方法。但问题的根本还在于，农户生产的自给性大，市场意识弱，没有把市场需求作为指导生产行为的第一因素。

10.3.3 非农产业就业中的农户行为

1. 剩余劳动力难以充分利用

调查表明，农户男、女劳动力平均每年分别有4.25个月和4.55个月的农闲时间。如果考虑非农闲时间的剩余劳动，其潜在剩余劳动时间要更高一些。农闲时间，男劳动力中，38.0%从事打工或做小生意，21.4%从事家庭养殖等可带来经济效益的活动，15.9%从事田间管理、果林管理等农业活动，10.5%无事可干。女劳动力中，41.3%从事家庭劳动，21.7%从事家庭养殖业，16.3%无事可做。统计结果和实际访问中所了解的情况说明，农村剩余劳动时间实际上大多数处于闲置状态。

2. 小农意识制约对非农产业的参与

访问中发现，相当一部分农民仍然抱着只要有饭吃有衣穿，就不愿到他乡打工就业，或冒风险进入非农行业的想法。调查农户中，28.4%从未考虑过到本地或外地企业打工。限制非农部门就业的因素中，认为本地企业少、无多余工作的占21.4%，认为农业劳动力缺乏、不愿去找工作的占31.2%，认为缺乏联系和相关技术的占21.9%。

10.3.4 资金获取和合作行为

1. 资金获取和使用行为

由于所调查区域农民手中资金积累很少，农民在生产中所需外部资金的获取以贷款为主。调查农户中，过去两年中曾有贷款的占59.3%。农户贷款具有如下特点：①农户贷款积极性不高。从获准贷款占申请贷款之比例（项目数占94.8%，总金额占92.5%）来看，贷款难度并不大，但还有40.7%的农户无贷款。这些农户中，70.4%认为不需要贷款。也有一些（20%）认为，贷款中的交易成本较高。②贷款农户平均收入水平低于无贷款农户，贷款农户人均年度总收入比无贷款农户低194.6元。③农户贷款的目的多为维持生计和农业简单再生产需要，农户贷款中，50%用于日常生活开支（包括看病、修房、结婚、日常花费等），33.0%用于农业再生产投入（包括购买化肥、农药、牲畜等）。用于开办工厂、经商等项目的不足10%。这些特征表明，农户利用外部资金扩大农业生产、发展非农经济的意识还非常淡薄。

2. 农民合作行为

基于新区域研究学派对区域网络的关注，作者分析了有关农户合作行为，结果表明：①多数农户（68.8%）具有某种形式的农户间合作。在该类农户中，96.5%认为农户间的无偿帮忙和互相交换是主要合作形式。这是农户中典型的非正式联系网络形式之一。②在有合作的农户中，60.9%同时与亲戚和非亲戚有合作关系，19.3%只与亲戚有合作关系，19.8%只与非亲戚有合作关系。这说明善于合作的农民多数并不区别其合作对象的亲疏。③在没有合作的农户中，绝大多数（80%）认为其主要原因是“不需要合作”。但也有 10%的农户认为，如果亲戚距离近一些，他们会与其合作的。

10.3.5　农户对其发展的自我分析

1. 贫富形成原因

农户对致富原因的分析，明显侧重于对当地农业资源条件的利用上（表 10.3）。“养殖及种植林果经济作物”是最主要的致富原因，如果再加上与农业生产有关的“劳动力多、地多”“有能力、勤快”和“原有基础好”（原有基础多与农业积累有关）等原因，这类影响的农户可达 60.9%。此外，38.9%的调查者认为到工商业、建筑业打工或自主经营小商业（表 10.3 中的“副业”指个体办或村办小型工厂、小作坊或商店），是致富的主要原因。

表 10.3　豫西山地丘陵区 10 县（市）农户对贫富形成原因的看法：1995 年（$N=332$）

序号	富裕原因	农户比重/%	序号	贫困原因	农户比重/%
1	养殖及林果、经济作物	35.0	1	没劳动力、地少、地差	33.9
2	工商业	30.1	2	无本钱、底子薄	20.0
3	劳力多、地多	12.1	3	没有养殖、种植经济作物	12.2
4	副业	8.8	4	病人多、孩子多、学生多	11.6
5	有能力、勤快	7.5	5	能力差、人懒、没文化	9.9
6	原有基础好	6.5	6	没技术、缺信息	6.1
			7	无打工和副业	4.4
			8	意外事件	2.0

农户为何处于贫困状态？农户的看法更加侧重于与农业生产有关的因素。其中，25.4%的农户认为“没劳动力”（无法利用农业资源）是贫困的主要原因。如果加上“地少、地差”“无本钱、底子薄”“没有养殖、种植经济作物”等原因，与农业生产有关者达 66.1%。另一类原因是家庭成员自然状况的影响。有 23.5%的农户将贫困归因于家庭病人多、孩子多、学生多，户主及家庭主要成员能力差、人懒和家庭成员的意外事件。相比之下，“没技术、缺信息”和“无打工和副业”的影响则十分次要。

2. 农户对改善目前现状的看法

调查的农户中，大多数（71.5%）对其目前的现状不满意。如何改变现状，农户十分依赖于畜牧养殖、林果和经济作物（表 10.4）。如此高的比例（89.7%）可能有调查时农户预期亚洲开发银行农牧业开发贷款引起的偏差。但是反映了一些农户通过种植、养殖致富示范效应的影响。此外，6.7%的农户认为打工、办企业、学技术是改善目前现状的主要途径。少数农户（3.0%，主要是贫困户）没有改善现状的看法，只能寄希望于下一代。

表 10.4 豫西山地丘陵区 10 县（市）农户对改善当前现状途径的看法：1995 年（$N=332$）

序号	看法	农户比重/%	序号	看法	农户比重/%
1	畜牧养殖、林果、经济作物	89.7	4	不知道如何改善	1.2
2	办企业、打工	5.8	5	学技术	0.9
3	靠下一代等	1.8	6	打井、修路	0.6

3. 农户所期望的近期家庭变化

调查结果表明，更多农户期望在家庭生活状况上发生变化。其中，“盖房子”“买家具、电器、交通工具”“孩子成才”“娶媳妇”“脱贫”“达小康水平”的期望占农户总数的 73.4%（表 10.5）。而期望在生产上变化（包括“发展林果业、养殖业”“农具和农业条件改善”“办工厂”等）的农户仅占 21%。这反映了农户生活需求（包括吃、住、结婚等）并没有得到满足时的心理状况。

表 10.5 豫西山地丘陵区 10 县（市）农户所期望近年家庭所发生的变化：1995 年（$N=332$）

序号	期望变化	农户比重/%	序号	期望变化	农户比重/%
1	盖房子	44.3	7	治病、还贷	3.0
2	发展林果业、养殖业	15.0	8	农具及农业条件改善	2.7
3	买家具、电器、交通工具	13.5	9	脱贫	2.7
4	孩子成才	6.9	10	没有期望	2.3
5	娶媳妇	4.8	11	达小康水平	1.2
6	办工厂	3.3	12	减轻负担	0.3

尽管所调查农户收入普遍不高，但均十分注重后代教育。表 10.5 中“孩子成才”为农户第四个最重要的期望。调查还表明，51.8%的农户希望自己的子女能够接受中专或大学教育，22.0%的农户认为“越高越好”。73.9%的农户希望通过上学使孩子走出农村，找到工作。然而，60.2%的农户在学生上学中存在这样或那样的问题，其中，64.1%的农户难以支付学生学费。

10.3.6 农户收入及其与环境关系的模型分析

依据生产函数，可以建立农户收入（Y）模型如下：

$$Y=a+a_1x_1+b_2x_2+b_3x_3+b_4x_4+b_5x_5+b_6x_6 \tag{10.1}$$

式中，x_1，x_2，x_3，x_4，x_5，x_6分别表示土地面积、劳动力数量、户主教育水平、全家非农打工时间、生产投资和粮食作物面积比例。为了区别因农户所在环境不同该模型的差异，我们以农户居住地地形为虚拟变量，对其收入与相关变量进行回归分析。结果表明（表 10.6），土地面积和劳动力数量对农民收入的影响，在平原地区大于丘陵区，丘陵区大于山区。生产投资的影响，也以平原地区最大。粮作比例占土地总面积的比例的影响，则基本上与此相反。这说明平原地区土地的农作条件明显高于丘陵和山地，投入同样的劳动和资金，可获得较好的收益。农业结构中，经济作物带来的收益，在丘陵地区最为明显。这是因为：①所调查的丘陵区农户种植经济作物和林果具有一定的优势；②该区粮作收益相对较低。与此比较，另外两个变量（户主教育水平和非农打工时间）的影响，因农户居住地环境差别带来的影响不大。

表 10.6　豫西山地丘陵区 10 县（市）农户收入与相关变量的回归结果：1995 年（$N=332$）

土地类型	土地面积		劳动力数量		户主教育水平		非农打工时间		生产投资		粮作面积比例	
	系数	T 值	系数	T 值	系数	T 值	系数	T 值	系数	T 值	系数	T 值
平原	0.780	8.713	0.301	2.209	0.103	0.722	0.612	2.047	0.769	8.409	−0.478	−3.808
丘陵	0.159	1.841	0.168	1.939	0.123	1.418	0.577	3.159	0.669	8.895	−2.228	−2.676
山地	0.088	1.076	0.075	0.911	0.099	0.211	0.761	4.223	0.668	10.876	0.107	1.300

注：平原、丘陵、山地分别指相应地形环境的农户；土地面积、劳动力数量和生产投资分别为调查年度农户拥有的该类指标数量，户主教育水平以受教育年限计，非农打工时间为全家总和（月份），粮食作物面积比例为粮食作物面积占总土地面积的比例。系数指回归系数，T 值为相应系数的 T 检验值。

10.4　农户行为对区域经济发展的影响

10.4.1　农户行为对区域发展的利弊影响

研究区域的不发达，在很大程度上归因于区内农户收入普遍较低。在该区域，农户经济状况改善的区域影响，也比发达区更为明显。根据以上分析和在农户访问中所得的信息，农户行为存在着不少不利于区域发展的因素。诸如，农户信息来源的局限性；信息获取的被动性；农业发展严重依赖自然条件；农村剩余劳动力转移存在意识障碍，农民对非农产业参与意识不强；一旦收入增加，农户更加期望家庭生活状况的改变，而不是着力于发展生产，等等。无须指责农户，这些不利因素，是他们长期的贫困或低收入水平、封闭的环境和小农生产方式造成的。

农户行为中积极向上，有利于区域发展的一面也不可忽视。例如，农民们长期生活在这种很低的水平之中，并无怨言，对改善生活状况有着强烈要求，并寄希望于凭借自己的劳动来达此目的。他们强调劳动力的作用和对当地条件的利用，注重农业生产；认识到工商业对致富的影响；善于利用非正式关系发展合作等。

10.4.2　农户行为影响的模型分析

农户作为生产单元，其生产可分为自给性和商品性两部分。农户的生产安排，服从于利益最大化原则（张启明，1997）。假如用以下简单模型来表示农户利益（π）（收益与成本之差）：

$$\pi = \max(\Sigma P_i Q_i - \Sigma W_j X_j) \quad (10.2)$$

式中，Q_i为农户所生产的 i 类农产品数量；P_i为相应农产品的价格；X_j为生产农产品所投入的 j 产品的数量；W_j为该类投入品的价格。其中，Q 可分为自给性 Q_1 和商品性产品 Q_2（即 $Q=Q_1+Q_2$）。农户生产行为及其影响可讨论如下：

农户在满足基本需要之前，其生产完全自给（$Q_2=0$）。此时，农户的货币性收益为零（$\Sigma P_iQ_i=0$）。投入品要么用自产型替代，要么靠外部援助（如政府救济等）。该类农户处于农区的低层，在所调查农户中占 26.6%。他们多数缺乏劳动力，政府应给予一定扶植。同时，还可发挥其他农户的帮带作用，促使其发展。

农户在满足基本需求之后，其生产产品部分面向市场（$0<Q_2<Q/2$）。此时，其利润的大小取决于产品价格和投入成本。其中，一部分农户出售农产品的目的，主要是用于购买农业投入品和其他家庭消费开支。他们的利润不高，也并不期望通过发展生产成为商品性农业生产大户。这类农户在调查中占绝大多数（63.4%）。他们是区域发展的基本力量。对该类农户，应重点培育其市场经济观念，转变传统的小农经济行为。

还有一部分农户的农业产品绝大多数面向市场（$Q_2>Q/2$）。他们或经营粮食作物，或经营畜牧业养殖、林果业种植，已成为商品生产性大户。尽管他们在调查农户中所占比例不大（9.9%），但却是农村经济发展的龙头。从上述模型可以看出，面向市场的农户，价格信息和销售市场信息，对其利润状况具有重要影响。除此之外，对该类农户还应提供技术支持。

10.4.3 欠发达农区发展的新思路

基于以上分析，在欠发达农区发展中，便会提出一些新问题：①区域发展的首要原则应为满足农户的基本需求，致富于民。②区域发展方向首先应充分利用当地资源，以农（业）养农（户）；其次发展农业产业化，通过后续农产品加工带动农业发展；再次，待经济有所发展后再考虑发展其他非农产业。③区域发展的决策、组织应集中于农户这一基本单元，必须适应农户特点，调动农户的积极性。利用农户之间的非正式合作关系的有利面，形成合作的力量和创新扩展的渠道。④客观对待不利于经济发展的农户行为。对于那些明显不利于经济发展的，可逐步引导改变。对于那些具有两面性的农户行为（如“孩子多”导致贫困与“劳动力多”导致致富的关系，对资源依赖的有利和不利等），则应认真研究。⑤目前农户消费并不能刺激区内经济发展，农户产品的市场主要在区外。这更加强了信息对农户和区域发展的重要意义。

10.5 结论及讨论

通过对豫西山地丘陵区农户行为的研究，本章回答了一开始所提出的问题。其中，着力分析了调查区 332 家农户与区域经济发展有关的行为特征及其影响。并在此基础上，探讨了如何利用农户行为，促进欠发达区域经济发展问题。作者发现，与其他区域发展研究方法相比，从农户行为角度分析区域发展，具有如下特点：①抓住了不发达农区经济发展中的最基本单元，使区域分析细化；②反映了区内统计数据所忽略的事实，以及在一些关键问题上农户实际行为与理性行为的差异；③揭示了农户行为与区域发展的矛盾和协调，便于提出符合区内实际的发展建议；④对区域发展的组织，可从农户角度着手，它比从政府角度组织更易于落实。

上升到理论层面，农户在欠发达农区经济发展中的作用，与企业在工商业占主导的区域中的作用，既具有相似之处，也有明显不同。与企业一样，农户利益与企业利益存在着矛盾（如农户利益最大化多与区域利益最大化不一致等）。但由于农户联系以区内为主，与企业，尤其是多区位企业的跨区域联系有很大不同（李小建，1999）。因此，区域利益应更多的是农户利益的集合。区域发展政策研究者更应该从人文关怀的角度（马润潮，1999）来注重对农户行为的研究。

作为探索性研究，本章在问卷设计中存在一些不适应区域发展研究之处。例如，并没有列出专项，请农户回答对区域发展的看法。此外，选择不同收入水平的农户进行分析，也应受到关注。

致谢：秦耀辰、千怀遂、金学良、冯兴祥、苗长虹、钱新强参与本章数据调查，乔家君在数据分析方面给予诸多帮助，特表谢意。

参考文献

费洪平. 1994. 产业带空间边际划分的理论与方法. 地理学报，49（3）：214～225

河南大学地理系. 1983. 豫西中部山地区自然条件与自然资源（专题研究）. 开封：河南大学学报丛书

李小建. 1998. 国有企业改革对区域经济发展的影响. 经济地理，18（3）：1～7

李小建. 1999. 公司地理论. 北京：科学出版社

陆大道. 1995. 区域发展及其空间结构. 北京：科学出版社

马润潮. 1999. 人文主义与现代主义之兴起及西方新区域地理学之发展. 地理学报，54（4）：365～372

仇保兴. 1999. 小企业集群研究. 上海：复旦大学出版社

谭崇台. 1999. 发展经济学的新发展. 武汉：武汉大学出版社

王丹红. 2000. 诺贝尔经济学奖获得者解决选择中的偏见与离散问题. 科学时报，3

王缉慈等. 2001. 创新空间：企业集群与区域发展. 北京：北京大学出版社

张启明. 1997. 农户行为分析与农业宏观调控政策. 中国农村经济，(6)：35～38

Antonelli C. 2000. Restructuring and innovation in long term regional change. In: Clark G L, Feldman M P, Gertler M S The Oxford Handbook of Economic Geography. Oxford: Oxford University Press. 395～412

Feldman M P. 2000. Location and innovation: The new economicgeography of innovation, spillovers, and agglomeration. In: Clark G L, Feldman M P, Gertler M S, eds. The Oxford Handbook of Economic Geography. Oxford: Oxford University Press. 373～394

Peet R. 1999. Theories of Development. New York: The Guilford Press

Scott A. 2000. Economic geography: The great half-century. In: Clark G L, Feldman M P, Gertler M S The Oxford Handbook of Economic Geography. Oxford: Oxford University Press. 18～44

第 11 章　欠发达区农户兼业演变

党的十六大报告中明确提出今后 20 年全面建设小康社会的目标（本书编写组，2002）。欲实现该目标，农村发展（尤其是农区经济发展）是最关键的问题。2001 年全国农村人口有 79563 万（占总人口的 62.34%），农村能否达到小康水平（尤其是全面建设的小康水平），是中国在相当长的一段时期内的主要任务。全国人民代表大会十届一次会议的《政府工作报告》，把发展农业和农村经济、增加农民收入作为经济工作的重中之重[①]。在农村经济发展中，农户兼业是一个重要的途径。因为，农户兼业化程度一般与区域经济发展成正相关关系（高强和赵贞，2000）。通过河南省 16 个村 1000 农户的调查分析发现，20 世纪 80 年代以来农户兼业化程度得到大幅提高，其增长可以划分为波动发展、快速增长、稳定发展三个阶段，这与中国的相关社会经济政策和农户兼业发展环境有着密切关系。农户兼业对农户经济及其差异的影响不断增大，尤其是二兼对农户经济带动明显。促进农户兼业，尤其是提高其质量和效益，对农村全面建设小康社会具有重要意义。

11.1　研究问题

有关农户兼业的确切内涵，目前尚未达成共识。美国学者把每年从事非农业劳动 100 天以上，或非农收入大于农业收入方称为农户兼业；日本学者把家庭成员中有 1 人及以上从事非农业生产即称为农户兼业（高强，1998）。本章根据国内学者的研究（杨俊青和吕小康，1998），把农户从事非农业经营活动称为农户兼业。农户兼业化是指农户总数中兼业农户所占比重越来越大的趋势（李苏，2000）。对农户兼业的作用，有学者（张晓明，1999）做了细致的总结，包括：①增加农户的家庭收入，改善生活水平；②充分利用劳动力资源，优化配置活劳力；③缓和就业矛盾，截留农村剩余劳动力；④有碍农业的规模经济；⑤不利于农业的集约经济；⑥促使农业劳动力素质下降；⑦阻碍农业社会分工等。在中国，由于目前农户兼业以非农业发展为特征，农户兼业以积极贡献为主，而对负面影响正积极加以引导。

对农户兼业与区域经济发展的关系，通常有两种观点：一种观点认为，随着经济的发展，农村专业化程度提高，农户兼业减少；另一种观点认为，经济越发达，增长越迅速，兼业化的程度就越高（高强，1998）。有学者（高强和赵贞，2000）根据农村住户调查资料，提出随着收入增长，兼业程度在深化。从农户投入看，以农业为主的兼业（一兼）农户拥有的土地和劳动力多，以非农业为主的兼业（二兼）农户少；生产经营费用亦如此；而从产出来看，总收入以二兼农户最高，从效率看，无论费用产出率、土

---

① 朱镕基总理《政府工作报告》摘要，2003. 经济日报，03-06. P2～3。

地产出率，还是劳动生产率都是如此。有学者（高强，1999）根据中国东、中、西部农户兼业化程度，得出了农户兼业化水平随经济发展程度而递减的规律。还有学者根据兼业化的发展，将其过程划分为：兼业化早期、中期、后期三个阶段（高强，1998）。也有一些学者调查了不同区域农户，得出了很有价值的成果（高强和赵贞，2000；胡荣华，2000）。

但是，这些研究并未揭示不同类型的兼业与区域发展的关系。从历史发展角度，这种关系处于不断变化之中。从空间角度，不同发展水平的区域两者的关系也应有所不同。本章将根据河南省 1000 多个农户的数据调查，对中国欠发达地区改革开放以来农户兼业化的发展演变，以及农户兼业与区域经济发展的定量关系等问题做初步分析。

11.2　数据来源及处理

本章数据来源于 1986～2002 年河南省农村 16 个固定观察点 1000 农户的实地调查。调查数据直接取自户主、企业家、村长等。这 16 个观察点是 1984 年国家为掌握农村发展状况而设立的，在河南省两万多个行政村的选取中，主要依据以下四个标准进行选定：①行政单元标准，每个地市有且仅有一个观察点；②地形地势标准，兼顾平原、丘陵、山区等类型；③人均收入标准，高、中、差不同级别收入均有分布；④其他标准，如隶属经济区类型、民族村域等。河南省设立农村固定观察点的基本概况见表 11.1。

表 11.1　河南省农村固定观察地点基本概况

项目	数据
调查农户数	1000 户（2002 年）
调查村数	16 个[a]
调查村地势状况	8 个平原村，4 个丘陵村，4 个山区村
隶属经济区域	13 个农区，3 个林区
经济发达程度（居所在县水平）	2 个上等，4 个中下等，4 个中等，6 个中下等（1984 年）
人均收入	2047 元（2002 年）
家庭平均规模	4.02 人（2002 年）

注：a：由于 1984 年焦作市、济源市隶属于新乡市，三市划开后还未增设新的观察点，故河南省 18 个地市仅有 16 个观察点。

资料来源：河南省农业厅 2002 年 12 月 15 日提供，本章除特殊声明外，所有数据均源于此。

调查数据基本可靠、有效。但由于调查对象对问题理解有误、调查员的笔误，以及录入员的机误等，有个别调查数据不符合实际，我们主要采用参照历史数据按照常规推理进行一定的修正。此外，1992 年的和 1994 年的数据因故暂缺，但对历史趋势的分析不会有很大影响。

11.3　农户兼业化演变

如果我们把以农业为主的兼业户占总户数的百分比称为一兼比率，把以非农业为主的兼业户占总户数的百分比称为二兼比率，把前两者的合计称为农户的兼业化程度，那么，根据农户调查数据，1986～2002年河南省农户兼业化的发展演化趋势（图11.1和表11.2）可总结出以下特点。

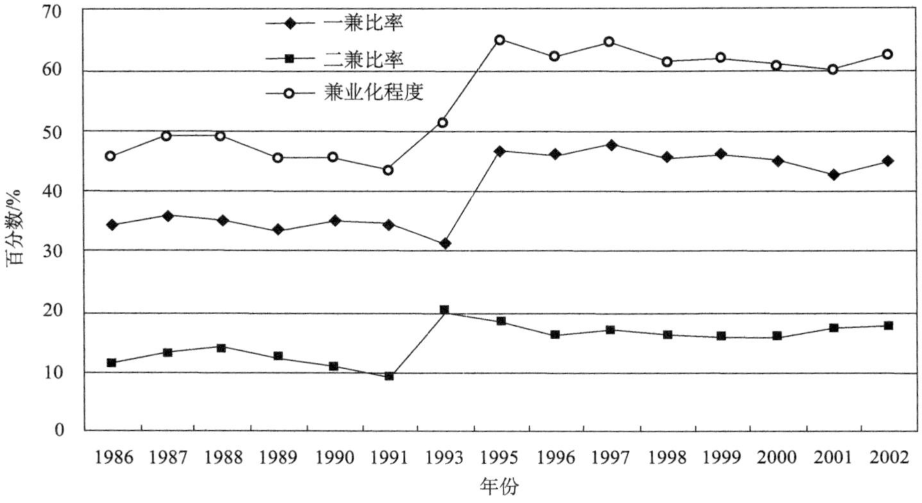

图11.1　河南省农户兼业化发展趋势

表11.2　河南省农户兼业化程度变化（1986～2002年）

项目	1986年	1987年	1988年	1989年	1990年	1991年	1993年	1995年	1996年	1997年	1998年	1999年	2000年	2001年	2002年
一兼比率（A）	34.44	36.00	35.40	33.36	34.96	34.27	31.40	46.70	46.20	48.00	45.50	46.20	44.80	42.60	44.94
一兼增长率		4.53	−1.67	−5.76	4.80	−1.97	−8.37	48.73	−1.07	3.90	−5.21	1.54	−3.03	−4.91	5.49
二兼比率（B）	11.25	12.96	13.71	12.24	10.80	8.97	20.10	18.10	15.90	16.70	15.90	15.60	15.70	17.20	17.32
二兼增长率		15.20	5.79	−10.72	−11.76	−16.94	124.08	−9.95	−12.15	5.03	−4.79	−1.89	0.64	9.55	0.70
B/A	0.33	0.36	0.39	0.37	0.31	0.26	0.64	0.39	0.34	0.35	0.35	0.34	0.35	0.40	0.39

11.3.1　农户兼业化呈增加趋势

1986年，河南省农户兼业化程度为45.7%，到2002年增长到62.3%，年均增长2.0%。其中，一兼比率年均增长1.7%，二兼比率年均增长2.7%。农户在从事农业生产的同时，在非农业领域的实践活动逐渐加强。

11.3.2 农户兼业化进程阶段明显

1979年以后，农村联产承包责任制的实施带动了农业的稳定发展，生产力的解放，使农民工商业意识得以萌发，农户兼业逐年增长。到20世纪80年代中期，已达到45%以上。研究阶段内农户兼业的演变大致可分为三个阶段：①波动发展阶段（1986～1991年），期间1988年之前农户兼业化程度逐年上升，之后由于指导思想的波动，影响农民在非农产业的发展；②快速增长阶段（1991～1995年），邓小平南行讲话之后，改革开放的新局面带来农民思想的进一步解放，非农产业获得快速发展，农户兼业程度出现大幅度增长；③稳定阶段（1995～2002年），20世纪90年代中期以后，中国市场产品趋于饱和，工商业竞争加剧，对农户兼业形成带来制约作用。与此相应，农户兼业程度处于稳定之中，并略微下降。

11.3.3 农户兼业结构以一兼为主

河南省农户兼业仍以一兼为主、二兼为辅（2002年一兼比例为二兼比例的2.6倍）。在农户兼业程度的变化中，16年间一兼上升了10.5个百分点，而二兼仅上升6.1个百分点（表11.2），反映了河南省农户兼业层次仍较低。从农户调查过程中，可发现河南省农户兼业时间较短，且多为季节性，这也印证了一些学者的调查实践（在陕西省宝鸡市陵塬乡856个兼业农户中，季节性外出占69.9%（高强和赵贞，2000））。但1986～2002年间二兼表现出较强的增长势头。

11.3.4 农户兼业化程度与社会经济环境密切相关

我们根据1986～2002年农户兼业化程度与河南省社会经济指标做相关分析，得出河南省农户兼业变化与其社会经济环境密切相关（表11.3）。其中，全省经济总量、人均量、乡村人口比重、城市化水平、居民消费等与农户兼业程度高度正相关，在城、乡消费中，城市消费对农户兼业趋向的吸引力更大。

表11.3 河南省农户兼业化程度与宏观社会经济指标的关系

指标	全省人均GDP	全省GDP	乡村人口比重	城市化水平	居民消费	农村消费	城市消费
兼业化与之相关系数	0.877**	0.999**	0.952**	0.996**	0.974**	0.908**	0.999**

** 表明显著度在0.01水平。

注：技术水平＝工业职工人均产值×工业资金产值率；城市化水平＝区域市镇人口/区域总人口。

11.4 兼业化对农户经济的贡献

11.4.1 兼业化程度对农户经济的贡献

1986～1991年，农户兼业化与农户家庭总收入呈负相关关系（表11.4），表明农户多从事低收入兼业，农户收入主要来源于农业，农户兼业在一定程度上影响了农业专业生产。1993 年，农户兼业对农户收入的贡献已由负转正；到 2002 年，兼业化程度与家庭收入的相关系数达 0.390，所调查的 1000 农户非农业收入平均为每户 4280 元，占家庭总收入（8001 元）的 53.49%（表 11.4）。

表 11.4 兼业化程度与农户经济及差异的相关系数

项目	1986 年	1988 年	1991 年	1997 年	2002 年
与农户家庭总收入的平均值	−0.596*	−0.479	−0.423	0.356	0.390
与农户家庭总收入的标准差	−0.635**	−0.444	−0.381	0.345	0.470
与农户家庭总收入的变异系数	−0.534*	−0.187	0.066	0.107	0.426

* 表明显著度在 0.05 水平；** 表明显著度在 0.01 水平。下表同。

11.4.2 兼业化程度对农户经济差异的影响

在 16 个调查村农户收入的绝对差异和相对差异中，兼业化程度的影响也十分明显（表 11.4）。1986 年兼业化水平与两者显著负相关。随着时间的发展，其负相关程度逐渐减小，最后对农户经济差异的影响也演变为正相关。

11.4.3 一兼比率对农户经济影响趋于弱化

1986 年，一兼比率与农户家庭总收入平均值、标准差、变异系数的相关系数分别为−0.543*、−0.599*、−0.548*，呈现出显著负相关，到 2002 年，上述指标已变为−0.381、−0.351、−0.242，一兼比率对农户经济的影响趋于减弱。

11.4.4 二兼比率对农户经济带动正日渐加强

1986 年，二兼比率与农户经济及差异呈现显著负相关（表 11.5），到 1997 年、2002 年二兼比率对农户经济的作用已由负转正，且影响程度在日渐加强，达到高度正相关。与此相关，二兼比率对农户收入差异的正向影响也十分明显。

表 11.5 二兼比率与农户经济及差异的相关系数

项目	1986	1988	1991	1997	2002
与农户家庭总收入的平均值	−0.617*	−0.473	−0.349	0.750**	0.831**
与农户家庭总收入的标准差	−0.617*	−0.406	−0.287	0.742**	0.815**
与农户家庭总收入的变异系数	−0.432	−0.187	0.082	0.243	0.710**

11.5 进一步讨论

通过对河南省 1000 户农户数据的分析表明，改革开放以来，欠发达区农户兼业化出现了十分明显的增长。经过 10 多年的发展，到 20 世纪 90 年代中期，兼业农户已占到农户的大多数。兼业农户数量的上升有明显的阶段性。这种变化除了与政策和发展环境关联外，还有其内在的发展趋势。就一典型农区而言，不同类型兼业农户随经济发展的变化大致可以分为 4 个阶段（图 11.2）。在农村经济发展的早期阶段，农业经济占主导地位，农户均从事农业生产。随着经济发展，少数农户开始兼业，出现一兼农户（阶段Ⅰ）。由于兼业非农产业可带来较高收入，促进一兼农户数量的增长；同时在一兼农户的发展中，有一些非农业所占比重逐渐超过农业，出现二兼农户；相应的，纯农户所占比例出现大幅下降（阶段Ⅱ）。第三阶段的特征是，随着二兼农户非农产业的进一步扩大，出现纯非农户。这时农户尽管仍生活在农村，但是，其生活完全依靠非农业收入。纯非农户、一兼和二兼的增长，促使纯农户数量进一步下降。第四阶段，随着农业机械化水平的提高，经营农业的规模会不断扩大，纯农户仍有下降但会稳定在一定水平；在农业产业化发展中有一些兼业户成为专业非农户，又有一些农户参与兼业，但兼业农户总体所占比例会相对稳定。这种农户兼业演变过程的假设，主要基于一般农村发展的分析，在一些特殊地区（如传统农业区转变为专业化农业区、工商业区等），情况会有所不同。

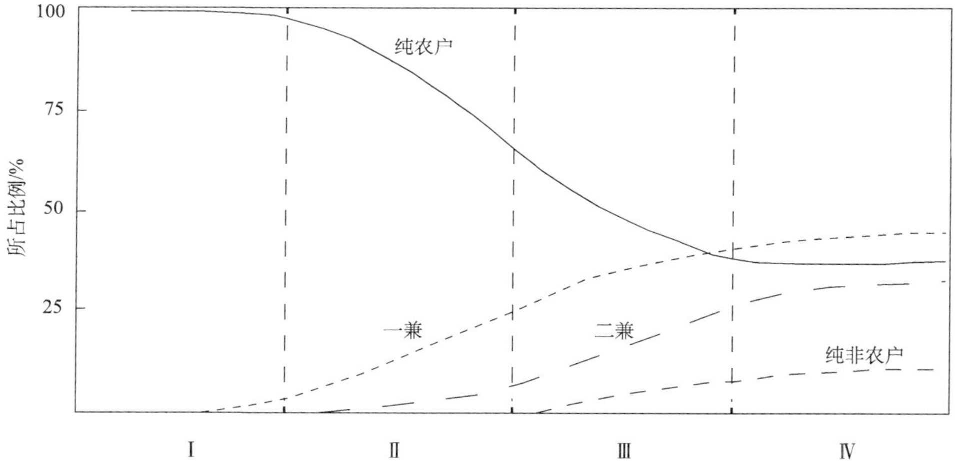

图 11.2　农户兼业变化阶段图示

按照以上对农户兼业的阶段假设，本章研究的农户兼业状况，应该处在第二、三阶段。尽管兼业数量已经增长到较高水平，但是兼业质量和效益仍然较低。河南省农户兼业时间较短，且多为季节性。绝大多数兼业农户仍以农业收入为主。农户兼业的进一步发展，会在数量稳定的基础上，不断提高质量和效益。

所研究农户兼业对经济增长的贡献，在 20 世纪 90 年代以后逐步增加。与此相关，兼业化程度对农户经济差异的影响亦逐渐明显。其中，一兼比率对农户经济的影响正趋于减弱，二兼比率对农户经济的影响程度在日趋加强。二兼农户正在成为农村经济发展的带头者。

毋庸置疑，农户兼业对农村经济和社会也产生了一定的负面影响，如农户办小工厂带来环境污染，由于受益差别，非农兼业对农业生产的冲击等。但是，总体来说，由于农村隐含着大量的剩余劳动力，农户兼业对农村（户）经济发展，进而对农村全面建设小康社会，具有重要意义。

欠发达区农户兼业状况，还受到农户行为的影响。例如，一些山区农户在农业剩余劳动力转移上存在意识障碍，农民对非农业参与意识不强等（李小建，2002）。相关决策者，应该加强这些地区工商业文化和创新精神的培育，以利于促进农户兼业水平的提高。

参考文献

本书编写组. 2002. 十六大报告辅导读本. 北京：人民出版社

高强，赵贞. 2000. 我国农户兼业化八大特征. 调研世界，(4)：29～31

高强. 1998. 国外农户兼业化研究述评. 世界农业，(11)：3～5

高强. 1999. 我国三大地带农户兼业形态研究. 经济地理，19 (1)：73～76

胡荣华. 2000. 农户兼业行为研究：以南京市为例的分析. 南京社会科学，(7)：87～92

李苏. 2000. 论农户兼业化向专业化的过渡. 社会科学家，15 (6)：60～63

李小建. 2002. 欠发达农区经济发展中的农户行为：以豫西山地丘陵区为例. 地理学报，57 (4)：459～468

杨俊青，吕小康. 1998. 论我国农户兼业化经营与农村经济产业化. 生产力研究，(1)：71～73

张晓明. 1999. 农户兼业行为初探. 学术交流，(5)：50～52

第12章　农户收入的地理环境影响

农业人口和农村地区在中国具有十分重要的地位。因此，在中国建立和谐社会的进程中，农村地区的发展起着十分关键的作用。因此，农区的发展问题逐渐引起学者们的重视，发表了不少相关研究成果（黄祖辉等，2005；张平，1992；万广华，1998；朱玲，1992；Liu，2006；Meng and Wu，1998；Knight and Song，1993；Wan and Zhou，2005；Wu and Zhu，2004）。在这些研究中，学者们认真地分析了农村经济结构（非农化）（朱玲，1992；Wu and Zhu，2004）、市场化程度（Meng and Wu，1998）、资金投入（Wan and Zhou，2005）、农村居民的要素禀赋，以及村庄外部市场环境（黄祖辉等，2005）等因素对农村收入差距的影响，并认为地理因素作为重要影响变量，其在解释农区差异中的重要性正在下降（Wan and Zhou，2005）。从理论角度，中国不同发展水平的农区，其经济发展的影响因素应有所不同。从宏观角度和农户微观角度分析，也可能得出不同结果。

河南是全国经济发展水平较低的省份，2005年农村人均纯收入为2870.58元，低于全国平均水平。河南省也是全国第一农业大省，不仅农业人口众多（乡村人口占69.35%）、农区面积广大（耕地面积811.03万 hm^2，占全国的6.24%），而且农业产值（第一产业产值占全国的8.24%，在31个省级单元中排名第二）和许多农产品（粮食产量占全国9.47%，排名第一；棉花产量占全国的11.84%，排名第三；油料产量占14.6%，排名第一）在全国占有重要地位（河南省统计局，2006）。在农村劳动力转移方面，河南省的劳动力输出居全国第一位。在农区的产业结构上，与东部沿海地区非农产业占较高比例、东北地区的大规模农场农业相比，小规模的农户型农业特点十分明显。因此，选择河南来研究经济发展水平较低、以传统农业为主地区经济发展与环境的关系，具有一定的典型意义。

农户收入是衡量农户经济水平和发展能力的重要指标，农区发展的重要目标是促进农户增收。通过对分层随机抽样选取的河南省不同类型的11个村的农户调查和定量分析，发现农户间收入差别很大，村际之间和同村农户之间均如此。全体样本农户收入的基尼系数达0.3936，有的村子已达0.4以上。模型分析表明，农区发展环境因素对农户收入具有重要影响。耕地面积、种植结构、经济基础、乡镇工商业发展水平、城郊区位、交通条件、兼业水平等因素在不同的地形类型和收入类型农户中，对收入提高产生一定的影响。低收入农户中，耕地面积较为重要，而在中等收入农户中，增加了种植结构因素，在高收入农户中，又增加了经济基础、工商水平、城郊区位和交通因素，由此验证了“区域发展阶段不同，影响因素有所不同”的理论假设。

12.1　研究问题

农户或农民收入在农区经济和社会发展中具有十分重要的作用。因此，相关文献十分关注农户收入的研究，从不同角度分析了影响农户收入的影响因素。这些成果可以概括为几个方面。①结构因素：认为农业结构（Wan and Zhou，2005；刘希凤和王联兵，2007）、农区的经济结构（朱玲，1992；Wu and Zhu，2004），以及与此相关的农民收入结构（王桂荣等，2006；贺梅英，2003）等对农户收入影响十分重要。在不少地区，工资性收入与农民收入关联密切（王桂荣等，2006；贺梅英，2003）。②政策因素：包括家庭联产责任制、农产品价格等（孟凡胜，2003），甚至还有人认为产权界定不清的一系列制度因素才是阻碍农户收入增长的基本因素（周其仁，2002）。③基础设施：认为农村基础设施建设的滞后严重制约农户收入增长（林毅夫，2001）。④要素禀赋与外部环境：通过对浙江一些村庄农户的量化分析，证明居民要素禀赋（包括劳动力、土地、资本和企业家才能）对村庄内部收入差距起着主导作用，而外部市场环境又影响着村庄间的收入差距（黄祖辉等，2005）。对全国1952～2003年数据的定量研究，也表明农业人均扶养比例的上升（即人增地减矛盾突出），以及农业技术进步缓慢对农民收入的不利影响（王韧，2006）。

以上研究对于揭示农户收入影响的内在原因均具有重要意义。但是，由于中国面积巨大，各地发展水平和发展环境又有明显差异。在某一类型的区域研究成果，在其他区域不尽成立。例如，影响宁夏、西藏农村人均收入的主要因素是牧业收入、传统种植业收入等（刘希凤和王联兵，2007；李祥妹等，2004），而广东省工资性收入和家庭经营纯收入则为农村居民收入构成的主要来源（贺梅英，2003）。因此，研究特殊类型区域的农户收入及其影响因素具有重要意义。

农区发展环境，即农村地区影响社会经济发展的自然、人文环境，是农区发展所有变量的集合，主要包括天然禀赋条件（如地形、耕地面积、土壤条件等），社会经济条件（如经济地理位置、经济基础、经济结构、种植结构、交通条件等）等。从理论上讲，处于不同发展阶段的区域，影响农民收入的决定因素有所不同。在完全依赖农业的区域中，生产力低下时种植业（或畜牧业）条件和劳动者体力对农户收入起决定作用；随着生产力水平的提高，作物种植结构对农民收入的影响力增大；农业技术的发展，高增加值的特殊类型经济作物（如有机农作等）对农区收入影响大幅提高。在工商业有一定发展的农区中，由于生产效率的差异，工商业地位在很大程度上影响农户收入。除此之外，随着市场经济的发展，在农区发展中交通、信息等基础设施的作用、技术的作用、人口的智力和经营能力等的作用，也会大幅增强。由此，可以大致做出推理，在经济发展水平较低的农区，天然禀赋环境在农户收入中发挥着较大作用，或者说是影响经济社会发展的基本因素（王守春，1995）。随着经济发展水平的提高和技术的变化，其他因素的影响会逐步上升。

12.2 数据来源

12.2.1 调查地抽样选择

研究数据来源于作者及其研究群体的调查。为了使调查地点具有代表性，我们在地点选择中采取了分层抽样方法。首先，根据我们收集到的河南省 1907 个乡镇的基本数据，选取了地形、通达性、土地类型和经济水平 4 个因子进行层次类型分析。根据乡镇主体地貌类型将地形因子分为平原、丘陵和山地；根据离最近的县城距离将通达性分为城郊（乡镇距所在县城在 5km 以内）、中等通达（乡镇距所在县城在 5～30km）和偏远（乡镇到所在县城的距离超过 30km）；根据占主导的土地利用情况将土地类型分为水田、旱地水浇地和园林草地；依据农民人均收入将经济发展水平分为高（高于全省平均水平 25%以上）、中（在平均水平±25%之间）、低（在全省平均水平 75%以下）3 类。理论上，依据以上 4 个因子的各 3 类划分，河南省的乡镇可分为 81 类，但实际上有 13 类中并无对应的乡镇存在。在余下的 68 类中，按照大数原则进行分层抽样的层次选择。根据对调查地点数量（10～15 个）的考虑，我们采取的分层方案为：舍去那些实际乡镇数占全省总乡镇数的比例小于 2%（42 个）的类别。这样余下的类别共计 10 种。通过对这 10 种类别分析，发现缺少水田类别。我们又在舍弃的类别中选择乡镇数量最多（36 个乡镇）的水田类别增列其中。这样，所选的 11 种类别共包含了 1562 个乡镇，占河南省乡镇总数（1907 个）的 81.91%，具有较高代表性（表 12.1）。

表 12.1　河南省乡镇分层抽样结果

类别代号	含义	乡镇数/个	随机抽样乡镇	村名
1	丘陵中等通达旱地水浇地中等收入农区	80	安阳市安阳县蒋村乡	石棺村
2	平原中等通达旱地水浇地中等收入农区	554	濮阳市台前县后方乡	大寺郭村
3	平原城郊旱地水浇地高收入农区	136	焦作市山阳区恩村镇	墙南村
4	平原偏远旱地水浇地低收入农区	45	开封市兰考县孟寨乡	北宋村
5	山地偏远园林草地低收入农区	48	三门峡市卢氏县瓦窑沟乡	上河村
6	平原偏远旱地水浇地中等收入农区	75	周口市鹿邑县辛集镇	董楼村
7	平原中等通达旱地水浇地低收入农区	209	平顶山市鲁山县张良乡	阎洼村
8	平原中等通达旱地水浇地高收入农区	226	漯河市郾城县阴阳赵乡	阴西村
9	丘陵中等通达旱地水浇地低收入农区	57	南阳市方城县清河乡	余庄村
10	平原城郊旱地水浇地中等收入农区	96	驻马店市新蔡县十里铺乡	祖岗村
11	丘陵中等通达水田中等收入农区	36	信阳市潢川县彭家店	陈湾村
	11 类总计	1562		

其次，我们在所选取的 11 个类别中，每类随机抽取 1 个乡镇作为调查村选取对象。

最后，我们于 2007 年 2 月实地调查了这 11 个乡镇。通过与这些乡镇负责人及熟悉各村情况的统计工作人员交谈，选取在地形、通达性、土地类型和经济水平这四个方面可以代表该乡镇特点的一个村子作为调查村（图 12.1）。

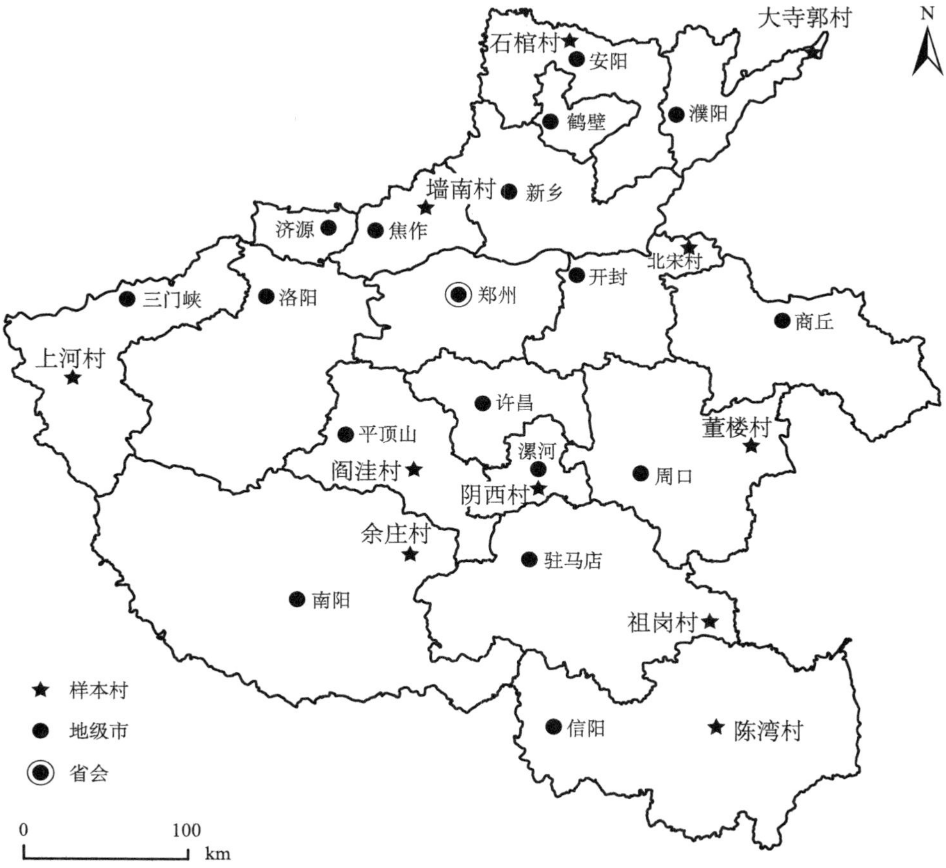

图 12.1　样本村位置分布示意

12.2.2　实地调查与数据整理

实地调查于 2007 年 4 月进行。在此之前，我们根据研究需要设计了调查问卷，并经多次讨论和调查实验后定稿。调查分为三个组。为了统一调查标准，我们对调查人员进行了培训，并选择第一个调查点集中调查。在调查中，要求调查者严格按照规程、认真获取真实可靠的数据，并实行当天数据的互相核查。调查结束后，经过筛选有效调查表，拟定了编码表并在 EXCEL 环境中输入数据。最后，经过内部一致性核查并纠正相关错误，形成了 1251 家农户、每个农户 556 个属性数据的数据库。该数据库为本章研究的基础数据。

12.3　农户收入的差异分析

根据对 11 个样本村 1251 户农户的调查结果的汇总和计算（表 12.2）可以看出，各村之间人均纯收入差异较大。在 11 个样本村中，人均纯收入最低的为开封市兰考县孟寨乡北宋村，2006 年人均纯收入仅 1210 元，而最高的焦作市山阳区恩村镇墙南村为 5222 元，极差达 4012 元。11 个村平均人均纯收入为 2806 元。多数（7 个）村的人均纯收入为 2000～3000 元。

表 12.2　样本村农户收入差异情况

村庄	调查人口/人	调查户数/户	基尼系数	人均纯收入/（元/人）	最低 10%人口人均纯收入/（元/人）	最高 10%人口人均纯收入/（元/人）
石棺村	476	118	0.3135	2961	801.54	7821.70
大寺郭村	478	121	0.3340	2252	427.91	5084.35
墙南村	483	118	0.3760	5222	738.27	14803.46
北宋村	453	111	0.4137	1210	95.22	3492.80
上河村	391	109	0.3316	2493	511.23	6087.89
董楼村	516	117	0.3429	2429	378.14	7204.81
阎洼村	451	103	0.3347	2442	466.64	6287.77
阴西村	459	107	0.3796	3616	699.22	10693.07
余庄村	431	106	0.3220	3215	630.16	7350.64
祖岗村	518	122	0.3827	2280	289.42	6040.31
陈湾村	525	119	0.3315	2718	524.28	6545.20
合计（平均）	5181	1251	0.3936	2806	393.33	8152.79

村内农户之间的收入差距也十分明显。所有样本村调查农户人均收入的基尼系数（采用几何法计算，下同）均在 0.30 以上，有 10 个村基尼系数为 0.30～0.40，另有 1 个村基尼系数在 0.4 以上。国内外相关研究中，有人认为国家层面的基尼系数在0.30～0.40 为比较合理的标准，但是对于一个具体的村庄而言，此标准并不一定适用。例如，平顶山市鲁山县张良乡阎洼村基尼系数为 0.3347，其收入最低 10%的人口人均纯收入仅 466.64 元，而收入最高 10%的人口人均纯收入为 6287.77 元，后者是前者的 13.47 倍，前者总纯收入仅占该村总纯收入的 1.86%，而后者则占 24.55%。在该村我们既可以看到住着楼房开着汽车的高收入群体，也可看到生活十分困难的极低收入群体。而基尼系数在 0.4 以上时，收入差距已十分明显。例如，开封市兰考县孟寨乡北宋村，其收入最低 10%的人口的纯收入只占到该村的 0.78%，而收入最高 10%人口的纯收入则占村纯收入的 28.66%，后者人均纯收入是前者的 36.68 倍。

农户收入结构[①]整体上以打工为主，其他兼业为辅，种地收入所占比例较小，但各村差异较大。据对样本村统计，整体上，种地纯收入只占总纯收入的20.08%，而打工纯收入占41.72%，兼业收入占29.59%，其他收入仅占9.27%。但是村际之间存在较大差异。在种地收入方面，最小比例仅2.49%，最大比例为39.25%，多数村在10%～30%。在打工收入方面，多数村所占总收入的比例在40%以上，最小为17.68%，最大为52.38%。兼业收入村际差异也同样很大，最小为11.67%，最高比例可达78.05%。近些年来，随着农业机械化水平的提高，分离出了较多的农村剩余劳动力，这些劳动力出于对个人和家庭收益最大化的考虑，许多人选择了打工和兼业。但是由于各村地理环境的差异性，农户对两者选择的比例有所不同，这是造成农户收入来源差异的重要原因。

据对各分项收入的贡献度计算（表12.3），农户收入差异主要源于兼业和打工。所有样本农户打工收入和兼业收入对总收入差异的贡献率分别为46.61%和31.61%，而种地和其他收入的贡献率较小。由于农业为非规模经营，各户之间的耕地面积差异较小，再加上农业收益较低，因而农户之间种地收入差异较小。而打工和兼业则不同，打工对劳动力的体能和素质有一定要求，各农户拥有的打工者数量不同造成农户之间打工收入差距较大。兼业往往同资源、城郊区位等因素有关，在资源丰富和城市近郊村，农户兼业比较普遍，而在其他村庄兼业则较少。由于兼业的内容不同和兼业农户的企业家素质不同，因而农户收入差距也较大。其他收入由于在农户收入中占较小的比例，因而对总收入的差异贡献也较小。

各分项收入差异对农户总收入差异的贡献率在各村之间差异明显。在种地收入方面，各村贡献率分布于1.08%～21.30%，平均值为8.32%。尽管整体上种地收入在整个农户中占比例较小，其平均的贡献率也较小，但也有村庄农业地位仍然重要（贡献率为21.3%）。打工收入差异对总收入差异的贡献率平均值为45.69%，最大值是最小值的4倍，但最小值也达17.95%，表明打工收入对农户收入差异产生着重大影响。兼业收入差异对总收入差异影响也较大，其贡献率平均为31.61%。其他收入差异对总收入差异的影响较小，其平均贡献率为11.48%，但其村际差异也较明显（表12.3）。

表12.3 样本村各分项收入差异对总收入差异的贡献率

村庄	种地纯收入	打工纯收入	其他兼业收入	其他纯收入
石棺村	2.12	26.01	57.04	13.98
大寺郭村	5.06	34.69	47.51	11.92
墙南村	2.92	17.95	58.31	19.49
北宋村	21.30	47.64	17.91	12.98
上河村	1.08	50.89	44.95	2.17
董楼村	7.59	36.30	46.60	8.65

① 为研究方便，结合调查村实际，我们将农户收入结构划分为种地、打工、其他兼业（简称兼业）、其他（包括转移性收入）。而一般的农户收入结构包括农业经营性收入、工资性收入、财产性收入和转移性收入。

续表

村庄	种地纯收入	打工纯收入	其他兼业收入	其他纯收入
阎洼村	2.03	43.79	19.26	34.12
阴西村	10.62	39.37	41.16	9.13
余庄村	15.06	71.63	6.16	4.57
祖岗村	7.44	64.58	12.47	14.76
陈湾村	16.34	69.78	9.06	3.04
平均	10.25	46.63	31.64	11.48

注：设某村农户总收入由 K 项收入构成，则各项收入的农户间差异对该村农户人均收入差异的贡献率 $S(Y^K, Y)$ 为（Shorrocks，1980）：

$$S(Y^K, Y) = [\mathrm{cov}(Y^K, Y)/\sigma^2(Y)] \times 100\%$$

其中，Y^K 为第 K 项收入；Y 为总收入；$\mathrm{cov}(Y^K, Y)$ 为第 K 项收入与总收入的协方差值；$\sigma^2(Y)$ 为总收入的方差值。

12.4　变量选择与模型建立

12.4.1　变量选择

农户收入受到诸多因素的影响和制约，这里主要分析农区发展环境的影响。农区发展环境主要包括地形、耕地面积、种植结构、经济基础、乡镇工商水平、城郊区位、交通、地形、村域兼业水平等因子。根据理论分析，上述因素均可能对农户种地收入、整时打工收入、除打工外的兼业收入或其他收入产生影响。各因子的含义及其赋值见表 12.4。

表 12.4　变量设计

变量	变量名称	定义
Y	人均纯收入	农户家庭总纯收入/家庭总人口，单位：元
D_1	中等收入虚拟变量	中等收入为 1，非中等为 0
D_2	高收入虚拟变量	高收入为 1，非高收入为 0
DD_1	丘陵虚拟变量	当农户所在村属于丘陵时为 1，非丘陵为 0
DD_2	平原虚拟变量	当农户所在村属于平原时为 1，非平原为 0
X_1	耕地面积	用家庭人均耕地面积代表，家庭人均耕地面积＝家庭总耕地面积/家庭总人口
X_2	种植结构	农户高产经济作物（指每亩纯收入在 1500 元以上的经济作物）种植面积/总种植面积
X_3	经济基础	用农户人均固有资产状况代表，农户人均固有资产状况＝当年住房、大件家具和农机具的财产总值/家庭总人口
X_4	乡镇工商水平	用农户所在乡镇当年第二产业总值代表（万元）
X_5	城郊区位	用距离最近的县城或城市的距离表示（km）
X_6	交通	用距离最近县乡公路及以上的距离表示（km）
X_7	村域兼业水平	村域兼业劳动力数量占总劳动力的比重（%）

由于地形为分类变量，因此，我们采用虚拟变量的方式将其引入方程。地形共分为三种类型：山区、丘陵和平原，因此，可设两个虚拟变量。DD_1 为丘陵虚拟变量，当地形为丘陵时，$DD_1=1$，当地形为非丘陵（即平原和山区）时，$DD_1=0$；DD_2 为平原虚拟变量，当地形为平原时，$DD_2=1$，当地形为非平原（即山区和丘陵）时，$DD_2=0$；当 $DD_1=0$ 且 $DD_2=0$ 时，表示山区。

类似的，基于不同的收入水平各因素影响会有所差异的假设，我们引入收入类型虚拟变量。这里，我们采用最优拟合方法，通过不断改变临界点以达到样本的恰当聚类结果（李小建等，2008）。根据多次试验的最优拟合结果，我们取人均收入在 2500 元以下为低收入农户，人均收入在 2500 元（含 2500 元）以上至 3500 元（不含 3500）为中等收入农户，人均年收入高于 3500 元（含 3500）为高收入农户。与此对应，我们假设 D_1 为中等收入变量，当收入取值为［2500，3500］（元）时，$D_1=1$，当收入在该区间以外时，$D_1=0$；D_2 为高收入虚拟变量，当人均纯收入取值在 3500 元以上时，$D_2=1$，而当人均纯收入在 3500 元以下时（含 3500 元），$D_2=0$；当 $D_1=0$ 且 $D_2=0$ 时，表示为低收入变量。

12.4.2 模型建立

利用农户调查截面数据，用普通最小二乘法（OLS）对 Y 和其他变量及其交叉变量进行线性回归，并剔除非显著变量，可得到以下的预估计模型。

$$Y=\beta_0+\beta_{D_1}D_1+\beta_{D_2}D_2+\beta_{DD_2}DD_2+\beta_{D_2DD_1}D_2DD_1+\beta_{D_2DD_2}D_2DD_2+\beta_{X_1}X_1+\beta_{D_1X_2}D_1X_2+\beta_{D_2X_2}D_2X_2+\beta_{D_2X_3}D_2X_3+\beta_{DD_2X_3}DD_2X_3+\beta_{D_2X_4}D_2X_4+\beta_{D_3X_5}D_2X_5+\beta_{D_2X_6}D_3X_6+\beta_{D_2X_7}D_2X_7 \quad (12.1)$$

式中，β_0 为常数项；其余各 β 为相应解释变量的系数。

12.5 模型分析结果

12.5.1 模型运算结果

利用 EVIEWS 软件，将式（12.1）的各参数进行估计，模型运行结果见表 12.5。

表 12.5 模型运行结果

变量	B	t	Sig.
	1545.2206	15.6810	0.0000
D_1	1469.2537	11.5467	0.0000
D_2	4638.4587	7.1811	0.0000
DD_2	−1106.3353	−5.7387	0.0000
D_2DD_1	−2771.6154	−5.1320	0.0000
D_2DD_2	−1831.9629	−3.3215	0.0009
X_1	596.2039	4.9013	0.0000

续表

变量	B	t	Sig.
	1545.2206	15.6810	0.0000
D_1X_2	10.7869	0.7043	0.0481
D_2X_2	132.3687	11.1177	0.0000
D_2X_3	0.1425	11.1568	0.0000
DD_2X_3	0.0376	3.6960	0.0002
D_2X_4	0.0506	2.9169	0.0036
D_2X_5	−59.3603	−5.4664	0.0000
D_2X_6	−73.3130	−0.8790	0.0379
D_2X_7	10.7832	4.1803	0.0000

注：调整 $R^2=0.836$，$F=181.7328$，$P=0.0000$，DW=1.909。

将上述系数代入式（12.1）中，可得到下列反映人均纯收入来源的模型。

$$Y=1545.22+1469.25D_1+4638.46D_2-1106.34\mathrm{DD}_2-2771.62D_2\mathrm{DD}_1-1831.86D_2\mathrm{DD}_2+596.21X_1+10.79D_1X_2+13237D_2X_2+0.14D_3X_3+0.04\mathrm{DD}_2X_3+0.05D_2X_4-59.36D_2X_5-73.31D_1X_6+10.78D_2X_7 \quad (12.2)$$

12.5.2　因子作用分析

耕地面积对农户人均纯收入具有显著影响。耕地是农业的主要生产要素，是发展种植业的物质基础，其面积大小是影响农户收入大小的重要因素。根据模型运算结果，在其他条件不变的情况下，耕地每增加 1 亩，人均纯收入增加 596.20 元。

种植结构显著影响农户收入。根据模型参数，在其他条件不变的情况下，中等收入农户经济作物比例每提高 1 个百分点，其纯收入增加 10.79 元，高收入农户经济作物比例每提高 1 个百分点，其纯收入增加 132.37 元，对于低收入农户而言，种植结构因素的影响没有达到显著水平。这意味着，由于农业结构调整具有一定的风险和需要较高的投入，低收入农户产业结构调整远远慢于中、高收入农户。而实际上，结构调整可增加农户的收入，种植收益较高的经济作物是农民增收的重要途径。

经济基础对农户收入具有显著影响，但主要表现在高收入农户。在其他条件不变的情况下，高收入农户人均固定资产每增加 1 元，其人均纯收入增加 0.14 元。农户经济基础状况影响着其进行扩大再生产投资的资本数量，在一定程度上也影响着获得外部资金（如贷款）的能力，同时经济基础又是农户发展能力的重要标志。但是，中低收入农户收入的增加与该因子无重要关联。这恰好从资金方面验证了经济基础对农户收入的影响：越富有的农户，其越有能力获得较高的收入；而越贫困的农户，其获得高收入的可能性越小。

乡镇工商水平对高收入农户收入的增加具有显著影响。农户所在乡镇经济越发达，农户收入增加的可能性越大，因为相对而言，工商水平较高的农区，农户兼业、发展个体经济和打工的机会较多，因而收入增加的可能性较大。对于高收入农户而言，假如其他条件不变，所在乡镇第二产业产值每增加 100 万元，农户人均纯收入增加 5.06 元。另据对调查样本的统计，高收入农户平均兼业率为 61.76%，而全体农户平均为 48.56%，高收入农户的兼业率明显高于样本平均水平。

地理区位对高收入农户具有显著影响。随着距县城距离的增加，农户收入递减，在其他条件不变的情况下，距离每增加 1km，人均纯收入减少 59.36 元。距离县城较近的农户收入较高的主要原因是兼业和打工的可能性增加、种植结构调整的可能性较大，获取农业结构调整信息的方便性增加及农产品市场价格中运费率下降。其中，农户的商品意识最为重要，相比较而言，城郊区位条件较好的农户，市场参与的主动性较强，而城郊区位条件较差的农户则较弱。

交通条件对高收入农户收入的增加具有显著影响。农户收入的增加主要依赖的是农户与外界联系的强弱，而与外界的联系则主要依赖交通运输。距公路线较近的农户，其生产的高附加值农产品可方便运出，运费率和运输时间都较有利于产品的市场销售，因而收入较高。在交通方便的地区，农户兼业也具有较方便的条件。对于高收入农户，在其他条件不变的情况下，距离县乡公路的距离每减少 1km，农户人均纯收入则增加 73.31 元。农区中的沿路经济十分明显，往往是距公路较近的村，人均纯收入较高。交通条件对中、低收入农户影响不显著的主要原因是这些农户对市场的依赖性较弱，收入主要依赖种地（多为低附加值农业）和打工，而种地和打工对交通的依赖性相对较弱。

村域兼业水平对高收入农户收入具有显著影响。兼业是农户在农业以外取得收入的重要渠道之一，和经营农业相比，其具有较高的收益，因此，兼业水平的高低直接影响农户的收入，但在模型中，只有高收入农户达到了显著水平，由此也可间接证明高收入农户收入中，兼业占重要地位。对于高收入农户而言，在其他条件不变的情况下，兼业水平每提高 1%，农户人均纯收入增加 10.78 元。

地形对农户收入具有显著影响。平原地区较非平原地区（山区和丘陵）人均纯收入低 1106.34 元，在所调查的样本村中，平原地区农户打工比例较小，而所调查的两个丘陵村打工者比例很大，同时耕地面积较大；1 个山区样本村兼业种植蘑菇的很多，同时打工者也较多，因而较平原收入高。但是在高收入农户群体中，丘陵地区较山区的农户收入低 2771.62 元，较平原地区低 939.65 元（D_2DD_1 和 D_2DD_2 系数之差）。这表明，在农户收入来源由以种植业收入为主转移到工资性收入和兼业收入为主的背景下，平原地区由于不能及时调整收入结构或由于资源因素的限制，其收入已经低于丘陵和山区。

12.6　结论与政策建议

通过对河南省 11 个样本村的实证研究，我们可以得到以下结论。农户收入差别较大，其来源主要在于打工和其他兼业。农户收入的较大差异不仅存在于村际之间，而且也存在于农户之间，也包括同村的农户之间。诚然，在经济发展过程中，农户收入不可避免地存在一定的差距，但从当前农区发展情况看，收入差距已经十分明显，如继续扩大，必将对和谐社会建设带来很大威胁。因此，提高低收入农户的收入与适当缩小收入差距应引起农区工作者的重视。

农区发展环境因素对农户收入具有重要影响。耕地面积、经济基础、乡镇工商业发展水平、城郊区位、交通条件等因素在不同的地形类型和收入类型农户中，对收入提高产生一定的影响。总的来看，在低收入农户的影响因素中，耕地面积较为重要，而在中等收入农户中，增加了种植结构因素，在高收入农户中，又增加了经济基础、工商水平、城郊区位、交通因素和兼业水平，这在很大程度上验证了本章提出的“区域发展阶段不同影响因素有所不同”的理论假设。根据样本村调查，地形对农户收入具有显著影响，传统上平原地区为高收入的概念已经发生变化。研究并未发现，地理因素对解释农户发展水平的重要性正在下降，相反，农区发展环境对农户收入和农区发展的影响仍然具有重要意义。因此，从影响收入的因素上分析，要提高农户的收入，除了发展劳务经济、鼓励兼业外，还应重视农区发展环境的优化。

与基于乡镇级的河南省农区发展研究相比（李小建等，2008），以农户为单元的研究结论同样支持农区发展环境因素对欠发达农区发展的影响处于变动之中的观点。但在乡镇研究的基础上，本章还进一步揭示了农业种植结构因素对中等收入农户的重要影响，交通条件和兼业水平对高收入农户的显著影响。除此之外，农户经济合作组织、政府的引导和激励措施也是农区发展环境的重要部分，农户之间也互为发展环境，但本研究问卷未曾包含，只能留待后续研究弥补。还有，本章研究的村子数量较少，影响从地理环境角度分析的代表性。如果能把农户分析与较大范围的村级数据研究相结合，则更有利于我们分析农区发展环境对农户收入的影响。

说明：本章调查地选择和调查问卷设计主要由李小建、乔家君、高更和完成；参加本项目调查的人员有乔家君、高更和、樊新生、鲁立新、李君、刘婷、时慧娜、王联锋、侯景伟、赵德华、李猛、范荣华、张雪峰、王丽、宋冰勇、王斌、王玉婵、吴孔坤、祝英丽、董爱华、葛真、朱开印；问卷编码主要由李小建、乔家君、高更和、李君、刘婷、时慧娜完成；问卷输入由各调查人员完成，数据核实中乔家君、时慧娜、高更和等付出了较多的劳动。

参考文献

河南省统计局. 2006. 河南统计年鉴 2006. 北京：中国统计出版社

贺梅英. 2003. 广东农村居民收入的变化及影响因素分析. 华南农业大学学报，(S1)：148～152

黄祖辉，王敏，宋瑜. 2005. 农村居民收入差距问题研究：基于村庄微观角度的一个分析框架. 管理世界，(3)：75～84

李祥妹，刘键，钟祥浩. 2004. 西藏自治区农牧民收入结构分析. 地理研究，23 (4)：561～569

李小建，周雄飞，郑纯辉. 2008. 河南农区经济发展差异地理影响的小尺度分析. 地理学报，63 (2)：113～121

林毅夫. 2001. 增加农民收入需要农村基础设施的牢固. 调研世界，(7)：3～4

刘希凤，王联兵. 2007. 影响宁夏农村经济收入因素的灰色关联分析. 宁夏工程技术，6 (1)：98～100

孟凡胜. 2003. 影响黑龙江省农民收入增长的主要因素. 哈尔滨商业大学学报（社会科学版），(1)：22～25

万广华. 1998. 中国农村区域间居民收入差异及其变化的实证分析. 经济研究，(5)：36～41

王桂荣，孟祥书，石玉芳，等. 2006. 河北省农村居民人均纯收入的影响因素分析. 河北农业科学，10 (4)：76～79

王韧. 2006. 中国农村居民收入决定特征及其影响因素变动：1952～2003 年. 数量经济技术经济研究，

(4)：3～13
王守春. 1995. 地理环境在经济和社会发展中的作用的再认识——对“地理环境决定论”批判的反思. 地理研究，14 (1)：94～103
张平. 1992. 中国农村区域间居民的收入分配. 经济研究，(2)：62～69
周其仁. 2002. 增加农民收入不能回避产权界定. 发展，(3)：44
朱玲. 1992. 非农产业活动对农户收入分配格局的影响. 经济研究，(3)：23～30
Knight J, Song L. 1993. The spatial contribution to income inequality in rural China. Cambridge Journal of Economics, 7 (2)：195～213
Liu H. 2006. Changing regional rural inequality in China 1980-2002. Area, 38 (4)：377～389
Meng X, Wu H. 1998. Household income determination and regional income differential in rural China. Asian Economic Journal, 12 (1)：65～ 88
Shorrocks A F. 1980. The class of additively decomposable inequality measures, Econometrica, 48 (3)：613～625
Wan G, Zhou Z. 2005. Income inequality in rural China: Regression-based decomposition using household data. Review of Development Economics, 9 (1)：107～120
Wu Z, Zhu Y. 2004. Income deferential and out-migration: The impacts of between-gap and within-gap. Journal of Chinese Economic and Business Studies, 2 (1)：27～37

第 13 章　农户自主发展能力

随着中国欠发达农区农户增收难、增收慢的局面日益突出，“三农问题”中不同行为主体发展能力逐渐引起了不少学者的关注，发表了一些很有参考价值的研究成果（刘祚详，2006；牛若峰，1995；李定轶，2006；Rozelle，1996；Brauw et al.，2002；Knight and Song，1993；Wan and Zhou，2005；Meng and Wu，1998；黄祖辉等，2005；Rozelle，1994；朱玲，1992；徐勇，2006；曾艳华，2006；李杰，2004；舒尔茨，2003；余长林，2006）。一部分学者从农村经济组织（刘祚详，2006）、农业产业化（牛若峰，1995）、制度性原因（李定轶，2006）、收入差距（Rozelle，1996；Brauw et al.，2002；Knight and Song，1993；Wan and Zhou，2005；Meng and Wu，1998；黄祖辉等，2005）、非农化（Rozelle，1994；朱玲，1992）、社会化（徐勇，2006）等外因解释农户增收难的问题，并把这些外因作为重要解释变量；另一部分学者认识到人的发展能力主要由教育、健康、技能培训等决定，土地等外部客观条件不是农民贫穷和农业经济增长的主要原因，人的知识和能力已成为社会财富的动力源泉（曾艳华，2006；李杰，2004；舒尔茨，2003）。这些成果中，多以定性研究为主，忽视农户作为经济发展主体的独立性和自主性。此外，相当一部分成果基于省级行政单元的时序统计数据（李杰，2004；舒尔茨，2003；余长林，2006），仅个别研究采用少数实地调研村域数据（黄祖辉等，2005）。本章基于河南省 11 个典型村域 1251 家农户的调研，从微观视角对不同地理环境下农户自主发展能力与农户持续增收的内在关系作初步探讨。

本章采用改进的信息熵值法和多元线性回归法对河南 11 个村 1251 农户调研数据进行处理，基于时空耦合的概念，定量分析了不同地理环境条件下农户自主发展能力与农户持续增收的内在关系，得出如下结论：①农户自主发展能力影响农户农业收入，但耕地和地形等地理因素的影响更为突出，且耕地增长的贡献度在山区最大，丘陵次之，平原最小，能力增长的贡献度恰好相反。②农户自主发展能力和家庭劳动投入显著影响农户非农收入，地理因素对家庭非农收入没有直接影响，地域通达性通过影响家庭自主发展能力间接影响家庭非农收入。③不同阶段农户自主发展能力对农户非农发展的贡献度不同。初级阶段，农户非农发展几乎完全依赖劳动投入的增长，能力增长几乎没有起作用；中级阶段，能力增长和劳动增长的贡献各半；高级阶段，能力的贡献度又跌至 15%。④农民非农收入报酬率的增长依赖农户能力增长和地域通达性提高。在低报酬阶段，能力的贡献度约占 2/3，但进入中下报酬阶段后，报酬的增长完全依赖地域通达性的增强，进入中上报酬阶段后，地域通达性的作用开始下降，到达高报酬阶段后下降到零，这时报酬的增长完全依赖能力的增长。

13.1 农户自主发展能力

13.1.1 农户自主发展能力概念

农户自主发展能力是指农户在经济利益驱动下，利用现有发展空间和发展机会，追求目标时展示一系列行为决策能力。反映了农户家庭人员发挥自身潜能，主动利用周围自然、经济和社会环境的综合能力，即所采用的“手段”“机会”“技能”，以及所持有的价值观和心态等。农户自主发展能力的内涵包括自主发展潜能和自主发展意识两个方面。

自主发展潜能包括农户的体能、素能、人际网，以及资本积累能力和主动获取信息的能力。农户体能是指家庭成员中主要劳动力的身体健康状况，是确保农户各种能力能否顺利实现的前提条件。农户素能主要指信息处理能力（即吸收、更新知识的能力）和创新能力（即获得新知识、扩充新知识的能力），具体指农户在受学校教育和社会锻炼中形成的技能和潜能，即具有适应市场经济、科技进步和时代迅速变化的综合性能力。人际网主要指农户在日常社会经济生活中形成的社交网络，它有助于延长农户自身的各种能力。资本积累能力主要体现农户现有的经济状况、筹资能力，是决定农户自我发展和自我决策的经济基础。信息获取能力是农户通过不同途径获取生产和生活的信息，在一定程度上体现了农户对外的视野和对所处社会经济的洞察力。

自主发展意识指农户在从事社会经济活动中所持有的价值观和心态，具体指农户对生活的态度、生活目标的设计、发展空间的拓展、市场经济参与度的认识。具有较高自主发展意识的农户，能够对自己所从事的活动进行一系列的比较、分析、判断，在确定自己发展取向的同时，合理地选择生活方式并设计自己的生活目标。

13.1.2 自主发展能力指标构造

在农户自主发展能力指标选取中主要考虑数据的可得性、可量性、可比性，同时遵循科学性、系统性与合理性的原则（乔家君，2008）。农户自主发展潜能的五项内容对应选择以下具体指标（表 13.1）。自主发展意识包括四个综合指标和相应的具体衡量指标（表 13.2）。

表 13.1 农户自主发展潜能衡量指标

分项指标	具体衡量指标
体能	医疗费用投资、主要劳动力身体与 5 年前相比变化状况体现
素能	以主要劳动力受教育的程度、农户对下一代的教育投资和村干部对农户能力的分层
人际网	体现在农户所能获取的社会资本上，具体指标包括村委会选举、农户所处的经济地位、社会地位、社会交往投资、对农户家庭帮助最大的人的个数；以及其与该农户不同关系类型的人员数
资本积累能力	村干部对农户的经济分层、农户家庭人均生活性消费水平、农户自家遇到重大开支时通过不同渠道能筹措到的资金额
信息获取能力	农户看电视时间、通信费用、外出远门次数、是否上网查信息等指标

表 13.2　农户自主发展意识的衡量指标

综合指标	具体衡量指标
农户对自己生活的态度	由农户对自己现在生活的满意程度和到城市定居的意愿组成
农户所处的发展空间	以农户现有耕地经营规模和农户家庭的劳均负担等指标来衡量
农户对市场经济的参与度	由农户主要粮食作物、经济作物的外卖率和农户进城购物的频率等指标构成
农户设计自己的生活目标	由 10 年来对非农业是否投资、开发利用当地资源的打算、家庭主要成员需要学习的技术和提高自家经济实力的措施组成

农户自主发展能力综合值采用改进的熵值法计算。该方法是根据指标间离散程度，利用信息熵来确定指标权重，已有研究表明（李小建和时慧娜，2008），改进的熵值法比较适合村域农户经济社会活动的量化评估。本章自主发展能力指标的具体计算过程如下。

第一，将各指标同度量化，计算第 j 项指标下第 i 待评对象指标值比重 p_{ij}。$p_{ij}=x_{ij}/\sum_{i=1}^{m}x_{ij}$。式中，$i=1$，2，3，…，$m$，$m$ 的取值为一个村的实际调查农户数；$j=1$，2，3，…，36，表示各指标。

第二，计算第 j 项指标的熵值 e_j。$e_j=-k\sum_{i=1}^{m}p_{ij}\ln p_{ij}$ 其中 $k=\ln$（$1/m$）。

第三，计算第 j 项指标的差异性系数 f_j。熵值越小，指标间差异性越大，指标就越重要。$f_j=1-e_j$

第四，定义第 j 项指标的权数 a_j。$a_j=f_j/\sum_{j=1}^{36}f_j$

第五，计算农户 i 的自主发展能力 C_i。$C_i=\sum_{j=1}^{36}a_jp_{ij}$。

13.2　空间增长与增长因素的贡献度

13.2.1　空间增长

基于时空耦合和时空转换概念，某时间断面的空间数据可以代替一定空间内随时间变化的序列数据，将随时间增长的概念引入空间，可以定义一个时间单元的经济随着空间单元的变化而增长的现象为空间增长。

假定在某个时间上，某空间单元的生产函数为 $Y=F$（X），其中，Y 为该空间单元的产出，X 为该空间单元的各种影响产出的因素向量。如果两个空间单元的影响因素相同，且它们之间的差异很小，我们可以比较两个空间单元的差异，讨论两个空间单元之间的产出变化和各种因素变化之间的关系。为此，对生产函数全微分得到

$$\Delta Y\approx\sum_{j=1}^{n}\frac{\partial F(X)}{\partial X_j}\Delta X_j \tag{13.1}$$

式中，ΔY 为两个空间单元之间的产出之差；ΔX_j 为两个空间单元之间第 j 种因素的投入之差。两端除以 Y 得到

$$\frac{\Delta Y}{Y} \approx \sum_{j=1}^{n} \frac{\partial F(X)}{\partial X_j} \frac{\Delta X_j}{Y} = \sum_{j=1}^{n} \left(\frac{\partial F(X)}{\partial X_j} \frac{X_j}{F(X)} \right) \frac{\Delta X_j}{X_j} \tag{13.2}$$

式（13.2）左端为产出的增长，右端括号中的项是要素 j 的产出弹性，另一项是要素 j 的增长。因此，产出的增长取决于各要素的产出弹性和各因素的增长。用 G_Y 表示产出增长，用 G_j 表示 j 要素投入增长，用 α_j 表示 j 要素的产出弹性，那么两个经济单元之间的经济增长与因素增长之间的关系可以简化为

$$G_Y = \sum\nolimits_{j=1}^{n} \alpha_j G_j \tag{13.3}$$

13.2.2　增长因素的贡献度

将式（13.3）两端同时除以 G_Y，得到 $\sum\nolimits_{j=1}^{n} \alpha_j G_j / G_Y = 1$，所以 $\alpha_j G_j / G_Y$ 就是因素 j 增长在经济增长中的贡献份额或贡献度。用 λ 表示贡献度，那么在一个时间单元上，两个空间单元的 j 因素增长的贡献度可以表示为

$$\lambda_j = \alpha_j G_j / G_Y \tag{13.4}$$

空间单元可以是地区，也可以是一地区内的不同个体，如企业或家庭，本章涉及空间单元是农户。根据上文中对空间增长和空间增长贡献度的定义，我们可以通过比较两个农户或两组农户来计算农户经济增长因素的贡献度。

13.3　数据调查及数据处理

本章数据来自国家自然科学基金重点项目课题组于 2007 年 3 月至 4 月对河南省 11 个村域 1251 家农户做的问卷调查（见本书 12.2）。所调查的村域农户经济发展概况见表 13.3。

表 13.3　调研村域的农户经济发展

指标	焦作市墙南村	郾城县阴西村	台前县大寺郭	兰考县北宋村	方城县余庄村	潢川县陈湾村	安阳县石棺村	卢氏县上河村	鲁山县闫洼村	新蔡县宋圈村	鹿邑县董楼村
总户数/户	1588	373	264	229	377	326	298	169	232	384	307
样本户数/户	118	107	121	111	106	119	118	109	103	122	117
家庭规模/（人/户）	4.09	4.29	3.95	4.08	4.07	4.41	4.03	4.00	4.09	3.65	4.31
打工兼业时间/（月/户）	119	166	149	119	187	213	176	118	167	206	173
耕地规模/（hm^2/户）	0.118	0.332	0.201	0.329	0.572	0.426	0.163	0.067	0.289	0.383	0.378
家庭纯收入/（元/户）	21358	15513	8895	4937	13085	11986	11933	9972	9988	8322	10469

续表

指标	焦作市墙南村	郾城县阴西村	台前县大寺郭	兰考县北宋村	方城县余庄村	潢川县陈湾村	安阳县石棺村	卢氏县上河村	鲁山县闫洼村	新蔡县宋圈村	鹿邑县董楼村
离城市距离/km	0.1	10	10	41	16	10	16	88	18	5	39
户主文化/年	9.05	8.95	7.81	8.00	7.27	6.78	8.64	8.00	6.86	7.27	6.23
地形	3	3	3	3	2	2	2	1	3	3	3

资料来源：据 2007 年 3～4 月的调查整理，下同。表中地形 1 代表山区，2 代表丘陵，3 代表平原。

13.4　农户农业发展模型

13.4.1　农户农业生产函数设定

本模型研究农户农业产出与农业投入之间的关系。农业生产投入主要是土地和劳动，所以农户 i 的农业生产函数可设定为 $y_i=f\ (m_i,\ l_i)$，其中，y_i、m_i、l_i 分别为农户 i 的农业产出，以及土地和劳动投入。不同的家庭具有不同的自主发展能力，从而对农业生产可能产生影响，所以农户自主发展能力应该进入生产函数，农户的生产函数变为 $y_i=f\ (m_i,\ l_i,\ C_i)$，其中，C_i 为农户自主发展能力。

不同地理环境会对农户生产造成影响。农户所处的地理环境涉及地形和地域通达性，地形分为山区、丘陵和平原，地域通达性可用农家离中心城市（县城）的距离来度量。考虑地理环境对农户生产的影响后，农户生产函数变为 $y_i=f\ (m_i,\ l_i,\ C_i,\ S_i,\ P_i)$，其中，$P_i$ 表示农户 i 家庭所在地区的地形。

在农户不同发展阶段，影响农户生产的因素可能不同，各因素对农户生产的影响程度也可能不同。考虑农户的发展阶段以后，农户的生产函数变为 $y_i=f\ (m_i,\ l_i,\ C_i,\ S_i,\ P_i,\ d_i)$，其中，$\mathrm{d}_i$ 表示农户 i 所处的发展阶段。变量 d_i 的作用不是用来解释农户发展，而是将农户发展生产函数变为分段函数。

13.4.2　变量定义

根据模型设定，选择 6 个变量：农户耕地面积、农户农业劳动投入、农户自主发展能力、离县城距离、家庭所在的地形和家庭发展阶段来解释家庭农业纯收入，如表 13.4 所示。其中，地形变量取山区、丘陵和平原 3 个值，用 P_1 和 P_2 两个虚拟变量将地形变量的 3 个值加以区分；采用最优拟合方法将农户农业收入分为 3 个组，年收入低于 1000 元的为低收入组，介于 1000 元和 5000 元之间的为中等收入组，高于 5000 元的为高收入组，并且用虚拟变量 d_1 和 d_2 将 3 个收入组加以区分。收入分组的原则是最优拟合，因为分组的正确程度与回归拟合程度正相关。

表 13.4　农业发展模型中的变量及定义

变量	定义
y	农户农业纯收入（元）
m	农户耕地面积（亩）
l	农户农业劳动投入（月）
C	农户自主发展能力（指数）
S	离县城距离（km）
P_1	丘陵属性变量，丘陵取 1，其他取 0
P_2	平原属性变量，平原取 1，其他取 0
d_1	中等农业收入属性变量，中等收入取 1，其他取 0
d_2	高农业收入属性变量，高收入取 1，其他取 0

13.4.3　计量分析

根据农户农业生产函数的设定，计量模型设定如下：

$$\ln y=\beta_y+\beta_m\ln m+\beta_1\ln l+\beta_A\ln c+\beta_s\ln S+\beta_{P_1}P_1+\beta_{P_2}P_2+\beta_{d_1}d_1+\beta_{d_2}d_2+\beta_{S_m}\ln S\ln m+\beta_{P_1m}P_1\ln m+\beta_{P_2m}P_2\ln m+\beta_{d_1m}d_1\ln m+\beta_{d_2m}d_2\ln m+u \quad (13.5)$$

上式中省略了表示农户的下标。根据上式，利用调查数据和 Eviews 软件得到的最小二乘回归结果如表 13.5 中模型 Ⅰ 所示，去掉不显著的解释变量后的回归结果如模型 Ⅱ 所示。保留两位小数，表 13.5 的回归结果意味着农户农业生产函数为

$$\ln y=28.7+068\ln m+9.95\ln C+0.78P_1+0.95P_2+0.88d_1+2.44d_2-0.45P_1\ln m-0.59P_2\ln m+0.34d_1\ln m \quad (13.6)$$

表 13.5　家庭农业模型

项目	模型 Ⅰ			模型 Ⅱ		
	修正后 $R^2=0.784$　$F=313$			修正后 $R^2=0.785$　$F=418$		
解释变量	B 系数	t 统计量	P 值	B 系数	t 统计量	P 值
常量	28.70202	2.537988	0.0113	28.03867	2.508700	0.0123
$\ln m$	0.682594	7.342261	0.0000	0.680719	7.345643	0.0000
$\ln l$	−0.008700	−0.312835	0.7545	—	—	—
$\ln C$	10.25212	2.079757	0.0378	9.951857	2.043613	0.0412
$\ln S$	0.011253	0.857462	0.3914	—	—	—
P_1	0.805845	7.668214	0.0000	0.775604	7.955438	0.0000
P_2	1.002808	9.321388	0.0000	0.946472	10.91816	0.0000
d_1	0.865015	9.584146	0.0000	0.878977	10.06227	0.0000
d_2	2.365037	8.353736	0.0000	2.439716	25.03512	0.0000
$P_1\ln m$	−0.461473	−3.999719	0.0001	−0.447286	−4.059634	0.0001
$P_2\ln m$	−0.620851	−5.418535	0.0000	−0.593802	−5.404961	0.0000
$d_1\ln m$	0.349741	4.727173	0.0000	0.335451	4.859965	0.0000
$d_2\ln m$	0.042258	0.307018	0.7589	—	—	—

注：被解释变量为农业收入的对数 $\ln y$；观测个数为 1029。

根据表13.5给出的回归结果可以得到如下结论：显著影响农户农业收入的因素是两个地理因素，即可耕地和地形，以及1个家庭因素，即农户自主发展能力。

农户农业劳动投入对农业生产没有显著影响这一结论说明，给定地形变量，土地和劳动的生产函数是里昂惕夫生产函数，即 $y=\min(a_m m^{b_m}, a_l l^{b_l})$，且土地是短缺要素，劳动相对剩余，因此，在给定地形的条件下，农业产出完全由耕地面积决定。

农户耕地面积对农户农业收入的影响最大，耕地对农业收入的影响可以通过式(13.6)两端对 $\ln m$ 微分得到

$$\frac{\partial \ln y}{\partial \ln m}=0.68-0.45P_1-0.59P_2+0.34d_1 \tag{13.7}$$

式(13.7)左端是耕地的产出弹性，即耕地增加百分之一所引起的家庭农业纯收入增加的百分点数。在山区的低收入和高收入家庭，耕地的产出弹性为0.68，即耕地增加1个百分点将引起农户农业收入增加0.68个百分点。在丘陵和平原，耕地的产出弹性分别降低0.45和0.59，说明山区耕地的产出弹性最大，丘陵次之，平原最小，也说明山区的耕地面积对农户农业收入影响更为明显。在农业生产中等发展阶段，耕地的产出弹性高出0.34，这说明在其他因素相同的条件下，中等农户对耕地的依赖性更强。

13.4.4　贡献度分析

根据式(13.4)，任何一种因素的贡献度取决于该因素的产出弹性、该因素在两个经济单元之间的增长，以及两个经济单元之间的产出增长。根据计量结果表13.5或式(13.6)，农户农业收入取决于耕地、地形和农户自主发展能力3个因素，我们需要计算这3个因素的贡献度。在不同的收入组，耕地的产出弹性不同，需要分组讨论，并且在每一个收入组，计算组内平均增长。组内平均增长的计算方法是将一个组的前一半农户当作一个空间单元，后一半农户当作另一个空间单元，将两个空间单元之间的增长作为组内平均增长。两个经济单元之间的投入因素增长和产出增长的数量指标可以从样本数据中计算出来。根据式(13.4)和式(13.6)以及样本数据，因素增长贡献度的计算结果如表13.6所示。

表13.6　家庭农业收入增长的因素贡献度　(单位：%)

项目	低收入组			中等收入组			高收入组		
	山区	丘陵	平原	山区	丘陵	平原	山区	丘陵	平原
耕地增长的贡献度	97	83	71	—	99	96	—	90	87
能力增长的贡献度	3	17	29	—	1	4	—	10	13

注：高收入组没有山区农户，中等收入组只有2个山区农户，没有代表性，故没有进行相关计算。

表13.6揭示了3个重要结论：第一，总体上，农业增长主要靠耕地增长，而不是能力增长，在农业方面地理因素比家庭因素的作用大得多；第二，在农业发展的中级阶段，地理因素的作用尤其突出；第三，在同一个收入组，耕地增长的贡献度在山区最大，丘陵次之，平原最小，能力增长的贡献度恰好相反。

13.5 农户非农发展模型

13.5.1 农户非农产出函数设定

本模型研究农户非农收入的决定及增长问题。农户非农收入包括打工收入和兼业收入，农户非农产出主要是劳动投入的函数，即 $Y=F(L)$（为了方便，省略了表示农户的下标），其中 Y、L 分别为农户的非农产出和劳动投入。不同的家庭具有不同的自主发展能力，进而对非农产出产生影响，所以农户自主发展能力应该进入生产函数，农户的生产函数变为 $Y=F(L, C)$。

地理环境可能对农户生产造成影响，考虑地理环境对农户生产的影响后，农户生产函数变为 $Y=Y(L, C, S, P)$，其中，S 为农户住址离城市的距离，P 表示农户所在地区的地形。

与农业发展模型类似，我们将每个农户置于不同的发展阶段来研究。考虑农户的发展阶段以后，农户的生产函数变为 $Y=F(L, C, S, P, D)$，其中，D 表示农户所处的非农发展阶段。变量 D 的作用不是用来解释农户发展，而是将农户发展生产函数变为分段函数。

13.5.2 变量定义

农户非农发展模型中的被解释变量是农户非农收入，解释变量涉及农户非农劳动投入、农户自主发展能力、离县城距离、地形和农户发展阶段 5 个变量（表 13.7）。采用最优拟合方法（李杰，2004）将农户发展划分为 3 个阶段：低水平阶段（年非农收入≤6000 元）、中等水平阶段（年非农收入介于 6000～10000 元，含 10000 元）和高水平阶段（年非农收入>10000 元）。

表 13.7 非农业发展模型中的变量及定义

变量	定义
Y	农户非农收入（元）
L	农户非农劳动投入（月）
C	农户自主发展能力（指数）
S	离县城距离（km）
P_1	丘陵属性变量，丘陵取 1，其他取 0
P_2	平原属性变量，平原取 1，其他取 0
D_1	中等非农收入属性变量，中等收入取 1，其他取 0
D_2	高非农收入属性变量，高收入取 1，其他取 0

13.5.3 计量分析

根据农户非农产出函数的设定，计量模型设定如下：

$$\ln Y=\beta_Y+\beta_L\ln L+\beta_c\ln C+\beta_s\ln S+\beta_{P_1}P_1+\beta_{P_2}P_2+\beta_{D_1}D_1+\beta_{D_2}D_2+\beta_{D_1L}D_1\ln L+\beta_{D_2L}D_2\ln L+u \tag{13.8}$$

上式中省略了表示农户的下标。根据上式，利用调查数据和 Eviews 软件得到的最小二乘回归结果如表 13.8 中的模型Ⅰ所示，去掉不显著的解释变量后的回归结果如模型Ⅱ所示。模型Ⅱ意味着农户非农产出函数为

$$\ln Y=28.23+0.46\ln L+9.19\ln C+1.79D_1+2.05D_2-0.42D_1\ln L-0.24D_2\ln L \tag{13.9}$$

表 13.8　家庭非农收入模型

项目	模型Ⅰ			模型Ⅱ		
	修正后 $R^2=0.768$　$F=393$			修正后 $R^2=0.769$　$F=590$		
解释变量	B 系数	t 统计量	P 值	B 系数	t 统计量	P 值
常量	28.9258	3.0921	0.0020	28.2274	3.0368	0.0024
$\ln L$	0.4633	14.1525	0.0000	0.4626	14.2598	0.0000
$\ln C$	9.4823	2.3273	0.0201	9.1929	2.2704	0.0234
$\ln S$	0.0021	0.2249	0.8221	—	—	—
P_1	−0.0428	−0.7826	0.4340	—	—	—
P_2	−0.0462	−0.8711	0.3839	—	—	—
D_1	1.7753	11.7713	0.0000	1.7871	11.9127	0.0000
D_2	2.0490	17.6157	0.0000	2.0505	17.7249	0.0000
$D_1\ln L$	−0.4208	−6.3219	0.0000	−0.4248	−6.4111	0.0000
$D_2\ln L$	−0.2419	−5.1627	0.0000	−0.2427	−5.2111	0.0000

注：被解释变量为非农收入的对数 lnY；观测个数为 1066。

根据表 13.8 给出的回归结果可以得到如下结论：显著影响农户非农收入的因素是两个家庭因素，即家庭劳动投入和家庭自主发展能力。地理因素对家庭非农收入没有显著影响。然而，进一步的相关性分析表明，地域通达性通过影响家庭自主发展能力间接影响家庭非农收入。直观上，近郊农户比远郊农户有更好的受教育条件和更加优越的信息获取能力，因此，农户自主发展能力与离城市的距离负相关。

根据式（13.9）对 $\ln L$ 微分，得到

$$\frac{\partial\ln Y}{\partial\ln L}=0.46-0.42D_1-0.24D_2 \tag{13.10}$$

式（13.10）意味着处于低发展水平的农户，劳动投入的产出弹性为 0.46，中等发展水平的农户为 0.04，高发展水平的农户为 0.22。

根据式（13.9）对 $\ln C$ 微分，得到 $\dfrac{\partial\ln Y}{\partial\ln C}=9.19$，这意味着农户自主发展能力提高 1 个百分点将引起农户非农收入提高 9.19 个百分点。

13.5.4　贡献度分析

据式（13.4），任何一种因素的贡献度取决于该因素的产出弹性、该因素在两个经济单元之间的增长，以及两个经济单元之间的产出增长。在我们的模型中经济单元是农户或农户小组。各因素产出弹性的数量指标可以从计量分析中得到，两个农户或两个农户小组之间的投入因素增长和产出增长的数量指标可以从样本数据中计算出来。

根据计量结果表 13.8 或式（13.9），农户非农收入取决于非农劳动投入和农户自主发展能力两个因素，我们需要计算这两个因素的贡献度。在不同的收入组，劳动的产出弹性不同，因此需要分组讨论，并且在每一个收入组，计算组内的平均增长。组内平均增长的计算方法是将一个组的前一半农户当做一个空间单元，后一半农户当做另一个空间单元，将两个空间单元之间的增长作为组内平均增长。根据式（13.4）和式（13.9）以及样本数据，因素增长贡献度的计算结果如表 13.9 所示。

表 13.9　家庭非农收入增长的因素贡献度　　（单位：%）

项目	低收入组	中等收入组	高收入组
劳动增长的贡献度	100	50	85
能力增长的贡献度	0	50	15

表 13.9 结论如下：在农户非农发展的初级阶段，农户非农发展几乎完全依赖劳动投入的增长（贡献度为 100%），能力增长几乎没有起作用（贡献度为 0%）；在农户非农发展的中级阶段，结果截然不同，能力增长和劳动增长的贡献各半；在农户发展的高级阶段，能力的贡献度又跌至 15%。直观上，从农户发展初级阶段到中级阶段的能力贡献度跃升存在两个原因，一是劳动的产出弹性下降（由 0.46 降为 0.04），二是能力增长的幅度增大。深层次上，劳动的产出弹性下降是关键原因，因为劳动产出弹性的下降导致农户在人口数量和质量之间的替代，用人口质量替代人口数量，人口质量的提高导致农户自主发展能力的提高，人口数量的下降导致劳动投入的下降。在农户发展的高级阶段，能力贡献度降低到 15%的原因可能是高级阶段农户的自主发展能力增长碰到了上限，这并不是因为农户的能力不能再提高，而是因为如果再提高农户将不再是农户，将成为非农户。例如，自主发展能力指标中包括受教育程度，当受教育程度达到大学水平时就已经不再是农民。

13.6　农户非农报酬率模型

13.6.1　农户非农报酬率函数设定

本模型研究农民非农产业获得的报酬率（打工月工资或兼业月收入）的决定及增长问题。该模型可以在上一个模型的基础上构建。在 13.5.1 小节中，农户家庭生产函数设定为 $Y=F(L, C, S, P, D)$，其中，D 表示家庭非农发展阶段的虚拟变量，发展阶段的划分标准是家庭收入的高低。在本模型中，我们用 T 代替 D，并重新定义。

定义 T 为表示非农报酬率水平的虚拟变量，它取低报酬率（月报酬≤400 元）、中下报酬率（月报酬介于 400～750 元，含 750 元）、中上报酬率（月报酬介于 750～1000 元，含 1000 元）和高报酬率（月报酬>1000 元）4 个值，并用 T_1、T_2和 T_3加以区分。将收入分组标准改变后，函数形式也会相应变化，农户家庭非农收入函数变为 $Y=G$（L，C，S，P，T）。假定该函数关于 L 和 C 是一次齐次的，那么两端除以 L 得到 $Y/L=G$（C/L，S，P，T）。等式左端就是劳动报酬率，右端中的 C/L 就是非农劳均能力，因为家庭非农劳动投入增加的一个主要途径是增加非农劳动人数，所以 C/L 在一定程度上反映家庭人均能力。我们用 W 表示报酬率，用小写字母 c 表示人均能力，所以农民非农报酬率函数设定为 $W=G$（c，S，P，T）。

13.6.2　计量分析

根据农民非农报酬率函数设定，计量模型设定如下：

$$\ln W=\beta_W+\beta_c\ln c+\beta_S\ln S+\beta_{P_1}P_1+\beta_{P_2}P_2+\beta_{D_1}T_1+\beta_{D_2}T_2+\beta_{sc}\ln S\ln c+u \tag{13.11}$$

根据式（13.11），利用调查数据和 Eviews 软件得到的最小二乘回归结果如表 13.10中模型Ⅰ所示，去掉不显著的解释变量后的回归结果如模型Ⅱ所示。模型Ⅱ意味着农户非农报酬率函数为

$$\ln W= 6.12+0.16\ln c-0.24\ln S+1.01T_1+1.4T_2+3.7T_3-0.05\ln S\ln c+0.37T_3\ln c \tag{13.12}$$

表 13.10　农户非农报酬率模型

项目	模型Ⅰ			模型Ⅱ		
	修正后 $R^2=0.786$　$F=301$			修正后 $R^2=0.785$　$F=557$		
解释变量	B 系数	t 统计量	P 值	B 系数	t 统计量	P 值
常量	6.1197	16.3603	0.0000	6.1499	46.1816	0.0000
$\ln c$	0.1619	2.0143	0.0442	0.1522	5.6672	0.0000
$\ln S$	−0.2059	−4.8205	0.0000	−0.2385	−6.0683	0.0000
P_1	0.1350	0.4427	0.6581	—	—	—
P_2	0.3046	1.0224	0.3068	—	—	—
T_1	0.6034	2.8638	0.0043	1.0082	28.6183	0.0000
T_2	1.0569	4.7015	0.0000	1.4046	39.7581	0.0000
T_3	3.4445	16.7207	0.0000	3.7039	26.3413	0.0000
$\ln S\ln c$	−0.0413	−4.6534	0.0000	−0.0471	−5.7443	0.0000
$P_1\ln c$	0.0172	0.2579	0.7966	—	—	—
$P_2\ln c$	0.0502	0.7673	0.4431	—	—	—
$T_1\ln c$	−0.0864	−1.9537	0.0510	—	—	—
$T_2\ln c$	−0.0746	−1.5810	0.1142	—	—	—
$T_3\ln c$	0.3152	7.2266	0.0000	0.3719	12.5477	0.0000

注：被解释变量为非农报酬率的对数 $\ln W$；观测个数为 784。

根据表 13.10 给出的回归结果可以得到如下结论：显著影响农户非农收入报酬率增长的因素是 1 个家庭因素和 1 个地理因素，家庭因素是家庭人均自主发展能力，地理因素是地域通达性。根据式（13.12），人均自主发展能力的月产出弹性为 $0.16-0.15\ln S+0.37T_3$，它随着离城市距离的增加而下降，离城市距离越远，其能力的价值越小，“春风不度玉门关”，这大概可以成为边远地区多出文盲的依据之一。另外，在高收入组，能力的产出弹性高出 0.37，意味着报酬越高，提高能力更具价值。

根据式（13.12），地域通达性的月产出弹性为 $-0.24-0.05\ln c$，它一般为负数，表明越是临近城市，非农劳动的报酬越高，近水楼台或地域临近性发挥作用。地域通达性除了以上述方式直接影响非农劳动报酬以外，还通过影响能力间接影响非农劳动报酬。

13.6.3　贡献度分析

根据式（13.4）和式（13.12），各收入组能力贡献度的计算公式为式（13.13）。利用式（13.13）并结合样本数据，因素增长贡献度的计算结果如表 13.11 所示。在低报酬阶段，能力的贡献度约占 2/3，但进入中下报酬阶段后，报酬的增长完全依赖地域通达性的增强，进入中上报酬阶段后，地域通达性的作用开始下降，到达高报酬阶段后下降到零，这时报酬的增长完全依赖能力的增长。

$$\lambda_c=\frac{0.16g_c-0.15\ln sg_c+0.37T_3g_c}{0.16g_c-0.15\ln sg_c+0.37T_3g_c-0.24g_s-0.15\ln cg_s} \tag{13.13}$$

表 13.11　家庭非农报酬率的因素贡献度　（单位：%）

项目	低报酬组	中下报酬组	中上报酬组	高报酬组
能力变化的贡献度	67	−78	3	100
距离差异的贡献度	33	178	97	0

13.7　结论及讨论

基于河南省 11 村 1251 农户的研究表明，农户自主发展能力，以及可耕地、地形两个地理因素显著影响农户农业收入，但它们的贡献度有明显差别。在现阶段的欠发达农村，在总体上，农业增长主要靠耕地增长，而不是能力增长，故在农业收入方面，地理因素的作用要明显大于农户自主发展能力因素。研究还表明，在同一收入组的农户中，耕地增长的贡献度在山区最大，丘陵次之，平原最小；而农户自主发展能力增长的贡献度恰好与此相反。

农户非农收入的影响因素与此有明显不同。研究表明，农户自主发展能力和家庭劳动投入显著影响农户非农收入，地理因素对家庭非农收入没有显著影响。然而，进一步的相关性分析表明，地域通达性通过影响家庭自主发展能力间接影响家庭非农收入。

对农户非农收入增长中各因素的贡献度分析表明，在农户非农发展的初级阶段，农户非农发展几乎完全依赖劳动投入的增长（贡献度为 100%），农户自主发展能力增长几乎没有起作用（贡献度为 0%）；在农户非农发展的中级阶段，结果截然不同，能力增长和劳动增长的贡献各半；在农户发展的高级阶段，能力的贡献度又跌至 15%。从农户发展初级阶段到中级阶段的能力贡献度跃升存在两个原因，一是劳动的产出弹性下降，二是能力增长的幅度增大。其中，劳动的产出弹性下降是关键原因，因为劳动产出弹性下降导致农户在人口数量和质量之间的替代，用人口质量替代人口数量，人口质量的提高导致农户自主发展能力的提高，人口数量的下降导致劳动投入的下降。在农户发展的高级阶段，能力贡献度降低到 15%的原因可能是高级阶段农户的自主发展能力碰到了上限，这并不是因为农户的能力不能再提高，而是因为如果再提高农户将不再是农户，将成为非农户。

显著影响农户非农收入报酬率变化的因素包括农户自主发展能力和地域通达性。两个因素的贡献度在农户收入的不同阶段有所不同。在低报酬阶段，能力的贡献度约占 2/3，但进入中下报酬阶段后，报酬的增长完全依赖地域通达性的增强，进入中上报酬阶段后，地域通达性的作用开始下降，到达高报酬阶段后下降到零，这时报酬的增长完全依赖能力的增长。

将该研究与同一区域的乡镇级数据研究作比较，农户层面的研究结论有条件地支持乡镇级数据的研究发现，即在农区的发展中，“随着经济水平的提高，传统地理因素（如地形、农业资源因素等）的影响逐渐被对经济积聚有明显影响的地理临近性等要素的影响所取代”的观点（见本书 34.5）。只是细化到农户收入类别的研究，进一步区分了农业收入与非农业收入的不同：地理因素对农户农业收入影响显著，对非农业收入则不显著。

农户是农区经济活动的主体。农户自主发展能力反映了农户作为农区最基本的经济组织，利用环境条件和机会自我发展的能力。随着农户经济发展水平的提高和环境条件的变化，农户自主发展能力的作用将进一步显现出来。同时，衡量农户自主发展能力的指标中，像农户素能、获取和处理信息的能力等指标将显得更为重要。进一步的研究应该考虑指标的结构变化。同时，农户自主发展能力对于从微观角度阐述农区发展也具有重要意义。联结农户与农区发展，有望建立农区发展的新理论。

参 考 文 献

黄祖辉，王敏，宋瑜. 2005. 农村居民收入差距问题研究：基于村庄微观角度的一个分析框架. 管理世界，(3)：75～84

李定轶. 2006. 论导致我国农民贫困问题的制度性原因. 北京市经济管理干部学院学报，21 (1)：28～32

李杰. 2004. 中国人力资本投资的内生增长研究. 世界经济，(4)：20～24

李小建，高更和，乔家君. 2008. 农户收入的农区发展环境影响：基于河南省 1251 家农户的分析. 地理研究，27 (5)：1037～1047

李小建，时慧娜. 2008. 基于农户视角的农区发展研究. 人文地理，(1)：1～6

刘祚祥. 2006. 新农村建设与农村经济组织自生能力研究. 农村经济，(11)：6～10

牛若峰. 1995. 产业一体化：市场农业发展的基本模式. 农业经济问题，(6)：7～11

乔家君. 2008. 中国乡村地域经济论. 北京：科学出版社

舒尔茨. 2003. 改造传统农业. 梁小民译. 北京：商务印书馆

徐勇. 2006. “再识农户”与社会化小农的建构. 华中师范大学学报，45（3）：2～8

余长林. 2006. 人力资本投资结构与经济增长——基于包含教育资本、健康资本的内生增长模型理论研究. 财经研究，32（10）：102～112

曾艳华. 2006. 农民发展能力的问题与对策. 经济研究，（6）：29～33

朱玲. 1992. 非农产业活动对农户收入分配格局的影响. 经济研究，（3）：23～30

Brauw A，Huang J，Rozelle S，et al. 2002. The evolution of china's rural labor markets during the reforms. Journal of Comparative Economics，30（2）：329～353

Knight J，Song L. 1993. The spatial contribution to income inequality in rural China. Cambridge Journal of Economics，17（2）：195～213

Meng X，Wu H. 1998. Household income determination and regional income differential in rural China. Asian Economic Journal，12（1）：65～88

Rozelle S. 1994. Rural industrialization and increasing inequality：Emerging patterns in China's Reforming Economy. Journal of Comparative Economics，（19）：362～391

Rozelle S. 1996. Stagnation without equity：Patterns of growth and inequality in China's rural economy. The China Journal，35：63～92

Wan G，Zhou Z. 2005. Income inequality in rural china：Regression～based decomposition using household data. Review of Development Economics，9（1）：107～120

第 14 章　农户务工区位选择

20 世纪 90 年代以后，民工潮逐渐成为中国社会经济发展的重大问题，务工队伍越来越庞大，农户务工成为一种重要的社会经济现象。据研究，农村劳动力流动就业的规模约为 1.2 亿，其中进城农民工约为 1 亿，跨省流动就业的农民工约为 6000 万（劳动和社会保障部课题组，2006）。中国目前正经历着人类历史上在和平时期前所未有的、规模最大的人口迁移活动，并成为世界上最大的人口迁移流（编辑部，2006）。

处于对这种重要社会现象的反映，学术界对该问题进行了较多的研究，有关剩余劳动力转移、农民工等的研究成果简直是汗牛充栋，相关研究所涉及的内容也十分丰富，经济学、社会学等学科对其进行了大量的研究，但是主要集中于务工的动因与机制、务工对劳动力输入地和劳动力流出地，以及整个经济社会发展的影响（Yang，2000）、农业劳动力转移的途径与模式（董文柱，2003）、对农民工合理流动的制度学分析、农民工培训和教育、国内外劳动力转移的比较、农民工流动与城市化、农民工非持久性迁移研究、农民工社会分层（李强，2000）、区域性农业剩余劳动力转移的现状、问题与对策研究（刘瑞芝，1998）等方面。国外学者在较早和新近对劳动力迁移的经济动因（Lewis，1954），以及个人特征（Stinner et al.，1993）、家庭特征（Massey，1993）、社区因素、关系网络（Portes，1993）和距离因素（Liang and Michael，1997）对劳动力迁移的影响进行了较多的研究。

地理学对务工空间问题研究的成果相对较少，研究内容主要集中于农民工的区域分布（蔡建明，1990）、区域差异（李玉江，1999）、流向（蔡昉，1998；李玲，2001）和农村剩余劳动力转移的空间途径（董文柱，2003）等方面，研究视角侧重于宏观的区域分析，研究方法多采用规范分析，研究数据大多是使用统计数据，基于农户微观视角的农户务工区位的研究成果较少，而此类研究是认识农户务工空间规律和农民工流动规律的基础。村落是农户务工的起点和终点，他们务工生活的城镇只是他们以村落为中心的活动空间的一个锚点。因此，研究务工者的空间行为，以村庄为中心来进行具有较大优势。本章主要从村域农户微观角度，探讨务工区位选择中的影响因素问题。研究发现，农户关系网络对打工地的选择具有关键作用，农户对打工地的选择是在能够预期取得一定收入的前提下，综合考虑个人、家庭和社区因素的结果，地理环境因素对打工地的选择具有重要影响。

14.1　数据来源与研究区域选择

14.1.1　数据来源

数据主要通过入户问卷调查获取。在国家自然科学基金重点项目的资助下，通过与当地政府部门的协调，由调查员按照问卷对务工农户进行了调查。调查之前，根据调查内容设计了调查问卷，并经过反复讨论和实地试验。调查员在河南大学环境与规划学院硕士研究生中和南阳师范学院环境科学与旅游学院本科生中择优选取，共12人。调查员经过严格培训后，在2006年2月农历春节时（2006年1月15日～2006年2月20日），对3个样本村回家过春节的农民工进行了面对面调查。调查员培训的内容包括问卷调查的目的、意义、访问技巧、注意事项等。本次调查共获取务工区位调查问卷303份，其中有效问卷288份。

调查问卷回收后，进行甄别，去除无效问卷，对有效问卷进行编号，将纸质问卷答案数据输入EXECL2000中，形成农户务工区位数据库，该数据库大小为：288×157=45216（288户，每户157个属性）。该数据库是本研究的基础，以下的模型运算和影响因子分析均建立在该数据库之上。

14.1.2　研究区域选择

河南省在我国中部农区具有一定的典型性和代表性（高更和等，2007），南阳市是河南省的农业大市，在农业和农区中具有较强的代表性，因此，我们选择南阳市作为研究的样本地区。2005年，南阳市人口达1075万，占河南省总人口的11%，是河南省18市中人口最多的市，但是城镇化水平仅为30%，低于全省平均水平，南阳市农民人均纯收入为2894元，排名第11位，居中等水平。2005年南阳市主要农业指标在河南省占据重要位置，如耕地面积、农林牧渔业增加值、油料产量在18市中居于首位，农业从业人员数量、粮食总产量、棉花产量居第二位，粮食播种面积虽然排名第四，但与第二相比相差甚少（河南省统计局，2006）。南阳市也是河南省农民工外出最多的地区

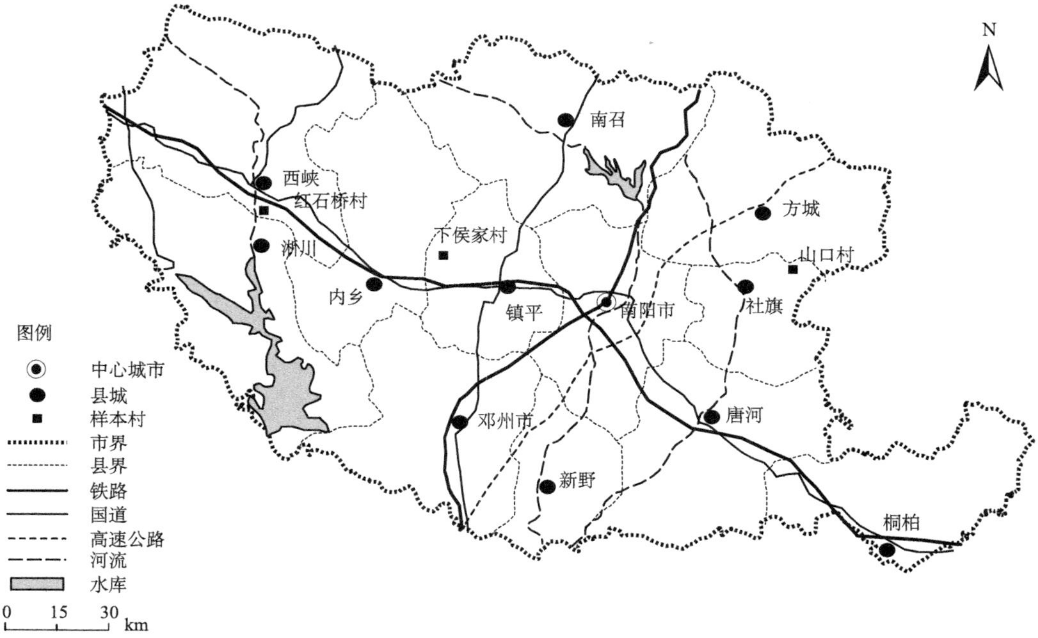

图14.1　河南省南阳市研究样本点分布示意图

之一。

在南阳市内，采用分层抽样方法对样本村进行选择。分层抽样方法是研究复杂对象的有效方法，鉴于研究的可行性，有必要对大样本数量进行简化，而分层抽样是简化样本数量的科学手段。研究首先将南阳市 214 个乡镇按地形（山区、丘陵和平原）进行分层，然后在各分层中进行随机抽样，以确定调查乡镇，最终选取的调查乡镇是社旗县下洼乡（山区）、镇平县曲屯镇（丘陵）和西峡县回车镇（平原）。在三个乡镇中，根据代表性原则、典型性原则和城郊区位条件，分别选取下洼乡山口村石河组、镇平县曲屯镇花栗树村下侯家组和西峡县回车镇红石桥村郭营组作为调查样本村（图 14.1）。

14.2　理论分析与研究假设

影响外出务工及务工区位选择的因素包括个人特征、家庭特征和社区特征等变量。农户外出务工的过程在空间上实际上是务工者由居住地到务工地的移动过程，是否移动、移动到哪里是由务工者决定的，而其决策与有关居住地的因素密切相连，这些因素包括长期生活在家乡所形成的个人特质和家庭特质，同时又包括居住地的社区特征，而务工地只是基于这些特征所作的一种选择。

务工者本人的性别、年龄、婚姻、学历等个人因素对外出务工及务工区位选择有重要影响。外出务工虽然能够取得一定的经济收入，但是用工单位对务工者本人的素质有一定的要求，务工过程本身也具有一定的风险性，因此，务工者具有一定的选择性。不同人的不同生理、经济、文化和社会特征，获取信息的不同途径，对待风险的不同态度，影响到对务工区位的决策。一般而言，男性较女性更富有冒险精神，因此其迁移距离可能较大；年龄较小者，由于身体强壮，后顾之忧较小，同时较具有冒险精神，对工资水平期望较高，因此其务工距离可能较远；已婚者，尤其是有小孩者，由于家庭负担较重，他们往往选择在离本地较近距离处务工；较高学历者，在较高收入的外地能较容易地找到工作且往往对自己充满自信，由此可能趋于在更远的地方务工。

务工区位选择不仅要考虑个人因素，同时也要考虑家庭因素。因为个人只是家庭成员之一，家庭利益往往要高于个人利益，个人务工决策的制定必须考虑家庭特征，个人是否务工也取决于家庭决策。如果家庭中有（较多的）老人和有（较多的）上学子女，作为家庭主要劳动力的潜在务工者可能不外出务工或在较近的地方务工，即家庭人口较多、家庭类型较为复杂、稳定型家庭、代数较多家庭的务工者其务工距离可能较近。有上学子女或上学人数较多的家庭，务工者处于对上学子女的照料，更可能选择在较近的地方务工。当家庭有较多的劳动力时，由于家庭管理成本较低，其务工者可能更趋于在较高收入的外地务工。人均耕地面积较大的家庭，可在当地取得较高的农业收入，因此其务工距离可能较小，或者不选择外出务工策略。总之，家庭特征变量是影响务工区位选择的重要因素。

社区因素也是影响农户外出务工和务工区位选择的重要因素。社区的交通条件、务工传统、经济发展水平、地形等因素均对务工区位选择有一定影响。经济发展水平较高的村，村民在本地就业的概率较大，因此往往选择就近务工。地形比较复杂的村（如山区），由于地形的影响和落后的交通以及较低的经济发展水平，村中的务工者在本地就业困难，因此趋向于选择在较远的地方务工。而近郊村的务工者由于在附近的城市中容易实现就业，所以往往选择在离本地较近距离务工，与此相对应，距离县城或城市越近，其在当地务工的概率越大。社区内部的务工网络能够为潜在或实际的务工者提供信息，提供各种形式的支援，从而降低迁移风险和成本，尤其是务工网络的示范功能，往往能引导务工者选择务工地。因此，关系网络往往对务工地的选择具有决定性意义。

由上面的分析可知，农户外出务工区位的选择受到性别、年龄、婚姻、学历等个人特征和家庭利益最大化、家庭类型、家庭劳动力数量等家庭特征及村经济发展水平、交通状况、关系网络等社区特征的影响。因此，我们的研究将从这三方面展开。为了进一步分析务工距离和务工区位选择的成因，我们做出了以下的研究假设。

（1）性别、年龄和婚姻状况不同，务工距离有明显差别。男性、年龄较小者、未婚者到较远地方务工的概率较大，相反，女性、年龄较长者和已婚者在较近地方务工的概率较大。

（2）高学历的人趋于在更远的地方务工，而低学历的人趋于在距离较近的地方务工。

（3）农户家庭中人口越多、劳动力越多，越趋向于到较远的地方务工。家庭代数越多、上学子女越多，农户中的务工者越趋于在较近地方的务工。

（4）人均耕地与务工距离成反比，即人均耕地越多，在附近务工的概率越大。

（5）务工者社会网络的引导对务工地的选择具有重要作用。

（6）经济发展水平越高，在附近地区务工的概率越大，经济越落后，在较远地方务工的概率越大。

（7）地形越崎岖，越趋于到较远的地方务工。反之亦然。

14.3 变量设计与说明

影响农民外出务工的因素可概括为个人、家庭、社区三大类变量，其中，个人特征变量包括务工者本人的性别、年龄、学历、婚姻状况等因子；家庭变量包括务工者所在家庭的人口规模、劳动力数（量）、家庭类型、家庭生命周期、人均耕地等因子；社区变量包括务工者所在村的经济发展水平、地形、城郊类型、关系网络、交通状况、城郊区位等因子。每个因子的具体含义、赋值统计方法见表14.1。

表 14.1 变量设计

序号	变量	赋值	含义
1	性别	男性，1；女性，0	务工者本人的性别
2	年龄	实际年龄，单位：岁	务工者从出生到调查年的实际年龄
3	学历	实际学龄，单位：年	务工者实际上学的年限，不包括短期培训
4	婚姻	结婚，1；未婚，0	务工者本人调查时的婚姻状态

续表

序号	变量	赋值	含义
5	家庭人口	实际人数，单位：人	务工者家庭调查时的实际人口数，包括未上户口的人口
6	劳动力数	家庭中的劳动力数量，单位：人	务工者家庭中，男性 15～60 岁，女性 16～55 岁的健康人口数量（不包括在读学生）
7	家庭类型	核心家庭，1；直系家庭，2；扩展家庭，3	根据家庭成员结构决定的家庭类型。因为被试者无单身家庭，故未考虑单身家庭因素
8	家庭生命周期	形成，1；扩展，2；稳定，3；收缩，4；空巢，5；解体，6	家庭从建立、发展到解体和消亡的过程①，可分为 6 个阶段（冯天立，1994）
9	人均耕地	家庭人均耕地面积，单位：亩/人	家庭人均耕地面积＝家庭总耕地面积/家庭总人口
10	家庭代数	家庭中的代际数量	家庭中由几代人构成
11	上学人数	家庭中上学子女数量，单位：人	包括所有上小学、中学和大学的子女
12	村经济发展水平	务工者所在村人均 GDP，单位：元/人	人均 GDP＝务工者所在村 GDP/村总人口
13	村地形	平原，1；丘陵，2；山区，3	务工者所在村地形类型
14	村城郊类型	城郊，1；非城郊，0	务工者所在村是城市郊区或非城市郊区
15	村关系网络引导	0～30	若为关系网络引导到该地务工，则其值为村到务工地距离的百分之一；若无则为 0
16	村交通状况	单位：km	村到最近公路的距离
17	城郊区位	单位：km	村到最近县城或城市的距离

如果模型中变量之间存在自相关，可能会造成对变量影响作用的估计正确性，有学者提出将±0.8 作为自相关阈值②。经过对上述因素的相关性检验，发现村城郊类型、交通距离、城郊区位与村经济发展水平有高度的相关性，因此，将村城郊类型、交通距离、城郊区位三个因子删除。

14.4　模型与讨论

样本务工者的务工地分布于北京、上海、天津、福建、广东、贵州、河北、河南、湖北、吉林、江苏、辽宁、山东、陕西、山西、浙江 16 个省市，主要集中于河南、广东两省，其分别占总务工者的 47.9％和 31.5％，其次为浙江、河北、天津、上海、山

① 可分为 6 个阶段。第一，家庭形成阶段，即从初婚到家庭主妇初育；第二，家庭扩展阶段，即第一个孩子出生至最后一个孩子出生；第三，家庭扩展完成阶段，即最后一个孩子出生到第一个孩子结婚或工作等原因离家；第四，家庭收缩阶段，即从第一子女离家到最后一个子女离家；第五，空巢阶段，即最后一个子女离家到配偶一方死亡；第六，家庭消亡阶段，从配偶一方死亡到双方死亡。

② 史天健，Kirsten H A. 调查研究技术与项目设计. 北京大学中国国情研究中心（内部资料），1999。

西、江苏、福建，再次为北京、陕西，其余省市分布较少。整体而言，务工地主要分布于制造业比较发达的广东省和务工者来源地附近的省份，沿海省份整体较多。西北地区、西南地区和东北地区分布极少，其原因与距离和制造业发达程度有关。此外，在新加坡务工 3 位，主要从事船员工作，由职业中介机构组织实施。

具体到国内，务工者分布在上述 16 个省市的 38 个地级市中。它们主要是南阳、广州、东莞、杭州、郑州、深圳、天津、邢台、上海等。

农户务工区位问题的核心是到哪个地方务工，我们可以从务工距离、务工地带（务工地所处的三大地带）、务工空间类型（务工地所在行政区域类型）等方面对此问题进行分析。

14.4.1　子模型 1：务工距离的回归概率参数估计

将务工距离分为本地（100km 内）和外地（100km 以外）两类（根据样本村位置和样本地区的范围大小，设定本地与外地的分界点为 100km），采用 SPSS13.0 中的二值逻辑回归（Binary Logistic Regression）模块进行分析，将个人因素、家庭因素和社区因素引入后，采用强迫法运算，可得到最终模型，其估计参数如表 14.2 所示。模型的拟合度较高，Nagelkerke R^2 为 0.836，模型中总百分率的符合率为 90.6%，达到了比较满意的结果，同时模型的显著性水平很高，为 0.000。

表 14.2　务工距离和务工地带二值逻辑回归模型参数

因子类	因子	务工距离模型		务工地带模型	
		系数	显著性水平	系数	显著性水平
	常数项	0.8715	0.8406	−0.0850	0.9761
个人因素	性别	0.7184	0.2979	0.4886	0.2994
	年龄	−0.0623**	0.0452	−0.0250	0.2952
	上学年限	−0.0785	0.5559	−0.0053	0.9538
	婚否	0.1969	0.7834	0.1231	0.8190
家庭因素	总人口	0.0925	0.8316	−0.0575	0.8597
	劳动力数	0.2279	0.5501	0.3756	0.1565
	家庭类型	1.5384*	0.0670	−0.3233	0.6234
	生命周期	0.2824	0.5820	−0.1389	0.7065
	人均耕地	0.4085	0.5780	−0.2277	0.5677
	家庭代数	−2.4330**	0.0118	−0.5364	0.4127
	上学人数	−1.0350*	0.0566	−0.3237	0.3734
社区因素	村经济发展水平	−0.0002	0.3724	−0.0002	0.2084
	村地形	0.6720	0.4706	0.2943	0.6379
	关系网络	1.0102***	0.0000	0.6795***	0.0000

注：①因变量：本地 0，外地 1（以 100km 为界）；非东部 0，东部 1；② * 显著性水平为 0.1①，** 显著性水平为 0.05，*** 显著性水平为 0.01。

① 因为是社会地理的研究，因此适当放宽了显著性水平的要求。

该模型中，年龄、家庭类型、家庭代数、上学人数、关系网络等因子达到了显著性水平。年龄因子系数为负，表明年龄与务工距离呈反方向变化，年龄越大在较远地方务工的概率越小，年龄越小在较远地方务工的概率越大。其形成主要与不同年龄务工者在家庭中的贡献有关，同时与务工者本人的观念有关。年龄较小者，对外面世界充满了好奇和憧憬，希望到外面闯一闯，同时无照顾家人的后顾之忧，而年龄较大者则需要照顾子女或年迈的父母。家庭类型因子系数为正，说明复杂型家庭中的务工者在较远地方务工的概率较大，而在较近地方务工的概率较小，因为复杂型家庭往往拥有比较多的劳动力。家庭代数因子系数为负，表明家庭代数越多，其务工者在较近地方务工的概率越大，因为作为务工者的劳动力需要照顾家人，家庭抚养成本较高。上学人数在此模型中达到了显著性要求，其系数为负，且系数较大，说明上学人数是影响务工距离的重要因子。上学人数与务工距离呈反方向变化，即上学子女数越多，父母在本地务工的概率越大，反之亦然。其原因可能是父母不仅需要为上学子女提供学费和生活费用，同时也需要提供生活方面和情感方面的照顾。如果父母在远处务工，则会为照顾子女带来很大不便。因此，有上学子女的父母或较多上学子女的父母在本地务工的概率较大，而没有上学子女的父母，则在较远距离务工的概率较大。关系网络因子的系数为正，且系数较大，表明关系网络是影响务工距离的重要因子之一。许多研究都表明，关系网络对务工地的选择具有重要意义。关系网络不仅为务工者提供信息，同时也可能为务工者提供资金帮助、生活照顾和情感支持。可以设想，在现在复杂的社会关系和信任危机中，在没有关系网络的情况下，一个寻找工作的农民在一个陌生的城市会面临多少不便和风险！只有很少的人才冒此风险。根据务工者样本统计，只有 11.8%的人是自己开辟找到务工岗位的，另有 1.1%的人是通过广播、电视、广告等媒体找到工作岗位的。经过政府和中介组织介绍务工的比例也只有 7%，绝大多数（80.1%）的务工者均由亲戚、同学、朋友、同族人、同村人介绍去务工，并一同前去。因此，关系网络在务工地的选择中具有决定性作用。

总之，影响农户务工距离选择的主要因素是年龄、家庭类型、家庭代数、上学人数和关系网络因子。年龄较大者、家庭类型较简单者、家庭代数较多者、上学人数较多者和关系网络较少者，选择在本地务工的概率较大，反之亦然。

14.4.2　子模型 2：务工地带的回归概率参数估计

按照我国三个地带的较新划分，我们将务工地也分为东部、中部、西部三大地带。由于到西部务工的人数很少，仅占到全部务工者的 2.1%，很难具有代表性，因此，我们研究的重点是在中部务工还是到东部务工，故采用二值逻辑回归模型进行分析。将个人因素、家庭因素和社区因素引入模型，可得到务工地带模型，其参数参见表 14.2。模型的拟合度较高，Nagelkerke R^2 为 0.763，总百分率的符合率为 84.5%，模型的显著性水平也很高，为 0.0000。

模型中只有关系网络因子达到了显著性水平，且其系数的绝对值也较大，这表明，关系网络因子对决定务工地带具有十分重要的影响。正如前面分析的那样，一个潜在的务工者在决定到哪里务工时，关系网络往往具有引导、示范、支持和保障作用，其对区位选择往往具有决定性的意义。

14.4.3　子模型 3：务工空间类型的回归概率参数估计

务工空间类型是按照行政区划分的务工地域类型，主要包括务工者所在的县域（简称县内）、县外市（南阳）内、市外（河南）省内和省外等 4 类。务工空间类型与务工距离有一定的相关性，但其空间内涵不同，由于务工空间范围逐步增大，可以将务工空间作为有序多元变量来处理，具体运行结果如表 14.3 所示。

表 14.3　务工空间类型的有序逻辑回归模型参数

因子类	因子	系数	标准误	Wald 值	自由度	显著性水平	95% CI	
							下界	上界
个人因素	性别	1.1152**	0.5026	4.9225	1	0.0265	0.1300	2.1003
	年龄	−0.0413*	0.0236	3.0628	1	0.0801	−0.0875	0.0049
	上学年限	−0.1095	0.0944	1.3465	1	0.2459	−0.2945	0.0755
	婚否	−0.6129	0.5213	1.3822	1	0.2397	−1.6346	0.4089
家庭因素	家庭人口	0.1769	0.3235	0.2991	1	0.5844	−0.4571	0.8110
	劳动力数	−0.1285	0.2744	0.2193	1	0.6396	−0.6662	0.4093
	家庭类型	0.3748	0.5962	0.3952	1	0.5296	−0.7937	1.5433
	生命周期	−0.1027	0.3842	0.0715	1	0.7892	−0.8558	0.6503
	人均耕地	0.4354	0.5615	0.6013	1	0.4381	−0.6651	1.5360
	家庭代数	−1.4211**	0.6594	4.6446	1	0.0312	−2.7136	−0.1287
	上学人数	−0.8203**	0.3751	4.7834	1	0.0287	−1.5554	−0.0852
社区因素	村经济发展水平	−0.0007***	0.0002	17.1768	1	0.0000	−0.0010	−0.0004
	村地形	1.8362**	0.7322	6.2890	1	0.0121	0.4011	3.2712
	关系网络	0.9673***	0.1068	81.9851	1	0.0000	0.7579	1.1767

注：①最终模型吻合显著性水平：0.000；②Nagelkerke R^2：0.801；③ * 显著性水平为 0.1，** 显著性水平为 0.05，*** 显著性水平为 0.01。

个人因素中，性别和年龄因子为影响务工空间的重要因子。性别因子的系数为正，表明在更大务工空间中男性的概率较高，而在较小的务工空间中女性较高。年龄因子系数为负，说明年龄较大者在较小空间中务工的概率较高，年龄较小者在较大务工空间中的概率较高。

家庭因素中，家庭代数和上学人数达到了显著性水平，这两个因子系数均为负，说明其与务工空间呈反方向变化。家庭代数越多，在更大空间务工的概率越小，家庭代数越少，在更大空间务工的概率越大，其形成主要与抚养成本、家庭感情纽带等原因有关。上学人数与此类似，上学人数越多，在更大空间务工的概率越小，上学人数越少，在更大空间务工的概率越大，而其形成的可能原因是抚育成本在多上学子女中较大的缘故。

社区因素中，村经济发展水平、村地形和关系网络因子均达到了显著性水平。村经济发展水平因子系数为负，说明经济越发达的村，在较小空间务工的概率越大，经济越落后的村在较大空间务工的概率较大。其原因可能是经济发达的村，附近有较多的就业岗位，可实现剩余劳动力的就地就业，而经济落后的村则不可能就地就业，为了增加收入，只能到较大的空间中务工。村地形因子系数为正，说明地形越崎岖，到更大空间务工的概率越大；地形越平坦，在较小空间务工的概率越大，因为平原村比较容易就地解决就业问题。关系网络因子为正，说明关系网络对务工空间具有正向的引导作用。

14.5　结论与政策建议

基于农户微观角度的务工区位选择研究是认识农民工流动空间规律的基础。本章利用 3 个样本村的实证研究表明，务工者不同的个人特征、家庭特征和社区特征对其务工地的选择具有重要影响。假设 1 中的婚姻假设、假设 2、假设 3 中的家庭人口数量假设、假设 4 被证伪，其余假设被证实，具体结论如下。

性别不同，其务工空间具有明显差别，男性更趋于在较大的空间务工，而女性则趋于在较小的空间务工。年龄不同，其务工距离和务工空间具有显著差异。年龄越小，越趋于在较远和较大空间务工，反之亦然。家庭类型不同，其务工距离具有明显差异，复杂型家庭在较远地方务工的概率较大，反之亦然。家庭代数和家庭中上学人数不同，其务工距离和务工空间具有显著差异，家庭代数越少、上学子女数越少，越趋于在较远的地方和较大的空间务工，反之亦然。村经济发展水平不同，其务工空间具有显著差异，村经济发展水平较低者在更大空间务工的概率较大。村地形不同，其务工空间具有显著差异，山区较平原更趋于在较大的空间内务工。另据研究（高更和等，2007），家庭代数、村经济发展水平和关系网络是影响农户务工地城镇规模类型选择的重要因素，家庭代数与城镇规模类型呈反方向变化，村经济发展水平是影响农户务工地城镇规模类型选择的重要反向因素。关系网络对务工者务工地的选择具有重要作用。

农户对务工地的选择是在能够预期取得一定收入的前提下，综合考虑个人、家庭和社区因素的结果，是理性的，地理环境因素对务工地的选择具有重要影响。与永久性迁移的迁移者选择性相同，非永久性务工迁移也具有一定的选择性，但是其形成原因主要在于削减家务管理成本和规避迁移风险，因此规范劳动力流动市场、降低迁移风险，以及农村社会化服务体系的完善和消除务工者的后顾之忧对农村剩余劳动力的合理流动具有关键意义。本章从务工区位选择角度进一步验证了“移民网络”（Massey et al.，1987）理论在非永久性迁移中的适用性，其政策含义是，对于没有或较少外出务工者的村，如果要发展劳务经济，对先期务工者的引导以及培育务工关系网络具有十分重要的意义，而当外出务工者发展到一定规模时，靠其自身的网络引导已经很容易使潜在务工者成为实际的务工者，因此，政府工作的重心应该放在种子务工者的培育上。

该研究以中部典型农区为研究样本，揭示出影响农户务工区位选择的主要因素及作用机制，所得结论在这类地区具有一定的普遍性，但能否运用于更大范围和其他地区，还有待于进一步研究。

参考文献

编辑部. 2006. 持续发展信息与动态. 中国人口·资源与环境,(6):168

蔡昉. 1998. 转轨时期中国劳动力迁移的区域特征. 当代亚太,(7):19~23

蔡建明. 1990. 中国省级人口迁移及其对城市化的影响. 地理研究,9(2):122~128

董文柱. 2003. 我国农村劳动力转移途径的再思考. 中国农村经济,(9):65~68

冯天立. 1994. 北京婚姻、家庭与妇女地位研究. 北京:北京经济学院出版社

高更和,梁亚红,李小建. 2007. 中部农区农户务工地城镇规模类型研究——以河南省三个样本村为例. 经济地理,27(6):922~926

河南省统计局. 2006. 河南统计年鉴 2006. 北京:中国统计出版社

劳动和社会保障部课题组. 2006. 当前农民工流动就业数量、结构与特点. 工人日报,02-14

李玲. 2001. 改革开放以来中国国内人口迁移及其研究. 地理研究,20(4):453~462

李强. 2000. 中国城市中的二元劳动力市场与底层精英问题. 清华社会学评论,(S):151~167

李玉江. 1999. 农业剩余劳动力转移区域研究. 济南:山东人民出版社

刘瑞芝. 1998. 九十年代河南农村剩余劳动力转移的经济分析. 中州学刊,(5):46~49

Lewis W A. 1954. Economic development with unlimited supplies of labor. Manchester School of Economic and Social Studies, 22: 139~191

Liang Z, Michael W. 1997. Market transition, government policies, and inter provincialmigration in China: 1983-1988. Economic Development and Cultural Change, 45 (2): 321~339

Massey D S, Alarcon R, Durand J, et al. 1987. Return to Aztlan: The social process of international migration from western Mexico. Berkeley: University of California Press

Massey D S. 1993. Theories of international migration: review and appraisal. Population andDevelopment Review, 19 (3): 431~466

Portes A. 1993. Embeddedness and immigration: Notes on the determinants of economic action. American Journal of Sociology, 98: 1320~1350

Stinner W F, Xu W, Wei J. 1993. Migrant status and labor market outcomes in urban and rural Hebei province. China Rural Sociology, 58: 366~386

Yang X S. 2000. Determinants of migration intentions in Hubei Province, China: Individual versus family migration. Environment and Planning A, 32: 769~787

第三篇　公司地理研究

第 15 章 公司地理的理论问题

公司地理是 20 世纪 60 年代初美国地理学家 R. B. 麦克尼首先提出的，其主旨是企图“使经济地理学中仅仅对物的分析转移到对人及社会组织机构的关注上来”（McNee，1960）。之后企业组织的跨国发展及全球化十分迅速，加之 20 世纪 70 年代地理学中的行为主义的促进，公司地理作为经济地理学的一个新研究领域逐渐活跃起来。

15.1 工业地理学的发展与公司地理

公司地理的出现是工业地理学发展的产物。而工业地理学的发展和公司地理的出现均与工业本身的发展有着不可分割的联系。

20 世纪以来工业地理学的发展，大致经过描述性研究、规范性区位分析、实证主义和行为主义方法诸阶段。20 世纪 50 年代中期之前，工业地理学的研究主要限定于单个制造业单位生产活动分布状况的描述。对其形成原因的解释，偏重于历史演变，尤其过分强调自然环境（如原燃料的可得性等）的作用，很少有人通过典型案例研究概括出一般性结论（Johnston et al.，1986）。

20 世纪 50 年代后期，随着廖什的著作《区位经济学》被译成英文出版，以及艾萨德、格伦哈特等人的研究，韦伯所开创的工业区位理论得以被重视和发展。这种工业地理学研究被称为规范性区位分析（Chapman and Walker，1987）。其规范性表现在：工厂的最佳区位是在一系列简化性的假设条件下求得的。例如，韦伯把他所认为的次要因素看作常数，不予考虑。虽后人研究时所考虑的因素逐渐增多，但仍与实际有一定距离。在逻辑方法上，这种研究主要从与工业区位选定有关的一些基本命题出发，演绎推理出结果。此外，这种理论深受古典经济学中的经济人概念的影响，认为区位决策者单一追求利润，他们具有所有经济学的有关知识。

各种假设条件限制着这种理论在实际中的应用，理想的经济人也很难与现实一致。20 世纪 60 年代的数量革命带来了实证主义的区位分析方法。与规范区位论不同，这种分析法强调空间结构的形成规律，主要用统计和数学模拟方法探索空间结构的模型。系统科学的兴起，将一系列基本空间概念联结起来形成综合空间科学。工业地理学的理论与实践在 20 世纪 60 年代得到进一步发展，研究重点由重视工业空间分布形式转移到强调其形成过程上来。

20 世纪 60 年代末，传统的区位论及当时十分流行的区位分析受到行为学派的冲击。实际上，对工业区位形成过程的探究，必将导致对区位决策者行为的分析。而对决策者行为的调查结果，又会证实个人行为的重要性。同样的区位影响条件，不同决策者会产生不同的区位结果。行为差异与前述区位纯数理分析上的矛盾，促使了工业区位研究中行为主义方法的兴起。

决策者行为包括孤立的个人行为和组织行为。工业组织的发展，使其结构及决策过程不断复杂化。工业组织的行为变得日益重要起来。为了研究工业组织行为和组织结构的空间意义，公司地理作为工业地理学的一个新领域而逐渐活跃起来。20 世纪 70 年代末以来，数量可观的工业地理学出版物涉及这个领域。

公司地理的发展又紧系于工业本身的发展。20 世纪 60 年代末，由于工业技术和通信手段的发展，国际性贸易集团的形成，以及世界性金融、资源和劳动力市场的开辟，促使了跨国公司及全球性公司的迅速扩张。自 20 世纪 90 年代，全球企业跨境并购无论在规模还是数量上，都保持着高速增长的态势，并在一系列的并购活动中，培养出一大批跨国企业。根据历年来联合国贸易和发展会议发布的《世界投资报告》，1998 年跨境并购为 411 亿美元，与 1997 年相比增长了 74%。到了 2013 年，全球投资协定达到 3240 个，跨境并购达到 3488 亿美元，相比 1998 年增长了约 7.5 倍①。不仅发达国家的跨国公司将其生产机构渗入其他发达国家和发展中国家，一些发展中国家的跨国公司也开始登上发达国家的国土。2013 年，全球跨国公司已经超过 8 万家，全球 5000 家大跨国公司的库存现金维持在高位，占其资产总额的 11%。来自发达国家的跨国公司的库存现金（包括短期投资）估计达到 3.5 万亿美元，而来自发展中和转型经济体的跨国公司的库存现金约 1 万亿美元。截至 2013 年，发展中国家的跨国公司（TNCs）的国外直接投资创造了历史新高，达 4540 亿美元。如果包括转型经济体，其占全球国外直接投资流出总量的 39%，这一比例在 20 世纪初仅为 12%。并且，发展中国家的跨国公司在不断收购发达国家的跨国公司在发展中世界的分支机构②。当今世界很少有不与跨国公司发生联系的孤立国家。在这样的条件下，要想弄清国家间的经济变化，要想弄清国家内区域之间的经济变化，要想弄清外资行为对接受投资地的影响并避免不利后果，都不能不对公司尤其是跨国公司进行研究。这是公司地理不断发展的社会经济背景。

15.2 公司地理的主要特点

15.2.1 强调对公司主题的研究

公司地理主要研究企业组织的空间格局及其与环境的相互关系。利用产业地理学、产业经济学和工业组织学等学科的有关知识，对产业组织结构形式、组织内各部门之间的不平等关系、组织间的关系与地理格局的关联，对企业与所在国家、区域的政治、经济和文化环境等进行地理学分析。在公司地理对企业组织的研究中，不同学者侧重不同，有的强调对大公司的研究，认为公司地理主要“研究多产品多分部企业的决策和结构对企业区位和区域经济发展过程的影响”（Hayter and Watts，1983）。例如，跨国公司对发达国家逆工业化与发展中国家工业化的影响便是一个研究的热题。有的认为小公

① 中国经济网．2015. 全球企业跨境并购新趋势．http://finance.eastmoney.com/news/1351，20150528511411745.html. 2015-05-28。

② 南开大学国际经济研究所．2014. 2014 年世界投资报告．http://www.nkiie.com/news1.asp? ArticleID=1312. 2014-07-13。

司增长和新公司形成的空间差异（Mason and Lloyd，1986），对一国之内就业状况的地理分布影响很大，尤其是区域不平衡发展中小公司的作用不容忽视。与这种仅仅以公司规模大小来区分研究对象的观点不同，一些地理学家试图用企业组织学中的势（实）力和分组构架概念包罗所有类型的组织。例如，泰勒和思里夫特根据控制与被控制关系，将公司分为先导公司、中间公司和滞后公司三个类型（Taylor and Thrift，1983），然后对每一类型中的单个公司之空间组织，每一类型所有公司之空间组织，以及不同类型公司间的相互关系问题进行研究（Taylor，1984）。

15.2.2　关注公司对环境的影响

公司地理的中心是承认“公司在一定程度上能够控制或改变其环境状况”（Hayter and Watts，1983）。20 世纪 60 年代，麦克尼曾根据对美国大公司的实际观察指出“重要的是，许多大公司（如汽车工业公司）的区域格局对于供应其零部件的小公司的区位选择，具有决定性的作用”（McNee，1960）。进而，大公司的活动可以直接或间接影响区域内的工业分布，这种影响小至一个工业小区，大至国际范围的工业格局。尽管国家和区域的有关政策可以限制或促进公司的发展，但在某些情况下，公司活动的主要原因却在政策之外，公司地理重视公司活动对环境的影响与传统工业区位理论强调环境因子对区位的影响形成明显对比。

15.2.3　重视公司内部因素的分析

公司地理重视公司内部因素对其决策的影响和公司内部结构的不均等性。传统的工业地理学注重成本和利润，认为“对所有从工厂后门进入和工厂前门运出的货物”的分析，可以解释“为什么工厂布局于此”（Ullman，1953）。由于行为主义方法的引入，研究者发现同样的公司区位条件，由于决策者对市场的观察能力及决策集团的偏好差异，会出现不同的区位结果。随着公司内部结构的复杂化，公司内部的中心-外围关系明显表现出来，一些部门在技术和生产联系上支配着其他部门，尤其是发达国家的跨国公司对发展中国家渗透，发展中国家的分支机构一般地位很低，常常以生产某些粗略加工品、劳动密集型产品及污染较重的产品为主，技术、资金均被设在发达国家的公司机构所控制。公司内部结构不均等性对区位的影响，用传统的工业地理学理论是无法解释的。

15.2.4　重视个案研究

公司地理十分重视个案的分析研究。公司地理在创立之初，深受实用主义的影响，多数学者的研究只是尽力去“发现事实”（McNee，1986）。这种传统被延续下来，公司地理对案例的研究逐步深化，由初始对从事大规模生产的公司（如钢铁、铝、汽车、化学等公司）的研究到电子工业等高技术部门的研究，由纵向一体化公司的研究到纵横合并而组成的跨行业多种经营大公司的研究。实例研究，为公司和国家决策提供参考意见，得到所研究公司及国家有关部门的重视。

15.3　公司地理的主要研究内容

15.3.1　公司增长的空间研究

公司地理提出以来，公司增长的空间研究一直作为一个主要专题。学者们根据工业经济学所提出的公司增长理论，探求伴随公司增长的空间扩张规律。例如，依据工业经济学理论，公司增长可分为内部增长、外部兼并、生产一体化和生产多样化四个方面。由于生产一体化是通过生产的前向关联（扩向资源）和后向关联（扩向深加工）的扩充来实现的，不同部门之间的产品联系便成为公司空间格局重要影响因素，生产多样化所带来的公司扩张则不必考虑以上因素。公司内部增长的过程中，新设工厂的区位多经过认真规划，靠近现存设施布局，而通过吞并、合并而形成的外部增长情形却不同，这些新并入的公司（工厂）已经存在，不可能对其区位进行规划。尽管公司吞并扩张多从经济、资本和技术上考虑，但不少研究仍证明这些外部增长一般由公司中心向外延伸（Chapman and Walker，1987）。也正是这种延伸的趋势，使区域性公司先扩为全国性公司，再扩为多国公司、全球性公司。

在公司增长的地理研究中，一些地理学家试图从大量实例中概括出其一般空间模式。到目前为止，作者所见到的模式有以下一些，如沃茨的市场区域扩大模式（Watts，1980）、哈坎逊的全球扩张模式（Hakanson，1979）、泰勒的组织变异及区位演化模式（Taylor，1987）、迪肯的全球转移模式（Dicken，1986）等。这些模式，从不同方面揭示了公司从小到大、从单厂到多厂（或多国）的区位扩张过程。其中，沃茨的市场区域扩大模式和哈坎逊的全球扩张模式论述较为全面，现简析如下。

沃茨的模式是1980年基于英国酿造业的研究提出的（Watts，1980）。他假设具有一个酿造厂的城镇是均匀分布的。这些工厂被设定生产固定产品，服务它们自己的限定市场区。由于这些工厂所在城镇的人口规模不同，它们的市场区及工厂规模是不相同的。规模较大的工厂生产成本较低，从而使位于较大人口中心的工厂增长较快。在市场竞争的环境中，那些生产成本较高的工厂逐步被迫关闭，或被兼并。最终导致公司规模及市场范围扩大。对于这个模式，需要指出以下两点：①该模式的理论基础是假设生产的规模经济大于其规模不经济，这在一般条件下是可行的。②该模式基于饮料生产部门，这个部门在生产上规模经济十分突出，在销售上又面向个体生活消费者，市场与人口关系十分密切。其他一些或生产上规模经济不突出，或产品销售对象为其他工业公司的部门，其市场区域扩大和公司空间扩张的模式会有所不同。

哈坎逊的模式展示了公司从区域到全国再到多国的发展过程（Hakanson，1979）。与沃茨的模式不同，这个模式仅关注了单个工业组织的空间扩张，并不考虑与该工业组织同部门的其他公司的情形。哈坎逊认为，公司的空间扩张，是由于“当地市场的增长速度低于公司所期望的速度”（Hakanson，1979）。在这种情况下，公司首先在其初始区位以外建立销售机构和生产厂家，向其他区域的市场渗透。之后，通过销售代理商向邻国市场发展。随着销售上升，公司在主要国际市场上建立起自己的销售机构。进而，由于运输成本增加和国家间贸易壁垒的设置，使公司仅在国内生产难以供应不断增长的国外市场的需求，于是便开始在国外主要市场建立附属生产厂家。十分明显，在这个模式中，市场占领被看做公司空间扩张的主要动力。实际上，在某些情况下，保证原材料供应或接近原材料，借助廉价劳动力等因素均可引起资本输出。哈坎逊模型的普遍性也同样受到限制。但忽略一些细节或个别情况，以上两个模型还是可以在某种程度上代表公司增长的区域扩张过程的。

15.3.2　公司内部结构的空间意义

公司（尤其大公司）内部各部门按一定结构组合成一体。这些组成成分的空间分布，形成相应的公司地理结构。20 世纪 70 年代以来，对于公司地理结构的研究，从区域范围延伸至国际尺度，从对制造业部门的关注扩展到包括研究和开发、销售和服务等非制造业生产部门。

公司内部结构形式很多，可分为功能型、产品结构型、区域结构型和控股分公司型四大结构形式。公司在其总部（董事会和主要经理执行机构）之下，若分为生产、人事、研究、市场、财经等功能机构，称为功能型结构；若分为以产品名称称谓的生产机构，称为产品结构型结构；若分为以区域名称称谓的机构，称为区域型结构；若似子公司形式进行机构划分，则称为控股分公司型结构（Chapman and Walker，1987）。

不同结构形式的公司地理格局有明显差异。功能型结构和产品型结构的公司地理分布相对较为集中，区域型结构公司各部门地理分布最为分散，控股公司型结构则可以十分广泛，也可以较为集中。作者曾对澳大利亚两个类型公司的结构与其地理分布的关系作了调查。博格-沃纳（Borg-Warner）公司为典型的产品型结构，在其公司执行机构之下，分为翻砂、压铸、钢铸、变速箱、车轴、机动船舶产品等分部。在地理分布上，这些部门绝大多数位于悉尼都市区，以利于不同部门间上下游产品的加工联系。与此不同，古德曼弗尔德（Goodman Field）有限公司则属区域结构型，公司活动十分分散。该公司总部设在悉尼市中心，以下分为澳大利亚区域分部、新西兰区域分部、亚洲区域分部（分部设在新加坡）、日本区域分部和欧洲区域分部。该公司以食品加工为主，食品在运输和销售方面的特性决定了该公司各个区域部分生产基本相似的产品（各式面包、黄油、乳酪等）来满足当地市场的需求。不同分部之间，并不存在如博格-沃纳那样的生产联系。

15.3.3　公司与环境相互作用的研究

公司与环境关系问题是公司地理新近理论研究的重点。20 世纪 80 年代以来，一些地理学家专门对此进行了研究（McDermott and Taylor，1982；Clarke，1985；Taylor，1987）。这些学者们的工作多借助组织理论中的权变理论（contingency theory），权变理论把组织（如公司）看做是复杂大系统中的亚系统，这个亚系统的内部结构是在不断与环境相互作用的过程中逐步形成的。在研究中，该理论强调的是组织内部结构。与此相反，传统工业地理学研究中则重视组织与其以外环境间的信息流和物质联系的研究，而组织内部结构则被作为“黑箱”处理。如果把以上两者结合，则可相互补充，更好地揭示组织内部结构与环境间的相互作用。这正是公司地理研究的出发点。

在这方面，P. 麦克德莫特（McDermott and Taylor，1982）、M. 泰勒（Taylor，1987）和克拉克（Clarke，1985）等做了很好的研究。研究认为公司内部是由各分支部门组成的，由于各部门所掌握的技术能力及隶属关系不同，它们之间的关系是不平等的，它们与环境的相互作用程度也是不同的。公司的环境可分为目标环境（task environment）和环境域（environmental domain）。目标环境是指与所研究公司群。它们包括顾主类组织（所研究公司产品的使用者和推销者）、供给类组织（原材料、资本、劳动力、设备以及工作场地的提供者）、竞争类组织（同一产品生产者或同一原材料使用者）和管理调节组织（包括政府有关部门和工会等）。由于各组织的实力不同，它们与所研究公司内有关分支部门（或整个公司）的相互关系是不平等的，存在着控制与被控制之别和控制或被控制的程度之别。环境域是所研究公司运行的国内、国际的政治、经济环境。它包括国家政治体制、货币控制与国家干预政策、国民生产总值、通货膨胀率、国际贸易、国际收支、工业品市场、劳动力市场等。与目标环境不同，它是一种潜在的环境。由于各国状况不同，以及它们之间在政治和经济上的依赖或被依赖关系，它们与所研究公司的关系也不相同。这两种环境均作用于公司组织结构上。在与不同的环境相互作用下，公司结构的差异化加大（或部门分化加剧）。由于公司各部门所控制的技术能力及所在的控制等级不同，形成公司内部控制与被控制等级网络。基于环境、环境域及公司结构三维坐标，可以把公司各部门活动所占据的空间以及与公司各部门具体物质联系和信息流的环境勾勒出来。这样，既可以通过公司内部结构分析其对环境的影响，又可以通过各不同层次的环境分析其对公司内部结构的作用。

以上理论分析框架的基本点是组织内关系及与环境关系的非对称性和不均等性（Taylor，1987）。这在跨国公司内很典型。例如，美国跨国公司的总部，主要研究和开发机构设在美国的主要城市，主要子公司及次要研究和开发机构多位于欧洲，其他子公司位于大洋洲或拉丁美洲，合资企业或装配生产机构位于不发达国家。澳大利亚跨国公司情形则不同。其总部处于半外围地位的环境，子公司主要位于新西兰和其他太平洋岛屿诸国，近期开始在东南亚和欧洲等地建厂。第三世界跨国公司的总部则处于外围环境，子公司主要位于其他第三世界国家。这些不同类型的跨国公司内部各部门间、各部门与其环境间的控制与被控制关系不同，也对所在区域产生不同的影响。

15.3.4 公司活动与区域发展研究

尽管公司地理以公司作为研究对象，但由于活动均落实在一定区域中，公司活动与区域发展具有密切关联。常规的区域经济发展研究多以区域作为整体，根据官方或（和）研究者自己实际调查所得的数据，选定一些定量方法，揭示区域发展规律，确定区域发展方向、战略及规划。这种研究从许多方向揭示了区域经济发展的基本形式，其重要作用不可否认。但是这种方法却忽略了在区域发展中扮演重要角色的公司活动。有一些区域经济变化现象，从区域资源、技术、劳动力及政府政策等方面很难作出解释，它源于控制这些经济部门的公司的决策。而这些决策又来自区域（或国家）之外的公司总部。区域研究方法的这种缺陷，促使地理学家从公司组织角度探求区域经济发展。

本书作者在 1990 年完成的博士学位论文中在对前人工业区域变化研究成果评述的基础上，提出工业区域变化的组织分析法。作者认为，组织变化是工业区域变化的核心。所谓工业是由大大小小的公司（工厂）组成的，工业中的任何变化都应该是这些公司变化的结果：由于公司从某一个部门的转产（停产）或在某一部门的扩张（收缩），才引起宏观经济上的结构变化；由于公司的区位变更或在某地设立（关闭）其分支机构，才引起工业的空间格局的变化。当然，公司的决策又受一系列环境因素的影响，但是，包括国家政策、技术变化等在内的环境，只是起影响作用，并不能取代公司自身的决策权。再者，跨国公司或者全球性公司所考虑的是全球的工业环境，为了整体利益，它可使某一局部的分支机构在当地环境并无变化的情况下停止生产，或使某地工厂在无利润的情况下运行。很明显，除非研究公司的决策行为，否则很难真正弄清区域工业变化的过程和原因的（李小建，1990）。

15.4　开展适应中国国情的公司地理研究

15.4.1　中国市场经济发展对公司地理研究的需求

改革开放以来，在我国的优惠政策吸引下，外国公司在中国投资建厂的数量和资金额均不断增长。在沿海开放区和经济特区，外资、合资和合作企业已初具规模。地理学家对这些三资企业进行研究的领域很广。例如，公司内部结构及公司内各生产地环境的比较研究，我国经济发展的暂时落后状态和跨国公司内不平等处理所带来的损失，跨国公司技术转让的区域趋向等。要弄清外国跨国公司的投资区域趋向，弄清这些公司对我国投资在其公司总体格局中的地位，建议有关部门采取有效措施，或吸引更多的投资，或避免可能出现的资金撤离。我国的经济发展是一个开放系统，是可逆的和可反馈的双向循环，只输入而无输出便会失去稳定，引进外资与资本输出同时并进，是一种规律性的发展倾向。抓住机会向外投资，有利可图。例如，目前有许多国家钢铁过剩，钢铁厂被迫关闭，我国由于钢铁紧张，还引进外资、耗费巨资新建大钢厂。有人估算，如把我国投入宝钢的钱转向海外，可以买到五个宝钢（孙月平，1989）。因此，随着引进外资数量的增加，我国必然会加大对外的直接投资，建立具有一定竞争能力的中国跨国公司。进行公司地理的研究，可以对我国向外投资的区位决策提供有益的建议。我国已经逐步建立市场经济体系。多数中、小工业企业（公司）的发展，在很大程度上是遵循市场经济规律的。对于这些工厂（公司）的行为研究，从微观角度揭示公司发展的内在因素及环境因素，揭示工厂（公司）形成和增长的区域差异原因，会对我国工业发展起重要促进作用。改革开放以来，我国工业企业的横向联合发展很快。截至 2012 年年底，中国大型工业企业数量达到 63314 家（中华人民共和国国家统计局，2013）。这些工业公司的空间格局呈现什么特征呢？公司内不同分公司（工厂）间的空间关系如何？通过这些研究，可以揭示与市场经济下公司地理的差异，建立具有中国特色的公司地理框架。

在我国进行公司地理研究的意义可从多方面分析。

首先，自主经营的公司在经济活动中的地位日益重要。国有企业的公司制度改造时期逐步摆脱过去的行政干预，真正决策自主。“抓大放小”的举措，还促进国有控股大型公司、巨型公司的形成。我国利用外资的全球份额进一步提升，已列世界第二位，它们已在投资地经济发展中起着重要作用，而这些外资多以公司形式注册。在农区经济中占有重要地位的乡镇企业，随着竞争的加剧，多数也会建立现代企业制度。这些自主经营的公司行为，只有进行公司地理研究才可揭示。

其次，随着我国经济实力的提高和公司规模的扩大，一些中国大公司也会逐步扩大对外国的投资。这样，可以充分利用各国的资源优势，建立强大的中国跨国公司。进行公司地理研究，可通过对公司对外扩张一般区位规律和各地区位优势的分析，为这些向外投资的跨国公司提供区位决策战略建议。

最后，我国经济地理学受传统计划经济体制的影响较大，过去一直注重政府行为与相关经济地理现象的研究，而不关注（或不重视）公司微观行为。而现实中，公司是社会经济中最重要的单元。只有通过对公司的研究，才更易于解释经济地理现象的形成原因。加强公司地理研究还可以缩小与国际经济地理学界研究方法与思维方式的差距。从而，使更多的成果进入国际经济地理学术领域。

15.4.2　经济全球化研究的需要

最近几十年来，由于国家开放政策、技术发展、运输方式的改进等，经济全球化迅速发展。全球贸易的增长率远远大于世界经济的增长，跨国的资本流动迅速增加，技术传播遍布各种经济体，大公司跨国建厂、跨国兼并日益活跃。全球化的趋势不可逆转，今后将在更加平等和更注重可持续发展的基础上，赋予全球化新的内涵和活力。2013年，全球FDI流入增长了9%，达到1.45万亿美元，各主要经济体——发达经济体、发展中经济体和转型经济体FDI流入均有所增长，同时，全球FDI存量增长9%，达到25.5万亿美元（UNCTAD，2014）。迎合经济地理学的这种发展趋势，我国一些地理学家对中国变化的某些方面做了一定研究。这些研究多以区域统计数据为分析依据，在解释区域变化原因时，多从地理条件、国家及区域有关政策方面着手。外国跨国公司及国内大型公司对区域的影响均有一定限度。即使如此，企业变化的组织研究仍是十分重要的：①对企业组织的区域变化研究，尤其是通过对典型地区企业组织行为的问卷调查分析，可以揭示国家及地方工业政策与企业执行人员之间的统一和矛盾，对国家和地方政策提出改进建议；②通过企业区域变化与组织变化的比较研究，弄清怎样的组织形式才能带来较好的区域效果；③从长远利益及区域相对平衡发展考虑，国家常常有计划地支持一些落后地区的发展。通过对企业布局行为因素的综合分析，建议政府在规划时创造吸引企业的环境，可使政策行之有效；④研究外国公司在中国投资对所在区域工业变化的影响，引导其向有利方向发展。

15.4.3　经济地理学学科发展的需要

20世纪50年代以来，我国经济地理学的发展经历了50年代的照搬原苏联理论，“文化大革命”期间的学科荒废以及70年代以来引进西方传统地理理论的过程。由于我国公司地理学起步较晚，加之其他一些原因，在该学科的研究方法和思维方式上，我国与国际上存在着一定的差距。我们应不失时机引进国外经济地理学中新出现的可以为我所用的理论和方法，在中国的研究实践中检验、修正和提高。因此，在我国经济地理学中引进公司地理研究是十分值得考虑的工作。计划经济转向市场经济，政府角色也随之变化，经济地理学在研究中更应该关注市场主体，从中发现经济地理现象的形成机理，促使经济地理学学科的发展。

参考文献

李小建. 1990. 工业变化与公司活动：澳大利亚工业地理研究. 天津：南开大学经济研究所博士学位论文

孙月平. 1989. 论我国企业集团向跨国公司的转轨. 亚太经济，(5)：54～59

中华人民共和国国家统计局. 2013. 2013 中国统计年鉴. 北京：中国统计出版社

Chapman K, Walker D. 1987. Industrial Location. Principles and Policies. Oxford: Basil Blackwell

Clarke I. 1985. Spatial Organisation of Multinational Corporation. London: Croom Helm

Hakanson L. 1979. Towards a theory of location and corporate growth. In: Hamilton F E E, et al. Spatial Analysis. Industry and the Industrial Environment, I: Industrial System. Chichester: John Wiley & Sons

Hayter R, Watts H D. 1983. The geography of enterprise: A reappraisal. Progress in Economic Geography, 7: 157～181

Johnston R J, Gregory D, Smith D M, et al. 1986. The Dictionary of Human Geography (2nd Edition). Oxford: Blackwell

Mason C, Lloyd P. 1986. New manufacturing firms in a prosperous UK sub-region: The case of South Hampshire. In: Scott M, et al. Small Firms Growth and Development. Vermont: Gower

McDermott P J, Taylor M J. 1982. Industrial Organisation and Location. Cambridge: Cambridge University Press

McNee R B. 1960. Towards a more humanistic economic geography. Tijdschrift Voor Economische en Sociale Geografie, 51: 201～206

McNee R B. 1986. One respective on the enterprise perspective. In: Taylor M, Thrift N. Multinational and Restructuring of the World Economy. London: Croom Helm

Taylor M J, Thrift N. 1983. Business organization, segmentation and lactation. Regional Studies, 17: 445～465

Taylor M J. 1984. The Geography of Australian Corporate Power. Sydney: Cromm Helm

Taylor M J. 1987. Technological change and the business enterprise. In: Brotchie J F, et al. The Spatial Impact of Technological Change. London: Croom Helm

Ullman E L. 1953. Human geography and area research. AAAG, 43: 55～66

United Nations Conference on Trade and Development (UNCTAD). 2014. 2014 World Investment Report: Investing in the SDGs: An Acting Plan. New York and Geneva

Watts H D. 1980. The Large Industrial Enterprise. London: Croom Helm

第 16 章 工业区域变化的综合研究

工业变化是 20 世纪 80 年代后一段时间工业地理学的重点研究课题之一。1984 年，国际地理学联合会“工业系统委员会”为突出其研究特点，易名为“工业变化委员会”。对于此领域的研究，学者们或重视区域变化（Hamilton，1978），或注重工业结构变化及地理影响（Robins，1981），或注重工业环境及劳动力市场的变化（Linge et al.，1989）、或注重工业组织的变化（Taylor，1984）等。本章拟将工业组织与工业区域变化、工业结构变化的研究加以结合，以弥补在工业区域和结构变化研究中忽视组织决策因素，以及在工业组织变化研究中忽视区域整体的不足，试图为工业区域变化的研究探求新的方法途径。基于统计数据和实地调查资料，本章应用这种综合方法研究了 20 世纪 70～80 年代澳大利亚的工业变化，并对当时澳大利亚国家着力培育的增长中心模式失败原因进行分析。澳大利亚的实地数据来源于作者 1988～1989 年在当地的调查访问。

16.1 研究方法讨论

16.1.1 工业变化与工业组织变化

工业变化含义很广，它“被广泛解释为包罗在不同尺度（区域、区域间、国家和国际）上的工业的构成、规模和区域格局的各种改变及其过程”（Hamilton，1978）。实际上，这种“广泛”的解释仍不广泛，它遗漏了作为工业重要组成部分的工业组织。近十年之后，同一作者在另一著作中分析了工业及工业企业的组织结构变化特点及其地理意义（Hamilton，1987）。概括地说，工业变化应包括结构变化（工业在整个经济中的比例及工业中各部门的比例变化）、组织变化（工业组织调整、工厂开办与关闭等）和空间格局（区域）变化。

对工业结构变化、区域变化与组织变化的关系，不同分析者从各自的立足点及目的出发，有着不同的解释。一些学者认为，“结构变化包含着公司组织的变化”，组织变化和空间变化是结构变化的两个主要组成部分（Fagan et al.，1981）。这种观点迎合当今多数国家结构调整研究的潮流，把工业变化的所有方面都概括于结构变化之内。这种观点偏重经济学，轻视社会学；偏重宏观经济，轻视个别公司的作用。本章认为，组织变化工业变化的核心。所谓工业是由大大小小的公司（工厂）组成的，工业中的任何变化都应该是这些公司变化的结果：公司从某一部门转产或在某一部门扩张（停产等），才引起宏观经济上的结构变化；公司的区位变更或在某地设立（关闭）其分支机构，才引起工业空间格局变化。当然，公司的决策又受一系列环境因素的影响。但是，包括地理条件、政府政策、技术变化等在内的环境，只是起影响作用，并不能取代公司自身的决策权。

16.1.2 区域系统与工业组织系统

将工业组织变化与工业区域变化联系起来研究时，存在着两个系统不重合的现象。工业组织有其自身的系统，一个公司可以仅拥有一个工厂，也可有多个工厂；这些工厂可以集中于一个区域，也可以分散在多个区域、多个国家。区域也有其自身的系统，从小区到大区到全国到国家间；与工业组织联系起来考虑，区域可以仅有一个公司在此生产，也可以有多个公司在此生产。从而形成了一个区域有一个（多个）公司进行生产，一个公司可在一个（多个）地区进行生产的排列组合（图 6.1）。

这种区域与公司组织间的不重合性使区域工业变化研究复杂化。区域工业的发展仅从区域内各种环境条件上分析已不能揭示其内在原因，因为支配公司发展的决策来自于区域或国家外的公司首脑机构。这个首脑机构与该组织内各区域的工厂和有关组织间形成了一个实实在在的经济帝国。为了这个帝国整体的利益，某一局部的工厂可以牺牲利润，甚至有时在无利润的情况下运行。在分析方法上，区域与公司组织间的不重合性影响了规范定量方法的应用。例如，地理信息系统用于区域工业变化的分析十分有力，但对区域变化与公司的区域网络的联结分析，便有了一定困难。当然，也正是这种不重合性存在加强了从公司组织角度分析区域工业变化的重要性。对于用局部条件、国家和区域政策解释显得不太得力的工业发展变化，从公司的整体决策方面考虑便可十分顺利地给予解释。后面提到的日本三洋电器公司澳大利亚沃东加生产厂的关闭便是一例。

16.1.3 研究方法

在对工业变化研究文献分析的基础上，本章将有关地理学家的观点概括为两大类：一是区域方法（Hamilton，1978，1987；Rich，1981），即侧重于区域单元上的统计数据的定量分析（包括结构分析），并不追究与这一变化相关联（或引起这一变化发生）的工业组织变化；另一类是企业（公司）地理的研究（Taylor，1984；Taylor et al.，1982，1986），这些学者们侧重于工业组织（单个或多个组织）的变化、组织间联系、组织内部结构及其区域影响，并不考虑（或不重视）公司所影响的区域内的整体情况。换言之，前一方法侧重于工业变化的结果，另一方法侧重于工业变化的过程，如将两者结合，则可相得益彰，更好地分析解释工业的结构变化和区域变化。

基于这种思路，本章的研究是以工业的结构和区域变化为基础，即先把区域作为一个整体，根据统计数据和本人调查所得资料，选择有关定量方法，弄清这些变化的基本形式。之后分析引起这些变化的工业公司的变化。根据对公司的访问资料，揭示公司行为与工业结构和区域变化的关联，把微观分析与宏观分析融为一体。

16.2 澳大利亚制造业结构变化分析

16.2.1 逆工业化分析

本章选择制造业就业人数变化、制造业就业人数占各部门总就业人数比例变化、制造业增值变化，以及制造业增值占国内生产总值比例变化 4 个指标来衡量制造业的下降。为了便于把澳大利亚与其他发达国家进行比较，本章采用综合评判法将所观察的11个经合组织主要发达国家（美、日、德①、法、英、意、加拿大、比利时、瑞典、挪威和澳大利亚）的4个指标各分为11个等级，分别给予相应的权分，然后将各权分相加，将四个指标综合衡量得出各国制造业下降的相对地位。

计算结果表明，1966年至20世纪80年代以来，澳大利亚在经合组织的11个主要发达国家中制造业下降程度，仅次于英国、瑞典和比利时，而高于其他所有国家。这个制造业并不十分发达的国家，其制造业的下降处于十分突出的地位。

16.2.2　制造业内部结构分析

为进行制造业内部结构变化的比较分析，本章根据联合国工业发展组织的定义（UNIDO，1986），采用结构变化（θ）和专业化（S_pI）两个指数。其表达式分别为

$$\theta = \arccos\left\{\frac{\sum_i S_it \cdot S_i(t-1)}{\sqrt{\left[\sum_i S_i t^2\right] \cdot \left[\sum_i S_i\ (t-1)^2\right]}}\right\} \tag{16.1}$$

$$S_pI = \left\{1 + \frac{\sum_i S_i \cdot \ln S_i}{\ln n}\right\} \times 100 \tag{16.2}$$

式（16.1）和式（16.2）中，S_i（$t-1$）和S_i（t）分别为制造业部门i在$t-1$年和t_i年在制造业总体中所占的比例；S_i为制造业中部门i在制造业总体中所占的比例（以小数表示）；n为制造业内总部门数。

根据统计资料所计算的这两个指数的结果表明，20世纪70年代～80年代以来，澳大利亚制造业的结构变化程度仅次于日本和挪威，居前述11个发达国家的第三位。然而，结构变化的结果，却反映为专业化程度的下降。澳大利亚的专业化指数由1975年的12.8下降为1985年的12.0；其他国家中，除挪威外，专业化指数均有不同程度的上升。

进而，对制造业各部门的研究表明，20世纪70年代～80年代以来，澳大利亚制造业中增长最快的部门与西欧、北美和日本这三个世界主要工业中心均不同。1970～1987年，澳大利亚的纸张和印刷部门发展最快，而电力及非电力机械部门则处于下降状态（然上述三个主要工业中心该两部门均增长迅速）。研究结果还显示出澳大利亚制造业仍集中于世界市场出口萧条的部门；世界市场销售增长迅速的产品，澳大利亚却较少生产。制造业结构上的缺陷，无疑对澳大利亚制造业竞争力的提高施以影响。

16.2.3　结构调整中的汽车工业分析

面临制造业的不振局面，战后以来，澳大利亚各届政府均在不同程度上对制造业的调整和提高予以关注。20世纪80年代工党重新上台后，雄心勃勃对钢铁、汽车等在澳大利亚制造业中占重要地位的部门加以调整，制定了有关的发展计划。其中，“载人汽

① 本章仅观察了德国西部的4个指标。

车工业计划”的主要目标是提高生产效率，降低国产汽车价格。为达此目的采取了如减少汽车型号、增加研究和设计投资、降低进口限制等具体措施。1985～1988 年，该计划已实施三年。尽管澳大利亚的汽车出口量有所上升，国内产汽车型号有所减少，但分析表明，该部门的发展并不乐观。汽车生产量不升反降（由 1985 年的 38.7 万辆降为 1987 年的 31.3 万辆），汽车价格指数上升幅度远大于平均消费品指数的上升幅度，汽车出口量上升中又隐含着澳元对日元和西德马克的大幅度贬值的内在作用。事实使得澳大利亚联邦工商部长也不得不承认，澳大利亚制造业调整的结果是令人失望的（Garran，1989）。

16.2.4 通用-霍登汽车公司（GMHA）的案例分析

为了从微观角度揭示制造业调整中的困难，作者对澳大利亚历史最悠久且曾很多年称霸汽车市场的通用-霍登汽车公司（General Motors-Holden Automotive Ltd）进行了调查访问。由于该公司生产地分散，影响其生产率的提高，20 世纪 70 年代以来在日本汽车公司的竞争面前节节败退。为改善这种状况，该公司在 20 世纪 80 年代初开始了大规模的调整（包括关闭低效率工厂、减少雇员、引进现代化生产和管理手段等）。然而，调整却步履维艰。公司遇到了来自地方（州）政府、工人和工会等方面强大的阻力。作者曾详细考察了 1980 年该公司所属的悉尼佩吉伍德（Pagewood）工厂在关闭过程中各方争斗情况。在相持近两个月的时间内，工厂几乎处于瘫痪状态。这一年该公司汽车销售量比上年下降 21%，加上雇员失业补助金的连连升级，该公司出现了 1.3 亿澳元的年亏损最高纪录。在这以后的几次大调整中，该公司均遭受类似损失。1988 年，该公司汽车销售量降至历史最低水平。

根据作者对澳大利亚一些制造业公司和社会情况的调查，将微观上影响制造业发展的不利因素归根于其“低工业文化”。这些低工业文化包括：①来自农矿资源的收入支撑着社会生活水平的提高，淡化了人们在制造业上奋斗的意识。在雇主方面，要使 50%的澳大利亚厂家达到世界级竞争水平，需要把全国制造业平均生产成本减少 30%，占地空间减少 40%，库存减半，平均每一雇员的销售量翻一番（Roberts，1989）。显然，所有厂商必须大干一番才行。然而，许多公司或乐于目前处境或难以忍受调整之苦，不愿调整和提高。在雇员方面，大家都想得到报酬，而不愿通过竞争取得，只好有福共享；一旦调整减员，便群起反对。②科学研究和生产脱节严重。该国具世界科学研究能力的 2%，但是专利申报仅占世界的 0.7%，高技术产品则只有世界的 0.1%（Bennett，1986）。一些科学领域（如生物工程等），澳大利亚的研究和发明在世界上十分领先，但其成果却难以在国内生产，不少成果被卖到国外。③教育方面的资料表明，在经合组织的 19 个国家中，17 岁青年就教或接受培训的人员比率，澳大利亚居倒数第 4 位，比居第一位的日本（为 96%）低 37 个百分点（Ergas and Lee，1988）。这种状况影响工人技术水平的提高。④澳大利亚不少企业管理人员对市场反应不敏捷。例如，澳大利亚生产菠萝，却大量进口菠萝罐头；日本游客因买不到澳大利亚制造的纪念品（如销售的土著飞镖及玩具树熊，多为中国台湾和韩国制造），返回国时仍钱袋鼓鼓。⑤由于社会保险良好，澳大利亚人消费甚高，多将收入购置住房、家具、服装或外出旅游，较少考虑积累和投资（Colbatch，1989）。即使利率上涨和高收入所得税大幅度削减，私人积累兴趣仍十分低落（Shand et al.，1989）。

不可否认，澳大利亚远离其他竞争对手及主要市场、资源型经济及狭小的国内市场均制约着其制造业的发展。澳大利亚的特殊联邦制度、工资仲裁制度和工会组织等，也对制造业施以重要影响。作者以上对微观方面的分析意在弥补制造业发展中被人忽略了的内在障碍。

16.3　制造业区域变化分析

在制造业区域变化分析中，本章采用移动-份额（shift-share）技术。在对有关此方法研究文献（Edward et al.，1978）评鉴的基础上，选定以下五个计算式：

相对净移动（NS）：$NS=E^t-E\ (N^t/N)$　　(16.3)

结构移动值（IMS）：$IMS=e\,(n^t/n-N^t/N)$　　(16.4)

修正结构移动值（MIMS）：$MIMS=e^t-e^t\cdot n^t/n^t\cdot N^t\cdot N$　　(16.5)

部门结构修正移动值（IMMS）：$IMMS=MIMS-IMS$　　(16.6)

竞争移动值（CS）：$CS=NS-IMS-IMMS$　　(16.7)

式（16.3）、式（16.4）、式（16.5）、式（16.6）和式（16.7）中，e、e^t分别为某区内某制造业部门在研究时段初、终的就业人数；E、E^t分别为某区内所有制造业部门在研究时段初、终的就业人数；n、n^t分别为所有区域某制造业部门在研究时段初、终的就业人数；N、N^t分别为所有区域所有制造业部门在研究时段初、终的就业人数。

移动-份额分析的基本原理是将某时段内某区之增长（制造业总体或部门）与所有区域之总增长水平相比较，从而得出某区的得（高于总增长）与失（低于总增长）。其中，相对净移动值（NS）表明了制造业各区间的地位相对变化（得与失）；结构移动值（IMS）表明按初始年某区制造业各部门状况所期望的得失值；修正结构移动值（MIMS）表明按终止年制造业各部门状况经一定换算所求出的期望得失值；部门结构修正移动值（IMMS）为衡量某区制造业结构变化的指标，若该值为正，说明区内在某时段内增加（减少）了所有区域总增长较快（慢）部门的比例，若该值为负，则情况相反；竞争移动值（CS）为排除制造业结构因素之外的得失值，或称区域发展相对优（劣）势引起的移动值。

16.3.1　统计区间的制造业变化

按澳大利亚区域政策变化所划分的三个阶段（1972/3～1975/6，1975/6～1982/3和1982/3～1986/7）及澳大利亚统计局所划分的统计区计算所得的两主要制造业集中州（新南威尔士和维多利亚，见图16.1）制造业就业人数的移动-份额分析表明以下结果。

（1）制造业由都市区向农村地区的移动在第一阶段最为明显；之后的两阶段悉尼仍为主要移出区，但墨尔本变为移入区，农村地区的移入量也有所降低。

（2）三个阶段中，悉尼的移出和农村地区的移入均主要受竞争移动值影响；墨尔本

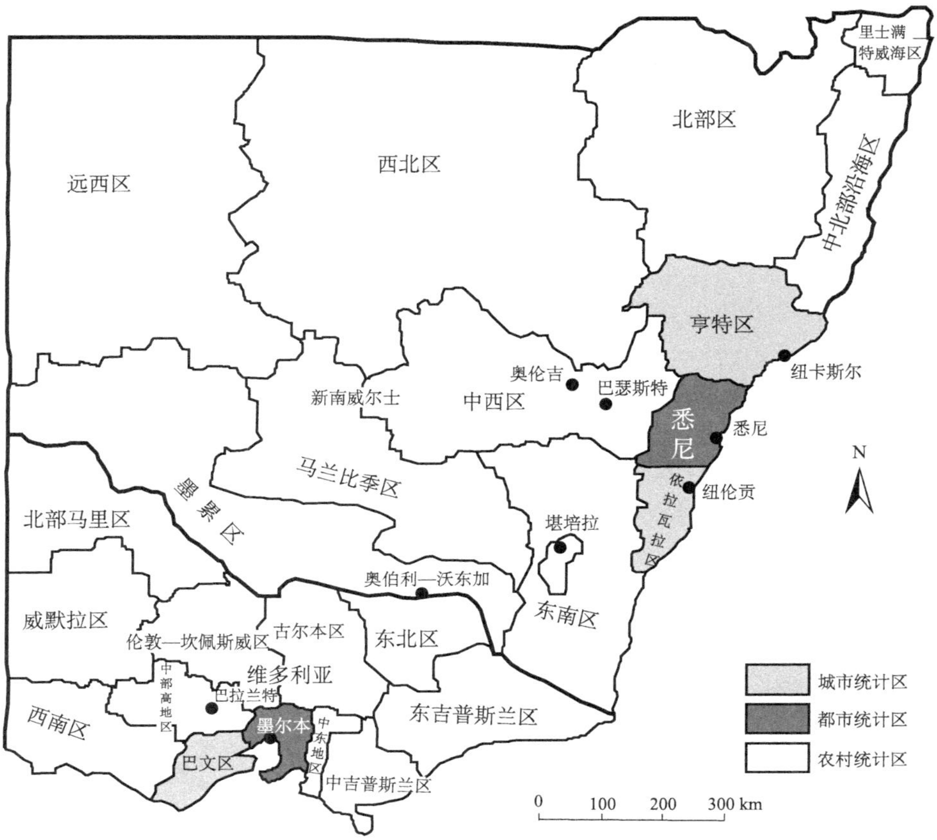

图 16.1　新南威尔士和维多利亚统计区及主要城市

第一阶段的移出和第三阶段的移入均主要受制于制造业结构状况。

(3) 前两个阶段，新南威尔士州各区的制造业多处于结构优势，而墨尔本区则相反；第三个阶段，新南威尔士的三个主要制造业区（悉尼、亨特和依拉瓦拉）处于结构劣势，墨尔本的制造业结构则处于有利地位。

与这些变化相关联的政府政策分析表明，第一阶段由于惠特兰政府热衷于分散化，不惜大量花费支持非都市区的发展，影响了制造业由都市区向非都市区的明显转移。1975 年自由党上台后区域政策的改变（削减对农村地区发展的援助），以及 1982 年工党重新执政后以部门政策取代区域政策，又减缓了上述区域变化趋势。1973 年工党政府对关税的大幅削减，使墨尔本受到较大打击（该区内高关税保护的服装、纺织和运输设备占较大比例）；而 1982 年以后工党政府的新的结构调整政策，又使墨尔本在结构上有所受益。悉尼区的净失，除受政策和制造业环境影响外，公司活动也起重要作用。

尽管在政府援助下非都市区制造业的地位有所上升，但直到 1986 年 7 月，两都市区仍集中了两州制造业就业人数的 78%（仅比 1972 年 3 月下降了 3 个百分点）。制造业空间分布过分集中的状况基本依旧。

16.3.2 非都市增长中心的实践分析

在澳大利亚非都市区的发展中，增长中心政策曾喧闹一时。20 世纪 70 年代工党执政期间，曾选择奥伯利-沃东加（Albury-Wodonga）、巴瑟斯特-奥伦吉（Bathurst-Orage）等近 10 个小城镇作为增长中心加以重点投资发展。其中，奥伯利-沃东加由新南威尔、维多利亚两州和联邦政府共同参与，在全国影响最大。

奥伯利-沃乐加和都市统计区、城市统计区、农村统计区①等 3 个类型区（图 16.1）3 个阶段（划分方法同前）的制造业就业人数的移动-份额计算结果表明：奥伯利-沃东加在 3 个阶段均为净得，其净得值占各阶段初始年制造业就业人数的比例分别为 44.5%、41.5%和 23.5%；两大都市区（悉尼和墨尔本）在三个阶段均为净失，其净失值占各阶段初始年制造业就业人数的比例分别为－1.34%、－1.26%、－0.9%。非都市增长中心随着政府及民众关注和经济援助水平的下降而逐渐增长缓慢，以及都市区下降幅度也明显变小；政府在增长中心花费巨大，而其实际增长距原定目标又相去甚远（1985 年该区制造业就业人数不足原定目标的 1/2）；其他增长中心不但没有按奥伯利-沃东加的“经验”而发展，反而相继销声匿迹，甚至连奥伯利-沃东加本身也逐渐被人搁置（1989 年国家地方政府部决定将该区发展问题交回当地政府负责）。一些事实表明，奥伯利-沃东加是一个失败的发展模式。

16.3.3 公司活动与制造业区域变化

在对奥伯利-沃东加这一典型地区制造业公司组织变化调查之后，作者进行了工厂关闭与开办、工厂的区位选择因素和典型公司的活动等方面的分析。各年份工厂开办与关闭的资料表明，政府优惠政策使区域经济显现出的活力随着优惠程度的降低而逐渐减退：近年来工厂的关闭数逐渐接近于新设工厂数。作者对百人以上工厂（分公司）的调查问卷结果表明，75%以上的工厂经理人员认为国家及州政府对该区区域发展援助停止后，再没有百人以上大厂在此建立。这从公司组织分析角度支持着前述本章对增长中心的结论。

为了揭示公司决策对小区域经济发展的影响，作者对日本三洋电器公司及其沃东加生产厂进行了个案研究②。日本三洋公司 1973 年在澳大利亚建厂，两个因素起着主要作用：一是当时彩电刚刚打入澳大利亚市场，需求看涨；二是澳大利亚政府的保护政策，尤其是对 18 英寸以上大屏幕彩电的进口限制③。这样，公司要想占领澳大利亚市场，就必须在此建厂。该公司之所以建厂沃东加，被认为是由于该地居于两大市场（悉尼和墨尔本）之间和具有一定质量的劳动力（Sydney Morning Herald，1981）。但经分析，作者认为政府的援助和在工薪、土地税等方面的优惠，以及新发展区较弱的工会组

① 都市统计区指两州首府所在统计区；城市统计区指两首府外以城市区人口为主的三个统计区；农村统计区包括以上五统计区以外其他统计区。

② 三洋澳大利亚有限公司财务经理布·山道尔（B. Sandel）先生在资料上给予帮助。

③ 据澳大利亚产业援助委员会信息，20 世纪 70 年代初澳大利亚与日本政府间秘密签订有自动出口限制协议（VER），迫使日本政府限制大屏幕彩电出口澳大利亚（IAC，1984）。

织有利于日本式管理，似乎起着更为重要的作用。

三洋沃东加厂建立后到 1976 年间，生产一直上升，就业人数达 385 人的高峰。之后，便逐步下降。最后于 1987 年 12 月完全停止生产。

沃东加厂的生产变化是澳大利亚市场环境变化和三洋公司，全球决策变化的共同反映。就市场而论，澳大利亚彩电需求趋于饱和，尤其对大屏幕彩电的需求下降甚快；三洋沃东加厂专门生产 18 英寸以上大彩电，必然首当受挫。此外，消费者逐渐偏好现代化的塑壳电视，而沃加东厂只生产木壳电视机，正与此相背。同时，澳大利亚市场狭小，却有 6 家（20 世纪 70 年代）大型跨国公司在此生产；竞争之下，或此或彼，必然引起一些生产厂家关闭。而澳大利亚政府对彩电进口政策的改变，也加重着在澳生产厂家的危机。该国彩电进口关税从 20 世纪 70 年代到 80 年代下降了 20 个百分点，且对来自发展中国家的产品免税，自动出口限制协议也被取消。这对跨国公司在发展中国家生产彩电进口澳大利亚市场，提供了便利条件。

在澳大利亚市场变化的同时，世界其他地区的彩电市场也在发生变化。在发达国家，市场有所收缩，并偏好于现代化、多样化的彩电；在发展中国家，彩电需求上升迅速。同时，各大彩电公司间的竞争也在加剧。为了在竞争中获胜，三洋公司逐步减少生产厂家，以集中技术力量进行高水平、大规模的生产。生产厂家何取何舍，又联系着各地的市场环境。前面分析的澳大利亚市场的变化，有许多不利于在此集中生产的因素。例如，要改变大型中小型彩电生产线，成本甚高；本身市场规模较小又远离其他主要市场，大量投资未必有利可图。同时，亚洲新兴彩电市场扩展甚快，且潜力很大。公司在接近亚洲市场的区位投资，既可就近占领亚洲市场，又可利用廉价运输和关税优惠，将产品输入澳大利亚，仍不失澳大利亚市场。同样原因，三洋公司在 20 世纪 80 年代中期还关闭了其在新西兰的生产厂家，以及世界其他地区的两家生产厂。而该公司的新加坡厂生产能力得到扩充，技术手段得以改进，作为澳新及东南亚诸国的主要彩电供应者。

三洋沃东加厂的不断收缩和关闭对增长中心的制造业冲击很大。其他机器及设备部门从 1981 年之后便一直处于下降之中，就业人数到 1986 年降到最低点。由此引起的失业者不得不到都市区其他有关工厂谋生。

16.4　结论与讨论

尽管 20 世纪 70 年代以来澳大利亚的工业变化受到国家工业结构政策和区域政策的影响，但是本章的研究表明，政府的结构调整政策及区域政策均没有实现政策制定者所预期的目标。澳大利亚的制造业在继续衰退，全国制造业极度不均衡分布的状况依然存在。

政策的不成功离不开澳大利亚的特殊工业环境。在这种环境中所衍生的一系列问题是很难在短期内解决的。例如，本章通过微观研究所揭示的低工业文化因素潜移默化，根深蒂固，政府根本不敢采取强硬措施来加强竞争，刺激工业发展。如果一旦这样做，政府将会失去选票而下台。区域间的不平衡发展，是公司对生产环境选择的结果。实践表明，人为地创造非发达区域的优惠生产环境，并不能真正促使这些区域的快速发展。

随着政府援助的停止，这些区域所呈现的一时繁荣也逐渐消失。

本章对澳大利亚工业发展的政策建议可简括为：①面对经济（尤其是工业）消沉的事实，澳大利亚政府应在经济发展和社会福利的选择中强调前者。在产业援助上，应把重点放在该国在世界上处于相对优势地位的资源加工型部门上，以较深入加工、较多增值的产品打入国际市场，形成其"拳头"产业。在区域发展上，应根据该国条件，着重于发挥区域潜力：政府对区域的援助应和区域本身发展潜力大小相一致。②亚太地区经济联系的日益发展以及澳大利亚与其他亚太国家发展条件的互补性，表明澳大利亚只有加强与亚太国家尤其是中国的经济联系，才能在经济上出现新的生机。

通过本章对澳大利亚工业变化的研究，作者认为将定量分析与组织微观分析相结合的研究方法是行之有效的。这种方法一方面提示了仅用统计数据定量分析所难以观察的公司组织行为特征，使工业变化的研究更具深度；另一方面，把公司活动放在广泛的工业结构和区域变化背景中，展现了政府区域和结构政策与单个公司决策之间的矛盾。抓住这种矛盾，可使地理学的研究更具政策参考意义。

尽管这种研究方法是以发达资本主义国家为背景，但它并不意味着仅仅适用于这类国家的情形。中国改革开放以来外国公司投资的增加，以及国内市场经济范围的扩大，使得工业地理学研究中对工业组织行为分析显得日益重要。例如，通过对区域工业组织行为的问卷调查分析，可以提示政策与工业企业决策者意向的统一与矛盾；通过对工业区域变化与组织变化的比较研究，可弄清怎样的组织形式才能带来较好的区域效果；通过对工业企业布局行为的综合分析，建议政策在规划时创造吸引企业的环境，促使落后地区工业资源优势得以发挥。当然，由于社会制度及工业发展环境的差异，这种方法的具体应用也应有所不同。

参 考 文 献

Bennett R. 1986. Australian Society and Government. Sydney：M. N. &B. Book Company

Colbatch T. 1989. Culture's fatal role in the economic decline of America. The Age，10-26

Edward J A，Harniman K F，Morgan J S. 1978. Regional growth and structural adaptation：A correction to the Stilwell modification. Urban Studies，15：97～100

Ergas H，Lee T. 1988. Industrial competitiveness and restructuring. The Australian Quaterly，60：94～108

Fagan R H，McKay J，Linge G J R. 1981. Structural change，the international and national context. In：Linge G J R. Structural Change in Australia：Some Spatial and Organizational Responses. Canberra：Department of Human Geography，ANU. 1～50

Garran R. 1989. Industry slower to respond than Senator Button thought. The Age，10-7

Hamilton F E I. 1978. Industrial Change. International Experience and Public Policy. London：longman

Hamilton F E I. 1987. Industrial Change in Advanced Economies. London：Croom Helm

IAC. 1984. Certain Consumer Electronic Equipment and Components No. 339. Canberra：AGPS

Linge G J R，Knaap G A. 1989. Labour，Government and Industrial Change. London：Routledge

Rich D. 1981. Structural Change in Australian manfacruring：An analysis of employment and productivity. In：Linge G J R. Structural Change in Australia：Some spatial and Organisational Responses. Canberra: Department of Human Geography, ANU. 143~188

Roberts P. 1989. Too many manufacturers back off from restructuring. Financial Review, 10-5

Robins P A. 1981. The regional impact of structural change in Australian manufacturing industry. The case of South Australia. In: Linge G J R, eds. Structural Change in Australia: Some Spatial and Organisational Responses. Canberra: Department of Human Geography, ANU. 189~218

Shand A, et al. 1989. What the world really thinks to our economy. The Weekend Australian, 8-12~13. P23~25

Sydney Morning Heral. 1981. The Albury-Wodonga 1981. A Special Herald Report. 6-2

Taylor M J, Thrift N J. 1982. The Geography of Multinationals. London: Croom Helm

Taylor M J, Thrift N J. 1986. Multinationals and the Restructuring of World Economy. London: Croom Helm

Taylor M. 1984. The Geography of Australian Power. Sydney: Croom Helm Australia

Unido. 1986. Industrial and Development. Global Report 1986. Vienna: UNIDO

第 17 章　跨国公司对区域经济发展的影响

随着日益增进的经济活动国际化，区域经济发展与世界经济的联系日益密切。由于跨国公司活动（尤其是跨国投资）在其中起的重要作用，跨国投资与区域经济发展关系已成为现代经济地理学研究的主题之一。在经济活动国际化的背景中，20 世纪 90 年代以来跨国直接投资向发展中国家的转移，令人注目（Ostry，1995）。总部设在瑞士日内瓦的联合国贸易和发展会议公布《全球投资趋势报告》的数据显示，2014 年中国成为全球外国投资的第一大目的地国，也是中国自 2003 年以来首次超越美国跃居世界第一[①]。本章根据跨国投资、组织结构、区域发展等方面的理论，以及包括中国在内的一些国家的研究实例，对跨国公司与区域发展之关系做一些理论探讨：①根据相邻学科的理论并基于前人的研究成果，提出跨国公司对区域经济影响、跨国公司与区域关系，以及两者关系的决定因素三层次研究思路；②以生产链、组织链和所有权关系三个关联系统和区域等级关系作为跨国投资的理论背景，导出跨国公司-区域综合分析方法；③跨国投资对区域发展影响具广泛性、层次性、区域性、多面性、差异性和时间性特点，跨国公司与投资地关系具互补性、竞争性和变化性特点，影响两者关系的主要因素为社会政治背景、结构状况和相对地位。

17.1　跨国公司与区域发展研究的理论背景

17.1.1　跨国公司对投资地的影响与两者联系

跨国公司对投资地经济发展的影响，涉及众多方面。1986 年，迪肯（Dicken）基于一些国家的实例，总结出以下 6 个方面：资本和金融、技术、贸易和产业联系、产业结构和企业家能力、就业、依赖和经济扭曲（Dicken，1986）。对于像中国这样的特殊类型的国家，跨国公司活动对其经济体制的转变和法律制度的建立也有一定影响（Li，1997）。从地理角度，由于投资活动分布的区域差异，将导致区域经济发展水平差异的变化。此外，其他与跨国公司活动发生直接或间接关联的领域，多少均会受其影响。

上述诸方面的影响，是投资者与投资地诸参与方相互作用的产物。跨国公司在投资活动中，与投资地政府有关部门、合资者、同类生产企业、生产关联企业、服务性企业等均发生一定联系。通过这些联系，各方相互作用，以其利用对方为自己牟得利益。尽管跨国公司在一地区投资的目的并不是为了促使区域发展，但当地各参与方为其利益而参与的结果，一方面扩大了投资影响的范围；另一方面，促成了对当地有利的影响效应。

---

① 参考消息网．2015．中国吸引外资规模跃居第一 2003 年以来首超美国．http://news.163.com/15/0131/09/AH9F50U700014AEE.html．2015-1-31。

17.1.2 三种联系系统

跨国投资看似简单，实际上综合着相互交错的多种关系系统。由于现代管理制度下管理权与所有权相分离，公司的空间组织包含着：不同组分之间的组织关系系统，即管理上的等级系统；生产关系（所有权关系）等级系统（Massey，1984，1995）。这两种关系都有地理轨迹。不同组分间可以是一国之内，也可以是多国之间的空间关联。如果说这种分析主要侧重公司内部的话，将视角扩大到公司之外，公司各组分还与其外部各组织机构（个体）之间产生关联。产品市场如此（Scott，1986），生产活动也不例外（Dicken，1994）。据此，本章认为，对于任一区域的跨国投资，均可以从生产链、组织链和所有权关系三方面进行分析（图 17.1）。

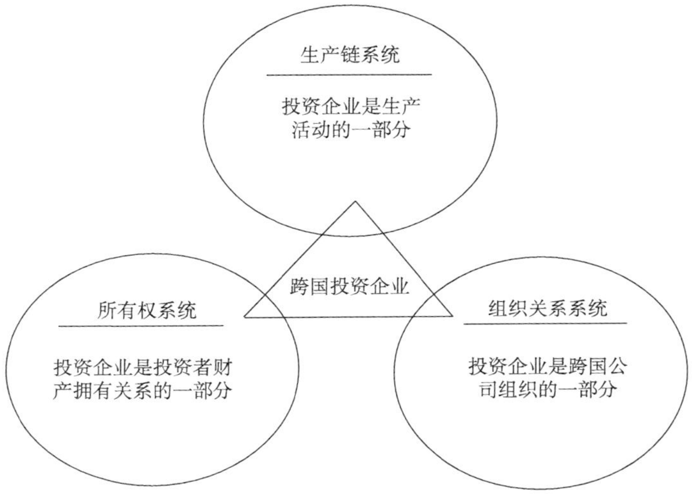

图 17.1 跨国投资企业的三种联系系统

1. 生产链（生产与销售活动关系系统）

跨国投资是跨国公司生产活动的一部分，所建工厂（或其他机构）为相关产品生产过程的一环节。从原材料、运输、逐次加工、组装，到制成品的销售，以及研究与开发和其他服务活动，每一环节均为成品提供相应的增加值（故又称增值链）。这些活动可以在公司内进行，也可在公司间进行。由于不同生产阶段具有不同条件要求，又由于不同区位地理条件存在差异，如果生产链上不同阶段的生产活动与各地区区位要素优势相配合，便可获得最大效益（Massey，1995）。这只是问题的一个方面。考虑劳动分工与各地条件，决不可忽视不同生产阶段在空间上必须联为一体才能完成生产过程（Walker，1988）。生产链中内部地理联系与各阶段的区域环境外部联系相互作用，是分析跨国公司与投资区域关系的背景之一。

对生产系统进一步探讨，可发现其内外部关系的非均等性。迪肯总结了诸多学者对生产网络的不均等性研究，认为被不同公司控制的生产系统各部分之间，有控制与被控制之别（Dicken，1994）。与此相关，被一公司所控制的生产联系各方，也并非均等。

在生产链系统中，投资企业与当地企业的生产联系状况，可作为跨国公司对投资地影响的重要标志之一。广泛和高强度的联系，可产生较高的乘数效应，利于刺激当地经济综合发展。否则，“飞地性”的外资企业对当地经济影响则十分有限。

2. 所有权关系系统

资金投入状况决定着跨国投资的拥有关系。外资企业可由一家或多家公司拥有（包括与当地的合股拥有），由此形成的拥有关系系统也简繁不一。这些拥有关系可通过在公司董事会中的地位，影响投资企业的重大决策。

按照马克思主义观点，所有权关系决定社会关系。据此观察空间上相互分离的跨国投资，可以借用空间化社会关系（spatialised social relations）概念（Massey，1995）。这样，所研究的空间上的所有权关系，便变成了权力关系地理、控制与被控制地理、影响与被影响地理。跨国公司总部控制着所拥有的全部生产设备，监控着所拥有的全部监控等级系统；而位于投资地的分支机构，则处于受控地位，其决策权和经济活动范围均有一定限制。

3. 组织链（组织关系系统）

跨国投资建立的机构，是跨国公司组织的一部分。在管理上，它与公司内其他机构有着一定联系。尤其是与公司总部、研究与开发机构（R&D），以及相关的生产机构的联系更为密切。通过这种联系，决定其在跨国公司网络中的地位。考虑公司网络系统的多层次性［如总部、管理机构、生产单元等（Dicken and Lloyd，1990）］，以及各层次的内、外部联系差别，可有助于投资企业的联系和地位分析。

公司内部结构还可以被看做是劳动技术分工中互相分离的劳动过程，以及与此相配合的管理机构的混合体（Scott，1986）。Taylor 认为，技术是“势力”（power）的重要标志之一（Taylor，1987）。这样，投资企业所掌握的技术状况便成为其在公司中地位的决定因素。一般而论，公司的核心是技术发明与控制部门，而具体进行生产活动的工厂则处于外围地区。

近年来，一些学者对以财产所有关系为依据来定义公司组织的界限提出怀疑，认为公司没有明确的边界。公司只是关系网中心的密集网络（Badaracco，1991）。跨国公司是“来自同一战略决策中心的合作生产手段，而这种合作使其跨越国界”（Cowling and Sugden，1987）。显然，这些学者更强调合作的作用，而不是财产所有制。这并不与我们的三种联系系统观点相矛盾，只是基于合作关系的组织关系系统，有时会包含前述的生产链系统（由于合作多与生产关联有关）。

17.1.3　区域等级关系

以上围绕投资主体的分析，只是问题的一个侧面。由于投资活动必发生于地理空间上，接受投资地状况具同等重要的讨论意义。一般而论，跨国投资企业所在地区在该国家中的地位，以及该国家在世界经济中的地位，均影响着跨国公司与投资地的关系。

区域之间的等级关系，克里斯塔勒的中心地理论（Christaller，1966）及其后人有关研究［如廖什（Losch，1954）等］已有阐述。这些理论基于对市场、运输和行政管理等的分析，认为以中心地为代表的区域之间存在着功能等级差别。高等级的区域拥有多种类型经济活动，或具有高层次的管理职能；而次级区域则具有较少和较低层次的经济活动，在政治或经济上受制于高一级的区域。这种功能划分是多层次的，其具体层次视不同区域状况而异。

与此种理论不同，梅西将空间看做是“该经济的相互交错的、差异的社会关系的产物”（Massey，1995）。这种分析强调区域之间的生产关系联系。与常规的用经济增长、就业等指标分析区域的观点不同，这种分析的结果更深入地揭示了区域之间的内在联系，尤其是势力关系（控制与被控制关系）。例如，按就业和经济增长指标，一些老工业区（老经济发达区）要滞后于新兴工业区；但从生产关系观点来看，新兴工业区的资金多来自老工业区，技术上也依赖于后者，故两者关系上老工业区仍起主导作用。

基于以上讨论，作者提出用政治、经济和社会关系三维坐标系，来讨论区域之间的关系（图 17.2）。任意两个区域之间，均可通过其在坐标系中的位置，表明相互关系。例如，区域 B 在政治地位上高于区域 A（$Y_2>Y_1$），经济实力和社会关系上也明显起主导作用（$X_2>X_1$，$Z_2>Z_1$），区域 B 对区域 A 的控制作用十分明显。然而，现实世界中，区域之间的关系十分复杂。有的区域仅在某一（两）方面起控制作用，在其他方面受制于对方。以区域 B 和区域 C 为例，区域 C 具较高政治地位，而其经济地位和社会关系均受制于 B 区域。因此，两个区域之关系，很难决然断定，要视研究目的而做进一步讨论。但一般而论，较高的经济地位和良好的经济基础更有利于加强与投资企业的经济联系。

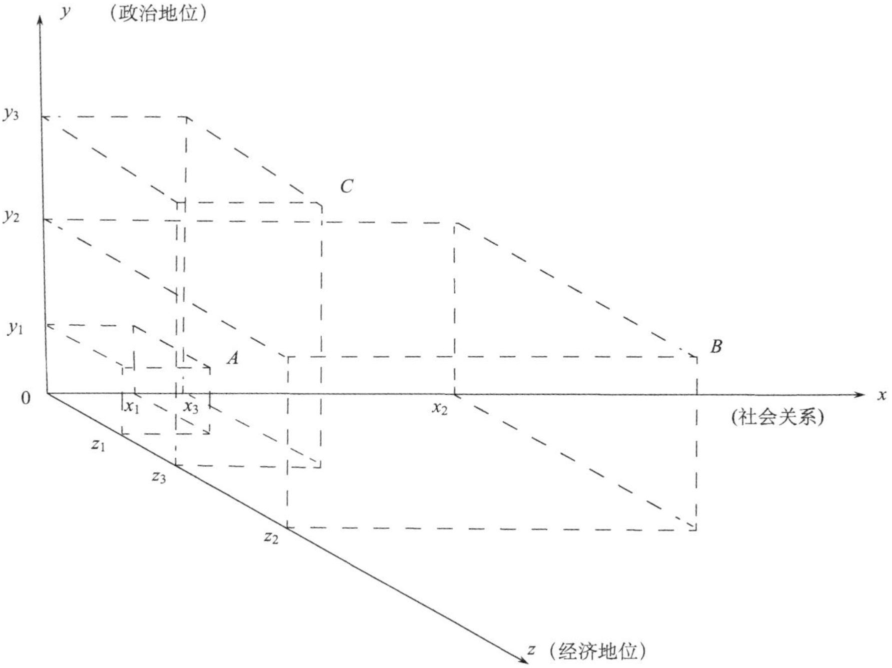

图 17.2 区域等级关系

17.1.4　跨国公司——区域综合联系

对照以上跨国投资企业关联系统和区域等级关系系统的讨论可以看出，跨国投资企业处于两类系统相结合的关键部位。区域系统可通过与跨国投资企业的联系，介入国际或全球生产系统；跨国公司通过投资企业与当地区域系统的联系影响区域生产活动，最终达到获取最大效益的目的。进而，两类系统均离不开地理空间。两者的区位之间是否具有一定相关性呢？

根据这种思路，可以构建组织-空间等级关系模型。Hymer 等的研究认为，跨国公司趋于将高级决策机构集中于发达国家的主要城市，将次一级管理功能集中于区域性中心，将生产活动分布于外围地区（Hymer，1972；Morgan and Sayer，1983）。尽管有人怀疑这种模型的普遍适用性，但纵观世界大型跨国公司的空间格局，相当高比例的跨国公司总部集中于少数城市。纽约、东京和伦敦为最重要的集中地，围绕着这三个中心为世界三大经济发达区的次一级中心（Dicken，1992）。这里仍集中一定的跨国公司总部或区域性总部。第三世界发展中国家，明显处于边缘地区。一国之内，区域之间也存在同类格局（Morgan and Sayer，1983）。可以认为，跨国公司空间结构与区域等级之间的这种相关性，可适用于多数情况。

尽管这种讨论并未涉及所有权关系系统和生产链系统，但一般而论，大都市区常汇集财富拥有者，外围区则以低收入阶层为主，故可以做出相应推理。就生产链而论，由于不同类型生产活动差别很大，似乎并不存在特定类型的控制区域，但信息和技术集中区的地位应更重要。

17.2　跨国投资公司与区域发展的关系

17.2.1　跨国公司对投资地影响特点

1. 广泛性

前已述及跨国公司影响投资地经济的很多方面。实际上，这些具体影响方面很难给予全面的概括。不少研究提出新实例。例如，影响基础设施（Kueh，1992）、区域差异（或城乡差异）（Buckwalter，1995；Urphy，1992）、自然环境和房地产价格（Ferrao，1994）、经济法律制度（Potter，1995）等。未来的研究，仍会发现前人所未曾涉及的方面。承认这种影响的广泛性的同时，还应看到不同区域、同一区域不同跨国公司之间，并非各种影响处于同等重要地位。

2. 层次性

根据与投资企业的关系，这种影响可有直接和间接之分。凡通过与投资企业直接联系（包括原料、燃料联系、半成品、零部件联系、劳动力及服务联系、信息联系、技术联系等）产生的影响，为直接影响；其他各种通过中间机构而产生的影响为间接影响。间接影响还可依据所通过的中间机构的多少，有层次之别。例如，一家跨国投资的汽车厂，需要与当地轮胎厂发生直接联系，由此产生相应的多方面直接影响；轮胎厂生产的增长，带动橡胶厂的发展；进而橡胶厂带动橡胶种植业和橡胶回收部门等的发展。尽管外资汽车厂对橡胶厂和橡胶种植业均产生间接影响，但它们位于不同的层次上。

3. 区域性

跨国投资常集中于某些区位上。发展中国家多集中于主要经济中心，尤其是全国首都和地方中心城市（Herrin，1987；Singh and Choo，1981）、沿海发达区（Li，1997；Leung，1990）。发达国家情况有所不同。欧洲不少国家的外资趋于城市区位，尤其是大都市区（Quevit and Dicken，1994）；而美国的外资则主要集中于人口规模较大的州和距离投资者较近的州（O'hUallachain and Reid，1992），其中，有些部门（如汽车工业）的外资企业位于非都市区，以利用农村劳动力（Mair et al.，1988）。投资企业的区域性，必然带来对投资地影响的区域性。

4. 多面性

跨国公司投资为城区带来的积极影响不容置疑。但是，其投资的目的是为了公司的利益，并非意在促进区域经济发展。其经济活动的结果，不可避免地会为区域带来负面影响。以就业影响为例，投资企业确实可直接吸纳一定的就业人员，间接带动相关企业就业人员的增加；但是，外资企业的建立也会取代一些原应由当地企业提供的就业机会。一般以出口为主的投资企业与当地竞争不太明显，而以占领国内市场为目的投资企业则会有明显的取代效应。服务业部门外资企业对当地就业的取代性也较大（O'Malley，1994）。其他如资金流入与资金回流，促进经济发展与转移价格避税①，技术引进与技术对外依赖（如只引进技术，不引进如何开发这种技术；尤其在第三世界国家，很少建立 R&D），积极的经济效果与消极的环境效果，贸易增长与外贸不平衡，规模经济与二元结构（Dicken，1992）等现象并存，也证实了跨国投资区域影响的多面性。

5. 差异性

首先，不同源地的跨国公司具有不同的区域格局。发达国家如此（O'hUallachain and Reid，1992；Harrington et al.，1986），发展中国家也如此（Leung，1990；Rogerson，1982）。不仅这种格局本身影响区域发展，而且不同源地跨国公司受本国政治、文化和经济结构的影响，在对区域的影响上也会不同。例如，港资公司利用亲属关系在珠江三角洲发展转包活动，促进了当地经济发展（Leung，1993），而美欧在中国投资则不具有如此特征。其次，公司规模、投资战略、所属产业部门所带来的影响的差别也很明显。大型跨国公司拥有较高技术水平，投资规模一般较大，且多具战略意义，故在同等情况下，其区域影响要比小型跨国公司大和长远；从公司投资战略和区位取向看，

① 据美国国会 1990 年研究，有半数以上外资企业 10 年内未付所得税。据估计有 350 亿美元的税收通过转移价格流失。

有服务当地市场和服务全球市场、市场取向和生产要素取向之分（Dicken et al.，1994），这些差异会在其区域影响中体现出来；就部门而论，投资于快速增长的产业（朝阳产业）要比投资于缓慢增长或衰退的产业（夕阳产业）具更大的区域影响。最后，在经济水平较高的地区，跨国投资易于借助广泛的联系，扩散其影响（Dicken et al.，1994）。以技术性影响为例，日本跨国公司对外投资的R&D机构，90%左右位于发达国家，其余位于新兴工业化国家（如新加坡、泰国等）（Florida and Kenney，1994）。相反，在不发达地区，多为加工型生产活动投资，技术扩散十分有限。

6. 时间性

跨国投资的区域影响程度，随着投资企业建立的时间而发生变化。一般情况下，经过一段时间后，投资企业可进一步熟悉当地环境，从而扩大其对当地经济的影响（Dicken et al.，1994）。此外，早期的跨国投资主要集中于某些特殊区位［如中国的经济特区、墨西哥的北部边境地区（Bagchi and Wheeler，1989）、美国东北部地区等］，其区域影响也主要限于少数地区。不过，投资企业的区位，随着时间而变化。例如，美国外资1979～1983年向南部和西部扩散（Bagchi and Wheeler，1989）；20世纪80年代后期，外资的空间扩散仍在继续（O'hUallachain and Reid，1992）。中国的港资也出现由南向北、由沿海向内地逐渐扩散的现象（李小建，1996）。随着这种区位变化，必然带来区域影响范围的扩大。

以上6个特点为前述理论分析的具体化。广泛性来自于跨国投资企业的错综复杂联系，层次性与生产链有关，区域性和差异性为区域系统（区域条件）与生产系统、组织系统相互叠置的产物，多面性则是跨国公司与区域目标利益不一致而又相互作用的结果。

17.2.2　跨国公司与投资地的关系

1. 互补性

跨国公司和区域各具有一定优势，而这种优势又为对方所需求。从而形成双方的互补关系。这正是其相互作用和建立联系的基础。例如，跨国公司拥有投资地所需的技术、管理专长、资金及市场营销能力等，投资地拥有跨国公司所需的市场、自然资源和劳动力等（Dicken et al.，1994）。跨国公司力图通过投资建立分支机构，以获取投资地的资源、占领该市场；区域则希望通过跨国投资为其带来所需的跨国公司优势。

在现实世界中，这种互补关系十分复杂。首先，跨国公司和区域对对方资源的需求程度并非等同。有时跨国公司对在某区域投资的需求性更强，有时区域对跨国公司投资更为渴望。前者可以德国大众汽车公司企图通过建立工厂进入美国市场为例（Dicken et al.，1990），后者的例子在我国不少地区均有存在。其次，在多数情况下，以上双方对对方的需求均有可替代性。例如，跨国公司投资可在多个区域选择（除非某区域拥有特殊资源，如特殊矿藏、特殊地理位置优势等），区域对资金的需求也并非仅限于外资来源或外资中某个跨国公司。这种替代性一方面减缓着对对方的依赖，另一方面通过多方相互作用，增加了跨国公司与区域之间互补关系的复杂性。

2. 竞争性

跨国公司在区域投资的目的，要么为了获取利润，要么为了获取特定资源，要么为了未来发展战略，总之是为了公司整体上的最大利益。区域引进外资的目的，则是为了弥补资金不足，提高技术水平，增加劳动就业等，总之是为了区域的利益。双方为各自的利益而竞争，最后达到双方都可接受的结果。当然，这种结果并不是双方利益的绝对折中，会有一方做出较大让步，另一方获得较大利益。

早在 20 世纪 80 年代初，McDermott 和 Taylor（1982）就提出企业组织与环境之间的不平等关系。跨国公司投资地的各参与方，组成该公司的局部运行环境。它们与跨国公司之间的关系也是不平等的。在一定情况下，总有一方起支配作用。支配地位的形成不仅与其掌握的，而对方又急需的资源状况有关，也受对方限制因素的影响（Dicken，1994）。究竟跨国公司与区域谁占支配地位，还难以给出一般性结论。有的学者指出，“政府作为群体确实已经失去了与多国公司的交易势力（bargaining power）”，国家之间的竞争加剧成为减弱其交易势力的重要作用力（Stopford et al.，1991）。地方社区在许多全球事务中，变得十分无力。地方有关机构除了提供吸引外资环境，促使当地公司加入跨国公司网络之外，其他可作甚少（Dicken，1994）。而在跨国公司网络中，当地公司很少有可能成为合作伙伴的主要成员，只不过处于被支配地位（Schoenberger，1991）。与这些观点相反，Gordon 认为，“跨国公司并非都十分强大，它们自己也不具备实力形成新的世界经济格局”（Gorden，1988）。公司之间的竞争加剧，也导致单一公司的交易力量减弱（Stopford et al.，1991）。这些观点的正确性及适应条件，还待以后实例研究进一步证实。

3. 变化性

跨国公司与投资地的关系随时间而变化。首先，全球经济环境、生产系统和跨国公司组织结构均在不断变化着。在西欧、北美和西太平洋沿岸三大经济中心格局中，后者的地位不断上升。1980～1993 年，东亚和西太平洋沿岸国人均 GNP 年平均增长速度达 6. 4%，远远超过世界各主要区域（World Bank，1995）。快速增长的趋势增加了这些区域对跨国公司的吸引力；经济实力的提高加强了其对跨国公司的交易力量。而生产系统和跨国公司组织，国际化的趋势越来越明显。甚至有人认为，按这种趋势发展下去，将不会再有国家产品、国家技术、国家公司和国家工业（Reich，1991）。这些变化，均带来跨国公司与投资地关系的相应变化。其次，跨国公司在区域的投资时间也改变着两者的关系。多数研究认为，跨国公司在一区域注入资金建立分支机构之后，其对区域的交易势力会逐渐下降，而当地政府的交易力量则会上升（Dicken，1994）。当然，也有人持不同观点，认为跨国公司的相对力量可随时间而增强（Kobrin，1987），这种分歧有多种原因，产业部门差异可为原因之一。例如，投入于自然资源开发型或大型基础设施型项目，会出现前者的情况，而投资于技术变化迅速的部门，则会证实后一观点。不管如何，从宏观、中观和微观角度，两者关系均在变化。

17.2.3 影响跨国公司与投资地关系的主要因素

1. 社会政治背景

跨国公司与投资地关系隐含着国家间的关系。跨国公司的跨国投资活动影响本国的对外政治和经济战略（Dicken，1994）；反过来，国家的政治、经济战略不仅影响跨国公司的投资去向，也会加强或减弱与投资地交易时的势力。在接受投资方，国家对外开放政策也起着同样的作用。而投资地政治的稳定和社会的安定，也会加强其对跨国公司的交易力量。此外，熟悉对方社会文化特点，在两者关系中也十分重要。例如，理解中国的“关系学”可促使投资者在与当地交易中获益，提高经营效果（Luo，1995）。

2. 结构状况

投资地经济和技术结构影响跨国投资企业与当地经济的联系。一般来说，发达地区经济技术结构易于使跨国投资企业与其联为一体，不发达地区则比较困难（Dicken et al.，1994）。例如，外国在美国一些地区的投资在很大程度上依赖当地的投入和市场（O'hUallachain，1984），投资区域便具有一定交易条件；反之，美国在墨西哥边境投资与当地经济结构无甚联系，其投入品及市场均在美国（South，1990），跨国公司便拥有较强交易条件。就跨国公司结构而论，垂直一体化联系较强者，难以与当地建立供应联系（Dicken et al.，1994）；反之，主要从事生产链中部分经济活动的跨国公司，在生产过程中必须与其他公司发生联系。在一定条件下，易于与投资地企业建立联系。跨国公司的具体结构十分复杂。如果将其简化为 4 种类型：生产分工结构（附国际部）、全球生产分工结构、全球地理分工结构和全球矩阵结构（Dicken，1992），那么，全球地理分工结构最易于与当地建立联系，全球生产分工结构则正与此相反，其他类型则介于两者之间。与当地的密切联系，一方面有利于地方经济的发展，另一方面也通过供求关系，增加地方对跨国公司的影响。

3. 相对地位

跨国公司与投资区域的经济实力、社会影响等，是决定两者关系的另一重要因素。有些大型跨国公司拥有超过 100 亿美元的资产和超过 100 亿美元的年营业额（Business Week，1996），其经济实力和社会影响超过世界大多数国家。这些公司在与国家（区域）交易中，往往财大气粗，具有相当优势。它们常会控制与投资地的关系。当然，国家（区域）的地位也不一样。有些国家经济实力雄厚，在世界上具重要影响；有些区域具有特殊的资源和市场。它们在与跨国公司的交易上并不会过分让步，最终可达到对其有利的结果。与大跨国公司比较，小跨国公司尽管也拥有资金和技术，但不具有特殊威慑力量。除非投资地对外资需求心切，它们在与投资地关系上不会明显控制对方。不过，由于具体情况复杂多样，特定区域两者的关系还应具体分析。

综合以上对两者关系特点和主要影响因素的分析，我们可参照 Gabriel（1966）的思路，将区域可以接受的外资条件（R）表示为愿意投资的跨国公司数量（F）、外资的特殊贡献（C）和区域对跨国公司的竞争地位（P_1）等的函数，即 $R=f$（F，C，$P_1\cdots$）。而跨国公司可以接受的条件（T）则为对外投资需求（I）、可以投资的区域数量（N），以及跨国公司对区域的竞争地位（P_2）等的函数：$T=f$（I，N，$P_2\cdots$）。两函数在某时点的均衡点便是该时点上两者相互关系的状态。

17.3 结论与讨论

跨国公司对区域经济影响的研究，对区域发展、区域规划和政策制定均有重要意义。然而，这种影响只是两者互相作用关系的一种体现。两者关系在理论上受生产链、组织链和所有权关系，以及区域等级系统的制约，在实践上具有互补、竞争和变化特点。三个特点的综合体现便是关系的非均等性。给定条件下，两者的联系中总有一方起支配地位。这一点可通过实例进一步证实。进而，何种条件决定这种支配地位，目前的研究结果并未给予回答。本章提出的社会政治背景、结构状况和相对地位 3 个主要影响因素，也只是初步地探索。由于进入中国的外国投资和区域经济发展的特殊关系，基于中国实例的进一步研究会对有关理论的形成起十分重要的作用。

研究跨国公司与区域发展的关系，涉及地理以外其他一些学科的理论，如国际经济和贸易理论、跨国公司组织理论、管理科学理论等。对这些有关理论不可照搬。要弄清真正涵义而为我所用。此外，其他学科对中国外资投资做了不少工作。尽管这些工作多以数据初步分析和描述为主，深层次的个例研究、区域研究很少见到，但仍可对进一步研究提供背景知识。在特定区域的研究中，一方面应特别注意通过典型企业调查分析微观上外资对区域影响、跨国公司与区域发展关系的真谛；另一方面，要把投资企业放在跨国公司的国际大背景之中。

通过以上的初步探讨，结合中国近年来引进外资的实践，提出如下建议：①各地方政府急于引进外资，甚至区域之间竞相出台优惠条件，易于被跨国公司所利用，从而提高其在两者关系中的地位。应引起有关机构注意。②投资企业与当地结构的关系十分重要。为此各地应注意投资部门在生产链中的地位，优先引进后向关联广泛而密切的生产企业，尽量少引进投入品主要靠进口的投资项目。③中国市场潜力巨大，经济增长迅速，并拥有跨国公司所需求的资源（如劳动力、自然资源等）。因此，不管跨国公司采用全球化战略、市场占领战略，还是要素取向战略，均会把中国作为主要投资目的地。认识这一竞争有利地位，各地在引进外资时要有自信心，不必做出太大让步。④为了提高与跨国公司交易时的实力，我们要保持政治稳定、经济开放，并逐步按国际惯例健全法律体制。此外，各地要了解跨国公司的社会经济背景和投资战略，以利用对方达到区域发展的目的。

参考文献

李小建. 1996. 香港对大陆投资的区位变化与公司空间行为. 地理学报，51（3）：213～223

Badaracco J L. 1991. The boundaries of the firms. In：Etzioni A，et al. Social-economics：Towards a New Synthesis. Armonk：M. E. Sharpe

Bagchi-sen S, Wheeler J O. 1989. A spatial and temporal model of foreign direct investment in the United States. Economic Geography, 65 (2): 113～129

Buckwalter D W. 1995. Spatial inequality, foreign investment, and economic transition in Bulgaria. The Professional Geographer, 47 (3): 288～298

Business Week. 1996. 1996 was one for the books: America's most valuable companies grew even more valuable. Business Week, 3-25

Christaller W. 1966. Central Places in Southern Germany. Englewood Cliffs: Prentice-Hall

Cowling K, Sugden R. 1987. Market exchange and the concept of attransnational corporation. British Review of Economic Issues, 9: 57～68

Dicken P, Lloyd P. 1990. Location in Space: Theoretical perspective in Economic Geography (3rd Edition). New York: HarperCollins

Dicken P, Quevit M, Savary J, et al. 1994. Strategies of transnational corporations and European regional restructuring: Some conceptual bases. In: Dicken P, Quevit M Transnational Corporations and European Regional Restructuring. Utrecht: N G S

Dicken P. 1986. Global Shift: International Change in a Turbulent World. London: Paul Chapman

Dicken P. 1992. Global Shift: The Internationalization of Economic Activity (2nd Edition). New York: Guilford Press

Dicken P. 1994. Global-local tensions: Firms and states in the global space-economy. Economic Geography, 70: 101～128

Ferrao J. 1994. TNC operation and host regional economies: A typology for Portuguese case. In: Dicken P, Quevit M. Transnational Corporations and European Regional Restructuring. Utrecht: N G S

Florida R, Kenney M. 1994. The globalization of Japanese R & D: The economic geography of Japanese R & D investment in the United States. Economic Geography, 70 (4): 344～369

Gorden D M. 1988. The global economy: New edifice or crumbling foundations. New Left Review, 168: 24～64

Grabriel P. 1966. The investment in the LDC: Asset with a fixed maturity. Columbia Journal of World Business, 1 (3): 113～120

Harrington J, Burns K, Cheung M. 1986. Market-oriented foreign investment and regional development: Canadian companies in western New York. Economic Geography, 62 (2): 1551～1566

Herrin A N, Pernia E N. 1987. Factors influencing the choice of location, local and foreign firms in the Philippines. Environment and Planning A, 21: 531～541

Hymer S H. 1972. The efficiency (contradictions) of multinational corporation. In: Paquet G. The Multinational Firms and the Nation-State. Don Mill: Collier-Macmillan

Kobrin S J. 1987. Testing the bargaining hypothesis in manufacturing sector in developing countries. International Organization, 41: 609～638

Kueh Y Y. 1992. Foreign investment and economic change in China. China Quarterly, 131: 637～690

Leung C K. 1990. Locational characteristics of foreign equity joint venture investment in China, 1979～1985. The Professional Geographer, 42 (4): 403～421

Leung C K. 1993. Personal contact, subcontract linkages, and development in the Hong Kong-Zhujiang region. A A A G, 83 (2): 272～302

Li X J. 1997. Foreign direct investment and its impact on China's economy: A research appraisal. The Journal of Chinese Geography, 7 (1): 33～45

Losch A. 1954. The Economics of Location. New Haven: Yale University Press

Luo Y. 1995. Business strategy, market structure, and performance of international joint venture: The case of joint venture in China. Management International review, 35 (3): 241～264

Mair A, Florida R, Kenney M. 1988. The new geography of automobile production: Japanese transplants in North America. Economic Geography, 64 (4): 352～373

Massey D. 1984. Spatial Division of Labour: Social Structures and the Geography of Production. London: Methuen

Massey D. 1995. Spatial Division of Labor: Social Structures and the Geography of Production (2nd Edition). New York: Rout ledge

McDermott P J, Taylor M J. 1982. Industrial Organization and Location. Cambridge: Cambridge University Press

Morgan K, Sayer A. 1983. The International Electronics Industry and Regional Development in Britain. University of Sussex, School of Urban and Regional Studies: Working Paper 34

Murphy A B. 1992. Western investment in East-Central Europe: Emerging patterns and implications for state stability. The Professional Geographer, 44 (3): 249～259

O'hUallachain B, Reid N. 1992. Source country differences in the spatial distribution of foreign direct investment in the United States. The Professional Geographer, 44 (3): 272～285

O'hUallachain B. 1984. Linkages and foreign direct investment in the United States. Economic Geography, 60 (3): 238～253

O'Malley E. 1994. The impact of transnational corporations in the Republicof Ireland. In: Dicken P, Quevit M. Transnational Corporations and European Regional Restructuring. Utrecht: N G S

Ostry S. 1995. Investment: The engine of transformation of the global economy. Business and the Contemporary World, 3: 126～138

Potter P B. 1995. Foreign investment law in the People's Republic of China: Dilemmas of state control. China Quarterly, 141: 155～185

Quevit M, Dicken P. 1994. Transnational corporations strategies and regional restructuring: Some lessons from the experience of EU countries and Central and Eastern European countries. In: Dicken P, Quevit M. Transnational Corporations and European Regional Restructuring. Utrecht: N G S

Reich R. 1991. The Work of Nation: Preparing Ourselves for 21st Century Capitalism. New York: Vintage Books

Rogerson C M. 1982. Multinational corporations in southern Africa: A spatial perspective. In: Taylor M, Thrift N. The Geography of Multinationals. London: Croom Helm

Schoenberger E. 1991. Globalization and regionalization: New problems of time, distance and control in the multinational firm. A A A G in Miami

Scott A J. 1986. Industrial organization and location: Division of fabor, the firms, and spatial process. Economic geography, 62 (3): 215～231

Singh M S, Choo C S. 1981. Spatial dynamics in the growth and development of multinational corporations in Malaysia. In: Hamilton F E I, et al. Spatial Analysis, Industry and the Industrial Environment, II. Chichester: John Wiley & Sons. 481～507

South R B. 1990. "Transnational" Maquiladora. A A A G, 80 (4): 549～570

StopfordJ M, Stranger S, Henley J S. 1991. Rival States, Rival Firms: Competition for World Market Shares. Cambridge: Cambridge University Press

Taylor M J. 1987. Technological change and the business cycle. In：Brotchie J F，et al. The Spatial Impact of Technological Change. London：Croom Helm

Walker R. 1988. The geographical organization of production-system. Environment and Planning D，6：377～408

World Bank. 1995. World Development Report 1995：Workers in an Integrating World. Oxford：Oxford University Press

第18章　跨国公司对区域经济差异的影响

众所周知，跨国公司（TNCs，Transnational Corporations）的直接投资会对投资国的经济发展产生影响。这种影响可能体现在东道国内的投资区域和其他区域的区域差异方面。跨国公司如何影响投资国的区域经济差异？跨国公司进入所产生的影响会加剧东道国经济发展的区域不平衡状况吗？对于这一问题，不同的学者持不同的观点。基于马来西亚（Singh and Choo，1981）、波兰、捷克斯洛伐克和匈牙利（Murphy，1992）、西班牙（Marquez，1994）和越南（Nestor，1997）的实证分析表明：跨国公司（TNCs）加剧了原已存在的区域差异；而Buckwalter对保加利亚的实证分析并没有提供支持上述结论的证据（Buckwalter，1995）。此外，O'Malley的研究揭示了20世纪70～90年代中期，外国直接投资倾向于减缓爱尔兰不同地区间工业化水平的差异（O'Malley，1994）。Dunning通过对西欧和北美一些国家的分析，认为跨国公司的区位策略对一个国家区域经济差异的影响因各国的具体情况不同而不同（Dunning，1993）。

中国是世界上第二大外国直接投资接收国（UNCTAD，1996），自从改革开放以来取得了快速的经济增长。由于其各地经济发展历史和基础条件都差别巨大，原本就存在较大的区域差异。改革开放以来，各地引进外资和经济增长又具有明显差别（胡鞍钢等，1995；陆大道，1995；覃成林，1997）。鉴于此，中国可作为研究跨国公司投资对区域经济差异影响的很好案例。

跨国公司投资影响着所投资国的区域经济差异。国际相关研究依据不同的国家实例得出不同的结论。本章作为20世纪末的研究成果，通过对中国的数据分析，认为跨国公司投资与中国区域经济差异之间存在着特殊关系：在开始的一段时间内，跨国公司投资缩小区域差异；之后，扩大区域经济差异。再后，随着跨国公司投资区位的变化，其影响也会发生相应的变化。本章提出跨国公司投资对投资国区域经济差异的影响处于变动之中的观点，对相关政策制定具有一定借鉴意义。

18.1　分析框架和研究方法

本章所使用的分析框架基于这一相关假设：跨国公司投资分支机构所在区域受到的影响大于其他地区。由此，需要弄清跨国公司是否有利于有关地区的经济发展。如果得出肯定的结论，那么跨国公司子公司的地理集聚可能会给这些地区带来很大的好处；跨国公司投资于发达地区会加剧国家内部的区域经济差异状况；反之，对区域差异状况会有所改善。然而，通过撤资和建立新工厂，跨国公司从中心区域向外围区域迁移会改善区域经济差异的状况。

然而，这种影响本身并不是静止的。跨国公司和东道国的讨价还价是动态的（Dicken et al.，1994），经过初始投资之后，谈判权的平衡会从一方移向另一方。随着这种变化，跨国公司将会更多或更少地融入当地的经济发展。因此，跨国公司与当地经济联系状况是另一个需要考虑的重要因素。

18.1.1 入境跨国公司的影响

通过直接投资，跨国公司可能对东道国的经济产生多方面影响。譬如，资本和金融、技术、贸易和贸易联系、产业结构和企业家精神、就业等（Dicken，1992）。此外，外国直接投资可能会增强比较优势，优化资源配置，提高技术效率及实现规模经济和范围经济（Young et al.，1994）。它也可能改善发展中国家的基础设施状况（Kueh，1992），促进以市场为导向的计划经济国家进行经济、制度和法律改革（Zhan，1993；Lardy，1994；Potter，1995）。这些影响可以通过跨国公司分支机构购买原料、零件和服务等直接联系进行扩散（Dicken，1992；Lan and Young，1994；Williams，1996；Kueh，1992）。然而，如果东道国政府在国家层面上实施本地政策进行干预（ILO，1981；Dicken，1994）及区域层面上经济发展水平和经济结构发生变化，那么这种状况会有所不同。

这种影响也存在着消极的方面。例如，所投资地区的资本收益可能主要体现在金融和财政方面；通过跨国公司所传递的技术可能并不适用于当地需求。更重要的是，外国跨国公司的高度参与将会削弱东道国的主权和自治权，同时也可能会“掏空（hollow out）”当地的经济。跨国公司会对东道国产生净收益还是净支出仍然是一个尚未解决的问题，对此不同的学者有不同的观点（Dicken，1992）。近期研究似乎更有利于跨国公司，尤其在东道国政府对跨国公司抱有敌意的地方也出现同样的结论（Lall，1993）。大多数政府对外国直接投资都表示欢迎（Dunning，1994），有学者认为“外国投资可以在任何一个国家的经济中发挥重要的积极作用”（Wang，1995）。但仍有少数国家并未为吸引外国直接投资进行周密部署（Glickman and Woodward，1988）。一些基于中国的实证研究强调，外国直接投资对中国经济发展具有重要贡献，同时认为其对中国经济发展具有一些消极影响（Kueh，1992；Zhan，1993；Lan and Young，1996；Cheng，1995；Leung，1993；Potter，1995；Lardy，1994；Zhang，1994；Wang，1995）。

18.1.2 跨国公司投资的区位

一般情况下，跨国公司倾向于在东道国的中心或者是较为发达的地区布局其子公司。一方面，跨国公司在这些地区可以较为便捷地获取信息，进而可以削减其高昂的交易成本（Williamson，1985；O'hUallachain and Reid，1992）；另一方面，这些地区具有如高质量的劳动力、高水平的技术和较高的增长潜力等其他有利的条件（Quevit and Dicken，1994）。除去中心地区之外，边境地区是另一个吸引跨国公司布局的地区（O'hUallachain and Reid，1992；South，1995）。

第三种跨国公司优先考虑布局的区位是与投资者具有较为亲密且可信赖的私人联系的地区，这种联系在决定跨国公司区位模式中起着重要的作用。对跨国直接投资在中国（Leung，1990，1993；Smart and Smart，1991；Li，1996；赵景华，1994）和东盟国家（Yeung，1997）的特定地区和区域的空间模式进行分析时发现，这种布局尤为明显。上述三种所提到的跨国公司布局的决定性因素，和有关的政府优惠政策一起，导致外国直接投资高度集中在中国东部沿海地区和东南沿海地区。与其他地区相比，这种不均匀的分布使得跨国公司布局的地区可以从跨国公司的投资中获取较多的利益。

18.1.3　区位迁移以及影响因素

跨国公司改变其区位会受到许多因素的影响。如果跨国公司对所在国家的投资机会更加熟悉或了解，它们可能会在更大的可能范围内使用更为精确的标准来选择新的投资地区。事实上，跨国公司所在地区的产品和市场状况决定着一个跨国公司的现有业务，而这些状况是动态变化的。此外，政府实施的新政策，尤其是那些针对特定区位的政策，通常会有效地说服外国公司进行区位迁移（Dunning，1993）。基于上述这些因素，跨国公司对区位改变所做出的回应可以减弱外国直接投资的地理集聚（Glickman and Woodward，1988）。

时间，同样也是一个关键的变量，它可以影响跨国公司和所在地区的关系。跨国公司投资需要花费一段时间才能和本地企业之间建立联系，尤其是后向联系（Dicken et al.，1994）。经过一段相对较长的时间之后，这种示范效应可能会更强。跨国公司将会继续去适应和发展它们的关系网络（Edgington，1995），反过来这种关系网络会对它们与投资地之间的关系产生影响。例如，在爱尔兰的国外高技术企业变得更多地融入本地经济的发展（O'Malley，1994）。

Ozawa（1992）基于许多国家的案例分析提出了一个“外商直接投资促进发展的动态范式”的假定。在他的模型中，跨国公司促使一个具有丰富劳动力资源的发展中国家通过一系列发展阶段，发展成为一个工业化的国家。随着一个国家这样的发展过程，较高的资本集约度会使其经济活动获得更多增加值。因此，本地企业和位于较为发达国家的跨国公司可能会把它们的现有业务迁移到欠发达国家其他低成本地区。虽然一个国家内复制发展阶段并非毫无问题，但是构成这种发展框架的基本理念应当是具有一定的普遍意义。

18.1.4　研究方法

研究外商直接投资对东道国区域影响主要是基于可获取的数据运用统计分析进行（Glickman and Woodward，1988；O'hUallachain and Reid，1992；Murphy，1992；Buckwalter，1995）。这种方法可以方便地绘制出外国直接投资的区位图和区位变化模式图，但这种地图并不能展示出跨国公司活动和投资地企业或东道国其他区域企业之间的关系。公司调查或访谈可以修正这一缺陷。因此，本章尝试使用“双重方法”，将统计分析和公司访谈信息相结合的方式对此进行研究。

18.2　外国直接投资与中国区域经济发展差异

18.2.1　跨国公司和外国直接投资

本章提到的跨国公司是指一个在至少两个国家（包含本国）进行经营的公司。根据这一定义，任何由中国以外的公司进行投资参股的都可以被称为跨国公司分支机构，这包括来自香港、澳门和台湾的公司，因为当前这些投资的资源在中国被归类为境外资本。而来自跨国公司的直接投资构成了外国直接投资的主要部分。

跨国直接投资的数据在统计出版物和其他官方渠道中较为稀少且难以获取。中国对外经济贸易合作部仅仅公布了一个大型外商投资企业（FIEs）的年度清单（中国对外贸易经济合作部，1985，1986，1992～1996）。下一节将使用我们自身调查的数据来讨论跨国公司的影响。与此同时，这些统计数据对于展示外商直接投资在中国区域经济发展中的作用提供了一个广阔的视角。正如 Dicken 所指出的那样，除去一些限制条件，外国直接投资数据显示了跨国公司活动的变化模式（Dicken，1994）。

18.2.2　对经济发展的重要贡献

在国家层面上，外国直接投资对中国经济发展的重要性在相关实证研究中已经被证实（Kueh，1992；Zhan，1993；Wang，1995）。Wang（1995）认为在资金补充、技术转移、对外贸易和企业管理等方面可以明显地看出外国直接投资对中国经济发展的贡献，这种贡献对于中国的现代化非常重要。在中国经济活动中，外商投资企业已经成为一个重要的组成部分。此外，外国直接投资对中国经济最重要的贡献在于它进入中国时带来了一种着重强调竞争、效率和自由市场的全新思维方式。基于增长模型的定量分析也表明外国直接投资对中国经济增长的贡献大体上是积极的（Wang，1995）。

外国直接投资高度集中在中国沿海省份和直辖市，尤其是上海、北京、天津、广东和福建。在 1979～1995 年间这些地区的人均累积外国直接投资是西部省份的数倍（图 18.1）。因此，外国直接投资对这些地区的经济发展具有更为重要的影响。表 18.1 表明了外国直接投资对中国 5 个经济特区（SEZs）、15 个沿海开放城市（OCCs）① 和广东省的一些影响。在过去的 10 年中，这些地区已经成为外国直接投资的主要接收地，在 1979～1995 年，它们分别集聚了全国实际累积外国直接投资的 16.22%、29.76%、30.66%。这些地区的外国直接投资在总固定资产投资中占有较高的比重，且这一比重高于全国平均水平，所占比重较高的地区是（所有）沿海开放城市（OCCs）和广东省，而经济特区（SEZs）更是高过全国平均水平约 2.3 倍。在厦门、北海、汕头和福州等城市，外国资本的贡献实际上已经成为主导。然而，外国直接投资对资本的形成，不仅沿海地区和内陆地区有所不同，而且在沿海开放城市之间也有所差异。在温州、宁波、连云港和秦皇岛等城市，由于它们早期较低的经济发展水平、外部联系的匮乏以及其他相关因素等，使得这些城市的外国直接投资在总体投资中占有较低的比重。

1995 年，外商投资企业对工业产值、出口和就业的贡献在许多城市较为明显，经济特区和广东省比其他地区更为显著（表 18.1）。这主要是由于两个方面的原因：一方面，城市和地区的地理位置。很明显地，外商投资企业占工业总产值（GVIO）、进出

① 在 1984 年，中国中央政府提出了 14 个沿海开放城市。1987 年，威海市，一个烟台市行政区划内的县级水平的城市被提升至地级市，与烟台市相当。此后，沿海开放城市的统计数据就将威海市包含在内（统计信息交流大会秘书处，1991）。

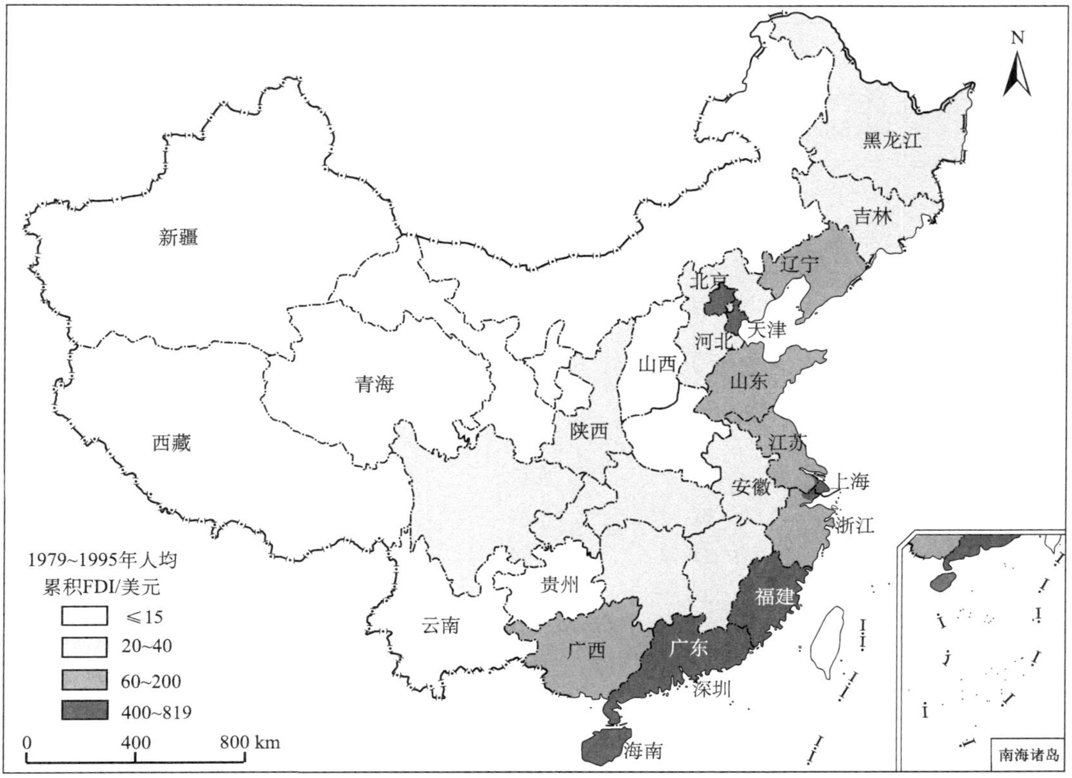

图 18.1　1979～1995 年人均实际累积外国直接投资在中国的区域差异

资料来源：1979～1985 年的实际外国直接投资数据来源于 Cheng (1995)；1987～1991 年的数据来源于中国统计信息和咨询服务中心 (1992)；其他年份的数据来自中国对外贸易经济合作部（不同年份）。

口和城市就业的比重在广东省和福建省的经济特区和沿海开放城市中（如深圳、珠海、汕头、厦门、福州、广州、湛江等）最为显著。另一方面，如深圳、珠海、秦皇岛、上海和广州等城市的外商资本所占比重较低，但是却达到了较高水平的产出，与之相比，其他地区的外商投资有着较低的产出比率。这与生产率、产业结构、投资时间的长短等因素的不同有关。

表 18.1　1995 年外国直接投资对中国区域经济发展的作用

城市或省份	1979～1995 年实际累计 FDI 份额/%	FDI 在固定资产总投资中的比重/%	外商投资企业输出在工业总产值中的比重/%	外商投资企业出口在总出口中的比重/%	外商投资企业就业在城市总就业中的比重/%	人均 GDP/元
经济特区	16.22	51.03	57.91	—	—	11168
深圳	5.22	39.66	72.09	52.13	34.62	23056
珠海	1.81	49.64	57.74	62.70	25.73	18885

续表

城市或省份	1979～1995 年实际累计 FDI 份额/%	FDI 在固定资产总投资中的比重/%	外商投资企业输出在工业总产值中的比重/%	外商投资企业出口在总出口中的比重/%	外商投资企业就业在城市总就业中的比重/%	人均 GDP/元
汕头	2.05	53.93	23.18	37.00	11.00	6524
厦门	4.04	82.41	68.14	41.71	39.61	20645
海南	3.10	44.48	19.45	9.67	4.68	5185
沿海开放城市	29.76	22.71	22.28	—	—	10764
大连	2.50	24.99	16.31	57.16	—	12058
秦皇岛	0.30	12.50	24.24	73.07	5.65	6626
天津	3.24	32.30	25.61	48.90	6.94	10284
烟台	1.55	32.36	8.19	69.05	6.12	9068
青岛	1.71	27.44	20.28	51.00	18.02	9378
连云港	0.19	11.52	8.08	38.95	8.25	4313
南通	0.63	18.80	15.96	53.66	22.07	5949
上海	8.81	16.94	27.98	31.00	6.92	18923
宁波	1.02	12.61	9.36	30.00	20.34	12117
温州	0.18	4.77	3.60	29.00	5.86	5783
福州	2.54	50.19	41.38	85.70	18.89	8958
广州	5.53	28.96	39.97	47.06	12.42	19370
湛江	0.60	17.99	14.74	40.05	—	4681
北海	0.91	71.11	11.67	39.39	4.18	6707
威海	0.42	19.82	6.98	—	6.16	13857
广东	30.66	36.52	37.15	45.53	14.11	7973
中国	100	15.65	11.94	31.51	3.35	4754

资料来源：1979～1984 年、1985～1991 年和 1992～1995 年的实际累计 FDI 分别来源于 Kueh（1992）、中国统计信息和咨询服务中心（1992）和中国对外贸易经济合作部（1992、1993、1994、1995、1996）；固定资产总投资、外商投资企业的出口、工业总产值和人均 GDP 数据来源于统计信息交流大会秘书处（1991～1995）；就业和出口数据来源于相关城市的统计年鉴。广东省和中国的数据分别来源于广东省统计局（1996）和中国国家统计局（1996a）。

附：人民币兑换率是 1 美元＝8.3507 人民币（1995）。GVIO＝工业总产值。

外国直接投资，连同其他的资本资源加速了沿海地区国内生产总值（GDP）的增长。1995 年，与国家平均水平的 4754 元相比，经济特区和沿海开放城市的人均 GDP 数值已经超过 10000 元。早期确立的经济特区（深圳、珠海和厦门）和广州市的人均 GDP 数值已上升至 20000 元左右，取代了上海市的地位（上海市的人均 GDP 在过去的几十年中一直是最高的）。汕头和海南相对略低的人均 GDP 数值主要是由于其特殊的行政区划特征，这包括汕头市除了正式划归为经济特区之外还有其他县市，海南省有大量农村地区。

18.2.3　早期阶段外国直接投资的分布：趋向于中心位置?

自 1979 年以来，在中国的外国直接投资可以划分为三个阶段：早期阶段（1979～1985 年）、波动发展阶段（1986～1991 年）和快速增长阶段（1992 年～至今）（赵晋平，1997；王志乐，1996）。在早期阶段，与其他许多国家一样，在中国的外国直接投资高度集中在部分省份和直辖市[①]（图 18.2）。广东、北京、福建和上海在 7 年中所接受外国直接投资总额占全国的 83.5%，与此相对应，其他 6 个省份（包括西藏、山西、宁夏、青海、云南和安徽）只有相当小的份额（每个省份不足 0.1%）。与许多其他国家不同的是，在中国最受优惠的地区既不是经济中心地区，也不是外围地区。广东省是一个中等收入水平的省份，然而，它占有了全国外商直接投资的 64.7%。尽管像上海和北京这样的经济中心城市吸引了大量的外国直接投资，但是福建省这样的外围地区也达到了同样的水平。图 18.2 的累积百分比曲线显示，人均 GDP 低于广东省的省份和那些人均 GDP 高于广东省的省份具有相似的外国直接投资份额。因此，从地理分布方面不能简单得出结论，即早期的外国直接投资增大或者缩小中国的区域经济差异状况。这种复杂的状况需要对各个省份或单独地、或组合地进行详细的分析。

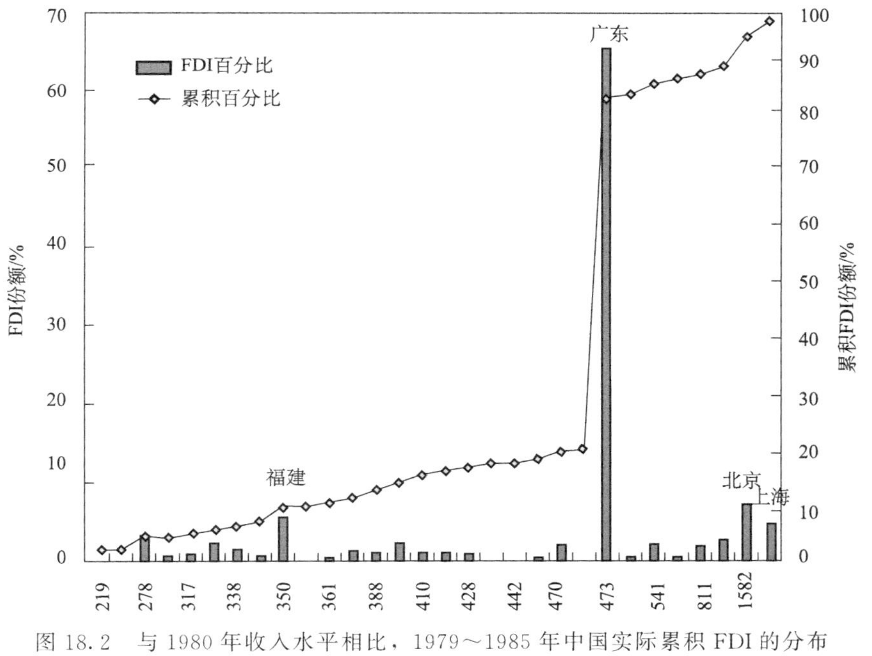

图 18.2　与 1980 年收入水平相比，1979～1985 年中国实际累积 FDI 的分布

资料来源：1979～1985 年实际 FDI 来源于 Cheng（1995）；人均 GDP 来源于中国国家统计年鉴（1996b）。

① 在 1997 年之前，中国的省级行政单元包括 3 个直辖市，5 个自治区和 22 个省份（包括台湾）。1997 年重庆市成为直辖市，但是这与本章的研究并不相关。

18.2.4　变化模式：1979～1995 年

使用变异系数（各省级单元外国直接投资数据的标准差除以平均值）来测量不同区域外国直接投资的差异。由于省级单元在人口尺度上存在巨大差异，该系数是基于人均外国直接投资进行计算的。计算结果显示，使用人均外国直接投资数据计算出的变异系数与使用外国直接投资数据计算出的变异系数相比，前者省际的变化幅度较小。这主要是因为一些人口稀少、偏远地区的省份具有数量较少的外国直接投资。但是，根据趋势可以看出，用人均数据的变化趋势与各地区总体数据的结果差别不大。

外国直接投资和人均外国直接投资计算得出的变异系数均有所下降，在 1979～1982 年分别从 4.31 和 3.14 下降至 1995 年的 1.67 和 1.50。在 17 年时间内，外国直接投资的扩散是较为显著的，当数据范围为 3 个不同时期时可以减少每年的数据误差。人均累积外国直接投资从 1979～1985 年的 2.32 下降至 1986～1991 年的 1.85 和 1992～1995 年的 1.51（表 18.2）。

表 18.2　1979～1995 年实际 FDI 的变异系数

年份	实际 FDI 数量	人均实际 FDI	人均实际累计 FDI
1979～1982	4.31	3.14	
1983	3.70	2.91	
1984	3.84	2.67	
1985	2.50	1.87	
1979～1985			2.32
1986	2.80	2.16	
1987	2.29	2.09	
1988	2.11	2.37	
1989	2.12	1.95	
1990	2.44	1.78	
1991	2.43	1.75	
1986～1991			1.85
1992	1.96	1.61	
1993	1.65	1.71	
1994	1.66	1.47	
1995	1.67	1.50	
1992～1995			1.51

资料来源：同图 18.1。

然而，一般情况下的扩散趋势并不能完全反映出特定年份的变化。例如，由于国家对 14 个沿海开放城市所实施的政策，这两个系数在 1984 年和 1985 年均有所下降。这一政策涵盖着 10 个以上的省份和直辖市（先前实施的经济特区政策仅仅使广东省和福建省获益），由此导致了整个沿海地区外国直接投资的增加。基于此，使用外国直接投资和人均外国直接投资计算得出的变异系数在 1986 年均有所上升，这就和政府政策具有相关关系。在 1986 年初期，中国政府颁布了第一部关于外商独资企业的法律（《中华人民共和国外资企业法》），并且在 1986 年 8 月施行的一系列“鼓励外商投资的规定”（《国务院关于鼓励外商投资的规定》）给予外国直接投资更多的优惠政策。这些法律和政策导致外国直接投资在一些已经集聚的省份和直辖市快速增长，如广东、上海和北京（1996 年 3 个地区的外国直接投资份额占全国总体的比重分别增长了 2%～5%）。在第二个时期也发现了一些年份（如 1988 年）这两个变异系数的动态变化。除此之外，由新确立的海南省[①]所引起的变化，使 1988 年外国直接投资额的系数有所降低（这是由于它在外国直接投资总额中较低的数量），但是人均外国直接投资额的系数有所提高（这是由于它较高的位居第三的人均外国直接投资数量），广东省在国外直接投资实际总额中所占的份额 1988 年下降了 3%（与 1987 年相对比，包含有海南），比其他地区缓慢。1989 年这种较为缓慢的增长继续持续。

与前两个时期相比，外国直接投资和人均外国直接投资的趋势在第三个时期相当模糊；前者的系数在 1993～1995 年之间有轻微的增长，后者则是较为曲折（表 18.2）。事实上，1992～1995 年实际外国直接投资在一些发展水平较高的省份和直辖市急剧增长，其他地区甚至出现相反的趋势（图 18.3）。如果将外国直接投资集中的省份和直辖市的前几名分组之后，这一集中状况更为明显（表 18.3）。表 18.3 表明 1992～1995 年那些高水平的省份和直辖市的人均外国直接投资在大多数情况下其增长高于国家平均水平（在 1992～1993 年位居前 5 位的地区增长较快，在 1993～1994 年位居前 7 位的和位居前 6 位的地区增长较快，在 1994～1995 年位居前 7 位的和位居前 5 位的地区增长较快）。这就说明人均外国直接投资总额系数的变化主要是因为在一些主要省份和直辖市外国直接投资集聚的增长，而不是因为外国直接投资从这些地区转移到其他低水平的省份和自治区。

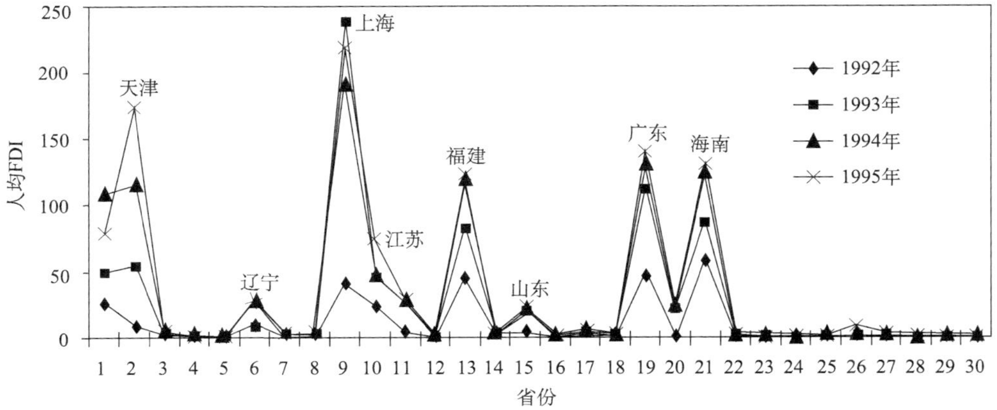

图 18.3　1992～1995 年中国 FDI 的区域变化

资料来源：同图 18.1。

① 1988 年海南被确立为一个省份；在此之前，它是广东省的一部分。

表 18.3 1992～1995 年国内及 FDI 集聚程度最高的省份/直辖市的人均 FDI 变化 （单位：%，以当前价格为基期）

项目	1992～1993 年	1993～1994 年	1994～1995 年
国内平均值	179	20	14
前 7 位的平均值（上海、天津、海南、广东、福建、北京、江苏）	171	22	15
前 6 位的平均值（上海、天津、海南、广东、福建、江苏）	177	21	14
前 5 位的平均值（上海、天津、海南、广东、福建）	189	14	19

18.2.5 1979～1991 年外国直接投资对区域经济差异的影响

为了检验外国直接投资对区域经济差异状况的影响，我们使用省域尺度上的人均 FDI、人均 GDP 和人均 GDP 变化的数据进行分析。这一分析建立的前提是：如果在给定时期内外国直接投资可以缩小区域人均 GDP 的差距，那么可以认为外国直接投资对减弱区域经济差异具有积极的作用①；反之亦然。由于在前两个时期，人均 FDI 的移动趋向于分散，并且在 20 世纪 80 年代中国区域差异的变化和下一时期的变化并不相同（胡鞍钢等，1996），对于第一个 13 年的变化在下面一起分析。

三个变量（1980 年的人均 GDP、1980～1991 年人均 GDP 增长率和 1979～1991 年实际的人均累积 FDI）的散点图结果显示（图 18.4），与其他地区相比，在收入较低的地区，外国直接投资对经济增长的影响较大。在人均 FDI 高于国家平均水平的 7 个省份和直辖市中，在这一时期收入稍低的海南、福建和广东（1990 年的外国直接投资分别占省际总投资额的 13.53%、12.74%、18.31%）的人均 GDP 达到了最高速度的增长，而其他收入稍高的地区（上海、北京、天津和辽宁的外国直接投资分别占总投资额的 3.73%、7.39%、4.54%、4.52%）的增长相对缓慢（图 18.4）。其中，30 个省级单元中，上海市的 GDP 增速最低。这主要是由于上海市较低的外国直接投资份额；另一方面是由于上海市大部分的外国投资是在 20 世纪 80 年代后期进入的，随之而来的外国直接投资的产出在这一时期并未完全实现。然而，其他因素，包括中央政府的财政关系、较多的地方国有企业和重工业等，也影响着上海的经济增长（Yeung and Sung，1996）。

图 18.4 也显示出一些人均 FDI 较低但是较接近平均水平的低收入省份（山东、陕西、广西和浙江）其人均 GDP 也在以较快的速度增长。

总之，对于人均 GDP 较低的省份，外国直接投资带来了快速的增长，人均 GDP 较高的省份和直辖市则增长缓慢，这就导致了区域经济发展的变化。实际上，正如胡鞍钢等（1995）所指出的那样，区域收入的差异在 1979～1990 年之间是缩小的。

18.2.6 1992～1995 年外国直接投资对区域经济差异的影响

经过 12 年的发展，1991 年广东省的人均 GDP 上升至第 4 位，如果将 3 个直辖市

① 区域差异可以使用很多指标进行测量。在这些指标中人均 GDP 是使用较为广泛的一个。

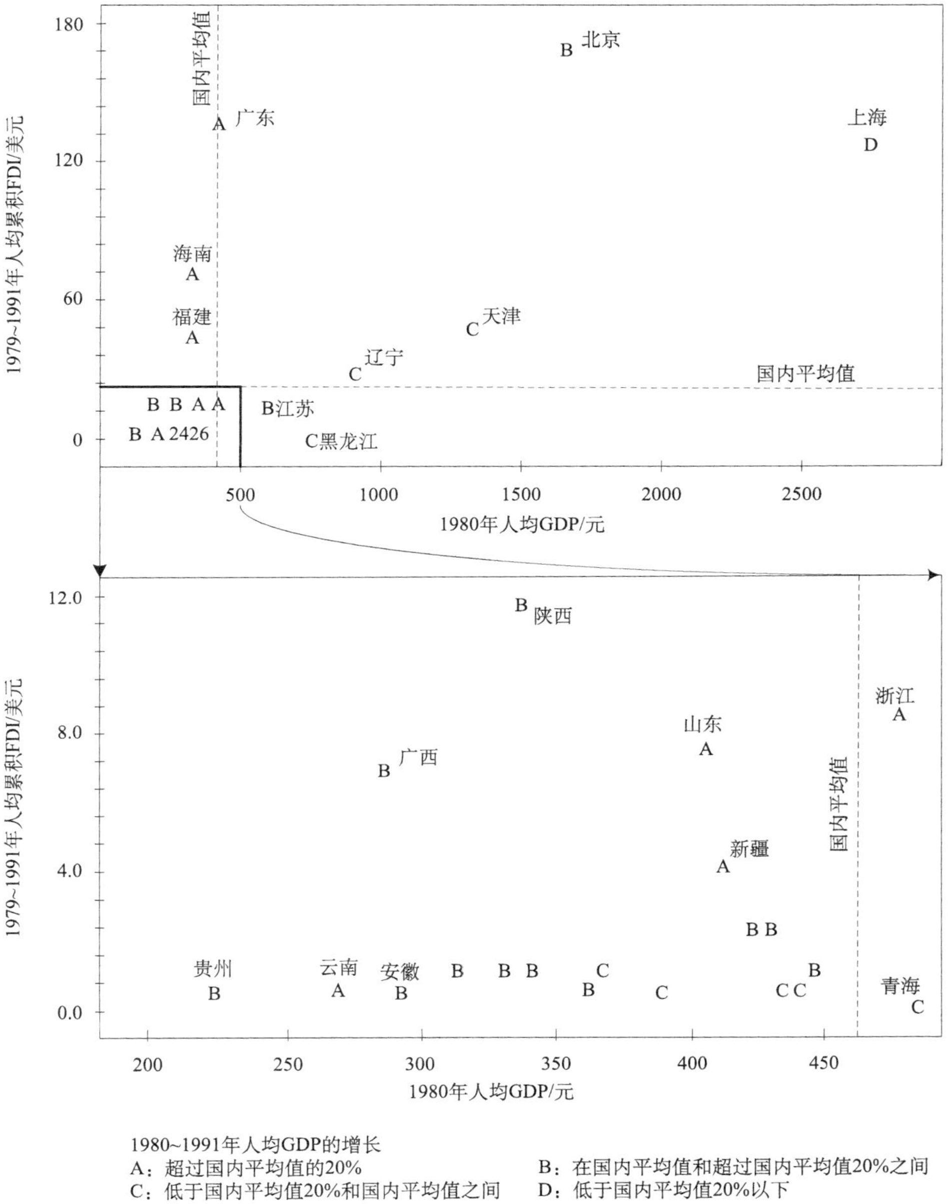

图 18.4　1979～1991 年 FDI 对中国区域经济差异的影响

注：图中的数据表示下降到特定值的观测值（省份）数量；下图是对上图遮挡部分的放大。

资料来源：同图 18.1 中的实际 FDI；人均 GDP 数据来源于中国国家统计年鉴（1996b）。

剔除在外，广东省在所有省份中是处于第一位。福建和海南则较接近国家平均水平（图 18.5）。

然而，1992～1995 年外国直接投资对 GDP 增长的贡献是模糊的。尽管如此，有三个因素似乎与此相关。第一，在这一时期具有较高的人均外国直接投资的四个省份和直辖市的增长速度高于国家平均水平。其中，1995 年福建省的外国直接投资占该省份总投资额的 49.51%，在 30 个省级单元的增长中居于首位，且 1995 年福建省的人均 GDP 位居第七；海南省投资额的 44.48%来自于外国直接投资，人均 GDP 增长速度比全国平均水平高 19%（仅仅低于图 18.5 中的 A 类 1%）；更重要的是，上海市和广东省作为收入最高的城市和省份（详见表 18.1，这两个地区的外国直接投资对总投资，特别是外商投资工业对总产值贡献都很明显），持续高速增长，这必然会扩大区域差距。第二，具有相对较高的人均外国直接投资和高于全国平均值的人均 GDP 的江苏、浙江和山东（山东除外，1991 年它比全国人均 GDP 仅仅低 6 元），在这一时期同样可能通过它们的快速增长而加剧区域经济差异。第三，具有较少外国直接投资和最低人均 GDP 的贵州省仍然处于增长缓慢的类别（图 18.5）。由此可见，贫富之间的差距确实在不断拉大。

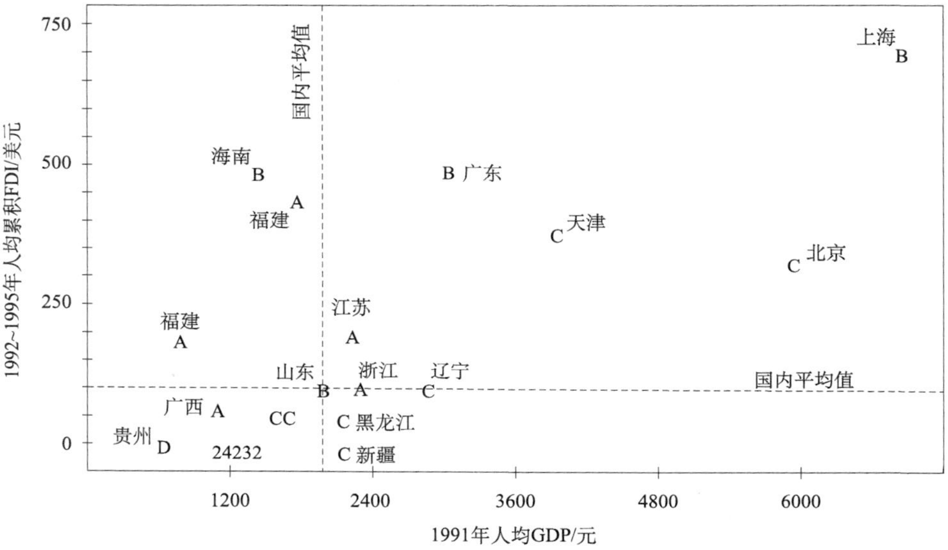

1980~1991年人均GDP的增长
A：超过国内平均值的20%　　B：在国内平均值和超过国内平均值20%之间
C：低于国内平均值20%和国内平均值之间　　D：低于国内平均值20%以下

图 18.5　1992～1995 年 FDI 对中国区域经济差异的影响

注：图中的数据表示观测值（省份）的数量下降的特定地点。

资料来源：同图 18.4。

图 18.5 也提供了支持这种观点的证据。北京、天津和辽宁的人均 GDP 和 FDI 均高于平均水平，而它们的增长并没有达到国家平均水平。但是这并没有缩小区域差距的扩大趋势，图上最高的地区（上海市）继续保持相对较高的水平和最低的地区（贵州省）继续保持相对较低的水平。通过全面的研究发现，自 1990 年以来区域之间的差距在不断加大（胡鞍钢等，1995），这就意味着 FDI 和其他一些因素，如政策、地方资本形成、前期的发展以及农村工业化水平等，使得 1992～1995 年间的区域经济差异状况不断加剧。

这两个时期的研究结果与之前描述的外国直接投资区域变化模式基本一致。外国直接投资的区域间差异正好与结论相符，即它导致了 1979～1991 年区域差异的不断缩小。与此相反，1992～1995 年外国直接投资的集聚加剧了区域经济差异。然而，在早期阶段，广东和福建（不是中国的经济中心）累积了大量的外国直接投资，其后一些高收入省市对外投资份额不高，这种状况可以在一定程度上减缓区域差异变化的速度。在 20 世纪 90 年代中期，由于一些外国直接投资高度集聚的省份进入高收入类别，外国直接投资的变化模式会对这些地区的区域经济差异造成更大的影响：外国直接投资的扩散可以缩小区域经济差异，反之亦然。

18.3　跨国公司投资的企业分析

18.3.1　跨国公司投资的时空演变

正如先前提到的那样，跨国公司在中国直接投资的数据难以获取，为了了解这一概况，本章的研究使用对日本和德国的 30 家大型跨国公司的调查数据（王志乐，1996）和来源于政府出版物（对外经济贸易合作部，多年份）的 200 家最大的美国投资公司的数据。根据我们对跨国公司的定义，这些数据只涵盖了跨国公司直接投资的一部分。然而，由于在中国投资的大型跨国公司主要来自日本、德国和美国，并且在区域经济发展中大型跨国公司发挥着重要作用。因此，这部分数据中所显示的变化也非常具有指导意义。

虽然跨国公司在中国的直接投资早在 20 世纪 70 年代末就已经开始，但是直到 20 世纪 90 年代也没有快速增长起来。根据王志乐对大型跨国公司的调查发现，到 1995 年世界 500 强企业在中国投资的 231 个项目中，只有 35 家是在 1991 年之前的 12 年中建立的（王志乐，1996）。在 1992 年，增加了 16 家。这意味着大型跨国公司数量快速增长的开始。在之后的 3 年中，每个年份依次增加 37 家、69 家、74 家。换而言之，从 1992 年开始的 4 年时间中，大型跨国公司增加的数量占先前跨国公司总数（1979 年开始）的 83%。来自美国的 200 家最大的投资也表现出相似的模式：1980～1991 年增长快速，总数达到 43 家，1993 年增加了 38 家，1994 年增加了 54 家，1995 年增加了 51 家。

跨国公司在中国的区位和外国直接投资的区位模式相同：趋向于沿海地区（表 18.4 所示）。然而，来自香港的跨国公司大多数布局在广东省（Li，1996），而 3 个直辖市（上海、北京和天津）和广东、江苏和辽宁省似乎更吸引来自美国、日本和德国的公司。如表 18.4 中的样本数据所示，美国、日本和德国的跨国公司有超过 70%的业务布局在这些直辖市和省份。

如果将这些在中国布局的跨国公司的时空特征与沿海省份和直辖市的经济状况相关联，那么下面的解释似乎是合理的。自 1992 年起，大型跨国公司直接投资的快速增长和它们高度集中在外国直接投资已经相对充足的地区，扭转了 1979～1991 年的外资扩散趋势。此外，拥有较多跨国公司投资的省份和直辖市一般具有较高的人均 GDP 数值（详见表 18.4 和图 18.5）。因此，正如我们先前所提出的，1992 年以来外国直接投资对区域经济差异的影响主要来自于跨国公司。在20世纪90年代早期，跨国公司是区域经济差异变化的主要推动力。

表 18.4　1980～1995年美国、日本和德国的跨国公司（TNCs）的布局

省份、直辖市或地区	来自美国TNCs的最大投资	占总体的比重/%	30家日本和德国的TNCs子公司的数量	占总体的比重/%
沿海地区				
上海	29	14.50	48	20.78
北京	28	14.00	41	17.75
广东	27	13.50	37	16.02
江苏	37	18.50	27	11.69
辽宁	12	6.00	15	6.49
天津	11	5.50	13	5.63
其他	33	16.50	25	10.82
小计	177	88.50	206	89.18
内陆省份	23	11.50	25	10.82
总计	200	100	231	100

资料来源：美国跨国公司的投资数量来源于不同年份的中国对外贸易经济合作部；日本和德国的子公司数据来源于王志乐（1996）。

18.3.2　案例公司的选择

文中对公司研究的目的是为了弥补统计数据中难以揭示的跨国公司对区域经济发展的影响，为了与这一主要目标相一致，案例公司是从制造业中进行选择的。之所以从制造业中选择案例公司是因为我们认为这些公司对区域经济发展具有许多的直接影响（尤其是技术方面），如通过产业链而产生的直接影响。我们在选择案例公司的时候考虑了四个主要因素。

（1）它们应当为大型跨国投资企业。

（2）它们的业务应当是存在一定影响（至少2年），这样可以揭示随时间推移的变化。

（3）它们应当代表不同的制造业。

（4）它们当前的公司应当来自于主要的跨国公司母国（日本、美国和西欧，尤其是德国）。

按照上述标准，最终选择了12个跨国公司子公司作为研究案例，这些公司来自上海、北京和天津这3个跨国公司进入较多的直辖市（表18.5）。它们中的大多数是1995年世界500强企业名单中的跨国公司的子公司；台湾地区的跨国公司被选为食品行业的代表。

表 18.5　12 家公司的概况

特征	描述
成立的年份	1980（1），1984（3），1985（1），1986（1），1991（1），1992（4），1994（1）
产业	电子和电子装备（2），通信装备（3），运输和升降机（4），食品（1），机械（1），化工（1）
跨国公司投资的母国	德国（3），日本（3），美国（3），比利时（1），瑞士（1），台湾（1）
年度销售额/百万	10～100（1），100～500（1），500～1000（1），1000～2000（3），超过 2000（5）
位置布局	北京（4），上海（4），天津（4）

资料来源：作者自己的调查。括号中的数据表示公司个数。

本章的调研人员来自于中国人民大学、南开大学和华东师范大学，在 1995、1996、1997 年使用相同的准则对这些公司的副总经理、总经理助理或其他高层管理人员进行访谈。访谈中所涉及的问题包括公司的经营状况、本地产业联系和它们的业务对当地人力资源开发、管理、技术和市场的影响。除此之外，来源于出版物的信息，如公司的年度报告、在《浦东开发》杂志上发布的公司简介和王志乐（1996）的文章，也用于改善小样本数据而导致的误差。同时，为了保守商业机密，在下面的讨论中这些公司并没有被明确提及。

18.3.3　对本地经济的影响

来自于 12 个公司的调查访问证据表明，技术的转移、管理的完善和雇员的培训是主要的影响方面。同样的，也存在一些间接的影响。

1. 技术转移

12 家外国投资的公司，其生产装备均得到升级，其中，2 家装备有 20 世纪 90 年代最先进的设备；同时，更有效率的产品生产技术从一些先进的国家被引进。通过跨国公司的进入，发达国家和欠发达国家之间的技术差距被大幅缩小。例如，汽车行业，在到访谈时为止的 20 年中，通过与跨国公司合作建立合资企业使得相关技术实现巨大的飞跃。然而，更为重要的是，有 2 家公司声称它们的技术转移是“动态的”，这就意味着技术的更新不需要（或较少的）额外费用。此外，样本公司中的 1/3 都已经在公司所在地建立起研发中心（R&D）。这些研发中心一般情况下都是对它们产品的某一部分进行研制，但是有一家研发中心例外，这家研发中心每年有 3000 万美元的研发投入，在其技术研发过程中发挥着关键的作用。这些公司的技术影响对独资企业和其他合资企业的影响是截然不同的。9 家合资企业所受到的影响明显大于 3 家独资企业，尤其是在本地技术创新方面。

2. 管理技能的改善

这个方面在被调研公司中也较为普遍。虽然合资企业的中方抱怨被引入的外国管理方式在西方标准下是相当过时的，但是多样化的现代管理方法通过跨国公司投资被引入是显而易见的。了解如何去管理一个现代化的公司是非常重要的，尤其是对中国的国有企业（SOEs）来说十分重要。之前是国有企业的 9 家公司通过合资企业在接受这种管理方式之后，其管理状况有所改善。目前，案例也显示出只有在合资企业中当地人才可能在较高的管理位置任职。

3. 培训项目

对雇员的培训项目在 12 个公司中十分普遍。接受培训的员工占全部雇员的比重在 80%～100%之间。除了在中国的员工培训，所有的公司都会安排一些雇员（主要是管理层和关键技术人员）到跨国公司母国去接受特殊培训。一些受访者认为，在特定领域的海外培训对提高他们的技能非常有用。合资企业均表示跨国公司投资之后，更多的培训项目被引入，并且表示培训之后劳动力技能水平有了显著地提高。

此次调查结果也显示一些间接影响。当然，上述 3 种类型的影响通过公司间的交流访问、会议、信息交流和媒体报道等已经被扩散到其他没有外国投资的企业。这种影响并不局限于公司所在地的区域。在其他省份的一些公司也可以同样受益。然而，最重要的间接影响是产业联系。国内原料和零部件的使用为相关产品提供了市场，反过来会促进公司的发展。例如，在被调研的两家拥有瑞士和比利时投资的公司中，它们对中国供应商的依赖分别是 100%和 40%；近几年这 2 个公司的扩展带动所有关联企业的发展。

第一，在同样的状况下合资企业的本地联系多于独资企业。除去食品公司，其他另外 2 家独资企业具有较少的本地联系。第二，在合资企业中，与跨国公司控股或两家以上中国公司控股的合资企业相比，中国公司控股的合资企业有着更大的本地影响。例如，一家上海合资企业，其公司份额的 60%被一家大型的中国公司占有，它的本地化程度由 1988 年的 20%上升至 1995 年的 68%；而另一家公司的中方有三家公司持有股份，其本地化程度在 1995 年仍旧保持在 20%。第三，本地化程度因产业不同而有所差异；食品产业最高（100%），然后是汽车产业（40%～87%）、通信产业（10%～60%）和电子产业（10%或少于 10%）。第四，投资的时间越长，更多地方参与的可能性越大，随着时间的推移，超过半数的受访公司经历了本地投资逐渐增加的过程。第五，产业联系可以帮助相关的中国公司从其他跨国公司吸引外国资本。一个典型的案例是上海市的一家汽车合资企业：由于该公司对零部件的需求，其他 4 家跨国公司分别在江苏和上海投资了 3 家零部件生产公司。

18.3.4 对区域经济差异的影响

跨国公司对所投资地区的经济发展具有十分重要的影响。由于它们主要集中在中国的经济中心（如北京、上海、天津）和其他一些沿海经济发达省份，这些公司不仅是在经济方面，而且在先进的技术和现代化的管理体系方面都产生重要影响。自从跨国公司进入这些直辖市和省份之后，这些地区与其他省份之间的交易地位进一步提高。

跨国公司的区位是否在整体上已经（或即将）从沿海城市向内陆省份转移仍旧是一个超出本章研究范围的问题，但是，有两个明确的相关因素：一是 1992 年以来大部分沿海地区跨国公司投资是快速增长的；二是跨国公司所投资的公司对其他省份（如四川省）的公司提供帮助，使技术趋于现代化，改善市场甚至于和外国公司一起成立合资企业等。这些活动可能会导致更多的跨国公司进入内陆地区。

18.4　结论与讨论

基于统计数据和公司信息对外国直接投资的一般分析和跨国公司的具体分析表明，跨国公司对中国和其他国家的当地经济的积极影响是相似的。然而，外国直接投资和跨国公司对区域经济差异的影响与来自许多国家的证据不一致。先前研究并没有证实在早期阶段外国直接投资可以缩小区域经济差异，或者说是大型跨国公司在扩大区域经济差异方面发挥着作用。但是，在中国，一方面相当规模的香港投资注入改革初期既不富裕也不是经济中心的广东省；另一方面是从 1979 年外国直接投资进入中国开始，到许多大型跨国公司对中国经济的中心进行投资之前有一个 10 年期的延迟，这两个方面是值得注意的。

为了解决本章开始时提出的问题，我们认为，中国改革开放 20 年间，外国直接投资表明，跨国公司对区域经济差异的影响不仅与其他国家间有所不同，而且会随着时间变化而变化。我们认为这种状况主要的影响因素是跨国公司子公司和东道国本地经济状况之间的关系。

某种程度上，基于中国的案例分析结果也支持跨国公司通过投资通道实现“增长扩散”的观点（Perroux，1973）。香港资本流入广东省及跨国公司在上海、北京和其他一些沿海省份和城市的直接投资均导致它们的经济快速发展。中国沿海地区和发达国家的差距通过这些发展而逐渐缩小。此外，外国直接投资扩散到其他省份也可以缩小区域经济差异。来自中国的实证研究可以与之前提到的 Ozawa（1992）的阶段方法相关联。在第一阶段，香港和台湾的跨国公司直接投资在广东省和福建省集聚；然后不断增加的成本导致它们迁移到其他成本较低的省份。与此相似，来自日本、美国和其他发达国家的大多数大型跨国公司起先认为它们的最优布局在上海、北京、天津和一些沿海省份，但预测其会从它们当前区位分散有待进一步的研究证实。

基于上述研究，我们提出了 4 条建议，以期对政策制定提供一定的借鉴。

（1）跨国公司在一些沿海地区的集聚应当被认为是受欢迎的，这是因为与其他地区相比，这些地区优越的基础设施和劳动力更可能促进跨国公司的技术转移。此外，随着时间的推移，跨国公司的投资倾向于由它们在中心区的初始位置向外扩散。不断增加的“松脚型”经济活动使跨国公司能够对影响其成本收益的诸多因素做出响应（Dunning，1997）。因此，内陆地区的低成本优势对跨国公司而言将会更为重要。

（2）在产出增加的同时，由于跨国公司还对投资地的管理系统、技术和市场产生更为积极的影响，跨国公司投资应该比其他外国直接投资更受欢迎，这对中国经济的转型非常重要。

（3）目前，三种类型的外国直接投资（独资、合资和合作经营）在中国正在流行，合资企业更有利于促进当地经济的发展。政府政策应该对此进行鼓励。

（4）根据外国直接投资的不同阶段模式，寻求资源的外国直接投资在沿海地区的布局已逐渐被持续增长的土地和劳动力支出所阻碍，对于这一状况，沿海地区应该集中于引进市场需求和战略资产需求的跨国公司，而内陆地区的省份应该尝试引进具有劳动力密集型和资源密集型产业的跨国公司。

学者们普遍使用外国直接投资数量的多少来预测它们对区域经济的影响（如 Singh and Choo，1981；O'Malley，1994；Buckwalter，1995），这是因为一般情况下，外国直接投资的产出和投入是相关的。然而，外国直接投资的多少并不往往都与它们对区域经济差异的影响相称。除去产业和公司的投入-产出比率差异，跨国公司的直接影响（如技术和管理）和间接影响也依赖于其他变量，而不只是外国直接投资的数量。对于这一问题，对跨国公司的深入研究会更有价值，它可以说明跨国公司投资的区域收益来源于许多方面。本章的研究也说明了企业在吸引外国投资的同时可能会对其他地区带来收益，而这些收益的各种维度都值得更为深入的研究。

参考文献

广东省统计局. 1996. 广东统计年鉴. 北京：中国统计出版社

胡鞍钢，王绍光，康晓光. 1995. 中国区域差距报告. 沈阳：辽宁人民出版社

陆大道. 1995. 区域发展及其空间结构. 北京：科学出版社

覃成林. 1997. 中国区域经济差异研究. 北京：中国经济出版社

统计信息交流大会秘书处. 1995. 沿海开放城市、经济特区和重要城市的统计数据. 深圳：统计信息交流大会秘书处

王志乐. 1996. 著名跨国公司在中国的投资. 北京：中国经济出版社

赵晋平. 1997. 中国的国际资本流入分析与展望. 管理世界，(3)：64～74

赵景华. 1994. 韩国外商来华投资企业考察. 中国工业经济研究，(8)：33～37

中国对外贸易经济合作部. 1985，1986，1992，1993，1994，1995，1996. 中国对外经济联系与贸易年鉴. 北京：对外贸易经济合作部

中国国家统计局. 1996a. 中国统计年鉴. 北京：中国统计出版社

中国国家统计局. 1996b. 改革开放十七年的中国地区经济. 北京：中国统计出版社

中国统计信息和咨询服务中心. 1992. 1979～1991 年中国对外经济统计. 北京：中国统计信息和咨询服务中心

Bradshaw M J. 1997. The geography of foreign investment in Russia 1993～1995. Tijdschrift voor Economische en Sociale Geografie，88：77～84

Buckwalter D W. 1995. Spatial inequality，foreign investment，and economic transition in Bulgaria. Professional Geographer，47：288～298

Cheng L K. 1995. Foreign Direct Investment in China. Paris：OECD

Dicken P，Quevit M，Savary J，et al. 1994. Strategies of transnational corporations and European regional restructuring：Some conceptual bases. In：Dicken P，Quevit M. Transnational Corporations and European Regional Restructuring. Utrecht：N G S

Dicken P. 1992. Global Shift：The Internationalisation of Economic Activity（2nd Edition）. New York：Guilford

Dicken P. 1994. Global-local tensions：Firms and states in the global space-economy. Economic Geography，70：101～128

Dunning J H. 1993. Original 1981. Multinational enterprises，locational strategies and regional development. In: Robson P. Transnational Corporations and Regional Economic Integration. London: Routledge

Dunning J H. 1994. Re-evaluating the benefits of foreign direct investment. Transnational Corporations, 3: 23～51

Dunning J H. 1997. How should national governments respond to globalization? International Executives, 39: 55～66

Edgington D. 1995. Japanese manufacturing companies in southern Ontario and NAFTA. In: Green M B, McNaughton R B. The location of Foreign Direct Investment. Aldershot: Avebury

Glickman N, Woodward D. 1988. The location of foreign direct investment in the United States: Patterns and determinants. International Regional Science Review, 11: 137～154

Harrington J, Burns K, Cheung M. 1986. Market-oriented foreign investment and regional development: Canadian companies in western New York. Economic Geography, 62: 155～166

ILO. 1981. Employment Effects of Multinational Enterprises in Industrialised Countries. Geneva: International Labour Origanization

Kueh Y Y. 1992. Foreign investment and economic change in China. China Quarterly, 131: 637～690

Lall S. 1993. Transnational Corporations and Economic Development. London: Routledge

Lan P, Young S. 1996. Foreign direct investment and technology transfer: A case study of foreign direct investment in north-east China. Transnational Corporations, 5: 57～83

Lardy N R. 1994. The role of foreign trade and investment in China's economic transformation. China Quarterly, 144: 1065～1082

Leung C K. 1990. Locational characteristics of foreign equity joint venture investment in China, 1979～1985. Professional Geographer, 42: 403～421

Leung C K. 1993. Pensonal contacts, subcontracting linkages, and development in the Hong Kong-Zhujiang delta region. A A A G, 83 (2): 272～302

Li X J. 1996. Hong Kong direct investment in mainland China: A spatial study with special reference to the locational behaviour of investors. Chinese Geographical Science, 6: 289～303

Marquez J M. 1994. Spatial and sectoral strategies of foreign direct investment in Spain. In: Dicken P, Quevit M, eds. Transnational Corporations and European Regional Restructuring. Utrecht: N G S

Murphy A B. 1992. Western investment in East-Central Europe: Emerging patterns and implications for state stability. Professional Geographer, 44: 249～259

Nestor C. 1997. Foreign investment and the spatial pattern of growth in Vietnam. In: Dixon C, Drakakis S, eds. Uneven Development in South East Asia. Aldershot: Ashgate

Ozawa T. 1992. Foreign direct investment and economic development. Transnational Corporations, 1: 27～54

O'Huallachain B, Reid N. 1992. Source country differences in the spatial distribution of foreign direct investment in the United States. Professional Geographer, 44: 272～285

O'Huallachain B. 1984. Linkages and foreign direct investment in the United States. Econmic Geography, 60: 238～253

O'malley E. 1994. The impact of transnational corporations in the Republic of Ireland. In: Dicken P, Quevit M, eds. 1994. Transnational Corporations and European Regional Restructuring. Utrecht: N G S

Perroux F. 1973. Multinational investment and the analysis of development and integration poles. Economies et Societes, 24: 831～868

Potter P B. 1995. Foreign investment law in the People's Republic of China: Dilemmas of state control. China Quarterly, 141: 155～185

Quevit M, Dicken P. 1994. Transnational corporations strategies and regional restructuring: Some lessons from the experience of EU countries and Central and Eastern European countries. In: Dicken P, Quevit M. Transnational Corporations and European Regional Restructuring. Utrecht: N G S

Rogerson C M. 1982. Multinational corporations in southern Africa: A spatial perspective. In: Taylor M, Thrift N. The Geography of Multinationals. London: Croom Helm

Singe M S, Choo C S. 1981. Spatial dynamics in the growth and development of multinational corporations in Malaysia. In: Hamilton F E I, Linge G J R. Spatial Analysis, Industry, and Industrial Environment: Progress in Research and Application. Chichester: Wiley

Smart J, Smart A. 1991. Personal relations and divergent economies: A case study of Hong Kong investment in south China. International Journal of Urban and Regional Research, (5): 216～233

South R B. 1990. Transnational "maquiladora". A A A G, 80 (4): 549～570

United Nations Conference on Tradeand Development (UNCTAD). 1996. World Investment Report 1996: Investment, Trade and International Policy Arrangement. New York: United Nations

Wang Z Q. 1995. Foreign Investment and Economic Development in Hungary and China. Aldershot: Avebury

Williams D. 1996. Analyzing the regional impact of foreign manufacturing firms. Tijdschrift voor Economische en Sociale Geografie, 87 (3), 259～265

Williams O E. 1985. The Economic Institutions of Capitalism. New York: The Free Press

Yeung W C H. 1997. Business networks and transnational corporations: A study of Hong Kong firms in the ASEAN region. Economic Geography, 73 (1): 1～24

Yeung Y M, Sung Y W. 1996. Shanghai: Transformation and Modernisation under China's Open Policy. Hong Kong: The Chinese University Press

Young S, Hood N, Peter E. 1994. Multinational enterprises and regional economic development. Regional Studies, 28 (7): 657～677

Zhan X J. 1993. The role of foreign direct investment in market-oriented reforms and economic development: The case of China. Transnational Corporations, 2 (3): 121～148

Zhang L Y. 1994. Location-specific advantages and manufacturing direst foreign investment in south China. World Development, 22 (1): 45～53

第 19 章　跨国公司投资的地方根植性

本章为20世纪末期的研究成果，针对影响跨国公司网络本地化参与的影响因素进行理论与实证分析。文献评述认为本地合作伙伴先前的经济实力和庞大的国内市场是两个还没有被探究的影响本地化的因素。本章主要利用在上海的实地访谈和调查数据来说明其对跨国公司在经营管理、产业联系，以及技术转让的影响。讨论了中国的政治文化背景、跨国公司抢占市场的动机，以及跨国公司最常见的参与模式——“合资企业”。研究表明当两种因素综合考虑时对合资企业的影响较显著。相关证据还表明，由于到研究时为止上海是跨国公司投资的新兴市场，因此跨国公司在上海的整体本地化水平要低于一些其他发展中国家。随着合资企业成为跨国公司投资的主要方式，预计未来几年跨国公司在上海的本地化程度将会提升。

19.1　研究背景

地区经济的发展能够通过企业之间的网络联系从一个地区扩散到另一个地区（Perroux et al.，1950；Hirschman et al.，1958）。而在国际之间，主要通过跨国公司的跨境投资实现扩散（Hirschman et al.，1958；Perroux et al.，1973）。在当前全球化时代，跨境资本流动已经成为无边界经济的显著特征（Chen and Yeung，1996，1998）。随着企业地方嵌入的观点兴起（Granovetter et al.，1985；Grabher et al.，1993），地理学家在最近的研究中用相关理论解释全球与地方关系（Amin and Thrift，1994；Dicken et al.，1994；Conti，1997）。这些研究表明，跨国公司在地方的强势嵌入应该产生巨大的溢出效应，并且给当地带来丰厚的收益，尽管在一些地区也会出现负面的影响（Amin and Thrift，1994）。研究还表明，在一些区域，跨国公司和本地企业间的网络联系要比其他区域的网络联系更紧密（O'hUllachain et al.，1984；Schoenberger et al.，1991；Dicken，1992，1994；Amin and Thrift，1994；Dicken and Quevite，1994；Young et al.，1994）。

跨国公司嵌入当地经济的程度是由多种因素决定的，包括跨国公司及其子公司的类型，跨国公司协调子公司的方式（Dicken et al.，1994），投资地区的经济发展水平以及地方政府采取的投资政策（Dicken，1992）。此外，本地机构也是重要的影响因素。Amin 和 Thrift 利用“制度厚度”的概念解释了“强制度存在”和“在局部地区内各制度政策的强烈相互作用”可以形成很强的本地嵌入（Amin and Thrift，1994），这些研究主要是基于发达国家的案例。在发展中国家，许多因素（如本地供应的产品质量和数量、出口平台的作用，以及知识产权保护的不足）都会抑制跨国公司和国内企业间网络联系的发展。因此，怎样将 Amin 和 Thrift 的观点应用到发展中国家？或者如何利用与一些发展中国家相关的特殊因素来增强跨国公司的本地嵌入？

作为一个发展中国家，中国的一些特殊因素会影响到跨国公司的本地嵌入。第一，在中国的文化中，商业行为强调社会网络与人际关系。顾客更倾向于与他们有紧密联系的企业进行交易。因此，强大的社会网络关系能够提供安全的供应与销售渠道（Zhao and Aram，1995）。这意味着，本地合作伙伴先前的经济状态可能会对跨国公司网络组织的构建产生强烈的影响。第二，国有企业已经支配了中国经济几十年。在计划管理体制的控制之下，它们已经与由同样政府部门主管下的其他国有企业建立了范围广泛的关系网络。随着国有企业作为跨国公司主要的本地合作伙伴（大多数跨国公司都将国有企业作为本地合作伙伴），企业原有的关系网络将继续影响到合资企业的本地嵌入。第三，由于中国政府的外商直接投资政策，使得合资企业成为最常见的资本进入模式，1980年以来的大多数年份，合资企业的数量已经超过合作企业和外商独资企业，其比重超过50%。相比其他模式，合资企业能够吸引更多本地机构参与到跨国公司的本地发展。第四，中国拥有世界五分之一的人口，自20世纪80年代以来保持着最快经济增长速度，并且正在成为世界上最大的市场。大多数跨国公司是为中国市场而来，在1994年由国家统计局进行的1066家外商投资企业全国性随机抽样调查中，约92%的样本企业认为庞大的中国市场是它们投资中国的主要动力（人民日报，1994），合资企业投资模式更容易发展地方联系（Dicken et al.，1992）。

中国独特的发展背景为调查本地合作伙伴先前的经济状态对跨国公司本地嵌入的影响提供了重要的案例支持。庞大的国内市场和跨国公司为争夺市场进行的投资之间的关系引起了另一个问题：合资企业在国内市场的绩效与其本地嵌入的关系。本章通过公司案例探究这两个影响因素对跨国公司本地嵌入的影响。当然，关注这个并不意味着之前提到的其他因素都不重要。

中国在世界上吸引外商直接投资的优势地位增强了本研究的意义。自1978年以来，中国决定进行改革和对外开放后，已采取了一系列的优惠政策来吸引外商直接投资，并最终吸引了大批跨国公司来华投资。外商直接投资的资本流动急剧增加，从1983年至1996年间年平均增长率为40.45%（以美元计）（Cheng，1995；国家统计局，1997）。自1993年以来中国成为仅次于美国的世界第二大外商直接投资接受国（UNCTAD，1996）。按照1995年的数据显示，外商投资企业贡献了全国15.65%的固定资产总投资、11.94%的工业总产值和31.51%的对外出口额（Li and Yeung，1998）。同时，通过外商投资对吸引国外先进技术、提升管理水平也产生了一定的影响（Li，1997）。

“嵌入性”是指经济发展受到各种经济参与者的对偶关系以及整体关系网络结构的影响的现象（Grabher et al.，1993）。跨国公司的本地嵌入是指跨国公司与它们的竞争对手（客户、供应商、区域性企业，以及在地域范围内它们掌控的公共组织）形成的关系网络（Granovetter，1985；Harrison，1992；Dicken et al.，1994），尤其是在某种程度上本地企业融入到跨国公司网络中。“本地”可以有多种含义，本章中，本地定义为一个小的地理区域，例如，上海。本地参与涉及许多方面，例如，Lall（1980）确定了10个类别的本地联系。本章主要关注的是材料和零部件供应的本地化、经营管理的本地参与、专业技术发展的本地参与（Fujita and Hill，1995），因为供应商的关系是“地方嵌入最重要的单一指标”（Dicken et al.，1994），而且后两个是中国吸引外商直接投资的主要目标。因此，外商投资企业产品的本地化程度是指在国内的原材料（包括其他外商投资企业在区域生产的产品）的投入与所有相关企业采购材料投入的比率来衡量。管理的本地化程度是由本地管理者占外商投资企业管理人员总数的比例来定义。技术转让中的本地参与程度则由外商投资企业有关的高级管理人员提供的经验判断进行估计。

19.2 案例区和跨国公司访谈

选择上海作为研究案例区基于以下几点理由，首先，由于它相对发达的基础设施、教育水平、优越的地理位置，以及国家促进浦东发展的优惠政策（Yeung and Sung，1996），吸引了世界上许多大型跨国公司的关注。从1979～1995年，在全国各省级单位中，上海人均累计外商直接投资排名第一（Li and Yeung，1998）。到1997年，世界500强企业中有超过230家以及1996年《财富杂志》评选的世界100强跨国企业中有55家已经在这里投资。这一时期，上海实现了经济的快速增长和转型（Yeung and Sung，1996；Yeung and Li，1999）。其次，对194家投资总额超过1000万美元的外商投资企业调查显示，合资企业占总数的81.4%（浦东新区管委会，1997）。再次，上海是中国最大的工业和经济中心，这里有许多对国内市场具有垄断实力的大型国有企业。这些国有企业先前已构建的关系网络为研究跨国公司的本地嵌入提供了非常重要的案例。最后，根据1994年随机抽样调查的81家外资企业显示，跨国公司投资上海的主要动机是为了抢占庞大中国的市场（Nyaw，1996）。

对外公布的统计数据和信息不包括在上海外商投资企业的本地化情况。然而，浦东新区管委会（1997）的调查提供了一些相关数据。调查是在1997年7月至8月间进行的，涵盖大多数浦东新区的外商投资企业（浦东新区管委会，1997；图19.1）。浦东新区是上海市跨国公司最集中的区域，经调查的194家外资企业占整个新区1996年外资投资企业的78%。在这组数据中，有67家外资企业提供了本地化生产和技术转让的本地参与的相关信息。67家外资企业涵盖了跨国公司参与的所有产业部门，占到194家外资企业的35.5%。虽然这组数据并没有提供有关管理本地化的相关信息，但这个调查结果仍然揭示了上海市外商投资企业的总体情况，该数据将在接下来的部分中使用。

为进一步获取信息，作者在1997年9月和10月间访谈了上海市政府经济研究中心和外国投资委员会的4名高级人员，浦东新区政府的5名官员，包括经济贸易局、国土规划局的相关负责人以及两个主要开发区（金桥和张江）的4名外资企业主管（1998年进行了电话采访，更新了信息）。这些访谈提供了跨国公司在上海投资方面大致的信息和经验数据。我们还对15家企业的副总经理、助理总经理或者其他高级管理人员进行了访问。选取67家企业中的15家作为访谈对象的准则是基于它们的产业基础（覆盖主要行业）、规模（产业内最大）、运营时间（至少三年以上），同时基于不同的本地化程度和股权结构。基于浦东新区管委会（1997）的调查结果和相关政府人员咨询，设计了调查问卷，问卷中的问题具有开放性，主要关注于合资企业的中方公司本地参与程度。在某种程度上，访谈数据反映了在上海的各种大型外资企业的基本概况。由于小规模样本企业的非随机选择，调查结果有一定的局限性，因此，需要谨慎解释相关结果。

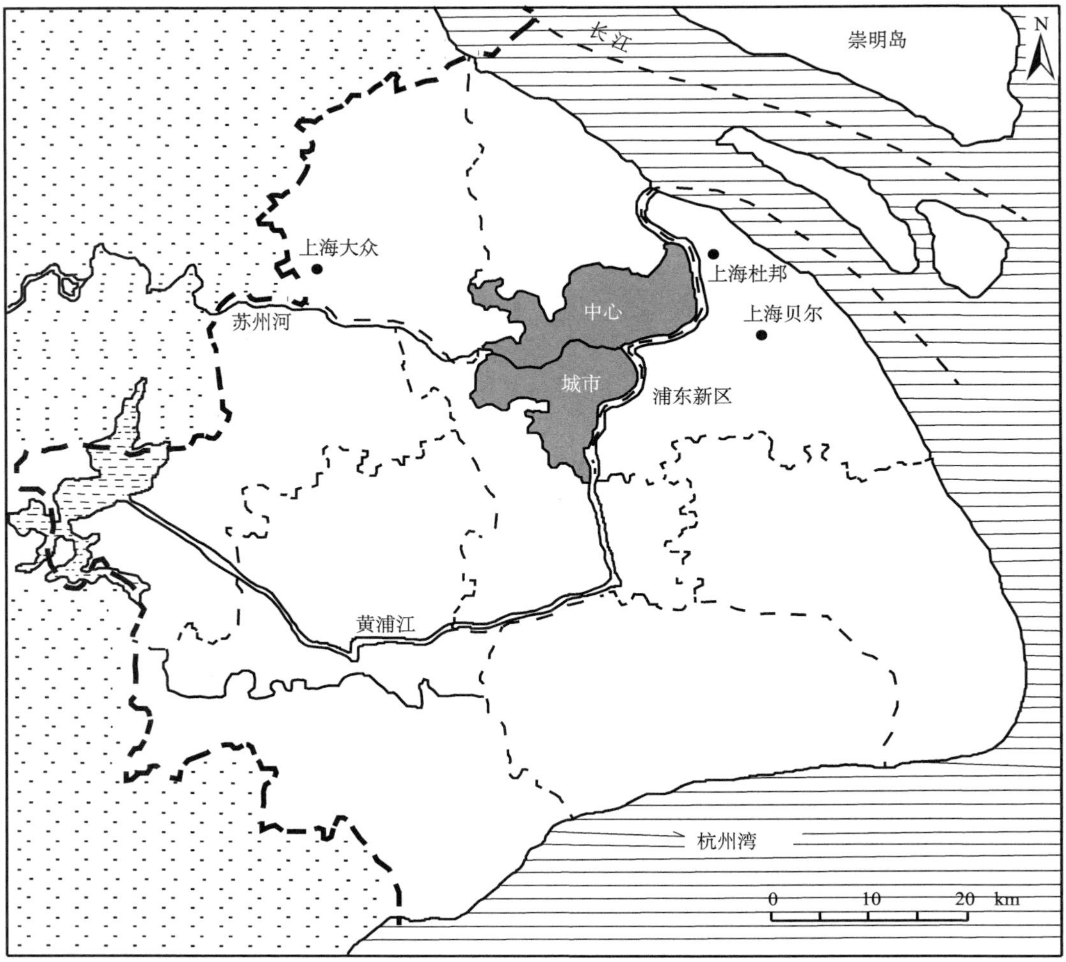

图 19.1 上海市及研究区的地理位置

在随后的讨论中，用来自于浦东新区管委会调查的 194 家外资企业数据、访谈政府官员，以及相关专家获取的信息来弥补这一限制。

19.3 企业管理的本地化程度

根据调查，在合资企业的中方所有权比例和企业关键岗位分配之间存在一种通用的模式。占有 70%以上的股权时，中方人员通常会拥有企业董事长和总经理两个位置。当股权降到 50%～70%会拥有两个位置中一个。如果多数股权属于外国投资者，那么本地人员将会担任企业的副董事长和副总经理的职务。这种情况在公司访谈中已经有了很好的说明（表 19.1）。

表 19.1　外资企业访谈中关键岗位的分配与本地所有权水平（$N=15$）

本地所有权水平（比例）	本地人员占据关键位置	本地人员占据其他管理岗位
70%及以上	公司董事长、总经理（2）	除了技术开发部门，大多数管理职位
50%～70%	董事长和副总经理（2）	除技术（1）或生产部门（1），大多数管理岗位
50%	公司董事长、总经理（1） 副董事长兼总经理（1）	除技术（1）或生产部门（1），大多数管理岗位
30%～50%	董事长和副总经理（7）	除技术或（某些情况下）生产部门，多数管理岗位
30%及以下	副董事长兼副总经理（1）	除了技术与生产部门，多数管理职位

注：括号里面的数字是样本企业部门职位占据的数量。

资料来源：作者的访谈。

由于大多数的外商投资企业的所有权是由跨国公司控制（如浦东新区管委会的调查 194 家外资企业中 71%的属这种情况），因此在管理中由中方控制的外资企业在上海并不常见。当然，本地控股较低的合资企业（本地股权低于 50%的企业）未必会抑制管理的本地化进程。例如，在表 19.1 中的 9 家此类合资企业，7 家企业拥有中方的董事长和副总经理。而且，被任命的本地管理人员占到了整个管理机构人数的 60%～80%。访谈进一步表明，本地管理者由于他们与本地商贸网络拥有紧密的关系，通常在国内业务中发挥着重要作用。当国内市场占总销售的大部分份额的情况下，本地参与显示出越来越重要的作用。随着实力较强的本地企业以他们的全部资产加入合资企业，那些原来的管理者由于更熟悉当地的情况几乎都继续担任他们的职务。上海外国投资委员会的一位高级官员估计，外资企业的本地化过程将快速推进。许多外商投资企业，包括一些外商独资企业，通过派遣有潜力的本地管理者去国外培训，开辟了向国外管理者学习的机会。因此，外商投资企业的本地经营时间越长，就会拥有更多的本地管理者。在受访谈的 15 家外资企业中都发现了本地管理者和技术人员来代替外籍工作人员的现象。这是一方面由于本地人员出色的管理能力（Kamis，1996；Nyaw，1996）；另一方面，与那些外籍人员相比，本地管理人员工资更低。

19.4　产品生产的本地化程度

一般来说，上海外商投资企业的本地后向联系较弱。通过对 67 家外资企业的调查数据分析，显示 45%的企业没有使用国内原材料，30%的企业使用了一小部分（低于 50%），仅有 25%的企业使用了较多的国内原材料和零部件（浦东新区管委会，1997）。访谈中我们发现，当地合作伙伴以前的生产状况、国内市场的规模和发展水平，以及投资持续的时间，都与生产的本地化程度有关。

规模较大且经营成功的本地合作企业通过提高合资产品的本地化程度来增强它们与对方谈判的实力。当本地合作企业此前的产品与合资企业生产的产品相类似时，这种情况就会出现。例如，表 19.2 中的合资企业 A-H 和企业 L 都拥有强大的本地母公司（无论是全国顶尖企业还是上海顶尖企业），在变成合资企业后没有改变它们主要的产品。

它们非常成功地实现了生产的本地化（本地化率达到70%～90%）。相比之下，合资企业J和K生产了不同于本地合作企业的产品，而且在经营三年之后其产品的本地化成分仍然较低。这是可以理解的，因为前一种情况本地合作企业通常已经拥有了较好的生产工艺和市场营销能力，它们既有的技术和供应网络能够使它们获得本地原材料从而降低生产成本。

表 19.2 受访企业的产品本地化生产程度（$N=15$）

合资企业（企业名称匿名）	企业股权的本地化程度/%	产品的本地化程度/%	本地合作伙伴的先前身份	目前在国内市场的业绩
A	60	70	N. L	V. G
B	75	>70	N. L	V. G
C	40	70	N. L	V. G
D	30	70	N. L	G
E	50	90	N. L	V. G
F	43	70	S. L	G
G	49	67	S. L	G
H	70	76	N. L	G
I	33	55	S. L	B
J	49	0	S. L/O	B
K	40	0	S. L/O	G
L	56	70	N. L	G
M	49.5	40	N. L/O	G
N	20	15	S. L/O	G
P	50	<10	N. L/O	B

注：本地合作伙伴的先前身份被分类为3组：国有企业（N. L），上海市属企业（S. L），其他企业。合资企业包含的多种本地合作伙伴的先前身份被注明。当前合资企业在国内市场的业绩用很好（V. G），好（G），差（B）和很差（V. B）来注明。最后两列的结果由企业自行评估。由于大多数跨国公司在投资之前做了市场投资调查，因此就不难理解企业的市场业绩没有处于最后一类的了（很差 V. B）。

资料来源：作者访谈。

在一些行业，国内巨大的销售额加快了生产的本地化进程，因为本地化生产可以降低成本，更好地满足当地消费者的偏好。在访谈的合资企业中，国内销售“好”和“很好”的产品几乎都有较高的本地化比例（表19.2），合资企业K是唯一的例外。该公司主要由一家大的跨国公司控制，其大规模的生产工厂主要位于那些能够为合资企业提供低成本零部件的国家（尽管不一定是低价格），一些中国不能生产的原材料同样需要进口。

原材料供应链上的本地化程度将随着时间变化而增加。在与15家外资企业的访谈中已经反映了这样的情况，虽然各企业之间生产的本地化程度增速不同，但仅有两家外资企业在运营之后生产的本地化程度变化为零。从没有本地供应开始，有两家企业在

10 年中生产的本地化程度已分别超过了 70%和 90%。来自 67 家企业数据显示，到 1996 年已经有 30 家企业的生产从刚开始的零本地化程度达到了 70%的水平。在过去的五年间，有 17 家企业的大部分原材料几乎都来自上海的本地供应（浦东新区管委会，1997）。由于大部分跨国公司是在 1992 年之后来到上海，这在一定程度上解释了上海外商投资企业整体较低的生产本地化水平。其他原因还包括一些跨国公司的国际化战略，产品相对较高的价格和激烈的竞争导致其在国内市场扩张缓慢，以及由于一些产品生产的特殊技术要求很难被本地工厂所掌握而造成了生产本地化存在困难。还有一小部分企业也出现这样的情况，即产品中的某些零部件进口的比本地生产的更便宜。

19.5　技术转让中本地参与程度

上海外资企业本地股权水平和技术转让存在这样的关系，当技术非常成熟且不会发生太大改变的情况下，合资企业通过共享要素为中方企业提供巨大的机遇来参与技术转让，这和之前的研究结论是一致的（Lan，1996）。表 19.3 显示的在技术转让中有一定程度的本地参与的 34 家外资企业中，仅有一家是外商独资企业，85%的合资企业中的中方股权超过 40%（浦东新区管委会，1997；作者访谈）。这些外资企业主要集中在如家用电器、汽车、摩托车部门，在这些部门技术已经普遍标准化（表 19.3）。

表 19.3　上海外商投资企业技术转让中的本地参与（外资企业数量，比例）

行业	外资企业总样本（数量，百分比）	技术进入阶段（数量，百分比）	技术吸收阶段（数量，百分比）	技术发展阶段（数量，百分比）
汽车、摩托车	12，100	3，25.0	7，58.3	2，16.7
电子通信	8，100	4，50.0	2，25.0	2，25.0
电子产品	8，100	5，62.5	3，37.5	
家用电器	13，100	2，15.4	10，76.9	1，7.7
机械与自动化设备	11，100	5，45.5	5，45.5	1，9.0
化学、建材材料	9，100	4，44.4	4，44.4	1，11.1
医药	5，100	3，60.0	2，40.0	
计算机，网络	6，100	5，83.3	1，16.7	
总计	72，100	31，43.1	34，47.2	7，9.7

注：技术进入阶段，技术只是被外商投资企业利用，并没有本地企业参与。技术吸收阶段，技术转让中出现不同程度的本地参与。技术发展阶段特点是研究机构和实验室的建立。

资料来源：浦东新区管委会（1997）和作者访谈。

表 19.3 中显示了外商投资企业经营的持续影响程度，先前的资产实力、技术状况、当前产品销售状况以及合资企业本地参与的业绩。例如，在过去十年间家用电器已经成为中国最大的消费品。并从发达国家购买了多条生产线。这些生产技术的引进给本地企业带来丰厚利润的同时，也缩小了本地与西方国家的技术差距。基于这样的技术来源增强了本地企业的协作实力，即使在外资占多数股权的合资企业，这个行业在技术转让中也是本地参与最强的（表 19.3 显示了技术转让的吸收阶段，10 家外资企业中 3 家拥有

同等股权，7 家本地股权达到 32％～45％）。这种情况在汽车和摩托车行业也比较普遍，多数本地合作企业在生产中已经遥遥领先其他相关产品。相比之下，制药和计算机行业在技术转让中本地参与程度最低，这是由于本地合作伙伴实力较弱，技术相对落后的结果（只有一家合资企业拥有相对较强的本地合作伙伴）。研发机构的设立同市场对新产品或改进产品的需求以及企业利润和经济实力密切相关，表 19.3 中组内排名靠前的 7 家外资企业在技术发展阶段均与其利润和销售额有关。

跨国公司间投资竞争的加剧给中方合作伙伴在技术转让中提供了有利的地位。这种情况存在于所有行业，因为每个参与的企业都会从众多跨国公司获取直接的投资。通用汽车（GM）就是典型的例子。在中国决定同跨国公司在上海浦东建立一个汽车生产厂后，通用汽车和世界上另外两个最大的汽车生产商参加了投标竞争。最终通用胜出，除了在 1998 年生产 1997 年版别克车模型外，还将在未来同时生产美国最新版别克车模型，并将同中方建立一个合资公司从事汽车设计和开发（人民日报，1996）。

19.6 企业案例分析

选取下面三个企业进行更深入的分析基于以下四个原因：首先，这些企业已在上海经营了相当长的时间（有两个企业已经超过 10 年，另一个则超过 5 年）。其次，它们占据了上海外商直接投资中汽车、电信、钢铁、电站设备、化工、电子电器 6 大主要行业中的 3 个。再次，这三个企业拥有不同的股权结构，有本地所有权占多数的，外商与本地同等股权的，还有外商股权占多数的。最后，这三家企业的外商投资者都来自于跨国公司世界 500 强。如无另外说明，在下面讨论中的信息主要是来自作者的访谈。

19.6.1 上海贝尔电话设备制造有限公司

这家合资企业是由两家大公司于 1983 年共同成立，中国邮电工业总公司拥有 60％股份，阿尔特卡朗讯贝尔电话制造有限公司拥有 31.65％的股份，另外 8.35％股份属于比利时政府。中国邮电工业总公司是由原邮电部完全拥有，拥有 42 家子公司和 32 家合资企业，分别位于中国 18 各省、市、自治区。自 1980 年以来，所有子公司和合资企业已经实现了超过 25％的年销售增长，有 15 家年销售额突破了 1 亿元（折合 1200 万美元）（陈少能，1995）。庞大的资产规模，对国内市场的有效掌控能力以及国内快速发展的电信市场，都给了这个本土企业在与比利时贝尔公司谈判中强大的谈判实力。除了充分参与企业管理和决策的制定，中方还得益于在多个领域高水平的本地化生产。

从 1984 年开始运营，上海贝尔公司取得了快速发展，已经成为先进的数字交换设备制造商领导者。1996 年，公司 1800 名员工取得了 45.6 亿元的销售额并且成为中国第五大外商投资企业。除了给当地带来巨大的利润和税收，本地合作企业的收益还延伸到自动化生产线和技术革新。由于原有的国内原材料供应网络、较低的生产成本和巨大的国内市场销售额促使原材料的国内供给由 1985 年的不足 10％，提高到 1988 年的 20％，1996 年增加到 70％。

乘数效应是非常显著的。首先，贝尔公司已为约 85 家国内供应商提供了市场（约

50 家位于上海），其中有一些是完全依赖该市场而生存。例如，上海有一家企业就为上海贝尔公司供应了超过 70％的集成电路板，该项供给的年采购额超过 3 亿元，使该企业成为中国电子显微加工企业中的顶级利润商。其次，随着上海贝尔公司强化了零部件供应的标准，激发了一些供应商提高产品质量、管理水平以及整体技术标准。1997 年 10 月，有 33 家供应商已经通过了 ISO9000 质量认证。最后是间接效应，一些工厂作为上海贝尔公司授权的供应商，在同其他潜在客户的谈判中已经获得了衍生优势。这种连锁效应推动了四家上海本地供应商向国际市场推销它们的产品。

就本地在技术上的收益而言，这家公司是一个很好的例子。早期，上海本地企业与发达国家在电子通信行业的技术差距还是很大的（通过访谈估计至少有 30 年的差距）。该公司一直试图通过各种方法来提高自身的研发能力，如在技术转让参与过程中学习，输送 50 名本地工程师去贝尔公司在欧洲的研发中心工作，与本地大学和科研机构加强联系合作等。本地技术人员在发展相关技术方面取得了很大的进步，最终于 1996 年在上海成立研发中心。为了开发一批具有知识产权的高科技产品，上海贝尔公司将其年销售额（1996 年为 3000 万美元）的 5％～7％的资金作为研发中心的经费。贝尔公司在上海的这家合资企业的贡献和价值在于极大地缩小了本地与国外的技术差距，就作者访谈对象估计，本地与国外先进技术的差距已缩短至几年的水平。

19.6.2 上海大众汽车公司

公司成立于 1985 年，是中国轿车制造业的第一家合资企业。合作伙伴包括上海汽车工业公司（SAIC）、中国汽车工业总公司、上海信托公司、德国大众汽车公司。资本投资的贡献对中国合作伙伴（主要是上汽集团）和德国大众公司是平等的。在董事会和执行管理委员会保持大致平等的人员搭配，中方担任公司总裁和总经理的职务，而德方担任商业执行总监和技术总监这两个重要的职位。作为本土企业，上海汽车厂（20 世纪 80 年代早期中国最大的客车生产商）为成为大众汽车公司的主要组成部分进行了彻底的改造，企业的中层人员在新的合资企业仍担任类似的职务。在我们访谈中了解到，合资企业中有 19 名德国人，而本地员工则超过 10000 人。由于产品成功的迎合了市场的需求，上海大众汽车的产量由 1985 年的 1733 辆剧增到 1997 年的 230443 辆，总销售额在 20 世纪 90 年代的前 6 年中，其在全国 200 家最大的外商投资企业中位居首位。

由于汽车工业生产联系的特点以及在上海市政府和德国大众汽车公司的共同推动下，大众汽车生产网络中本地参与的成分急剧增加。虽然双方组建合资企业的动机不同，但是都意识到生产的国产化提升有助于双方达到各自的目标：大众汽车想拥有更大的中国市场份额，而本地合作伙伴希望建立一个具有国际竞争力的汽车产业（王志乐，1996）。上汽集团作为主要的本地合作伙伴，是一个由上海市政府控股的国有企业，因此，20 世纪 80 年代末上海市政府和德国大众汽车就开始采取措施来支持和协调汽车生产的国产化。另一个主要动机是 1988 年中央政府为了缓解政府财政收入不足，批准通过了向大众汽车销售者征收购置税的方案（每辆车约 28000 万元，折合 3400 美元）。在随后的几年，德国大众公司既帮助潜在的供应商雇佣已退休的专家，同时鼓励相关的外资企业对这些供应商进行投资。因此，首个新款汽车“桑塔纳 B2”的国产化成分由

1987年的5.7%增加到1990年的60.1%，在1997年达到了92.9%。新款“桑塔纳2000”，由1995年开始生产时的69.7%的国产化率，提升到1997年的84.0%。到1997年年底，大众汽车使用的材料和零部件来自于270家国内企业，其中，67%为上海本地企业。

来自于大众汽车的本地化效益是显而易见。大众汽车和它的国内供应商提供的直接就业机会估计接近50000个岗位。作为中国最大的外资企业，上海大众汽车公司和它的供应商为上海工业总产值和上海市税收贡献了相当大的份额。上海汽车工业集团主要由上海大众汽车公司和零部件供应商组成，在过去两年的时间里有五项指标排在全国前列，包括纳税、利润、营业额、资本流动和国产化率。此外，其他企业与大众公司之间的联系也促进了整个汽车行业大发展以及上海其他相关产业的发展。随着汽车国产化程度不断推进，60家外资企业与本地供应商建立了合资企业，120家企业向供应商转让了技术。通过引进、吸收和消化国外技术，上海企业提升了汽车制造和设计的整体技术水平，这也推动了上海大众在1992年设立了技术开发中心，并开始在本地设计新的汽车款型，从而使得上海成为中国汽车制造技术的中心之一。

就上海大众汽车公司对其他行业产业的乘数效应而言，塑料行业或许是一个典型的例子。20世纪80年代之前这个行业在上海属于相当落后且规模很小的行业，企业规模非常小且多为乡镇企业或村集体企业。由于现代汽车制造需要利用许多塑料零部件，上海大众汽车的发展创造了这样的需求并且促进了这个行业的成长。现在，塑料行业使用最先进的设备和技术来生产高质量的产品，例如，在1996年，这个行业超过15%的产品出口到国际市场（上海市统计局，1997）。

19.6.3　上海杜邦农业化学有限公司

相比于前两个公司，这家公司绝大部分股权（80%）由美国杜邦公司所有。这个农用化学产品制造商没有较多的供应链，外资公司在技术转移中比较敏感。然而，正像前面描述的两个案例，这家合资企业同样拥有强大的本地合作伙伴，上海亚太农业化工集团有限公司，这家国有企业由上海市政府控制，拥有超过2.4亿元的资产（约合3000万美元），在上海投资了三个大工厂和一个研发机构，它也通过合作或联盟的方式与其他省份的十几个企业建立了紧密的联系。这家合资企业生产与本地合作企业相同类型的产品，由于国家政策强调农业的发展，农业仍然是中国一个巨大且重要的经济部门，所以产品拥有巨大的国内市场。

自1992年投产经营以来，杜邦公司的产品就深受中国农民的欢迎。在1996年的时候销售总额就达到1.5亿（1800万美元）。本地合作伙伴的经济效益和营销优势以及中国巨大的市场促使杜邦集团在上海设立了研发实验室。这是1997年杜邦集团在亚太地区设立的唯一的研发机构。该机构的雇员主要来自本地专业人员，这导致了技术转让中高水平的本地化参与，所有的七个部门都拥有本地管理者。此外，尽管在本地生产主要化学合成品还比较困难，但是生产的本地化程度在1996年已达到15%。

19.7 结论与讨论

作为促进全球化的一个重要因素，跨国公司的本地嵌入可以从不同的视角进行研究。本章主要关注于跨国公司在投资地内的本地合作伙伴的一些特征。通过在上海的实地访谈和调查数据显示，强势的本地合作伙伴，连同其他影响因素，都会深刻地影响到合资企业在经营管理、产业联系和技术转让中的本地嵌入。合资企业生产的产品与它们的本地合作伙伴相类似的时候，因为本地强势企业通常在生产链和技术比较好的相关行业拥有广阔的关系网络，它们先前拥有的人际关系同样能够应用到合资企业。通过政府政策可进一步增强本地化的优势条件，鼓励本地企业参与到跨国公司的经营网络中。当前跨国公司在上海的合作伙伴主要是国有企业，而政府对国有企业拥有较强的控制力，所以政治因素起着主要作用。因而，鉴于中国商业行为的传统习惯，强势的本地合作伙伴可能代表着各种类型的本地企业、政府部门等一系列本地机构。从这个视角来看，本研究的发现，从某种程度上响应了 Amin 和 Thrift（1994）早期提到的观点。然而，在与其他发展中国家相比较时应该谨慎看待这项研究的结果，因为在加强跨国公司本地嵌入的过程中，中国的文化和政策能够起到强化本地合作伙伴（国有企业）的作用。

联系到跨国公司抢占市场的动机，上海的案例彰显了外商投资企业的市场业绩与本地嵌入之间的关系。一方面，外商投资企业的国内市场由本地嵌入进行扩展。例如，在本地合作的参与中，跨国公司利用本地合作伙伴（或本地人）先前的销售网络展开产品营销，通过增加生产的本地化程度来降低生产成本；企业技术进步的本地参与，特别是在本地设立研发中心，使产品更加适应当地消费者偏好。另一方面，外商投资企业市场的拓展推动了本地嵌入的发展，国内市场不断扩张的销售网络需要雇佣更多本地人员，巨大的销售额产生的丰厚利润支持着新产品的开发和本地研发机构的设立。作为影响跨国公司本地嵌入的重要影响因素，合资企业的市场业绩是吸引外商直接投资的关键，这种情况可能与出口导向型的外商投资有所不同。

上海合资公司的案例研究表明，在全球经济背景下，跨国公司的本地嵌入对区域经济发展具有重要作用。随着本地在生产联系、管理和技术转让中的参与程度不断提高，合资企业的增长趋势已经扩散到整个地区经济。从1992～1996年，上海国内生产总值年平均增长速度为14.2%（上海市统计局，1997）。这期间本地企业管理能力也得到很大提升。通过在外资企业工作，许多本地人已经成为了现代企业管理者。根据多位政府官员和有关专家的估计，经过20～30年的跨国公司投资，上海与发达国家在汽车、电信、电子行业的技术差距将大幅度缩小。此外，跨国公司会促使上海进一步成为国际经济、贸易和金融中心。1996年外资企业出口额已占到了出口总额的31%。通过与位于上海的世界各大跨国公司的商业联系，诸多国际银行和贸易企业都已经在这个城市设立了分公司。

与其他发展中国家相比，上海本地化的总体水平要低于菲律宾（Hill，1982）、新加坡（Lim and Fong，1982）和印度（Lall，1980）。这主要由于多数跨国公司投资从90年代才开始流向上海，而且外资工厂发展本地供应商则需要时间（Dicken，1992）。

调查的案例企业证明了长期的投资可促使本地化提升（Li and Yeung，1999）。例如，上海大众和上海贝尔公司比菲律宾汽车公司和新加坡的电子企业取得了更高的国产化水平（Hill，1982；Lim and Fong，1982）。因此，在未来几年将会有愈来愈多的上海本地企业参与到跨国公司的贸易网络中。随着跨国公司的发展，上海将进一步从本地嵌入中受益，并将成为全球经济中一个现代化的国际性都市。

参考文献

陈少能. 1995. 世界著名跨国公司在浦东. 上海：华东师范大学出版社

浦东新区管委会. 1997. 浦东外国直接投资原因的调查报告. 上海（非公开内部资料）

人民日报（海外版）. 1994. 外资快速增加的主要因素，3-28

人民日报（海外版）. 1996. 通用汽车来到中国，3-30

上海市统计局. 1997. 上海统计年鉴. 北京：中国统计出版社

王志乐. 1996. 著名跨国公司在中国的投资. 北京：中国经济出版社

中国国家统计局. 1997. 中国统计年鉴. 北京：中国统计出版社

Amin A, Thrift N. 1994. Living in the global. In: Globalization, Institutions, and Regional Development in Europe. Oxford: Oxford University Press

Cheng L K. 1995. Foreign Direct Investment in China. Paris: OECD

Conti S. 1997. Interdependent and uneven development: A systemic view of the global-local dialectic. International Geographical Union Bulletin, 47: 195～204

Dicken P, Mats F, Andres M. 1994. The local embeddedness of transnational corporations. In: Globalization, Institutions, and Regional Development in Europe. Oxford: Oxford University Press

Dicken P, Michel Q. 1994. Transnational Corporations and European Regional Restructuring. Utrecht: N G S

Dicken P. 1992. Global Shift: The Internationalization of Economic Activity (2nd Edition). New York: Guilford Press

Dicken P. 1994. Global local tensions: Firms and states in the global space-economy. Economic Geography, 70: 101～129

Fujita K, Hill R C. 1995. Global Toyotaism and local development. International Journal of Urban and Regional Research, 19 (1): 7～22

Grabher G. 1993. The Embedded Firm: On Socioeconomics of Industrial Networks. London: Routledge

Granovetter M. 1985. Economic action and social structure: The problem of embeddedness. American Journal of Sociology, 91: 481～510

Harrison B. 1992. Industrial district: Old wine in new bottle? Regional Studies, 26 (5): 469～483

Hill H. 1982. Vertical inter-firm linkages in LDCs: A note on the Philippines. Oxford Bulletin of Economics and Statistics, 44: 261～271

Hirschman A O. 1958. The Strategy of Economic Development. New Haven, C T: Yale University Press

Kamis T L. 1996. Education for the PRC executive. The China Business Review, 23 (4): 36～45

Lall S. 1980. Vertical inter-firm linkages in LDCs: An empirical study. Oxford Bulletin of Economics and Statistics, 42: 203～226

Lan P. 1996. Technology Transfer to China Through Foreign Direct Investment. Aldershot: Avebury

Li X J, Yeung Y M. 1998. Transnational corporations and their impact on regional economic imbalance:

Evidence from China. Third World Planning Review, 20 (4): 1～23

Li X J, Yeung Y M. 1999. Inter-Firm Linkages and Regional Impact of Transnational Corporations: Company Case Studies from Shanghai, China. Geografiska Annaler B, Human Geography, 81 (2): 61～72

Li X J. 1997. Foreign direct investment and its impact on China's economy: A research appraisal. Journal of Chinese Geography, 7: 33～78

Lim L Y C, Fong P E. 1982. Vertical linkages and multinational enterprises in developing countries. World Development, 10: 585～595

Nyaw M. 1996. Investment environment: Perceptions of overseas investors of foreign-funded industrial firms. In: Shanghai: Transformation and Modernisation under China's Open Policy. Hong Kong: The Chinese University Press

O'h Ullachain B. 1984. Linkages and foreign direct investment in the United States. Economic Geography, 60: 238～253

Perroux F. 1950. Economic space, theory and applications. Quarterly Journal of Economics, 64: 89～104

Perroux F. 1973. Multinational investment and the analysis of development and integrated pole. Economies et Societes, 24: 831～868

Schoenberger E. 1991. Globalization and regionalization: New problems of time, distance and control in the multinational firms. Paper presented at the Annual Meeting of AAG in Miami, April

United Nations Conference on Trade and Development (UNCTAD). 1996. World Investment Report 1996: Investment, Trade and International Policy Arrangement. New York: United Nations

Wang Z Q. 1995. Foreign Investment and Economic Development in Hungary and China. Aldershot: Avebury

Yeung Y M, Li X J. 1999. Bargaining with transnational corporations: The case of Shanghai. International Journal of Urban and Regional Research, 23 (3): 513～533

Yeung Y M, Sung Y W. 1996. Shanghai: Transformation and Modernization under China's Open Policy. Hong Kong: The Chinese University Press

Young S, Hood N, Peters E. 1994. Multinational enterprises and regional economic development. Regional Studies, 28 (7): 657～677

Zhao L M, Aram J D. 1995. Networking and growth of young technology-intensive ventures in China. Journal of Business Venturing, 10 (5): 349～370

第 20 章　跨国公司与投资地关系

本章为 20 世纪末的研究成果，通过对中国最大的经济中心之一——上海的研究，探讨跨国公司与投资地之间的关系。自 1993 年以来，中国已成为全球第二大吸引外资的国家（Unctad，1996），而上海，作为中国最强的经济中心，人均累积外商直接投资位居中国首位（广东虽然累积外商直接投资总额第一，但人均位居上海之后，见 Li and Yeung，1998）。更重要的是，这座城市近期已吸引世界多数大型跨国公司的注意，经济增长和结构转型很快（Tian，1996；Yeung and Sung，1996；Olds，1997）。除了探讨双方关系的独特性，包括地方对外商直接投资的渴望，跨国公司对进入中国这个具有巨大潜力的市场和获得地方资源的渴望，本章还将探讨：①研究区内跨国公司和地方参与者间的力量关系；②各种公司特性，如所有权结构、地方参与者以前的经历、技术密集度、投资期限等，对相互作用影响的差异；③最初投资后讨价还价力量的变化；④权力关系对地方经济的影响。

20.1　研究背景

伴随着全球化的加速发展，区域经济发展越来越密切地与跨国公司的全球发展战略关联。通过跨境投资，跨国公司对投资地经济的影响越来越大，并使经济增长在投资地扩散开来（Perroux，1973）。跨国公司对投资地经济的影响包括很多方面，如资本和金融、技术、贸易和产业联系、产业结构和企业家精神、就业和经济依赖（Dicken，1992）等。接受投资还可以增加比较优势、提高资源配置效率和技术效率、获得规模和范围经济（Young et al.，1994），改善基础设施（Kueh，1992），推动经济、制度和立法改革（Zhan，1993；Lardy，1994；Porter，1995）等。回顾这些文献，尽管有不同观点，但很多学者强调投资地所获得的利益。不过跨国公司的影响存在区域差异，既表现在国家间，也表现在一国之内不同区域之间。

在投资地，跨国公司和地方政府（或地方公司）间的相互作用由双方的势力关系决定（Dicken，1994）。相关各方间的谈判力量决定着外国直接投资（FDI）产生的利润和成本的分配。跨国公司和地方参与者之间存在讨价还价；地方政府官员和地方公司管理人员在战略取向方面也会不一致（Guthrie，1997）。不过跨国公司和地方参与者之间各个方面的相互作用不会消除讨价还价方面的区域差异。当跨国公司准备进入经济中心时（Dunning，1981），跨国公司之间在这些区位的激烈竞争和地方公司的强大（经济中心有适宜它们成长的环境）会使地方公司在与跨国公司交易时处于有利地位。所以，即使其他因素相同，经济中心的地方参与者会比其他地方的参与者拥有更强的谈判力量。在更大地理尺度上，学者们的研究表明强国和弱国，发达国家和发展中国家与跨国公司的关系也存在差异（Pitelis，1991）。但在国家之内的区域层面，还没有文献探讨这个问题。不过，相关研究已给出有价值的参考。例如，地方社区面对全球化力量时的相对无力，地方机构除了提供更有吸引力的商业环境或努力推动地方企业进入跨国公司网络之外，能做的事情很少（Dicken，1994）。对很多地方公司来说，加入跨国公司生产网络后，往往处于不太重要的地位（Schoenberger，1991）。

对已有文献的评述可以提出以下几个问题。如果一个地区拥有跨国公司所需资源，这个区域在谈判过程中就拥有较强的议价能力吗？区域如何利用它的议价能力，从跨国公司获得积极影响？如何理解跨国公司和地方合作者之间的讨价还价关系？

为了研究跨国公司和发展中经济投资地的关系，学者们（主要来自商业研究领域）使用的度量指标有外商投资企业[①]的所有权结构（Fagre and Wells，1982；Pan，1992）、控制程度、盈利能力（Lecraw，1993）等。这些度量多关注单个企业。除企业之外，还有一些其他指标更适合探讨投资地和跨国公司相互关系的区域特征。

20.2　影响讨价还价关系因素

跨国公司和投资地的讨价还价关系受很多因素影响，如双方对资源的相互需求，各方实现其潜在谈判力量的约束，参与方的谈判地位（Dicken，1992）等。尤其是以下五个因素值得探讨。

20.2.1　投资地的资源和市场

区位优势，由一个区域的自然资源、相应的劳动力、合适的基础设施、政府刺激、稳定的政治氛围和完善的市场等（Dicken，1992），是吸引跨国公司跨境投资的最重要因素。

这些因素的质量和数量是投资地与跨国公司讨价还价的基础实力。除此之外，投资机会的唯一性（Gabriel，1966）、优势投资机会的创造（Nixson，1988）也可增加投资地的谈判力量：当某一公司特别想接近某一区位时，最终的谈判，跨国公司可能会做出让步（Dicken，1992）。的确，政府通过直接或间接行动，越来越成为影响跨国公司区位决策的重要力量（Dunning，1997）。

20.2.2　跨国公司控制的资源和机会

跨国公司拥有技术、管理技巧、资本、营销能力和其他机会（Dicken，1992），这是很多区域想得到的，尤其是发展中国家。如果地方公司不能达到这些要求，区域就特别需要跨国公司，这就增加了跨国公司的谈判力量（Gabriel，1966）。的确，在发展中国家经济现代化过程中技术日益重要，跨国公司的技术能力对最后的谈判结果具有重要影响（Fagre and Wells，1982；Gomes-Casseres，1990；Lecraw，1993）。

---

① 本章中外商投资企业或子公司指在中国的一项外商直接投资，而不管外商股权比例多少。

20.2.3 各方的竞争

多数政府将外国直接投资视为“好消息”（Dunning，1994），几乎没有政府无吸引外资的计划（Glickman and Woodward，1988）。潜在投资国（区域）间对FDI的竞争越激烈，投资国或投资地的谈判地位就越弱势（Dicken，1992）。相反地，如果很多跨国公司单独竞争投资机会或想获得投资地控制的资源，跨国公司的谈判力量就越弱。换句话说，投资地的谈判力量将随着其他渠道跨国公司投资可得性的增加而增加（Lecraw，1993）。

20.2.4 投资地和跨国公司的情况

投资地的经济、政治、社会中心地位将增加其谈判力量，因为很多证据表明跨国公司倾向于将附属机构布局于投资国的这些地方。另一方面，跨国公司的跨国度、技术密集度、母国的国际地位也会影响公司的竞争优势和谈判地位。

20.2.5 合资企业中地方合作者的状况

在中国，跨国公司投资的主要模式是建立合资企业。由于中国还是国家主导的经济体制，中国的地方公司，政府所有的程度越高，在和外国合作者谈判时，拥有的谈判力量就越强。在国有合作者中，合资之前规模比较大，经营比较成功的企业，与跨国公司谈判时，就比小企业或不太成功的企业拥有更强谈判力。

20.3 讨价还价度量

合资企业的所有权结构常被用作度量跨国公司和地方合作者讨价还价结果的重要指标。一方在股权结构中拥有的比例越高，说明他相对于合作方拥有较强的谈判力量。很多情况下是这样，但四个方面的原因也会挑战这种现象。

第一，资本短缺是发展中国家经济增长中的主要问题，这也是这些国家吸引跨国公司资本进入的主要原因。这意味着在所有权结构方面，地方合作者无法和跨国公司竞争。从这点看，跨国公司比地方合作者拥有较强的谈判力量。第二，某些控制和利益，包括提名董事会成员的权力、政府的特殊管制、税收等等，无法直接和所有权相连。第三，跨国公司利用它的谈判力量不是为了提高股权比例，而是为了获得某些其他东西。相同的，地方合作者也会以低的股权比例换来先进技术。最后，一些相对发达地区，由于更加开放的政策（如允许外国投资者在合资企业里拥有较高比例股权），跨国公司所控制的所有权比例会高些。例如，Pan（1996）的研究指出，中国三个直辖市（北京、上海、天津）的外国投资者比其他地方的投资者更可能拥有高比例股权份额。这不能解释为在与跨国公司谈判时，三个直辖市比中国其他省份拥有谈判力量较低。

除所有权之外，管理和技术方面的控制度也不是度量讨价还价结果的敏感指标。发展中国家现存的技术水平远低于跨国公司的技术水平。所以，一般来说，地方合作者无法在这些方面与跨国公司竞争。

从投资地的角度，度量指标应该反映区域（包括区内的地方公司）是否获得想要的资源，或地方公司是否从跨国公司进入中获益，并能持续发展。从这个观点出发，考虑到中国的政治和经济体系，本章使用三种度量，即投资地跨国公司数量增长、所有权结构和地方化程度。

第一种度量以以下两个方面为基础。①投资地跨国公司数和增长率，可以一定程度上反映着跨国公司间的竞争；②中国每个区域都在吸引 FDI，跨国公司的数量和快速增长反映着吸引力，或特定区域的谈判力量。这种度量应该小心应用，因为地方政府和地方企业为了使自己更具吸引力会做出很多让步。处于这种考虑，使用这种度量时，需要进行区域 FDI 政策的比较。

第二种度量之所以使用，是因为，在其他因素相同情况下，高比例所有权会给所有者争得更多利益。不过在解释所有权模式时要小心，如上文提到的理由。

第三种度量在评价地方获得的实际利益时最重要。中国的国家政府和区域政府通常使用地方化程度，表征在吸引 FDI 方面取得的成就。由于到目前为止，政府在制订经济政策，控制国有企业方面仍居领导角色，国有企业是跨国公司主要的地方合作者（尤其在上海、北京和天津），地方拥有较强谈判力就可以达到较高程度的地方化。具体来说，地方化包括原材料、零部件供给中地方所占份额、管理中的地方参与程度、地方在技术发展中的参与和知情程度（Fujita and Hill，1995）。

20.4　上海讨价还价力量的来源

20.4.1　中国的资源和市场机会

上海拥有的讨价还价筹码是和中国的国家状况相连。1980 年以来，快速的经济增长和拥有世界 1/5 人口，使中国成为世界上最大的市场。有吸引力的国内市场增加了投资地政府的讨价还价能力。除此之外，其他因素，如廉价土地、低劳动力成本、丰富和多样的自然资源、政府前瞻性的政策也增强了中国面对跨国公司时的实力。中国国家统计局 1994 年对 1066 家外商投资企业的随机调查证实，潜在市场，丰富的人力资源和政策刺激是吸引 FDI 到中国投资的主要因素（人民日报，1994）。

20.4.2　上海的重要地位

第一，上海位于东西流向的长江出海口，而长江流域拥有中国 1/3 的人口，40%的 GDP。同时，上海又位于中国海岸带，国家最重要经济带的中部。这种战略区位（T 字形交汇处）使上海与中国的经济发达区域紧密相连，腹地范围很大（Yeung，1996）。从国际上说，中国上海北边临近日本、韩国，南边临近中国香港、中国台湾和新加坡，是西太平洋地区的中枢节点。这种独特的地理区位，被想要实现全球化运作的跨国公司看好，这极大地提升了上海在讨价还价中的地位。

第二，在推动现代中国的发展过程中，上海有辉煌的发展历史，在技术水平和基础设施上均有良好基础。在 20 世纪前半期，引领着中国工业化和城市化的发展。西方商业主义和地方行动的神奇结合，产生了蓬勃的企业家精神，这极利于创新（Yeung，

1996)。在技术能力方面，上海市拥有的高等教育和研究机构，以及技术人员、工程师和科学家数量位居全国第二（Nyaw，1996）。这其中原因之一是越来越多内陆省份的专业技术人员来上海寻找更好的工作机会。作为中国最大的产业中心，经过几十年的发展，上海的基础设施已有很大改善。它的港口是在中国最大（不包括香港），城市电信设施为中国最好之一。

第三，上海引领全国很多工业品生产。例如，1996 年它生产着中国 49.7%的缝纫机，31.5%的发电设备，26.6%的自行车，15.5%的乙烯，14.4%的钢，13%左右的家用洗衣机、摩托车和塑料，11.5%的化纤（上海市统计局，1997）。而且，上海还有很多超大型企业，在一些行业拥有某种垄断势力（Mok，1996）。这对跨国公司很有吸引力，因为这些企业已建成国内营销渠道，可通过地方合作者控制市场。

第四，国家的优惠发展政策，特别是推动浦东发展的政策，使上海的地位远高于中国很多省份。拥有中央政府赋予的比经济特区更特殊的政策，浦东被指定为要恢复上海以前的角色，即成为中国重要的国际金融、贸易和经济中心。随后，改善上海基础设施，加速技术转移，推动第三产业增长的工程项目会大量开工。

第五，上海和中央政府具有特殊联系。中国国家领导人中，许多在他们的职业生涯中都曾担任上海市的党政领导。这些特殊的个人关系对上海的发展有很大好处。

自前文所述，中国在世界地位的不断提升，上海在中国地位的不断提升，给上海带来了较强的讨价还价能力。上海远不是一个平常的、第三世界国家的城市，它被很多跨国公司看好，并将以此撬开中国这个巨大的市场。不过，上海也受到一些跨国公司的挑战，因为这些公司拥有先进技术和优质资产①。不完善的法律制度也会降低上海在股权谈判中的地位。北京、天津和中国其他重要经济中心对 FDI 的竞争也会削弱上海的讨价还价能力。所以，跨国公司和上海的关系远比表面上看起来的复杂。

20.5 跨国公司的上海直接投资增长

在中国开始经济改革后的 10 年间，在吸引外资方面上海落后于广东和其他南方省份。20 世纪 90 年代早期浦东和长江经济带被指定为吸引外资区域，之后上海吸引外资的地位就发生了改变。单就 1992 年一年，上海实际吸引的 FDI 数量就几乎和 1979～1991 年的总量相当。上海实际吸引外资占中国的比例由 1991 年的 4%增加到 1996 年的 9%。更引人注目的是，在上海市区及郊区投资的大型跨国公司数量远超过北京、广东和其他省份（表 20.1 和表 20.2）②。

① 根据我们的调查（见附录），与跨国公司拥有的其他资源相比，上海更看重技术、管理方法和资本。例如市政府制订了一个指南，鼓励公司以市场换技术，以市场换资本，以市场换现代管理方法。实践甚至表明技术转移成为政府对跨国公司政策的首要目标。

② 以下讨论基于 1997 年 9 月作者对上海对外经济贸易委员会工作人员的访谈（见附录，一些数据在 1998 年 5 月又通过电话进行了修订），有数据来源说明的除外。

表 20.1　大型制造业外商投资企业的区位（1979～1994 年）和 1980～1995 年来自美国、日本和德国的跨国公司

省市区	外商投资企业中外商注册资本超过 1 亿美元（1 亿美元，占总数%）		外商投资企业中外商注册资本超过 5000 万美元（1 亿美元，占总数%）		30 家日本和德国跨国公司的附属企业（数量，占总数%）		美国跨国公司的 200 家最大投资（数量，占总数%）	
上海	563	81	662	56	48	21	29	15
北京	130	19	248	21	41	18	28	14
广东	0	0	60	5	37	16	27	13
其他	0	0	210	18	105	45	116	58
总计	693	100%	1180	100%	231	100%	200	100%

资料来源：大型制造业外商投资企业数来自 Tian（1996）；30 家日本和德国跨国公司附属企业数来自王志乐（1996）；美国跨国公司的投资数来自中国对外贸易经济合作部各年统计。

表 20.2　50 家世界 100 强工业跨国公司在上海的直接投资

	描述
第一次投资时间	1980～1992（15），1993（10），1994（6），1995（12），1996（7）
母国	美国（19），日本（11），德国（9），荷兰（3），韩国（3），英国（2），法国（2）
项目规模	1980～1995：79 个项目，总投资 19 亿美元，平均单个项目 2400 万美元 1996 年：21 个项目，总投资 12.5 亿美元，平均单个项目 5990 万美元
区位（基于主要项目）	浦东新区 17 个：其中金桥 9 个，其他发展区 8 个 徐汇区 10 个：都在漕河泾高新技术园区 其他 12 个区和 6 个郊县 23 个：其中松江工业区 1 个，闵行经济开发区 4 个
行业	汽车，电信，电器，钢，电站设备，化学

注：括号里的数字是各类别跨国公司的数量。当一个跨国公司有多个投资项目时，它在上海的区位由主要（或最大）项目决定。

1. 大型跨国公司的快速增长

截至 1997 年年底，财富杂志世界 500 强工业公司有 230 家在上海有投资；100 强跨国公司中，有 55 家。除了几家跨国公司，如德国大众是 1983 年来上海外，大多数跨国公司是到 90 年代才来上海投资。在 90 年代早期，浦东新区发展，中国法制环境的改善（特别是在知识产权保护方面）和中国政府鼓励大力投资于高新技术产业的推动下，1992 年以后大型跨国公司投资上海的步伐加快。世界 100 强工业跨国公司，已有 50 家在上海有投资，其中 70%是在 1993～1996 年来到上海的（表 20.2 和图 20.1）。

2. 三个来源地

50 家跨国公司主要来自美国、日本和西欧世界三大核心区域，占总量的 94%（表 20.2）。来自这些国家的跨国公司更可能拥有上海所需的先进技术。

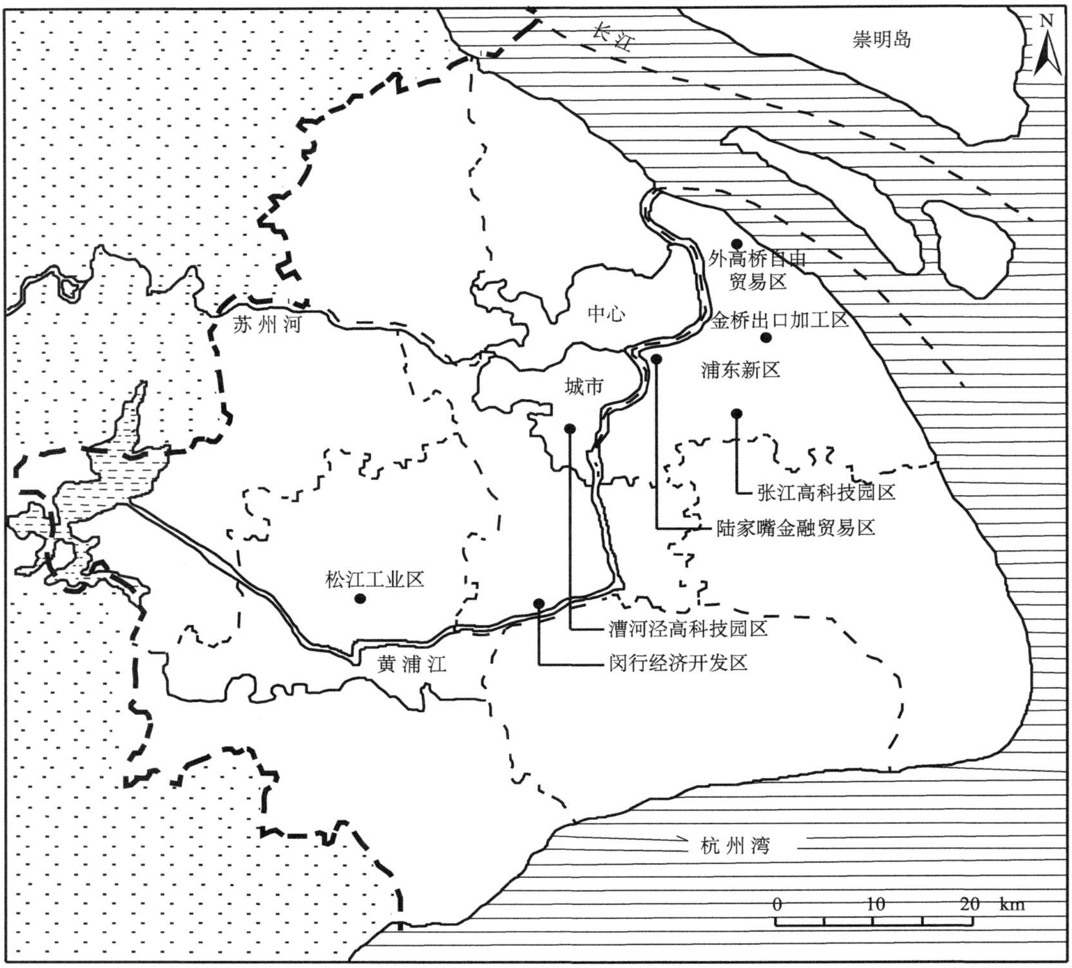

图 20.1　上海主要发展区域（高科技园区）

资料来源：Yeung，1996。

3. 投资规模巨大

20 世纪 90 年代之前，大规模的跨国公司投资就倾向于投资到上海。如 1979～1994 年间，超过 5000 万美元注册资本的项目，上海占到全国总量的 56%（表 20.1）。证据也显示，投资规模越大，上海越占主导地位（表 20.1，超过 1 亿美元投资项目中上海所占百分比很高）。90 年代初，投资上海的项目规模更加增加。1996 年平均单个项目投资额是 5990 万美元，有 4 个项目投资额超过 2 亿美元。1997 年前三个季度，平均单个项目的投资额增加到 8900 万美元，有 7 个项目投资额超过 1 亿美元。大型投资项目中，和通用汽车建立的合资企业投资额达 19 亿美元，和日本电气股份有限公司（NEC）建立的合资企业投资额达 12 亿美元。

4. 技术层次较高

在地方政府看来，世界 50 强跨国公司投资企业的技术水平和知识密集度较高。这些企业拥有最新的，甚至最先进的生产设备，相应地，它们也使用着相对先进的技术。技术转移在汽车制造、电信和电子行业比较显著。

5. 良好业绩

世界 50 强跨国公司在上海运营得都很好。多数企业扩大了产出，赚取了利润。根据获得的数据，1996 年世界 50 强跨国公司投资的 19 家合资企业，都在上海 50 家销售额最大外商投资企业行列。利润方面更令人吃惊。例如，上海三菱电梯三年间赚取的利润就等于它的总投资 1700 万美元；它的主要效率指标是 10 年前的 10 倍，多年位居中国首位。同样的，上海贝尔电话设备制造有限公司，在过去 13 年间，产品市场份额一直在扩大。自其开业 10 年来，这一公司对上海市政府的税收贡献是政府投资额的五倍（地方合作者是一家国有企业）。上海大众到 20 世纪末的 8 年都是全国所有外商投资企业中产值最高的。

依据最初的举措，上海没有比其他区域做出更多让步，就比中国其他省市区吸引到更多大型跨国公司，大规模的跨国公司投资项目。访谈的政府官员和公司管理人员估计，多数外商投资企业运营很好，也给地方合作者带来了利润。证据表明，在与跨国公司谈判时，与中国所有其他地方相比，上海拥有更强的讨价还价能力。

20.6　上海与跨国公司的讨价还价分析

20.6.1　讨价还价力量和所有权结构

1. 所有权结构

根据官方数据，在所有权结构中，外商相当一部分占有股权（表 20.3）。根据对 194 家外商投资企业调查，71％的企业，外商占大部分股权（浦东新区管委会，1997）。外方拥有过半股权的企业数不仅远超过地方拥有过半股权的企业数，而且在不断增加（表 20.3）。其他数据也显示，同一时期完全归外商所有的企业比外商投资

表 20.3　上海外商投资企业所有权结构中外方控制的比例，1992～1995 年（单位：％）

外方所有权	1992 年	1993 年	1994 年	1995 年	1992～1995 年
＞50％	40.0	26.9	78.6	78.3	53.8
50％	6.7	15.4	7.1	13.0	11.5
＜50％	53.3	57.7	14.3	8.7	34.6
合计	100	100	100	100	100

注：只统计合同投资额超过 1000 万美元的制造业企业。

资料来源：中国对外贸易经济合作部（1993～1996 年）。

企业增长得快，这类企业在全部外商投资企业中所占比例由1991年的13.7%增加到1995年的28.1%（上海对外经济贸易委员会，1992～1996）。这一现象和很多因素有关，包括更加开放的政府政策（可接受多种形式的外资）、跨国公司的资本实力等。

分行业部门观察所有权结构，会发现一些有意思的现象。外方控制所有权主要集中在两个行业。一类是产品技术含量高的部门，如精密仪器、化学、医药和医疗器械、电信、机械、电子、电器。另一类是拥有较大地方市场，包括食品饮料（它也有秘密配方）、建筑和装饰材料。相比较而言，地方主要在拥有较大比较优势，如纤维和纺织业，或有较长生产历史如印刷、塑料、电池等行业，占有大部分股权。

2. *所有权谈判*

调查和访谈（见附录）表明，在企业建立谈判过程中，关于所有权的讨价还价主要围绕资本能力、技术水平和营销能力展开。如果一方在这三方面都比对手强得多，这一方通常会建立全资企业，或为了利用另一方的一些优势，放弃一小部分所有权（通常在25%以下）。对于这类企业，跨国公司拥有绝对优势地位，很少有例外。例如，为扩大投资规模和开拓国际市场，两个地方公司与一家美国公司、一家香港公司建立了合资企业，新成立的每个企业里，地方公司只占25%的股权。

对一些合资企业，地方和外方都有一定的讨价还价能力，所有权的最终安排就由上面提到的三个方面中的一方决定。例如，由于拥有先进技术，跨国公司就在所有权安排中占较大比例。这在化学、电信、医药、电器行业很普遍。这里，一个有意思的发现是，地方也愿意合资企业由跨国公司控制，因为在这种情况下，跨国公司更可能采用先进技术。同样的，熟悉（一些情况下是控制）地方市场渠道，增强了地方讨价还价的能力。地方拥有过半股权的企业多是因为这个原因，包括一些位于上海的中国大型外商投资企业（如上海贝尔、上海日立）。因为巨大的销量是实现相关生产规模经济所必需的，地方就拥有了所有权谈判筹码。这种情况特别适合在国内市场拥有一定垄断势力的地方国有企业。一些情况下，每一方在三个方面都不是很强，讨价还价的结果可能是近乎相等的所有权。双方各占50%左右所有权的合资企业多是由于这个原因。

就所有权来说，显然，跨国公司总体上比其上海的合作者拥有较强的讨价还价能力。这个观点需要说明一下。第一，如前文指出的，一些地方公司认为技术转移比所有权安排更重要，所以在所有权谈判中并不是特别强烈地、一定要拥有大部分股权。第二，虽然地方在资本形成方面拥有劣势，很多地方公司还是成功占有大部分股权。第三，低的所有权比例并不意味着地方公司不能获得所需的东西。地方利益可用其他手段保障。的确，一些例子表明地方即使拥有较低比例股权，仍能和跨国公司成功讨价还价。

20.6.2 管理地方化

根据访谈政府官员介绍，上海外商投资企业关键职位的分配和所有权之间存在着通行模式。控制70%以上所有权，中方一般会占据董事会主席和总经理的位置。所有权比例下降到50%～70%，可能只占据这两个位置中的一个。如果外方投资者拥有大部分所有权，投资地一方就占据副主席和副总经理职位。这种状况可通过上海的访谈公司看出（表 20.4）。在北京和上海的其他访谈也显示同样的结果。

表 20.4　访谈外商投资企业的所有权和关键职位的分配

地方拥有的所有权比例	地方所占据的关键位置	地方所占据的其他管理位置
70%及以上	董事长和总经理（2）	除技术发展部门外的多数管理岗位
50%～70%	董事长和副总经理（2）	除技术（1）或生产部门（1）外的多数管理岗位
50%	董事长和总经理（1） 副董事长和总经理（1）	除技术（1）或生产部门（1）外的多数管理岗位
30%～50%	董事长和副总经理（7） 副董事长和副总经理（1）	除技术和（一些情况下）生产部门外的多个管理岗位
30%及以下	副董事长和副总经理（1）	除技术和生产部门外的多个管理岗位

注：括号里的数字表示此类样本公司的数量。

资料来源：作者调查。

显而易见，中方拥有的所有权比例越高，占据的重要岗位就越多。不过中方拥有的所有权比例低并不妨碍管理的地方化。例如，表 20.4 所列，中方所有权低于 50%的 9 个合资企业中，7 个拥有中方提名的董事长和副总经理。在公司所有管理岗位中，中方提名人员占到 60%～80%。访谈也进一步表明，通常，中方经理在国内营销方面发挥重要作用。一些实力较强的地方公司，如果是全部纳入到合资企业里，以前的管理人员多数还担任类似职位，因为他们有熟悉人事关系的优势。

随时间推移，管理地方化发展很快。很多外商投资企业，包括一些外方独资公司，也鼓励管理地方化的一些安排，如派有潜力的管理人员去国外培训，给他们提供学习机会，和优秀管理人员一起工作。外商投资企业运行的时间越长，地方管理人员就越多。用地方管理人员和技术人员替代外派人员在 15 个访谈公司中都有发现。这归因于中国整体，尤其是上海讨价还价能力的提升，地方管理人员管理能力的显现（Kamis，1996；Nyaw，1996），以及地方管理人员支付的薪酬远低于外派人员等。

20.6.3　地方产业联系

地方产业联系包括前向和后向联系。但是，对快速增长的经济来说，后向或供给联系更重要（Dicken，1992）。公司调查和访谈中使用地方化程度度量后向联系。与国外供货相比，外商投资企业的地方化水平较低。在 194 家外商投资企业中，对 67 家进行的访谈表明，它们中的 45%并不使用地方供货商，30%用很少一部分，只有 25%使用的地方供货多于进口原材料和零部件（浦东新区管委会，1997）。不过，与北京和天津相似的外商投资企业相比，上海的企业，地方化表现还是很出色，尽管营运的时间较短（表 20.5）。

表 20.5 上海、北京和天津重要外商投资企业供货地方化比较

行业	上海/%	北京/%	天津/%
电话设备	70	20	30
电子和电器	70	20	40
汽车	90	50	60

注：重要企业选择是根据它们在各自行业产值中的排名。

资料来源：作者调查。

关于地方化和所有权的关系，我们在上海调查的证据显示，如预期一样，较高的地方所有权比例能够提高本地化水平；4 个地方拥有大部分所有权的合资企业，地方化程度都比较高（超过 70%）（表 20.6）。不过，表 20.6 也显示，产品地方化程度较高（超过 50%）的 10 个合资企业中，半数是由跨国公司控制所有权，有一家企业，外方和地方拥有的所有权比例相等。这表明，即使地方拥有少数所有权，也会出现地方化程度较高。事实上，我们在调查中发现，地方合作者以前的状况，地方市场的规模和发展，合资企业存在的时间都会影响地方化程度。

表 20.6 访谈公司（15 家）的地方化

合资企业（公司名字是缩写）	地方拥有的所有权比例/%	地方化程度/%	地方合作者以前的状况和数目	当前的地方市场
A	60	70	NL（1）	VG
B	75	超过 70	NL（1）	VG
C	40	70	NL（1）	VG
D	30	70	NL（1）	G
E	50	90	NL（1）	VG
F	43	70	SL（1）	G
G	49	67	SL（1）	G
H	70	76	NL（1）	G
I	33	55	SL（1）	N
J	49	0	SL/O（6）	N
K	40	0	SL/O（3）	G
L	56	70	NL（2）	G
M	49.5	40	NL/O（5）	G
N	20	15	SL/O（4）	G
P	50	10 以下	NL/O（3）	N

注：将地方合作者以前的状况分成三类：国家领先（NL）、上海领先（SL）、其他（O）。当前的市场分成三种情况：很好（VG）、好（G）、不好（NG）。这两列的结果由访谈公司评定。括号里的数字是地方合作者的数量。

资料来源：作者调查。

大型、管理成功的中方合作者对合资企业的地方化，有较强的讨价还价能力，即使跨国公司控制着所有权。特别是当只有一家中方合作者，或中方合作者以前生产的产品与新成立的合资企业生产的产品相似时，尤其如此。例如，表 20.6 中 A～H 的合资企业都有很强的中方母公司（或是国家重要企业或者上海重要企业），它们成为合资企业后，并没有改变其主要产品。它们在本地化方面（70%～90%）就很成功。这很容易理解，因为这些中方合作者通常有较好的产品技术和市场营销能力。原有的技术水平和供给网络使中方合作者可以利用地方供给降低成本，从而增强了中地方合作者的讨价还价能力。与此对照，样本公司中，多个地方合作者，反而削弱了其联合讨价还价能力，因为不同公司有不同的利益。这类合资企业（表 20.6 中的 J～P 公司），本地化水平都很低。

大规模的国内销售也可加速生产本地化，因为本地化可以降低成本。在某些行业，也可更好地满足地方消费者的需求。访谈的合资企业中，当地销售的“好”和“非常好”多与高比例的地方供应相连（表 20.6）。合资企业 K 是个例外。这个公司由一家大型跨国公司控制，公司所需零部件由跨国公司规模化生产工厂以低成本供应（但不一定是低价格）；生产必需的原材料也是进口，因为它们不在中国生产。

在地方合作者的讨价还价压力下，供应链的本地化会随时间推移而加强。这可从受访的两组公司中看出。我们的访谈表明，除两个地方化程度为零的公司，其他所有公司在上海开业后，地方化程度都有提高，虽然速度不同。开始时，没有地方供应商，10 年后它们中的两个，地方化程度分别到达 70%和 90%。这两家合资公司各有 200～300 家地方供应商。对 67 家公司的访谈发现，30 个案例中有 70%在 1996 年开业时地方化程度为零。17 个主要依赖地方供应商的公司多是在上海运营 5 年以上的（浦东新区管委会，1997）。这也可部分解释，为什么上海的外商投资企业本地化程度低，因为大部分跨国公司是在 1992 年后才来到这里。其他的原因，包括一些跨国公司采用的国际化战略；一些产品由于价格比较高和市场竞争激烈，市场扩展缓慢；一些产品地方化困难，因为需要特殊技术，而地方公司目前很难采用。个别案例表明一些产品的组件，进口比在当地生产更便宜。

20.6.4　技术转移中的地方参与度

就外商投资企业技术转移中的地方参与度来说，上海的研究证实了以前研究中的两个发现。一是与其他所有权结构相比，跨国公司更可能把最先进的技术转移给其在发展中国家的全资子公司或持有多数股权的公司（UNTCT，1987）。14 个合资企业中，与其母公司技术差距不到两年的，只有一个企业是地方拥有多半所有权，另一个企业是双方各拥有一半所有权（浦东新区管委会，1997；作者访谈）。另一个发现是，合资企业的共享特征为地方参与技术转移提供了很多机会，但转移的往往是比较成熟且多年不变的技术（Lan，1996）。34 个外商投资企业中，地方显著参与技术转移的（表 20.7），只有一个是外商独资企业，85%的企业地方拥有超过 40%所有权（浦东新区管委会，1997；作者访谈）。这些外商投资企业主要集中在家用电器、汽车和摩托车（表 20.7）等技术大多标准化的部门。在这种情况下，地方还是有很多方法获得技术，如通过训练学习、在工作中学习、通过共享学习，甚至通过探索研究学习。而在上一种情况下，先进技术仍由跨国公司控制。地方都认识到，无论所有权结构如何，跨国公司的直接投资都给上海带来了相对先进的技术。

多数研究公司认为，随着时间的推移，地方在技术转移中的参与度在增加。除营运时间外，还有很多其他因素，如以前的经济实力和技术差距，当前市场的规模，合资企业的绩效也会影响到地方在技术转移中的参与度。这些因素的影响可在表 20.7 中发现。例如，家用电器 10 多年来一直是中国销量最大的消费品之一。巨大的市场导致许多生产线被发达国家购买。这为中方公司带来了巨大利润和更强的经济实力，也缩小了与西方国家的技术差距。从这些因素获得的讨价还价能力增强，使这个行业成为技术方面地方参与度最高的行业，即使在外方拥有大部分所有权的企业（表 20.7 里的 10 家外商投资企业，3 家拥有相等所有权，7 家地方拥有 32%～45%的所有权）。汽车和摩托车行业情况相似，多数当地合作者在生产相关产品方面实力很强。相比之下，由于地方合作者实力较弱和技术的特殊性，医学和计算机行业技术转移中地方参与度的较低。研发机构的建立尤其受市场对新产品或改善产品需求，企业利润以及经济实力的影响。处于技术发展期的 7 个外商投资企业，如表 20.7 所示，都是盈利和销售在上海排名靠前的企业。

表 20.7　上海外国投资企业技术转移中的地方参与度（外国投资企业数，百分比）[a]

行业	FIEs 总数（数量和百分比）		技术获得阶段（数量和百分比）[b]		技术吸收阶段（数量和百分比）[b]		技术发展阶段（数量和百分比）[b]	
汽车和摩托车	12	100%	3	25.0%	7	58.3%	2	16.7%
电信	8	100%	4	50.0%	2	25.0%	2	25.0%
电子	8	100%	5	62.5%	3	37.5%		
家电	13	100%	2	15.4%	10	76.9%	1	7.7%
机械和自动化设备	11	100%	5	45.5%	5	45.5%	1	9.0%
化学和建筑材料	9	100%	4	44.4%	4	44.4%	1	11.1%
医药	5	100%	3	60.0%	2	40.0%		
计算机（网络）	6	100%	5	83.3%	1	16.7%		
总计	72	100	31	43.1	34	47.2	7	9.7

注：a 指占行业总量的百分比；b 在技术获得阶段，外商投资企业只是使用技术，没有地方参与。技术吸收阶段，地方参与度差异明显。技术发展阶段的突出特征是建立研究开发实验室或部门。

资料来源：浦东新区管委会（1997）和作者调查。

投资跨国公司间的激烈竞争使地方合作者在技术转移中处于有利地位。各产业部门都是如此，因为每一个行业都有跨国公司的直接投资。一个典型的例子是通用汽车(General Motors)。自中国宣布计划与一家跨国公司在上海浦东建立一个新汽车厂后，通用和其他世界两大汽车生产商都加入了投标。最终，通用汽车获得成功，条件是它将生产 1997 别克车型，并承诺未来将生产和美国车型相似的汽车，并将和中方成立一个合资公司进行汽车设计和开发（人民日报，1996；作者的访谈）。

20.6.5　跨国公司和上海的相互作用

我们和上海市政府有关部门的官员，两个主要开发区合资企业的管理人员，15 个大型外商投资企业高级管理人员的访谈表明，跨国公司和地方政府在签署投资合同之前的讨价还价十分激烈，且非常费时，尤其是和大型跨国公司讨价还价。每年政府都会出版外商投资指南，列出优先吸收外商直接投资的产业①。投资于这些行业的跨国公司将会享受相关优惠待遇，但很少有跨国公司简单地顺应这一指南。相反，它们大多先做市场调查，然后研究相关产品的商业贸易、整体投资环境，寻找潜在合作伙伴和进行可行性研究，最后才来到谈判桌前同当地政府谈判。根据我们的访谈，这个过程通常需要 5 年左右的时间。地方政府这边，如果目标行业没有多少投资者，或某个跨国公司能够给当地经济带来很大益处，政府通常更愿意与跨国公司合作。在政府帮助下，工厂可以迅速地、高质量地建成。还有其他一些妥协政策，如允许跨国公司控制股权或提出特殊的、非原来设定的政策。讨价还价特征可总结为以下三个方面。

1. 地方能力的增长

证据显示，20 世纪 80 年代早期，上海几乎无法选择跨国公司。由于中国才开始改革开放，很多大型跨国公司还没准备投资中国。一些国家的跨国公司也因它们国家与中国的关系而受约束，或限制它们直接投资，或禁止它们对中国的技术转移。曾有一个典范的合资企业的母公司代表中国寻找在全球的合资投资伙伴，在寻找了西欧、北美和日本后，只找到一家来自中等发达国家的跨国公司，愿意在合理条件下进行投资。早期合资企业的成功运营、基础设施的改善、法律体系的完善，加上更加开放的政策已经改变了跨国公司对上海形象的认识。现在上海比以前就有了更多选择。

上海讨价还价能力的提升也来自跨国公司间的竞争。多个跨国公司竞争一个项目，如前文中的通用公司案例，或几个外商投资企业在中国生产相似产品（这已成为越来越普遍的情况，例如电器和通信设备行业），都增强了上海在技术转移方面与跨国公司谈判的能力。事实上，上海已经拒绝了几个跨国公司的投资建议，由于低技术、高污染、或其无法接受的条款。不过，这并不意味着上海比跨国公司拥有更强的讨价还价能力。

2. 双方选择近乎平等

多数访谈跨国公司表示，在投资上海之前，它们已将上海与北京、天津和其他可能投资的区位进行了比较。同样，超过半数以上访谈中方合作者表示，它们也可以在潜在投资者中选择最佳跨国公司。20 世纪 90 年代，上海从不接受带着不可接受条件的投资者。例如，一家世界 100 强跨国公司希望以独资方式在上海投资。上海方面表示欢迎这家公司但要求合资。最终这家公司投资于另一个城市，而上海则与另外一个拥有相同技术的公司建立了合资企业。FDI 给双方带来的互惠互利也可以证明这个判断。通过外国直接投资，上海提升了关键工业部门的技术水平，而很多跨国公司则进入了中国市场并赚取了利润。

3. 关于所有权结构变化的谈判

多数和大型跨国公司合资的企业都获得了成功，跨国公司的母公司就想提高它们在

① 例如，汽车、电信、钢铁、电站设备、精细化工和电器 6 个行业多年被上海列为优先吸引外资的行业。

资本投资中的份额。这种情况下，地方往往处于支配地位。访谈显示，当地各方通常会竭力维持每一方最初的投资比例，特别是限制外国股权不能超过50%。三分之一的受访公司表示，跨国公司要求增加他们的股份。增加资本时，地方合作者坚持要维持最初的股权比例。来自浦东新区管委会的数据表明，20世纪90年代以来，资本投资超过1000万美元的145家制造业合资企业中，48家企业扩充了资本，但只有20家改变了资本投资比例。在这20家公司中，只有三个从本地股东控制变为外国股东控制。

20.7 结论与讨论

研究跨国公司和投资地间的讨价还价关系是一项艰巨任务。原因之一在于，评价讨价还价关系的度量存在争议（讨价还价能力本身无法度量，多数代理指标度量的是讨价还价的结果）。此外，讨价还价过程的内部信息很难获得，特别是在中国更是如此。在分析了使用所有权结构作为讨价还价能力度量的缺陷之后，本研究使用了三种度量。这三种度量是以区域为基础选择的，以便于比较讨价还价能力的区域差异。

通过这些度量指标和现场访谈数据，以及获得的第二手资料，有以下发现。

第一，一些区域与跨国公司的讨价还价能力比其他区域强。总的来说，在中国，上海与跨国公司的讨价还价能力比其他省市区要强。这归结于中国的区域政策和上海自身的发展条件。许多大型的、运营成功的国有公司位于上海，也起重要作用。与跨国公司相比，近年来上海在吸引跨国公司方面几乎没有做出实质性让步。但利用其在中国的战略地位和中国巨大的市场潜力作为讨价还价手段，上海还是获得了巨大利益，尽管在资本所有权方面还处于较弱地位。

第二，一个区域讨价还价能力的变化不仅和合作的跨国公司能力有关，而且和其他竞争（或潜在竞争）区域的能力有关。例如，中央政府支持上海浦东新区发展的优惠政策和其他支持，肯定对其他区域与跨国公司讨价还价产生负面影响，尽管不是有意的。随时间推移，跨国公司的持续投资和本地化的提升，使上海成为中国最受外国投资喜爱的区域。这反过来增强了上海与跨国公司的讨价还价能力。此外，不断从跨国公司投资中获得的利益也增强了上海的经济实力。这样，通过跨国公司全球-本土的互动实际上增加了区域经济的不平衡（Li and Yeung，1998）。

第三，在上海，跨国公司和地方合作者之间讨价还价的关系不同受很多因素影响。所有权结构取决于双方资本实力的竞争、技术水平和营销能力。本地化程度受地方合作者以前的经营状况、国内市场的规模和发展、地方管理人员能力等因素的影响。地方拥有的所有权比例对地方化有影响，但不是决定性的。研究表明，经济实力较强的合作者（在合资企业成立之前，通常已经是运营成功的地方大公司），已为其产品建立了强大的国内营销网络，可以显著增强其讨价还价能力。与这类合作者建立的合资公司大多在生产联系、管理知识和技术专长方面地方化程度较高。

第四，与近期一项研究发现一致（Dicken，1994），随时间的推移，上海的讨价还价能力在不断增强。现在，上海比以前对跨国公司有了更多选择，供应链、管理和技术转移方面地方的参与度也在提高。换句话说，跨国公司投资的时间越长，当地获得的利益就越大。

第五，在区域比较方面，本章提出区域讨价还价概念，认为区域的优势可以转化为公司层面的讨价还价优势。当然，这并不意味着一个区域与跨国公司的讨价还价能力是同质的。中国的政治和经济体制强调区域利益，这种情形和其他国家的区域不一样。而且，随着中国渐进式政治体制改革的推进，经济的市场化，许多国有企业将成为股份制公司。政府对经济发展和单个企业的控制正在放松。因此，地方利益正走向多元化，地方管理者在与跨国公司打交道中不一定受中央政府直接控制。鉴于这种情况，应谨慎使用此研究框架。

本章中度量讨价还价能力的代理指标由情景决定。进一步的研究应该关注哪一方控制着关键组织问题的决策，如采购、生产、销售、扩张、利润分配等。

本章表明，尽管发展的时间较短，上海的跨国公司直接投资在 20 世纪 90 年代增长很快。第一手的访谈和调查数据，加上获得的第二手资料，证明了中国最大城市，上海地方公司讨价还价能力的增强，通过合作发展提高了地方化程度。上海的案例研究阐明在中国，全球-地方相互作用的机制和理念，这是当前全球化时代，发展中国家经常面临的主题。

附录：相关数据和访谈

没有关于跨国公司和地方参与者之间讨价还价关系的统计数据和信息。通过上海浦东新区管委会，对 194 家合同投资超过 1000 万美元的大型制造业外商投资企业的调查，获得了以上提到的一些度量信息（浦东新区管委会，1997）。这次调查，在 1997 年 6～7 月进行，对浦东新区的外商投资企业进行了到目前为止最广泛的调查。浦东新区是上海跨国公司布局最集中的区域，调查的 194 家外商投资企业占该区 1996 年外商直接投资总额的 78%。虽然只有一些外商投资企业给了相关数据，加上我们的访谈数据，调查结果还是反映了这座城市的整体情况。

1997 年 9 月和 10 月，作者访谈了上海市政府外商投资委员会和经济研究中心的 4 位高级研究人员，浦东新区管委会的 5 位高级官员，包括经济贸易局、规划和土地局的主任，两个主要开发区（金桥和张江）的 4 位管理人员。这些访谈提供了关于上海跨国公司投资很多方面的概况信息，并形成了一些经验判断。然后基于研究目的和数据可得性，确定了抽样判定法。依据规模大（行业最大）、产业部门（覆盖主要产业）、较长的营运时间（至少三年）、多种所有权结构等，选择了 15 家公司。选定之后，访谈了这 15 家公司的副总经理，总经理助理或其他高级管理人员。基于调查和从其他政府部门获得的信息，访谈中询问的问题主要集中于合资企业里跨国公司和地方的相互作用，及其对经济发展的意义。访谈结果为本章分析提供了重要信息。参考另一个调查结果（浦东新区管委会，1997）和地方政府官员给出的经验判断，又调查了相关专家以弥补小样本的缺陷。调查数据另一个缺陷是，由于可得性困难，对 15 个公司的 18 个访谈中，有 17 个是关注地方参与者。他们的观点可能并不完全被他们的合作跨国公司所认同。

在 FDI 三种通常的进入模式中（合作、全资和合资经营），合资经营最重要。194 家大型外商投资企业调查显示，合资经营占总样本的 81.4%（浦东新区管委会，1997）。所以样本公司主要来自合资经营企业。

为了将上海和其他类似区域进行比较，本章使用了以前进行的两次访谈数据。1995 年 4～5 月和 1996 年 5 月，作者和北京的中国人民大学和天津的南开大学的两名博士研究生、硕士研究生，访谈了这两个市政府的外资经济委员会和政策研究部门①。根据它们列出的每个直辖市的10大优秀外商投资企业，成功访谈17家（每个直辖市7家）企业，包括这次上海访谈中涉及的问题。

参考文献

陈少能. 1995. 世界著名跨国公司在浦东. 上海：华东师范大学出版社

对外贸易经济合作部. 中国对外经济联系与贸易年鉴（多年）. 北京：对外贸易经济合作部

浦东新区管委会. 1997. 浦东外国直接投资结果的调查报告. 上海（非公开内部资料）

人民日报（海外版）. 1994. 外资快速增加的主要因素，03-28

人民日报（海外版）. 1996. 通用汽车来到中国，03-30

上海对外经济贸易委员会. 1992. 上海对外经济贸易统计年鉴. 上海：上海对外经济贸易委员会

上海市统计局. 1997. 上海统计年鉴. 北京：中国统计出版社

王志乐. 1996. 著名跨国公司在中国的投资. 北京：中国经济出版社

中国国家统计局. 1997. 中国统计年鉴. 北京：中国统计出版社

中国统计信息和咨询服务中心. 1992. 1979～1991年中国对外经济统计. 北京：中国统计信息和咨询服务中心

Chen J H. 1993. The environment for foreign direct investment and the characteristics of joint ventures in China. Development Policy Review，11：167～250

Cheng L K. 1995. Foreign Direct Investment in China. Paris：OECD

Corbridge S. 1986. Capitalist World Development：A Critique of Radical Development Geography. New Jersey：Rowman and Little field，Totawa

Dicken P. 1992. Global shift：The Internationalization of Economic Activity (2nd Edition). New York：Guilford Press

Dicken P. 1994. Global-local tensions：Firms and states in the global space-economy. Economic Geography，70：101～128

Dunning J H. 1981. Multinational enterprises，locational strategies and regional development. In：Dunning J H. International Production and the Multinational Enterprise. London：Allen and Unwin

Dunning J H. 1985. Multinational Enterprise，Economic Structures and International Competitiveness. Chichester：Wiley

Dunning J H. 1994. Re-evaluating the benefits of foreign direct investment. Transnational Corporations，3：23～51

Dunning J H. 1996. The geographical sources of the competitiveness of firms：Some results of a new survey. Transnational Corporations，5：1～29

Dunning J H. 1997. How should national governments respond to globalization? International Executive，39：55～66

Fagre N，Wells L T. 1982. Bargaining power of multinationals and host governments. Journal of International Business Studies，13：9～32

Ferrao J. 1994. TNC operation and host regional economies：A typology for the Portuguese case. In：Dicken P，Quevit M. Transnational Corporations and European Regional Restructuring. Utrecht：N G S

① 虽然广东是中国各省份中吸引FDI总量最大的（自1979～1996年，累积吸引外资509.48亿美元），但它和上海在很多方面不是一个比较量级。上海、北京、天津是同一类型行政区，具有更多的相同特征。

Fujita K, Hill R C. 1995. Global Toyotaism and local development. International Journal of Urban and Regional Research, 19: 7～22

Gabriel P. 1966. The investment in the LDC: Asset with a fixed maturity. Columbia Journal of World Business, 1: 113～120

Glickman N, Woodward D. 1988. The location of foreign direct investment in the United States: Patterns and determinants. International Regional Science Review, 11: 137～154

Gomes C B. 1990. Firm ownership preference and host government restrictions: An integrated approach. Journal of International Business Studies, 21: 1～22

Gordon D M. 1988. The global economy: New edifice or crumbling foundations?. New Left Review, 168: 24～64

Guthrie D. 1997. Between markets and politics: Organizational responses to reform in China. American Journal of Sociology, 102 (5): 1258～1304

Hill H. 1982. Vertical inter-firm linkages in LDCs: A note on the Philippines. Oxford Bulletin of Economics and Statistics, 44: 161～171

Jenkins R. 1987. TransnationalCorporations and Uneven Development: The Internationalization of Capital and the Third World. Methuen: New York

Kamis T L. 1996. Education for the PRC executive. The China Business Review, 23: 36～39

Kobrin S J. 1987. Testing the bargaining hypothesis in the manufacturing sector in developing countries. International Organization , 41: 609～638

Kueh Y Y. 1992. Foreign investment and economic change in China. China Quarterly, 131: 637～690

Lall S. 1980. Vertical inter-firm linkages in LDCs: An empirical study. Oxford Bulletin of Economics and Statistics, 42: 203～226

Lan P, Young S. 1996. Foreign direct investment and technology transfer: A case study of foreign direct investment in north-east China. Transnational Corporations, 5 (1): 57～83

Lan P. 1996. Technology Transfer to China through Foreign Direct Investment. Aldershot: Avebury

Lardy N R. 1994. The role of foreign trade and investment in China's economic transformation. The China Quarterly, 144: 1065～1082

Lecraw D J. 1993. Bargaining power, ownership, and profitability of transnational corporations in developing countries. In: Lall S. Transnational Corporations and Economic Development. London: Routledge

Leung C K. 1993. Pensonal contacts, subcontracting linkages, and development in the Hong Kong-Zhujiang delta region. A A A G, 83 (2): 272～302

Li X J, Yeung Y M. 1998. Transnational corporations and their impact on regional economic imbalance: evidence from China. Third World Planning Review, 20 (4): 1～23

Lim F Y C, Fong P E. 1982. Vertical linkages and multinational enterprise in developing countries. World Development, 10: 585～595

Mok V. 1996. Industrial development. Shanghai: Transformation and modernization under China's open policy. In: Yeung Y M, Sung Y W. Hong Kong: The Chinese University Press

Nestor C. 1997. Foreign investment and spatial pattern of growth in Vietnam. In: Dixon C, Drakakis-Smith D. Uneven Development in South East Asia. Aldershot: Ashgate

Nixson F. 1988. The political economy of bargaining with transnational corporations: Some preliminary observations. Manchester Papers on Development, IV: 377～390

Nyaw M K. 1996. Investment environment: Perceptions of overseas investors of foreign-funded industrial firms. In: Yeung Y M, Sung Y W. Shanghai: Transformation and Modernization under China's Open Policy. Hong Kong: The Chinese University Press

Olds K. 1997. Globalizing Shanghai: The 'Global Intelligence Corps' and the building of Pudong. Cities, 14: 109～123

O'h Uallachain B. 1984. Linkages and foreign direct investment in the United States. Economic Geography, 60 (3): 238～253

Pan Y. 1996. Influences on foreign equity ownership level in joint venture in China. Journal of International Business Studies, 27: 1～26

Perroux F. 1973. Multinational investment and the analysis of development and integration poles. Economies et Societes, 24: 831～868

Pitelis C. 1991. Beyond the nation-state? The transnational firms and the nation-state. Capital and Class, 43: 131～152

Potter P B. 1995. Foreign investment law in the People's Republic of China: Dilemmas of state control. China Quarterly, 141: 155～185

Quevit M. 1994. Transnational Corporations and European Regional Restructuring. Utrecht: N G S

Reid R A. 1992. Source country differences in the spatial distribution of foreign direct investment in the United States. The Professional Geographer, 44: 272～285

Schoenberger E. 1991. Globalization and regionalization: new problems of time, distance and control in the multinational firms. Paper presented at the Annual Meeting of A A G in Miami, April

South R B. 1990. Transnational 'Maquiladora'. A A A G, 80 (4): 549～570

Stopford J M, Stranger S, Henley J S. 1991. Rival States, Rival firms: Competition for World Market Shares. Cambridge: Cambridge University Press

Sung Y W. 1996. Shanghai: Transformation and modernization under China's open policy. Hong Kong: The Chinese University Press

Tian G. 1996. Shanghai's role in the economic development of China: Reform of foreign trade and investment. Praeger Connecticut: Westport

United Nations Centre on Transnational Corporations (UNCTC). 1987. TransnationalCorporations and Technology Transfer: Effects and Policy Issues. New York: UNCTC

United Nations Conference on Trade and Development (UNCTAD). 1996. World Investment Report 1996: Investment, Trade and International Policy Arrangement. New York: United Nations

Wang Z Q. 1995. Foreign Investment and Economic Development in Hungary and China. Aldershot: Avebury

Williams D. 1996. Analyzing the regional impact of foreign manufacturing firms. Tijdschrift voor Economische en Sociale Geografie, 87: 259～265

Yeung Y M. 1996. Introduction. In: Yeung Y M, Sung Y W. Shanghai: Transformation and Modernization under China's Open Policy. Hong Kong: The Chinese University Press

Young S, Hood N, Peter E. 1994. Multinational enterprises and regional economic development. Regional Studies, 28 (7): 657～677

Zhan X J. 1993. The role of foreign direct investment in market-oriented reforms and economic development: The case of China. Transnational Corporations, 2 (3): 121～148

Zhang L Y. 1994. Location-specific advantages and manufacturing direct foreign investment in south China. World Development, 22 (1): 45～53

第21章　大公司空间扩张区位变化

公司由小到大的规模增长，常伴随有公司活动地理范围的扩张。学者们曾基于对公司空间增长实际的研究，抽象概括出一些公司空间变化模式，如沃茨的市场区扩大模式，泰勒的组织形变及区域演化模式，哈坎逊的全球扩张模式，以及迪肯的全球转移模式等（李小建，1999）。这些模式从不同侧面解释了公司由地方性小公司到区域性公司、全国性公司、跨国公司的演变过程。根据国际学术界相关研究，总结出大公司空间扩张中，具有接触扩散和等级扩散两规律。但以中国为例的实例研究表明，中国特殊的体制和文化背景，影响公司扩张，除呈现这些规律外，作者提出了通道扩张的假说。本章对公司有关区位扩张规律进行探讨，并结合中国实际加以分析。

21.1　公司空间扩张规律

公司空间扩张是一种经济现象，应该遵循社会经济现象地理扩散的一般规律。公司空间扩张又是一个组织行为，这种扩张又受制于组织的决策行为、组织内外部网络和发展战略。这两种作用力共同作用于公司空间扩张过程中，但前者使这一过程呈现某些规律，后者又使其偏离这些规律。

21.1.1　社会经济现象的地理扩散规律

地理现象的空间扩散研究曾得到不少地理学家的关注。在哈格斯特朗1952年的经典研究之后（Hargerstrand，1952），地理学家的研究涉及疾病、组织、建筑风格、技术创新等的扩散。在源地和扩散地的关系上，最为常见的是接触扩散（contagious diffusion），即地理扩散过程是由近及远进行的（Moriill，1968）。根据这一观点，源于任一源点的地理扩散均具有距离衰减效应。另一种扩散规律是等级扩散（Hudson，1969），即经济或社会现象的扩张是沿着一定等级规模的地理区域进行的。这种扩散过程并不一定（多数情况下完全不是）按地理邻近性，而是按区域（或城市）的重要等级跳跃式的扩散的。

21.1.2　公司空间扩张规律

作为一种经济现象，公司空间扩张也应该遵循以上两条规律。研究发现，公司的销售区发展、新工厂建立以及兼并活动发生的区位也具有接触扩散和等级扩散特点。不管是公司国内扩张，还是国际扩张，这两条规律均起一定作用。接触扩张在公司空间扩张中较为常见。尤其在各地社会经济条件差别不大的情况下，公司常常就近扩大市场，进而建立起生产机构。这种扩散在服务型的公司中表现更为典型。以美国第二大家庭装修公司洛氏公司（Lowe's Companies）为例。该公司年销售收入562亿美元（2014财务年），在美国 20 个州拥有 460 家商店，销售各种家庭装修用品。在公司空间扩张中，由近及远的特色十分突出：1921 年公司在北卡罗来纳州的北威尔克斯保罗（North Wilkesboro）建立后，逐渐北扩；到 20 世纪 40 年代末，已扩延至华盛顿特区、西弗吉尼亚州；20 世纪 60 年代初又西扩肯塔基州、北扩宾夕法尼亚州；20 世纪 60 年代中后期东扩至大西洋海岸；20 世纪 70 年代初南扩至墨西哥湾；20 世纪 70 年代中后期又西进阿肯色州和路易斯安那州；20 世纪 80 年代又继续西扩，抵俄克拉荷马州和得克萨斯州（Laulajainen and Stafford，1995）。

公司等级扩张常按市场规模，首先进入最大的市场（都市区）、接着进入次大市场，以此类推。并不考虑这些市场的距离是否邻近。实际上，等级扩张是公司对环境（社会经济条件）区域差别所采取的对策。世界著名销售商 LVM 公司进入日本各地的先后顺序，便具有等级扩散特点。依次从东京，到大阪、名古屋、京都，再到规模较小的城市（Laulajainen，1992）。

21.2　外国跨国公司在中国投资区位扩张规律

对部分来自美国和日本的跨国公司在中国投资区位变化研究，发现它们也遵循以下两种扩散规律。根据有关文献所提供的资料（王志乐，1998，1999），作者对在中国投资项目相对较多（大于 5 家）的日、美跨国公司的投资区位变化分析表明，8 家具有等级扩散特点，6 家具有邻近扩散特点。

21.2.1　等级扩散

基本符合这一扩散规律的有日本的日立公司、松下公司、长野工业株式会社（NKK）和美国的联合技术公司、摩托罗拉公司和朗讯公司等。与其他国家的实例研究有所不同，中国的特殊政治环境使得这些跨国公司的投资区位出现少许偏差。即 20 世纪 80 年代投资的跨国公司多选择最早对外开放的广东、福建为初始区位，然后，再进入北京、上海等国家最大的城市。20 世纪 90 年代这些跨国公司投资则多直接进入最大的城市，然后向次等城市扩散。这主要是由于 20 世纪 80 年代（尤其是 80 年代早期）国家开放政策区域差异很大，仅这些少数地区具有吸引外资的优惠政策，90 年代开放政策的区域差异则明显缩小。

日立公司是世界规模庞大的跨国公司之一。该公司早在 1982 年就进入中国，20 世纪 80 年代投资的两个区位分别为福建和广东（深圳），这也是我国对外开放的优惠政策所致。20 世纪 90 年代，其区位变化为：1992 年在北京建立日立华胜信息系统和日立电梯；1993 年在上海建立上海日立电器；之后，日立公司开始投资于大型省会城市，先后在哈尔滨、西安、长沙、沈阳等地建立起企业；20 世纪 90 年代中期以后，日立公司投资扩散至省会之外的主要城市，如江苏的苏州、辽宁的大连等（图 21.1a）。需要说明的是，日立公司为生产经营多种产品和服务的公司，在公司扩张过程中，不同类别的投资项目对区位有不同的要求条件，这也使其区位演变过程偏离等级扩散。例如，20 世纪 90 年代日立公司第一个投资项目为计算机系统和软件开发，而中国的相关产业在北京发展基础较好。且北京中关村电子产业已在全国具较大影响（北京科技咨询业协会等，1998）。加之，北京作为首都的政治影响，故日立公司选址北京。1995 年在西安投资火力电站设计，1996 年和 1997 年在沈阳和大连投资输变电设备及核能设备，也与这里的工业基础和市场有关。

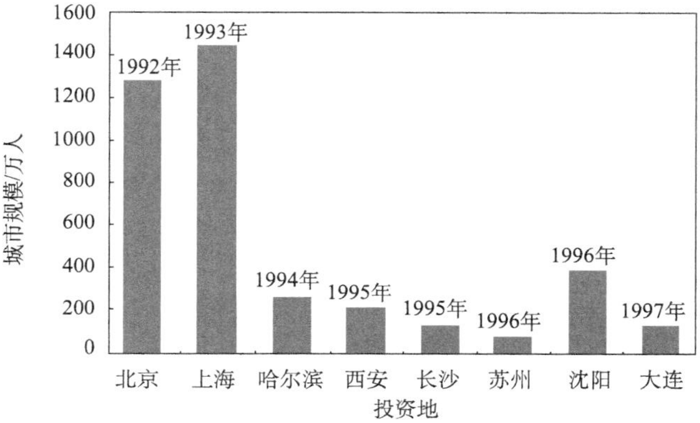

a. 日立公司

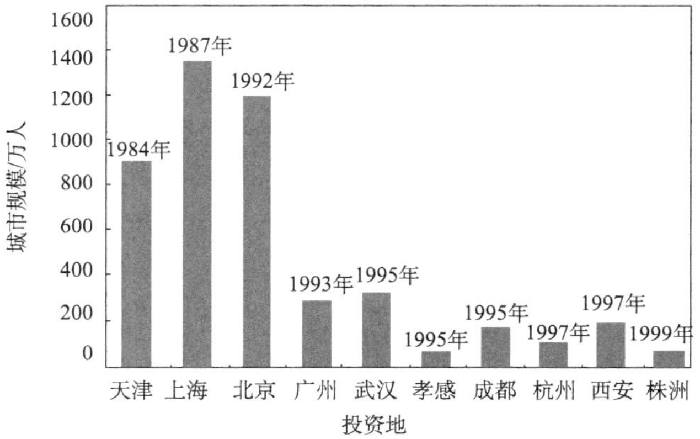

b. 联合技术公司

图 21.1　日立公司和联合技术公司在中国投资的区位扩张（王志乐，1998，1999）

美国的联合技术公司（United Technologies）是一家综合性大型工业跨国公司，业务涉及航空航天、建筑和汽车工业，产品遍布世界各地。2010 年，联合技术公司营业额超过 500 亿美元，在全球拥有超过 20 万名员工，其中一半以上在美国本土以外的世界各地工作，在《财富》杂志 2010 年评出的全球 500 强企业中位列第 130 位[①]。该公司在中国投资的第一个项目是在 1984 年。1984 年以来，其投资区位的扩张也大致符合等级扩散规律（图 21.1b）。但是，由于其投资涉及部门多，而各部门又与相关区位工业基础相关，使这种等级扩散并不十分严格。联合技术公司在中国投资集中于四大部门。

① 数据来源于联合技术研究中心（中国）有限公司好搜百科：http://baike.haosou.com/doc/4251531-4453888.html。

一是来自该公司的奥的斯子公司（Otis）投资的电梯生产，主要集中于天津、北京、广州、上海和杭州，以接近不断增长的沿海地区的市场；二是来自开利子公司（Carrier）投资的空调设备生产，也主要集中于上海、天津、深圳等沿海地区；三是来自汽车零件（UT Automotive）子公司的投资，主要分布于湖北、天津、上海等汽车工业生产地；四是来自普惠飞机制造子公司的投资，主要分布于成都、西安、株洲等具有相应工业基础的区位。

联合技术公司第一个投资项目为1984年奥的斯在天津的投资。当时，之所以首先进入天津，是由于北京电梯厂已与瑞士迅达公司合资，天津电梯厂具有积极的合资意向。由于天津电梯厂的生产基础条件较好，将厂房、设备全部作为股份投入可以减少美国公司的建设时间；原有的销售渠道也可得以利用，从而为打开市场奠定了基础。天津又是中国北方最大的临海城市，邻近北京。这些条件，均促成天津成为联合技术公司投资的第一个区位。

21.2.2 邻近扩散

日本和美国的跨国公司在中国投资区位扩散中，符合这一规律的公司不多。大致符合这一规律的公司有：日本的日本电气股份有限公司（NEC）、索尼公司、五十铃公司和美国的杜邦公司等。以下以NEC公司为例。

NEC公司是世界最大电器制造公司之一，多年名列全球500家大公司的前50名以内。1997年，由于亚洲金融危机的影响，其地位有所下降。2012年在财富世界500强排行榜中排名第271位[①]。该公司在中国的第一个投资项目是1989年在天津建立的“天津日电通讯技术有限公司”。该合资企业以局用交换机的安装维护为主要业务。之所以选择在天津，除了天津的城市规模和经济基础之外，环渤海地区与日本的历史渊源和距离邻近性也起有一定作用。

20世纪90年代，NEC在中国的投资扩张区位变化，基本具有邻近扩散特点。第二个投资地北京，紧邻天津。这项于1991年与首钢总公司合资的项目（首钢日电电子有限公司），主要从事大规模集成电路的设计、开发、生产（包括芯片加工、组装、测试）和销售。高技术密集的北京区位，为NEC在中国电子产业的发展奠定了良好的基础。接着，公司开始向内陆拓展。于是选择了技术力量较为雄厚的武汉作为公司的投资区位。武汉不仅是中国最主要的光纤通信技术基地之一，而且该区位具有极强的辐射力，以武汉为轴心，画半径为1000km的圆，可以把中国2/3的省会城市包含在内（王志乐，1998）。这些因素促使NEC从80年代末期就同武汉有关部门接触，探讨建立合资企业。终于于1993年建立了“武汉NEC中原移动通信有限公司”。

此后，NEC的投资区位继续南扩至广州，东扩至上海，西扩至广西（图21.2）。之后，又计划在西安建立生产卫星微波通讯设备的合资企业。可以看出，该公司的这些扩张，大致具有邻近扩散的特点。

---

① 数据来源于NEC好搜百科：http://baike.haosou.com/doc/6119236-6332381.html。

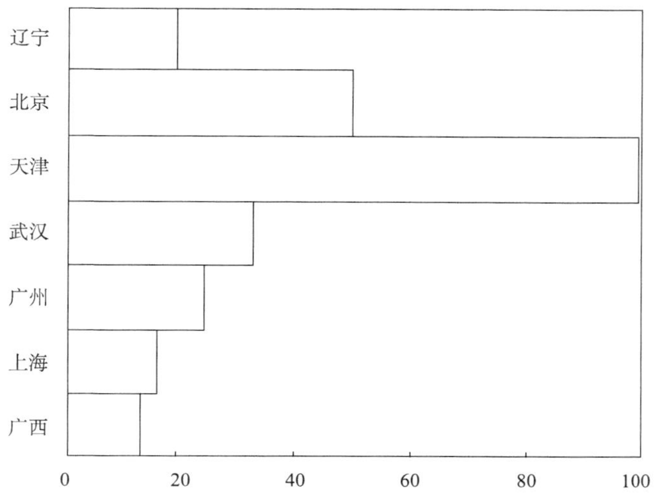

图 21.2 NEC 在中国的投资区位变化（1989～1997）

注：本图绘制时，将第一个投资区位赋值 100，假设投资区位顺序为 i，第 i 个投资区位的值为 $100/i$。以此绘出的图形可直观表示出投资区位的先后顺序。

21.3 进一步讨论

以上实例表明，外国跨国公司在中国投资区位的空间扩张中，既具有大致符合一般规律的一面，也有脱离这两个规律、呈现复杂变化的一面。这种情况，与中国经济环境区域差异、外资投资时的决策行为，以及各地吸引外资的积极性和引资方式等均有关系。与跨国公司相比，中国国内企业（尤其是国有企业）的区位扩张，情形就更为复杂。例如，中国传统文化注重人际关系，在公司新区位选择或兼并其他公司时，熟悉的人际关系（如亲属关系、朋友关系等）易于带来这些活动在相应区位发生。此外，在中国几十年的中央计划经济下，国有企业占主导地位。这些国有企业常隶属中央某一部门，其相互作用的企业对象常受国家指令安排。同一隶属关系的企业之间常发生较多关联（原材料、产品、信息等）。改革开放后，尽管企业权力有所扩大，但其扩张（尤其是兼并）中的行政干预仍然存在。从而使隶属关系在企业空间扩张中具有重要影响。根据中国实际情况，作者提出中国公司空间扩张的通道扩张假想。

所谓通道扩张，是指公司空间扩张沿通道延伸。密切的人际关系形成公司空间扩张的人际关系通道；相同的隶属关系或计划体制下长时间的互相作用关系形成机构（或体制）通道；产品生产或服务之间的关联形成生产通道；地理区域的邻近性形成距离通道。这些通道共同作用于公司的空间扩张过程之中。但各种类型的通道扩张的重要性，各种通道的综合影响情况，还有待实际上的定量研究结果来证实。

参 考 文 献

北京科技咨询业协会等. 1998. 中关村十年之路. 北京：改革出版社

李小建. 1999. 公司地理论. 北京：科学出版社

王志乐. 1998. 日本企业在中国的投资. 北京：中国经济出版社

王志乐. 1999. 美国企业在中国的投资. 北京：中国经济出版社

Hagerstrand T. 1952. The propagation of innovation waves. Lund Studies in Geography (B)：Human Geography，(4)：3～19

Hudson J. 1969. Diffusion in a central place system. Geographical Analysis，(1)：45～58

Laulajainen R. 1992. Louis Vuitton Malletrer：A truly global retailer. Annals of the Japan Association of Economic Geographers，(38)：55～70

Laulajainen R，Stafford H. 1995. Corporate Geography. Dordrecht：Kluoer Academic Publishers

Morrill R. 1968. Waves ofspatial diffusion. Journal of Regional Science，(8)：1～19

第 22 章　企业联系与跨国公司的区域影响

外商直接投资的产出通常情况下与其投入规模成正比，因此，通常使用外商直接投资规模来表征外国直接投资对区域经济的影响（Singh and Choo，1981；Murphy，1992；O'Malley，1994；Buckwalter，1995）。但外商直接投资的规模并不总是与其对区域经济发展的影响一致（Li and Yeung，1998）。第一，行业和企业间的投入-产出率不同，投入产出率高的行业和企业可能对地方经济发展的影响更大些。第二，除投资外的其他影响，如技术和管理方面的影响，就不能通过外商直接投资总量来反映。第三，由外商投资企业的示范效应和产业联系而产生的间接影响总是被忽略。第四，投资地之外的一些地方也可能受外商投资企业的影响。这种影响也无法从获得的外商直接投资数据中看出。

公司案例研究有助于上述问题的解决。本章试图通过上海的两个公司案例来证实跨国公司投资对区域经济发展的间接影响。这两个案例反映了当前在中国的外商投资企业的企业联系网络状况。该案例研究还可验证企业间的联系是技术和管理技能传递的最重要渠道（Dicken，1992），尤其可以说明跨国公司对那些并没有外商直接投资区域的影响。

这项研究具有一定的代表意义。自 1993 年以来，中国已成为世界第二大外商直接投资接受国（UNCTAD，1996）。上海是中国最大的工业和经济中心，其在吸引跨国公司直接投资方面一直处于领先地位。截至 1997 年年底，财富杂志认定的世界 500 强企业中已超过 230 家企业投资于上海，或世界前 100 名的跨国企业有 55 家企业投资于上海。在 1997 年前三个季度中，世界 100 强企业中有 36 家投资或再投资于上海，投资合同额超过 39 亿美元。平均每个项目的规模达到了 5990 万美元，其中 7 个项目超过 1 亿美元；两个最大的项目分别是 19 亿美元和 12 亿美元（作者调查）。进入 20 世纪后，跨国企业在上海设立地区总部的速度明显加快。2002 年年末，上海市政府认定的跨国企业地区总部仅有 16 家，而到 2004 年 12 月，此类总部累计已达 104 家。截至 2005 年 6 月，有企业在上海投资的国家和地区已达 116 个，世界 500 强在上海落户的有 491 家。从 2002 年上海市政府认定首批跨国公司地区总部到 2004 年年底，落户上海的跨国公司地区总部 104 家，其中世界 500 强企业的地区总部 33 家。总部企业在上海的投资涵盖了汽车、通信、钢铁、石化和精细化工、家电、电站设备等行业[①]。截至 2014 年年底，世界 500 强企业均在上海布局有区域中心[②]。

---

① 深圳特区报．世界 500 强 491 家落户上海．2008．http://sztqb.sznews.com/html/2008-01/30/content_48901.htm．2008-01-30。

② 郭震洲：上海创新不强 因世界 500 强、大国企在上海占主导．2015．http://finance.ifeng.com/a/20150627/13802580_0.shtml．2015-06-27。

本章通过20世纪末调查的两个公司案例的分析，揭示了跨国公司直接投资的区域影响要比直接投资数据本身显示的要大得多。这些影响远超出外商投资的企业和区域。与合资方是国家部委的企业相比，合资方是地方政府的合资企业，区外的供应商会少一些。通过外商投资企业的外部联系网络，国内相关的很多企业实现了产业增长、技术转化、管理改善、就业增加。相关区域的政府应该采用适当的措施发展这些联系，尤其是那些在吸引跨国公司投资有困难的区域。

22.1　跨国公司的影响和企业联系

通过直接投资，跨国公司影响着投资地的经济发展。这种影响表现在多方面，如资本、技术、贸易、产业结构和就业（Dicken，1992），比较优势、资源配置效率、规模经济和范围经济（Young et al.，1994），基础设施建设（Kueh，1992），经济、制度和立法改革（Zhan，1993；Lardy，1994；Porter，1995），等等。通过产业联系，尤其是通过和跨国公司子公司或附属机构（subsidiaries）的后向联系，如提供原材料、零部件和服务等，外商直接投资对区域经济发展的影响得以扩大。已有很多研究强调这种间接影响的重要性（Dicken，1992；Kueh，1992；Young et al.，1994；Williams，1996）。Dunning（1985）发现这种间接的正面效应在大的、发达经济区中比其他区域强。Dicken认为跨国公司和国内企业的联系网络，核心区比边缘区密集和宽泛。例如，美国境内的外商投资大多依赖美国的投入和市场（O'h Uallachain，1984），而墨西哥境内的跨国投资企业（South，1990）和当地企业的联系很少。不过，这种情况可能因东道国的地方政策（ILO，1981；Dicken et al.，1994）和区域的经济发展水平与产业结构不同而有所不同。事实上，中国的一些区域，跨国公司的企业联系就很密集（Lan and Young，1996）。

跨国公司和地方企业的联系会随时间而发展。政府的推动和跨国公司寻求降低生产成本的努力都会促使生产的地方化。跨国公司的分支机构（TNC subsidiaries）和地方企业发生联系是需要花费时间的，尤其是和地方企业的后向联系。跨国公司也在不断地调整和发展其网络（见北美的例子，Edgington，1995），这又反过来影响与投资地的关系。由于搜集信息度量这类动态效应十分困难，急需全面深入的解剖研究。值得一提的是，O'Malley（1994）通过爱尔兰的案例发现：随着时间的发展，外资高新技术企业与本地经济的联系会越来越密切。

学者开始利用已出版的统计数据（O'Malley，1994），或通过调查采访（Lall，1980；South，1990；Lan and Young，1996）研究外国直接投资的间接影响。但到目前为止，还没有使用企业案例研究，来探讨跨国公司对投资地之外区域的影响。

22.2　公司选择和访谈

在中国，有关企业联系的数据很难获得，政府也很少收集和发表相关信息。为了选择访谈公司，1997年10月，作者访问了上海市外商投资委员会和经济研究中心的四位相关人员。这些访谈使作者了解了上海的跨国公司投资状况、外商投资企业和其他企业联系的一般情况，并形成经验判断。基于这些信息，选择上海大众和上海贝尔公司进行深度案例研究。之所以选择这两个公司，基于以下考虑。第一，它们在上海运行的时间较长，都是在 1980 年代早期投产，是上海最早一批的外商投资企业。第二，上海吸引外资最多的行业有六个，分别是汽车、电子和通信、电器、电站设备、化学、钢铁。这两个公司所在的行业在上海吸引外商直接投资最多。第三，这两个公司是各自行业产出量最大的企业（表 22.1）。第四，在外商投资企业中，它们的地方化水平相对较高。第五，它们的母公司都是世界 500 强跨国企业。

表 22.1　案例公司在上海相关行业的产出份额

行业	总产出/10 亿元	案例公司所占份额/%
电子通信设备制造	13.31	34.28
配电设备制造	5.34	85.36
机动车制造	41.27	58.9
汽车制造	24.85	97.83

资料来源：上海市统计局（1997）和作者调查。

在中国对外贸易经济合作部和上海市外国投资委员会相关人员的帮助下，1998 年 1 月，作者访谈了上海市政府国产化办公室的负责人和两个公司相关部门的管理人员。这些访谈主要集中于合资企业和国内企业间的联系。除此之外，也从其他渠道收集了两个公司的外部供应商信息。

企业间的联系包括后向联系和前向联系，但后向联系或供应商联系对区域发展更重要（Dicken，1992）。这些联系有多种形式，本章主要关注案例公司和其供应商之间的原材料、技术、管理和信息的联系。

22.3　上海大众

上海大众汽车制造有限公司成立于 1985 年，是中国第一家客车制造合资企业，由中方（主要是上海汽车工业总公司）和德国大众各投资 50%组建。在董事会和执行管理委员会里，双方人员数相等。总裁和管理总经理是中方人员，而德方人员占据另外两个重要位置，即商业执行总经理和技术执行总经理。作为一个地方企业，上海汽车制造厂（中国 1980 年代早期最大的客车制造商），全部转型成为上海大众汽车制造有限公司的主要组成部分，原来的中层管理人员被重新安排到新公司的相似岗位上。根据我们当时访谈的情况，上海大众一万多名本地员工中有 19 个德国人。

基于双方达成的协议，上海大众汽车制造有限公司要完成的目标包括采用德国大众最新的技术生产客车和引擎，实现管理现代化，“将上海建成为中国的汽车中心，促进中国汽车业的发展”等（Liu，1992）。在这些目标的引导下，上海大众汽车制造有限公司开始生产德国大众的车型，随后逐步降低进口零部件［completely knocked down (CKD) parts］比例。这些预先设定的发展方向鼓励生产的国产化，从而扩大了跨国企业和国内企业的联系。

自成立以来，上海大众汽车制造有限公司就一直是中国重要的汽车生产商。2010年10月22日，随着一款红色途观的出厂，上海大众第600万辆轿车正式诞生。同年，上海大众汽车产销量双双突破百万大关，成为中国汽车工业史上首家年产销突破百万辆的轿车生产企业。上海大众旗下的桑塔纳、帕萨特新领域、POLO、途安、朗逸和途观均称为热销车型。由于成功迎合了市场需求，2013年第1000万辆轿车下线，成为国内首家产量突破千万辆的轿车生产企业，还以152.7万辆的年销量位居国内乘用车市场销量第一，占大众集团2013年全球970万辆销量的15.6%。

22.3.1 汽车业的特殊性

汽车行业本质上是一个装配行业（Dicken，1992）。由于要利用其他行业生产的多种零部件，汽车行业的带动效应非常大。在生产组织上，正如Lall（1980）描述的，汽车制造商总是专注于生产技术相似的活动，如车身制造、发动机或变速器等，而将技术差别较大的领域，如电子、玻璃和橡胶生产，留给其他企业生产。并且，汽车制造商并不涉足所有技术相似的活动。一些产品，如活塞、紧固件、燃料喷射等，多由大型专业化企业生产，以供应整个行业，而一些简单的、劳动密集型产品，如焊接、机械加工和各种配件，通常由小的承包商完成。

在地理上，一些生产，如车身组装、喷绘、内饰和总装，需要区位临近，而很多其他零部件可在不同的地方进行生产。因此，企业间的联系网络是非常广泛和复杂的，包括相关企业所在区域内的联系，这一区域和其他区域供应商的联系，供应商所在区域的内部联系等。随着全球跨国生产体系中丰田生产方式（JIT）的扩张，企业间的联系越来越地方化（Fujita and Hill，1995）。

22.3.2 企业联系的变化

上海大众的中方合资——上海汽车厂，生产能力有限（1978年的年产量是7571辆），它的供应商主要是上海汽车工业总公司控制下的一些工厂。上海大众汽车制造股份有限公司成立后，供应商的选择就走向全国。接受访谈的管理人员回忆说，在和德国大众谈判过程中，中方和德方为寻找合资企业的供应商，调查了每一个潜在的供应企业。这打破了以前由行政管理部门不同和行政管理区域不同而形成的分割障碍，上海大众汽车和更多、更高质量的供应商建立了联系。此外，随着其生产规模的不断扩大，其供应商网络也在不断扩张，并开始利用多种渠道保障每一个零部件的供应，也进一步提升了其地方化水平。1988年为上海大众提供零部件的供应商有168家，到1997年这一数字增加到276家。

地方化为上海大众企业间联系的扩张做出了重大贡献。自合资企业建立之初，合资双方都认识到提高地方化水平将有助于大众汽车占领中国市场，同时，也为地方合作者建立起一个具有国际竞争力的汽车企业（王志乐，1996）。合资企业的合同里包括有地方化过程的计划。因此，上海市政府和德国大众都设立了相应的工作组，以支持和协调上海大众汽车生产的地方化。1988年，中国政府批准了关于由上海大众生产的汽车销售量的本地化税（每辆车 28000 元），以缓解其资本短缺。多年来，德国公司不断介绍退休专家到潜在的供应商工厂里工作，并鼓励相关外国公司投资这些企业。这些努力显著提高了汽车生产的地方化水平。以第一款车——桑塔纳 B2 为例，1987 年其国产化率是 5.7%，1990 达到 60.1%，1997 年年底达到 92.9%。另一款桑塔纳 2000，1995 年国产化率是 69.7%，1997 年年底达到 84%。2003 年国产化率达到 98.9%[①]。

22.3.3 企业联系的区域模式

我们可以从上海大众供应商的数量看出企业联系的区域分布（图 22.1）。很明显，上海是上海大众供应网络最密集的地方，1997 年，全国 276 家国内供货商有 64%位于上海市和上海市周边。更为重要的是，在上海生产的零部件，其附加值普遍高于其他地方生产的产品（表 22.2）。除上海之外，沿海省份和直辖市的供应商较多，内陆省份供应商较少。7 个有供应商的内陆省份中（吉林、陕西、四川、湖北、安徽、贵州和湖南），贵州有 10 多家企业为上海大众供应零部件，是继上海和江苏之后的第三大零部件供应地。

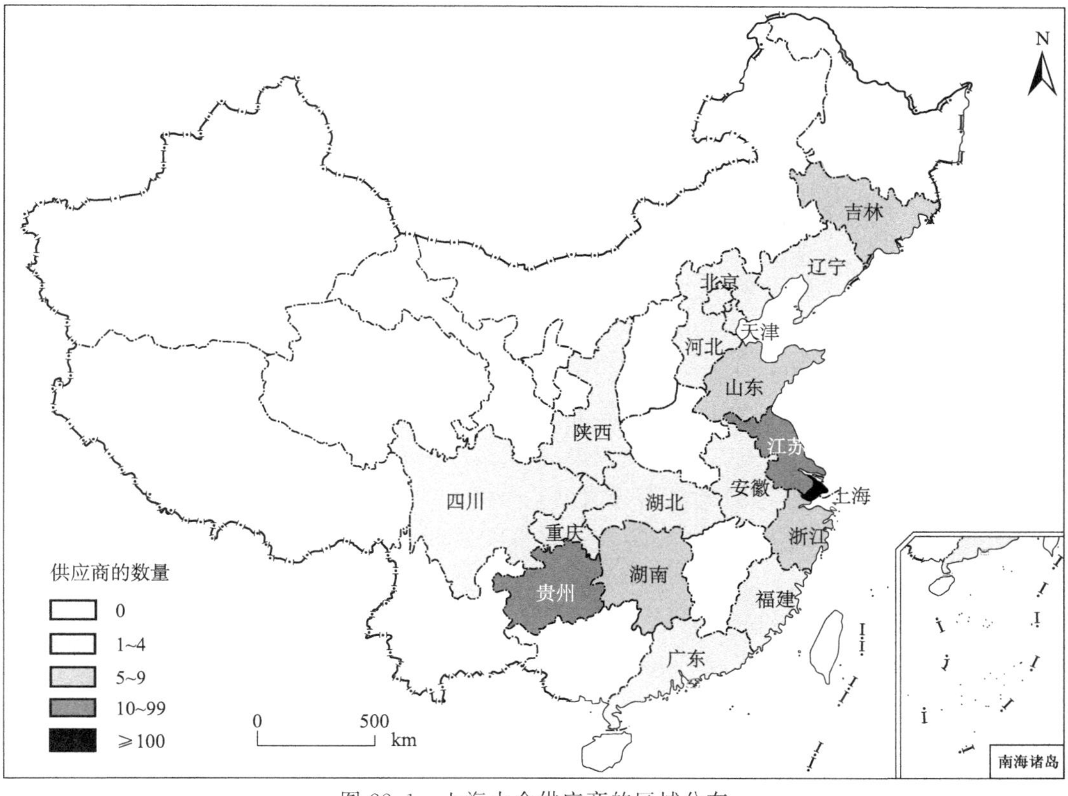

图 22.1　上海大众供应商的区域分布

资料来源：作者调查。

① 北京娱乐信报．追溯中国车业（六）上海大众率先尝试国产化．2004．http://auto.sina.com.cn/news/2004-06-11/68905.shtml．2004-6-11。

表 22.2　上海大众主要供货区域供给的零部件类型

区域	主要零部件
上海	除了下述的所有零部件
江苏	塑料部件，模具，安全带，火花塞，油箱，保险杠，门锁，收音机
贵州	消音器，各种类型的开关，锁具，铸件，天线，挡风玻璃垫圈，封底漆，窗户升降装置
浙江	塑料制品，玻璃，隔音毡
山东吉林	低温驱动器，汽缸零部件
湖南	发电机，启动马达，活塞环，塑料部件，空调压缩机
湖北	铸成品，门锁，保险杠
广东	收音机和卡式播放机，汽化器，轮胎
福建	开关
河北	电池，油漆

资料来源：作者调查。

这种区域模式的形成受很多因素的影响，其中，技术能力的影响最为关键。当上海大众选择新的供应商时，它首先考察的是潜在供应商的技术能力。上海市是中央政府指定的三大汽车生产基地之一，也得益于其十分发达且与之相关的制造行业（Yeung and Sung，1996），所以，在上海有 177 家供应商也就不足为奇。其他省份的企业之所以被选中，是因为其能生产质量更好的产品。这些企业主要有两类，一类隶属于中国汽车零部件公司的企业，这些企业主要分布在吉林和湖北。这些企业在上海大众成立之前就已生产相关产品。另一类隶属于飞机制造部的企业，主要位于贵州和湖南。他们的制造设备相对先进，生产的产品质量相对较高。

政治考虑和生产组织的变化也影响着上海大众供应商的区域分布。在中国，行政管辖区内经济总产值通常是评估区域政府的一个重要指标。所以，上海市政府多年来一直鼓励大众在本地建立供货商。在生产组织方面，上海大众在 20 世纪 80 年代引入了“及时生产方式”“及时配送系统”的管理方式，促使供应商和上海大众临近布局。为了保证对上海大众的及时供货，一些距离较远省份（如贵州、湖南和北京）的供应商就在上海郊区建立工厂。由此，上海市的地方供应商数量，从 1988 年的 91 家（占总供应商数量的 54.2%）增加到 1997 年的 177 家（占总供应商数量的 64.1%）。除了上海汽车工业集团，其他供应商企业数量扩张最为迅速（表 22.3）。

表 22.3　上海大众国内供应商的区域变化

区域	1988 年（数量，占比%）	1997 年（数量，占比%）
上海汽车工业集团	24，14.30	36，13.0
其他上海企业	67，39.9	141，51.1
其他省份	77，45.8	99，35.9
合计	168，100	276，100

资料来源：作者调查。

22.3.4 企业联系的意义

由于在汽车行业生产链中的特殊性，上海大众汽车有限公司对地方经济影响效应是非常显著的。正如上文所提到的，通过生产扩张，上海大众与很多地方企业建立了供货联系。由这些企业提供的直接就业机会就有 50000 个左右。作为中国销售额最大的外商投资企业，上海大众和它的供应商，对上海的经济总产值和上海市政府的税收贡献很大。上海汽车产业总公司，主要依赖上海大众和其供应商，1997～1998 年两年中 7 个指标连续位居国家首位，包括纳税、利润、总产出、资本流通和地方化。此外，与上海大众的企业联系也推动了整个汽车行业以及其他相关产业在上海的发展。例如，自 1990 年起，许多全球大型汽车生产商和汽车零部件生产商，像美国的福特（Ford）、联合信号（Allied-Signal）和埃梯梯（ITT），德国的博世（Bosch）、吉凯恩（GKN），在上海均有相关投资项目。1992 年，福特和一个中方合作人建立了一家合资企业，生产各类汽车玻璃。1994 年，联合信号在上海浦东新区投资 2.74 亿美元，建立了全资子公司，生产涡轮增压机。ITT 也成立了合资企业生产刹车设备。1989 年，吉凯恩开始生产传动轴。1996 年，全球最大的汽车零部件生产商之一——博世，与一批中国企业签署了投资额高达 27 亿英镑的合资合同。

在上海大众对其他相关产业的影响方面，玻璃、塑料行业最为典型。1980 年之前，这个行业很落后，生产规模很小，已有的企业主要是乡镇企业。由于现代汽车制造需要使用大量玻璃部件，上海大众创造的这种需求促使玻璃行业的发展。现在这个行业拥有世界上最先进的装备和技术。例如，1996 年，上海该产业 15%以上的产品出口到国际市场（上海市统计局，1997）。

这种影响的区域差异可通过供应商的数量、生产规模和产品结构反映出来。江苏省有 40 家供应商，它主要供应技术水平相对低的小的零部件。浙江也是这种情况。这两个省份的供应商，70%以上是小规模的乡镇企业。与此相反，贵州、湖南、吉林和湖北供应的是比较复杂的产品。这些产品多和二级供应商相连。这些省份的供应商大多是大规模的国有企业。这些供应商对地方经济发展的影响也很大。

企业联系对区域的影响表现在很多方面，如经济增长、技术更新、管理水平的提高等。在某种程度上，技术和管理方面的影响对中国更重要。这种影响可从上海大众供应商的挑选程序中看出。在选择供应商时，上海大众首先要考察供应商的产品、产品设计和技术能力。如果满意，上海大众会给供应商提供零部件生产的技术标准。然后这两个企业签订“试供应”合同，并附加详细的供应条件。如果生产的零部件被证明达到标准要求，供应商才开始制造这些产品。然而，在某些情况下，供应商需要改变产品设计的技术规范，直到达到上海大众的技术标准。在订单第一次送货之前，上海大众的专家还要进行第二次检查。这次考察主要关注产品程序、设备、管理和成本。第一次供应的零部件（通常是小规模合同）要经过精细测试。产品只有在实际运行中表现良好，才会继续下面的订单。只有顺利通过整个监测程序的企业才能成为正式供应商。整个程序一般要持续 1～2 年（Liu，1992）。而这个过程实际是供货商技术和管理方面提升的过程。

值得注意的是，上海大众有一个政策，同一零部件要有 1 家以上的供应商。一方面，保证供应（预防运力不足和其他不可预见的问题，如某些地区电力供应紧张）；另一方面，促进供应商之间的竞争。这种竞争无疑会对供应商产生压力，迫使它们不断进行技术革新和提高生产效率。

至 20 世纪末，在上海大众的供应商中，有 60 家已经与外国公司建立了合资企业，有 120 家引进了发达国家的技术。通过引进、吸收、转化海外技术，汽车行业生产和设计的整体技术水平得以提升。因此，上海大众在 1992 年建立了一个技术研发中心，开始联合设计一款地方新车型。1994 年，桑塔纳 2000 就在上海大众诞生。由于使用功能和外观设计的改进，这款新车型很受消费者喜爱。这也奠定了上海引领中国汽车技术发展的地位。

因为要供应产品给上海大众，供应商们就要不断进行质量改进，并增强其产品研发能力。由此，从给上海大众供应零部件开始，后来这些供应商就逐渐为多家汽车组装企业提供产品。据上海市政府相关官员估计，在上海大众的 276 家供应商中，这类多客户的供应商，在上海本地大约有 60 家，在上海以外有 80 多家。桑塔纳国产化就像个孵化器，实现了“引进一个车型，改造一个行业”。桑塔纳国产化的成功，则为上海大众后续新车型的开发及全国的整车企业上马探索了路径。桑塔纳后续的多种改款车型开创了中国汽车合资自主研发的先河。现在，上海大众汽车零部件配套体系几乎为中国所有汽车厂商提供服务。后来进入中国市场的许多跨国汽车公司在投产初期，零部件本土化率就在 40%以上。正是有了这样完善的配套体系，才有奇瑞、吉利的成长。例如，为上海大众提供配套的几百家零部件企业，同时承担着奇瑞的配套工作。而上海大众在这个基础上也逐渐建立了独立的研发体系。2008 年，由上海大众自主设计和研发的 A 级车 Lavida 朗逸成功上市，长期占据国内 A 级车畅销榜首位。2011 年，上海大众与德国大众合作开发的基于德国大众新一代 B 级平台、面向中国市场的全新帕萨特上市，这是中国轿车企业首次直接参与国际一流汽车制造商的全新产品开发，也标志着上海大众的研发工作正逐步融入大众汽车集团全球开发体系。经过 30 年的发展，桑塔纳的“共同体”已经由过去以推进国产化为主要任务的松散联合体，发展成为上海大众和它配套企业的经济联盟。同时，成员单位也发生了变化，不再局限于零部件供应商，而是吸收了经销商和服务商，转变为实体上的利益和命运的共同体①。

22.3.5 贵州的例子

很久以来，贵州都是中国最贫穷的地方之一。它的外商直接投资额居于中国较低省市区行列（Li and Yeung，1998）。在这种背景下，与上海大众的企业联系所产生的影响很值得探讨。

1960～1970 年，中国政府为战备目的在偏远地区投资了很多大项目，包括贵州的山区。这些项目（或企业）主要是航空航天产业。20 世纪 70 年代后期，政府转向发展经济而不是战备准备，这些企业不得不寻求产品的民用化。由于它们拥有相对先进的装

① 陈墨．从上海大众读中国汽车合资三十年．2013．http://www.txweekly.com/index.php? m=content&c=index&a=show&catid=16&id=1772．2013-11-11。

备、技术和发展能力，在 20 世纪 80 年代早期它们就开始生产轻型汽车。它们的背景和产品质量使得上海大众 1986 年在贵州选择了 16 家供应商。这些企业提供 32 种零部件，占上海大众总产值的 6%。这些需求估计给贵州当地带来了 1 亿多元的工业产值（贵州年鉴编委会，1987）。更重要的是，给上海大众供货的企业提高了它们的技术发展水平，它们也为很多其他汽车生产商，如天津大发和广州标志，生产 200 多种零部件（贵州年鉴编委会，1988，1989）。

贵州由此成为中国汽车零部件的主要货源地之一。1996 年，仅汽车零部件的产出就占全省机械总量的 40%（贵州年鉴编委会，1997）。而且这些生产又带动其他相关行业的发展，这种影响应该比统计数据显示的要大得多。

22.4 上海贝尔

上海贝尔电话设备制造有限公司是 1983 年由两个大的公司——中国邮电工业总公司（拥有 60%的股权）和阿尔卡特贝尔电话设备有限公司（拥有 31.65%的股权，另外 8.35%属于比利时政府）投资组建。中国邮电工业总公司隶属于中国邮电部，在中国 18 个省（市、区）有 42 家分公司，32 家外国投资合资企业。自 1980 年以来，所有分公司和合资企业销售额年均增长 25%以上，其中 15 家分公司年销售额超过 1 亿元（陈少能，1995）。由于国内地方市场的有效控制和快速增长的电信市场，都促使上海贝尔公司快速发展。自 1984 年开始运营以来，公司已取得长足的进步，不久就成为高级数字交换系统的领导制造商。连续 7 年位居全国 10 大外商投资企业行列。1996 年，上海贝尔公司拥有 1800 名员工，年销售额达到 45.6 亿元，成为中国第 5 大外商投资企业。上海贝尔拥有贝尔实验室中国研究中心和数个重要的全球研发中心，可全面进入阿尔卡特朗讯全球技术库，开发服务于中国和阿尔卡特朗讯全球客户的独创技术，并且在多项新技术开发中居于主导地位。公司拥有技术先进、制造能力达到世界一流水平的生产制造平台，公司销售服务网络遍及全国和海外 50 多个国家。2012 年，上海贝尔顺利完成收购安弗施（RFS）无线射频系统业务，迈入拓展全球化业务的新纪元。上海贝尔已成为集研发、产业化供应链和信息技术服务中心于一体的阿尔卡特朗讯在全球的旗舰。上海贝尔的研发中心是阿尔卡特朗讯全球三大研发中心之一，同时，上海贝尔拥有阿尔卡特朗讯在亚太地区唯一的研创中心，研创中心人均专利数在阿尔卡特朗讯集团内连续多年排名第一。上海贝尔的研发不仅针对中国市场，而且面向世界，同时直接参与阿尔卡特朗讯的全球策略研究，以及新产品从概念、原形设计到开发的全过程。截至 2014 年年底，上海贝尔在上海、北京、南京、成都、青岛成立了五个研发中心，研发人员超过 5500 人，产品覆盖固定网络、移动网络、宽带接入、智能光网络、多媒体解决方案和网络应用等领域①。

---

① 数据来源于上海贝尔百度百科：http://baike.baidu.com/link? url=AO6da1H23GG2OjUOnmjNtVN89IBMrXeSToXWqYdisNBIZA2vwMY7yefRQ9yiiRTxXfEP3d1ZyhBnM2ckn09Iut_QaiI057dw-O9jk2DDiboCwa4wADzxPcQYurytGttldniCUnhMbYxZiVzFjjK7LVe2B9gNT3cfXOyzzwH6MtDdO8NOoSZ7kQlYMAR0m_HL。

22.4.1　公司供应商的发展和区域分布

尽管有其他原因，上海贝尔公司寻找国内供应商的主要目的是降低生产成本。在其生产起步阶段，公司几乎进口所有零部件。由于零部件成本太高，在与竞争对手以同样的价格销售产品时，公司总是遭受损失。为了降低成本，提高竞争力，零部件供应的地方化变得十分有必要。为了实现这个目标，首先要实现集成电路（IC）生产的本地化，因为它占整个生产成本的30%～40%。上海一家公司在引进生产64k位内存芯片技术后，成功满足了上海贝尔生产IC的需求。其他零部件的生产也开始本地化。截至1997年年底，上海贝尔的主要产品（S12数字交换系统）的本地化率超过70%，S12-J系列新一代交换机本地化率达到62%。自1987年后的十年间，1000多种、涵盖15个类别的不同规格组件，已可以在国内生产。这些组件包括超大规模集成电路，精密混合机，微型冷凝器，继电器，连接器，大电流和高频电磁过滤器，各类信号电缆，多层印刷电路板（PCBs）和原材料，金属和化学物质等。

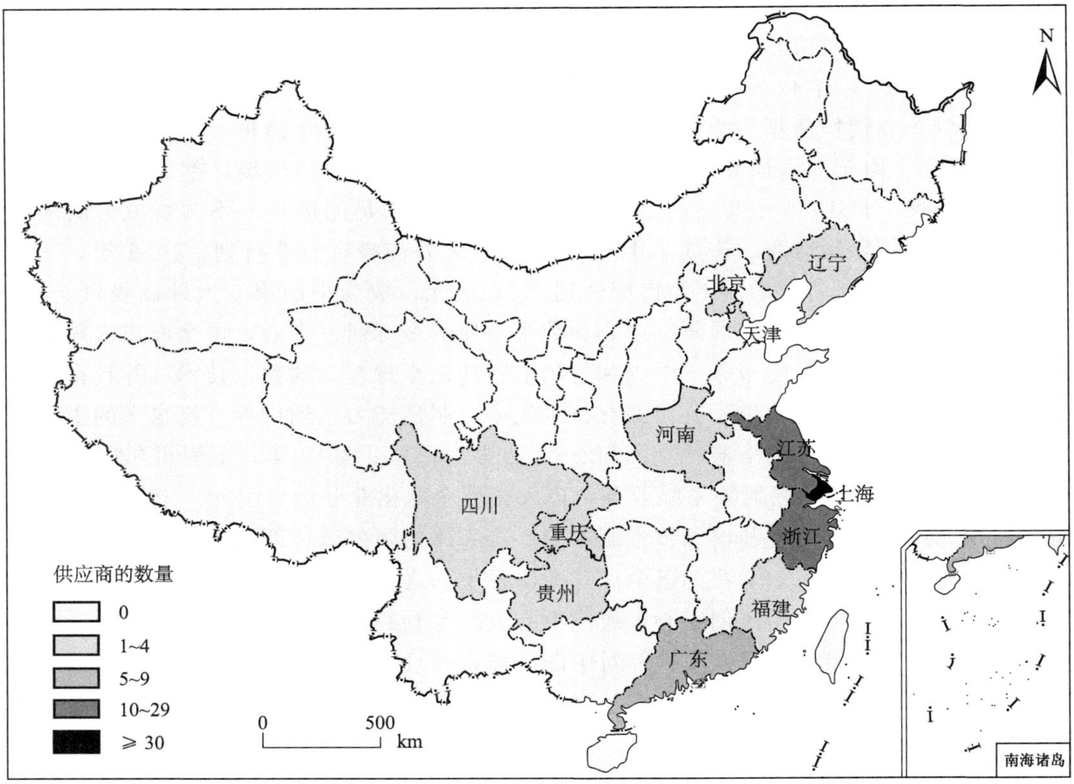

图 22.2　上海贝尔供应商的区域分布图

资料来源：作者访谈。

从地理上讲，与上海大众类似，由于接近上海贝尔的区位优势和发展相关产业相对优越的氛围，上海成为供应商最集中的地方（Nyaw，1996）。在上海贝尔的85家国内供应商中，近 50%的供应商位于上海（图 22.2），并且这些位于上海的供应商都是资本和技术密集型的（表 22.4）。它们对地方化的贡献更多表现在价值创造方面，而非数量方面。除上海外，江苏和浙江也是供应商集中分布的地方，但它们主要生产小组件，多是规模较小的乡镇企业。相比较而言，其他省市区的供应商大多是大中型的。换句话说，在这些地区，单个企业与上海贝尔公司的联系可能要强于江苏和浙江供应商的联系。不过，与上海大众不同的是，从上海贝尔的案例中未发现供应商逐渐向上海市集中的趋势。这显然与两家公司的所有权结构不同有关。上海大众合资的一方是上海市政府，主要代表上海市的利益；而上海贝尔完全由国家邮电部控制，它与多个区域的子公司的利益有关。

表 22.4　上海贝尔主要供货区域供给的零部件类型

区域	主要零部件
上海	超大规模集成电路，精密的混合机，通信电缆，电子元件
江苏	小部件（如螺栓，螺母等紧固件）
浙江	小部件
广东	混合机，印刷电路
北京	集成电路
辽宁	电容器
四川	混合机，通信电缆
河南	电容器
贵州	钽电容器
福建	电容器
天津	通信电缆

资料来源：作者访谈。

22.4.2　企业联系对地方经济发展的影响

企业联系对地方经济发展的影响显著表现在就业、利润和税收方面。上海贝尔和它的供应商共提供了 20000 多个就业机会。仅上海贝尔就占领中国数字交换系统市场的三分之一。在开业后的 10 年间，上海贝尔公司给上海市政府的税收贡献是中央政府最初投入资金的 5 倍。

尽管不太明显，但同样重要的是，在不同层面上的企业联系影响地方经济的发展。

首先，上海贝尔为 85 家国内供应工厂提供了市场，其中一些工厂完全依赖这个市场生存。例如，上海贝尔需要的 IC，70%多由上海本地一家公司生产。这保证了这家公司每年 3 亿多元的收入，每年 1 亿多元的利润，并在中国微处理机公司中占据首位。1980 年代，四川的两个供应工厂一度面临着市场问题，后来通过为上海贝尔供应电缆和混合机，这两个公司逐步强大起来。而且，附近的一个测试公司也从这个市场中获益。

其次，上海贝尔为所需的组件设定了高标准，通常是从 3～4 个候选公司中选择一家供应商。这也促使供应商改善产品质量，改进管理水平和提高整体技术水准。到 1997 年 10 月，有 33 家供应商通过了 ISO9000 国际质量体系认证。根据上海贝尔公司的计划，其所有供应商都要在 1998 年年底通过这个认证。

最后，通过更为间接的影响，一些工厂在被上海贝尔授权为供应商后，就拥有了与其他潜在客户进行谈判的优势。这种关联效应推动了几家供应商把产品打入国际市场。据上海贝尔公司的受访者说，1980 年代后期和 1990 年代早期，很多候选供应商处于亏损状态，后来由于上海贝尔提供的市场才得以盈利。开始时，上海贝尔使用这些供货商 60%以上的产品。随着它们产品质量的提高，这些企业又开发了新的客户。后来，即使上海贝尔压缩了订购规模，它们还是能满负荷生产。

在对本地技术影响方面，上海贝尔公司也提供了一个良好典范。开始时，中国与发达国家在高级数字交换系统方面存在很大的技术差距，据受访者估计有超过 30 年的差距。但是，当地技术人员通过技术转移和海外培训学习，实现了技术大跃进。目前，他们不仅知道如何利用这些技术，还试图改进某些零部件性能。自 1992 年以来，该公司尝试过多种方法，以提高当地的研究和开发能力，如派 50 位本地工程师去欧洲贝尔技术研发中心工作，并与当地的大学和研究机构建立合作等。最终，1996 年，在上海建立了一个研发中心。为发展一批拥有自主知识产权的高新技术产品，上海贝尔公司每年将销售额的 5%～7%作为研发经费。

这个合资企业最大的贡献是缩小了中国和发达国家在电信技术方面的差距。据受访者的估计，现在的差距已缩小至 1～2 年的时间。这主要归结于以下几个方面。第一，经过十多年的运行，这个合资企业的技术水平已有很大提高，可以进行进一步的研究和开发。第二，中国市场销售额的快速增长，使其获得巨额利润，有足够的财力支撑其高额的研发费用。第三，激发了中国合伙人强烈的研发能力。第四，来自其他跨国公司的市场竞争，如西门子等，用同样先进的技术生产相同的产品，这也强化了研发动机。

22.5 结论与讨论

本章中的两个案例公司都与国内众多供应商形成了广泛的企业联系，尤其是上海大众。这种广泛的网络联系是诸多因素共同作用的结果，其中中国政府实施本地化的政策和公司降低成本的考虑起关键作用。中方持有大部分股份和中方合作伙伴较强的实力也强化了中方的谈判能力（Pan，1996；Yeung and Li，1999），从而进一步强化利用国内供应商的行动。从地理上讲，虽然企业联系覆盖很多区域，但主要集中于公司所在地。与合资方是地方政府的合资企业相比，合资方是国家部委的合资企业拥有较多区外供应商。

通过这两个公司的案例研究进一步表明，跨国公司对区域直接投资的实际影响要比一般外商直接投资的影响更大。首先，这种影响远不止一个外商投资企业。就像经济学家和地理学家（Hirschman，1958；Dicken，1992）描述的，通过供应联系，产业增长、技术转移、管理改进和技术创新就在很多地方企业中传播开来。其次，这种影响也超出了所投资地区。很明显，跨国公司直接投资的区域受益最多。上海经济在 20 世纪 90 年代快速增长，就在于有众多跨国公司在此投资。不过，这两个公司的案例研究也证明，其他省市区也能从跨国公司在上海的投资中受益。

在某种程度上，这两家公司反映了这两个行业的一般情况。根据我们以前对北京吉普汽车有限公司和中国汽车工业总公司的访谈，发现汽车行业内其他主要合资企业也拥有和上海大众一样的企业联系。而电子和电信行业内其他合资企业在企业联系方面就不同于上海贝尔，不过这主要归因于合资企业的本地化水平不同（浦东新区管委会，1997）。其他研究表明，多数情况下，这两个行业最后的总装公司使用由众多其他公司大规模生产的、质量好的零部件（Dicken，1992）。

与其他发展中国家相比，这两个案例公司的企业联系网络并不是特别强大。印度的两大卡车公司（Lall，1980 年）和新加坡的三大电子公司（Lim and Fong，1982）的国内企业联系网络，分别比上海大众和上海贝尔的国内企业联系广泛得多。这可能跟产品的差异性，每种零部件供应商的数量，以及本地化水平等因素有关。根据其他国家的实证研究以及我们访谈对象的观点，更多国内供应商的出现是可能的。鉴于企业联系对经济发展的重要影响，相关地区的政府应该采取适当措施以开发和扩展这些联系。

跨国公司在中国的直接投资已经呈现出显著的区域差异。就外国直接投资额来说，上海和其他沿海省份占全国较大份额，而中西部的省份所占份额很小（Li and Yeung，1998）。这种区域模式源自投资者对中国投资环境的判断。由于西部地区基础设施落后，发展水平较低，阻碍了跨国公司的直接投资，鼓励该地区的企业加入到沿海地区外商投资企业的供应商网络中可视为一种可行的选择。

本章仅揭示了两个跨国公司投资企业供应链的最重要部分。由于时间和资金限制，无法对这两个案例公司的直接供应商进行研究。这些间接联系可以追溯到几个层次。关于公司间网络关系的更详尽研究可以揭示跨国公司投资的乘数效应。如果不是很困难，这是一个迷人又重要的研究议题。这样的研究还需单独进行。

参 考 文 献

陈少能. 1995. 世界著名跨国公司在浦东. 上海：华东师范大学出版社

贵州年鉴编委会. 1987. 贵阳：贵州人民出版社

贵州年鉴编委会. 1988. 贵阳：贵州人民出版社

贵州年鉴编委会. 1989. 贵阳：贵州人民出版社

贵州年鉴编委会. 1997. 贵阳：贵州人民出版社

浦东新区管委会. 1997. 浦东外国直接投资结果的调查报告. 上海（非公开内部资料）

上海市统计局. 1997. 上海统计年鉴 1997. 北京：中国统计出版社

王志乐. 1996. 著名跨国公司在中国的投资. 北京：中国经济出版社

Buckwalter D W. 1995. Spatial inequality，foreign investment，and economic transition in Bulgaria. The Professional Geographer，47：288～298

Dicken P，Quevit M. 1994. Transnational Corporations and European Regional Restructuring. Utrecht：N G S

Dicken P. 1992. Global Shift：The Internationalization of Economic Activity（2nd Edition）. New York：

Guilford Press

Dunning J H. 1985. Multinational Enterprises, Economic Structures and International Competitiveness. Ames: Wiley Chichester

Edgington D. 1995. Japanese manufacturing companies in southern Ontario and NAFTA. In: Green M B, Mcnaughton R B. The Location of Foreign Direct Investment. Aldershot: Avebury

Fujita K, Hill R C. 1995. Global Toyotaism and local development. International Journal of Urban and Regional Research, 19: 7～22

Hill H. 1982. Vertical inter-firm linkages in LDCs: A note on the Philippines. Oxford Bulletin of Economics and Statistics, 44: 261～271

Hirschman A O. 1958. The Strategy of Economic Development. New Haven: Yale University Press

ILO. 1981. Employment Effects of Multinational Enterprises in Industrialized Countries. Geneva, International Labour Organization

Kueh Y Y. 1992. Foreign direct investment and economic change in China. China Quarterly, 131: 637～690

Lall S. 1980. Vertical inter-firm linkages in LDCs: An empirical study. Oxford Bulletin of Economics and Statistics, 42: 203～226

Lan P, Young S. 1996. Foreign direct investment and technology transfer: A case study of foreign direct in vestment in north-east China. Transnational Corporations, 5: 57～83

Lardy N R. 1994. The role of foreign trade and investment in China's economic transformation. China Quarterly, 144: 1065～1082

Li X J, Yeung Y M. 1998. Transnational corporations and their impact on regional economic development: Evidence from China. Third World Planning Review, 20 (4): 351～374

Lim L Y C, Fong P E. 1982. Vertical linkages and multinational enterprises in developing countries. World Development, 10: 585～595

Liu W. 1992. Technology Transfer, Technological Capability and Late Entry into the International Automobile Industry: A Case Study of Shanghai-Volkswagen Automotive Corporation in China. Unpublished Ph. D. thesis, University of Sussex

Murphy A B. 1992. Western investment in East-Central Europe: Emerging patterns and implications for state stability. The Professional Geographer, 44: 249～259

Nyaw M K. 1996. Investment environment: Perceptions of overseas investors of foreign-funded industrial firms. In: Yeung Y M, Sung Y W. Shanghai: Transformation and Modernisation under China's Open Policy. HongKong: The Chinese University Press

O'huallachain B, Reid N. 1992. Source country differences in the spatial distribution of foreign direct investment in the United States. The Professional Geographer, 44: 272～285

O'huallachain B. 1984. Linkages and foreign direct investment in the United States. Economic Geography, 60 (3): 238～253

O'malley E. 1994. The impact of transnational corporations in the Republic of Ireland. In: Dicken P, Quevit M. Transnational Corporations and European Regional Restructuring. Utrecht: N G S

Pan Y. 1996. Influences on foreign equity ownership level in joint venture in China. Journal of International Business Studies, 27: 1～26

Park S O. 1997. Rethinking the Pacific Rim. Tijdschift voor Economische en Sociale Geografie, 88: 425～438

Porter P B. 1995. Foreign investment law in the People's Republic of China: Dilemmas of state control. China Quarterly, 141: 155～185

Singh M S, Choo C S. 1981. Spatial dynamics in the growth and development of multinational corporations in Malaysia. In: Hamilton F E I, Ling G J R, eds. Spatial Analysis, Industry, and Industrial Environment: Progress in Research and Application. Chichester: Wiley

South R B. 1990. Transnational "maquiladora". A A A G, 80: 549～570

United Nations Centre on Transnational Corporations (UNCTC). 1987. Transnational Corporations and Technology Transfer: Effects and Policy Issues

United Nations Conference on Trade and Development (UNCTAD). 1996. World Investment Report 1996: Investment, Trade and International Policy Arrangement. New York: United Nations

Williams D. 1996. Analyzing the regional impact of foreign manufacturing firms. Tijdschrift voor Economische en Sociale Geografie, 87: 259～265

Yeung Y M, Li X J. 1999. Bargaining with transnational corporations: The case of Shanghai. International Journal of Urban and Regional Research, 23 (3): 513～533

Yeung Y M, Sung Y W. 1996. Shanghai: Transformation and Modernization under China's Open Policy. Hong Kong: The Chinese University Press

Young S, Hood N, Peters E. 1994. Multinational enterprises and regional economic development. Regional Studies, 28: 657～677

Zhan X J. 1993. The role of foreign direct investment in market-oriented reforms and economic development: The case of China. Transnational Corporations, 2: 121～148

第 23 章　大型劳动密集型企业快速扩张区位选择

富士康在中国内地的区位变化，尤其是短期内新建区位的迅速增加，提供了大型劳动密集型企业快速扩张区位选择的特殊案例。对富士康的研究表明，富士康在中国内地的扩张符合企业空间扩张的一般规律，经历了 1988～1996 年企业初始扩张阶段的接触扩张和 1997～2003 年布局沿海大城市的等级扩张。但宏观经济政策和所处的外部环境使企业扩张偏离一般规律，表现出多样性和复杂性。主要表现在 2004 年以后企业在中西部地区有选择性地快速超常规扩张。这种扩张是多种因素共同作用的结果，劳动力、地价、交通、政府作用在企业的不同发展阶段影响强度不同。富士康快速扩张离不开强有力的政府作用，企业所带来的利益驱动政府给予企业特殊支持，中国特殊的强政府体制使世界上十分罕见的企业扩张和区位选择得以实现。

23.1 研究问题

企业规模由小到大，由单工厂企业向多工厂模式转变，是企业发展的较普遍过程。伴随着企业活动地理范围的扩张，企业决策主体为了追逐最大化的经济利益，根据自身需要和相应的约束条件，对影响区位选择的要素进行综合评价，选择最佳投资区位。不同类型企业在发展中表现出不同的扩张过程。

改革开放以来，大批劳动密集型企业依托我国丰富的低廉劳动力在沿海发展起来。随着沿海地区要素成本的上涨、资源环境保护和产业结构升级，劳动密集型企业逐步向中西部地区转移和扩张。富士康是其中的典型代表。从 1988 年成立之初的单厂单产品到如今的多厂多区位并广泛涉足 6C 产业领域，富士康已布局于中国大陆 19 个省市，员工数也从 9000 人增加到 140 万人。近 10 年来富士康在中国中西部地区的扩张尤为迅速，在有些区位，短短数月富士康新厂区就正式投产，并在 2～3 年内成为数十万人的生产企业。这种情况在世界上十分独特。从区位选择、建厂、招工到投产，中国强有力的政府对推动这种扩张起着重要作用。

目前企业扩张研究中针对这种快速扩张的案例企业的相对较少。现有研究多从宏观角度分析企业扩张动因及企业区位选择的影响因素，忽视了不同类型企业的差别性。富士康的快速扩张是鲜见的，对其研究有重要的理论意义。对富士康在中国内地的空间扩张进行分析，探讨我国特殊政治体制下富士康扩张的原因、影响因素，可揭示富士康快速扩张的动力机制，为劳动密集型企业的发展提供借鉴。

23.2 理论基础

23.2.1 相关研究综述

寻找企业增长的空间扩张规律是公司（企业）地理研究的主要内容（李小建，2006）。企业空间扩张反映了企业随时间发展的历程，伴随着企业原有区位向其他经济区位的扩散和辐射。传统的区位理论主要从经济利润最大化的角度分析企业区位选择（刘静和迟柏龙，2008；李杰，2008），认为区位选择主要受成本影响，主要指劳动力及运输成本（陈嘉等，2014）。在非经济因素（决策者行为、区域政策、特殊考虑等）的作用下，区位选择追求的是某种程度上的满足（李小建，2002，2006），集聚经济、制度和政策以及创新（刘静和迟柏龙，2008）等因素对企业区位选择也越来越重要。区位理论认为企业区位选择倾向于大中城市或者接近最佳区位（接近大中城市）（祁新华等，2010）。不同行业或生产环节企业区位选择时影响因素作用强度也不同（宋周莺和刘卫东，2012）。制造业企业布局主要考虑原材料、能源、成本、交通运输、劳动力、地方政策、企业周围生活条件状况、社会文化、环境保护等（韩国立和张保霞，2007；陶哲雄，2008），向中西部转移是成本导向而非市场导向（杨菊萍和贾生华，2011）。而服务业企业是市场导向型，对政策制度也较敏感（贺灿飞等，2011）。零售业主要考虑人口规模、交通和购买力等（肖琛等，2013）。高新技术企业主要考虑人才与教育、资本与风险投资、人文环境、地方政府服务等（袁义才，2001）。

劳动密集型企业以普通服装、食品、日用百货、电子制造为代表。依托低成本的发展策略使要素成本差异成为区位选择的主要原因。集聚效应、优惠政策等因素也间接发挥着重要影响（魏玮和毕超，2010）。随着交通仓储技术的改善，本地市场规模的作用在下降（张学良和孙海鸣，2008）。区域间劳动力成本差异相对缩小，也使其他因素的作用相对增强（魏玮和毕超，2010）。相比于一般企业，劳动密集型企业区位选择更为复杂，主要体现为候选厂址信息不完整和不同决策者的偏好性（张培勇和刘明，2013）。

在中国特殊的政治体制下，政府对资本、土地等企业所需的重要资源有很大程度的控制权，在考察中国企业的行为时，要综合考虑地方政府的作用（田伟，2007）。地方经济发展状况是衡量地方政绩和地方领导人能力的重要指标。吸引企业投资能够有效解决就业、创造税收、带动相关产业发展，是最快也是成效最明显的促进地区经济发展的方式。企业为当地带来的益处驱动政府采取措施吸引企业，为企业扩张提供有利条件。企业有望获得政府的低息贷款、税收优惠或特殊的生产许可等扶持机会，从而实现规模的超常规扩张或维护现有的市场垄断地位（李晓波，2008）。政策因素是企业迁移最重要动因（杨菊萍和贾生华，2011），企业扩张在很多时候是政府影响下的被动选择（朱松等，2013），但也会主动通过其政治行为谋求有利于自己的外部环境，从而影响政府政策与法规制定和实施过程（田志龙等，2004）。政府在税收及资本等方面的优惠政策、对基础设施的投入，以及对当地生活条件的改善间接影响着企业区位选择（赵丹丽，2009）。区域发展战略引导和促进企业科学合理地进行区位选择（刘静，2010）。在某种意义上，制度因素比经济因素或者硬环境更重要（刘静，2010）。企业网络概念指出企业和政府之间的非经济关系对企业经济行为产生巨大影响，政府行为是企业面对的最为重要的网络关系对象。企业规模扩张的动力根源在于政府和企业两个行为主体对企业边界的认知态度趋同（李晓波，2008）。

23.2.2 分析框架

区位理论蕴含了企业空间布局的原理，企业空间布局的研究结论解释和指导着企业怎样进行布局更为合适。基于区位理论，结合富士康的企业性质和所处的外部环境，提取成本、劳动力、交通条件和政府作用等因素，构建富士康扩张的影响因素分析图（图23.1）。

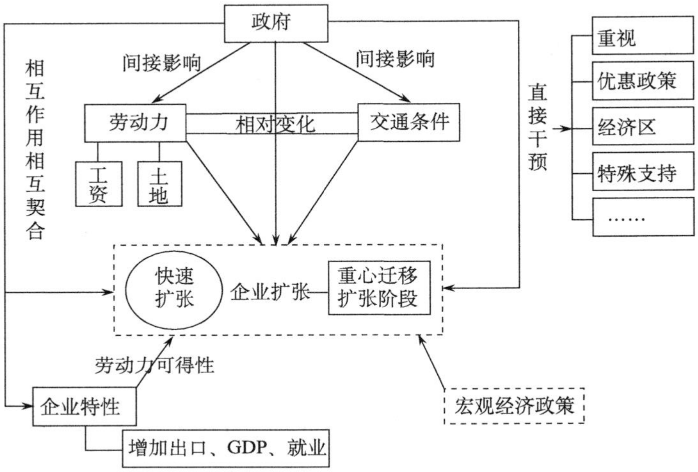

图 23.1　分析框架

不同类型企业区位选择影响因素不同。对电子制造企业来说，产品主要用于出口且时效性强，对交通要求相对较高。劳动密集型企业追求低成本，对生产要素成本（工资、地价等）的上涨较为敏感。劳动力资源丰富且便于获得是企业扩张的必要条件，短期足够劳动力的可得性是劳动密集型企业快速扩张的制约因素，强有力的政府作用可以缓解这一问题。各地政府的竞争使企业扩张成为政府和市场共同作用的行为，表现为以行政手段引导企业扩张和区位选择。

政府和企业行为均符合利益驱动机制。企业投资可以带来经济指标的增长、带动就业、产生示范和连锁效应，满足地区经济发展和政府政绩的需要。低成本和高利润是企业的目标，因此企业争取低价获取生产要素和政策优惠。企业利益和政府利益相互作用、相互契合促进企业扩张的产生。政府作用包括国家宏观经济政策和区域政府对企业扩张的直接与间接干预。政府通过直接干预，如提供各项优惠政策、积极招商引资、建立特殊经济区等措施，加速企业扩张，并作为“看不见的手”间接影响成本因素和交通条件。各要素在不同阶段的相对优劣势的变化造成企业扩张备选区域的差异，影响企业的扩张和区位选择。不同地区政府干预强度的差异性也增加了企业扩张的复杂性和区位选择的不确定性。

23.3　富士康概况

富士康科技集团是台湾鸿海集团在中国大陆投资设立的高科技企业集团。鸿海集团于 1974 年创立于台湾肇基，1985 年创立自有品牌富士康，1988 年富士康开始投资中国大陆。目前在全球拥有 200 余家子公司和派驻机构，12 个事业群，约 130 万员工，涉足电脑（computer）、通信（communication）、消费性电子（consumer electronics）、数位内容（content）、汽车零组件（car parts）、通路（channel）6C 产业多个领域，是全球最大的 OEM 生产商、电子产业科技制造服务商。2005 年首次进入《财富》全球 500 强（居第 371 位），2013 年位列第 30 位。

劳动密集型、出口外向型的企业性质决定富士康可以带动投资地 GDP、出口额、税收等经济指标快速增长，解决当地剩余劳动力问题，产生集聚和连锁效应，满足当地政府政绩的需要。富士康的概念设计和核心部件均来自西方工业国，从设计、研发、品牌、信息来源到运输及销售渠道，均需依靠国外供给商和进口商，产品附加值虽高，但处于制造业下游的不利地位，缺乏对设计、营销等高利润阶段的介入，对劳动力成本以及其他情况导致的成本上涨反应敏感。

表 23.1　布局位置及投资年份

地区	省份	城市	年份	地区	省份	城市	年份
珠三角	广东	深圳	1988	长三角	江苏	南京	2007
长三角	江苏	昆山	1995	珠三角	广东	惠州	2008
环渤海	北京	北京	2002	长三角	浙江	嘉善	2008
长三角	浙江	杭州	2003	中西部	四川	成都	2009
长三角	上海	上海	2003	中西部	重庆	重庆	2009
珠三角	广东	中山	2004	中西部	河南	郑州	2010
中西部	山西	太原	2004	长三角	浙江	宁波	2010
环渤海	山东	烟台	2004	珠三角	广东	东莞	2011
环渤海	天津	天津	2005	中西部	湖南	长沙	2011
珠三角	广东	佛山	2006	中西部	湖南	衡阳	2011
中西部	湖北	武汉	2007	长三角	江苏	阜宁	2011
中西部	广西	南宁	2007	中西部	山西	晋城	2012
环渤海	辽宁	沈阳	2007	中西部	内蒙古	鄂尔多斯市	2012
环渤海	辽宁	营口	2007	中西部	河南	鹤壁市	2012
环渤海	河北	廊坊	2007	中西部	河南	南阳市	2013
环渤海	河北	秦皇岛	2007	中西部	贵州	贵阳	2013
长三角	江苏	淮安	2007	中西部	安徽	安庆	2014

资料来源：据富士康官方网站、富士康宣传资料、报纸杂志以及网络数据整理。

1988年，富士康在深圳设立第一个生产基地（表23.1）。从企业成立到2008年，富士康的投资重点一直集中于沿海地区。随着沿海地区出现的成本上涨和社会问题，内陆地区后发优势的相对增强，富士康陆续向内陆地区扩张。金融危机冲击中国沿海制造业，富士康遭遇订单缩水及加薪困境，2008年之后富士康在中西部地区迅速扩张发展起来，2008～2014年新建了16个占总数约50%的富士康厂区。

23.4 空间扩张特征

富士康的扩张可表现为新建区位的增加、营业额的增长和员工数的增多。富士康现布局于中国大陆19个省市，并在新近6年间新建了与过去20多年同样多的厂区，新建区位涉及10个省市。富士康营业额从1996年的8亿元到2012年的7651亿元、2013年的7549亿元，营业额年平均增长率（已扣除价格影响）为52.7%。营业额持续增加但增长率波动较大，自1996年保持着40%以上的增长率，2007年降为20%，2009年出现负增长（－5.6%），之后缓慢恢复（图23.2a）。富士康员工数量总体上持续增加，从1996年的0.9万人到2012年的139.7万人，十余年间增长了150多倍。特别是近10年来，员工增长迅速（图23.2b）。伴随企业增长，富士康的空间扩张及重点迁移可见图23.3。

23.4.1 重心迁移

重心迁移仅考虑厂区所在城市的位置，因各厂区有些年份数据不齐全，未考虑权重。对上述四个年份的厂区分布情况进行标注，利用ArcGIS和CAD进行计算，得到1996年、2003年、2008年、2012年富士康的分布重心（图23.3）。

1996年，企业建立初期，富士康仅在广东深圳和江苏昆山建厂，其投资重心在福建北。2003年，布局重心迁移到安徽省。2008年，布局重心向安徽西北方移动。2012年，重心移动到湖北省，这一阶段的企业区位变化大致显示出沿海向中部地区迁移。

23.4.2 空间扩张阶段

1. 扩张初始阶段（1988～1996年）

这一阶段企业扩张较慢，仅在广东深圳和江苏昆山建厂。这些区位与台湾交通便捷，较为符合接触扩散的规律（李小建，2002）。改革开放是富士康投资大陆的契机。沿海的发展创造了就业机会，吸引了大量内地剩余劳动力。当时台湾工人的基本工资每月超过2500元，而深圳流水线上的工人每月500元。充足的廉价劳动力、较低的土地价格以及深圳等地对外实施优惠政策，富士康开始向大陆扩张，并集中在两个一线城市附近。

2. 布局沿海大城市（1997～2003年）

该阶段企业主要在沿海大城市（北京、上海、杭州）布局，扩张较慢。发达地区这

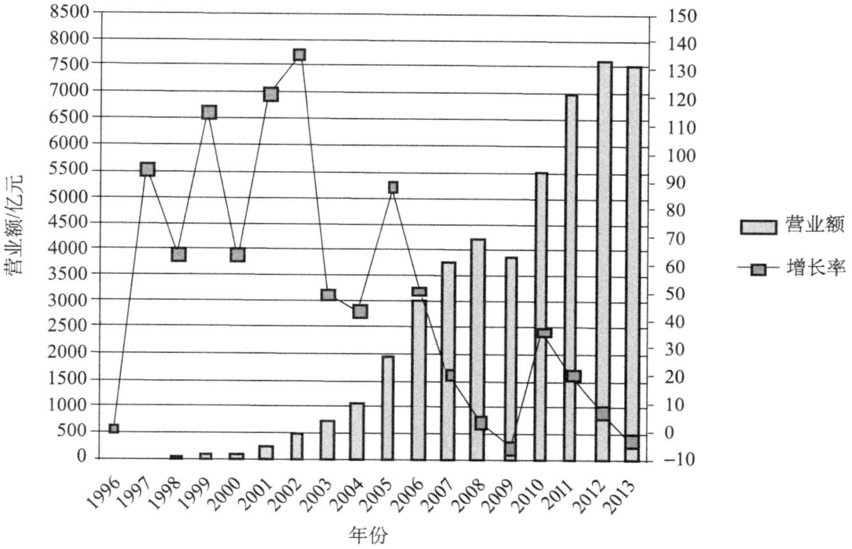

a

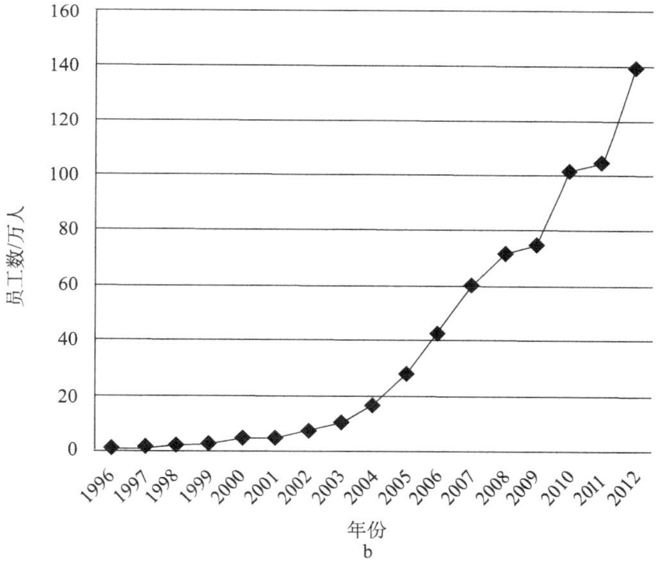

b

图 23.2　富士康营业额及员工数

些主要经济中心基础设施和对外交通在全国处于优势地位，劳动力主要来自其他地区的流动人口，成本并不高。区域环境对企业扩张产生重要影响，较为遵循等级扩张的模式（李小建，2002）。

3. 集中在沿海布局（2004～2008 年）

这一阶段，富士康在沿海地区迅速扩张，涉及除福建外的沿海其他省份。影响企业扩张的各因素处于较为均衡状态，企业延续原有的扩张路径。

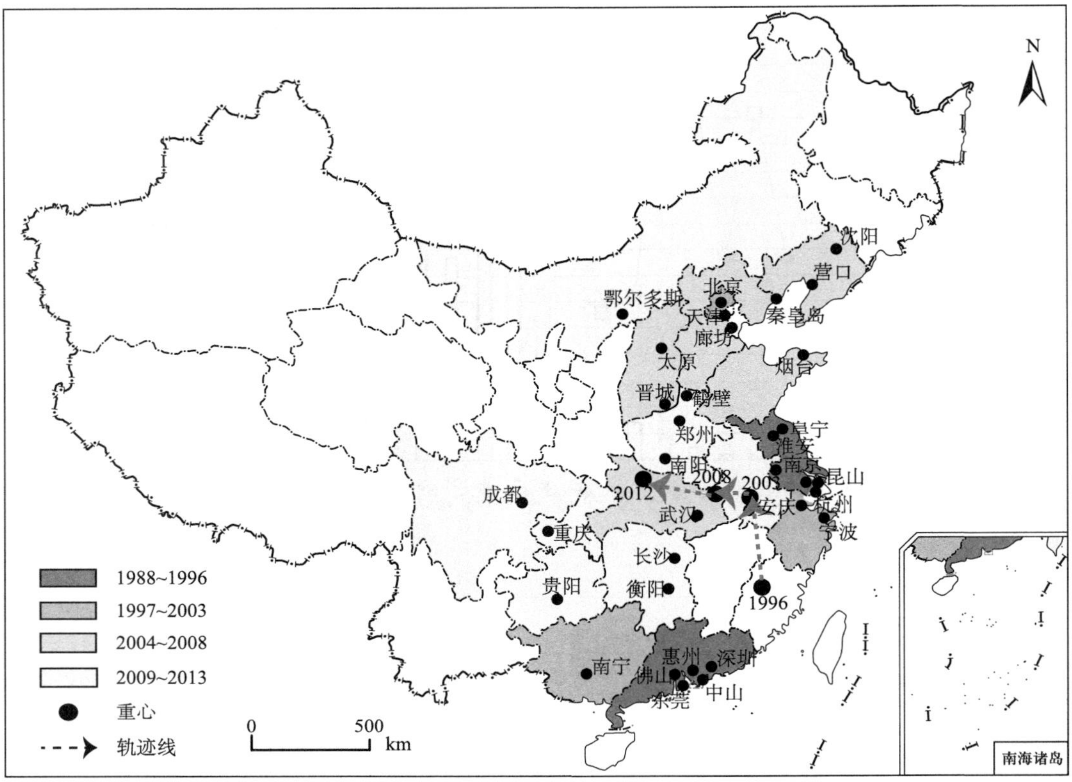

图 23.3　富士康扩张图

4. *加速布局中西部*（2009～2013 年）

这一阶段富士康扩张迅速，在成都、重庆、贵阳、郑州、长沙等中西部地区大量建厂。这些地区的优惠政策成为吸引富士康投资的重要因素。

富士康扩张初始，在台湾母公司临近的深圳和昆山建立生产机构，就近布局的特点明显，符合接触扩散的规律。随着企业的发展，信息获取能力增加，企业沿着一定等级规模的地理区域如北京、上海等大城市新建生产区位。2004 年以来，富士康逐渐偏离接触和等级扩张的模式，有选择性地快速在中西部地区扩张。

23.5　空间扩张影响因素分析

低成本是企业普遍追求的目标，要素成本的区域差异是企业扩张的原因。交通条件影响着物流成本和运输时效性。政府通过直接的行政机制作用于区位决策，或间接作用于其他因素对区位选择产生影响。成本、交通、政府等因素相互作用影响企业扩张，强有力的政府作用推动企业快速扩张。

23.5.1　成本因素

企业成本主要包括原材料成本、人力成本、土地成本、固定资产成本、管理成本等。富士康原材料购入成本几乎比一般竞争对手少 10%。固定资产和管理成本与区位关系较小，因此，企业要想获得高利润就需尽量选择人工成本和土地厂房成本较低区位。

1. *劳动力状况*

富士康大部分的产品生产过程需要人工完成，一线员工所占比重在 90% 以上。生产过程分解详细，劳动力门槛相对较低。因此，工资和劳动力数量状况非常重要。如果用近 10 年各省市 14～65 岁人口占全国平均数的比重表示各地可用劳动力的数量，用各地平均工资和 2014 年最低工资水平衡量工资成本，可以大致看出富士康区位选择与劳动力状况的关系（表 23.2）。从表中可以看出，相对而言，相对平均工资（即各省市平均工资与全国水平的比值）高低影响较为复杂。一些平均工资较低的省份（如陕西、吉林、海南、新疆、宁夏），由于劳动力数量限制，并未有富士康投资。

表 23.2　各地区劳动力供应状况

地区	14～65 岁人口比重	相对平均工资	2014 年最低工资	是否布局	地区	14～65 岁人口比重	相对平均工资	2014 年最低工资	是否布局
广东	7.49	1.48	1305	√	福建	2.77	1.16	1135	×
山东	7.33	1.22	1230	√	山西	2.66	1.02	1140	√
河南	7.03	0.87	1100	√	贵州	2.56	0.93	940	√
四川	5.98	0.96	1100	√	吉林	2.24	0.85	1220	×
江苏	5.97	0.57	1290	√	重庆	2.08	1.18	975	√
河北	5.45	0.6	1180	√	甘肃	1.97	1	1110	×
湖南	4.81	1.09	1160	√	内蒙古	1.95	1.03	1050	√
湖北	4.47	1	1100	√	上海	1.61	2.44	1620	√
安徽	4.45	0.64	1060	√	新疆	1.59	0.9	1340	×
浙江	4.04	1.21	1275	√	北京	1.43	1.83	1400	√
辽宁	3.47	1.1	1100	√	天津	0.95	0.7	1500	√
广西	3.41	0.68	1015	√	海南	0.63	0.9	975	×
云南	3.34	1.09	1105	×	宁夏	0.46	0.92	1225	×
江西	3.17	0.79	1065	√	青海	0.42	1.27	1060	×
黑龙江	3.15	1	1005	×	西藏	0.22	1.94	900	×
陕西	2.9	0.51	1010	√					

2. *土地成本*

富士康生产设备、厂房需要较大空间，同时还要考虑员工的生活空间，需要较大面积的土地，如深圳龙华占地 1.3km²、昆山占地 2km²、北京占地 0.8km²、太原占地 1.6km²、烟台占地 3.3km²、武汉占地 3.3km²、廊坊占地 3.5km²、重庆占地 1.2km²、成都占地 10km²、郑州占地 10km²等。土地取得成本是企业成本的重要组成部分。

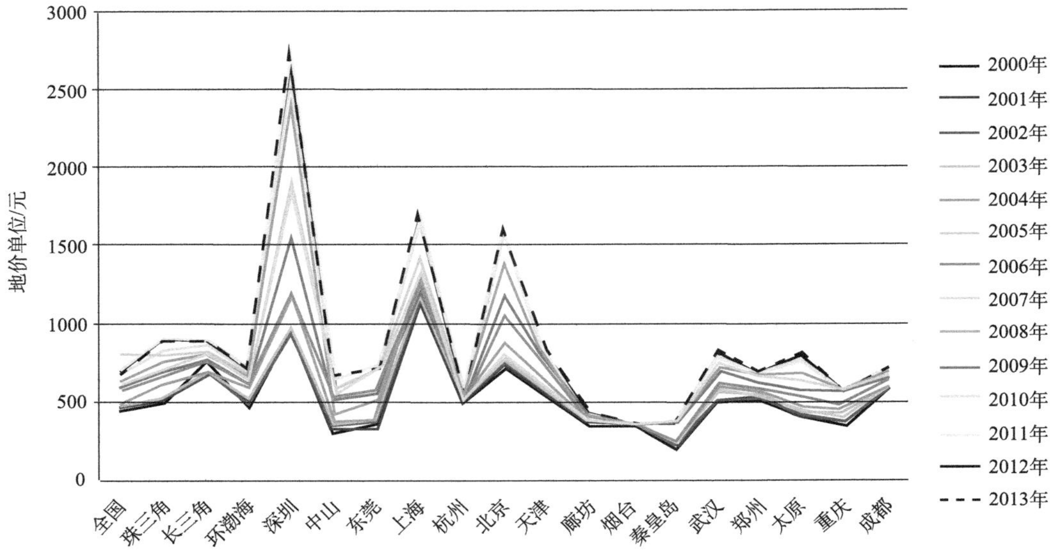

图 23.4　各地区工业地价水平

各地区工业地价水平差别较大（图 23.4）。深圳、上海、北京、天津等沿海地区工业地价一直高于全国平均水平。中西部地区地价较低且各地水平相当。从地价方面考虑，中西部地区具有吸引企业投资的优势。富士康扩张初期并未布局中西部地区是因为沿海地区的优惠政策、交通和劳动力资源优势弥补了高地价带来的成本增加。富士康同时布局在工业地价相差很大的地区，一方面是因为投资年份不同，地价水平有差别；另一方面是因为中国特殊的体制——地方政府拥有土地的使用权，大型企业可以通过划拨或者转让的方式获得大量廉价土地。富士康布局在地价相对较高的地区或者在地价相似的地区进行选择主要是因为其他影响因素增强了这些地区的吸引力。

23.5.2　交通条件

高科技电子产品价值高，市场范围覆盖全球，对运输时限的要求较高，70%靠空运。富士康的多数产品及所需原材料，如液晶面板、芯片等，均为高附加值产品。富士康的“零库存”策略也要求区位选择需接近交通便利的地区以降低物流成本。

富士康在中西部地区的快速扩张与当地空运的发展密不可分。富士康在成都设厂是因为在成都生产的平板电脑和电池可以通过密集的国际航线从成都双流机场及时运到国外。郑州富士康生产的苹果手机从厂区运往新郑机场再通过全货机航线（超过 20 条）运往美国芝加哥等地。烟台富士康产品空运出口的首选机场是青岛流亭机场。富士康在北方地区生产的产品从天津机场运往世界各地。电子产品价格波动大，多耽搁一天，都会增加意想不到的生产成本和经营风险。交通条件和运输的时效性是富士康区位选择需要考虑的基本因素。

23.5.3　政府作用

政府在企业扩张中发挥着直接或间接的作用。政府作为国有银行的控制者，影响企业资金的取得成本。政府对土地资源的配置享有行政垄断权（王箐和魏建，2011），影响土地的取得成本。特殊的经济区域、政府提供的优惠政策是影响富士康区位选择的直接因素。帮助招工、低价转让土地、协助建厂、高效率完成建厂流程和完善基础配套设施也吸引富士康投资。

一些省份的政府（如四川、湖北、山西、广西、河北等）非常重视对富士康的引进，提供了包括财政补贴、土地征用、配套设施建设、税收补贴、帮助招工等措施。廊坊富士康从项目选址到正式开工仅用了 100 天，成都用 80 余天，重庆用 53 天。郑州从签订商务意向书到开工投产只用 63 天，2010 年 8 月第一条生产线正式投产，2011 年年底员工数达 13 万人，2013 年年底员工超过了 30 万人。这些数字反映了政府在吸引富士康上所表现的积极作用。短期内招聘大量员工是富士康的特殊需求，这一问题的解决离不开自上而下的政策体制。一些省份政府通过将招工作为政治任务向下分配、组织学生去富士康实习、对中介机构和员工设置招工补贴等方式帮助企业获取所需劳动力。

此外，政府设立的保税区、开发区等也有一定吸引力。富士康在各省市至少有一个厂区设立在综合保税区或者经济技术开发区（图 23.5），这些厂区占所有厂区的 60%。

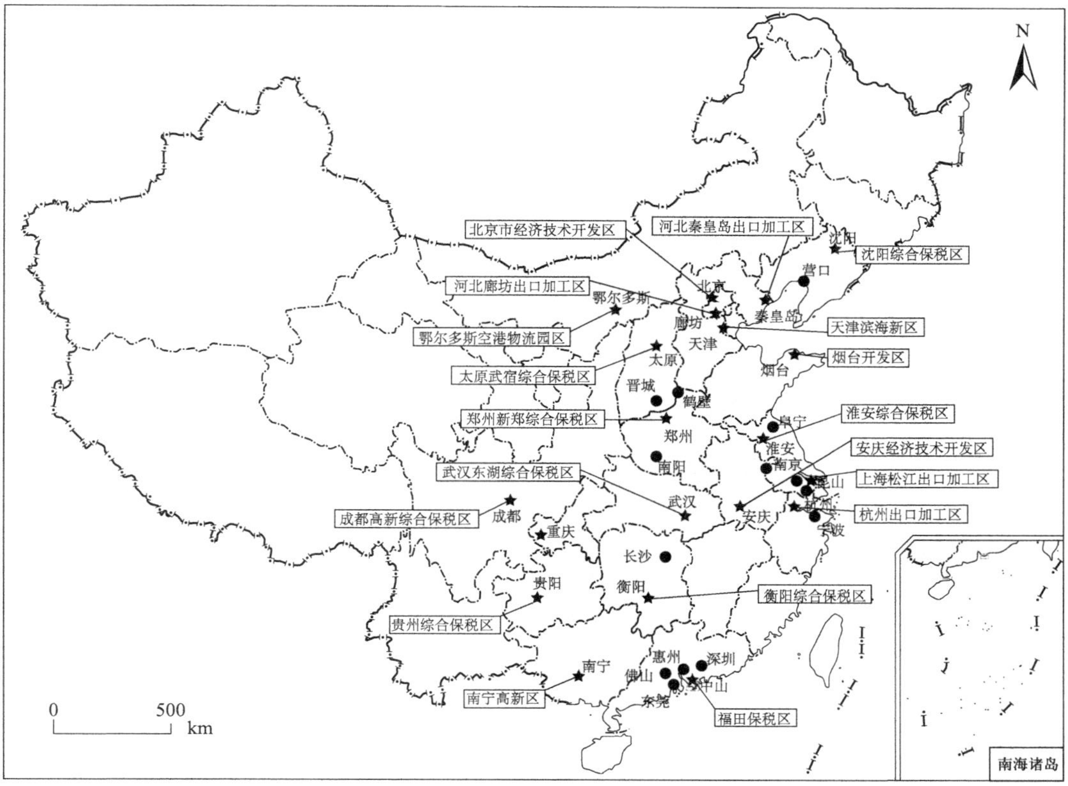

图 23.5　富士康厂区所在经济区

劳动力、地价、交通、政府对企业区位选择的影响相互交织，在社会经济发展以及企业发展的不同时段，这些因素具有不同的耦合方式。随着收入水平的提高，内陆潜在的消费市场对富士康也是一个吸引因素，富士康未来的转型升级策略离不开中国强大的内需市场。

23.6 结论与讨论

富士康扩张是多种因素共同作用的结果。富士康扩张符合中国整体经济发展的路径——先东部再中西部，先沿海后内陆。富士康的扩张过程表现出阶段性，各阶段的主导影响因素不尽相同，经历了从政府政策主导到区域环境再到政府政策为主导的扩张过程。综合看富士康扩张各阶段，特别是加速布局中西部地区过程中，政府起着举足轻重的作用。政府作用强度逐渐增大，是因为在新的产业转移浪潮中，富士康满足了中西部地区招商引资和经济发展的需求，利益驱动政府为富士康的扩张提供机制通道。

我国正处于产业结构重新调整和劳动密集型产业重新布局的时期，因此对劳动密集型企业扩张的研究有助于产业转移和区域产业结构调整。劳动密集型企业的快速扩张是企业自身战略发展、成本优化和优惠政策相互作用的综合结果。改革开放早期，沿海地区率先发展，依靠劳动密集型产业取得经济快速成长。随着改革开放深入及经济发展，面对日益出现的成本上升和社会问题，劳动密集型企业在沿海的发展受到制约，其扩张只能选择经济相对不发达的中西部地区。在国家大背景下，如劳动力成本持续升高，交通等基础设施条件趋于同质化，宏观经济政策也已惠及全国大部分区域，地方政府作用的差异性是影响企业扩张的新的关键因素。目前偏远地区无明显政策优势，劳动密集型企业向中西部扩张的可行性在减弱，转型升级才是最好的出路。

参考文献

陈嘉，韦素琼，陈松林. 2014. 1991 年来台商在大陆直接投资区位选择及驱动机制. 地理学报，(6)：838～849

韩国立，张保霞. 2007. 制造企业的选址决策. 决策探索（下半月），(8)：58～59

贺灿飞，李燕，尹薇. 2011. 跨国零售企业在华区位研究——以沃尔玛和家乐福为例. 世界地理研究，(1)：12～26

李杰. 2008. 企业区位选择的影响因素研究综述. 江汉论坛，(8)：40～43

李小建. 2002. 公司地理论. 北京：科学出版社

李小建. 2006. 经济地理学（第二版）. 北京：高等教育出版社

李晓波. 2008. 我国企业的扩张动力：基于政-企网络关系的思考. 经济体制改革，(2)：62～65

刘静，迟柏龙. 2008. 创新对企业区位选择影响研究. 当代经济研究，(6)：62～65

刘静. 2010. 我国企业区位选择与区域布局问题探讨. 当代经济研究，(7)：54～57

鲁明泓. 1999. 制度因素与国际直接投资区位分布：一项实证研究. 经济研究，(7)：57～66

祁新华，朱宇，张抚秀，等. 2010. 企业区位特征、影响因素及其城镇化效应——基于中国东南沿海地区的实证研究. 地理科学，(2)：220～228

宋周莺，刘卫东. 2012. 信息时代的企业区位研究. 地理学报，67（4)：479～489

陶哲雄. 2008. 制造企业选址问题研究. 商业时代，(18)：54+90

田伟. 2007. 考虑地方政府因素的企业决策模型——基于企业微观视角的中国宏观经济现象解读. 管理世界，(5)：16～23

田志龙，高勇强，卫武. 2004. 中国企业政治策略与行为研究. 管理世界，(12)：98～106

王箐，魏建. 2011. 中国转轨过程中的企业扩张行为. 当代经济管理，(5)：9～12

魏玮，毕超. 2010. 区际产业转移中企业区位决策实证分析——以食品制造业为例. 产业经济研究，(2)：46～54

肖琛，陈雯，袁丰，等. 2013. 大城市内部连锁超市空间分布格局及其区位选择——以南京市苏果超市为例. 地理研究，32 (3)：465～475

杨菊萍，贾生华. 2011. 企业迁移的动因识别——基于内容分析法的研究. 地理科学，31 (1)：15～21

袁义才. 2001. 关于高新技术企业选址理论的探讨——兼论深圳吸引高新技术企业的区位优势与不足. 特区经济，(11)：17～19

张培勇，刘明. 2013. 基于 ANP/D-S/TOPSIS 的劳动密集型企业内迁选址决策方法. 机械设计与制造工程，(3)：35～40

张学良，孙海鸣. 2008. 交通基础设施、空间聚集与中国经济增长. 经济经纬，(2)：20～23

赵丹丽. 2009. 政府对于企业选址的作用. 经营管理者，(11)：3

朱松，杜雯翠，高明华. 2013. 行业景气程度、政府支持力度与企业扩张决策——基于中小企业调查问卷的分析. 财经研究，(10)：133～144

第 24 章　香港大陆投资的区位变化

由于特殊的地理位置和历史渊源，中国改革开放以来，大批的香港资金以直接投资形式流入中国大陆，港资已成为大陆外资的最主要源地（改革开放之后的 10 多年港资占大陆海外直接投资的 60%以上）。对于这种特殊现象，经济学家和管理学家从各自的视角作过不少研究。但是，香港对大陆投资的区位变化及其原因（尤其是从所投资公司决策行为角度）的研究较少。而该领域研究，对于大陆各地加快吸引香港投资的进程，将具有十分重要的意义。本章通过对统计数据和公司调查结果分析表明，香港在大陆直接投资（本章主要采用工业投资数据）的省际差别很大。区域格局变化为，1989 年之前香港直接投资集中于我国南部和沿海地区，之后向其他省份扩散；然而对工业直接投资的趋势并不明显。基于 20 世纪 90 年代中期对香港公司的调查，从对投资主体（香港公司）对大陆各地投资环境的意境地图和潜在投资区位分析，20 世纪 90 年代后半期香港工业投资会向北部和内地转移。除广东、福建以外，对港资有吸引力的省份除长江流域的一些省、市外，还包括华北经济条件较好的省、市。最后，对各地吸引港资提出若干建议。

24.1　文献评述、研究方法与数据

24.1.1　文献评述

到研究时为止，没有专门文献通过对公司投资行为的调查，研究香港在大陆投资的区位变化。从其他侧面研究港资在大陆分布的成果也不多见。英文文献中，Leung（1990）曾研究了 1978 至 1985 年在大陆海外直接投资中的合资企业的区位特点，提到香港和大陆合资企业集中于广东，亲属关系对此格局起决定作用。Smart 和 Smart（1991）也从人际联系角度研究了香港在中国南部的投资，在区位决定因素上得出相似结论。进而，Leung（1993）通过对香港的大陆转包活动区位的分析，仍强调原存亲属关系和工商联系的作用。与这些学者们的研究不同，香港工业总会曾 1990 年、1991 年和 1993 年对其成员进行 3 次在大陆投资的调查（Federation of Hong Kong Industries，1990 年，1991 年，1993 年），其中以 1993 年的调查内容最为丰富，涉及样本企业所投资的工厂数、其厂址区位，以及投资者对长江流域投资的态度。这些成果给本研究以启迪和参照，奠定了本研究的起点。但是它们均没有分析香港投资区位变化（尽管香港工业总会有三个年份的调查结果，但可比性较差），也没有对影响投资的区位因素进行较全面的研究。

24.1.2　研究方法与数据基础

本研究采用宏观和微观兼顾，统计数据定量分析与有关公司调查相结合的方法。在两者互相印证的基础上，重点通过对投资主体——香港公司的调查，分析投资者对大陆投资的空间行为。由于数据收集困难，统计数据采用国家统计局公开发表的 1987～

1991 年各省份（包括省、市、区，下同）港澳直接投资协议额资料（国家统计局贸易物资司，1992）和从中国统计信息咨询服务中心有偿调用的 1992～1993 年该项目资料。这些数据经过鉴别核对，具有较高可靠程度。可作为分析区域变化的基础。

公司调查资料来源于作者 1994 年第四季度在香港的工作。根据香港政府工业署的资料（Industry Department，1993），样本企业取自在工业中占比例最大的纺织与服装业和电子工业两大部门（表 24.1）。它们也是香港在大陆投资量最大的两个工业部门（Federation of Hong Kong Industries，1993）。为获取这两个部门在中国投资的企业名录，从《香港工业总会会员录》（Federation of Hong Kong Industries，1994）中选取在大陆有投资的 240 家公司作为样本（不包括少数就业人数在 100 人以下的公司）。利用传真分批发出问卷给公司总经理或部门经理。随后打电话请求、催问对方填写问卷。三周内共收回问卷 55 份（回收率 22.9%）。经审核，均为有效问卷。

表 24.1　调查部门与调查公司情况

部门	就业人数占制造业比例/%	大陆投资公司数	样本公司	回收有效回卷	回收率/%
纺织与服装业	42	101	90	19	21.1
电子工业	10.6	164	150	36	24.0

24.2　香港在大陆投资空间变化的统计分析

24.2.1　省际变化分析

根据有关统计资料计算，1987～1993 年全国 30 个省份引入港澳直接投资[①]协议额占全国的比例表明，各省份所占比例在 7 年间有升有降，波动很大。

除了个别省份（如江苏、浙江、安徽、山东）保持上升势头外，其他省份这 7 年间变化趋势并不明显。就各省份在全国所占地位而论，7 年中广东一直居第一位，福建由 1987 年的第 6 位跃入 1988 年的第 3 位之后，一直居第二位。其他年份均居前 10 位的省份包括海南、江苏、山东、上海和辽宁。而北京、天津、河北、黑龙江、浙江、河南、湖北、广西、四川则在有些年份进入全国前 10 名之列。从 20 世纪 90 年代以来的发展趋势看，北京、上海的香港直接投资增长速度明显加快。北京占全国的比例从 1991 年的 1.66%，上升到 1993 年的 5.55%；上海的比例则从 1991 年的 1.75%上升到 1993 年的 6.13%。1993 年，在北京的香港直接投资达 40.6 亿美元，上海达 44.8 亿美元，分别为 1992 年的 4.8 倍和 2.4 倍，远超过同期广东、福建的增长率（分别增长 75.7%和 62.7%）。

香港大陆直接投资的省际差异变化可通过表 24.2 分析。20 世纪 90 年代以前 30 个省份中香港直接投资的变差系数在逐步增大，1991 年以后又逐步减小。这反映了各地引进港资的差异从加大到减少的变化过程。同样，30 个省份中吸引港资额前 5 名和前

① 由于资料原因，这里所依据的为港澳两地数据，考虑澳门投资所占比例甚少（如 1992 年澳门大陆直接投资协议额仅占香港的 3.7%），故引用该数据不会引起太多偏差。

10 名在全国所占比例的变化也表现为先升后降，以 1989 年为最高。这说明 20 世纪 80 年代末以来，香港投资的重点省份在全国的地位有所下降，港资逐步向多个省份扩散。

表 24.2 1987～1993 年香港在大陆直接投资的省际差异变化

项目	1987 年	1988 年	1989 年	1990 年	1991 年	1992 年	1993 年
变差系数	2.20	2.75	3.06	2.99	3.09	2.20	2.17
前 5 个主要省（市）所占全国比例/%	79.20	74.84	84.90	81.74	80.34	71.29	69.73
前 10 个主要省（市）所占全国比例/%	92.69	91.44	93.76	92.63	90.91	85.94	87.77

资料来源：国家统计局贸易物资司，1992。

24.2.2 沿海、内陆变化分析

表 24.3 显示了 1987 年以来我国沿海、中部和西部地带引进香港直接投资的明显格局变化。1989 年之前，沿海 12 个省份引进资金的比例递增，后出现徘徊下降。与此相对应，中西部地区所占比例则以 1989 年为界，由降转升，其中，中部地区上升更为显著。

表 24.3 1987～1993 年香港大陆直接投资的区域所占比例变化：沿海、中部和西部

（单位：%）

项目	1987 年	1988 年	1989 年	1990 年	1991 年	1992 年	1993 年
沿海 12 省、市、区	74.48	93.86	94.93	94.37	92.92	88.88	90.61
中部 9 省	13.08	4.23	3.44	2.74	5.51	7.25	6.9
西部 9 省、区	12.44	1.9	1.63	2.89	1.58	3.84	2.49

资料来源：国家统计局贸易物资司，1992。

24.2.3 南、北变化分析

为了分析香港在大陆直接投资的南北变化，表 24.4 选取最有代表性的南部、长江流域和北部一些省份的数据。可以看出，1989 年以来，全国引进港资最多的两个南部省份（广东和福建）所占比例出现显著下降。同期，长江流域 6 省份上升十分明显；北部 6 省份也在波动中出现大幅度上升。

表 24.4 1987～1993 年香港在大陆直接投资的区域所占比例变化：南部、中部和北部

（单位：%）

项目	1987 年	1988 年	1989 年	1990 年	1991 年	1992 年	1993 年
广东、福建	42.86	57.49	72.25	67.47	66.51	50.42	50.65
浙江、江苏、上海、湖北、湖南、四川	15.77	10.8	10.31	11.27	13.27	24.72	19.55
山东、河南、河北、北京、天津、辽宁	22.75	16.84	8.21	14.39	12.91	13.23	16.44

资料来源：国家统计局贸易物资司，1992。

以上分析结果可以归纳为：20 世纪 80 年代末开始，香港在大陆直接投资出现明显扩散。这种扩散的总体趋势表现为：逐步由沿海省份向内陆省份（目前主要是中部地区）转移，由南部重点省份向北部地区转移，且这种转移有递转征兆，即长江流域首先出现明显增加，继而北部省份增幅加大并超过长江流域。这种变化可简单表述为港资的“内进”和“北上”。这一现象既与大陆各地全方位开放的吸引外资政策和投资环境改善有关，也反映了港资在大陆 10 余年的发展，加深了对北方和内地的了解。而港资对第三产业的投入增加，则直接导致了投资地的扩散。有关资料表明，我国引进外国直接投资中工业的比重在 80 年代趋于上升（由 1984 年的 22%升至 1990 年 85.1%），90 年代以来则不断下降（1992 年降为 56.5%）。根据本研究中对一些大公司（如长江集团、怡和集团等）的调查，其在北部省份的投资中第三产业所占比重很大。如果仅仅从工业部门看，香港对大陆投资的“北上”和“内进”并不明显，这将从以下对工业公司调查结果所证实。

24.3　香港在大陆投资区位变化的企业分析

本研究的调查问卷涉及所调查工业公司在大陆的初始投资区位及其随后的新工厂区位，以比较区位变化。初始投资区位的调查结果表明（表 24.5），在 55 家公司投资于大陆的 64 个工厂区位中，有 92.2%位于广东，其中又以深圳和东莞两地最为集中。这与香港工业总会 1993 年的调查结果（广东占 90%）相差不大（可旁证调查样本对总体具显著的代表性）。广东之外，其他初始投资区位涉及北京、上海、福建和山东（均为引进港资的重点省、市）。从表中还可看出，香港投资的初始区位并无明显的时间变化规律。1978～1993 年，广东以外地区初始建厂的数目并无增加。

表 24.5　香港对大陆工业投资初始所建工厂的区位

地区	1978 年	1980 年	1982 年	1983 年	1984 年	1985 年	1986 年	1987 年	1988 年	1989 年	1990 年	1991 年	1993 年	*	总计
广东	1	4	4	6	3	4	4	9	7	7	3	4	1	1	58
深圳	1	2	1	1	1	2	2	4	4	3	2				23
东莞			1	2		1	1		1		1	1			8
其他地区		2	2	3	2	1	1	5	2	4		3	1	1	27
北京		1									1				2
上海		1													1
福建									1						1
山东												1			1
总计	1	6	4	6	3	4	4	9	8	7	4	5	1	1	63

* 年份不详。

新建工厂区位与初始投资区位相比较（表 24.6）表明：位于同一城市的新工厂区位占多数，其次为非同一城市但无明显北移的区位，两者合计，新建工厂并没有发生区位北移的公司占建有新工厂的公司总数的 77%。而所调查的公司中，发生区位北移的公司仅 9 家，地位并不明显。但广东省外的北移均发生在 1993 年以后，且 1995 年有所增加。这说明 20 世纪 90 年代初的香港对工业投资仍无“北上”迹象，1995 年之后才有此征兆，且有发展趋势。

表 24.6 香港对大陆工业投资新建工厂区位与初始工厂区位的比较

项目	1978 年	1986 年	1987 年	1988 年	1989 年	1990 年	1991 年	1992 年	1993 年	1994 年	1995 年	*	总计
位于同一城市	1	1	2	1	2	1	3	4	2	1	2	1	21
没有北移					1	1	1	1	3	2			9
广东省内北移					1	1		1		1			4
广东省外北移									1	1	3		5
总计	1	1	2	1	4	3	4	6	6	5	5	1	39

* 年份不详。

从沿海、内地角度分析，55 家公司投资的初始区位均位于沿海地区（表 24.6）。新建工厂的 39 家公司中，仅 1 家拟于 1995 年在湖南建厂，转向内地。从对企业调查结果的分析，可以认为，香港工业公司对大陆投资区位由广东向北移动和由沿海向内地移动均不明显，但存在这种潜在趋势，90 年代中期将逐步显现出来。

对这种区位格局，本章着重从投资主体（香港公司）的行为角度对此作以解释。

24.4 香港公司对大陆投资的空间行为分析

公司投资的区位选择，受制于投资动机的支配。对公司投资动机的调查结果表明，46 家公司将“降低生产成本”作为在中国投资的最主要动机，8 家公司将“打入中国市场”作为最主要动机（表 24.7）。为便于比较，我们按公司所选择动机的先后顺序，进行加权综合评判，得出各动机的综合评分。四个动机中，“为中国现代化作贡献”无明显区位意义；“进入中国市场”也因到研究时为止，多数产品以出口外销为主，而使其区位意义并未真正得以体现。比较而言，另外两个主要动机则直接影响着公司对区位因素的考虑。

表 24.7 香港工业公司投资大陆的主要动机

动机	(1)*	(2)*	(3)*	综合评分
降低生产成本	46	6	1	461
进入中国市场	8	25	5	292
为中国现代化作贡献	2	7	21	209
为家乡做好事	5	3	9	153
其他	1	0	0	9

* (1)、(2)、(3) 分别代表公司第一、第二和第三选择的数量，下表同。

表 24.8 为所调查公司初始投资时所考虑的主要因素。可以看出，“接近香港”“廉价劳动力”“良好运输条件”和“优惠政策”前 4 个重要因素均与“降低生产成本”有

关。至于“个人关系”因素，一方面具有一定经济意义（如熟人好办事，可减少交易成本），另一方面则为在信息缺少情况下，公司对区位信息获取的一种手段，即在初始区位决定中，公司可通过亲属、朋友和熟人关系的中介，了解当地利于降低生产成本的区位因素。随着各地吸引外资宣传活动的展开和信息的发展，其中介作用会有所降低。“文化接近”虽然对投资者管理带来许多方便之处，但与以上前 4 种因素相比较，其对生产成本的影响要次要得多，故其综合评分位居第 6 位。这种初始区位所考虑因素的状况，可很好地解释香港投资初始区位多集中于广东的格局。

表 24.8　香港工业公司初始投资区位所考虑的因素

区位因素	(1)*	(2)*	(3)*	综合评分
接近香港	29	11	2	551
廉价劳动力	15	10	9	466
良好运输条件	9	14	13	444
优惠政策	6	10	7	336
个人关系	10	2	2	262
文化接近	5	4	7	238
其他	2	0	1	35

* 同表 24.7。

从表 24.9 中可以看出，所调查公司新建工厂所考虑的主要区位因素中，均直接或间接与降低生产成本有关。其中，列居首位的是劳动力因素，而现存工业与新建工厂的产业联系以及更优惠的政策也起着一定作用。与表 24.8 相比较，新建工厂区位中考虑接近香港的因素有所下降，一些公司开始表现出对市场地和原料地的关注。由于有了初始区位建厂的经验，新建工厂所选的区位多更优越，对于生产的组织和降低成本更加有利。

表 24.9　香港工业公司大陆新建工厂所考虑的因素

区位因素	(1)*	(2)*	(3)*	综合评分
廉价劳动力	12	5	6	334
有技术劳动力	1	10	7	266
个人关系	9	1	2	248
较好工业关系	8	3	3	238
更优惠政策	8	5	3	234
接近市场	2	4	3	171
接近原料地	1	6	1	121
其他	2	0	0	39

* 同表 24.7。

值得注意的是，在新建工厂的区位因素中，“个人关系”仍起着主要作用。这反映了厂商追求低成本的动机与获取信息渠道不畅的矛盾，也与投资地环境的不确定性有关。这种过分对人际关系的依赖，限制了厂商区位选择的视野。由表 24.10 可见，在多数工厂的区位选择中，并未作比较研究，只是出于降低成本或其他需要，经人介绍或主动找熟人了解情况后，便决定在某处投资建厂。即使进行区位比较研究的公司，也以在广东省内的不同区位比较为主，其次为现区位与其他国家（如新加坡、越南、马来西亚、印度、泰国、菲律宾等）和中国澳门的比较，而真正在中国境内进行多省份区位比较的公司很少。

表 24.10　香港工业公司对投资区位的比较

类别	公司数	所占比例/%
没有区位比较	30	55.6
在广东省内作区位比较	13	24.1
广东与其他省份区位比较	2	3.7
与其他国家（地区）区位比较	9	15.7

香港厂商的投资动机、投资时所考虑的主要因素、中国各地投资环境信息不畅，以及厂商对区位比较研究的行为，决定了到目前为止其在大陆的工业直接投资仍主要集中于广东，且向内地移动不明显。但随着我国各地开放程度加大（尤其是中部地区经济特区的建立），以及广东省生产成本的上升，以降低成本为主要动机的香港投资者们，必然会寻求更为有利的区位，其投资向广东以外地区的扩散是毋庸置疑的。

24.5　香港公司对投资环境的感知分析

24.5.1　对所投资区位环境的综合评估

香港投资者对大陆投资的回报率要求较高，据调查公司所得信息，所期望的回报率平均为 2.57%，最高为 50%，最低 10%。而实际操作运行中，1/3 的厂家未达到其期望的回报率。这当然与多方面因素（如自身管理、市场变化、技术水平等）有关，而所在地的环境状况也十分重要。

根据所调查公司对大陆投资环境的评估，有 56.4%的公司对其工厂所在地的投资环境表示满意或十分满意，有 43.6%的公司对投资环境有意见。对投资环境满意者中，所称主要满意方面包括劳动力低廉且供应充足、地价低、政府激励措施好，以及当地的承诺可兑现等。对当地环境所表示的不满，则主要反映在政策变化快、收费多，政府吸引外资的措施不力，开发区管理不好，海关不便，交通、通信等基础措施不能适应发展需要等；也有少数公司对当地的教育水平低、人际关系复杂和犯罪问题表示忧虑。这种对投资环境的评估意见主要反映了厂商对广东区位的看法。

24.5.2　在非广东投资的环境障碍

表 24.11 为香港投资者所反映的除广东以外内地其他地区投资环境中的主要问题。可以看出，“距香港太远”成为最主要的不利因素。作者在对一些公司管理人员的访问

中，他们也表现出对此因素的关注。由于对大陆投资的工厂多数仍受香港公司的控制和管理，距离和旅行便捷性便十分重要。一旦需要，香港公司管理人员数小时可到达位于广东的工厂；若投资其他地方，香港公司的控制会困难许多。

在广东以外地区投资的第二个主要不利因素是缺少人际关系的中介和缺少对当地情况的了解，尽管现在已有不少地方来香港举办引资招商会，但对大型公司影响较大。一般的工业公司通过招商会投资的不多，他们多通过可信赖的人的引介。不过，随着信息联系的扩展和中国市场经济规范化，这种情况会有所改变。

对香港投资者来说，他们对政府的激励措施和政策的落实总有担心，这在表 24.11 中也反映出来。一些投资者认为，大陆政策不错，但下面具体执行时会打折扣。

此外，内地的办事效率低也影响着香港投资者。

表 24.11　广东以外地区投资的不利因素

不利因素	(1)	(2)	(3)	综合评分
距香港太远	33	3	1	478
缺少人际关系	12	3	4	233
缺少信息	8	1	1	216
政策落实不可靠	7	2	4	185
政府激励不够	8	1	1	175
效率较低	4	5	1	135
其他	3	0	0	39

24.5.3　近期投资的可能性区位

根据所调查公司对拟投资省份的重要性评定，进行综合权重处理的结果表明（表 24.12），广东、上海、北京是香港工业最热衷于投资的省市，福建、天津、海南、四川、湖南、浙江、山东、广西、江苏、湖北 10 省份，可称为香港工业热衷于投资的地区。表 24.12 中所列的其他 9 省份，可被称为香港工业可能投资区。这些省份均距香港较远，多数位于长江以北地区。根据这些省份所采取的措施，可望在近期内会有一些香港公司在此投资。需要说明，由于所调查公司数量有限，其他未列入表 24.12 的省份，也并非香港工业不愿投资区，只是相对而言，其吸引力较为次之。

比较表 24.12 中各省份的名次与其所在的地理位置，可以认为，沿海地区仍是未来一段时间内香港投资的重心，但内陆一些省份也已得到投资者的关注。从南北位置分析，邻近香港的南方省份（如广东、福建、海南等）仍在吸引港资中占重要地位，但长江流域的省份（如上海、四川、湖南、浙江、江苏、湖北等）也显示出较大的投资可能性。按照这种港商投资趋势，20 世纪 90 年代中后期，香港工业投资的北上与内进会更加明显化，中部地区引进港资在全国的地位会得以上升。

表 24.12　香港工业公司拟投资省份及其名次、权重评估

省份	(1)	(2)	综合评分	省份	(1)	(2)	综合评分
广东	21	1	326	江苏	1	0	35
上海	5	12	262	湖北	1	1	29
北京	3	5	126	贵州	0	1	22
福建	2	1	65	黑龙江	0	1	22
海南	2	2	56	内蒙古	0	0	20
天津	1	0	56	辽宁	1	0	1
四川	1	2	52	吉林	0	0	14
湖南	2	1	50	河南	0	1	13
浙江	2	1	44	陕西	0	0	11
山东	0	3	39	云南	0	0	9
广西	0	1	38	江西	0	0	3

24.6　创造吸引港资环境建议

为了吸引香港直接投资，大陆各省份应真正理解投资者的空间行为，创造一个投资者认为具有吸引力的环境。根据作者对香港公司大陆投资行为的调查研究，建议在以下几方面应引起各地关注。

（1）认识大陆建厂企业的特性，建立方便的关系渠道。由于大部分产品外销，香港多数工业公司（尤其是中小型公司）在大陆投资建厂后，香港总部在原料购入、市场销售、技术设备引进，以至于生产管理等方面起着控制作用，这与第三产业的投资是截然不同的。因此，期望吸引投资的地区一定要考虑这一生产组织和生产联系的特性，创造一个便于香港总部和其大陆工厂进行沟通联系的渠道。这种联系不仅仅限于通信联系，还应包括交通运输。毗邻香港的地区可借水陆运之便，而远离香港的地区，航空运输便十分重要。方便、安全的航空服务可以大大缩短内陆地区与香港的距离，如果再加上其他吸引外资的措施，定会吸引香港投资者。

（2）理解香港投资者的动机，帮助厂商降低其生产成本。本研究表明，香港对大陆投资的最主要动机是降低生产成本。了解香港投资者的这一特点，就要在投资环境中注意创造相应的条件。就中国各地的现状，劳动力土地价格为影响成本最主要因素。根据香港投资者行为，在劳动力要素上，除了价格低廉之外，劳动力的素质也十分重要。为此，要求各地的基础教育和职业教育均要达一定程度。在土地要素上，要在降低土地使用价格的同时，关注厂址周围的环境，建立完好的基础设施。考虑投资者的总成本基准和成本可替代性，以及区位选择上的惰性，广东以外劳动力和土地价格所降低的成本，要远远大于运输和管理所增加的成本，才有可能吸引香港投资者考虑在这些区位的投资。

（3）保持政策的稳定性，并真正落实。通过对香港投资者行为的调查结果，显示出在大陆投资所承担风险较高。调查企业仅有 6%认为承担风险较低，83%认为承担风险较大，11%认为承担高风险。对有关公司的访问还证实这些风险，除了市场风险外，政策多变引起的风险影响很大，由于从传统计划体制向市场经济过渡和中国对外开放过程中有许多开创性和探索性问题，因此便带来政策的不稳定性。但这并不是问题的关键。依香港投资者的观点：大陆吸引外资的政策有区域差异，这些政策的落实情况更有区域差异，而投资者所接受到的政策不稳性，区域差异最大。由此，各地应尽量保持有关政策的稳定性，拟制定的政策要能够真正落实，使每一个办事人员和决策者一样，在引进外资上具有同样的认识和积极性。

（4）加强内地与香港的管理沟通。在大陆建厂的企业在管理上的控制作用缺乏地方化。因此，建议各地加强管理上与香港地区的沟通和信任。为此必须提高内地管理者的管理水平，使这些人熟练掌握现代管理方法，熟悉港方投资者的行为特征和心理特点；同时，要建立法律上的保障体制，约束内地管理者的行为，杜绝徇私舞弊行为。

（5）通过多种渠道宣传投资环境。促成港资投入，不仅要创造适宜投资者行为的环境，而且要宣传所创造的环境。否则，投资者根本认识不到有关环境信息。分析港商对投资环境感知的意境地图，便会发现信息获得程序起着重要作用。有些地区实际投资环境并不差，但香港投资者却知之甚少。为此，各地尤其是距香港较远的地区，应通过各种媒介，宣传当地投资环境的优越性。为提高宣传效果建议地方政府构建区位投资收益模型。通过将当地区位要素输入模型，给投资者以投入收益的定量分析结果。这比空洞的宣传更具说服力，它易于吸引投资者关注，使投资者得到量化的数据，并形成实实在在的环境感受。

参考文献

国家统计局贸易物资司. 1992. 1979～1991 中国对外经济统计大会. 北京：中国统计信息咨询服务中心

Federation of Hong Kong Industries. 1990. Hong Kong offshore Investment. Hong Kong: Federation of Hong Kong Industries

Federation of Hong Kong Industries. 1991. Survey of investment in China. Hong Kong: Federation of Hong Kong Industries

Federation of Hong Kong Industries. 1993. Survey of investment in China. Hong Kong: Federation of Hong Kong Industries

Federation of Hong Kong Industries. 1994. Member's directory 1994. Hong Kong: Federation of Hong Kong Industries

Industry Department. 1993. Hong Kong's manufacturing industries1993. HongKong: Industry Department

Leung C K. 1990. Locational characteristics of foreign equity joint venture investment inChina, 1978-1985. Professional Geographer, 42 (4): 403～421

Leung C K. 1993. Personal contacts, subcontracting linkages, and development in the Hong Kong-Zhujiang delta region. A A A G, 83 (2): 272～302

Smart J, Smart A. 1991. Personal relations and divergent economies: A case study of Hong Kong investment in south China. International Journal of Urban and Regional Research, 5 (2): 216～233

第 25 章　外商直接投资对中国沿海地区经济的影响

中国对外开放以来，外商投资数量增长迅速。1992 年以来，每年进入中国的外商直接投资已仅次于美国，居世界第 2 位（UNCTAD，1996）。这些投资不仅对中国经济整体发展产生多方面的影响（Li，1997；Kueh，1992；Potter，1995），而且通过其区位分布，影响中国的区域经济发展。相关的研究已论及转包活动对珠江三角洲工业的影响（Leung，1993），外资对珠江三角洲城市化模式的影响（薛凤旋和杨春，1997），外资与各地 GDP 的相关分析（陆大道等，1997），韩国投资与山东沿海地区的发展（李文彦，1999），跨国公司对区域经济差异的影响（Li and Yeung，1998）和对特殊地区（浦东）经济发展的影响（Li，1999），外资企业区域关联的案例分析（Li and Yeung，1999）；学者们对全国外资进入的区域差异（Leung，1990；焦华富，1997）、香港投资区位及空间行为（Li，1996）和广东省内外资区域格局及形成原因（许学强和李胜学，1995）的研究，也间接涉及这一问题。然而，纵观这些研究，外资与区域经济发展的一些关键问题答案并不清晰：①外资对中国区域经济增长的影响程度如何？在影响区域经济的诸变量中处于何种地位？②这种影响的区域扩散如何？③中国吸引外资的主要目的之一是引进现代技术和管理方法，从区域角度看这种效应如何？本章研究表明，外商直接投资对沿海地区经济增长具有显著影响，但并非是促使这些地区经济增长的最主要影响变量。大企业调查表明，外资影响通过产业关联在投资地和非投资地扩散；外资对沿海地区技术水平和管理水平的提高有重要促进作用。与其他国家相比，中国早期外资并不集中于经济最为发达的省份，而具缓和经济差异的作用；但随着这些省份已成为发达地区，其影响方向便发生改变。

25.1　外商直接投资与区域经济发展的理论简评

外资与投资地关系有两种不同观点。多数学者认为跨国投资可为投资地带来好处（Young et al.，1994），通过直接投资渠道，使发达地区的经济增长在投资地扩散（Perroux，1973）。与此相反，另一些学者认为跨国投资以剥削投资地为特征，对投资地带来诸多负面影响（Corbridge，1986；Jenkins，1987）。持第一种观点的人较多，多数国家均把外国直接投资看作“好事”（Duning，1994），并制定相应吸引政策。

外资对区域经济的影响包括许多方面（李小建，1997）。其中，如通过资本形成，促进经济增长；通过生产活动的介入，带动技术、贸易、产业结构的变化，促进就业等，有不少研究谈及（Dicken，1992）。这些影响可通过产业关联（尤其是后向关联）产生乘数效应。该效应在经济发达国家（地区）比其他地区更为广泛、明显，来自西欧（Dicken and Quevit，1994）、美国（O'h Uallachain，1984）和墨西哥（South，1990）等国的实例均证明这一点。

一般情况下，外商投资地所接受到的影响更大。因此，投资区位成了研究外资与区域发展的重要方面。研究表明，外商直接投资集中于东道国的经济中心区，尤其是首都或地方首府（Leung，1990；Dicken and Quevit，1994），以利用这里的信息获取优势和相对较好的技术基础条件。但是，不同来源国的外资集中地又有差异，交通运输和信息条件使边界地区成为另一类外资集中地（Leung，1990；O'h Uallachain and Reid，1992）。在东亚的实例研究中，人际关系因素还带来外资在侨乡的集中（Leung，1990；李小建，1996）。来自多个国家的研究证实，这种集中分布的外商投资会随时间逐步向其他地区扩散（焦华富，1997；李小建，1996；Dicken and Quevit，1994；O' h Uallachain and Reid，1992；Bradshaw，1997；Nestor，1997）。

25.2　研究思路及数据

沿着以上理论思路，本章首先分析外商直接投资的区域分布，接着审视集中分布区（沿海地区）外资对经济增长的影响，进而用企业调查资料讨论统计数据所忽略的对技术和管理的影响，以及所产生的间接影响。

依据来源和规模，中国的外资可分为两类：一类以海外华人中小资本为主，集中于广东、福建等地，对投资地的影响以经济增长和扩大就业为主；另一类为跨国公司投资，集中于主要经济中心，对区域的影响除经济增长和就业外，还有明显的技术和管理带动。本章在企业案例分析中侧重于后者。

为进行相关分析所建立的中国各省、市、区外国直接投资数据库主要依据官方统计资料（中国对外贸易经济合作部，1993～1997；国家统计局贸易物资司，1992），仅1979～1984 年取自 Kueh（1992）的估算。企业案例选自上海、北京和天津。这些企业均为制造业企业，选定的主要依据为部门特征（覆盖本地主要外资进入的制造业部门）、在本地本行业的地位（最大或次大）、建立时间（至少 3 年以上）、所有制结构（从中方控股到外方控股）等（表 25.1）。所调查的企业数量取决于在当地的调查时间和企业调查的难度。调查的问题集中于外资企业对当地经济的影响。

表 25.1　样本企业特征（总数=29 家）

项目	特征
建立时间	1980～1985（8）1986～1990（6）1991～1994（15）
工业部门	汽车制造（2）通信（7）电子及家用电器（10）制药（2）建材（2）食品（1）电梯制造（2）机械（3）
来源国别	美国（7）日本（7）欧洲国家（8）亚洲他国（7）
规模（年销售额，亿元）	0.1～1（4）1～10（12）>10（13）
中方控股	>50%（11）50%（4）<50%（14）
地理分布	上海（15）北京（7）天津（7）

注：括号中数字为企业数。

资料来源：作者调查。

作者于1995年、1996年和1997年分别对这些公司的总办主任、副总经理或总经理助理等进行了访问①。访问结果构成本章25.4和25.5两部分分析的主要依据。

25.3 外商直接投资的区域分布及变化

已有文献对中国外资区域分布的研究，多依据某年份的资料（Leung，1990；焦华富，1997）。为避免年份波动偏差，本章使用1979～1996年累计外商直接投资数据。图25.1表明如下外资分布特点。

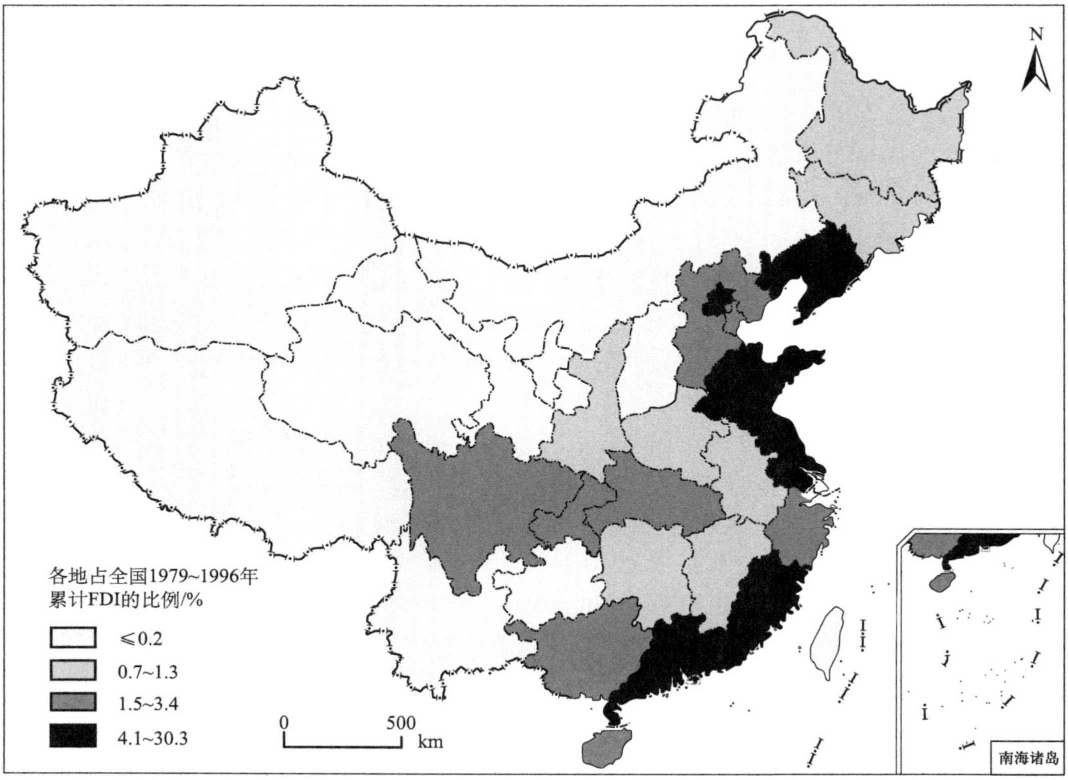

图25.1 1979～1996年中国实际利用的外国直接投资分布

资料来源：1979～1984年来自文献（Kueh，1992）；1985～1991年来自文献（国家统计局贸易物资司，1992），1992～1996年来自文献（中国对外贸易经济合作部，1993～1997）。

1. 东重西轻

18年累计外商直接投资在全国地位最重要的省、市，全部集中于东部沿海地区；西部省、区在全国地位微不足道。沿海12个省、市、区，除河北排名13外，其他均排前11名。12个省、市、区合计占全国的比例近85%。其中，广东（30.3%）、江苏

① 参与访问的有覃成林、周曙云、熊世伟等。

（11.4%）、福建（10.5%）、上海（8.7%）、山东（6.6%）、辽宁（4.3%）和北京（4.1%）占全国的比例均超过 4%。与此比较，广大中西部地区 18 个省、区（重庆市暂未单列）总计占比例仅 15%。多数省、市所占比例在 1%以下，其中，西藏几乎无外商直接投资，青海、宁夏占全国的比例仅 0.01%和 0.02%。

2. 南多北少

在沿海地区内，南部的广东、福建合计占全国累计外国直接投资的 40.8%，约与以北从浙江到辽宁的 8 个沿海省、市的总和相当。

3. 区域变化

与 20 世纪 80 年代前半期相比，80 年代后半期中国南部两外资集中省份（广东、福建）在全国地位明显下降；长江三角洲（上海、江苏、浙江）和环渤海省、市（山东、河北、天津、辽宁、北京）则明显上升（表 25.2）。90 年代，广东的地位仍以下降为主；福建上升到 1992 年高峰后出现下降；长江三角洲上升十分突出；而环渤海地区则以波动为主，并无显著上升。与此相比较，内陆地区尽管比例有所上升（焦华富，1997），但在全国的地位仍然很低。

表 25.2　1979～1996 年外国直接投资的区域变化（各地占全国的比例）（单位：%）

年份	广东	福建	两省合计	上海、江苏、浙江	山东、河北、天津、辽宁、北京
1979～1986	61.22	5.33	66.55	9.78	14.34
1987	41.64	3.55	45.19	19.58	22.00
1988	34.46	4.88	39.44	18.44	24.94
1989	36.60	12.35	48.95	17.94	20.52
1990	45.20	8.94	53.96	11.30	24.62
1991	44.94	9.93	54.87	12.06	21.60
1992	33.12	13.21	46.33	20.28	18.94
1993	27.68	10.59	38.27	25.98	17.39
1994	28.40	11.22	39.62	22.30	20.75
1995	25.57	10.94	38.51	25.30	19.42
1996	27.86	9.79	37.65	25.58	20.88

资料来源：同图 25.1。

中国外资分布的格局，与其他国家具有相似性，即集中地（沿海地区）原有经济和技术条件较好，又为中国的边界地区，易于和相邻国家（地区）接触。中国与其他国家相比也有差异性，即中国的特殊区域开放政策（在广东和福建首设 4 个经济特区）和海外华人与广东、福建的亲属关系，使原不太发达的广东和福建成为外资最为集中的地区。这种区域分布格局是分析外资区域影响的基础。早期外资在非发达区集中（在区域投资中占重要地位），有利于减缓中国省际区域差异（Li and Yeung，1998）。

25.4 外商投资与沿海地区经济增长的定量分析

25.4.1 分析模型

多数关于外商投资对经济增长的经验研究，均以综合产出是生产要素（劳动力、资本和技术）的函数为理论依据构造模型（Wang，1995）。与仅选取外资作为解释变量的模型相比，该模型可更为客观地度量外资相对于其他变量的影响程度。资本可分为国内投资和外资。考虑到发展中国家由农业向第二、三产业的资源转换对产出的影响，以及出口是增长的“引擎”的理论，Wang（1995）在对中国和匈牙利的分析中增加了结构变化和出口两变量。基于前人经验，并考虑投资对产出的滞后影响，本章的分析模型为

$$G = a + b_1 L + b_2 \mathrm{RT} + b_3 \mathrm{FCI} + b_4 \mathrm{FCI}_{t-1} + b_5 \mathrm{DCI} + b_6 \mathrm{DCI}_{t-1} + b_7 X \quad (25.1)$$

式中，G 为国内生产总值（GDP）年增长率；L 为劳动力因素，取从业人员年变化率；RT 为资源转换因素，取第二、三产业增加值在 GDP 中的比重；FCI 为外国投资变量，取实际利用的外资占 GDP 的比重［这里 GDP 代表社会总产出，用外资和国内投资分别占产出的比重作为投资变量，被不少学者所采用（Wang，1995）］；FCI_{t-1} 为滞后一年的外国投资变量；DCI 为国内投资变量，取扣除外资的全社会固定资产投资总额占 GDP 的比重；DCI_{t-1} 为滞后一年的国内投资变量；X 为出口变量，取出口额占 GDP 的比重。

分析数据依据全国及相关省、市的统计年鉴（1997 年）和前述外商投资数据库。由于分省可靠的外商投资数据始于 1983 年，至 1996 年仅 14 年时间。该样本容量不易再增加变量个数，故实际利用外资不再分解为外国直接投资、对外借贷和其他外商投资。实际上，1979～1996 年实际利用外资中，外商直接投资占有 62%的份额；且 20 世纪 90 年代以来此比例更大（1991～1995 年占 71%）。实际利用外资数据主要反映的是外商直接投资的影响。

25.4.2 区域选择

本章以外商直接投资与当地经济规模的关系为指标，确定定量分析的区域。1979～1996 年全国外商直接投资与 1996 年全国 GDP 之比为 0.025 美元∶1 元。高于此比值的省、市依次为海南（0.144）、广东（0.078）、福建（0.068）、天津（0.051）、上海（0.050）、北京（0.042）、江苏（0.032）。海南于 1988 年建省，资料系列短。故 6 省、市被选作定量分析区。

25.4.3 模型结果分析

经过反复多次回归、检验，得出全国及 6 省、市的模型（表 25.3）。该相对最优模型中多数变量对经济增长具显著水平，仅全国和北京市的模型中使用少数不能通过显著性检验的变量（去掉这些变量，R^2 和 DW 均远离可接受水平）。其结果可做如下分析：①全国总体水平上，外商投资对经济增长的影响不显著（取 $T = 0.10$）。该结果与他人同类研究一致（Wang，1995；贺执中和盛欧，1997）。②6 省、市模型中外商投资与

GDP 增长呈显著正相关。尽管由于各模型 R^2、F 值和 t 统计值不同，不能完全相比，但可以看出广东省外资影响最为明显：假若其他变量不变，外资在 GDP 中的比重每增加一个百分点，可带来当年 2.93 个百分点和次年 1.63 个百分点的 GDP 增长率。福建、上海外资对经济增长的带动效应也十分明显（其弹性系数分别为 1.92 和 1.27）。江苏的情况比较复杂。从出现的滞后 1 年外资的负面影响，以及该模型仅解释了 66.3%的经济增长来看，其经济增长中有其他重要影响因素未包括在内。③外资因素在投资当年的影响比滞后 1 年的影响更为重要。④6 省、市外资变量对经济增长的影响程度均大于国内投资；而全国总体状况则与此相反，国内投资影响显著。⑤尽管外资在这些省份对经济增长影响具有重要意义，但均不是经济增长的最主要影响变量。广东、福建、上海、江苏的劳动力变量的影响（b_1）均大于外资影响（b_3、b_4），而北京、天津、上海的经济结构变化影响（b_2）具最重要地位。⑥出口因素在模型中以负相关出现。这可能是由于中国的出口以低附加值产品为主。其他低收入发展中国家也常出现出口与增长的负相关（Ram，1987）。

表 25.3　外商投资对投资集中区的经济增长影响的模型分析（$N=14$）

变量	全国	广东	福建	上海	江苏	北京	天津
a	−3.07	142	3.77	−339	−91.4	−135	−213
	(0.34)	(1.58)	(1.05)	(−1.15)	(−1.44)	(−1.4)	(−3.79)
b_1	1.21	5.63	2.80	3.83	7.72	0.446	−1.47
	(0.79)	(2.87)	(3.61)	(2.23)	(2.56)	(1.02)	(3.76)
b_2		−2.03		3.99	1.19	1.74	2.21
		(−1.67)		(1.32)	(1.49)	(1.68)	(3.47)
b_3	0.511	2.93	1.92	1.27	3.45	0.999	0.374
	(0.76)	(1.84)	(3.86)	(1.87)	(2.11)	(1.81)	(2.37)
b_4		1.63			−2.96		
		(1.62)			(−2.15)		
b_5	0.956	0.827					0.404
	(2.71)	(4.29)					(2.89)
b_6	−0.626	−1.43		−0.53		−0.254	0.166
	(−1.91)	(−2.17)		(−1.83)		(−1.26)	(1.52)
b_7		−0.313	−0.562	−1.05		−1.24	
		(−1.43)	(−2.26)	(−3.09)		(−1.96)	
R^2/%	54	91.6	74.1	79.7	66.3	50.2	97.6
F	2.63	7.76	9.54	5.48	3.93	2.31	40.54
DW	2.20	1.44	2.04	2.01	2.14	2.33	2.34

注：括号中数据为 t 统计值。

25.5　外商直接投资影响的企业分析

所调查的 29 家企业对当地经济增长的影响十分明显。29 家企业中有 8 家为全国最大 50 家外商投资企业，1996 年总销售额近 600 亿元。其中，上海大众汽车有限公司和摩托罗拉（中国）电子有限公司年销售额达 240 亿元和 160 亿元。调查企业近 3 年的年均增长速度均在 15%以上。无疑，这些企业以其宏大的生产规模、惊人的增长速度，促进投资地的经济增长。更为重要的是，企业调查证实了外资影响的扩散及其对投资地管理和技术水平提高的影响。

25.5.1 外商直接投资影响的扩散

表 25.4 表明，29 家企业除两家外，均使用数量不等（15%～100%）的国产零部件和原材料，其中，15 家（占 51.7%）企业的国产化在 50%及以上，10 家（占 34.5%）在 70%及以上。样本企业较高程度的国产化，受多种因素影响：①国家鼓励国产化政策。尤其是中方控股企业多为国家参股，政府影响较大。此外，中方控股企业的中方多为国有大型企业，原有技术水平较高，且有广泛供货网络。故表 25.4 中此类企业的绝大多数（73%）具 50%以上国产化水平。②部门影响。食品制造、建材、家用电器、电梯制造等部门的平均国产化较高，通信设备（尤其是卫星通信）、医药和机械行业则较低。③样本企业建立时间相对较长。由于多数跨国公司投资中国以占领市场为主要动机[①]，较长运营时间可促使厂商发展国内供应商，以降低生产成本，进一步扩大市场。

表 25.4　外商投资企业零部件及原材料国产化（分企业，国产化比例）

部门	中方股权比例									
	>50%			50%		<50%				
汽车制造业	60%			90%						
通信设备	70%	70%	20%	10%		0%	0%	30%		
电子，家用电器	70%	70%	30%	30%	10%	30%	30%	70%	70%	40%
制药	70%					15%				
机械	30%					50%	10%			
建材						90%	67%			
电梯制造	50%	60%								
食品						100%				

注：国产化比例以价值计；表中每个百分比表示相应的一个企业的国产化比例。

资料来源：作者调查。

通过生产联系，外商投资企业的影响在投资地及相关地区扩散。零部件订购为国内厂商提供了发展机遇。29 家企业中 5 家拥有百家以上国内零部件供应厂。这些供应厂半数以上位于本市区，其他主要位于邻近省区。也有一些位于距离遥远的省份，如上海大众在贵州、湖南、湖北、四川有 20 家，上海贝尔在广东、四川有 7 家国内零部件供

---

① 据国家统计局 1994 年 3 月对全国 1066 家外商投资企业的抽样调查，中国市场潜力是外商最为重要的投资动机（见《人民日报》海外版 1994 年 3 月 28 日第 1 版）。

应厂。这些大型外资企业多数具有一个企业带动一个产业，甚至多个产业；带动一个地区，甚至多个地区经济发展的效应。

外商投资企业的国产化还促使其他跨国公司进入邻近地区，与国内企业建立合资企业。例如，天津摩托罗拉公司带动英国 BOC 公司、日本三井高科技公司共约 2 亿美元的投资。上海大众汽车公司带动 60 家汽车零部件合资厂家。上海贝尔带动上海贝岭微电子制造公司的建立，该公司 1996 年销售额达 40 多亿元。周庄镇是江苏江阴市的一个普通村镇，由于大众公司带动，德国公司相继与中方建立江南庆玛曼模塑有限公司、江南庆玛曼箱包厂和江南庆玛曼大型模具厂等，目前已形成“中国江阴德国工业园”。

25.5.2　外商直接投资对管理水平提高的影响

所调查的企业均有一批当地人员参与管理。据粗略估算，29 家企业中，当地人员任中等以上管理人员的比例约 80%。其中，主要决策的当地参与程度与中方所占股份比例有关。中方具 70%以上股份时通常占据董事长、总经理两重要职位；当 50%～70%时，常拥有两重要职位之一；当 25%～50%时，多获得副董事长、副总经理职位；当小于 25%时，则很少获得高层职位。实例还表明，管理人员的当地化随企业建立时间而增加。

通过参与，当地管理人员学习、掌握了跨国公司先进的管理方式。其中，在改善劳动组织和加强销售服务体系、严格控制产品质量和成本方面更为明显。以 1996 年销售额居中国外商投资企业第 5 位的北京吉普汽车有限公司为例，中方在参与管理中学习和消化了美方的管理方式。在领导和决策体制上，把董事会作为最高权力机构；在财务管理上，发挥“管理会计”功能；在生产过程上，实行均衡生产；在质量管理上严格执行 TQC；在劳动人事上，实行聘用制、合同制和职能工资制。其他与大型跨国公司合资的企业的情形与此基本类似。

25.5.3　外商直接投资对技术水平提高的影响

29 家企业中，90%以上引进使用先进技术。这些技术，有 50%以上填补了国内该领域的空白。作者调查及其他相关研究均表明（慕海平，1994），外资所带来的技术进步效应在光纤光缆、通信设备、自动化仪器仪表、彩色显像管、电梯、大规模集成电路、微型电机、轿车、药品、新型建材等方面最为明显。北京市工业部门通过引进外资，使 63%的企业技术装备达到 20 世纪 80 年代后期国际水平；用了不到 8 年时间，完成了 20～30 年的技术进步路程。天津市随着跨国公司投资，形成了以摩托罗拉为中心的通信、电子产业技术优势；上海市大型跨国公司的带动，加强了其 6 大支柱产业的技术优势。

外资企业的技术转移方式以一次性转让为主，其次为引进硬件技术为主，两者合计占调查企业的 58.6%（表 25.5）。这种引进方式尽管也有利于技术水平提高，但关键部分仍被跨国公司所控制。与此相比，约占 1/5 的企业采用动态性技术引进。该类企业可不断更新技术，当地技术人员也适当参与技术引进。4 家大型跨国公司投资企业在中方促进下，建立起研究与开发（R&D）机构。它们对投资区域技术开发能力的提高具有重要意义。对这4家跨国公司调查表明，R&D的设置与其在中国的市场拓展和盈利状况具明显联系。成功地占领国内市场，使其从中获取丰厚的收益，为高投入的R&D奠定了基础；而继续开拓中国及邻国市场，需要开发适合消费者偏好的新产品，从而提出对R&D的需求。

表 25.5 外商投资企业的技术转移

转移方式	企业数	占比/%
引进动态技术，免费更新	6	20.7
一次性转让，开发受限制	10	34.5
主要引进硬件技术	7	24.1
建立R&D机构	4	13.8
以中方技术为主	1	3.4
无技术注入	1	3.4
总计	29	100

资料来源：作者调查。

由于外商投资企业对产品零部件质量需求较高，通过供货联系，这些企业的技术辐射也十分明显。例如，北京吉普汽车有限公司、北京飞利浦公司等分别带动了北京市几十家配套厂，使其技术和产品质量迅速达到国际标准。上海大众、上海贝尔、上海理光的技术辐射达数十家至近300家国内企业。

所调查企业谈及对区域经济的负面影响不多。所谈及的负面影响包括中方在核心技术上介入困难，一些公司使用的技术并不先进；一些公司使用在发达国家淘汰的泰罗式管理方式；跨国公司转移价格影响当地的税收；个别企业受外方控制，国产化进展缓慢。此外，外资企业对当地同行国内企业冲击明显。

25.6 结论与讨论

本章的模型分析表明，外商直接投资对经济增长的影响在中国具有明显的区域差异：全国总体水平上，外资对经济增长的影响不显著；而在外资占当地经济规模比例超过全国平均值的6个省、市，外商投资变量与GDP增长呈显著正相关。广东、福建、上海、江苏的外资对经济增长均具较高的影响弹性系数（1.27～3.45）。但是，外商直接投资并非是促使这些地区经济增长的最主要影响变量。承认这些事实，有利于客观地认识外资的作用。

从较大的区域尺度看，与国际上同类研究结果相似，中国外资集中于经济发达的东部沿海地区。但就省份而论，由于开放政策、边界邻近因素和密切的海外亲属联系，广东、福建这两个原经济并不发达的省份成了最为集中的外商投资地之一。这种经济格局，有利于减缓中国区域经济的省际差异。但是，随着两省经济的迅速增长和发展水平的提高，外资在这里及其他沿海发达地区的集中，会加大中国区域经济的省际差异。

对大型企业的调查表明，外商直接投资的影响也以有利于当地经济发展为主。大型外资企业对沿海地区经济增长，以及技术和管理水平的提高，有明显带动作用。不仅如此，通过与当地其他企业的产业关联，这些影响向更多的国内企业扩散，产生更大的乘数效应。企业实例还显示，作为发展中国家，中国的外资企业国内联系较为广泛。这主要是由于所调查的大型外资企业多以占领中国庞大市场为建立目的，有利于国产化水平的提高。当然，并非所有外商投资企业均具有如此影响（本章以大型企业为主的分析可能夸大外资的积极影响，即使在大型企业中，也有企业根本无技术引进）。外资对区域经济的负面影响，也有发现。区域决策者应充分利用外资促进当地经济发展，尽量限制其不利影响。

和多数国家一样，中国的外商直接投资具有从原集中地向其他地区扩散的特点，尽管这种扩散重点发生在相对发达的东部沿海地区内。随着这种扩散，其对区域经济发展的影响相应发生变化。此外，本章实例还揭示了外商投资通过产业关联对非投资地的影响，这些影响近及邻近省份，远及中西部偏远地区。认识这种影响，可以建议在那些目前难以吸收外商直接投资的中西部地区积极发展与东部沿海地区大型跨国公司投资企业的生产联系，以此带动区域经济增长和管理、技术水平的提高。并通过这种带动，创造吸引外商直接投资的环境条件。

参考文献

国家统计局贸易物资司. 1992. 1979～1991 中国对外经济统计大全. 北京：中国统计信息咨询服务中心

贺执中，盛欧. 1997. 我国经济增长中的外商投资. 世界经济文汇，(3)：31～37

焦华富. 1997. 中国外商投资的地域结构研究. 地理研究，16 (3)：32～38

李文彦. 1999. 中韩经济合作. 北京：经济管理出版社

李小建. 1996. 香港对大陆投资的区位变化与公司空间行为. 地理学报，52 (3)：193～206

李小建. 1997. 跨国公司对区域经济发展影响的理论研究. 地理研究，16 (3)：101～111

李小建. 1999. 跨国公司与中国投资地经济发展. 二十一世纪双月刊（香港），51：148～158

陆大道，等. 1997. 1997 中国区域发展报告. 北京：商务印书馆

慕海平. 1994. 我国利用外国直接投资的现状及对策. 管理世界，(1)：152～157

许学强，李胜学. 1995. 改革开放以来广东省利用外资的时空差异特征. 地理学报，50 (2)：128～137

薛凤旋，杨春. 1997. 外资：发展中国家城市化的新动力——珠江三角洲个案研究. 地理学报，52 (3)：193～206

中国对外贸易经济合作部. 1993～1997. 中国对外经济贸易年鉴. 北京：中国对外经济贸易出版社

Bradshaw M J. 1997. The geography of foreign investment in Russia, 1993-1995. Tijdschift voor Economische en Sociale Geografie, 88 (1)：77～84

Corbridge S. 1986. Capitalist World Development：A Critique of Radical Development Geography. New Jersey：Row man & Little field

Dicken P. 1992. Global shift：The Internationalisation of Economic Activity (2nd Edition). New York：Guilford Press

Dicken P, Quevit M. 1994. Transnational Corporations and European Regional Restructuring. Utrecht：N G S

Duning J H. 1994. Re-evaluating the benefits of foreign direct investment. Transnational Corporations, 3

(1): 23～51

Jenkins R. 1987. Transnational Corporations and Uneven Development: The Internationalization of Capital and theThird World. New York: Methuen

Kueh Y Y. 1992. Foreign investment and economic change in China. China Quarterly, (131): 637～690

Leung C K. 1990. Locational characteristics of foreign equity joint venture investment in China, 1978-1985. Professional Geographer, 42 (4): 403～421

Leung C K. 1993. Personal contacts, subcontracting linkages and development in the Hong Kong-Zhujiang region. A A A G, 83 (2): 272～302

Li X J. 1997. Foreign direct investment and its impact on China's economy: A research appraisal. The Journal of Chinese Geography, 7 (1): 33～45

Li X J, Yeung Y M. 1998. Transnational corporations and their impact on regional economic imbalance: Evidence from China. Third World Planning Review, 20 (4): 351～374

Li X J, Yeung Y M. 1999. Inter-firm linkages and regional impact of transnational corporations: Company case studies from Shanghai, China. Grografisca Annaler B, 81 (2): 61～72

Nestor C. 1997. Foreign Investment and Spatial Pattern of Growth in Vietnam. In: Dixon C, Drakakis-smith D. Uneven Development in South East Asia. Aldershot: Ashgate

O'h Uallachain B. 1984. Linkages and foreign direct investment in theUnited States. Economic Geography, 60 (3): 238～253

O'h Uallachain B, Reid N. 1992. Source country differences in the spatial distribution of foreign direct investment in the United States. Professional Geographer, 44 (3): 272～285

Perroux F. 1973. Multinational investment and the analysis of development and integration poles. Economies et Societes, 24: 831～868

Potter P B. 1995. Foreign investment law in the People's Republic ofChina: Dilemmas of state control. China Quarterly, (141): 155～185

Ram R. 1987. Exports and economic growth in developing countries: Evidence from time-series and cross-section data. Economic Development and cultural Change, 36 (1): 51～72

South R B. 1990. Transnational "Maquiladora". A A A G, 80 (4): 549～570

Unctad. 1996. World Investment Report 1996. New York: United Nations

Wang Z Q. 1995. Foreign Investment and Economic Development in Hungry and China. Aldershot: Avebury, 324～329, 250

Young S, Hood N, Peter E. 1994. Multinational enterprises and regional economic development. Regional Studies, 28 (7): 657～677

第 26 章　大型国有企业空间网络变化

改革开放以来，中国逐渐从计划经济向市场经济转变，不断开展增大企业自主权、提高生产效率的企业改革，使得大型国有企业空间网络发生了较大变化。源于中国大型农业机械公司——中国一拖集团有限公司的访谈数据显示，企业网络密度在不断增强，但销售地域空间有所缩小。除了销售和原材料供应外，企业在管理、技术和其他方面的空间网络联系均在拓展。在这些变化的背后，有许多政治和经济因素在起主要作用，人际关系居次要地位。与韩国的大企业和在其他亚洲国家的国有企业相比，中国的国有企业（国企）在网络形成和演化机制方面不同。在国有企业得益于不断扩张的空间网络的同时，有些市场的萎缩亦不容忽视。

26.1　研究背景

在中国改革开放之前的几十年中，国企决定着中国经济的命脉。1978 年之后，国企经历了一系列的企业改革，如扩大企业的自主权（1978～1984 年）、实行合同责任制（1984～1986 年）、转化企业经营机制（1987～1993 年）、建立现代企业制度（自 1994 年起）（董辅礽等，1995）。这些改革导致国企发生了许多变化，并引起了许多学者的关注（Huang and Kalirajian，1998；Chen，1998；Nolan and Wang，1999；Mo and Li，1998；Raiser，1997）。然而，多数研究强调了企业改革的机制和社会经济效果，而非其空间特征（李小建，1998，2000；Li，2001）。相反，许多地理学研究多强调中国改革的区域影响（Wei，1999；Ma and Wei，1997；Zhao and Tong，2000；Marton，2000），但是忽视了国有企业改革在其中的作用。有关国企改革和区域发展之间的关系，一个关键问题是企业联系的空间网络发生了变化（Li，2000）。

然而，在经济地理学中，在工业和商业网络方面有着丰富的文献（Conti，1993；Amin and Thrift，1994；Park，1995；Dicken，1998；Yeung，1997a，1997b；Yeung，2000a）。这些文献通过对发达国家和发展中国家的研究，验证了无论是跨国公司还是小企业，都存在着网络联系。它们极其强调网络形成研究中的社会和制度机制（Yeung，2000a）。遗憾的是，中国的国有企业并未被纳入网络研究范畴中。中国的国有企业是在一个非常独特的（某种意义上是独一无二的）环境下运行的。第一，政府政策发生了重大的变化。在过去的计划经济体制下，国有企业相当于政府的一个单元，其运行完全服务于国家利益。企业改革政策旨在提高国企的自主权，促使它们依据市场规则运行。第二，改革开放的 1978～2000 年，GDP 年均增长率高达 9.61%，中国经济已经取得了快速增长。这为企业扩张提供了大量的机遇。第三，中国文化强调私人关系；客户更喜欢和具有历史悠久的，与自己关系较好的公司合作（Zhao and Adam，1995；Smart and Smart，1991）。加上中国加入世界贸易组织后的全球化趋势不断加快，这些因素对国企网络的影响更大。

显然，前两者和经济全球化均促使国有企业网络的变化，而第三者起相反作用。在以上提到的政治、经济及文化力量的作用下，国有企业该如何重塑其地理网络？它是否与其他国家的企业网络模式不同？各影响因素对不同国有企业构建网络的影响强度有多大？在中国经济、政治转型的独特背景下，中国企业的网络发展过程与中国在其他发展中国家的企业不同吗？

本章旨在通过对中国国有企业——中国一拖集团有限公司空间网络变化的深入调查，对以上问题有所回答。超过5万员工的一拖集团有限公司位于中国中部地区——河南省洛阳市（其前身是成立于1959年的中国第一拖拉机厂，1997年重组为当前的公司）。之所以选择以该公司作为案例的原因有三。第一，规模之大决定了其在农机行业中的特殊地位。作为中国百强工业企业之一，该公司自成立以来一直是中国最大的拖拉机生产商，直到2000年，已经生产大中型拖拉机50万辆（占全国市场份额的43%）。第二，该公司的体制改革过程折射了国家的企业改革历程。第三，作者在河南省工作了近20年，且与洛阳市政府官员接触较多。考虑到获取企业数据的极端困难，尤其是在中国的企业间联系方面，这种友好关系有助于搜集数据（Li and Yeung，1999；Yeung and Li，2000）。

为搜集相关信息，作者及其研究生先后在1992年7月、1993年6月、1998年4月和2000年6月对中国第一拖拉机集团有限公司进行了访谈。访问对象包括公司副总经理，董事会办公室主任，市场部门和研究部门的负责人等。这为详细分析过去20年不断变化的网络联系提供了可能。公司联系网络形式很多（Lall，1980；Hill，1982；Conti，1993）。本章主要关注公司内部、公司与其同行之间在管理、原材料和技术等方面的网络联系。

26.2 国有企业空间网络

20世纪50年代，学者们首次对空间网络联系进行了研究（Perroux，1950；Hischman，1958），之后，大批学者从不同角度对其进行了分析（Lall，1980；Lim and Fong，1982；Mc Dermott and Taylor，1982；Conti，1993；Dicken，1998；Amin and Thrift，1994；Dicken and Quevit，1994；Young et al.，1994；Hanink，1995；Harland，1995；Yeung，1997a，1997b，2000a）。除了单纯的经济要素外，政治及文化环境作为商业网络发展的重要决定性因素被纳入进来（Yeung，1997a，1997b，2000a）。在经济全球化背景下，企业扩展与其他市场参与者合作网络的可能性更大（Dicken，1998）。大量、密集的网络通过利用各方面的优势、各类型专业知识的互补，促进了公司和区域经济的增长（Amin and Thrift，1994）。然而，基于发达市场经济国家的研究发现，在20世纪80年代～90年代，许多公司的原材料供应商数量有所下降（Farmer and Von Amstel，1991；Griffiths，1992）。这可能涉及技术及管理等因素，如确保即时供应（JIT）的需求、严格质量保证承诺的需求、取消双重采购政策和降低通信成本的需求等（Lamming，1993）。东亚及东南亚不同的政治及文化背景已形成了不同类型的网络，如日本的集团公司、韩国的大企业、中国在亚洲其他国家的家族企业，以及东南亚的裙带资本主义企业（Yeung，2000b）等。韩国财团组织（大企业集团公司）的发展在很大程度上归功于政府的支持（Wade，1990）。中国的商业体系则强调人际关系在塑造商业网络中的作用（Zhao and Adam，1995）。政府作用和个人关系都与中国国企网络有着密切联系。诚然，中国商业体系并不等同于当代中国的商业。在中国，私人关系在构建商业网络方面发挥着毋庸置疑的作用。然而，国有企业利用关系的方式具有独特性。例如，亲属关系对海外华人家族企业的影响很大，但对中国的国企并非如此。在严格的计划经济体制下，国家当局在很大程度上决定着企业间的合作关系。国企的市场营销是由国家计划委员会负责的，销售与分配是由商务部执行的，原材料和零部件是由物资部供应的（蒋一苇，1993）。中国向市场经济的过渡过程中，源自于改革前的人际关系可能还会发挥作用。

明显影响农业机械行业大型国有企业，尤其是中国拖拉机制造商空间网络，还有其他四个因素。

第一，在过去的 20 年中，农业作为中国的一个产业部门，已经发生了巨大的变化。1970 年年末，家庭联产承包责任制实施。由农村社队管理的耕地被划分成小块，并根据家庭规模的大小分配给了农户。每家农户对其耕地都有自主经营权。由于劳动力资源丰富、耕地面积小、资本匮乏，在农业生产时，农民通常使用自身家庭的劳动力。这在很大程度上影响了拖拉机的销售市场，间接影响着拖拉机生产企业。

第二，中国政府的企业改革政策支持大型国有企业的扩张。20 世纪 80 年代期间，大多数大型国有企业通过联合经营扩大了对外联系（蒋一苇，1993）。主要有两种联合经营方式。第一种是，通过业务合作，进行贴牌生产。第二种是，原材料和零部件供应商与下游的生产商之间通过协议进行合作，或企业之间在业务、技术和信息等方面产生联系。这一战略被 1990 年年初成立的集团公司所取代。而改革前，工厂是企业的主要形式，改革有利于促进管理网络的空间范围进一步扩张。

第三，紧随 21 世纪全球议程（环发 1992 号）的出台，中国发布了自己的 21 世纪议程（中国 21 世纪议程领导小组，1994）。20 世纪 90 年代，可持续发展被作为国家战略。作为这一战略的一部分，各级政府出台了退耕还草、还林的政策。这一政策在具有丘陵景观或生物重要性的地区（如西北、西南和东北的主要复垦区）的影响尤其明显。这可能导致拖拉机销售区域的变化。

第四，除了政治因素外，对于商业网络的组织而言，空间亦相当重要（Yeung，2000b），尤其是对中国巨大的地区差异和经济增长的区域变化，空间性更为重要。改革开放初期，中国沿海地区的经济增长较内陆地区快。尤其是当地民营企业和外资企业，为沿海地区提供了高质量的产品和良好的服务，带来了发展动力。因此，这些地区更可能成为中国一拖集团有限公司的供应商。相反，中国一拖集团有限公司在传统内陆地区的供应商，多为在生产和销售方面遭受了种种挫折的国有企业。它们由于缺乏在技术开发和产品创新方面的投入，其供应商的位置岌岌可危。

26.3　管理网络

在计划经济体制下，中国第一拖拉机厂先后直属第一机械工业部（1953～1959年）、国务院第八机械工业部（或农机部）（1959～1970年），1970年后，归河南省政府（中国第一拖拉机厂，1985）管理。作为生产单位，该厂主要负责生产管理。商业部和物资部分别负责销售和分配，材料和零部件供应。中国一拖集团有限公司所有的生产部门都位于洛阳市，因此，管理网络仅限于运营，也均位于本地（图26.1，底层）。

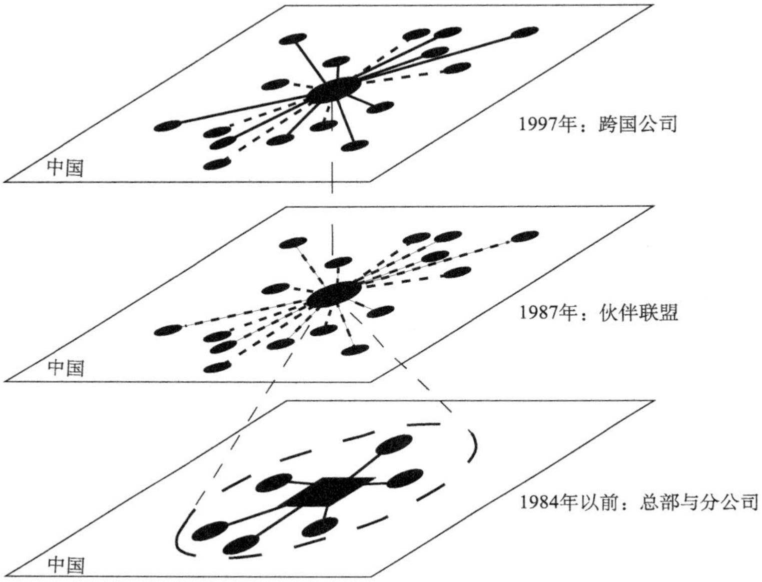

图26.1　一拖集团管理网络空间扩展的示意图

注：虚线代表供求等松散联系，实线代表管理联系。

随着中国逐渐向市场体制迈进，20世纪80年代，中国一拖集团有限公司和其他企业之间的联系得到发展。1985年，该工厂与17个企业、研究机构、大学进行合作，以推动新产品的开发。这些合作伙伴位于6个省份。在自愿互利的原则下，它们在经济、技术和生产方面建立起了合作关系。尽管没有发展管理网络，但合作关系为中国一拖集团有限公司的成立建立了基础。

1987年，关系网络的发展导致17个省、市、自治区的50家企业、研究机构和大学与第一拖拉机厂建立了合作关系。这促使了第一拖拉机工程机械协会的成立。在协会中，第一拖拉机厂与其他成员之间存在三种形式的联系。

（1）第一拖拉机厂对其他成员拥有人员、融资、股份、生产、供应和销售等运营管理的权利。

（2）第一拖拉机厂在战略规划、生产计划、技术要求、销售和服务方面与成员之间存在联系。

（3）第一拖拉机厂仅与成员之间存在供应关系。但是，所有成员都是个体企业，在第一拖拉机厂和这些成员之间不具有平等的关系。

在 20 世纪 90 年代，一些成员完全或部分地被第一拖拉机厂收购。1992 年，“中国第一拖拉机工程机械联营公司”更名为“中国第一拖拉机工程机械集团公司”。随着“公司法”的出台，1997 年，再次更名为“中国一拖集团有限公司”（以下简称为“一拖集团”）。一拖集团拥有 6 个专业厂，5 个分公司和 13 个下属子公司，部分拥有 11 家公司。35 个成员单位分别位于河南、河北、江苏、辽宁、浙江、上海和广东。因此，公司的管理结构分为三个层次。

（1）顶层：决定重大问题，如战略规划、运营方向和投资策略。

（2）行政层：执行顶层设计的战略，监测和评估各个子公司和分公司的绩效。

（3）实施层：负责工厂、子公司、分公司的日常管理。

因此，35 个成员与总部和行政部门的管理联系形成了较为复杂的网络。空间范围亦得到扩展（图 26.1，顶层）。到 21 世纪初，管理联系已扩展至其他国家。例如，第一拖拉机有限公司（大部分股权为一拖集团控制的上市公司）收购了位于百慕大群岛华晨中国机械控股有限公司 90.1%的股份。为满足客户的需求，一拖集团在中国各个区域设置了 380 个服务站点，在东欧、美国、澳大利亚、东南亚等有自己的营销和服务点。一拖集团主体和成员之间的管理联系变化可从以下四方面解释。第一，中国政府的过渡政策起到了根本性的作用。随着计划经济机制向市场经济体制的过渡，国家或省级政府逐渐释放了对一拖集团的直接控制权。公司因此获得管理自身业务的权利。第二，国家及省政府一向支持公司的发展。政府部门甚至有时参与一拖集团合并企业的谈判，偶尔会向被合并者施压。第三，网络的扩展是一个加工工厂（中国第一拖拉机厂）发展为现代公司的重组过程。作为一个市场经济中的公司，一拖集团必须考虑如何在激烈的竞争中生存。广泛的网络联系可使其获取各方的优势。第四，计划经济时期建立的联系或人际关系，在后来，深刻影响着管理网络的发展。大多数准成员在计划经济时期都与中国第一拖拉机厂有过某种合作关系。

26.4　供应商网络

一拖集团的原材料供应网络中至少需要 14 个大类中的 4000 种不同类型的材料，包括钢铁、有色金属、铸造炉料和化学品。在以往计划体制时期，这些材料完全需要通过国家政府的分配计划获得。1980 年以来，第一拖拉机厂逐渐提高了自身在自主采购中的比重。在 1999 年，这些供应商分别位于 24 个省、市和自治区（图 26.2）。从 1980 年以来原材料联系的变化中可发现两个特征。

首先，从 1984～1997 年，供应商的数量从 278 个增加到 428 个［尽管在数量上略有下降，但 1999 年仍有 412 个（图 26.2）］。因此，联系数量在持续的增长，联系网络的范围和密度在持续增加。

其次，供应联系的平均距离在下降。为了测量平均距离，本章使用了以下公式（张晓平，1999）：

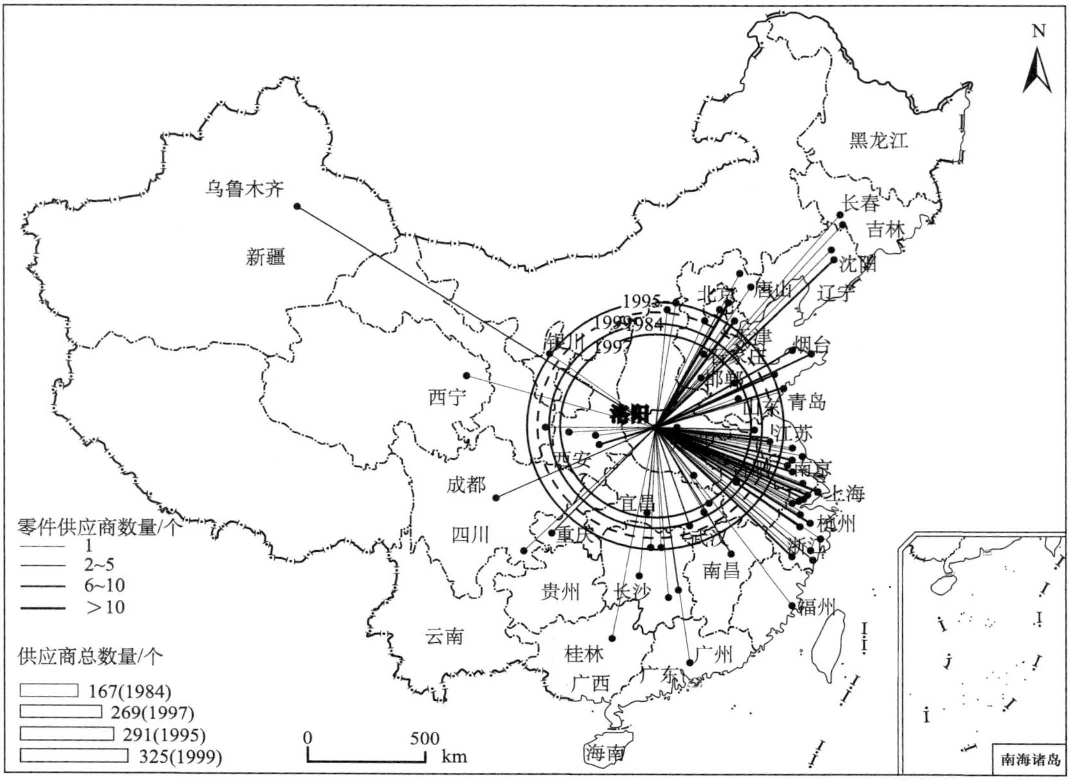

图 26.2　1999 年一拖集团的原材料供应者网络

注：同心圆是指 1984 年、1997 年和 1999 年，一拖集团与供应商的平均距离。

$$D = \sum (n_i d_i) / \sum n_i \qquad (26.1)$$

式中，D 指供应联系的平均距离；n_i 指省内供应商的数量；d_i 指洛阳与省内供应商的距离 i（为简单起见，洛阳和省会之间的距离用直线表示）

结果表明，1984～1997 年，供应联系的平均距离从 714.9km 下降到 673.4km，1999 年为 458.9km。这反映了在市场体系下，公司减少了在原材料供应方面的运输成本。例如，河南省材料供应商的数量，从 1984 年的 59 个急剧上升至 1997 年的 96 个，再到 1999 年的 200 个。

零部件的供应网络变化——可总结为以下三点。

首先，随着时间的推移，零部件供应商的数量在增加。相比 1984 年，1999 年总数（325）增加了近一倍（图 26.3）。这反映了在市场经济体制下，中国一拖有限公司延伸外包的行为。

其次，与原材料供应联系变化不同，从零部件联系的平均距离变化比较复杂：1984 年，平均距离为 523.5km，1995 年第一次上升至 570.6km，然后在 1997 年下降至 492.9km，之后在 1999 年回升至 542.0km。这或许可这样的客观情况来解释，即一个零部件供应商需要一定的技术和生产条件。发展一个零部件设备厂家需要一定的时间。

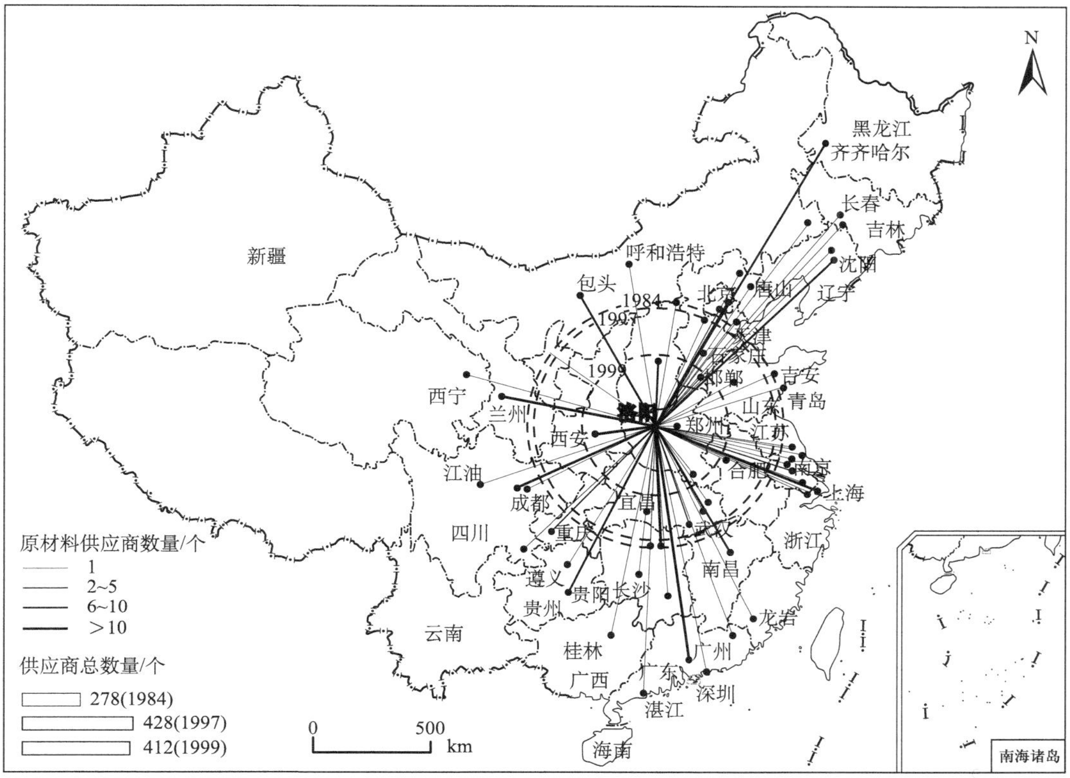

图 26.3　1999 年一拖集团零部件供应商的网络

注：同心圆是指 1984 年、1995 年和 1999 年供应商与一拖集团的平均距离。

同时，每单位价值的零部件运输成本通常低于其材料成本。

最后，零部件供应商从中国过去的老工业基地转移至新近发展的地区。东部沿海地区各省和直辖市（山东、上海、江苏和浙江）的数据表明，供应商在数量和份额方面均在增加，而老工业基地（黑龙江、吉林、辽宁、北京和天津）却经历了一个低迷时期（表 26.1）。这一转变与前述提到的经济发展区域差异是密切相关的。中国的沿海比内陆具有更长的商业史，人们对市场体系更为熟悉。中国东部沿海企业主要生产品质相对高且价格相对低廉的产品。这些企业更可能取代中国一拖有限公司以前位于老工业基地的供应商。

表 26.1　零部件供应商从工业基地向新发达地区的转移

省或自治区	1984 年		1995 年		1999 年	
	供应商数	占总量的%	供应商数	占总量的%	供应商数	占总量的%
山东、上海、江苏、浙江	32	19.2	126	43.3	142	43.7
黑龙江、吉林、辽宁、北京、天津	24	14.4	24	8.2	21	6.5
合计	167	100	291	100	325	100

资料来源：作者调研。

除了经济发展的区域差异，中国一拖集团有限公司供应商的网络演化可以用其他三个因素解释。第一，自20世纪90年代中期，中国市场从卖方转移至买方。因此，中国一拖集团有限公司已经能够从所有可能的企业中选择供应商。第二，追求效率的动机驱使企业购买低成本、高质量的零部件。供应商数量的增加，为企业寻找同一类型供应商提供了更多的选择机会。换句话说，企业多样化采购可以利用供应商的竞争。第三，空间邻近性和集聚经济促使企业附近供应商数量的增加。这进一步说明河南省原材料供应商数量的显著增加。

26.5　销售网络

在计划经济体制下，中国第一拖拉机厂的销售完全是由国家政府控制的。1980以后，农村家庭联产承包责任制的实施减弱了政府市场控制权力，因此，中国第一拖拉机厂不得不做自己的市场销售。为了获取市场信息并宣传其产品，在20世纪80年代初该厂派出1000人到农村。这些工作团队遍布在中国的东北、北部、东部、南部、中部、西北、西南17个省106个县。这种策略导致了其产品销售的区域变化（图26.4）。

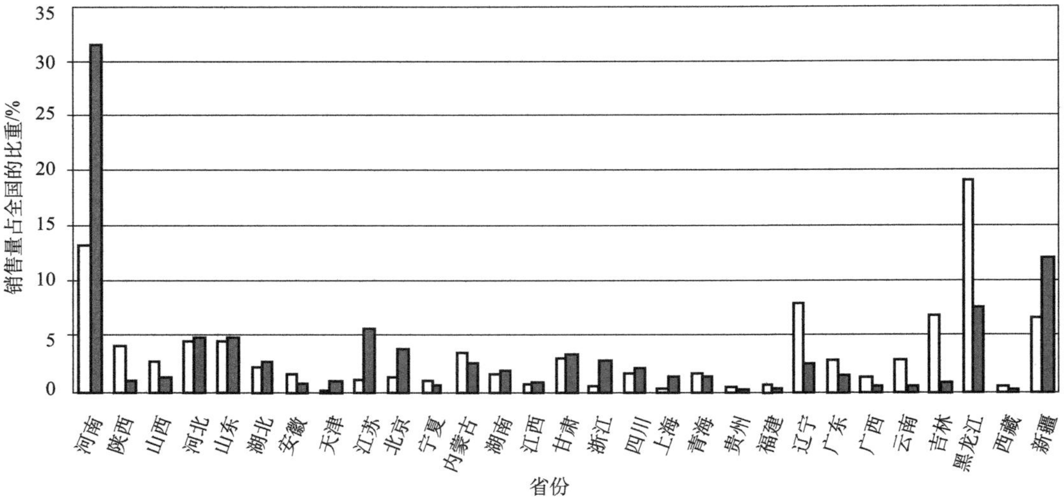

图26.4　1958～1984年和1997～1999年各省大中型拖拉机销售量的比较

根据我们的访谈，中国第一拖拉机厂产品主要运往中国东北和西北地区以满足国家复垦的需要。统计数据显示，中国东北地区（黑龙江、吉林和辽宁）占据了中国第一拖拉机厂27年（从1958～1984年）中全国总销量的34.18%。特别是，黑龙江省作为其产品的主要采购区占了全国总销量的19.17%，在中国西北，新疆消费占6.70%（表26.2）。这种空间格局很大程度上受国家维护社会稳定鼓励移民在边疆省份垦荒的政治策略影响。

表 26.2　1958～1984 年和 1997～1999 年一拖集团大中型拖拉机主要销售区域

省份	1958～1984 年全部的百分比/%	1997～1999 年全部的百分比/%	份额变化
东北			
黑龙江	19.17	7.53	−11.64
吉林	6.96	0.88	−6.07
辽宁	8.05	2.40	−5.64
西北			
新疆	6.70	12.05	5.35
西南			
云南	2.90	0.43	−2.46
广西	1.37	0.45	−0.92
贵州	0.49	0.09	−0.39
四川	1.54	2.06	0.52
中部			
河南	13.13	31.45	18.32
东部沿海			
山东	4.66	5.15	0.49
江苏	1.27	5.82	4.55
浙江	0.39	2.64	2.25
上海	0.12	1.08	0.96
全国	100.00	100.00	0.00

资料来源：作者调研。

改革开放以来，中国西北部的新疆的销售份额持续增大，但在中国东北的各省，西南地区四分之三的省市销售份额有所下降（表 26.2）。这主要是因为政府的可持续发展政策导致了大规模的土地复垦的停止。此外，另一个解释是东北地区经济的衰退。首先，由于国有企业的困难造成政府收入不足，限制了政府对农民购买拖拉机的补贴（通常是拖拉机成本的 1/3）。其次，与天津拖拉机厂和俄罗斯的拖拉机生产商的竞争有关。在供应东北市场方面，这些竞争对手都有短距离运输的优势。显然，新疆销售量的持续增加是因为国有金融的支持。鉴于该地区的动荡，这种金融支持将极有可能继续。

反过来，东南部省份和直辖市，如山东、江苏、浙江和上海，大中型拖拉机占全国的总销售份额在增加（表 26.2）。市场份额上升的主要原因在于，改革开放背景下，该地区经济快速增长。在一些快速增长的区域，农村土地被转移到专业农户手中。为经营手中的耕地，高效生产的农民需要拖拉机和其他农业机械。

总之，一拖集团的平均销售距离越来越短。图 26.5 说明了 1958～1984 年和1997～1999 年之间，销售份额变动的省份。X 轴是将洛阳到每个省省会的距离按升序排列的情况。于是，趋势线清楚地显示了从远距离市场到近邻市场的转变，这种变化在很大程度上是由政府的政策造成的。从出于国家安全战略考虑而鼓励边疆省份垦荒到可持续发展政策的退耕还林、还草、保护生物多样性景观，这种政策变化导致边疆省份拖拉机销售市场明显萎缩。

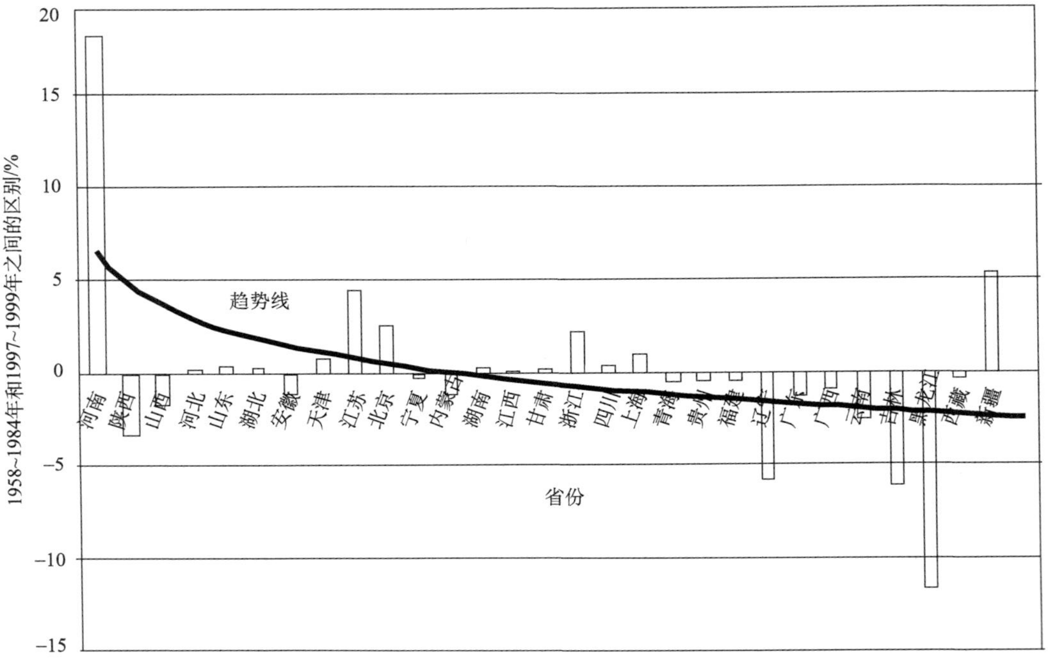

图 26.5　1958～1984 年和 1997～1999 年一拖集团生产的大中型拖拉机销售的区域格局变化

此外，这种变化的其他两种解释如下。

第一，经济增长和发展状况的差异（如东部省份销售量的增长，表 26.2）。

第二，一拖集团采用的营销策略，强调就近开拓市场（如河南省销售量的增长，表 26.2）。

26.6　技术网络

计划时期的技术网络：在 20 世纪 50 年代，中国第一拖拉机厂技术联系的主要对象是原苏联，并从那里获取大部分设备。此外，其主要的产品——履带式拖拉机，最初也是由原苏联设计。在 20 世纪 60～70 年代，该厂与外界的联系较少。技术的部分改进主要是由中国第一拖拉机厂内部的技术人员实现的。

改革时期的技术网络：从 20 世纪 80 年代开始，中国一拖集团有限公司的技术联系开始拓展。在这个时期内，该厂从美国、德国、意大利、英国和日本引进了新技术。不仅有硬件技术的购买，更重要的是还有很多软技术的引进。例如，1986 年的 LF90 系列轮式拖拉机制造技术就是来自于意大利的菲亚特（Fiat）。经过 5 年的探索，一拖集团在 1991 年实现了东方红 90 系列轮式拖拉机的批量生产。这种新型拖拉机安装的是一拖集团生产的 LR100/105 系列柴油机，但该技术是从英国的里卡多（Ricardo）引进的。

在国内，此前由中国机械工业部下属的洛阳拖拉机研究所和第四设计院在 1995 年被合并到一拖集团。通过上述两个机构与一拖集团的拖拉机和卡车研究所的合并，一个强大的技术中心——一拖集团技术中心成立了。该中心与 6 个著名的技术研究机构建立了联合技术开发的关系，并与 8 所大学建立了培训和联合技术开发的关系。这些研究机构和大学分布在洛阳、北京、天津、上海、长春、武汉和西安。因而，技术联系的空间已扩展至国内主要的技术研发中心。这种技术网络的扩展，第一，由中国的改革政策诱导——鼓励国内企业和外国公司，以及制造企业和研究机构、大学之间的技术合作。第二，公司重视销量好的产品中的技术因素。因此，一拖集团积极建立并保持了与那些要么具有先进技术，要么有开发新产品能力的组织机构的联系。第三，那种在计划经济时期就已有的技术联系，在市场经济时期被保持并得到进一步发展。

26.7　结论与讨论

为了阐明前面提出的问题，本章以一拖集团为例揭示了改革时期其网络联系的复杂变化。一方面，管理和技术联系空间范围扩大，网络间联系密度增强。另一方面，与洛阳距离较近省份的销售量增加，销售联系的平均距离缩短了。由企业改革实现的计划体制向市场体制的过渡，导致了从偏远省份到东部沿海经济发达省份的市场的变化。但供给联系走的却是一种特殊的道路。虽然整体上供应商的数量在增加，但原材料供应联系的平均距离大幅度减小。然而，上述现象在零配件的供应联系中并不明显。相反，其网络联系从老工业基地转移到了新近快速发展的沿海地区。

一拖集团不断变化的空间网络表明，企业改革政策使国有企业从计划控制中释放了出来，并使其受益于网络联系。网络的扩展可利用从多方面获取的丰富信息、获取不同区域的比较优势，从而得到企业的青睐。市场领域的变化，零部件供应地和原材料供应距离的缩短也是企业采取的合理化策略。但是，值得注意的是在走向市场经济后，一拖集团的市场在地域上缩小了，并且引起了整体销售额的变动。对于决策者而言，需要考虑重新拓展偏远省份的原有市场，因为这些地区的拖拉机在几年后需要更新。

本章给出了一些与发达国家不同的发现。在中国，原材料联系的差异——供应商数量的增加，可以反映出中国国有企业的特殊行为。首先，政府放权后，国有企业在第一时间通过市场竞争机制选择了它们的供应商。因而，它们尝试尽可能地利用各方面的优势。再者，在政府部门鼓励大型国企拓展，并期望它们在全球化市场经济中具有竞争力的情况下，国企倾向于扩大规模。随着中国加入 WTO，很多企业开始寻求扩大已有的联系。因此，国企的网络联系会在将来继续扩展。

中国从计划经济体制向市场经济体制的转变，给国企提供了一个特殊的拓展其网络联系的环境。中国本土的国有企业与华人在国外的华人企业的差异明显。在国内环境中，政策和经济因素在管理、技术和原材料供给联系方面，深刻影响着一拖集团空间网络的变化。人际关系的作用处于次要地位。但这并不是意味着“关系”在中国大陆不如在亚洲其他国家或者地区经济领域内重要。以下三个方面可以对此做出解释。首先，国企可能不同于其他经济形式。中国的事实表明，“关系”在民营企业（Zhao and Adam，

1995)、外资企业（Smart and Smart，1991）和乡镇企业的经济网络的形成中具有很重要的地位。其次，公司规模也会影响其对“关系”的运用。上述论据源自于中小企业公司。最后，更重要的是，过去的20年是中国的一个特殊时期。在国企拓展网络关系的过程中，政治和经济上的巨大变革弱化了包括“关系”在内的其他因素。然而，随着中国进入市场体制，政策和经济因素的变化趋于稳定，“关系”在国企发展中的重要性会日益凸显。

本章结论可与另一种企业网络形式进行对比，即在经济学和经济地理学中表述的韩国财阀（chaebols）。事实上，韩国大型企业和中国的国有企业都曾得到过政府的大力支持。同样的事实是，中国的国有企业在网络变革中具有不同的制度环境。特别是：

（1）1949～1978年，中国政府对国企网络的建立进行严格管控。

（2）1978年后，中国的政策发生了巨大变化。

（3）国有企业现在面临着特殊的情形——一方面要遵从市场规律，另一方面还要服从政府制约。例如，国有企业的所有者从未被指定。相关的政府部门（多数情况下、国家或省级）实际上扮演了所有者的角色。通过任命国企关键领导人，使其更好地遵循政府的政策和意图。

（4）巨大的区域性差异、区域经济转型和结构调整，在网络的形成中也起着重要的作用。在这些方面，很多的中国国有企业网络是否代表了一种新的公司网络——政治经济导向的网络？

假设问题的答案是积极的，但需要来自各个行业更多的案例研究。此外，本研究只对一些形式的联系进行了研究。在没有研究的联系中，信息流是一个非常重要的线索。因为数据获取的困难，我们未能对其进行分析。在经济和社会转型期，更多深入的研究无疑会更好地阐明大型国企空间网络的变化。

附注：在20世纪90年代中期之前，中国的集团公司是相当松散的联盟，其成员之间几乎没有资本联系。

参考文献

董辅礽，唐宗焜，杜海燕. 1995. 中国国有企业制度变革研究. 北京：人民出版社

蒋一苇. 1993. 我的经济改革观. 北京：经济管理出版社

李小建. 1998. 国有企业改革对区域经济发展的影响——以河南为例. 经济地理，18（3）：1～6

李小建. 2000. 国有企业的制度改革//陆大道，刘毅. 1999年中国区域发展报告. 北京：商务印书馆. 65～78

张晓平. 1999. 国有大型企业网络变化及对区域经济发展的影响——以中国一拖为例. 地理科学进展，18（2）：176～185

中国21世纪议程领导小组办公室. 1994. 中国21世纪议程：中国21世纪人口、环境与发展白皮书. 北京：中国环境科学出版社

中国第一拖拉机厂. 1985. 中国第一拖拉机厂的历史. 洛阳：中国第一拖拉机厂

Amin A，Thrift N. 1994. Globalization，Institutions，and Regional Development inEurope. Oxford：Oxford University Press

Chen A. 1998. Inertia in reformingChina's stateowned enterprises: The case of Chongqing. World Development, 26 (3): 479～495

Conti S. 1993. The network perspective in industrial geography. Geografiska Annaler B, 75 (3): 115～130

Dicken P. 1998. Global Shift: Transformation the World Economy (3rd Edition). London: Paul Chapman.

Dicken P, Quevit M. 1994. Transnational Corporations and European Regional Restructuring. Utrecht: Netherlands Geographical Studies

Farmer D H, Vonamstel P. 1991. Effective Pipeline Management: How to Manage Integrated Logistics. New York: Gower

Griffiths J. 1992. Lean supply chain management. Proceeding of BPICS 27th Annual Conference. Birmingham

Hanink D M. 1995. The International Economy: A Geographical Perspective. New York: John Wiley & Sons

Harland C M. 1995. Networks and Globalization: A Review of Research. Warwick: University of Warwick

Hill H. 1982. Vertical inter-firm linkages in LDCs: A note on thePhilippines. Oxford Bulletin of Economics and Statistics, 44: 261～271

Hirschman A O. 1958. The Strategy of Economic Development. New Haven: Yale University Press

Huang Y, Kalirajan K P. 1998. Enterprise reform and technical efficiency of China's state owned enterprises. Applied Economics, 30 (5): 585～592

Lall S 1980. Vertical inter-firm linkages in LDCs: An empirical study. Oxford Bulletin of Economics and Statistics, 42: 203～226

Li X J, Yeung Y M. 1999. Inter-firm linkages and regional impact of transnational corporations: Company case studies fromShanghai, China. Geografiska Annaler B, 81 (2): 61～72

Li X J. 1993. Industrial linkages and rural industrialization: A case ofHenan Province, China. Chinese Geographical Science, 3 (3): 255～263

Li X J. 2000. China's enterprise reform and spatial networks of large state-owned enterprise: The case of First Tractor Co Ltd. Paper presented at the 29th IGC, 14～18 August 2000, Seoul, Korea

Li X J. 2001. Globalization and response of large state-owned enterprises: Company case studies from central China. Chinese Geographical Science, 11 (2): 120～128

Lamming R. 1993. Beyond Partnership: Strategies for Innovation and Lean Supply. New York: Prentice Hall

Lim L Y C, Fong P E. 1982. Vertical linkages and multinational enterprises in developing countries. World Development, 10: 585～595

Ma L J C, Wei Y. 1997. Determinants of state investment in China, 1953-1990. Tijdschrift voor Economische en Sociale Geografie, 88 (3): 211～225

Marton A M. 2000. China's Spatial Economic Deveopment: Restless Landscapes in the Lower Yangzi Delta. London & New York: Routledge

Mcdermott P J, Taylor M J. 1982. Industrial Organization and Location. Cambridge: Cambridge University Press

Mo P, Li S. 1998. Contract responsibility systems and productive efficiency: A case study on state-owned enterprises in China. Bulletin of Economic Research, 50 (4): 323～341

Nolan P, Wang X. 1999. Beyond privatization: International innovation and growth in China's large state-owned enterprises. World Development, 27 (1): 169～200

Park S O. 1995. Networks and embebbedness in the dynamic types of new industrial districts. Progress in Human Geography, 20 (4): 476～493

Perroux F. 1950. Economic space, theory and applications. Quarterly Journal of Economics, 64: 89～104

Raiser M. 1997. How are China's state-owned enterprises doing in the 1990s? Evidence from three interior provinces. China Economic Review, 8 (2): 191～216

Smart J, Smart A. 1991. Personal relations and divergent economies: A case study of Hong Kong investment in south China. International Journal of Urbanand Regional Research, 15 (2): 216～233

UNCED (United Nations Conference on Environment and Development). 1992. Agenda21: Action Plan for the Next Century. Rio de Janeiro: UNCED

Wade R. 1990. Governing the Market: Economic Theory and the Role of Government in East Asian Industrialization. Princeton NJ: Princeton University Press

Wei D. 1999. Regional Inequality in China. Progress in Human Geography, 23 (1): 48～58

Yeung H W C. 1997a. Transnational economic synergy and business networks: The case of two way investment between Malaysia and Singapore. Regional Studies, 32 (8): 687～706

Yeung H W C. 1997b. Business networks and transnational corporations: A study of Hong Kong firms in the ASEAN region. Economic Geography, 73: 1～25

Yeung H W C. 2000a. Special issue on industrial and business networks in Asia. Environment and Planning A, 32: 191～304

Yeung H W C. 2000b. Guest editorial: A crisis of industrial and business networks in Asia. Environment and Planning A, 32: 191～200

Yeung Y M, Li X J. 2000. Transnational corporations and local embeddedness: Company case studies from Shanghai. Professional Geographer, 52 (4): 624～635

Young S, Hood N, Peters E. 1994. Multinational enterprises and regional economic development. Regional Studies, 28: 657～677

Zhao L, Aram J D. 1995. Networking and growth of young technology-intensive ventures in China. Journal of Business Venturing, 10: 349～370

Zhao X, Tong S P. 2000. Unequal economic development in China: Spatial disparities and regional policy reconsideration, 1985-1995. Regional Studies, 34 (6): 549～561

第 27 章　中部中小企业集群竞争优势

20 世纪 70 年代末改革开放以来，乡镇企业得到迅速发展。但 90 年代以来国家宏观大环境的改变和企业自身发展的乏力直接威胁着乡镇企业的生存，一些企业被迫关闭。而唯有在市场力的作用下自发形成的小企业集群，像一颗颗璀璨的明星闪耀着五彩的光辉，令人刮目相看。例如，河北省清河县的羊绒业集群（王缉慈，2001）、河南省孟州市的皮毛加工产业群（李小建，1993）、偃师市翟镇的针织业集群（文婷和李小建，2003）、虞城县南庄村的钢卷尺产业集群等。这些集群没有改革开放政策惠及的优越区位，没有城市工业那样雄厚的经济基础，没有北京中关村那样的高新技术产业，没有大型跨国公司的进入，没有发达地区那样多的高素质人才，但面对环境的瞬息万变，也都能表现出巨大的适应性。它们为何具有如此强大的生命力？其竞争优势的来源何在？国际上的企业集群文献中，竞争优势形成问题成为研究焦点之一（Martin and Sunley，2003）。但在研究中，国内外学者选择的案例大多集中在先决条件较好的发达国家或发达地区，且多集中在高技术产业，而对在市场力的作用下自发形成的中国中部农区村级层次企业集群的研究相对很少。本章试图对此做初步探讨。

中国中部农区企业集群的竞争优势来源既具有一般企业集群的共性——它是规模经济、分工经济和网络联系三者共同作用的结果，又具有其特殊的个性——模仿创新的普遍发生、中原文化背景、制度扶持和较低的劳动力、土地等要素成本起着决定作用。本章以河南省虞城县南庄村钢卷尺企业集群为例，详细分析中国中部农区企业集群竞争优势的内在来源。

27.1　中部农区企业集群的竞争优势来源

27.1.1　企业集群竞争优势来源的共性

企业集群是指属于某种特定产业及其相关支撑产业的众多企业和机构因共性和互补性而相互联系并在一定地域范围内集聚所形成的群体（Porter，1998，2000；仇保兴，1999；冯德连和王蕾，2000）。其地理边界是由企业及相关机构的相互联系与依赖内在决定的，并不局限于行政边界。本章的企业集群竞争优势是指该集群与周围区域相比所具有的高得多的收益递增速度。其竞争优势来源可通过收益递增理论和网络组织理论来分析（李二玲和李小建，2005）。

追溯历史渊源，收益递增理论可以分为将收益递增归因于规模经济的马歇尔学派、新增长理论、新经济地理学理论（以克鲁格曼为代表的）和将收益递增归因于分工经济的亚当·斯密（Adam Smith）、杨格（Arthur Young）以及杨小凯的新兴古典经济学理论。收益递增源于规模经济还是分工经济，是经济学界从古典到现代一直争论的问题。笔者认为，规模经济和分工经济是收益递增来源的两个侧面，两者在市场经济下相互依赖、相互加强。克鲁格曼认为，报酬递增本质上是一种区域和地方现象，而且支持收益递增的市场、技术和其他使报酬递增的因素在规模上既不是国际的，也不是国内的，而是通过区域和地方经济集聚过程形成的（保罗·克鲁格曼，2001）。所以对于企业集群所在区域而言，规模经济和分工经济的双重作用体现得更为明显。规模经济能引起经济的持续增长，分工经济能带来生产率的提高，企业集群收益递增来源是规模经济和分工经济的叠加。但由于协调（或组织）成本和交易成本的存在，规模经济和分工经济是有一定限度的，并会发生冲突。而集群企业之间的网络组织关系不仅可以使企业获得资源共享、风险共摊、优势互补、专业化分工合作等方面的收益，即有效地实现集群的规模经济和分工经济，而且还可以缓和由分工深化而引起的交易成本与分工经济、由扩大规模而引起的协调成本与规模经济之间的两难冲突；即减缓了由规模经济和分工经济而带来的负面矛盾，扩大了两者发生作用的范围，成为集群有机体的调和剂。所以集群的收益递增速度必然大于其周围非集群区域的收益递增速度，其静态的竞争优势就表现为规模经济、分工经济和网络联系三者共同作用的结果。规模经济是集群点元和面的外延扩大；分工经济能引起个人和企业生产率提高，使集群内点的内涵增加；而网络联系是集群内各行为主体之间的向心力、凝聚力，是区内线的致密性。三者的相互作用构成了企业集群不可比拟的强度和韧度，是企业集群经济增长的三个维。

企业集群动态的竞争优势可以表现为集群内大量新企业的衍生、分工的逐步深化和网络创新的普遍发生三个方面。它其实是静态的竞争优势在时间轴上的保持和增强。规模经济、分工经济和网络联系三者动态上的数量增加和协调互动是企业集群发展的驱动力所在。

作为企业集群的一种类型，中国中部农区企业集群也应具有一般企业集群竞争优势来源的共性。但是，由于特殊的发展环境，该类型集群也会具有一些特殊性。

27.1.2　中部农区企业集群竞争优势来源的特殊性

为了分析中国中部农区企业集群竞争优势的来源，我们于 2002 年 11 月和 2003 年 12 月对豫东平原上典型的乡村地域——河南省虞城县南庄村的钢卷尺企业集群进行两次实地调查。样本企业的选择依据以下原则：①调查的生产经营企业数量超过其总数的 1/10；②调查的企业要具有代表性：既兼顾不同规模（如大、中、小企业兼顾），又兼顾不同类型（如垂直一体化企业和中间产品生产企业兼顾，生产经营企业和家庭组装户兼顾）。据此，选择了 23 家生产经营企业和 10 户家庭组装户进行了实地访谈。同时，还对稍岗乡政府、钢卷尺行业协会及其他配套产业的企业进行了调查访问。调查结果表明，该农区企业集群不仅具有规模经济、分工经济和网络联系，其竞争优势来源还表现在以下特殊方面：高频度全方位模仿性创新的发生、中原文化背景、制度扶持和较低的劳动力、土地等要素成本（图 27.1）。

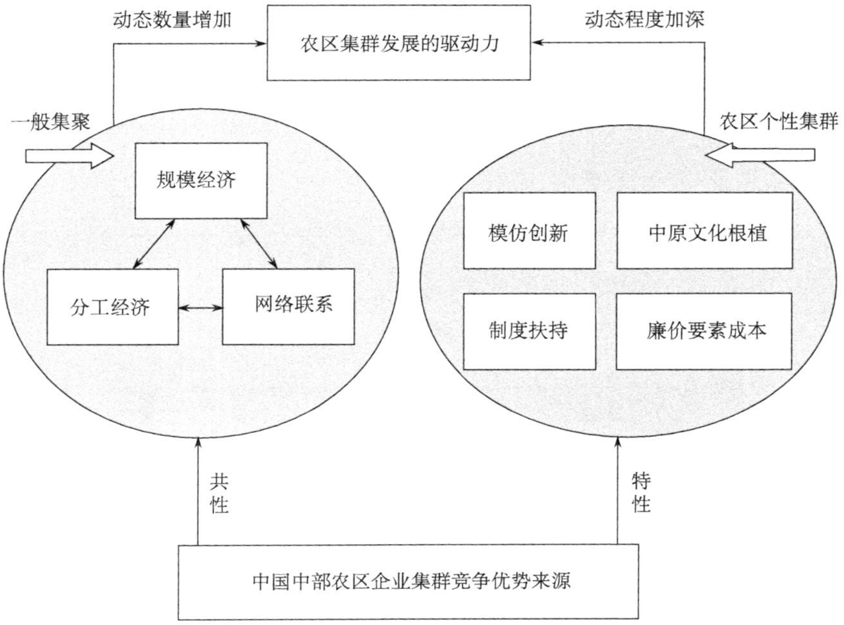

图 27.1　中国中部农区企业集群的竞争优势来源示意图

27.2　南庄村钢卷尺企业集群案例分析

南庄村地处河南省虞城县稍岗乡，北靠 301 国道，南隔乡政府与陇海铁路相距不足 4km。自 1993 年第一家企业创办以来，该村钢卷尺工业发展迅速，并逐渐辐射到周围 10km 范围的村镇。截至 2002 年年底，集群内钢卷尺生产经营企业已达 228 家，家庭组装户 150 多户，吸引外来人口 6000 多人。年产卷尺 5 亿只，占全国 70%以上的钢卷尺市场份额，远销俄罗斯、韩国、土耳其等 20 多个国家和地区，实现产值 4.2 亿元，占全乡工农业总产值的 80%以上。2002 年南庄村农民人均纯收入突破 10000 元。916 位常驻居民中，80%直接或间接地从事钢卷尺生产经营活动。这个曾经属于国家级贫困县的贫困村，农民收入已远远高于河南省及虞城县的平均递增速度增长(图 27.2)。到 2002 年，该村人均纯收入分别是河南省和虞城县的 4.5 和 6.2 倍。昔日的穷乡僻壤之所以能击败国内 29 家国有企业，逐渐发展成为全国最大的钢卷尺产销基地，其根源就在于适应时代潮流的新型企业组织方式——企业集群，在本地的形成和发展。

27.2.1　企业集群内的规模经济

南庄村钢卷尺企业集群内存在明显的内部和外部规模经济。此前的企业集群研究多偏重企业外部的规模经济，其实，企业内部的规模经济也非常重要。南庄村集群以小企业为主，其中，三个较大的龙头企业领导着战略、技术和行业行为的潮流，在集群内起

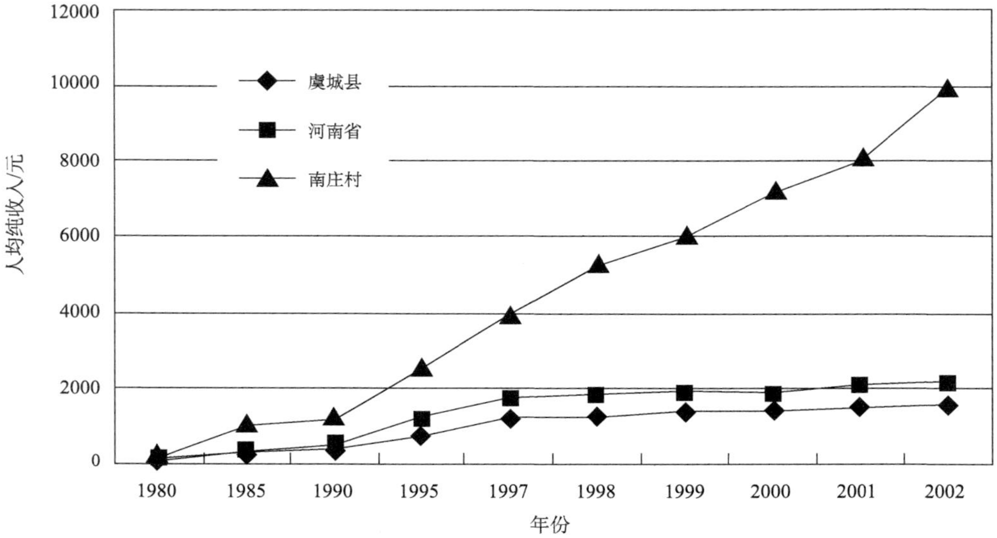

图 27.2 改革开放以来南庄村与河南省及虞城县农民人均纯收入比较情况

资料来源：作者调查。

核心主导作用。在这些企业带领下，小企业为了追求内部规模经济，想方设法购进关键设备和技术，由家庭作坊式的手工业向机械加工业转变。调查中，当问及“企业在成长过程中，规模是扩大还是缩小”，90％的调查企业回答是“扩大”；98％的企业将利润主要用于扩大再生产。因为只有规模大了，才能培养出自己强硬的品牌，才有降价让利的空间，才会在激烈的竞争中抵御风险、站稳脚跟。内部规模经济不仅包含着规模和经营范围的扩大而带来的成本降低，而且还含有速度经济的内容。即不仅依靠企业的生产能力，而且还依靠利用生产能力的强度。集群内许多企业（如江华、华新量具有限公司等大企业及一些家庭组装户）在生产任务紧迫时，凭借身处集群专业技术工人雇佣的便利，实行“人停机器不停”的“三班倒”，按生产任务决定雇佣人数，大大降低了企业的生产和管理成本。

集群企业所享有的外部规模经济包括区域性和行业性两方面。南庄村企业集群形成之初，其城市性基础设施几乎为零。第一家企业华新量具有限公司就是因为南庄村缺乏电力供应，才不得不在虞城县城建厂，后来为了享受集群的外部规模经济又迁回集群。电力、交通、通信等基础设施是经济发展的命脉，面对钢卷尺行业蓬勃生长的嫩芽，稍岗乡政府深深意识到了这一点。几年来，乡政府自筹资金铺修了环村油路，建造了高压电站，架设了电视、通信光缆线路，建立了大型批发市场等。如果没有这些生产环境的改善，企业的投入成本将会非常高昂。

南庄村的行业性外部规模经济表现为浓厚的行业氛围。在该村，人们会听到家家机器的轰鸣声，乡邻之间的串门、聊天也都是谈论钢卷尺这一主题。孩子在钢卷尺生产的耳濡目染下长大，几乎不需要培训即可通晓该行业的通用知识。辅助工业和劳动力市场也因为当地需求的扩大而得以生存。浩浩荡荡的销售大军常年奔波在全国各地，成了连接生产和市场的纽带。他们各自带回的大量市场、技术和需求信息在南庄村溢出扩散，经过综合、碰撞促使创新产生。在“江华”“红叶”“黑豹”等知名品牌的共同打造下，区位品牌已经形成。调查中，当问及“企业集中的好处”时，38%的企业回答内容包含“知名度高”或“名气大”，40%的企业回答“共同形成钢卷尺市场”。

27.2.2　企业集群内的分工经济

南庄村企业集群内的分工经济是随着规模的扩大而产生的，它包括企业内部的分工经济和企业外部的分工经济。早期，各中间产品均是从外地购买，各组装户业主既是生产者又是管理者。随着规模的扩大，业主雇佣了家庭以外的工人而从生产中分离出来，各自从事专职工作实现内部分工合作，生产能力和生产效率大幅提高。江华、东方等龙头企业都很重视实践中的“熟能生巧”，并制定了相应的措施。例如，工人的工资与工龄挂钩，新进工人由师傅传授技巧，从而限制工人改换工作。为了长期留住有经验的技术工人，他们还专门建造了职工家属楼，夫妻双方均在本厂就能分得一套。

随着集群内家庭组装户的增多，各中间产品和辅助工业的当地需求随之增多，导致专门从事某一环节生产和服务的企业纷纷建立。由图 27.3 可以看出，南庄村钢卷尺的生产存在着规模经济和分工经济的巨大潜力。各企业主购入原材料后（由于经济基础薄弱，需要上亿元资金的带钢生产商不在集群内），从事磕条、淬火、拉漆、印字、制盒、制簧、组装、成品包装、销售、运输等工艺过程的生产，专业化分工精细，他们相互结成网络共同完成钢卷尺的生产和众多家庭组装户的配件供应。截至 2002 年年底，仅南庄村固定资产投入 100 万元以上的尺盒厂就有 20 家、尺条厂 16 家、尺簧厂 10 家、垂直一体化的钢卷尺厂 8 家。另外，还有配套关联企业 42 家。同行企业相互竞争，比质量、比价格，争先创新。竞争的结果虽然降低了价格（其实是让利于家庭组装户），但也造就了集群内不怕失败、吃苦耐劳、勇往直前的企业家精神。市场筛选，优胜劣汰，倒闭的企业主积极寻找市场空间，试图东山再起；正在运行的企业也竭力挖掘一切潜力去提高自己、参与竞争，致使整个集群的创新不断涌现，知识水平和行业标准不断提高。

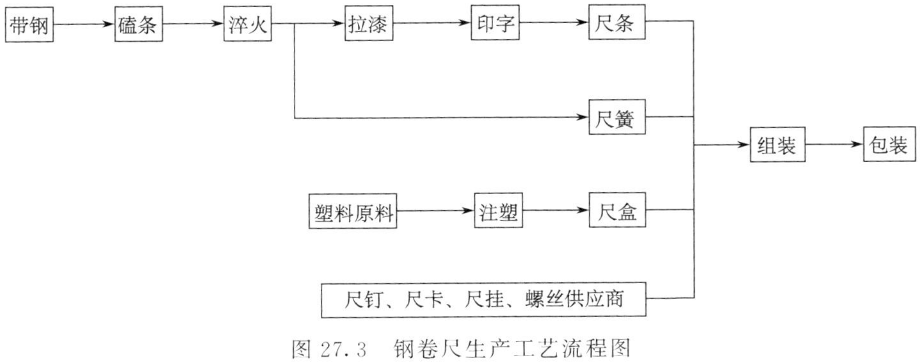

图 27.3　钢卷尺生产工艺流程图

27.2.3　企业集群内的网络联系

南庄村企业集群的规模发展现已遍及整个稍岗乡，并基本形成钢卷尺行业的本地生产网络。如图 27.4 所示，该网络中最主要的是生产性企业（它包括钢卷尺生产企业、中间产品生产企业和家庭组装户）之间极为紧密的网络联系；企业与政府、中介机构、服务机构等的联系较弱，中介机构功能近期有所退化；企业与大学、科研机构（不在集群内）的联系较少；集群内的配套产业包括运输队、集装公司、大型批发市场等，相关产业有塑料厂、纸箱厂、涂漆厂、电镀厂、五金器具厂等。互补企业分工合作，构成投入-产出联系；同行企业相互竞争，优胜劣汰，形成集群内的待下岗机制。据调查，垂直一体化生产厂 50%的中间产品和专业化尺条厂、尺簧厂、尺盒厂 80%的产品销于集群内部，而各组装户 90%以上的零部件购于集群内部。各中间产品生产商在生产任务不足时也从事组装工作。南庄村的钢卷尺吸引了国内外众多客户。

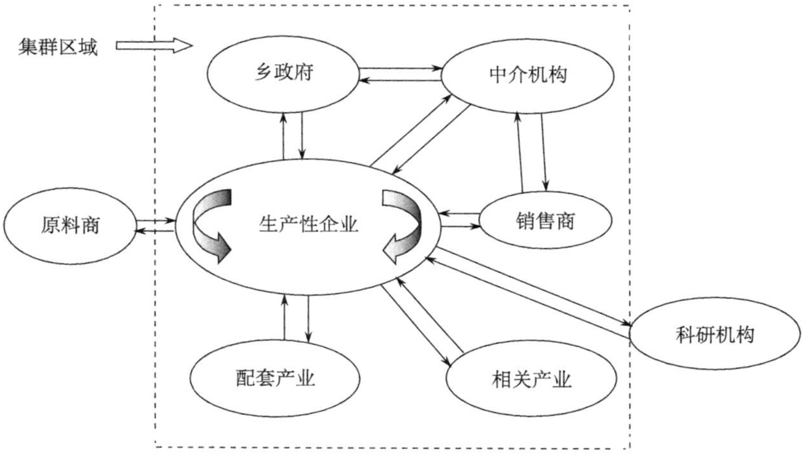

图 27.4　钢卷尺企业集群网络联系图

集群内的企业主大多来自本乡，地方“根植性”强化了他们的“关系网络”。相同的道德行为法则减少了许多机会主义行为，从而大大降低了企业的交易成本。例如，企业之间的生产交易几乎不需要用合同来约束，有时可以赊账购买，双方打一个白条即可。生产厂急需配件半小时内即可在集群借到，过一时再还上。集群内较大的订单可以根据交货时间灵活地组织分包给若干个中间产品厂商（如江华量具有限公司在集群内就有 7～8 个下转包厂）。相互串门成为人们交流与沟通的主要渠道，市场、技术、管理、人才信息是主要交流内容。乡邻之间的浓浓人情使各企业心甘情愿笑纳一切参观访问和技术请教，当然利润的驱使也使他们对自己的核心技术保密。生产上遇到的技术难题，他们共同讨论、共同克服。纯朴厚道的老传统使他们互帮互助，大大提高了他们的合作效率。

27.2.4　企业集群内的模仿性创新

企业集群长期的竞争优势表现为集群创新能力的不断生长。缺乏许多先决条件的南庄村企业集群的自主创新能力较弱，因此，它们主要是依靠模仿性创新来培养自己的创新能力。

1. 企业集群为模仿创新提供了便利条件

一般来讲，模仿是普遍的，而创新是罕见的，模仿创新既降低了创新的难度，又降低了创新产品的市场风险。所以，模仿和模仿性创新是企业发展和赢利的极其重要的途径，也是企业集群形成、发展和升级的有效手段，尤其是在企业和集群的起步阶段，更是如此。而集群则为其成员企业的模仿创新提供了先决的便利条件，如：①集群内模仿创新源可不断产生并快速传播；②集群内创新知识的迅速扩散和溢出使模仿者具有模仿行为所必备的初始专业技术知识；③集群内模仿者的蜂拥而至，使模仿创新具有成功的概率基数；④集群内紧密的网络联系和频繁的网络学习是模仿创新广泛而迅速发生的有效途径。因此，模仿创新和企业集群是相互促进的关系。

2. 模仿创新推动集群创新能力螺旋上升

对于钢卷尺行业，要保护率先创新者的知识产权，模仿产品与模仿源相比必须有 7 种不同（或创新）。所以，模仿创新并不是单纯的模仿，它同样需要投入一定的研究开发力量，对率先者的技术进行再开发，属于一种渐进性创新行为。企业集群内一项成功的率先创新总要引来许多后续的模仿跟进者，而模仿跟进者依靠知识的积累创造出自己的核心技术，又成为后续模仿的率先创新者，其创新成果又会被进一步模仿。在这种一轮又一轮不断模仿的过程中，新工艺得以不断改进，新产品性能不断提高，集群的知识水平也不断上升。这种创新过程带动了企业集群创新能力的螺旋式上升。该过程可做如下直观说明。

初始创新源的产品技术可以分为以人力资本为载体的部分 H 和不以资本为载体的技术部分 A。由于对其主体人的依附性，H 是依靠人与人之间的网络联系或人员的流动（跳槽）来传播的。嵌入产品的技术部分 A 是依靠其可模仿性和投放市场后模仿者的破译技术能力来扩散的。两种知识传播渠道保证了创新源的迅速扩散。设企业集群内初始创新源的所含技术为 A_0，每次模仿创新所增加技术为 A，经过 k 次模仿创新后的技术为 A_k，则 $A_k = A_0 + kA$。

借用 Mansfield 创立的创新技术扩散的传染模型（仇保兴，1999）来描述集群内的技术扩散，设集群内最终将有 N^* 个企业参与模仿、采用创新技术，则传播速率：

$$\omega(t) = \frac{N^*}{1 + \exp(-\eta - \Phi t)} \tag{27.1}$$

式中，$\Phi = b_1 + b_t M + b_3 K + \varepsilon$（$\varepsilon$ 为误差项），M 是采用创新技术后的利润，K 是采用创新技术所需的投资，二者均为常数。创新技术在企业集群内的扩散过程遵循的是一条逻辑扩散曲线（仇保兴，1999）（图 27.5），其速度 ω 起初很缓慢、急剧增加到拐点后下降。

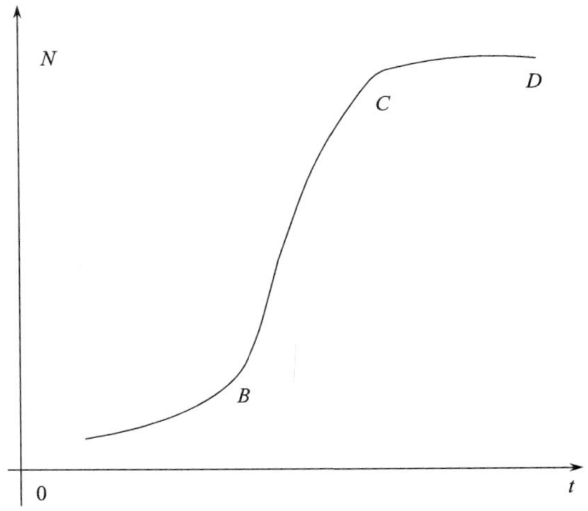

图 27.5　技术创新逻辑扩散曲线

设在时间 t 内有 N_t 个企业采用创新技术，其中，有 N_{t_1} 个企业在此基础上有不同的创新，即模仿创新速度为 $V=N_{t_1}/N_t$，则 t 时间后的技术 $A_t=A_0+AN+1$。

以模仿创新战略为主的企业集群其技术创新的轨迹是一条空间螺旋曲线（图 27.6），在水平面上它以角速度 ω（非匀速）在底园（集群边界）旋转（即创新技术在集群内以 ω 速度扩散），同时它又以速度 V（设为匀速）向上运动（创新水平增加）。两个运动的合成即为一条螺旋线。其螺距 $h=A_0+AVN_t$，为第一轮模仿创新过后集群技术创新能力的增加。

由于角速度 ω 为非匀速，其逻辑曲线如图 27.5，所以

$$N_t=\int_0^t \omega(t)\,\mathrm{d}t=\int_0^t \frac{N^*\,\mathrm{d}t}{1+\exp(-\eta-\Phi t)}=N^*\int_0^t [1+\exp(-\eta-\Phi t)]^{-1}\mathrm{d}t \tag{27.2}$$

则

$$h=A_0+AVN^*\int_0^t [1+\exp(-\eta-\Phi t)]^{-1}\mathrm{d}t \tag{27.3}$$

由式（27.3）可知，当模仿创新速度 V 较大、传播速度 ω 处在图 27.5 的 BC 段时，集群的技术创新能力提高最快；当传播速度处在 CD 段时，模仿创新处于饱和状态，创新能力提高 h 后第一轮模仿创新结束，开始第二轮的模仿创新，如此循环往复。由于每一个模仿创新，其技术扩散——再创新的过程都是螺旋上升的，各个模仿创新相互传播、相互渗透，致使整个集群内的通用知识水平增高，技术创新能力螺旋式上升（如图 27.6 中 M 点的轨迹）。

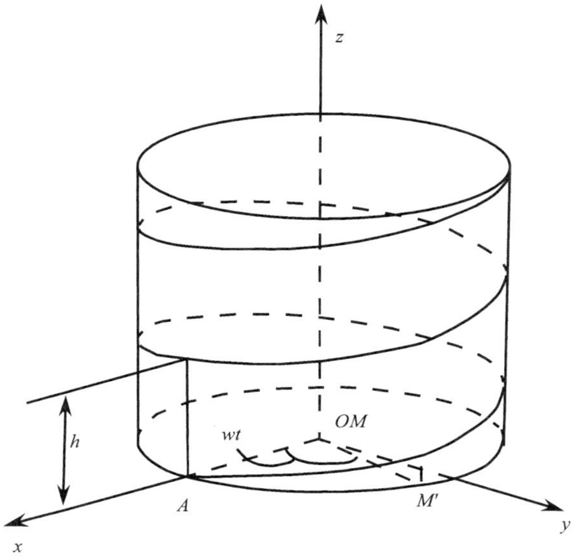

图 27.6　企业集群技术创新能力螺旋线

3. 南庄村企业集群中模仿创新频繁发生

南庄村企业集群的创新过程主要是以模仿创新为主，甚至初始创新源都来自模仿创新。调查中，当问及技术来源时，70%的调查企业的回答是“模仿”；当问及企业的创新来源时，77%企业的回答内容中包含“模仿创新”。集群内较大企业的模仿多来自集群外部，而小企业的模仿多来自集群内部，并且小企业比较大企业更加依赖模仿。新产品一出现，经验丰富的业主们只要一拆一看，就知道如何制造，如何改良，并迅速模仿创新。

模仿创新促进了南庄村企业集群的产生和发展壮大。该集群起源于一个很偶然的事件。20 世纪 70 年代末，一村民在路过商丘市卷尺厂时捡到报废的尺条，他截成段卖给当地的学生，引起周围人的纷纷效仿。众多模仿者中创新的发生使产品质量和价值不断提升，该创新又引起四邻的争相模仿。这种群起效应促进了钢卷尺工业由手工作坊式的原始积累到机械化的加工工业再到资源整合的规模化、分工化。调查中，当问及企业创办的动机时，68%企业的回答内容包含“模仿他人经验”。20 年商海中的摸爬滚打使每个企业主积累了丰富的经验，并使他们以犀利的目光和敏锐的头脑去寻找每一个模仿创新空间。尤其是几个龙头企业的业主，他们积极参加各种各样的交易会，宣传和推销自己的产品，搜集市场信息、广采产品新样。市场上每出现一个新型钢卷尺，他们都会迅速知晓并购买回来，组织自己的技术人员去求反破译其中的技术秘密，研究设计产品如何生产、如何取长补短加以创新。而他们的创新成果一经投放市场，又会立即引起周围人的模仿，并在此基础上思考自己的创新。由于模仿具有时滞性，在集群内第一轮模仿创新者总能得到一定时间内的垄断利润，当大量的其他模仿者进入并造成利润大幅下降时，第一轮模仿创新者又会收集各第二轮模仿者的创新，并进一步综合、筛选形成自己第三轮的模仿创新。所以，南庄村的钢卷尺总能赶超时代步伐，稳步前进。但随着知识经济的到来，仅靠集群内的通用知识是远远不够的，他们也遇到了“模仿不了”的难题。如，江华总经理王胜喜在和外国老板打交道时，买了一把美国全新数字技术生产的钢卷尺，面对这一全新技术领域他既束手无策，又非常高兴。立即去北京请相关教授来破译这把钢卷尺。就这样，南庄村的钢卷尺科技含量越来越高，产品成本越来越低，品牌质量也越来越好。

南庄村的模仿创新不单单体现在产品上，还体现在机械设备和管理方式上。1998年江华投资48万元进口了一台德国淬火炉，技术先进但有些功能利用起来不太方便，王胜喜凭借自己多年的实践经验，与相关制造厂联合研究，扬长避短，终于仅以10万元的成本生产出来自己的高温淬火炉，并在集群内得以推广。据调查，目前南庄村已能自制全部生产设备，其节约成本均在40%以上，大大降低了企业的生产成本和进入门槛。由此可见，模仿性创新在南庄村钢卷尺企业集群的形成、发展、升级和演变过程中起着非常重要的作用。

27.2.5 中原文化背景

南庄村企业集群的竞争优势来源还有赖于其所处的中原文化背景。

1. 企业家文化

博大精深、风格独特的中原文化是中华民族文化长河的源头，从《愚公移山》到老子的《道德经》，培育了中原人吃苦耐劳、朴实忠厚、奋进创新、勇往直前的优秀品格和创业精神。南庄村企业集群十多年的迅速扩张很大程度上归因于本地企业家资源的大量涌现和创新的产业文化氛围。贫穷的现状和能人的财富示范效应，使南庄村的每一个家庭都崇尚创新，或努力创办新公司，或给邻居们打工。

2. “共富观”

儒学伦理的“仁、义、礼、智、信”使人们有了统一的行为准则，其核心思想“仁”注重全体性而非个人的满足，造就了中原人的“共富观”。当问及创业动机时，东方量具有限公司老板许秀章一语道破：“是贫穷，有志气的人都想带领乡亲们共同致富，而工厂一般比土地能淘出更多的金子”，调查中此选择项被38%的企业选中。可见，“带领乡亲们致富”是他们追求的一种天经地义的完美人格。而崇尚“能人”、效仿“贤士”又加速了这种共同富裕的进程。

3. “家族化”

以家庭联产承包责任制为标志的农村改革使家庭在经济活动中的地位上升，“家族而居”的农村传统文化使南庄村企业集群起步于家庭小作坊式经济，创业者或管理者以一种“家长”作风对企业实施“权威管理”，这种以血缘、地缘和人情关系为基础的“家族化”组织方式使企业在形成之初具有强大的凝聚力和信任关系，大大降低了企业的管理成本，推动了企业集群的产生。不过，“家族化”的组织管理方式中，企业的技术、管理和销售要职一般是由家族内部成员担任，这有悖于能者善用的原则。目前，44%的调查企业已转变为“公司制”管理方式。

4. 民俗文化

农民多年形成的生活、生产、社会习惯和行为特点等地区民俗文化使集群成员具有趋同的价值判断和意识形态，提高了交流和沟通的效率，缓解企业之间的冲突，减少了机会主义行为。熟识的人际关系产生的信任与承诺，对南庄村集群来说不仅是一种重要的社会资源，又是一种具有资源配置功能的经济资源。同处一地的企业主之间长期交往而结成的“哥们儿”义气，使他们追求一种“人格化交易”（阮学金和张军，1999），即强调人情的作用而非单纯的利益最大化。当问及“企业交易中，若人情与利益发生冲突你该如何？”时，几乎所有的企业均选择“二者折中，稍偏向人情”。正是这种“人格化交易”，不仅实现了平等互利，还克服了诸多不确定性带来的资金、技术甚至政治风险而造成的心理压力。

27.2.6　制度扶持

南庄村企业集群的竞争优势很大程度上来源于乡镇政府的制度扶持。财政收支分级包干制度的实施使企业的纳税成为政府的主要财源，企业和区域经济的健康发展是政府官员的主要政绩，而市场制度的不完善和竞争的不确定性又使企业积极寻求政府的保护，企业与政府相互依赖。政府为了其共同利益积极参与集群建设，并对企业进行监督、引导、协调和间接管理，为集群内的经济活动提供良好的软硬环境和制度安排。政府为扩大集群规模、扶持企业发展，采取“放水养鱼”政策，简化企业审批手续，降低企业进入门槛，规定企业按月或按季度缴税，其标准远远低于城市同行业企业，新建企业前几年甚至可以不缴税。

稍岗乡政府在集群网络中也起着重要作用。乡政府在改善硬环境的同时也着力改善了软环境：对所属职能站所约法三章，不准对企业卡、拿、要，并在集群内设立治安报警点；成立稍岗乡钢卷尺协会，通过章程约束来规范内部竞争，协调企业之间的分工协作关系。集群每月要向外发放集装箱 800 个，乡政府成立了集装箱办公室，组织专门的运输队伍，有条不紊地把各企业的产品运达指定地点，不仅节省了企业大量的时间和精力，而且大大降低了运输成本。

27.2.7　较低的要素成本

农村中大量剩余劳动力和低廉的地价为集群的规模扩张提供了成本优势。钢卷尺生产属于劳动密集型产业（李小建等，2000），劳动力稍作培训即可上岗。技术工人工资每月大约 500 元，虽还不及发达地区同行业企业工人工资的一半，但他们与周围从事其他职业的人相比已得到很大的满足，所以工作起来积极性非常高。在南庄村钢卷尺集群，企业规模扩张所需的工厂用地，其地租按亩产 250kg 小麦的价格收取，亦即每亩工厂用地的租金每年仅 300 元左右。另外，由于整体上稍岗乡经济发展水平较低而社会网络所决定的地方根植性又较强，在集群的内部交易中，各种配件让利的空间非常大。这种种原因导致南庄村的钢卷尺生产具有极强的成本优势。据估计，南庄村钢卷尺与外地的竞争对手相比，同类同质的产品成本大约能降低10%～20%。

27.3　结论与讨论

缺乏许多优越条件的中国中部农区企业集群，一般不是由政府自上而下设计或推动的，而是在市场机制作用下自发形成的。究竟何产业、在何地能够形成集群？其最初原因是多方面的，如偶然事件的发生、地方传统文化、资源禀赋条件、个人特殊的人际关系等。这些初始的优势因“循环累积”和“路径依赖”，使得集聚一旦发生，就会产生自增强机制，并具有“锁定”效应。因此，在适宜的环境条件下，集聚的规模不断扩大，分工不断细化，网络联系不断加强。规模经济、分工经济和网络联系三者共同作用的结果构成了企业集群无可比拟的静态竞争优势，三者动态上的数量增加和协调互动是企业集群发展的驱动力所在。

中国中部农区企业集群的竞争优势来源不仅具有上述共性，还具有自己特殊的个性，如模仿创新的频繁发生、中原文化背景、制度扶持和较低的劳动力、土地等要素成本在企业集群的形成、发展、演变和升级过程中也起着非常重要的作用。

南庄村企业集群就是在上述共性和个性竞争优势来源的共同作用下蓬勃发展的。当然，产权明晰的企业制度（集群内全部生产性企业为个体私营）、小企业对市场的快速适应和全方位满足等，也是集群企业频频击败僵化停滞、管理不善、激励微弱的国有企业而立于不败之地的部分原因。

参考文献

保罗·克鲁格曼. 2001. 克鲁格曼国际贸易新理论. 黄胜强译. 北京：中国社会科学出版社

冯德连，王蕾. 2000. 国外企业群落理论的演变与启示. 财贸研究，(5)：1～5

李二玲，李小建. 2005. 企业集群的竞争优势研究. 河南大学学报（社会科学版），45（3）：9～14

李小建. 1993. 河南农村工业发展环境研究. 北京：中国科学技术出版社

李小建，葛震远，乔家君. 2000. 偶然因素对区域经济发展的影响. 人文地理，15（6）：1～4

仇保兴. 1999. 小企业集群研究. 上海：复旦大学出版社

阮学金，张军. 1999. 乡镇企业的社区性格和空间集聚. 地理学与国土研究，15（1）：23～29

王缉慈，等. 2001. 创新的空间：企业集群与区域发展. 北京：北京大学出版社

文娉，李小建. 2003. 非正式因素影响下的中小企业网络学习与区域发展. 人文地理，18（3）：73～76

Martin R，Sunley P. 2003. Deconstructing clusters：Chaotic concept or policy panacea. Journal of Economic Geography，3（1）：5～35

Porter M E. 1998. Clusters and new economics of competition. Harvard Business Review，76（6）：77～90

Porter M E. 2000. Locations，clusters，and company strategy. In：Clark G L，Feldman M P，Gertler M S. The Oxford Handbook of Economic Geography. Oxford：Oxford University Press

第 28 章　产业联系与农村工业化

中国农村工业的高速发展在许多方面是世界上十分独特的现象。它吸引着国内外众多学者的关注（Byrd and Lin，1990），其中，少数地理学家也对此进行了研究（陆大道等，1990；曾尊固和陆诚，1990；苗长虹，1997；樊杰和陶普曼，1998）。然而，在这些研究中，很少有人从企业组织角度，基于详细的企业调查研究而得出结论。20 世纪 90 年代初，邓小平南行讲话进一步促进中国的改革开放，农村工业得到快速发展。为此，本章重点通过 1992 年对河南近 200 家农村工业企业的调查访问，对产业联系与农村工业化的关系加以研究。尽管该研究已过去多年，但当时是中部农区农村工业的大发展时期，调研结果具有一定的历史意义。

28.1　理论思路及企业选择

产业联系指发生在不同生产、经营、管理及辅助单位之间的物质和信息流，以及其他形式的接触。在本章研究中，产业联系重点包括生产经营者之间的商品和货物流动、服务联系、技术转让和资金流动等。

产业联系与区域发展的关系是区域发展理论研究的一大焦点，区域发展的一些重要理论的建立，多基于这一根本点。由于不同分析者从各自的审视角度加以研究，所得结论也明显迥异。增长极理论的创立者皮鲁认为，区域间的控制与被控制状态及产业联系决定着外围区的增长，企业间的联系可使增长极扩散，使增长遍及整个国家（Perroux，1971）。与此相反，依赖理论和中心-外围论者则认为，区域间的联系，尤其是发达区与不发达区的联系，将导致剩余价值由外围区（不发达区）向区域和国家中心转移（Frank，1969；Szentes，1976；Johnson，1986）。然而，在不发达的第三世界国家，产业联系所产生的影响很难扩大。

不同的分析者基于各自的理论构架和推理，并运用区域上的一些统计数据来支持其观点。然而，产业联系归根到底是发生于企业之间，区域发展也是区域内各企业发展状况的综合体现，在以上两者关系分析中基于企业调查访问所得的资料便显得十分重要。由于中国农村工业在全国发展较快，且扩及广大的一向不发达区域，如果能通过企业调查资料证明产业联系与中国农村工业化的关联，不仅对以上理论讨论有重要意义，而且也有利于农村工业发展的实践。

为了选择所调查的农村工业企业，根据统计资料，将河南 1991 年各县（包括县级市）乡镇及乡镇以下工业人均产值以最短距离法分为五个等级：最高、较高、中等、较低和最低。然后，依据以下两原则进行选点：①调查地应具有代表意义，既兼顾不同发展水平，又兼顾不同发展类型（平原、山区，以及资源型、劳动密集型、技术型等）；②调查地可达性，在经费及时间限制下，不宜分散。最后选定巩县（今巩义市）、孟县

（今孟州市）、新安、尉氏和宁陵县为调查区（表 28.1）。

表 28.1　调查区基本情况及调查企业

县（市）	1991 年人均农村工业产值/(元/人)	发展水平	发展条件	调查企业数/个
巩义	3695	最高	丘陵区，靠近郑州、洛阳	52
孟县	2260	较高	平原，农业发达	29
新安	781	中等	山区，矿产资源丰富	21
尉氏	472	较低	平原，农业较好	42
宁陵	234	最低	平原，资源缺乏，农业一般	34

资料来源：河南省乡镇企业局。

为了在相对集中区调查较多企业，在每个调查区（县或市），我们选择乡镇企业发展最好的一个乡（镇）和两个村，对所选乡（镇）村的主要工业企业均进行调查访问，前后共调查企业 178 个。据事先印制的调查表，每个企业获取数据（包括描述性资料转换成的数据）88 个。这些数据经整理后，作为我们进行分析的基本资料。

除了 5 个调查区之外，我们还访问了河南的 4 个亿元村，并对其中的临颍县南街村进行了典型案例分析。

28.2　产业联系类型

根据调查分析，在农村工业企业中占重要地位的产业联系类型有以下 5 种。

1. 资源-加工联系

资源-加工联系即资源原材料与加工工业之间的联系。调查中发现，这种联系主要发生于自然资源富集区和工业相对发达区之间。在自然资源富集区，尤其是山区，大多数工业企业主要从事矿产开采和粗加工，其产品则多供应本区以外的工业企业，这种产业联系多具有区域意义。例如，新安县仓头乡，共有各级工业企业 54 家，均从事煤矿和硫黄矿开采，其产品 90%以上销往本县以外其他地区，该县的庙头村，10 家工业企业中有 7 家基于当地原材料（煤、石料和铁矿等）工业。这些原材料经初步加工后，供应全国范围内的一些企业需求。但位于山区的资源富集区，交通不畅在很大程度上制约着这种联系的发展。

2. 农产品-加工联系

在农业相对发达区，作为商品的农产品既可以在产地加工，也可以运往产地之外的其他工厂。然而，由于商品性农业相对发达区为工业的发展提供了前提条件，加之农村工业发展初期多以“小而全”的形式出现，因此，农产品与其加工业的联系多在区域内发生。以孟县缑村镇为例，这里农村工业中的主导企业均为基于本地农产品的加工业，其所用原材料（粮食、水果、肉类、麦秸等）95%以上来自本县。

大农业范围内的牧副业产品，与加工工厂的联系则以区域间为主。牧副业发达的山区，经济多不发达，制约着有关加工业的发展，故产品多输往其他区域。孟县的桑坡村，有毛皮加工厂 30 家，从外县、外省运来的原料毛皮占总原料的 90%以上。

3. 零部件-半成品联系

零部件-半成品联系即某工业企业的成品作为另一工业企业的生产投入品而形成的联系。它既包括工业企业为另一工业企业生产零部件产品，又包括工业企业对另一工业企业产品的进一步加工。它既发生于农村工业与城市工业之间，又存在于农村工业企业之间。但由于农村工业企业技术设备等条件的限制，城乡工业之间这种联系较多。在交通便捷的农村地区，农村工业企业可通过生产技术简单或污染较为严重的产品生产，供应城市工业。例如，巩义位于郑州、洛阳之间，与两城市距离不超过 100km，且铁路、公路交通均十分便利，生产零部件、半成品的农村工业比较发达。这里生产的纯碱、氯化铭、铸钢件及各种机械配件，不仅供应郑州、洛阳，还有一部分销往省外。

4. 资金联系

资金联系可发生于农村工业之间，也可发生于农村工业与其他企业、金融机构之间。在所调查的农村工业企业中，资金联系多限于所在县域之间，尤其是工业企业与金融机构之间。只有少数企业通过外资贷款、中外合资、外向联合及与大企业合并等形式，吸引城市和其他相对发达地区的资金。例如，孟县东韩村的河南凯祥实业有限公司为了开发当地的玉米资源，经过详细论证，得到 200 万元的外资贷款，建成万吨玉米淀粉生产线。临颍县南街村 1991 年与一日本公司合资建立耐可达彩色印刷有限公司，生产本村所需用的食品包装袋等。

5. 技术联系

技术联系即与农村工业企业所发生的技术合作、技术转让和技术指导等联系。这种联系的跨度较大，不局限于县内及与邻近城市间，可遍布全国甚至跨国界。在所调查的 178 家农村工业企业中，40%从城市工业企业或科研机构、高等院校得到过技术转让或技术指导。在这种联系中，农村工业企业均为接受方。

在调查企业中，相当一部分技术联系的发生受人际关系的影响。由于同学、同乡、战友、亲戚从中介绍而形成技术联系的占城乡技术联系企业总数的 30%。这种联系渠道受多种因素制约，很难使技术需求与供应达一最佳状态：先进的技术由于信息不灵而得不到应用，一般技术则由于人际关系影响而推广使用。

除了以上五种联系外，农村工业企业的信誉联系也值得一提。某些农村工业企业为了占领市场，常通过联营或与大企业合并等方式，或借助大企业名声，或用大企业名牌产品商标，来吸引消费者和商业经营者。

28.3　产业联系与农村工业发展

根据调查，产业联系与农村工业发展水平之间存在着较为密切的关联。区域内产业联系对农村工业发展的影响可以临颍县南街村为例。表 28.2 以企业所生产产品的销售地为例，列举了区域间产业联系与农村工业发展的关系。十分明显，在农村工业相对发达区（人均农村工业产值较高区），其产业联系范围较广。大多数企业的产品销往所在县、省以外，甚至销往国际市场（如巩义）。与此相反，在农村工业相对落后区，其产品主要在当地或所在省县销售。

表 28.2　产品联系与农村工业发展水平

县（市）	1991 年人均农村工业产值/(元/人)	产品销售地所占比例/%			
		县内	省内	省外	其他
巩义	3695	12.0	36.0	42.0	10.0
孟县	2260	26.9	34.6	34.6	3.9
新安	781	45.0	30.0	10.0	15.0
尉氏	472	5.6	87.0	5.0	2.5
宁陵	234	80.7	6.5	9.7	3.2

注：产品销售地数据基于 1992 年对 178 家农村工业企业的调查资料。

产业联系对农村工业发展的促进作用主要表现在以下几方面。

1. 企业产品占领较大的市场

这种情形在经济欠发达地区（如河南）表现尤为突出。因为在当地经济发展水平的约束下，居民一般消费水平较低，仅靠当地市场很难激励工业企业的生产热情。来自调查区域的资料表明，农村工业企业（尤其是大型企业）的创办动机很少是为了本地市场需求。这样，为了占领市场，很多企业便不惜花费到外地推销产品，从而扩大其产业联系的范围及强度（销售量）。

2. 农村工业引进较为先进的技术

对农村工业企业技术来源的调查表明，区域间产业联系发达的巩义市，所调查企业中直接从城市获取技术的占 67%，反之，宁陵县的农村工业企业与城市的技术联系则十分微弱（23%）。利用城市较为先进的技术，极大地促进了农村工业的发展。例如，巩义市的竹林村，从天津市一家企业引进技术，并高薪雇用该企业技术人员作技术指导，从而成为河南的第一家氰化钠生产厂家，其产品供不应求，1991 年年产值达 350 万元。根据市场潜力及该厂生产规划，到 1996 年，该厂产值将达 3000 万元。巩义孝南村的净水剂厂，从东北吉林市某国家大厂引进净水剂提取技术，现已成为“星火计划”国家净水剂定点厂之一。

3. 产业联系可以产生乘数效应

在一个主导工厂建立后，通过产业的前向关联和后向关联，促进相关的上下游生产厂家建立，带动整个区域经济的发展。临颍县南街村是通过产业联系而高速发展的典型例子，将做专门讨论。其他类似的例子还包括孟县缑村和新乡的刘庄村。所调查区域内产业联系发展较好者，其主导企业的生产均以农产品为基础。在矿产品富集区，还没有发现区内产业联系发展很好的例子。

4. 逐步改进管理经营体制

中国传统的农业文化，与现代化工业文化差距较大。农村工业发展伊始，多以家庭、亲友以及之间的联合为经营基础，经营者即为所有者。产业联系所带来的信息流，以及随着城市及国外资本的流入而对投资企业管理方针的参与，逐步改变了一些企业的组织结构及管理体制。例如，孟县东韩村的“凯祥实业有限公司”、缑村的“河阳实业公司”，巩义小关的“河南豫州水泥有限公司”等，均在人、财、物、产、供、销诸方面进行了大胆改革，管理水平大有提高。

28.4　典型案例分析

南街村位于河南中部的临颍县城南 500m，紧邻京深公路。这里农业发展条件较好，然而矿产资源贫乏。由于合理开发当地农业资源，形成了密切的产业联系（图 28.1）。该村经济发展迅速。1991 年，全村各业生产总值达 1.03 亿元，平均每人 34190 元。按到 1992 年 10 月为止的产值预测，1992 年全村各业总产值至少突破 2 亿元。也就是说，截至 1992 年年底，全村人均各业总产值将达 6 万元以上。突破 1985 年发达工业国的该项指标（据世界银行资料，1985 年所有发达市场经济国家的

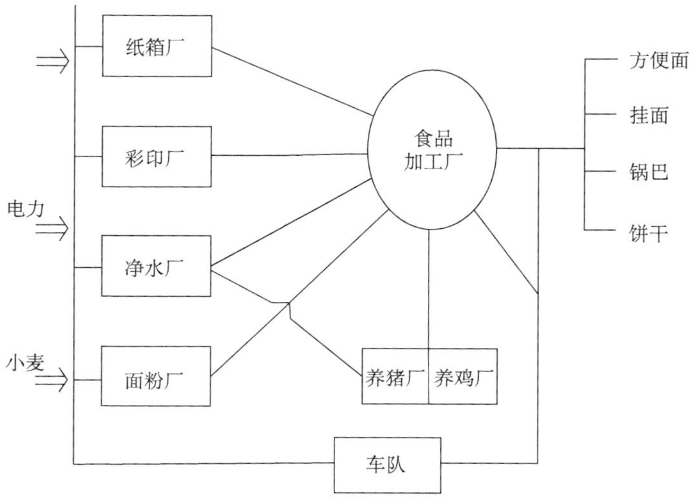

图 28.1　临颍县南街村产业联系

人均国民生产总值达 11810 美元)。其发展速度及经济规模均在内陆省份具有十分突出的地位。

工业在南街村的发展中具有十分重要意义。1991 年工业产值占全村各业产值的 97.9%。在该村工业发展中，产业联系起了关键作用。20 世纪 80 年代初，农村经济政策刚刚改革之时，本村建立起一个面粉加工厂和一个砖瓦厂。由于附近农业较为发达，粮食加工业发展势头看好。这两个厂的利润主要用于购买新面粉加工机械。面粉厂的生产规模逐步扩大，其质量也逐步提高。市场范围不断向外延伸，销路打入北京。在和北京某大食品加工厂的联系中，南街的决策者看到食品加工工艺并不十分复杂。如果能引进技术建立自己的食品加工厂，不仅所产面粉可直接得以利用，而且也可以在河南食品（糕点）市场占据一席之地。于是，南街糕点厂于 1986 年建立起来。一开始仅生产各式糕点，之后开始向方便面、锅巴等方面扩展。到 80 年代末，其方便面生产能力已居全国各厂家之冠，成为该村的主导企业。

伴随着主导企业的发展，与此相关联（主要是后向关联）的企业逐步建立和发展起来。由于方便面等食品成箱包装的需要，1987 年建立了纸箱厂，由于食品单件包装的需要，1991 年与日本合资建立耐可达彩色印刷有限公司，为了满足糕点生产中对奶、肉类的需求，同时也为了使面粉加工时的副产品（麸皮等）得以利用，1988 年建立了养鸡场和养猪场，同年，还建立了冷库和运输队。前者用于储存肉蛋及其他糕点生产原料，后者用于原料和产品的运输。现在，全村大小近 10 家工厂，由于产业联系密切成为一体。1992 年成立“河南中原工贸公司”，以企业化统一管理各家工厂。

由于南街各厂家配套合理，加之决策者经营有方，其增长速度很快，未来发展潜力十分可观。从 1985 年以来，该村各业总产值基本上呈每年翻番的趋势增长。截至 1992 年年底，全村产值突破 2 亿元的基础上，到 1995 年再增长到 3 亿元是完全可以实现的。

28.5　区域模式

据调查分析，产业联系与农村工业发展之间存在着三种区域模式。

模式 A：主导产业带动相关联行业的发展（图 28.2a）在该模式中，主要为了满足本地需要，资源型（资源开采、冶炼和粗加工）工业首先在某一农村区建立起来（t_1）。由于该工业的发展积累一定资金之后，区域内的企业家便开始通过与外区域的联系，引进较为先进的生产技术并创办新的工业部门。经过几年的发展，区域内的主导产业部门逐步被确立起来（t_2）。原创办企业在主导产业建立中多起资金积累作用。为了减少运输、保证生产稳定增长及实现集聚效益，伴随着主导产业的发展，其前向关联和后向关联部门也得以建立和发展（t_3）。一段时期后，便形成了区域内各产业关联紧密的产业综合体（t_4）。这时，尽管各企业与区域外也发生联系，但区域产业综合体作为一个整体，对外的产业联系更显得重要。这种模式的实例，除南街村外，还见于调查区域中的巩义市竹林村、新安县庙头村。当然，这些村子在模式的发展阶段上是有差异的。

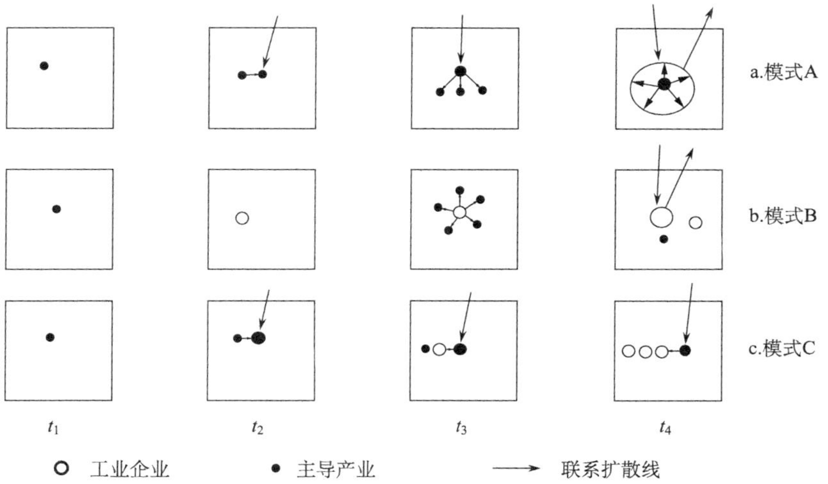

图 28.2　产业联系与农村工业发展的三种模式

模式 B：产业联系与区域专业化（图 28.2b）主要通过技术联系（技术模仿和技术转让），使某种生产在一农村区域迅速扩散，从而形成区域专业化生产。初始，由于某种原因（传统技术或亲友传授，或从城市引进等），村子开始建立起某种产品加工厂（t_1）。由于区域条件对该种生产十分有利，工厂盈利并扩大其生产规模（t_2）。其他村民见有利可图，便通过各种途径，从第一家工厂处学得技术并建立起类似的工厂。结果是家家办厂，形成专业化村（t_3）。在各厂家竞争中，必各显神通。其中，某厂家由于经营有方，看准市场，从外地引进先进技术，进行大规模生产。最终将导致现代化生产取代家庭工厂（t_4）。这种模式以孟县桑坡村为典型。该村皮毛加工传统在 20 世纪 80 年代得以扩散，现已为典型皮毛加工专业村。现代工厂建立及对小家庭工厂的合并趋势已经出现。

模式 C：产业多次转换（或主导产业不断转换）由于多数乡村工业发展条件并不十分独特，加之当地企业家对市场预测不足，20 世纪 80 年代以来从未形成较为稳定的主导产业。在该模式中，初始的工厂多建立在当地资源基础上（包括矿产资源和农产品资源），形成当时的主导部门（图 28.2c，t_1）。随着资金积累、市场变化及对市场认识的变化，企业家或建立新工厂取代生产市场不佳的老产品厂家，或改换老厂厂名、设备，生产新产品，老的主导产业被新的主导产业所取代（t_2）。若干年以后，这种状况由于市场变化将再次发生（t_3，t_4）。其结果是，产业大的转换经常发生，并伴随着不断出现结构变化和组织调整。例如，巩义市小镇工业企业原以煤炭开采为主，以后伴随煤炭开采业的下降，出现一些大型耐火材料和水泥烧制企业，现在又有一些企业转向小型机械等的制造。新乡县刘庄村的主导企业也由农产品加工转向机械制造，进而转向制药、电子等行业。

28.6 结　　语

实例分析表明，产业联系在农村工业发展中起着十分重要的作用，农村工业发展水平较高区，产业联系一般均比较发达；同时，农村工业现代化程度越高，产业联系亦越显重要。因此，促使产业联系发展，疏通产业联系中的障碍应在农村工业化政策中有所体现。

区域内的产业联系，无疑可通过乘数效应，带动农村工业各部门以至于整个经济的发展（如南街村）。但是，区域间的产业联系，对于落后地区农村工业的发展，对于农村工业的结构调整，对于农村工业现代化和城乡工业一体化更显得十分重要。为了改变中国经济的二元结构局面，区域间的产业联系应给予特殊关注。同时，市场机制是产业联系发展的主要渠道。完善的市场机制，可促使产业联系的发展。此外，有远见能力的企业家在产业联系扩展中的作用也不容忽视。

参考文献

樊杰，W. 陶普曼. 1998. 中国乡镇企业外向型经济发展的基本态势及省际差异. 地理学报，53（1）：13～23

陆大道，等. 1990. 中国工业布局的理论与实践. 北京：科学出版社

苗长虹. 1997. 中国农村工业化的若干理论问题. 北京：中国经济出版社

曾尊固，陆诚. 1989. 江苏省乡村经济类型的初步分析. 地理研究，8（3）：78～84

Byrd W A，Lin Q S. 1990. China's Rural Industry：Structure，Development and Reform. Oxford：Oxford University Press

Frank A G. 1969. Capitalism and Underdevelopment in Latin America. London：Penguin

Johnston R J，et al. 1986. The Dictionary of Human Geography（2nd Edition）. Oxford：Basil Biack-well

Perroux F. 1971. Note on the concept of "growth pole". In：Livingstone I. Economic Policy for Development：Select Reading. Harmondsworth：Penguin

Szentes T. 1976. The Political Economy of Undevelopment（3rd Edition）. Budapest：Publishing House of the Hungarian Academy of Sicence

第 29 章　金融地理学理论探索

金融地理学始于 20 世纪 50 年代（Myrdal，1957），但从 80 年代以来才迅速兴起，现已成为经济地理学的重要分支之一。国际上不少学者进行了卓有成效的研究，发表了一批很有分量的成果（Corbridge et al.，1994；Porteous，1995；Leyshon and Thrift，1997；Martin，1999；Laulajainen，2003）。与国际上十分活跃的状况相比，金融地理学在中国国内的研究尚属刚刚起步。一些学者已经认识到金融地理学研究的重要性，开始介绍国际相关研究状况（金雪军和田霖，2004；武魏等，2005），并结合中国实际，在信息对金融中心影响（Zhao et al.，2004）、区域金融发展影响因素（金雪军和田霖，2004）、区域金融中心重组（赵晓斌和王垣，2005）、银行业空间系统变化（李小建等，2006）等方面做了一些有益的探索。中国特殊的国情，为金融地理学的研究提供了很好的平台。为了促进相关研究的发展，很有必要从理论视角对国际进展进行一定深度的分析，并结合中国特点，对金融地理学发展进行认真思考。

基于本人对国际文献和中国实际的了解和思考，本章从金融机构的空间结构、空间发展过程和金融机构与环境的关系等方面分析了金融地理学的主要研究内容。金融地理学主要理论问题包括地理存在论、金融变化的区域经济影响观点、区域金融系统演化模式、金融地理的路径依赖、金融全球化与地方关系等；在此基础上，从环境对金融地理影响、全球化与区域金融系统、行政格局与金融体系、金融系统与区域发展、金融企业地理等方面提出中国金融地理研究的切入点。

29.1　金融地理学主要研究内容

货币和金融业是揭示空间经济的主要切入点之一。20 世纪 80 年代以来，国际上有不少学者关注货币、金融业区位与空间经济的研究。这些成果涉及金融地理学的诸多方面（Corbridge et al.，1994；Porteous，1995；Leyshon et al.，1997；Martin，1999；Laulajainen，2003），诸如金融空间中的经济、社会和文化因素影响，货币空间与社会权力，货币与全球空间秩序变化，金融中心发展，国际银行业中心与空间经济，金融系统的空间结构，地方金融系统与区域产业发展，私有化与金融空间结构，全球化、管理与金融空间组织变化，国际金融市场的地域根植性，金融企业家、风险资本与区域发展，等等。对这些纷繁复杂的研究，必须从一定视角进行梳理。本章将其归纳为以下研究侧面。

29.1.1　金融机构的地理研究

金融地理学的客体是金融机构。所以，金融地理学应该把金融机构的空间结构、空间发展过程和金融机构与环境的关系作为主要研究内容。已有研究，多数是围绕这一框架进行的。但仍有一些问题并未给予足够重视。在这一框架下，金融地理学可包括以下层面。

1. 不同金融机构区位研究

不同金融机构具有不同的区位特征。这是其本身功能特征与社会经济现象的空间格局相互作用的结果。例如，银行与证券交易机构、外汇交易机构的区位会有明显差别：前者会相对较为分散，而后两者会较为集中（Martin et al.，1999）。甚至不同银行间也会有所不同。例如，商业银行与政策性银行相比，会更加倾向于在居民区、企事业集中地等直接客户地布局分支机构。进一步分析，同一金融机构内部的不同组分，其区位也有明显差别。例如，银行的服务网点（支行、分理处、储蓄所等）会较为分散，而银行的总部和区域总部的区位会较为集中。这一点，与生产性企业的情况有些类似（李小建，2002）。对金融机构区位的研究，20 世纪 90 年代曾有一些理论成果。例如，Porteous 对银行区位模型进行了很好的理论分析（Porteous，1995）。通过对距离对银行贷款监督成本影响的模型分析，他认为，如果市场潜力的空间分布是不均匀的，在不考虑价格竞争的情况下，将产生银行的集聚。其结果有点类似霍特林（Hotelling）对企业的空间分析模型（李小建，1999）。近年来关于金融中心的研究文献很多，其中一些也与金融机构区位有关（赵晓斌和王垣，2002；Clark，2002；Zhao et al.，2004）。但是，总的来说，对金融机构微观区位的理论研究成果并不多。也许西方主流地理学家的注意力已经转向全球金融等更能引人关注的问题，但金融机构微观区位仍很重要。

2. 金融机构空间系统研究

与以上讨论不同，金融机构空间系统侧重于金融机构之间关系的空间研究。例如，有些国家（如英国、澳大利亚、加拿大等），形成了全国性的银行系统。全国性（或国际性）的银行通过其遍布各地的分支机构，组成复杂的空间系统。而另外一些国家（如美国、德国、意大利等），则长期以地方性银行为主。由此形成区域分割的金融空间系统。尽管后一类型的国家近年来随着政府金融管制的放开，也开始趋于向全国性金融系统发展，但历史上形成的格局仍有一定影响。对这一问题，西方学者的关注较多（Martin et al.，1999；Clark and Wojcik，2005）。但是，计划经济下的特殊金融空间系统，以及由计划向市场转型过程中的金融空间系统变化，却几乎仍为空白。

除了国家尺度外，国际甚至全球金融系统也引起了不少学者的关注（Clark，2005）。但国家之内的区域金融空间系统研究不多。少数相关研究侧重于一国之内区域之间金融服务的差异（Klagge et al.，2005）、城市内金融机构区域差异问题（Marshall and Martin，2005；Marshall，2004）。另外，金融企业本身的空间系统研究，对公司空间格局理论十分重要。但并未引起重视（Clark，2005）。很少有相关成果问世。

3. 金融机构与区域关系研究

该研究层面涉及金融机构发展与环境的关系问题。以上讨论中，有一些已经与此有所关联（如金融机构区位、金融中心形成等）。以下关于外部影响的讨论也会考虑这一问题。这里，主要侧重金融机构空间系统与区域的关系。一般来说，一个区域可以仅有一个金融机构运营（这里的金融机构指相同拥有关系的一个金融企业，如中国工商银行，而不是指其分支机构），也可以有多个金融机构；这些金融机构可以是地方性的（如中国的城市银行等），也可以是全国性的。从金融企业角度，一个金融机构可以仅在一个地区运营（如地方银行），也可以在全国、甚至世界多个地区运营。通常情况为，一个区域会有多家金融机构，而这些机构中有一些并不限于仅在本区运营。这样，金融机构的空间系统与区域之间就形成了十分复杂的交错关系。对这种关系的研究曾有一些关注。例如，Martin 认为，地方和区域银行系统与全国性银行的分支系统相比，与当地的经济联系会更为密切，会更受制于也更投身于当地经济（Martin et al.，1999）。但不同情形下的实例和理论研究也还比较薄弱。

该问题的另一层含义是区域金融的研究。区域金融为一区域金融系统的集成，不仅包括各种金融机构，而且包括与此相关的区位条件、经济发展、文化和制度环境等。其研究视野除了一区域的金融系统形成演变之外，还包括区域之间金融的差异，区域间的金融联系等。我国经济学界关于金融地理的研究多属于区域金融学的范畴，主要涉及金融发展与区域经济发展关系研究（徐明圣和郭凯，2004）。例如，认为 1978～2000 年中国各地区金融发展与经济增长密切相关，金融发展差距可以部分解释各地区经济增长差异（周立和王子明，2002）。其次是金融产业区域发展差异分析。例如，通过数据揭示了全国各省、自治区、直辖市的证券市场投资的块状结构特点（田霖和金雪军，2004），探讨了河南、山西、浙江的金融成长差异，并认为区域金融成长差异的原因包括地理环境、金融人格和自组织 3 个方面（金雪军和田霖，2004）。但区域金融还有一些领域未曾涉及。

29.1.2　外部影响的金融地理

与金融机构区位研究相比，外部影响的研究比较活跃。众多的金融地理学成果涉及这一领域。也许，这正是伴随 20 世纪后期以来的经济地理学思维的转向，地理学家更加重视因果关系探索的一种表现。对外部影响的金融地理研究，主要包括以下内容。

1. 政府调节法规变化的影响

由于金融对国家经济至关重要，而金融机构又不会自觉地从政府和民众角度来运营，由此政府要么完全控制金融机构（如计划经济下的中国），要么不断制定相关法规来约束金融机构的行为。由于近几十年来，多数国家政府调节的导向是放松管制，相关文献也多涉及放松管制的影响。例如，美国在西部开拓时，由于与东部已开发地区的金融中心距离遥远，便鼓励建立地方或州域银行系统。并由此建立了相关法案（如 1927 年 McFadden Act，1933 年的 Glass-Steagall Act 等）。各州也通过相关立法限制跨州银行发展。在此背景下，形成了美国地方和州域银行系统。但到 20 世纪 70 年代，各州开始逐步放开对金融的限制，尤其是 1974 年美国联邦 Riegle-Neal Act，使得银行跨州设立分行的限制为之松绑，由此不需经由多家银行控股或各州互惠的方式，即可达成跨州经营银行业务的目的。从而带来了全国性银行系统的发展（Martin et al.，1999）。从世界角度，20世纪八九十年代以来，在诸多国家出现了金融调节法规的转变。这一浪潮始于美国和英国，而后迅速扩及其他发达国家和发展中国家。伴随政府放松控制，促进一些国家金融机构的私有化（Martin et al.，1999）。各个国家不同时段所实行的不同调节法规，会对其金融系统带来不同的空间影响。不少学者关注这一课题，发表了一些很有意义的成果（Martin et al.，1999；Clark and Wojcik，2003；Carnevalo，1996）。其中，计划经济和转型经济国家的制度对金融系统影响更为直接，也更为突出。所影响层面不仅包括国家，还包括不同尺度的区域（李小建等，2006）。

与制度相关联，国际金融地理研究中常常提及布雷顿森林体系（Bretton Woods System）术语。它是对国际金融系统具有重要影响的几个重大事件之一。其背景为1944年7月，二战中的44个同盟国在美国新罕布什尔州的布雷顿森林村召开会议，通过了《国际货币基金协定》和《国际复兴开发银行协定》，总称布雷顿森林协定。布雷顿森林体系下的汇率制度，最突出的特点就是"双挂钩"，即美元与黄金挂钩，其他货币与美元挂钩。布雷顿森林体系的建立，使国际货币金融关系领域从动荡混乱状态进入了相对稳定时期，美元作为主要国际支付手段和储备货币，在当时背景下，弥补了过去清偿能力不足，消除了影响国际间商品货币流通的各种障碍。从地理学家的角度，该体系对金融国际化，以及国际金融地理的发展、国际金融中心的形成均具有重要影响。

2. 技术变化的影响

对金融地理来说，最主要的是有关信息处理和通信方面的技术变化。包括计算、微电子、远距离通信数据处理系统（telematics）等相关技术。它们不仅改变了金融交易的方式，而且改变了货币和金融的形式以及金融机构本身的一些特性。例如，随着非实物化的进程所出现的电子和虚拟货币，以及相关的电话银行、直接借贷、电子转账、屏幕交易、计算机化的套汇交易等，使我们逐渐进入一种无货币的社会。货币实际上正在变成一种信息，在复杂的电子通信网络中传输。伴随着货币形式的变化，货币交易过程大为简便，所需时间大大缩短。不少情况下变为即时交易。由此带来了一些新的货币和金融产品的出现［包括证券化票据及其衍生性金融商品，如货币或股票的选择契约（options）、远期契约（forwards）、期货（futures）、交换选择权（swaps）等］。这些新的金融产品带来较大规模、较高风险的投资，并促进金融体系的组织结构发生变化。例如，出现大的投资主体（如保险基金、养老基金、股票基金等），产生电话"呼叫中心"，以及出现零售金融商业（Martin et al.，1999）。

除了以上从机制角度的影响之外，技术变化对金融地理学的影响还表现在其他诸多方面。例如，对传统地理因素对金融格局影响程度改变的影响、对信息对金融中心作用增强的影响、对国际金融中心增长的影响、对金融企业内部空间系统的影响、对不同金融机构关系的影响，以及对金融网点布局的影响等。

3. 经济全球化的影响

经济全球化与金融全球化关系十分密切。两者互为促进，很难分清孰因孰果。这里我们侧重经济全球化对金融地理的影响。经济全球化对金融地理有诸多方面的影响，例如：①促进区域金融多元化。经济全球化带来各国、各地区联系的加强。例如，国内市场对外开放，不可避免带来外资银行及其他金融机构的进入，促进国内、区内金融机构的多元格局。并进而促进金融机构间竞争的加剧。②对金融中心发展的影响。例如，国际跨国公司（包括国际金融企业）的中国总部集中在北京和上海布局，对这两个城市作为全国重要金融中心的控制地位，起着十分重要的作用（Zhao et al.，2004）。③促进金融全球化。以贸易、投资、服务等为主要标志的经济全球化，尤其是投资的全球化，必然带来金融的全球化。不仅各国金融联系不断加强，更重要的是，以少数全球金融中心（纽约、伦敦、东京）、一些不同等级国际金融中心为主干的全球金融体系逐步形成。④区域金融风险增加。伴随经济全球化，在给地方经济带来有利影响的同时，也带来了新的威胁。例如，东南亚金融危机所暴露出的对国家或地区金融体系的冲击，便引起了人们的高度关注。⑤出现新的金融地理形式。其中，境外金融或离岸金融便是这种新形式之一。它是 20 世纪 70 年代以来，随着经济全球化的发展和对金融交易的方便性要求的提高，为了全天候进行金融交易和逃避关税等的需要而快速发展起来（Roberts，1994）。目前，在世界金融体系中已经占有一定地位。

29.2　金融地理学主要理论问题

金融地理学在诸多领域均有一些理论贡献，但代表性的理论又不十分突出。以下根据本人所掌握的文献及其对相关问题的把握，选择其中的一些问题做分析。为以后他人研究起着“抛砖”的作用。

29.2.1　地理存在与否的辩论

伴随着技术的发展，地理区位对经济活动的影响必然发生变化，这是各个经济部门均存在的问题。但是，由于金融产业的特殊性和信息技术的巨大变化，使得该部门对地理因素的讨论更具有重要意义。地理存在与否的讨论源于 1992 年 O'Brien 在国际金融关系上提出的“地理已死”观点（其原意为“地理区位在国际金融关系中对经济发展状况的决定不再重要，或不如以前重要”）（O'Brien，1992）。之后，Cairncross（1997）从电子通信对距离成本影响角度，提出与此类似的“距离已死”观点。地理学家多数不同意这一观点。认为该观点夸大了技术变化和全球化对空间的影响。尽管新技术和全球化对传统区位因素的影响有所改变，但地理区位对全球金融业的布局仍起着重要作用。广泛引用的论据是金融活动仍在向某些区位集中（Martin et al.，1999）。在相关的解释中，除了有人认为在这些中心布局更接近客户和基金外（Martin et al.，1999），还有研究强调诸如社会文化联系等根植性的作用（Martin et al.，1999；Agnes，2000），以及信息获得性的影响（Zhao et al.，2004）。该问题仍是金融地理学中的一个热点问题。研究的重点侧重于在新的条件下地理对金融中心的影响及金融地理差异的深层机理。

29.2.2　金融变化对区域经济的影响

前已述及，金融与区域经济关系十分密切。除了金融本身就是区域经济的一个重要部门之外，金融还以其产品（如资金等）的独特性质对区域经济产生重要影响。在这一课题上进行具体的理论研究，又涉及诸多侧面。例如，①金融发展与区域经济关系的量化研究。不少学者认识到两者关系密切，并做了一些经验研究。但究竟在某一区域两者量化关系如何？随着经济发展阶段的变化这种关系又是如何变化的？以中国河南为例的研究曾揭示经济发展与银行网点数量的关系（李小建等，2006），但缺乏广泛意义上的比较。②金融体系发展包括金融国际化对区域经济差异的影响。在这方面，从不同的角度，有一些不同的结果。例如，有人认为金融全球化是避免未来收入差别增加的一种重要途径（Clark，2003）。但其他研究则指出金融系统的变化加强了区域发展的不平衡（Martin et al.，1999）。③特殊地区的金融问题。金融地理长期以来多关注全球金融体系、国际及全国金融中心等，忽视金融薄弱地区的研究。近来，一些文献开始关注边远地区和大城市中的金融薄弱区（或被排斥在外的金融地区，即 deprived area）（Klagge and Martin，2005；Marshall，2004）。这些研究通过国际比较，指出一些国家（如英国）金融过度集中对一些地区带来明显不利，但并未引起相关国家政府的高度关注。但总的来说，相对优势较为薄弱地区的金融问题仍是研究的薄弱领域。

29.2.3 区域金融系统演化模式研究

这是金融地理的重要理论侧面之一。基于一些发达国家的实践过程，英国学者 Dow 总结了伴随着其组织变化的银行业空间演化过程。即银行业空间系统演化分为 6 个阶段：①服务当地社区的金融中介；②经营者信誉带来市场拓展但仍限于本地；③银行系统向全国发展；④依据国内向海外拓展；⑤在全国市场上与非银行金融机构竞争；⑥放松管制带来国际竞争并最终导致相关活动在金融中心集中（Dow，1999）。该过程可概括为，银行系统开始于当地或区域银行阶段，通过全国性银行的分支分散阶段和金融活动在特殊区位集中形成区域性和全国性金融中心阶段，达到国际发展和向国际金融中心集中阶段（Martin et al.，1999）。作者认为，该演化模式的核心内容是银行组织形式的空间拓展和金融活动的地理集中。无疑，该理论构架对后人起了重要的奠基作用。但是，有以下几点需在后续研究中给予特殊关注。一是不同的背景下模式的演化会有很大差别。例如，完全计划经济下的银行业空间演化一开始就是国家银行阶段，而转型时期的特殊政策又会导致演化过程发生特殊改变。二是，不同地理尺度的银行演变也会有所不同，如对中国国内的大区、省和地市的研究，在同一时间段内，也可能会有所差别（Li and Zhou，2006）。

29.2.4 金融地理的影响因素及路径依赖

金融地理的形成和变化，有诸多影响因素。例如，区域居民收入水平（Corbridge et al.，1994），经济增长状况、信息获得性（Porteous，1995），政府调节政策、银行业所使用的技术变化、经济全球化（Martin et al.，1999），社会、文化和制度因素（Leyshon and Thrift，1997）等。这些因素在不同区域，以及不同时段、不同环境条件下，对金融地理有着不同的影响。但什么条件下何种因素影响突出、这种影响可否量化并总结一般规律，还有待继续研究。另外，除了这些因素之外，是否还有新的因素，也是个研究议题。显然，与这些因素的综合相关联，路径依赖对金融体系中心-外围的形成具有重要的影响（Corbridge et al.，1994；Porteous，1995）。但也有研究对这种路径依赖提出质疑。例如，通过对德国的资本市场结构中地理研究，克拉克等认为，就公司之间拥有关系的集中度来说，德国实例并不支持路径依赖，即不断集中的趋势（Clark and Wojcik，2005）。通过该研究结果的启示，我们完全可以以科学态度，对前人的相关研究结果进行审视和批判性的验证。

29.2.5　金融全球化与地方的关系

金融全球化是金融地理学最为热衷的课题之一。金融地理学的文献多数涉及这一课题。劳拉詹南的《金融地理学》甚至开宗明义，主要关注国际金融，国内问题只有在与国际有关时才涉及（Laulajainen，2003）。在金融地理全球问题的研究中，全球化与地方的关系十分值得关注。除了经济地理学本身性质决定应对区域问题关注之外，对于发展中国家该问题又具有特殊意义。尤其是东亚国家和地区，银行业在经济结构中的地位又远大于世界其他国家（Wojcik，2000）。在理论层面，金融全球化与地方的关系可追随经济地理学中全球化与地方化的一般框架（李小建，2002）。但金融全球化中的主体跨国银行（MNBs）的跨国经营又有一些特殊之处。例如，银行内部产品联系十分密切，且产品空间移动便捷；新发展地区的信用风险对银行跨国发展影响很大；各国对银行业进入的法规又与生产性企业有所不同等。跨国银行与当地的关系比起生产性跨国公司要更为复杂。相关理论包括：空间化的马克思资本积累和货币循环理论，地方、区域、国家资本通过金融系统转向全球资本；水银理论，认为货币在全球的流动按照水银流动的规律，包括汇聚（地方性金融系统）、沿通道快速流动（金融流动）、遇阻重新汇聚（区域或全球金融中心）、有害性（金融管理不当同样有害，如 20 世纪末金融市场的网络股泡沫）等（Clark，2005）；价值链理论，认为地方金融的发展中，与金融相关联的部门的状况起着重要作用（Grote et al.，2002）。这些理论各有特点，均值得认真研究。

29.3　中国金融地理研究

中国的金融地理研究可从多方面着手。根据作者对国际文献和中国现状的了解和思考，提出以下一些研究切入点。尽管其中有些方面具有重要实践意义，但本人更强调它们的理论视角。

29.3.1　特殊环境对金融地理的影响

中国特殊的国情为金融地理学的研究提供了良好的条件。例如，近几十年来，与金融业发展相关的制度的巨大变迁远非发达国家的实际经验所及。随着我国金融体制改革的深化，金融企业运行的机制发生了深刻的变化。中国区域差异巨大，改革开放以来各地的经济发展速度又有很大不同。有一些过去相对落后的地区迅速增长，也有一些过去相对发达地区却增长缓慢（陆大道等，1997）。中国加入世界贸易组织后，经济全球化的影响逐渐加大，到2006年年底，外资银行进入中国的地区限制将被取消。尽管中国的银行业近年来技术更新十分迅速，但与发达国家的银行业相比，中国居民在接受银行服务的偏好上，仍习惯于直接的人工服务，电话银行、网络银行还未被广大消费者所接受，等等。对这些环境条件的影响，可从单一因素入手，也可选择特殊区域对所有因素进行综合研究。基于中国实例的科学分析并与国际相关结论比较，完全有可能归纳出有意义的理论结论。例如，作者曾在中国银行区域系统演化和银行业区位决定因素方面进行了一些探索（李小建等，2006；Li and Zhou，2006）。

29.3.2 全球化对区域金融系统影响

随着中国加入世界贸易组织相关协议的落实，尤其是跨国银行和其他跨国金融机构在中国经营区域限制的取消，它们将不断进入中国各个地区。这些机构对中国区域金融系统的影响，可从多方面研究。例如，全国各地全球化对区域金融系统影响的差异分析，跨国银行进入后对区域金融结构的影响，跨国银行对区域金融系统影响的演变，跨国银行与当地银行的关系分析，政府及当地社会经济条件与全球化影响的关系等。与此相关联，外资银行进入地区的空间演进过程、区域金融系统的规模与开放的关系等，也有希望做出创新成果的理论议题。从实践的角度，跨国银行的进入，可以通过竞争加快当地银行系统的现代经营进程，可提供更多的信贷渠道以利于经济的发展，当地居民可以接受更好的进入服务；但也为当地的金融系统带来竞争威胁，为政府监管带来不便。各地如何根据当地的社会经济条件，充分发挥外资金融机构进入后的有利影响，限制其不利影响，也是一项很有意义的研究。

29.3.3 行政格局与金融体系

中国传统计划经济下形成的特殊政治与经济关系，对区域金融系统产生着特殊的影响。尽管银行体制改革力图淡化两者的联系，但传统的积淀仍发生着作用。尤其是各地政府从地方经济发展角度出发，会尽力发挥其行政职能对银行业的影响。而银行的地方社会文化根植性，又会加强与当地的各种联系。所以，中国行政格局与金融系统的关系，也许当数世界上最为复杂者之一。地理学家应该抓住这种特殊现象，研究金融区与行政区的联系与矛盾、政府在区域金融体系中的特殊作用、社会文化根植性与金融联系等。从而，在区域金融体系的政治经济学研究方面提出一些创新观点。

29.3.4 金融系统与区域发展

前已述及，金融系统与区域经济的关系，中国经济学家已经做了一些很有意义的研究。研究具体展示了两者关系的密切程度。但从理论角度，两者的密切关系本已是一个无可非议的论题。在原有的研究基础上，金融系统与区域发展的关系，可以另辟蹊径，寻找学术性切入点。例如，从工业经济向知识经济演进过程中，金融对经济系统的影响会有什么样的差别？中国各地经济结构的巨大差异，正好提供了一个对此论证的良好实例。通过时空转换，有望提出具有启发意义的观点。此外，从拥有关系的区域特点上看，金融企业主体可分为当地金融企业和大区性、全国性、国际性金融企业。这些不同企业对地方经济发展的影响是否有别？有什么样的差别？与基于其他国家的研究结论有何不同？也是很有理论意义的研究。还有，金融机构服务当地经济发展的机理，并未引起地理学家的应有关注。而这一问题的研究，不仅具有明显的实用价值，其理论意义也很重要。

29.3.5 金融企业地理

从理论上讲，金融企业作为企业的一种类型，应该遵从企业地理的一般理论。但由于到目前为止对金融企业研究较少，且近些年来金融企业发展迅速，随着制度、技术变化和全球化进程的加快，出现了一些新的特点。因此，用 20 世纪形成的一些企业地理理论套用到金融企业，并不一定符合实际。这也引出对金融企业地理研究的需要。其研究议题可以包括：①金融企业组织演变与空间扩张的关系，以及其空间扩张的一般规律；②金融企业组织结构与环境的关系，尤其是不同环境是如何影响金融企业组织结构的；③金融企业内部不同组织部门的区位特点，包括总部、研究机构、区域总部、分支机构等的区位影响因素；④不同所有关系的金融企业的空间结构差异，如跨国金融企业，中国国内的国有金融机构、股份制银行、私有银行，以及许多地方性金融机构（如城市银行、农村信用社等）的空间结构差异。在这些研究中，均可以与一般的公司地理理论进行比较，从而发现其独特之处。

总之，金融地理学在经济地理学中具有十分重要的意义。甚至有的学者认为 21 世纪应该是金融资本占主导的世纪，因此，经济地理学家应像 20 世纪关注工业地理一样来关注金融地理（Clark，2005）。因此，希望中国经济地理同行，尤其是年轻学者们，以创新的思维，勇于探索这个新领域，共同构建能在国际产生影响的中国金融地理学。

参考文献

金雪军，田霖. 2004. 金融地理学：国外地理学科研究新动向. 经济地理，24（6）：721～725

金雪军，田霖. 2004. 金融地理学视角下区域金融成长差异的案例研究. 河南师范大学学报，31（2）：37～40

李小建. 1999. 经济地理学. 北京：高等教育出版社

李小建. 2002. 公司地理论（修订版）. 北京：科学出版社

李小建，周雄飞，卫春江，等. 2006. 发展中地区银行业空间系统变化：以河南省为例. 地理学报，61（4）：414～424

陆大道，薛凤璇，等. 1997. 1997 中国区域发展报告. 北京：商务印书馆

田霖，金雪军. 2004. 金融地理学视角下的证券市场投资潜力分析. 世界地理研究，13（1）：102～108

武魏，刘卫东，刘毅. 2005. 西方金融地理学研究进展及其启示. 地理科学进展，24（4）：19～27

徐明圣，郭凯. 2004. 我国区域金融发展与区域经济增长关系的实证分析. 财经问题研究，（7）：26～32

赵晓斌，王垣. 2002. 中国加入 WTO 对国内金融中心区域重组的影响. 国外城市规划，（5）：31～37

周立，王子明. 2002. 中国各地区金融发展与经济增长实证分析：1978-2000. 金融研究，（10）：1～13

Agnes P. 2000. The "end of geography" in financial services? Local embeddedness and territorialization in the interest rate swaps industry. Economic Geography，76（4）：347～366

Cairncross F. 1997. The Death of Distance：How the Communications Revolution will Change Our Lives. London：Orion Business Books

Carnevali F. 1996. Between markets and networks：Regional banks in Italy. Business History，38（3）：84～100

Clark G L. 2002. London in the European financial services industry：locational advantage and product complementarities. Journal of Economic Geography，2：433～453

Clark G L. 2003. Pension security in the global economy：Market and national institutions in the 21st century. Environment and Planning A，35：1339～1356

Clark G L. 2005. Money flows like mercury：The geography of global finance. Geografiscka Annaler B，87（2）：99～112

Clark G L，Wojcik D. 2005. Path dependence and financial markets：The economic geography of the German model，1997～2003. Environment and Planning A，37：1769～1791

Corbridge S，Martin R，Thrift N. 1994. Money，Power，and Space. Oxford：Blackwell

Dow S C. 1999. The stages of banking development and the spatial evolution of financial systems. In：Martin R. Money and the Space Economy. London：John Wiley & Sons

Grote M H，Lo V，Harrschar E S. 2002. A value chain approach to financial centres：The case ofFrankfurt. Tijdschrift voor Economische en Sociale Geografie，93（4）：412～423

Klagge B，Martin R. 2005. Decentralized versus centralized financial systems：Is there a case for local capital markets? Journal of Economic Geography，5（4）：387～421

Laulajainen R. 2003. Financial Geography-A Banker's View. London：Routledge

Leyshon A，Thrift N. 1997. Money Space：Geographies of Monetary Transformation. London：Routledge

Li X J，Zhou X F. 2006. Institutional reforms and the spatial evolution of banking system in a less developed region of China since 1978. Working Paper Series，Oxford University Center for the Environment，May（WPG 06～12）

Marshall J N. 2004. Financial institutions in disadvantaged areas：A comparative analysis of policies encouraging financial inclusion inBritain and the United States. Environment and Planning A，36：241～261

Martin R. 1999. Money and the Space Economy. London：John Wiley & Sons

Myrdal G. 1957. Economic Theory and Underdevelopment Region. London：Gerald Duckworth

O Brien R. 1992. Global Financial Integration：The End of Geography. London：Royal Institute of International Affairs

Porteous D J. 1995. The Geography of Finance：Spatial Dimensions of Intermediary Behaviour. Aldershot：Avebury

Roberts S. 1994. Fictitious capital，fictitious spaces：The geography of offshore financial flows. In：Corbridge S，Martin R，Thrift N J. Money，Power and Space. Oxford：Blackwell

Wojcik D. 2000. The East Asian banking sector：Overweight. Environment and Planning A，32：4～8

Zhao X B，Zhang L，Wang D T. 2004. Determining factor of the development of a national financial center：The case of China. Geoforum，35：577～592

第30章 发展中地区银行业空间系统变化

本章基于对中国发展中地区的河南省的第一手调查数据，对经济水平较低、受外部影响较小，但增长迅速的内陆省份银行业空间系统变化进行了量化分析和解释。结果表明，与国际上发达国家相同，中国发展中地区的国有银行业逐步向中心城市集中。其中，作为区域中心的地级城市的地位上升最为突出。其形成原因主要与制度变化有关；而区域经济的发展差异又是促进该趋势的直接诱因。这一观点通过混合OLS模型模拟得到证明。城市内部的银行业区位变化具有一些与发达国家的不同之处。区域经济快速发展带来了中心城市的迅速拓展。同时，经济结构调整又带来了城市内不同地区经济发展水平的变化。由此形成了银行业区位的不断扩散，新兴快速增长的地区迅速吸引了一批银行的建立。对郑州市58家银行网点的调查表明，在1978年之前，银行网点设立十分遵循计划体制的安排；而在1979年以后，邻近地段"人均收入水平高"决定着相当一部分银行网点的布局。这从微观角度佐证了河南省的分析结论。金融系统的集中格局为非中心地区经济发展带来的不利影响，应该给予关注。

30.1 研究背景

市场经济下，银行区位与区域经济发展具有密切关联，全球化、私有化、政府放松管制和技术变化，带来了全球及许多国家金融系统的空间变化。在中国，改革开放以来的市场化进程，不断冲击着计划经济体制下的国有银行管理模式。为了应对加入世界贸易组织后外资银行进入带来的激烈竞争，国有银行进行着一系列面向市场的改革。这种特殊的制度背景，再加上经济的快速发展且地理差异明显，为研究银行业空间系统的变化，提供了难得的实例。本章基于对中国河南的调查数据，对银行业空间系统的变化做一量化分析和解释。并将其发现与国际上的文献相比较，分析中国特定环境条件下的特殊地理过程。

货币和金融业是揭示空间经济的主要切入点之一。20世纪80年代中期以来，国际上有不少学者关注货币、金融业区位与空间经济的研究，发表了一批很有分量的成果(Corbridge et al.，1994；Dow，1999；Leyshon and Thrift，1997；Martin，1999；Laulajainen，2003)。这些成果涉及金融地理学的诸多方面，其中，银行业空间系统的演化，作为金融地理学中的重要研究论题之一，不断吸引着众多学者的关注。金融地理学领域中的重要文献，不少涉及这一论题（Corbridge et al.，1994；Dow，1999；Leyshon and Thrift，1997；Martin，1999）。基于欧美发达国家实例的一些研究表明，在全球化快速发展的大背景下，世界银行业空间系统正在发生新的变化（Martin，1999）。英国、美国和欧洲其他一些国家，均出现金融服务业逐步集中分布现象。国际性金融中心（如纽约、伦敦）的地位在不断加强（Sassen，2001）；国家内部金融业也趋于向中心城市集聚。在这些金融业集聚的城市内部，银行高层管理机构或继续向一些区位集中（如纽约、法兰克福），或形成新的金融区（如伦敦）。

这种现象的形成有多种原因，主要包括：①经济全球化使银行企业从全球（大区域）视野寻找其竞争优势区位，由此促使具有这种优势的区位成为众多银行公司的集中地。②先进的通信技术加强了银行内部的密切联系，使中心区位的控制作用进一步加强；同时，客户对电子化服务的接受，也带来了银行网点的布局革命。③近年来一些发达国家对银行业管制的宽松化，从制度上改变了银行业区域分割局面，使企业从更大范围考虑市场；而国有银行的私有化和所有制多元化，带来银行业的竞争加剧，从而促进企业进一步提高效率开拓市场，这也在一定程度上鼓励其集聚布局。

与国际上十分活跃的状况相比，金融地理学在我国国内的研究尚属刚刚起步。一些学者已经认识到金融地理学研究的重要性，开始介绍国际相关研究状况，并结合中国实际，在信息对金融中心影响（赵晓斌等，2002）、区域金融发展影响因素（金雪军和田霖，2004）、区域金融中心重组（赵晓斌和王坦，2002）等方面做了一些有益的探索，但还未见到银行业空间系统研究的相关成果。

中国金融业的发展处在与发达国家既相似又有不同的背景之中。其相似之处表现为：①中国的开放政策加快了经济活动全球化的进程，外资银行在一些特殊区域（如上海的浦东等）建立分支机构已有十余年的历史，中国银行也不断向国际市场拓展。按照2001年11月中国加入世界贸易组织时的承诺，中国将在5年时间内，分批允许国外银行在国内城市建立其分支机构，经营人民币业务（段永宽，2003）。②伴随着经济实力的增强和国际交流的拓展，中国的银行在技术手段更新上也发生了快速变化。网络技术正在影响着银行内部和外部的联系。③1978年以来，中国银行业运营的政策环境发生了，并正在发生着较大变化，它们深刻影响着银行业空间系统的变化（段永宽，2003）。

在以上相似的背景之下，中国银行业的空间系统运营环境又有一些独特之处：①制度的巨大变迁远非发达国家的实际经验所及。20世纪80年代以来，中国的经济体制逐渐由计划经济转向市场经济。在传统的计划经济体制下，银行被作为一种准行政性的机构，其网点的设置与行政管理系统高度一致，省、市、县对应着相应的分行、支行。90年代之后，市场经济体制逐渐引入，银行业开始走向市场，银行的商业功能逐渐显现出来。②中国区域差异巨大，改革开放以来各地的经济发展速度又有很大不同。有一些过去相对落后的地区迅速增长，也有一些过去相对发达的地区却增长缓慢（陆大道等，1997）。区域经济格局的这种变化在很大程度上引导着银行业空间系统的变化。③虽然中国加入世界贸易组织后，经济全球化的影响逐渐加大，但到2004年，外资银行还未进入中国大多数地区。也就是说，除沿海地区一些城市外，中国大多数地区外资银行对国内银行的竞争还是潜在的。④尽管中国的银行业近年来技术更新十分迅速，但与发达国家的银行业相比，在银行网络整合和技术升级上还存在一定差距（陈威和唐齐鸣，2003）。中国居民，尤其是内陆地区居民在接受银行服务的偏好上，仍习惯于直接的人工服务，电话银行、网络银行在有些地区还未被某些消费者所接受。

中国银行业运营的独特背景，会带来相应的银行业空间系统变化的独特之处。由于中国中部地区受全球化的影响远小于沿海地区，技术变化对银行业格局变化的影响也有滞后，银行业空间系统变化更大程度上反映了制度和区域经济格局变化的影响。本章选择中部地区的河南省为例，对近50多年来银行业的空间系统变化加以分析，重点揭示在这种变化背后制度和经济发展的特殊作用。提出不同于发达国家案例的政治经济学解释（Polese and Shearmur，2004），丰富国际学术界的相关讨论。

30.2　研究区域与数据来源

30.2.1　研究区域与银行选择

本章选择河南作为研究区域，主要基于以下几方面的原因：①位于中部地区，经济发展水平较低。2003年人均GDP为7570元，在全国位居中下等地位，仅略高于中部6省（河南、湖北、湖南、安徽、江西、山西）的平均值7256元（中国国家统计局，2004）。②外资数量少，传统上受计划经济影响较深。河南引进的外资数量在全国处于较低水平。1983～2003年河南实际利用外资数量在中部地区还不足湖北的1/2，仅略高于经济规模远小于此的山西和安徽。2003年河南的外贸依存度为中部地区最低（中国国家统计局，2004，1999）。③近几年经济增长迅速。1996～2003年河南GDP年均增长率为13.1%，尤其是1999～2003年来，年均GDP增长率高达13.5%。明显高于全国平均水平，居中部6省之首（中国国家统计局，2004）。较低经济水平、较快经济增长、特殊的制度变迁使得河南成为研究发展中地区银行业空间系统变化的一个很好案例。

四大国有银行（中国工商银行、中国银行、中国建设银行、中国农业银行）是1949年以来中国发展历史最久的银行，它们至今仍是中国（尤其是发展中地区）占主导地位的银行。以河南为例，2002年和2003年四大国有银行资产规模分别占全省银行机构总和的52%和45%，存贷款比重分别占全省总量的62%、50%、60%、49%（表30.1）。

表30.1　2002～2003年河南省四大国有银行所占地位　（单位：亿元人民币，%）

项目	2002年		2003年		2002年		2003年	
	资产额	所占比重	资产额	所占比重	存款比重	贷款比重	存款比重	贷款比重
中国农业银行	1127.61	14	1204.82	12	17	17	17	17
中国银行	697.58	9	817.65	8	9	7	10	7
中国建设银行	876.84	11	1001.28	10	14	8	13	8
中国工商银行	1407.15	18	1551.32	15	22	18	20	17
四大国有银行	4109.18	52	4575.07	45	62	50	60	49
股份制银行	829.34	11	1303.47	13	13	9	15	12
其他机构	2894.79	37	4263.07	42	25	41	25	39

注：股份制银行包括交通银行、中信实业银行、光大银行、广东发展银行、招商银行、浦东发展银行等。其他机构包括全省城市商业银行、市级城市信用社、农村信用社，以及农业发展银行、国家开发银行等。

资料来源：中国人民银行济南分行编．中国人民银行济南分行金融年鉴2003，2004．北京：中国财政经济出版社，2003，2004。

30.2.2 数据获取

1. 调研1950年以来的区位数据

2004年7月，作者通过对河南省银行监管局负责人和相关部门的访问，了解河南省银行业体制沿革和区位变化的背景，并获取1950年以来，河南省各主要银行的所有网点的区位数据。

2. 访谈四大银行决策人员了解区位变化概况

2004年7月，我们访问了四大国有银行负责人，了解相关银行的空间系统变化概况，以及他们作为银行经营的决策者如何考虑网点区位及区位变化。这些高层信息对具体网点的调查提供了参照。

3. 抽样调查网点区位决定因素

2004年7月，按照12%左右的比例，随机抽样选取了郑州市四大国有银行的50家网点。随后，考虑到一些网点集中地段的特殊情况（如郑州市二七商圈、文化路北段、经三路等），又在这些地段的国有银行共增加了8家网点，使得总计调查网点增至58家（表30.2）。

表30.2 河南省四大国有银行的网点样本分布

银行	网点总数	样本数	百分比/%
中国工商银行	143	20	14.0
中国农业银行	105	13	12.4
中国银行	68	11	16.2
中国建设银行	107	14	13.1
总计	423	58	13.7

2004年7～8月，作者与研究生一起对所选取的网点进行了调查，访谈对象为网点负责人。之前，根据对四大国有银行决策人员和4家不同银行网点的访谈，设计了调查问卷。问卷包括银行基本情况、该网点的区位选择因素、经营状况、存在问题等。根据回答情况，利用SPSS软件进行分析处理，作为研究的主要依据数据。

在数据调查的基础上，利用ArcGIS系统下的河南省和郑州市的空间数据，建立了四大国有银行的区位数据。其中，在郑州市的银行网点进行空间定位时，又用电话进行了其具体位置的核实。根据这些结果，形成了四大国有银行网点的空间分布图（图30.1，图30.3）。在研究中，根据数据情况对河南省的分析采用了规范计量分析法，而对郑州市的分析采用了问卷调查实证分析法。在研究结论上力求使两者互相印证。

30.3 银行业空间系统的变化

30.3.1 河南省银行业网点的区域变化

银行业体制改革为其空间系统的变化提供了基本背景。1949年以来，中国银行业体制变化可大致分为 4 个阶段：①1949～1978 年为完全计划经济下的“大一统”国家银行阶段（全国由中国人民银行集中经营）；②1979～1985 年为改革开放初始环境下的国有银行专业化分化阶段（四家国有银行相继成立）；③1986～1992 年为专业银行为主体的银行运营阶段；④1993 年以来为社会主义市场经济下的商业银行发展阶段。在一段时间内，不同银行之间曾具有专业分别。但进入商业化之后，这种分别逐渐淡化，再加上不同银行的细化分析结果对银行本身较为敏感，故本章只做四大国有银行区位变化的总体分析。由于中国工商银行的前身为中国人民银行，故 1979 年之前的中国人民银行经营网点也包括在分析之中。

河南省第一家国有银行（中国人民银行）建立于 1951 年。从 20 世纪 70 年代末到 80 年代中期，四大专业银行才逐步建立起来。其中，中国人民银行的经营性机构逐步转属中国工商银行。50 多年来，河南省四大国有银行的空间系统变化具有以下特点：①网点数量逐步增加，影响范围逐步外扩。四家银行新增网点的数量在 1949～1978 年，平均每年 8.0 家，逐步增加到 1979～1985 年的 93.9 家和 1986～1992 年的 228.4 家。1993 年以后，其他银行的进入对其带来了一定的竞争，但每年仍为 162.8 家。②地级城市在四家银行中的地位不断上升，县及县以下区域的地位则持续下降。地级城市银行业网点的数量在全省的比例由 1949～1978 年的 14.7%，上升到 1979～1985 年的 26.8%、1986～1992 年的 42.6%，以及 1993～2003 年的 56.8%；后者则相应地由 69.8%分别下降到 66.2%、48.9%和 31.7%。③省会城市（郑州）的地位先降后升。改革开放之初的几年，其拥有的银行网点由过去的 15.5%下降到了 7.0%；之后，逐步增至 1986～1992 年的 8.5%和 1993～2003 年的 11.5%（表 30.3）。应该指出，1979 年郑州市地位的下降在很大程度上是由中国农业银行的建立引起的。该银行主要面向农业，其网点区位多数位于城市郊区、县城或乡镇所在地。1979～1985 年河南省郑州以外建立的农业银行网点有 344 家，占四大国有银行新建网点总数的 50.8%。因此，排除这一特殊因素，郑州市其他银行的实际地位并没有下降。④四大国有银行空间系统地区分化显著。1978 年之前，国有银行在县域的机构设置十分均匀，不管其人口和经济实力，一个县有一个银行机构；地级城市内的金融机构虽然因工商业状况不同而有差别，但并不明显。1979 年以后，这种状况逐步改变。第一，各个行政单元之间的银行网点数量出现明显差异：除省会之外的地级行政单元中，到 2003 年年底，银行网点最多的洛阳达 387 个，是数量最少的鹤壁市的 4.7 倍；考虑人口因素后，三门峡、焦作两市每万人拥有的网点数分别达 0.80 和 0.78，而商丘、周口两市则分别为 0.22 和 0.23。第二，地级中心城市与所辖县域之间的网点数量比例出现明显差别：多数城市的地位不断增强（如洛阳市 1979～1985 年新建银行网点市区与所辖县域的比例为 27.5∶72.5，到 1986～1992 年和 1993～2003 年分别变为 69.4∶30.6 和 91.0∶9.0），但也有少数增长并不明显（如周口市 1979～1985 年新建银行网点市区与所辖县域的比例为 38.6∶61.4，到 1986～1992 年和 1993～2003 年分别变为 31.5∶68.5 和 39.1∶60.9；三门峡市的情况与此类似）（图 30.1）。⑤从体制的角度，省会城市为河南省四大国有银行的总部所在地，地级城市为各相应的分行驻地，县城则有各相应的支行。省行与地市分行、县支行之间，依次具有等级控制关系。这种状况自从这些银行成立以来一直延续着。

表 30.3　1951～2003 年河南省四大国有银行新建网点的区位（单位：个，%）

项目	1951～1978 年	1979～1985 年	1986～1992 年	1993～2003 年
省会城市	35（15.5）	46（7.0）	136（8.5）	206（11.5）
地级城市	33（14.7）	176（26.8）	681（42.6）	1018（56.8）
县域	157（69.8）	435（66.2）	782（48.9）	567（31.7）
总计	225（100.0）	657（100.0）	1599（100.0）	1791（100.0）

资料来源：作者调查。

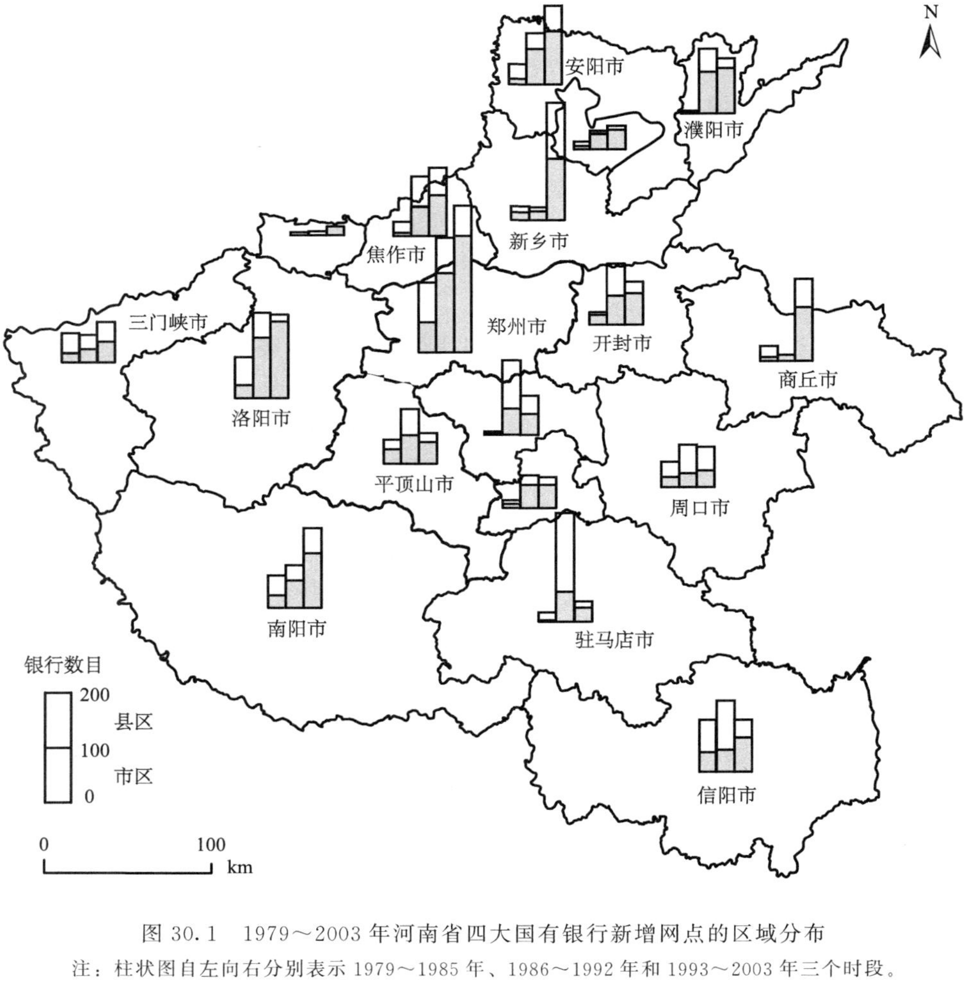

图 30.1　1979～2003 年河南省四大国有银行新增网点的区域分布

注：柱状图自左向右分别表示 1979～1985 年、1986～1992 年和 1993～2003 年三个时段。

资料来源：作者调查。

30.3.2 中心城市银行业网点的变化

1. 1979 年以来网点数量迅速增加

1951～1978 年，郑州市建立的银行网点总数仅仅为 35 家，平均每年 1 家。仅仅相当于 1992 年一年的新建网点数。其中，1954 年增加最多（8 家），而很多年份（如 20 世纪 60 年代中期和 1971～1978 年）受制于当时的政治经济环境甚至没有新增一家网点。

1979 年以后，郑州市网点数量增加十分迅速。至 1997 年的 19 年间，共有 383 家网点先后建立，是前 28 年总和的 11 倍。平均每年增加约 20 家。其中，每年新建网点超过 20 家的年份主要集中在 90 年代。增加最多的年份为 1993 年，达 82 家。这与当时经济快速发展的大背景，尤其是着力发展中心城市的策略有一定关联。21 世纪来，由于四大国有银行内部实施的“扁平化”机构改革（即减少中间机构，撤销储蓄所），以及数家股份制银行进入对市场的分割，四大国有银行网点数量基本处于稳定状态（图 30.2）。

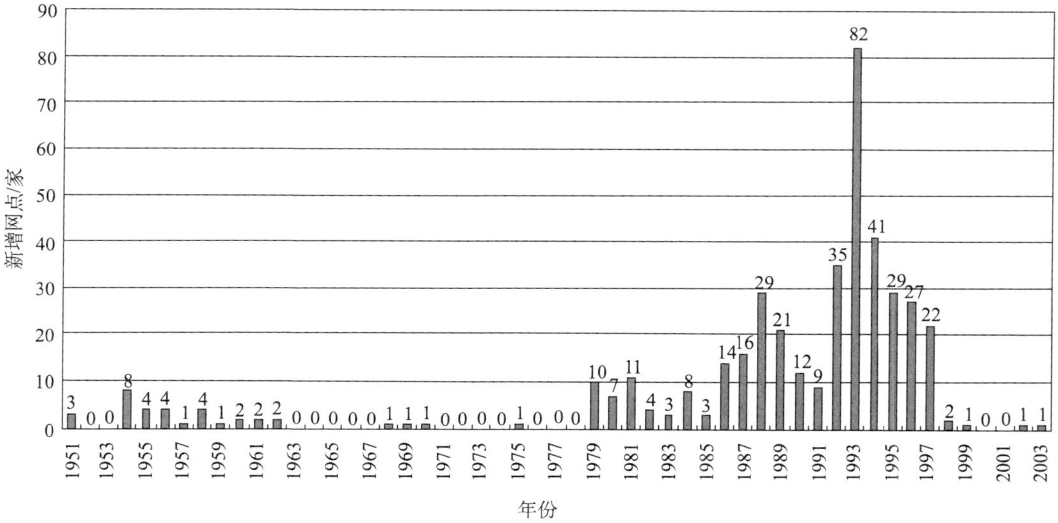

图 30.2 1951～2003 年郑州市四大国有银行新增网点变化

资料来源：作者调查。

2. 网点布局呈局部集中和总体扩散特点

据图 30.3，郑州市四大国有银行网点的区位变化表现为：1978 年之前数量少且主要集中于市区内的主要干道上，靠近当时的主要国有工厂和行政区政府区位，沿建设路、棉纺路、金水路形成零星线状格局；1979～1985 年，增加网点除了市中心区位外，由于中国农业银行的经营，有一部分（20%）位于郊区行政中心所在地，从而形成片状散布格局；1986～1992 年银行区位散布各主要街区和主要道路，且围绕着人口聚集区逐步形成簇群式格局；1993 年以来，内部的簇群化继续加强，但开始随城市外延而向外扩展，高收入区、大客户区（如金水路、黄河路及其周围地区，大学路、陇海路一带）银行网点更加集中化，形成东西两大片集中区。

a.1978年

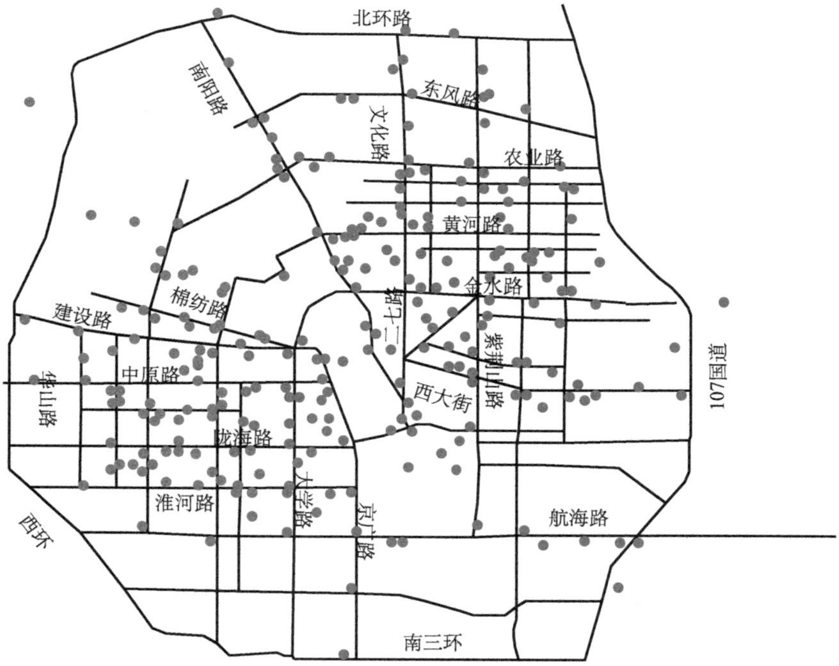

b.2003年

图 30.3　1951～2003 年郑州市四大国有银行网点区位分布

资料来源：作者调查。

30.4　银行业空间系统变化的宏观影响因素

河南银行业空间系统的变化，是多种因素共同影响的结果。其中，如前述分析，制度和区域经济差异起着更为重要的作用。1951～1978 年，行政因素在银行系统空间变化中起决定性作用，这一作用我们定义为区域行政效应或行政捆绑效应；1979 年以后，经济因素在银行系统空间变化中起决定性作用，这一作用我们定义为区域经济效应或经济“捆绑”效应。

30.4.1　理论分析

1979 年之前银行机构的设立与行政区划严格关联。银行不能根据自己经营需要设立机构，因此行政单位的区位分布在很大程度上决定了银行网点的区位分布。或者说，任何一个区域的银行网点的数量在很大程度上由行政单位的数量决定，银行网点的数量与行政单位的数量高度正相关。因此，区域银行网点函数可设定为

$$N = N(A), \quad N'(A) > 0 \tag{30.1}$$

式中，N 为区域内银行网点数量；A 为区域内行政单位数量。

1979 年以后逐步放松了行政区划对银行设点的约束（放松了行政捆绑），银行有越来越多的选址自由，银行选址越来越注重利益目标，行政捆绑逐步被经济“捆绑”所取代。相应的，区域内银行网点的数量不再是行政单位的函数，而是经济变量的函数。由此可以设定，区域 GDP 是决定区域内网点数量的主要因素，且银行网点的数量与 GDP 正相关，区域银行网点函数为

$$N = N(Y), \quad N'(Y) > 0 \tag{30.2}$$

式中，N 为区域内银行网点数量；Y 为区域 GDP。式（30.2）可以由银行企业与银行产业的行为推导出来（见附录）。式（30.2）的含义是，从地段来看，区域 GDP 的分布密度决定了银行网点的分布密度；从时段来看，区域 GDP 的分布密度的变化决定了银行网点的分布密度的变化。

30.4.2　经验分析

为了验证以上理论分析结果，我们利用《河南统计年鉴》中河南各相关区域的 GDP 数据，以及所调查的河南省 18 个地市、3 个年度（1985 年、1992 年和 2003 年）的银行网点数据，使用 Eviews 软件，分别用混合 OLS 和固定效应法 FE 做了计量模拟。在使用混合 OLS 时，模型设定为

$$N_{it} = \beta_0 + \beta_1 Y_{it} + \beta_2 A_{it} + \beta_3 D_{03} Y_{it} + u_{it} \tag{30.3}$$

式中，N_{it} 表示 i 地区 t 年的四大国有银行网点数；Y_{it} 表示 i 地区 t 年的 GDP；A_{it} 表示 i 地区 t 年的县级行政区划数；D_{03} 为虚拟变量，2003 年取 1，1985 年和 1992 年取 0。增设这一变量的原因是在 1992 年以后四大国有银行以外的其他银行进入银行系统，到

2003 年这些银行已有一定份额。据式（30.3）得到的回归结果（表 30.4）可概括出两个重要结论。

表 30.4 混合 OLS 模拟结果（1）

（被解释变量：四大国有银行网点数 N；观测个数为 54）

解释变量	系数	t 统计量	P 值
C	5.512170	0.305534	0.7612
Y	1.458452	6.384285	0.0000
A	2.043982	0.987717	0.3280
$D_{03}Y$	−0.948898	−4.570662	0.0000
$R^2=0.849278$		$F=93.91214$	

结论 1，决定因素的转变。1985 年以后，国民收入对银行布点有显著影响（Y 对应的 t 统计量很大），行政区划对银行布点无显著影响（A 对应的 t 统计量很小），行政捆绑已经被经济捆绑所取代。

结论 2，影响程度的转变。1992 年以后，国民收入对四大国有银行布点仍有显著影响，但影响程度明显减弱（$D_{03}Y$ 对应的 t 统计量反映了这一事实）。

由于行政区划的影响不显著，去掉该变量后的回归结果如表 30.5 所示，依据该结果可得出 1985 年和 1992 年的回归方程式（30.4）以及 2003 年的回归方程式（30.5）。两式的含义为：在 1985 年或 1992 年，GDP 每增加 1 个亿，国有银行就增加约 1.6 个网点，在 2003 年，国有银行仅仅增加约 0.5 个网点，这是由于 1992 年以后其他银行的进入对四大国有银行产生了明显的挤出效应。

表 30.5 混合 OLS 模拟结果（2）

（被解释变量：四大国有银行网点数 N；观测个数为 54）

解释变量	系数	t 统计量	P 值
C	19.65033	1.789853	0.0794
Y	1.574200	8.029594	0.0000
$D_{03}Y$	−1.047130	−5.747459	0.0000
$R^2=0.846337$		$F=140.4477$	

$$N=19.7+1.6Y \tag{30.4}$$

$$N=19.7+0.5Y \tag{30.5}$$

以上两式，混合 OLS 模型给出的拟合优度达 0.85，可信度较高。但为了防止因遗漏重要的解释变量而出现谬误，考虑式（30.3）中应包含各地区不同而又不随时间而变的非观测变量 F_i，方程（30.3）变为

$$N_{it}=\beta_0+\beta_1 Y_{it}+\beta_2 A_{it}+\beta_3 D_{03} Y_{it}+F_i+u_{it} \tag{30.6}$$

对式（30.6）取关于时间的差分：

$$\Delta N_{it} = \beta_1 \Delta Y_{it} + \beta_2 \Delta A_{it} + \beta_3 D_{03} \Delta Y_{it} + \Delta u_{it} \qquad (30.7)$$

用 OLS 对式（30.7）进行估计，得到固定效应模型分析结果（表 30.6），该结果进一步证实了结论 1（ΔY 和 ΔA 对应的 t 值反映了区域经济影响显著和行政区划影响不显著）和结论 2，并使结论 2 的含义更加清晰（当 D_{03} 取 1 时，ΔY 对应的是 2003 年 GDP 与 1992 年 GDP 的差额，$D_{03}\Delta Y$ 对应的 t 值反映了在这段时间内区域经济影响程度显著下降）。

表 30.6　固定效应模型模拟结果

（被解释变量：四大国有银行网点数 ΔN；观测个数为 54）

解释变量	系数	t 统计量	P 值
ΔY	1.816892	10.04108	0.0000
ΔA	−2.691692	−0.406377	0.6862
$D_{03}\Delta Y$	−1.525994	−8.269501	0.0000
R^2=0.510161		修正 R^2=0.490952	

注：取差分后观察个数本应该减少，但我们在这里增加了 1978 年的数据。由于是取差分，差分数据反映的是 1978 年以后的变化。

30.5　银行区位选择的微观因素

在对郑州市 58 家银行网点的调查中，我们列举了 10 个微观区位选择因素（表 30.7）。每个因素对样本网点选址影响的重要程度用 5 分制来表示：5 代表最重要，4 代表重要，3 代表一般，2 代表不重要，1 代表无关。在调查中，让网点负责人对每一因素进行重要性打分，数据整理后，得到区位影响因素的重要性评估。

表 30.7　郑州市四大国有银行网点区位影响因素（58 家样本）　（单位：%）

区位影响因素	无关	不重要	一般	重要	最重要
交通便利	5.2	5.2	10.3	53.4	25.9
地租、水电、人力成本	5.2	44.8	25.9	19.0	5.2
网点的可获得性	19.0	31.0	25.9	20.7	3.4
靠近机关、企事业单位	10.3	31.0	12.1	25.9	20.7
人均收入水平高	8.6	13.8	15.5	17.2	44.0
靠近商业、交易中心、餐饮娱乐场所	22.4	20.7	19.0	5.2	32.8
政府区域开发政策导向	43.1	17.2	13.8	17.2	8.6
模仿因素	70.1	12.1	6.9	10.3	0
计划体制下的行政命令	60.3	17.2	5.2	12.1	5.2
靠近居民点	15.5	12.1	15.5	22.4	34.5

30.5.1 微观区位选择因素的总体分析

根据对 58 家银行网点的调查结果分析（表 30.7），在 10 个影响银行网点选址的微观因素中："交通便利，人均收入水平高，靠近居民点，靠近机关、企事业单位，靠近商业、交易中心、餐饮娱乐场所"五个因素是银行选址时较为重要的影响因素。认为其重要和很重要的占整个样本网点的百分比分别为 79.3%、61.2%、56.9%、46.6%、37%。十分明显，这些因素均直接或间接与银行客户数量和规模有关。

而对"地租、水电、人力成本，网点的可获得性，政府区域开发政策导向，模仿因素，计划体制下的行政命令"等因素，多数银行网点均认为不重要或无关。认为其不重要和无关占整个样本网点的百分比分别为 50%、50%、50.3%、82.2%和 77.5%。这些因素之所以对银行区位影响不大，主要是因为，银行占地空间有限，地租、水电所占成本比例很低；人员的可流动性和网点的可获得性均很困难，故在选址时考虑不多；银行在政府主导的开发区中，一般只有一家分支机构，政府区域开发政策的导向对其整体没有很大影响；被调查银行网点中改革开放后，尤其是在 20 世纪 90 年代以后建立的占多数，故在总体上计划体制下的政策对其产生的影响便显得十分微弱。

30.5.2 微观区位选择因素的时段差异

由于中国近 50 多年来银行业运营环境以及银行企业本身的性质变化很大，分析不同时段银行网点区位选择原因便具有特殊意义。为此，将被调查网点分为 1978 年之前、1979～1992 年、1993 年后三个时段进行进一步分析（表 30.8）。结果发现，有些区位因素在各个时段均起重要作用；还有一些因素，在不同时段其重要性发生明显的变化。

表 30.8 分时段各影响因素分析（认为重要和最重要的网点数量及占总量的百分比）

影响因素	1951～1978 年		1979～1992 年		1993～2003 年	
	数量/个	所占比重/%	数量/个	所占比重/%	数量/个	所占比重/%
交通便利	4	80	19	82.6	23	76.7
地租、水电、人力成本	1	20	4	17.3	9	30.0
网点的可获得性	0	0	6	26.1	8	26.7
靠近机关、企事业单位	1	20	10	43.3	16	53.3
人均收入水平高	0	0	15	65.2	17	56.7
靠近商业、交易中心、餐饮娱乐场所	1	20	9	39.1	12	12.4
政府区域开发政策导向	1	20	5	21.7	9	30.0
模仿因素	1	20	5	21.7	4	13.4
计划体制下的行政命令	4	80	3	13.4	3	8.7
靠近居民点	2	40	16	69.6	15	50.0

"交通便利"始终是一个十分重要的区位影响因素。在三个时段中认为重要和最重要的网点分别占各时段总样本的 80%、82.6%、76.7%。同样，"靠近居民点"和"靠

近机关、企事业单位”在三个阶段的影响也很重要。

“人均收入水平高”作为一个区位影响因素，只是在改革开放之后才显出其重要影响。认为其重要和最重要的网点占总样本的比例，在 1978 年之前为 0%，之后的两个阶段迅速上升至 65.2%和 56.7%，反映出银行作为真正意义上的企业后，市场因素在银行网点选址时占据重要的地位。

与以上因素相反，“计划体制下的行政命令”因素的影响在三个时段中出现明显下降。认为重要和最重要的网点占各时段总样本的比例分别为 80%、13.4%、8.7%。这反映了在 1978 年以前的银行网点选址时，十分遵循计划体制的安排，几乎不受市场导向的影响。其后，其影响大幅减弱。

以上“人均收入水平高”和“计划体制下的行政命令”等微观因素的时段差异进一步证实了改革开放以后行政捆绑被经济捆绑所取代的宏观结论。

30.6　结论与讨论

与国际上发达国家银行业区位变化相同，中国发展中地区的国有银行业区位集中化趋势明显。改革开放以来，伴随着银行网点数量的大幅增加，银行业逐步向中心城市集中。其中，作为区域中心的地级城市的地位上升最为突出。其形成原因主要与制度变化有关。政府放松对银行区位的严格约束，是这一格局形成的前提条件。而区域经济发展的差异，又是促进其形成的直接原因。本章通过理论分析和计量模拟，证实了这一结论。

城市内部的银行业区位变化，中国发展中地区具有一些特殊之处。区域经济快速发展带来了中心城市的迅速拓展。同时经济结构调整又带来了城市内不同地区经济发展水平的变化。由此形成了银行业区位的不断扩散，新兴快速增长的地区，迅速吸引了一批银行的建立。对银行网点的调查表明，在研究时段内，“交通便利”在银行网点设立中一直具有重要影响。在 1978 年之前，银行网点设立十分遵循计划体制的安排；而在 1979 年以后，邻近地段“人均收入水平高”作为一个重要区位影响因素，决定着相当一部分银行网点的布局。

在金融系统集中化的过程中，出现了一些令人关注的问题，如中小企业，尤其是非中心区的中小企业在发展中面临一些金融困境（Klagge and Martin，2005）。这种现象在中国也已出现。金融控制的地理和制度上的集中，如贷款权限审批上移，确实对地方经济发展带来了不利，甚至经济较为发达的非中心区（如全国经济实力百强县之一的河南省巩义市）也遇到了资金获取的困难。如何恰当地处理金融系统的集中与分散的关系，应该是一个十分值得研究的课题。

银行业区位研究是金融地理学的重要内容之一，发达地区银行业区位会有一些与发展中地区不同之处，即使发展中地区之内也会因环境不同而有差异。在不同地区金融业区位研究基础上，可以总结金融业区位的一般规律，从而为建立中国特色的金融地理学奠定基础。

附录：银行网点函数的推导

假定 GDP 数量为 Y 的区域内有 N 个相同的银行网点，每个网点的利润函数如下：

$$\Pi = r\frac{Q(Y)}{N} - C\left(\frac{Q(Y)}{N}\right) \tag{30.8}$$

式中，r 为存贷款利率差额；$C(\cdot)$ 为银行企业长期成本函数；$Q(Y)$ 为存款函数。假定 $Q'(y) > 0$，即随着 GDP 的增加，存款也增加。利率由中央银行决定，是外生的，对于银行系统来说，区域 GDP 也是外生的。假定银行产业的网点个数由产业竞争决定。由于银行有布点的自由，所以竞争的结果将导致每个网点的利润为零或接近为零。零利润条件为

$$rQ(Y) = NC\left(\frac{Q(Y)}{N}\right) \tag{30.9}$$

该条件决定了区域网点数量，它是区域 GDP 的函数，即 $N(Y)$。将 $N(Y)$ 代入零利润条件得

$$rQ(Y) \equiv N(Y)C\left(\frac{Q(Y)}{N(Y)}\right) \tag{30.10}$$

据上式对参数 Y 微分，并利用零利润条件可以得

$$N'(Y) = N\frac{Q'}{Q} \tag{30.11}$$

由于 N、Q 和 Q' 均大于零，所以

$$N'(Y) > 0 \tag{30.12}$$

参考文献

陈威，唐齐鸣. 2003. 我国国有商业银行与在华外资银行比较研究. 经济师，(10)：210～211

段永宽. 2003. 加入 WTO 背景下国有商业银行深化改革与金融创新研究. 成都：西南财经大学出版社

金雪军，田霖. 2004. 金融地理学视角下区域金融成长差异的案例研究. 河南师范大学学报，31 (2)：37～40

陆大道，薛凤璇，等. 1997. 1997 中国区域发展报告. 北京：商务印书馆

赵晓斌，王坦，张晋熹，等. 2002. 信息流和“不对称信息”是金融与服务中心发展的决定因素：以中国为例. 经济地理，22 (4)：408～414

赵晓斌，王坦. 2002. 中国加入 WTO 对国内金融中心区域重组的影响. 国外城市规划，(5)：31～37

中国国家统计局. 1999. 新中国五十年统计资料汇编. 北京：中国统计出版社

中国国家统计局. 2004. 中国统计年鉴 2004. 北京：中国统计出版社

Corbridge S, Martin R, Thrift N. 1994. Money, Power, and Space. Oxford: Blackwell

Dow S C. 1999. The stages of banking development and the spatial evolution of financial systems. In: Martin R. Money and the Space Economy. London: John Wiley & Sons

Klagge B, Martin R. 2005. Decentralized versus centralized financial systems: Is there a case for local capital markets. Journal of Economic Geography, 5 (4): 387～421

Laulajainen R. 2003. Financial Geography——A Banker's View. London: Routledge

Leyshon A, Thrift N. 1997. Money Space: Geographies of Monetary Transformation. London: Routledge

Martin R. 1999. Money and the Space Economy. London: John Wiley & Sons

Polese M, Shearmur R. 2004. Culture, language, and the location of high-order service functions: The Case of Montreal and Toronto. Economic Geography, 80 (4): 329～350

Sassen S. 2001. The Global City: New York, London, Tokyo (2nd Edition). Princeton: Princeton University Press

第四篇　经济地理学的小尺度研究

第 31 章　经济地理学研究中的尺度

尺度在地理学研究中具有十分重要的作用。但不同的分支学科对尺度的强调和运用又有所不同。自然地理学和地图与地理信息系统研究中，对尺度十分关注（彭建等，2003；鲁学军等，2000）。人文地理学研究中，相关问题讨论不多。国际文献中，对人文地理学中的尺度问题还存在一些争论（Marston et al.，2004）。本章通过分析尺度在经济地理学中的作用，以及经济地理学研究中的尺度变化，强调在具有宏观视野的同时，我国经济地理学应加强微观研究。微观研究可沿着三个层面展开：①在研究对象的空间尺度上从小区域或点位入手；②对研究对象进行分解，抓住其中最基本的单元，借助微观研究解释、揭示宏观现象；③对宏观（中观）对象的研究中，注意微观视角，即利用相关技术，构造精细的宏观模型。

31.1　尺度的概念

尺度是个含义很广的概念，不同的学科有不同的解释。地理学家认为，尺度是地理事件和地理过程表征、体验和组织的等级（Jonston et al.，2000）。不同的地理分支学科具有不同的考虑。

31.1.1　地理学科不同分支中的尺度

在地图学与地理信息科学中，尺度被用于定义地图尺寸与地表实际大小之间的关系，即对现实世界的抽象和简化程度。与此相关联，在地图和遥感影像中，不同尺度还可反映所包含的信息数量，以及该影像中地物的复杂程度。

自然地理学常运用等级关系尺度。认为自然地理现象可细分为不同的垂直等级系统，每一等级又可分为若干水平子系统。任一子系统是其下所有等级系统的“总和（合成）”，又是其上等级的部分。每一个等级均可通过时间和空间尺度与其他等级进行区分（Mcmaster and Sheppard，2004）。例如，大陆系统、地区系统和地方系统之间的关系便是如此。

人文地理学中的尺度在形式上也具有等级性，但其内涵上具有相对性。不同部门、不同时间，尺度的概念会有所不同。例如，钢铁工业与微电子工业、工业与商业中的尺度含义会有不同，信息时代与农业时代的尺度也会不同。人文地理学中的尺度可概括为三个特点：①尺度的单元并不固定，其边界可随时间而发生变化（如行政单元边界的变化）。进而，其空间单元内部的一致性，与其他同尺度单元的相对重要性均可变化。②因果性并非由最低（小）尺度开始，它可以在任一尺度发生。人文地理学并不接受自然科学中普遍存在的方法论以及社会科学中的理论选择。③尺度具有可替代性。这种可替代性带来更加自由的研究思路（Sheppard and Mcmaster，2004）。

31.1.2 尺度的三个侧面

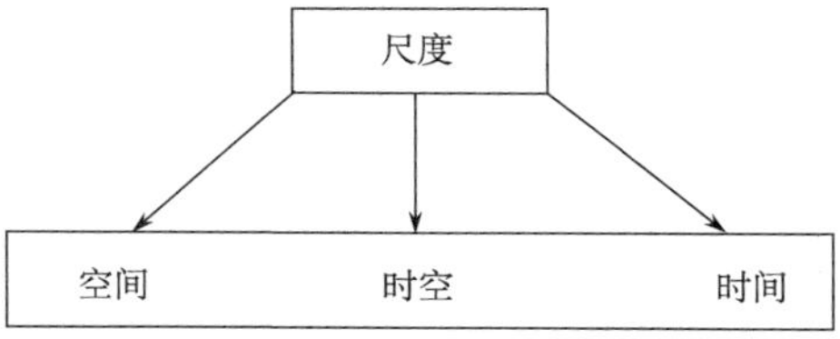

图 31.1 地理尺度的三个侧面

依据以上地理学尺度的定义，地理学家在对地理事件和地理过程研究中，不仅要涉及其空间特征还要涉及形成这些特征的时间概念。空间与时间相伴而发生。由此，地理尺度不仅包括空间侧面，还包括其时间侧面以及两者所叠加的时空侧面（图 31.1）。

31.1.3 空间尺度的五种类型

地理学家所涉及的空间尺度有多种类型。这里谈及其中的五种，即地图尺度、观察尺度、测量尺度、运行尺度和解释性尺度（图 31.2）。地图尺度指用比例尺表示的地图与地面实际之间的关系，大比例尺常与小范围对应。观察尺度指所研究对象的空间范围，大尺度研究指对大区域的研究。测量尺度也叫分辨率，指研究对象的最小可分辨部分。例如，遥感影像中的像素，地图中的可显示地物精细程度。运行尺度（operational scale）指某种地理过程运行环境的空间范围。例如，城市内部就业的郊区化过程涉及城市不同分区；外资投资问题就涉及国内国外。解释性尺度（construction scale）：依研究对象不同而采用不同的空间视野（图 31.2）。

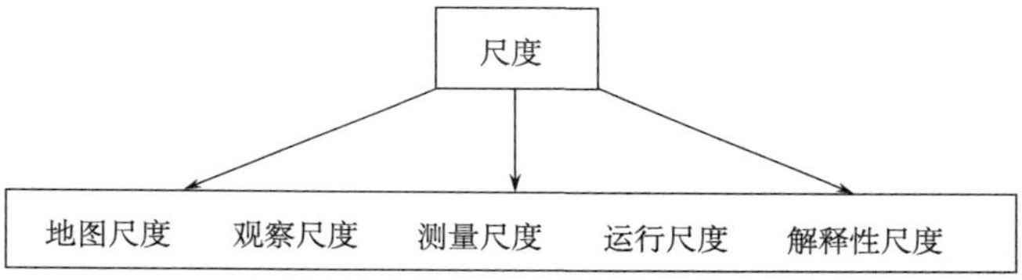

图 31.2 地理尺度的五种类型

31.2 尺度在经济地理学研究中的意义

31.2.1 对尺度重要性的不同观点

在人文和经济地理研究中，由于研究主题的主观性、空间（时间）单元大小的相对性、空间（时间）边界模糊性、数据可获得性、结论的普适性等原因，使得尺度问题远比自然地理中更难于定义、理解和分析，由此带来国际学术界对尺度的不同观点。其中，多数学者强调尺度在人文地理学研究中具有重要意义。例如，泰勒（P. Taylor）认为，这三种尺度：全球、国家和城市，已经自然存在，就像社会科学中将人类活动分为经济、社会和政治一样。这种空间组织已定（Taylor，1982）。阿格纽（J. Agnew）谈及区位可能产生的影响，显现出了地方、国家和全球空间等（Agnew，1993）。进而，马斯顿（S. A. Marston）总结到，尺度已成为每一个激进人文地理学家为通晓相关文献所必须关注的概念（Marston et al.，2004）。

与以上观点相反，也有学者认为全球、国家和地方尺度并不如所说的那样存在（Smith，2003）。甚至，并不存在尺度之类的东西（Thrift，1995）。观点不同，反映了学者的视角和研究目的的差异。

31.2.2　尺度对经济地理学研究十分重要

1. 带来社会科学对空间的关注

近几年来，来自不同领域的社会科学家受经济地理学的影响，在研究中关注尺度问题，从而带来了社会科学中的"空间转向"（spatial turn）或"地理化"（geographicalizing）。以经济学科为例，一些主流经济学家逐步改变其对经济空间现象的忽视，从不同尺度关注经济活动，形成了"新经济地理学"学派。

2. 孕育了经典经济地理学理论

经济地理学中的不少经典理论，均在一定程度上与尺度有关。例如，韦伯区位论的提出，离不开对原料、市场、生产地之间空间距离的分析；克里斯泰勒中心地理论中，更是展示了不同等级市场区中的尺度问题：近距离购买日常用品，较远距离购买耐用品或高档商品。

3. 交通与通信条件变化对尺度研究提出新要求

通信技术和交通运输条件的飞速变化、生产技术的发展，以及生产和营销组织的现代化，逐步改变着传统的尺度观念，为经济地理学中的尺度研究提出了新要求。例如，小区的发展、工商业的具体区位，更加密切地与远距离的国际政治经济背景相关联。不同尺度的问题更易于互相交错，使尺度研究趋于复杂化。

4. 尺度选择影响经济地理探求结果

尺度不同标志着对研究对象细节了解的程度不同。小尺度上测得的格局在大尺度上不一定存在，在小尺度上占主导的过程在大尺度上不一定占主导地位。同样的道理，有些地理特征（如全球变化特点），只有在大尺度上才能分析出来。也就是说，研究范围和尺度不同，会导致不同的研究结果。

31.2.3　全面理解经济地理学中的尺度问题

经济地理学中的尺度，可以从多方面来理解。例如，从研究对象所涉及的空间范围而论，可有大小尺度之分；从研究对象之间的关系而论，又可有总体局部、高低层次之分；从研究视角考虑，又可有宏观到精细研究之分。而就某一侧面而论，不同尺度之间又有多重关系。以下以经济地理学中常用的全球、国家、区域、地方这四个尺度为例，来说明之（Herod，2003）。

1. 梯级等级关系

不同尺度间的关系就如梯阶，从下到上具有依次进程之别。以此观点，全球高于国家，国家高于区域，区域高于地方。经济地理学研究中，大型跨国公司的组织结构具有此特征（图 31.3 a)。

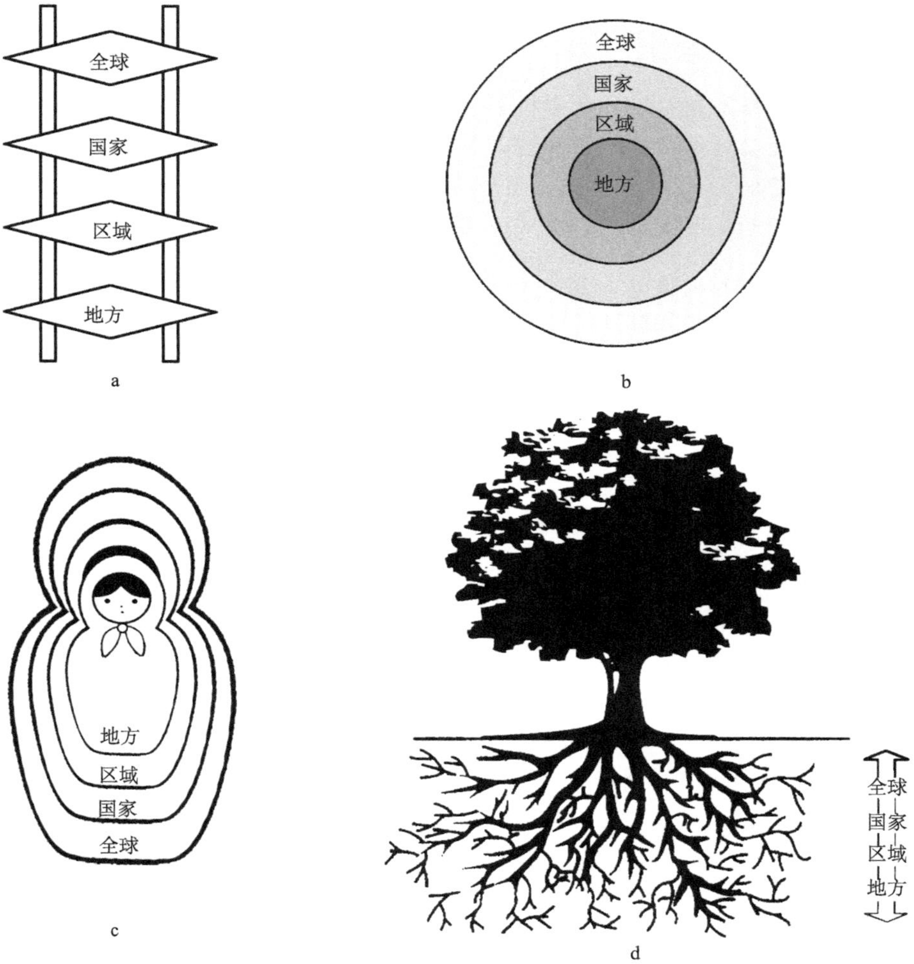

图 31.3　经济地理学中对尺度的不同理解

资料来源：据 Herod（2003）资料改绘。

2. 包含等级关系

不同尺度间具有包含与被包含之分。即全球包含国家，国家包含区域，区域包含地方。进而，全球包括国家、区域和地方（图 31.3b)。比较典型的例子是经济发展的区域环境，它们从地方到全球具有如此包含关系。

3. 嵌套等级关系

每一尺度独立于其他，不同尺度间严格依次相关，形成密切联系的整体。与前两类情况不同，某尺度只与与之紧邻（或大或小）的尺度发生关联，而不与其他尺度发生跨越式关联（图 31.3c）。

4. 复杂等级关系

不同尺度间难以分割，互相关联形成一个整体。如蚯蚓洞、树根一样，将不同土壤层相互关联（图 31.3d）。该类型中，全球与国家、区域、地方之间相互关联，难以严格区分。现实世界中，社会网络和企业网络便具有如此特征。

31.3　经济地理学研究中的尺度变化

经济地理学发展中，不同尺度的研究贯穿其中，再加上尺度本身含义的多样性，梳理经济地理学发展中的尺度变化是一件艰难复杂的工作。以下仅从研究视野范围角度大致分析其尺度变化的轮廓。

第一，以实地考察为主的微观尺度研究。尽管经济地理学作为一门独立学科出现较晚，但在该学科出现之前的地理学研究中，也包含着不少经济地理学内容。在相当长的时期内，地理学的研究侧重于微观尺度层面。早期的地理相关文献，如荷马的《伊利亚特》和《奥德赛》，我国学者的《山海经》和《禹贡》等，均有一些对诸如山脉、矿物、地方史志等的记载。随着生产力的发展，人类远足的能力有所提高，出现了游记性的地理描述。例如，我国著名的《徐霞客游记》，描绘了所到之处的地貌、地质、水文、气候、植物、农业、矿业、手工业、交通运输，以及名胜古迹、风土人情等自然、人文、经济现象。

第二，跨国及洲际探险带来了尺度拓展。从地理大发现开始，地理学家的研究视角进一步向较广的尺度拓展。该时期内，探险家们从欧洲出发，足迹遍及非洲、美洲、大洋洲和亚洲的不少地区，由此带来了地理学家对新世界的认识。相关地理成果中，对其他国家景观的描述，国家间资源条件与经济发展的比较等，占有一定地位。

第三，以国家和区域为主要研究对象。19 世纪以来的一段时期内，国家和区域成为地理研究的重心。洪堡、李特尔均强调区域是地理研究的框架，受其影响，德国学者李希霍芬运用方志学或区域研究的相关方法对德国一些经济问题进行了分析，施吕特尔阐述了德国的文化景观。法国学者白吕纳在研究区域人与地基础上提出人地相关论。英国学者奇泽姆在分析英国经济地理基础上，著书《商业地理手册》，斯坦普组织人员用了约 10 万个工作日对英国土地利用进行了调查（普雷斯顿·詹姆斯，1982）。这种基于国家和区域的地理研究成果，为经济地理学的理论研究，以及国家和区域经济发展的实际需要均做出了重要贡献。

第四，宏观和微观结合与宏观精细化研究。20 世纪中期以来，伴随着经济活动全球化，经济地理学研究的视野更加广大，许多问题被放在全球视野的框架中。与此同时，由于地理信息系统和高速度计算技术的应用，又为地理学家的微观精细研究提供了条件。这时的地理研究尺度出现了两大特征：①多种尺度研究兼具，既有全球、洲际的研究，也有国家及区域的研究，还有小区及更为细小的点位的研究；②宏观精细化研究，即从宏观角度发现大尺度规律，再从微观角度研究规律的小尺度特征。

31.4　经济地理学中的微观研究

31.4.1　宏观与微观研究的关系

经济地理学研究中，不同尺度的成果均具有重要意义。但是，不同尺度的成果之间又具有密切关联。例如，宏观是各微观的综合，是个体的组分、结构、性质、功能和多样性的联系与相互作用的辩证统一。宏观尺度的研究离不开对微观尺度地理事实的了解。尤其是在内部运行机理上微观侧面的剖析更具有重要意义。同时还应该注意到，仅仅立足微观尺度的研究在一些情况下，难以把握地理现象的总体规律。例如，从地方角度研究区域经济发展，是很难理出更大尺度的区域经济空间变化特征的。

微观是宏观的组成部分，但宏观并不是微观的简单相加。各微观单元的有机关联，整体功能才能很好地发挥。与此相关联，宏观尺度的研究成果，也不是微观尺度成果的简单综合。两者均有其特定的作用，不能互相替代。

31.4.2　中国经济地理学研究中的尺度回顾

受原苏联经济地理学影响，20 世纪 50 年代以来，中国地理学家适应计划经济的需要，结合国家建设在流域规划、资源调查、区域规划、地区工业布局、国土整治、农业区划等方面进行了卓有成效的研究。这些研究视角侧重于宏观层面的经济分析，研究空间范围侧重于较大的区域或以至于涵盖整个国土。在大量实际研究的基础上，中国地理学家进行相关理论总结，发展了具有宏观特色的经济地理学（王铮和杨妍，2002）。

与此相关联，中国经济地理学近几十年来微观研究相对薄弱。西方经济地理学者 20 世纪以来形成的微观研究侧重并未很好地在我国发展起来。小尺度的微观区域分析或点位分析、研究对象的微观经济分析（如企业分析、个人行为分析）等，并未受到应有的重视。这种状况在一定程度上影响着与国际主流经济地理学家的对话与交流。

31.4.3　加强经济地理学的微观研究

基于中国特殊国情形成的宏观研究传统，在中国的社会主义市场经济条件下，仍有继续发扬光大的空间。计划手段和政府在中国经济以至于在中国区域经济格局中，仍发挥着重要的作用。作为一个快速发展中的大国，适当加强经济空间格局的政府干预，更有利于全国经济持续健康的发展。但应该注意，经济地理学家在这种国家决策咨询的实践活动中，应加强其理论视角的凝练，不断推出可启迪国际学术界的相关理论成果。

中国经济地理学中微观研究相对薄弱的状况，应该引起同行学者应有的关注。随着中国社会主义市场经济制度的建立，微观个体（个人、企业、农户）在经济活动中的作用越多越重要。缺乏对经济活动基本单元的关注，不易于很好地揭示经济空间格局的形成机理。国际学术界在经济地理学的理论构建中，通过微观层面的精细研究，带来了农业区位论、工业区位论和中心地理论等古典区位论的建立。新经济条件下沿着这一途径的深入探究可望在中国特殊背景下的微观经济空间理论发展上有所建树。

中国经济地理学的微观研究，可沿着三个层面展开：①在研究对象的规模尺度上从小区域或点位入手；②对研究对象进行分解，抓住其中最基本的单元；③对宏观（中观）对象的研究中，注意微观视角，即对宏（中）观问题的精细化研究。

立足小区域或点位的研究有利于揭示经济地理现象的微观内部机理。以人地关系这一经济地理学的核心论题而论，近年来人们从哲学层面的定性研究走向不同层面的量化探索。其中，微观尺度的精细解剖，对于深入认识和解释其内部机理，具有十分重要的作用。笔者曾根据对 482 块农田的调查，研究了地形对山区农村人地关系的影响。探索了不同高度、坡度、坡向、坡位条件下，山地农田系统人工能量的转换效率。这一研究，不仅尝试了从微观角度量度人地关系中的能量流和物质流，而且为更好地协调山区人地关系提供了科学依据（李小建和乔家君，2004）。

在经济空间格局形成中，企业和农户作为重要的基本单元，起着关键作用。其中，外资企业的进入，促进了沿海开放地区的发展。基于对外资企业的跟踪调查，可以剖析外部力量与当地的博弈关系，以及外资对投资地经济发展的影响过程（Li and Yeung，1999；Yeung and Li，1999）。20 世纪 80 年代中期以来，中国的国有企业在特殊的背景下，发生着重大改革。这些改革从多方面深刻影响着老工业基地地区的经济发展。对相关企业的深入调查分析，可以揭示特殊的制度变迁与区域经济发展的关联，参与国际经济地理学术界制度转向的讨论（Li，2002）。农村工业企业是中国的特色企业群体，它们在广大农区的经济发展中起着重要作用，富有专业化特色的中小企业集群在农区发展中显示了巨大生命力。研究中小企业集群竞争优势的形成，并与世界其他国家产业集群进行比较，可以展示特殊背景下产业集群的形成和成长机理，为国际上相关理论研究做出贡献（李小建和李二玲，2004）。农户不仅是一个家庭组织单位，也是欠发达农区重要的生产单元。从农户行为角度研究区域发展，对区域发展现状分析、区域发展目标制定，以及区域政策实施等，均具有特殊意义（李小建，2002）。

在区域可持续发展研究中，地理学家扮演了重要角色，发表了许多有见地的成果。但是，大多数学者在研究中，把区域看作一个整体。然而，从可持续发展角度，区域并非均质体。把区域作为一个整体忽视了区域内各细微尺度的差异。其研究成果并不能很好地反映所研究对象的实际情况，应用性成果在付诸实施时也会有一定困难。如果对不同的区域均从微观视角入手，借助地理信息系统和遥感技术，利用高速计算机，从点位角度研究区域可持续发展问题，便可收到较好的效果（Li et al.，2001）。

参考文献

李小建. 2002. 欠发达农区经济发展中的农户行为. 地理学报，57（4）：459～468

李小建，李二玲. 2004. 中国中部农区企业集群的竞争优势研究. 地理科学，24（2）：136～143

李小建，乔家君. 2004. 地形对山区农田人地系统投入产出影响的微观分析. 地理研究，23（6）：717～726

鲁学军，励惠国，陈述彭. 2000. 地理时空等级组织体系初步研究. 地球信息科学，(1)：59～66
彭建，王仰麟，景娟，等. 2003. 中国东部沿海滩涂资源不同空间尺度大的生态开发模式. 地理科学进展，22 (5)：513～523
普雷斯顿·詹姆斯. 1982. 地理学思想史. 李旭且译. 北京：商务印书馆
王铮，杨妍. 2002. 理论经济地理学. 北京：科学出版社
Agnew J. 1993. Representing space：Space，scale and culture in social science. In Duncan J，Ley D. Place Culture Representation. London：Routledge
Herod A. 2003. Scale：The local and global. In Holloway S L，Rice S P，Valentine G. Key Concepts in Geography. London：Sage Publications Ltd
Jonston R J，Gregory D，Pratt G，et al. 2000. Dictionary of human geography 4th edition. Oxford：Blackwell Publishers Inc.
Li X J. 2002. Thechanging spatial networks of large state-owned enterprises in reform-era China：A company study. Tijdschrift voor Economische en Sociale Geografie，93 (4)：383～396
Li X J，Peterson J，Liu G，et al. 2001. Assessing regional sustainability：The case of landuse landcover change in the Middle Yiluo catchment of the Yellow River basin，China. Applied Geography，21 (1)：87～106
Li X J，Yeung Y M. 1999. Inter-firm linkages and regional impact of transnational corporations：Company case studies from Shanghai，China. Geografiska Annaler B，81 (2)：61～72
Marston S A，Jones Ⅲ J P，Woodward K. 2004. Human geography without scale. Paper presented at the IBGPRGS plenary sessions of the 30th IGC. Glasgow，18 August
Mcmaster R B，Sheppard E. 2004. Introduction：Scale and geography inquiry. In Sheppard E，Mcmaster P B. Scale and Geographic Inquiry. Oxford：Blackwell Publishing Ltd
Sheppard E，Mcmaster R B. 2004. Scale and geographic inquiry：Contrasts，intersections，and boundaries. In Sheppard E，Mcmaster R B，eds. Scale and Geographic Inquiry：Nature，Society，and Method. Oxford：Blackwell Publishing Ltd
Smith R G. 2003. World city actor-networks. Progress in Human Geography，27 (1)：25～44
Taylor P. 1982. A materialist framework for political geography. Transactions of Institute of British Geographers，NST：15～34
Thrift N. 1995. A hyperactive world. In Johnston R J，Taylor P，Watts M. Geographies of Global Change：Remapping the World in the Late Twentieth Century. Oxford：Blackwell
Yeung Y M，Li X J. 1999. Bargaining with transnational corporations：The case of Shanghai. International Journal of Urban and Regional Research，23 (3)：513～533

第 32 章　20 世纪 90 年代中国县域经济空间差异

中国区域经济差异研究引起了不少国内外学者的关注（胡鞍钢和邹平，2000）。这些研究，相当一部分基于全国省级行政单元的数据（杨开忠，1989；国家计委国土与地区司，1994；Fan，1995；胡鞍钢等，1995；Zhao，1996；陆大道等，1998；覃成林，1997；Wei，1999；王绍光和胡鞍钢，1999；Zhao and Tong，2000），仅个别研究使用了少数省份的县级数据（厉以宁等，1999）。基于省份数据的研究，较好地展示了区域经济大格局的变化，却忽略了省内区域经济的非均质性，尤其是一些跨越省级的经济地域特征很难展现出来。就与区域政策的关系而论，同样的区域政策会在同一省份的不同区位上产生不同的结果。为此，学者们已经认识到从县级资料对全国进行地区差异分析的重要性（厉以宁等，1999；王绍光和胡鞍钢，1999）。但以前由于县级数据获取十分困难，制约着相关的研究。本章收集了 20 世纪 90 年代两个年份的县级数据，结合地理信息系统空间分析，从新的角度对中国区域经济差异做一初步探讨。结果表明 1990～1998 年中国县域经济发展相对差异明显变小，但沿海地区与内陆地区的差异则出现扩大；经济增长较快的县域自一些增长中心向外扩延，逐步形成沿海岸带、京广线和长江沿岸三大经济增长轴；但沿海发达区内存在十分不发达县域；经济不发达县域主要位于西部地区，与环境较差的山区、寒区、旱区和省际边界地区有关；全国县域经济基础和增长可分为基础好增长较快型、基础差增长较快型、基础差缓慢增长型、基础好缓慢增长型。

32.1　理论背景及数据分析

32.1.1　中国区域经济差异讨论的主要观点

关于中国地区经济差异的变化，基于省际人均国内生产总值（GDP）的分析结果表明，改革开放以后出现趋同现象，但 20 世纪 90 年代以来出现扩大趋势（胡鞍钢和邹平，2000；Chen and Fleisher，1996；Zhao，1996；胡鞍钢等，1995）。如何看待这种变化，有两种不同观点。一种认为，中国正处在大规模工业化和城市化的初期，国家优先目标应当是谋求经济的快速增长（陆大道等，1998），解决地区差异问题不应当成为国家的头等大事（侯勇智和胡长春，1995）；另一种认为，当前地区差异已经太大，如果再扩大会引起灾难性的政治后果（胡鞍钢等，1995）。缩小区域差距的措施很多，可归结为市场调节和政府干预两大类（王绍光和胡鞍钢，1999）。2000 年中国实施的西部大开发政策，似乎是对区域经济差异过大的观点的肯定。

然而，笼统地基于对东（沿海）、中（内陆）、西部三大地带的分析，忽略了三大地带内的巨大差异。沿海地区内部，仍有处于贫困线以下的人口集聚区；西部地带中，也有经济相对发达的地域。省际之间的分析结果，明显优于三大地带的分析。但仍存在分析单元过大的弊端。

基于更小的地理单元的分析，是否可以揭示出与省际分析不同的区域经济差异特征？区域经济增长具有由点及面扩展特征，县域分析可否展示这种特征？就区域政策的制定及实施而论，较小区域的分析是否比省际分析更具实践意义？本章力图回答这些问题。

32.1.2 指标及数据讨论

由于GDP较好地反映了区域的发展程度，它被广泛用于区域经济差异研究之中（王绍光和胡鞍钢，1999）。作为对基于县级单元研究的尝试，为了在较短时间内做出成果，本章选取1990年和1998年的数据。这两个年份各县、县级市、区（以下统称县域）人均GDP，主要来源于各省、市、自治区的统计年鉴。对于统计年鉴中未提供相应数据的省份，通过统计系统的朋友帮助进行了补充，同时根据各县域GDP与常住人口数据计算人均数据。

需要说明，1990年相当一部分省份仅提供了国民生产总值数据。考虑到这些省份的国民在省外（国外）所创造的生产总值十分有限，国民生产总值数据与GDP差别不大，故使用了人均国民生产总值数据。

本章研究中使用了数字化的县域界线数据。该数据基于不同年份的测绘资料，经与最新出版的各省、市、区行政区划图比较，有99个县名出现了变化。其中，91个为县改市后的名称变化，8个为县名本身变化。但是，县域界线变化不大。故运用该图形数据进行1990年和1998年的经济差异变化分析，基本可行。

在分析中，对省辖市的数据做了如下特殊处理。①如果两年份市辖各区统计资料齐全，将各区分别处理；②如果两年份市辖各区统计资料不全，将市区统一考虑，各区均为市区统一数据。用该方法处理的省辖市共计62个，占全国2469个县级单位的2.51%，由于各省辖市的地理范围较小（多数小于县级地域），故这种处理在空间上不会产生大的偏差。

32.2 1998年中国县域经济空间格局

1998年中国县域经济发展水平的空间格局为高低交错（图32.1），但大致具有如下特征。

（1）低于全国平均水平的县域数明显多于高于全国平均水平的县域数。图32.1表明人均GDP低于全国平均水平的县域处于控制地位（在全国不含港澳台的2443个县域中占66.3%）。这种数据分布反映了高于全国平均水平的县域中，有些人均GDP处于极端高水平。这些极端数据加大了数据总体的离散程度（图32.2）。其实际含义，便是出现了较大的县域经济发展水平差异。

（2）经济发展水平较高的县域集中于沿海、江、线、边地带。从图32.1可以看出，经济发展水平高于全国平均状况的县域主要集中于东部沿海、沿长江地带、沿京广线地带和北部沿边地带。其中，东部沿海地带最为突出，由北向南可分为6个地区：①辽中

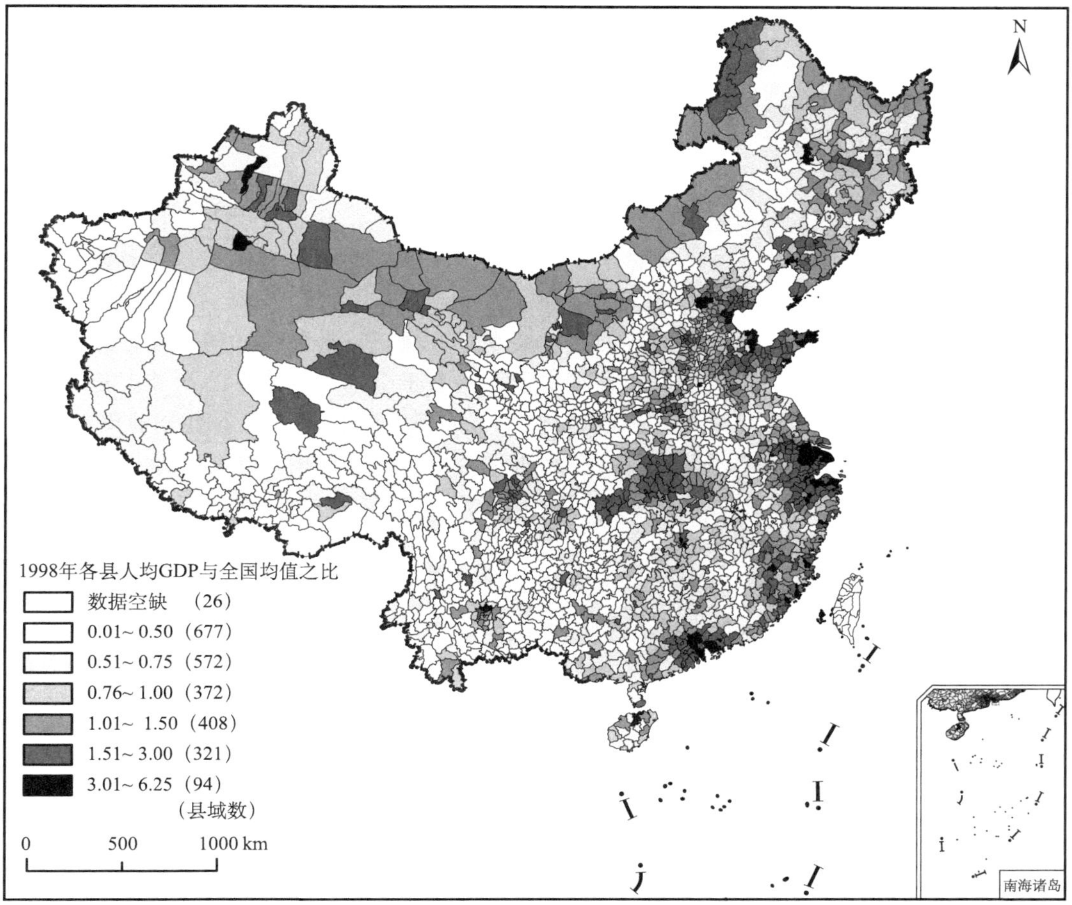

图 32.1　1998 年中国县域经济发展水平

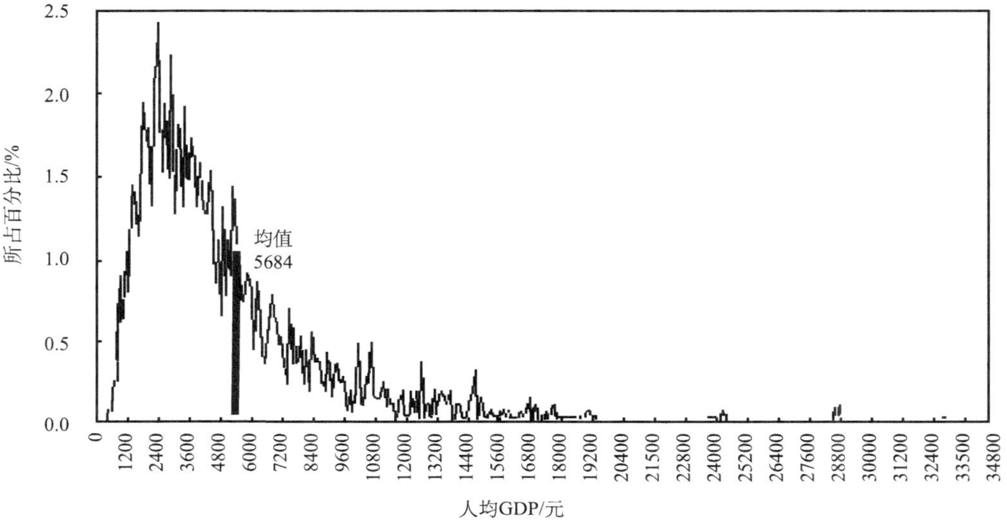

图 32.2　1998 年中国县域人均 GDP 数据分布

南区，有 32 个县域高于全国均值；②京津唐区，包括北京、天津、河北环渤海区，有高于全国均值的县域 38 个，其人均 GDP 平均值是全国平均水平的 2.5 倍；③山东半岛，有高于全国均值的县域 50 个；④沪宁杭区，包括上海、江苏东部和南部、浙江北部，有高发展水平县域近 140 个，其中，高出全国平均水平 3000 元以上者约 100 个，人均 GDP 在全国均值 3 倍以上的县域数为 67 个；⑤福建中东南区，有高发展水平县域数 68 个，人均 GDP 为全国均值的 2 倍；⑥珠江三角洲区，有高发展水平县域数 72 个，人均 GDP 比全国均值高出 3000 元以上，部分地域（如深圳市）高于全国平均水平值 2 万元以上。

内陆地区的沿长江和京广线地带的高发展水平县域，只是断续显现出来。沿长江地带在湖北中部和成都、重庆附近，明显集中了一些高于全国平均水平的县域。湖北中部以武汉为中心，东西延伸的该类县域数达 32 个；成都平原和重庆附近也分别集中了 21 个和 6 个该类县域。沿京广线地带的高发展水平县域，从北向南依次为石家庄附近、郑州附近、武汉附近、长沙附近地区。

北部沿边区包括黑龙江、内蒙古北部边境地区，以及甘肃北部和新疆东部。这里高发展水平县域平均高于全国平均水平 1.5 倍左右。

（3）经济发展水平较低的县域集中于中西部地区。人均 GDP 比全国水平低 50％以上的县域明显集中于京广线以西地区（图 32.1）。其中，西南地区（包括广西、云南、贵州和四川大部、西藏东南部），绝大多数县域人均 GDP 不足全国均值的 50％，有些县域还不足全国均值的 10％。陕西、山西、豫西、鄂西、湘西是另一片低水平县域，其情况与西南地区相类似。

纵观低发展水平县域的分布，可以看出，除了集中于山区、寒区和旱区之外，省际边界地区是另一类值得关注的区位。例如，陕甘、陕蒙、川陕、鲁豫、鄂豫、皖豫、浙闽、闽粤等边界地区，均明显出现呈带状分布的低发展水平县域。这一点，曾有学者在对部分省际边界分析中提到（Wei，1999）。而全国性的分析更是展现了其普遍意义。尤其是一些经济较为发达省份之间（如苏鲁、浙闽、闽粤间），也出现了不发达走廊。

（4）沿海发达区内部存在着不发达县域。尽管沿海地区较高发展水平县域十分集中，但是，可以明显看出仍有一些不发达县域点缀其中。有两种情形：①6 个高发展水平区内有较低县域，如辽宁的凌海市（4339 元）竟比近邻盘锦市低 15021 元；河北大城县（5467 元）不及东北邻的天津市的 1/3；山东惠民县（3879 元）仅为东邻东营市的 15.7％；在全国工业发达的沪宁杭区，浙江缙云县人均 GDP 仅为 4164 元，不及义乌市的 1/4；位于福建泉州市（16929 元）北邻的仙游县（3728 元）比全国平均水平还低 2156 元；在珠江三角洲区，广东佛冈县人均 GDP 为 3185 元，比南邻的花都市低 18074 元。②6 个高发展水平区间存在一定数量的不发达县域，如辽中南和京津塘区之间有 16 个发展水平较低的县域；山东半岛与沪宁杭区之间有一个带状分布的低水平区（有 29 个县域）；有 7 个低发展水平县域把福建中东南和珠江三角洲区隔开。

32.3　20 世纪 90 年代中国县域经济空间变化特点

第一，高发展水平县域沿一定规律扩延。比较 1998 年（图 32.1）和 1990 年（图 32.3）中国县域经济发展水平的空间格局，可以看出，高发展水平的县域从几个中心向外扩延。这些中心包括沿海地区的北京-天津、胶东、上海、厦门、深圳；内陆地区的武汉、郑州、长沙、成都、昆明。沿着这些中心，其周围地区的高发展水平县域在 1998 年明显多于 1990 年。其中，上海和深圳两中心的向外扩延最为突出。这种扩延现象，回应了增长极和增长中心理论中的扩散效应（Perroux，1971；李小建和苗长虹，1993）。

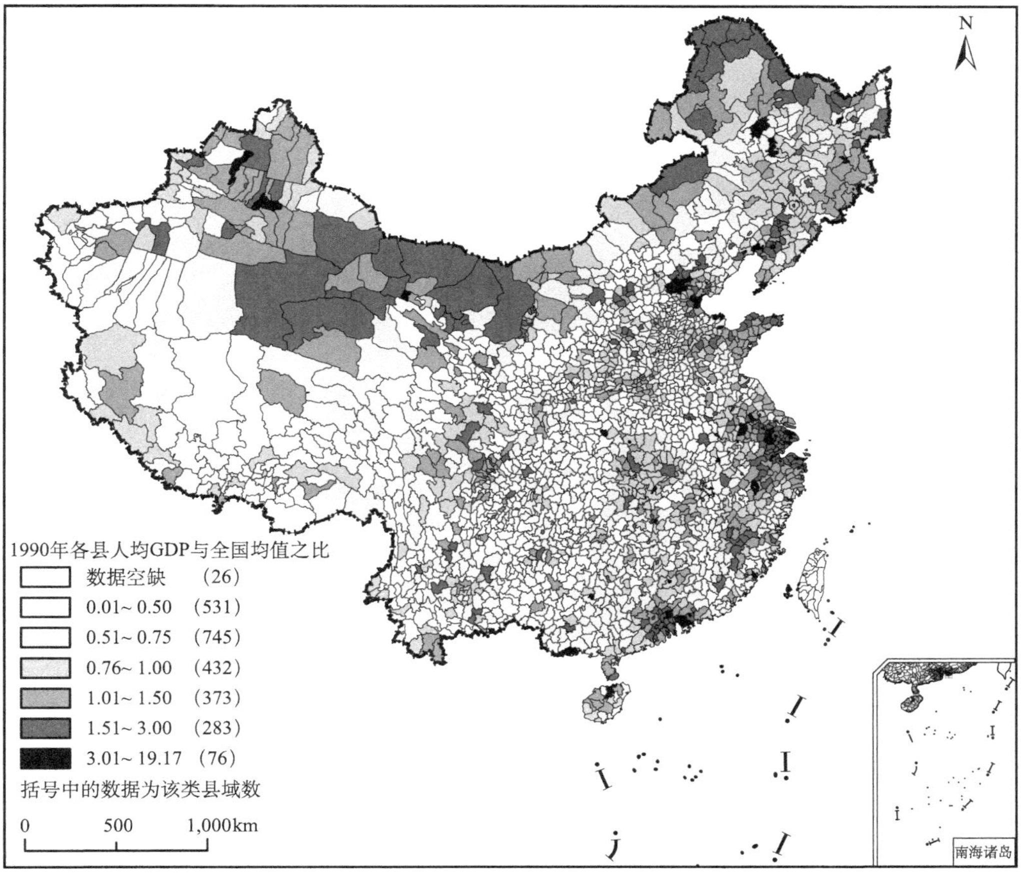

图 32.3　1990 年中国县域经济发展水平

第二，经济增长轴基本显现。以上各增长中心在 20 世纪 90 年代的向外扩延，在空间上使全国的经济增长轴逐渐显现出来（图 32.3）。尤其是全国 90 年代人均 GDP 绝对量增长较快县域，呈轴线分布的格局更为明显（图 32.4）：①沿海岸带增长轴：沿海五大经济增长中心向外扩延形成沿海地区较快增长县域连片发展；②京广沿线增长轴：沿着京广线，大致呈条带状分布着一些 90 年代人均 GDP 增长量较多的县域；③长江沿岸增长轴：尽管中间有一些间断，但在上海、南京、武汉、重庆、成都一带的长江沿岸，已呈带状汇集了高增长县域。

在以上三大经济增长轴中，沿海岸带的增长最为显著。在全国人均 GDP 绝对增长大于 5900 元的 489 个县域中，66.9%位于沿海地带（图 32.4）。各县域人均 GDP 的相对变化（增长比率）也呈现大致相同的格局。

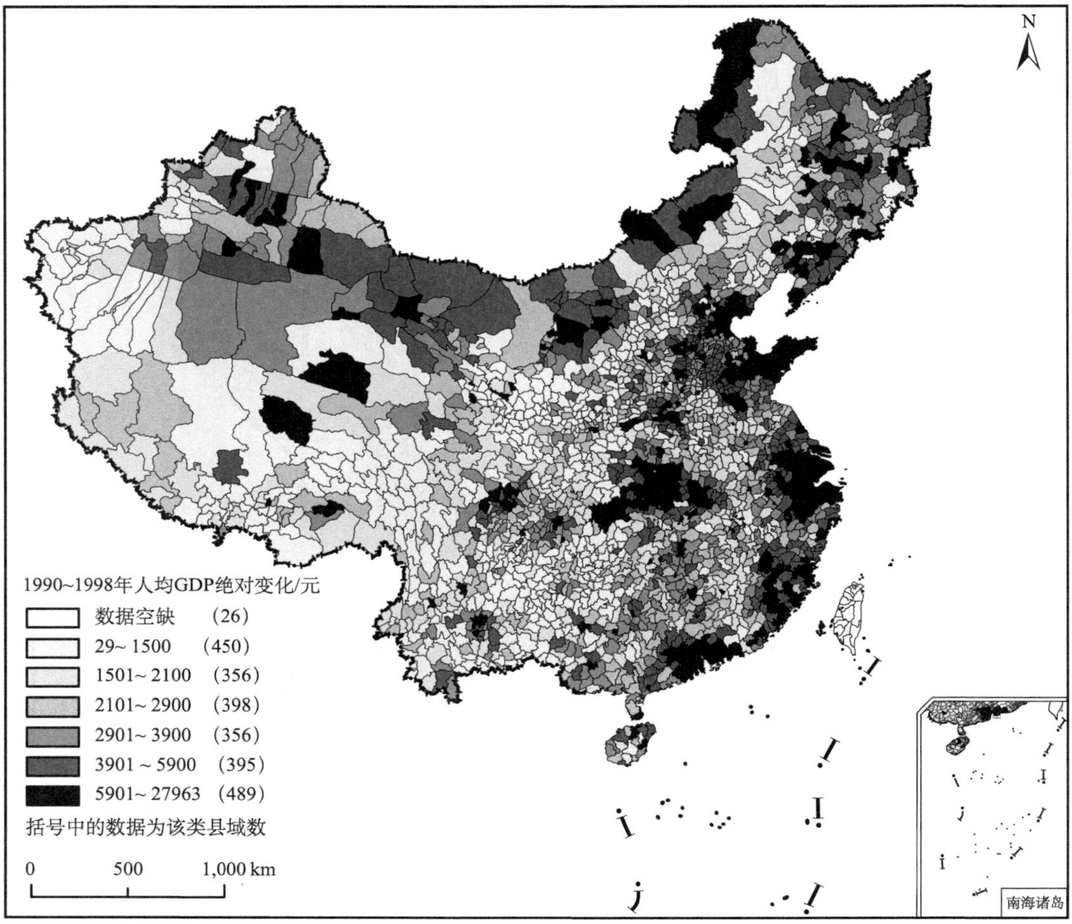

图 32.4 中国县域人均 GDP 绝对量变化（1990～1998 年）

第三，低增长县域在空间上明显扩大。比较图 32.1 和图 32.3，可以看出 1998 年低经济发展水平的县域多于 1990 年。统计表明，人均 GDP 低于全国均值 50%以下的县域，1990 年为 531 个，到 1998 年增加到 677 个。在空间分布上，这些低增长县域主要位于京广线、西藏中部、青海中部之间的区域（图 32.4）。该区域内，除了成都、重庆、昆明、南宁、贵阳、拉萨等城市周围区外，绝大多数县域的人均 GDP 增长量为全国最低。

第四，县域经济差异变化趋势。首先，全国总体上，20 世纪 90 年代县域经济发展水平的绝对差异有所扩大。以县域人均 GDP 的标准差变化与基于省际数据分析的结果相似。然而，90 年代县域经济发展水平的相对差异变化，则呈现与省际分析不同的结果。1990 年县域人均 GDP 的变异系数为 1.06，1998 年减少为 0.87（表 32.1）。

表 32.1　中国县际经济差异变化与省际经济差异变化比较

项目		1980 年	1985 年	1990 年	1995 年	1998 年
省域人均 GDP	标准差	518	735	1156	3686	5411
	均值	581	1000	1871	5338	7457
	变异系数	0.89	0.74	0.62	0.69	0.72
县域人均 GDP	标准差			1517		4951
	均值			1430		5684
	变异系数			1.06		0.87

其次，沿海与内陆地区比较，90 年代县域经济发展水平的绝对差异和相对差异均在扩大。如表 32.2 所示，1990～1998 年，沿海 12 个省、市、区县域人均 GDP 平均增长 6488 元，年递增率达 20.12%，内陆 18 个省、市、区县域人均 GDP 平均增长 3132 元，年递增率为 13.09%。分析县域经济高发展水平相对集中的沿海地区与内陆地区的差异，结果表明，1990～1998 年，沿海 125km 宽的带状区与其以内内陆地区县域人均 GDP 的绝对差异和相对差异也同样处于扩大之中。但是，其绝对差异扩大量的沿海内陆差距要明显高于按省份划分的两者差距（表 32.2）。

表 32.2　中国沿海与内陆县域经济发展差异变化（1990～1998 年）

项目	沿海 12 个省份县域	内陆 18 个省份县域	沿海 125km 带状区县域	沿海带状区以内的内陆地区县域
1990～1998 绝对增长量平均值	6488	3132	8184	3425
1990～1998 年平均增长率/%	20.12	13.09	21.94	17.61

32.4　中国县域经济增长类型简析

根据 1990 年各县域人均 GDP 与全国均值比较和 20 世纪 90 年代各县域人均 GDP 增长与全国平均值的比较，以 1990 年人均 GDP 高于全国均值为高基础，反之为低基础；1990～1998 年增长高于全国平均水平为增长较快（或高增长），反之为增长较慢（或低增长），可将全国 2443 个县域（数据空缺者除外）划分为以下 4 种类型（图 32.5）。

1. 基础好增长较快型（高基础高增长型）

东部沿海有四大区（指 10 个以上县域连片分布区）：①津沽区，包括天津市及所辖

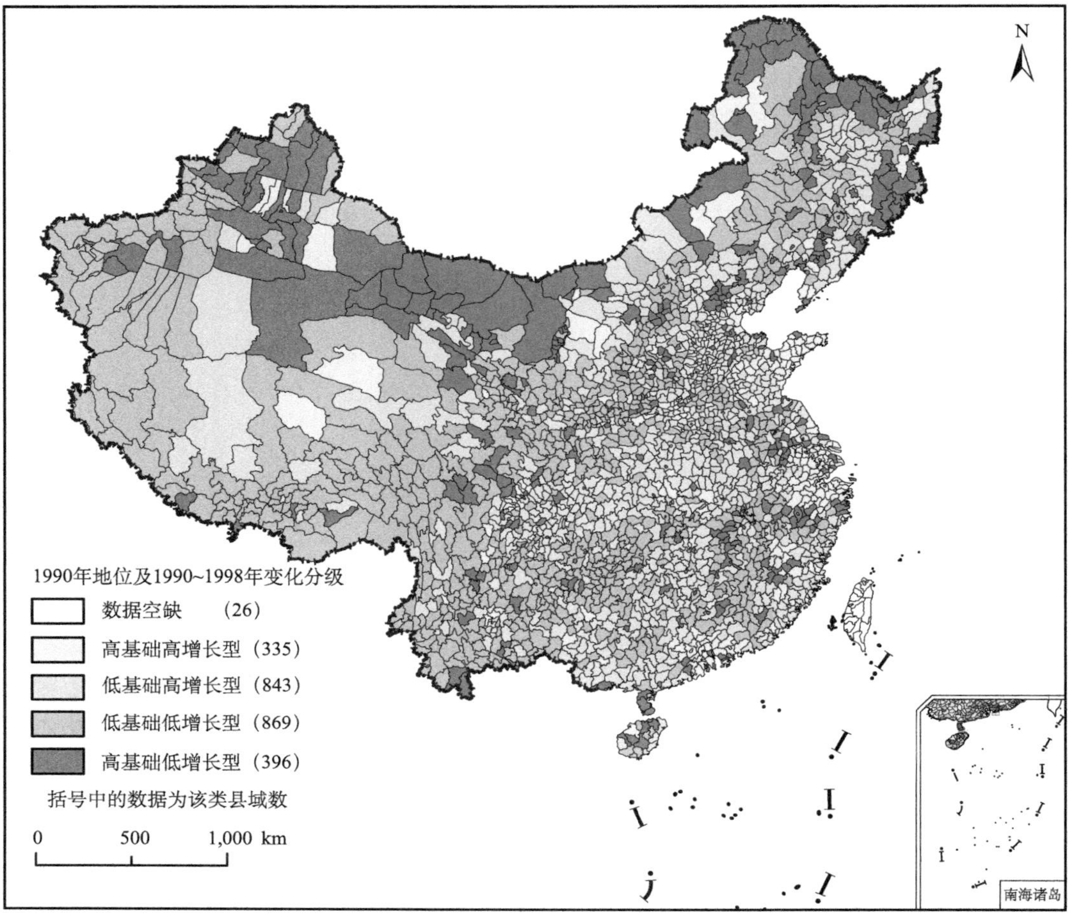

图 32.5　20 世纪 90 年代中国县域经济发展类型区

县市、河北邻近地区，共有此类县域 16 个。②山东半岛与冀南区，包括山东省大部，河北省南部一部分地域，县域数为 43 个。③长江三角洲区，包括上海市、江苏中南部、浙江北部，县域数达 100 多个，占全国该类型的近 1/3。④珠江三角洲区，有此类型县域 32 个。

中西部地区主要分布于：①河南中北部区，包括河南省的郑州、焦作、济源等地域，共有此类县域 13 个。②川中区，包括四川省成都市、德阳市及所辖县市，共 16 个县域。

2. 基础差增长较快型（低基础高增长型）

该类型主要集中于中国中部地区。大致可分为四大区：①冀晋鲁区，包括河北省、山西东部、山东西部，县域数为全国该类型的 1/4 稍弱。②长江沿岸带，包括四川省东南、重庆市、湖北和安徽省中部。该区县域数占全国该类型的 25%强。③湘桂粤区，包括湖南大部、广西南部、广东西部，有县域数 95 个。④东北区，包括黑龙江南部、吉林中部和辽宁北部，县域数仅为 34 个。

3. 基础差增长缓慢型（低基础低增长型）

该类型主要分布于中西部大多地域，大致可分为四大区：①新疆、西藏西部沿边区；②大渡河西南广大地域，包括西藏大部、四川西部、云南省、贵州、湖南西部等；③长江以南，京广线以东，沿海带以西部分地域，包括江西省大部，湖南东部；④山西、陕西、宁夏、甘肃、青海五省（区）大部，四川北部等。

4. 基础高增长缓慢型（高基础低增长型）

主要分布于西北、东北、北部沿边境区，有县域数达 114 个，占全国该类型县域总数的 28%。其余县域主要散布于中国各地，相对集中于四川西北、北京、长江三角洲的外围区。

上述各类型区并非集中分布，而是相互交错的。例如，高基础高增长型中，也有其他类型；高基础慢增长型中，也有高基础高增长型；基础差类型中，出现经济发展较快区与较慢区相互交织。

32.5　结论与讨论

（1）20 世纪 90 年代中国县域经济发展水平空间差异变化，展现了与省际分析不同的状况。1990～1998 年县域人均 GDP 的绝对差异出现扩大，而相对差异则明显变小。沿海与内陆地区比较，90 年代县域经济发展水平的绝对差异和相对差异均在扩大。以沿海 125km 宽的带状区所划分的沿海-内陆地区绝对差异，比人们所采用的按沿海省份、内陆省份所衡量的绝对差异扩大趋势更为明显。

（2）沿海与内陆地区县域经济发展水平差距的扩大，证实了中国政府出台的西部大开发政策的适应性。但是，从另一方面看，政府出台向中西部倾斜的政策，并不能等于宣布了学术研究中区域差异是否过大讨论的终结。学术研究应为生产实践服务，但行政政策并不能代替学术研究。中国区域经济差异是否超过可容忍的限度，科学的学术研究仍有一定的意义。

（3）90 年代县域经济增长分析揭示了省域分析所不易揭示的区域经济增长空间转移现象。经济增长较快的县域自一些增长中心向外扩延，逐步形成全国的沿海岸带经济增长轴，京广线经济增长轴和长江沿岸经济增长轴。在这三大经济轴中，沿海岸带的经济增长最为显著。这种经济空间扩散现象印证了增长极（增长中心）的扩散效应，以及据此引申的“点-轴”经济增长模式（陆大道，1995）。

（4）基于县域经济分析，本章展示了沿海发达区内存在不发达县域。有一些沿海县域人均 GDP 不足全国平均值的 50%，且紧邻人均 GDP 高于全国 3 倍以上的县域。沿海发达区内的区域经济差异也不容忽视。

（5）全国总体上，经济不发达县域主要位于中西部，尤其是西部地区。这些地区多为山区、寒区、旱区等环境条件较差区。与省际边界叠加，还可发现，不发达县域还存在于省际间地带。跨省地带经济发展，应引起相关省份的关注。

（6）基于 1990 年县域经济状况和 20 世纪 90 年代变化，本章将全国县域分为 4 种类型：基础好增长较快型、基础差增长较快型、基础差增长缓慢型、基础好增长缓慢型。由于数据所限，这种分类十分简单。但比起省域分析，可以为区域政策的制定和实施提供进一步的参考。

参考文献

国家计委国土与地区司. 1994. 中国地区发展报告. 北京：中国环境出版社

侯勇智，胡长春. 1995. 东中西部的协调发展. 经济工作者学习资料，73：13～29

胡鞍钢，王绍光，康晓光. 1995. 中国地区差距报告. 沈阳：辽宁出版社

胡鞍钢，邹平. 2000. 社会与发展：中国社会发展地区差异研究. 杭州：浙江人民出版社

李小建，苗长虹. 1993. 增长极理论分析及选择研究. 地理研究，12（3）：45～55

厉以宁. 1999. 区域发展新思路. 北京：经济日报出版社

陆大道. 1995. 区域发展及其空间结构. 北京：科学出版社

陆大道，薛凤旋，等. 1998. 1997 中国区域发展报告. 北京：商务印书馆

覃成林. 1997. 中国区域经济差异研究. 北京：中国经济出版社

王绍光，胡鞍钢. 1999. 中国：不平衡发展的政治经济学. 北京：中国计划出版社

杨开忠. 1989. 中国区域发展研究. 北京：海洋出版社

Chen J，Fleisher B. 1996. Regional income inequality and economic growth in China. Journal of Comparative Economics，22：141～164

Fan C C. 1995. Of belts and ladders：State policy and uneven development in post-Mao China. AAAG，85（3）：421～449

Perroux F. 1971. Note on the concept of "growthpoles". In：Livingstone I. Economic Policy for Development：Selected Reading. Harmond sworth：Penguin Books Ltd

Wei Y. 1999. Regional in equality in China. Progress in Human Geography，23（1）：48～58

Zhao X，Tong S P. 2000. Unequal economic development in China：Spatial disparities and regional policy reconsideration，1985～1995. Regional Studies，34（6）：549～561

Zhao X. 1996. Spatial disparities and economic development in China，1953～1992：A comparative study. Development and Change，27（1）：131～160

第33章　20世纪90年代河南经济空间结构变化及其效应

经济空间结构是经济地理学和区域经济学研究的重要论题之一。国际学术界早期的研究成果，如杜能的农业区位论、韦伯的工业区位论、克里斯泰勒的中心地理论、皮鲁的增长极理论等，奠定了空间结构研究的理论基础。20世纪50年代以来，由于经济建设实践的需求，中国学者们在经济空间结构方面进行了卓有成效的研究。例如，陆大道提出的点轴模式（陆大道，2001），叶大年提出的对称分布理论（叶大年等，2001），陆玉麒提出的双核结构理论（陆玉麒，2002）。这些理论模式在不同空间尺度上为中国经济布局提供了理论借鉴。在实证研究方面，学者们也作了不少工作（陆大道，1999；胡序威等，2000；陆玉麒，2000；甄峰等，2000；张景秋和杨吾扬，2002；万家佩和涂人猛，1991；陈修颖和陈国生，2001；俞勇军和陆玉麒，2003），这些研究从不同侧面关注了区域经济空间结构，对后续研究产生了很有意义的启迪。

在中国经济空间结构的研究中，有诸多问题有待深入。例如：①在理论层面，对微观地域的空间经济演化缺乏探讨。尽管较大尺度的观察有利于揭示空间结构变化的宏观特点，但微观角度的研究对于分析这些特点的形成具有重要意义。②在区域角度上，对中国欠发达地区的研究不足。由于所处的经济阶段不同，欠发达地区在区域联系、经济扩散条件等方面与东部发达地区存在差距，因此，欠发达地区的经济空间结构布局与演化应该与发达地区有所不同。探讨欠发达地区的经济空间结构演化规律，对这些地区在有限经济资源状况下的经济布局具有重要实践意义。③区域经济空间结构的经济效应，是个非常重要的研究问题，但很少有学者涉及。

基于以上分析，本章的研究主要集中于以下两方面：①欠发达地区的经济空间结构的长时期演化；②区域经济空间结构模式的经济效应。我们以县域为基本空间单元，以人均GDP为衡量指标，分析了河南省经济空间结构演变过程，结果表明，20世纪90年代以来，河南省经济正处于空间集聚过程，经济空间结构呈现出明显的中心-外围模式。通过建立模型对河南省经济空间集聚格局的经济增长效应的分析表明，总体上河南省县域间经济增长的空间相关性不显著。只有在高水平县域集聚区，县域经济增长与相邻县域呈显著的正相关关系，表现出区域之间的经济溢出效应。

33.1　河南省经济空间结构演变过程

人均GDP（国内生产总值）由于可以较好地反映区域经济发展水平，而被广泛用于区域经济差异和经济空间结构研究中（李小建和乔家君，2001；王绍光和胡鞍钢，1999）。利用河南省1980年、1990年、2000年各县（市）（包括地级城市的市区）的人均GDP，按全省平均水平的150％、100％、50％、＜50％，可将各县市相对地划分为经济发达、次发达、欠发达和落后等 4 种类型（表 33.1、图 33.1）[①]。

表 33.1　河南省区域经济发展水平分类及其标准（人均 GDP）　（单位：元）

县域经济类型	1980 年	1990 年	2000 年
发达	[475，1395)	[1636，4600)	[8166，21360)
次发达	[317，475)	[1091，1636)	[5444，8166)
欠发达	[158，317)	[545，1091)	[2722，5444)
落后	(120，158)	(410，545)	(2240，2722)

注：发达县域人均 GDP 大于等于全省平均水平的 150%；次发达县域人均 GDP 小于全省平均水平的 150%，大于等于全省平均水平；欠发达县域人均 GDP 小于全省平均水平，大于等于全省平均水平的 50%；落后县域人均 GDP 小于全省平均水平的 50%。

从图 33.1 分析知，1980 年，总体上河南省经济空间结构呈现出较低层次的空间均衡。表现在以下几个方面：①经济发展落后的县域在数量上占主体，达 83 个，占全省总数的 65%。②豫北地区经济发展水平较高。焦作、新乡市区和它们其所辖的部分县域，以及安阳、鹤壁市区形成全省经济发达县域和次发达县域集聚区。③其他经济发达的区域主要是各地级市的市区，空间分布比较分散。这些市区既是各地的行政中心，又是经济中心，并且大都被经济水平落后的外围县域所包围。

1990 年，河南省经济空间结构与 1980 年相比发生了显著的变化。焦作、新乡、安阳、鹤壁市形成的豫北经济带进一步加强。同时，以郑州、平顶山、许昌为中心的豫中地区经济已经崛起，成为经济发达或次发达县域集中分布区。豫西三门峡市沿陇海铁路的所辖县市经济开始快速增长。

与 1990 年相比，2000 年豫北地区经济发展水平较高的县域数量减少，而豫中地区经济发展水平较高的县域数量增加。总体上，豫北、豫西、豫中经济发展高水平县域在地域上连接，形成河南省强大的经济中心。经济发展水平落后的县域数量增加，经济发展水平两极分化加剧。落后县域主要集中在豫东南地区。总体上，河南省经济空间结构呈现出明显的中心-外围模式。

33.2　河南省经济空间集聚格局及其经济效应

33.2.1　空间自相关与河南县域经济集聚格局

空间自相关（spatial autocorrelation）是指同一个变量在不同空间位置上的相关性。许多地理现象由于受到在地域分布上具有连续性的空间过程的影响而在空间上具有自相关性。度量空间自相关性的方法有很多，如 Geary 比率、Moran's I 系数。从功能上，这些方法都分为全域型（global spatial autocorrelation）和局域型（local spatial autocorrelation）两种，全域型用于判断整个研究区域某一要素或现象在空间上是否有聚集

① 本章以河南省 2000 年行政区划为标准，全省共有 127 个市县（市），以下同。

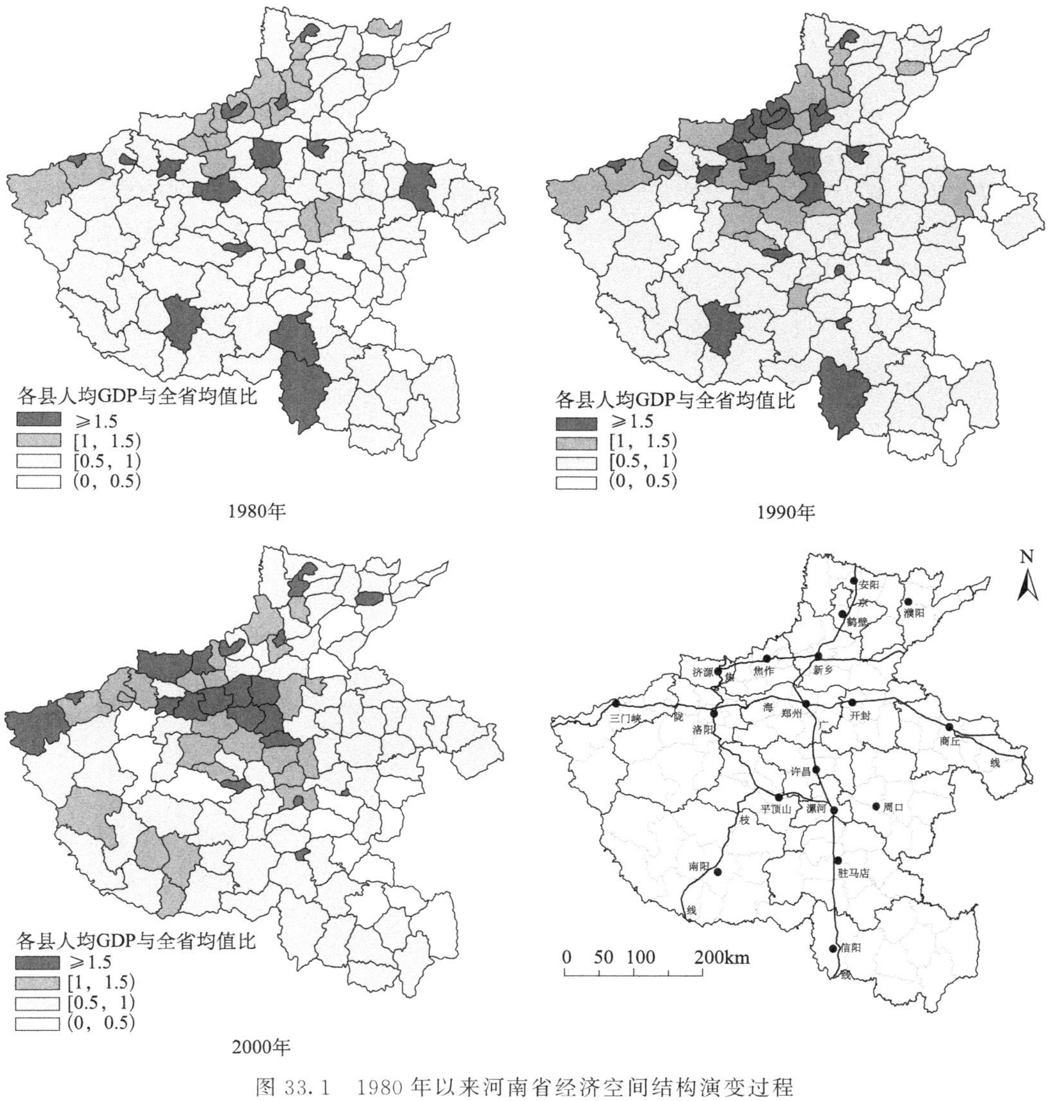

图 33.1　1980 年以来河南省经济空间结构演变过程

特性存在，但其并不能确切地指出聚集在哪些地区。而局域型用于反映在整个大区域中，一个局部小区域单元上的某种地理现象或某一属性值与相邻局部小区域单元上同一现象或属性值的相关程度，所以能够推算出聚集地（spatial hot spot）的范围。对经济空间结构进行分析，采用 Moran's I 系数比较合适（Anselin，1995）。近年来，该方法已经广泛地应用于社会经济数据的分析，来探测社会经济现象的空间模式（Long，2000；陈斐和杜道生，2002；刘德钦等，2002；梁艳等，2003；吴玉鸣和徐建华，2004；樊新生和李小建，2005）。如果以人均 GDP 为衡量指标，则所研究区域（河南省）的全域型 Moran's I 的公式可作如下定义：

$$I = \frac{n}{\sum_i \sum_j W_{ij}} \cdot \frac{\sum_i \sum_j W_{ij}(X_i - \bar{X})(X_j - \bar{X})}{\sum_i (X_i - \bar{X})^2} \tag{33.1}$$

式中，X_i 为所研究县域 i 的人均 GDP；X_j 为县域 i 的相邻县域 j 的人均 GDP；X 表示所有县域人均 GDP 的平均值；$i=1, 2, \cdots, n$ $(n=127)$；$j=1, 2, \cdots, m$；W_{ij} 为空间权重矩阵 W 中的元素，空间权重矩阵 W 定义了县域之间特定的空间依赖。任一元素 W_{ij}，其目的是定义县域 i 与县域 j 的相互邻接关系，便于把有关属性数据放到所研究的地理空间上来进行分析对比。矩阵表示如下：

$$\begin{vmatrix} W_{11} & W_{12} & \cdots & W_{1n} \\ W_{21} & W_{22} & \cdots & W_{2n} \\ \cdots & \cdots & \cdots & \cdots \\ W_{m1} & W_{m1} & \cdots & W_{mn} \end{vmatrix} \tag{33.2}$$

上述权重矩阵的元素 W_{ij} 取值规则为

$$W_{ij} = \begin{cases} 1 & \text{县域 } i \text{ 和县域 } j \text{ 相邻} \\ 0 & \text{县域 } i \text{ 和县域 } j \text{ 不相邻} \end{cases} \tag{33.3}$$

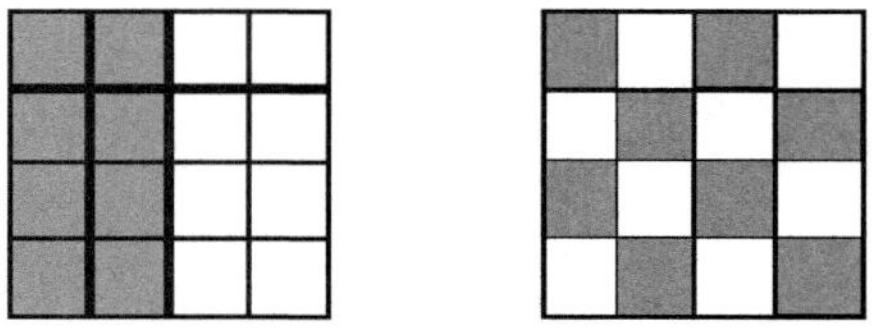

图 33.2　空间自相关正负结果示意图

本章采用的相邻规则为：如果县域 i 和县域 j 在地域上有共同边界，则定义为相邻，$W_{ij}=1$；否则，定义为两县域不相邻，$W_{ij}=0$。依照以上步骤计算出的 I 值介于 -1～1 之间。大于 0 为正相关，且 I 值越大，表示空间分布的相关性越大，即在全域空间上有聚集分布的现象（图 33.2）；I 值越小，表示空间分布相关性小；而当 I 值趋于 0 时，即代表此时空间分布呈现随机分布的情形；I 值小于 0 为负相关。

根据以上方法计算的结果表明，1990 年河南省县域人均 GDP 的 I 值为 0.35 [$z(I)=3.415$]，2000 年河南省县域人均 GDP 的 I 值为 0.481 [$z(I)=2.251$]。对 I 值进行显著性检验，在 5%显著水平下，$z(I)$ 值都大于临界值 1.96 [$z(I)$ 为 I 值的正态标准化值]①。

这表明，在统计上，河南省 1990 年和 2000 年县域人均 GDP 之间有很强的空间正相关性，相同经济发展水平的县域在地域上有显著的集聚特征。如果用人均 GDP（x_i）作为衡量县域 i 经济增长水平的指标，则县域 i 人均 GDP 的局部空间自相关指标的计算公式为

$$\text{LMI}_i = Z_i \sum_{j=1}^{m} W_{ij} Z_j \tag{33.4}$$

式中，Z_i 表示县域 i 人均 GDP 与全省县域人均 GDP 均值 $\bar{x}$ 的离差，即 $Z_i=(x_i-\bar{x})/$

① 具体检验方法见文献：刘德钦，刘宇，薛新玉，2002。

s，$s^2=\sum_i(x_i-\bar{x})/(n-1)$ ，Z_j 表示县域 i 的相邻县域 j 的人均 GDP 与全省县域人均 GDP 均值 $\bar{x}$ 的离差。W_{ij} 是二元对称空间权重矩阵的元素；$j=1$，2，…，m。如果 $LMI_i>0$，表明县域 i 与其相邻县域人均 GDP 间存在正相关关系，LMI_i 值越大，正相关性就越强。

如果 $LMI_i<0$，表明县域 i 与其相邻县域人均 GDP 间存在负相关关系，LMI_i 绝对值越大，负相关性就越强。LMI 值大于零的县域在地域上的集中分布区，可以是人均 GDP 都比较低的县域集聚区，也可以是人均 GDP 都比较高的县域集聚区。

从局部空间自相关指标的计算公式知，LMI 的计算分为两部分，一是县域 i 人均 GDP 与全省县域人均 GDP 均值的离差 Z_i，二是相邻县域人均 GDP 与全省县域人均 GDP 均值离差的加权平均值 $\sum_j W_{ij}Z_j$ 。由于各个部分的值都可能取正值（+）、负值（—）、零，如果不考虑零，可得到四种组合关系（++，+—，—+，——）。据此，可将各县域分为四种类型（樊新生和李小建，2005）：①HH 型（high-high）。$LMI_i>0$，县域 i 与相邻县域人均 GDP 都高于全省平均水平。②LL 型（low-low）。$LMI_i>0$，县域 i 与相邻县域人均 GDP 都低于全省平均水平。③HL 型（high-low）。$LMI_i<0$，县域 i 人均 GDP 高于全省平均水平，而相邻县域人均 GDP 低于全省平均水平，成为孤立的高经济发展水平县域。④LH 型（low-high）。$LMI_i<0$，县域 i 人均 GDP 低于全省平均水平，而相邻县域人均 GDP 高于全省平均水平，这些县域一般处于 HH、HL 类型县域的边缘，因此可称为“边缘县域”。

采用以上方法分别对河南省 1990 年和 2000 年的县域进行类型划分（图 33.3 和图 33.4）。可以看出，1990 年 HH 型县域集中在豫中地区和豫北地区，如郑州、焦作、新乡市和它们所辖的外围县域；LH 型县域集中分布在 HH 型县域外围，如洛阳所辖县域，许昌、漯河、平顶山市所辖县域，南阳市所辖县域，以及新乡、安阳、濮阳市所辖县域；LL 型县域集中分布在商丘、周口、信阳等豫东南地区和豫西南地区；HL 型县域主要是除安阳、鹤壁、新乡、焦作、郑州、三门峡以外的 12 个地市的市区。与 1990 年相比，2000 年各经济类型县域的空间格局没有大的变化，唯一比较明显的变化是焦作、新乡市区由 HH 型变为 HL 型，以及它们部分所辖县由 HH 型变为 LH 型，从而导致 HH 型县域数量有所减少。

33.2.2 河南省 1990～2000 年县域经济增长效应

以上根据每个县域人均 GDP 和相邻县域人均 GDP 的关系，把所有县域分成了四种类型，并分析了它们在地域上的集聚格局。那么这种集聚格局对经济增长是否有促进作用？具体说来，高经济发展水平县域集聚区能否促进其内部县域的经济增长？孤立的高经济发展水平县域能否保持自己的增长趋势？高经济发展水平县域集聚区和孤立的高经济发展水平县域对相邻县域的经济增长是否有空间溢出效应？本章构建一个线性回归模型来回答这些问题。

假设所考察县域（i）研究时段（t）的人均 GDP 增长率为 r_{it}，与此相邻的县域（n）研究时段的人均 GDP 增长率为 r_{nt}，再假设所考察县域人均 GDP 增长只与该县域

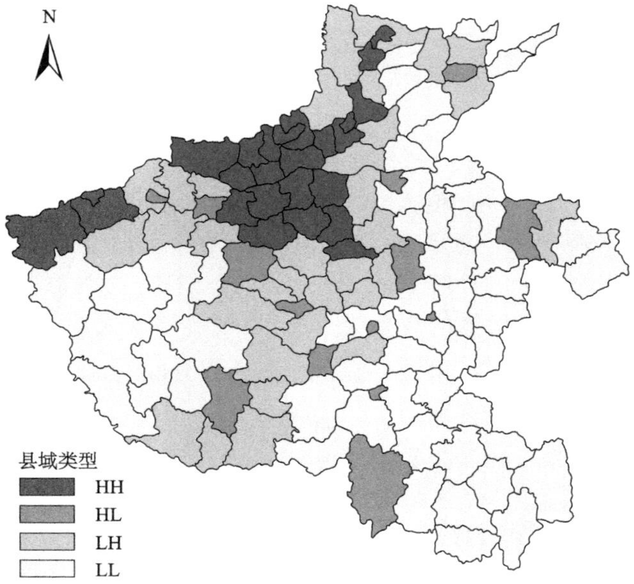

图 33.3　1990 年各类型县域空间格局

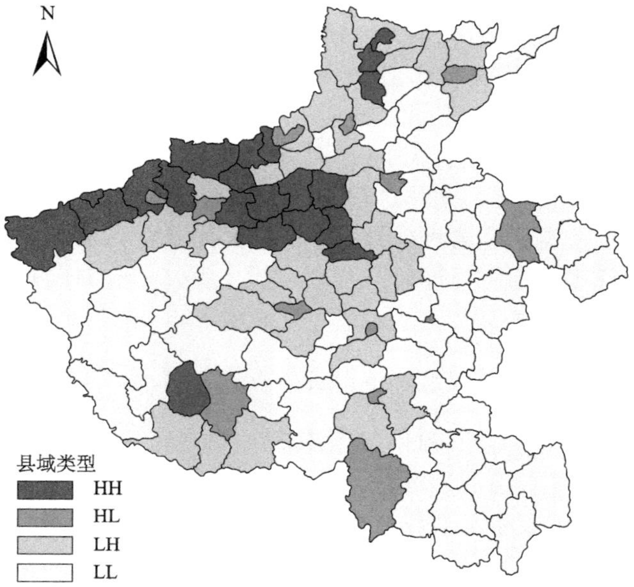

图 33.4　2000 年各类型县域空间格局

前一时期的人均 GDP（$Y_{i(t-1)}$）以及相邻县域同一时段内人均 GDP 增长率有关，暂不考虑其他因素，则可建立以下线性回归模型：

$$r_{it} = \alpha_i + \beta_i r_{nt} + \gamma_i \ln(Y_{i(t-1)}) + \varepsilon_i \tag{33.5}$$

以 1990 年为基期，2000 年为终期，利用以上模型，以每个县域 1990～2000 年人均 GDP 平均增长率为因变量，相邻县域人均 GDP 增长率和 1990 年县域人均 GDP 为自变量，可分别对 HH、LL、HL、LH 四种县域类型人均 GDP 增长进行回归估计（表 33.2）。

表 33.2　各类型县域回归结果

变量	回归系数值	t 检验值	样本数 n	临界 $\|t\|$ 值
α^{HH}	−30.99	−1.746		
β^{HH}	3.889	2.020	25	1.708
γ^{HH}	0.726	2.489		
α^{LL}	33.474	2.979		
β^{LL}	−3.826	−2.065	53	1.671
γ^{LL}	0.024	0.107		
α^{HL}	−13.199	−0.583		
β^{HL}	3.561	1.813	15	1.753
γ^{HL}	0.084	0.161		
α^{LH}	−22.07	−1.258		
β^{LH}	4.937	1.863	34	1.697
γ^{LH}	0.181	0.538		

注：HH、LL、HL、LH 四种空间增长模型的回归方程的 R^2 分别为 0.29、0.079、0.131、0.106。

根据回归结果，可进行以下分析。

1. HH 型县域集聚区

每个县域 1990～2000 年人均 GDP 平均增长率与相邻县域人均 GDP 增长率和 1990 年该县域人均 GDP 都呈正相关关系。说明高经济发展水平县域的空间集聚进一步促进了集聚区内部县域经济的增长。例如，郑州市和它所辖的外围县域 20 世纪 90 年代以来人均 GDP 增长比较快，已经成为河南省经济发展水平最高的地区（图 33.1）。

2. LL 型县域集聚区

每个县域 1990～2000 年人均 GDP 平均增长率与本县 1990 年人均 GDP 则呈负相关关系，与相邻县域人均 GDP 增长相关性不显著。这些县域集中分布在洛阳、三门峡、南阳之间的豫西中部山区，信阳、周口、商丘等豫东、豫东南地区，这些地区的资源禀赋、区位条件、经济基础在全省处于劣势地位，区域内部缺乏经济发展的动力，也很难接受到外围高水平地区的经济辐射带动。

3. HL 型孤立的高发展经济水平县域

这类县域经济增长与自身的前一时期的经济水平相关性很强，而与相邻发展水平较低的县域人均 GDP 增长相关性不显著。这些区域主要是各个地市的市区。这些市区经济发展水平高于外围县域，但是经济规模还不够大，辐射功能弱，对外围低水平县域经济带动不明显。

4. LH 型县域集聚区

这些县域一般处于 HH、HL 类型县域的边缘。从回归结果看，这些县域人均 GDP 增长率与前一时期的人均 GDP 呈显著的正相关关系，而与相邻高水平县域人均 GDP 增长率的相关性在统计上不显著。表明低发展水平的县域没有受到外围高发展水平县域的带动作用。

因此，从四种类型县域经济增长看，每个县域 1990～2000 年人均 GDP 增长率都与其 1990 年的人均 GDP 存在显著的统计相关性，除组合类型 LL，其他 3 种均呈正相关关系。而与相邻的县域人均 GDP 增长率相关性不显著，只有在 HH 类型中呈现显著的正相关性。

33.3 结　　语

从空间分布特征看，20 世纪 90 年代河南省经济发展水平较高的县域日趋集中，经济正处于空间集聚过程。模型分析表明，高经济发展水平县域集聚区内部的县域经济增长之间存在显著的相关性，集聚进一步促进了这些县域经济的增长。而经济增长低水平县域集聚区、孤立的高经济增长水平县域以及“边缘县域”经济增长与各自相邻县域经济增长的相关性不显著。因此，经济扩散效应只发生在高水平县域集聚区内部。

河南经济的发展变化是否代表所有欠发达地区，还需要通过比较才能判定。但是通过对河南的研究，似乎可以大致判定在快速发展背景下，欠发达地区经济的空间变化：中国欠发达地区的经济正处于空间集聚的过程，但集聚带来的经济效应只在经济发展水平较高集聚区内部比较明显。与国际理论比较，显现出了区域发展早期阶段的特征（Friedman，1966）。

在中国区域发展中，应该研究这种趋势。利用适当的区域政策，促进经济发展的集中布局，逐步形成自己的经济增长极，带动整个区域发展。尤其是在条件合适的地区，应当选择主导产业，培育产业集群。同时，通过接受发达地区的产业转移提高竞争力（李小建等，2004）。

参考文献

陈斐，杜道生. 2002. 空间统计分析与 GIS 在区域经济分析中的应用. 武汉大学学报（信息科学版），27（4）：391～396

陈修颖，陈国生. 2001. 湖南省区域开发的空间模式研究. 经济地理，21（4）：394～398

樊新生，李小建. 2005. 基于县域尺度的经济增长空间自相关性研究. 经济经纬，(3)：57～60
胡序威，周一星，顾朝林，等. 2000. 中国沿海城镇密集地区空间集聚与扩散研究. 北京：科学出版社
李小建，乔家君. 2001. 20 世纪 90 年代中国县际经济差异的空间分析. 地理学报，56 (2)：136～145
李小建，覃成林，高建华，等. 2004. 我国产业转移与中原经济崛起. 中州学刊，(3)：15～18
梁艳，钟耳顺，朱建军. 2003. 我国省级人均 GDP 增量变化的空间特征分析. 中南大学学报（社会科学版），9 (3)：355～359
刘德钦，刘宇，薛新玉. 2002. 中国人口分布及空间自相关分析. 理论研究，(6)：1～6
陆大道. 1999. 区域发展及其空间结构. 北京：科学出版社
陆大道. 2001. 论区域的最佳结构——提出“点-轴系统”和“T”结构以来的回顾与再分析. 地理学报，56 (2)：127～135
陆玉麒. 2000. 江苏沿江地区的空间结构与区域发展. 地理科学，20 (3)：284～290
陆玉麒. 2002. 区域双核结构模式的形成机理. 地理学报，57 (1)：85～96
万家佩，涂人猛. 1991. 湖北省域经济的空间结构及发展战略. 湖北大学学报（自然科学版），13 (4)：388～394
王绍光，胡鞍钢. 1999. 中国：不平衡发展的政治经济学. 北京：中国计划出版社
吴玉鸣，徐建华. 2004. 中国区域经济增长集聚的空间统计分析. 地理科学，24 (6)：654～659
叶大年，赫伟，徐文东，等. 2001. 中国城市的对称分布. 中国科学（D 辑），31 (7)：608～616
俞勇军，陆玉麒. 2003. 江西省经济区位特征及其区域发展空间结构研究. 经济地理，23 (4)：462～466
张景秋，杨吾扬. 2002. 中国临海地带空间结构演化及其机制分析. 经济地理，22 (5)：560～563
甄峰，顾朝林，沈建法，等. 2000. 改革开放以来广东省空间极化研究. 地理科学，20 (5)：403～410
Anselin L. 1995. Local indicators of spatial association-LISA. Geographical Analysis，27 (2)：93～115
Friedman J. 1966. Regional Development Policy：A case study of Venezuela. Cambridge：The MIT Press
Long G Y. 2000. Measuring the spillover effects：Some Chinese evidence. Papersin Regional Science，(79)：75～89

第 34 章　农区经济发展差异的乡镇尺度分析

随着中国经济的快速发展和城乡差距的扩大，中国农区经济发展问题逐渐引起了学者们的重视，发表了不少很有价值的研究成果（张平，1992；朱玲，1992；Knight and Song，1993；Meng and Wu，1998；万广华，1998；Wu and Zhu，2004；Wan and Zhou，2005；黄祖辉等，2005）。在这些研究中，学者们认真地分析了多种因素对农村收入差距的影响，并认为地理因素作为重要的影响变量，其在解释农区差异中的重要性正在下降（Wan and Zhou，2005）。从理论角度，中国不同发展水平的农区，其经济发展的影响因素应有所不同。在不同尺度的区域层面上的分析，也可能得出不同结果。

本章根据对河南省乡镇数据的分析，从较小尺度对经济发展水平较低的农区农民收入的影响因素做一量化分析，分析表明，地理因素对农区经济发展具重要影响。在较低经济发展水平的乡镇，地形和农业资源条件具有显著的影响；而在相对较高经济发展水平的乡镇，地理位置以及与此相伴生的基础设施条件的影响更为显著。模型分析表明，地形显著影响乡镇的人均收入，而且随着收入的增加，其影响程度递减。人均土地面积显著影响非农产业发展水平较低乡镇的人均收入。对非农产业比重低于 20% 的乡镇，人均土地每增加 $1hm^2$，人均收入就增加约 96 元。地理位置影响着相关农区经济的发展，尤其是对收入较高的农区的影响十分明显。全省高收入乡镇的 70% 集中在河南中部地区，正好与中原城市群的空间范围相吻合。就单个乡镇而论，离县城的距离显著影响高收入乡镇的人均收入。地理因素对欠发达农区经济发展的影响处于变动之中。随着经济水平的提高，传统地理因素（如地形、农业资源因素等）的影响逐渐被对经济集聚有明显影响的地理临近性等要素的影响所取代。因此，不能简单地认为地理因素对经济发展的影响在下降。

34.1　农民收入影响因素的一般性分析

相关文献对影响农民收入影响因素的分析可以概括为：①结构因素：认为农业结构（Wan and Zhou，2005；刘希凤和王联兵，2007）、农区的经济结构（朱玲，1992；Wu and Zhu，2004），以及与此相关的农民收入结构（贺梅英，2003；王桂荣等，2006）等对农户收入影响十分重要。在不少地区，工资性收入与农民收入关联密切（贺梅英，2003；王桂荣等，2006）。②政策因素：包括家庭联产责任制、农产品价格等（孟凡胜，2003），还有人认为产权界定不清等制度因素阻碍农户收入增长（周其仁，2002）。③基础设施：认为农村基础设施建设的滞后严重制约农户收入增长（林毅夫，2001）。④要素禀赋与外部环境：通过对浙江一些村庄农户的量化分析，证明居民要素禀赋（包括劳动力、土地、资本和企业家才能）带来村庄内部收入差距，而外部市场环境影响着村庄间的收入差距（黄祖辉等，2005）。对全国 1952～2003 年数据的定量研究，也表明农业人均扶养比例的上升（即人增地减矛盾突出），以及农业技术进步缓慢对农民收入的不利影响（王韧，2006）。

这些因素及其影响在不同地区有明显差异。因此，从影响因素区域差异的角度，研究其对农民收入差异的影响，可以得出类似的结论。例如，Meng 和 Wu（1998）通过对 5 省 1000 农户的研究，认为农户收入区域差异主要与区域市场化程度有关；此外，要素收益率的区域间差异也对农户收入有明显影响。柯尼特（J. Knignt）等对全国 2400 个县域的分析表明，人均收入受地形、农业类型、区位、非农业地位影响明显；非农业地位又与农业的成功发展有关（Knight and Song，1993）。Wan 和 Zhou（2005）运用 3 省（广东、湖北、云南）9 村 766 个农户数据，分析收入差异的决定因素，得出地理仍然是收入差异的重要决定因素，但其作用在下降；资金投入新近出现作为一个十分重要的决定因素；农业结构的影响比劳动力和其他投入更为重要。

以上研究对于揭示农民收入影响的内在原因均具有重要意义。但是，由于中国面积巨大，各地发展水平和发展环境有明显差异。在某一类型的区域研究成果，在其他区域不尽成立。例如，影响宁夏农村人均收入的主要因素是牧业收入、传统种植业收入等（刘希凤和王联兵，2007），而在广东省，工资性收入和家庭经营纯收入则为农村居民收入构成的主要来源（贺梅英，2003）。因此，研究特殊类型区域的农户收入及其影响因素具有重要意义。

从理论上讲，处于不同发展阶段的区域，影响农民收入的决定因素有所不同。在完全依赖农业的区域中，生产力低下时种植业（或畜牧业）条件和劳动力强壮与否对农户收入起决定作用；随着生产力水平的提高，作物种植结构对农民收入的影响力增大；农业技术的发展，高增加值的特殊类型经济作物（如有机农作等）对农区收入影响大幅提高。在工商业有一定发展的农区中，由于生产效率的差异，工商业地位在很大程度上影响农户收入。除此之外，随着市场经济的发展，在农区发展中交通、信息等基础设施的作用、技术的作用、人口的智力和经营能力等的作用，也会大幅增强。由此，可以大致做出推理，在经济发展水平较低的农区，地理环境在农户收入中具有较大作用。这里，地理环境指研究区域特定的自然条件和社会经济条件。

与此相关联，细微尺度上的分析比起大区域的总体研究，更能揭示发展程度差异对农区发展影响因素差异的影响。基于中国国情，村级研究是农区数据可获取的最小尺度。如果把省及多省区域作为大尺度、把县及地级市层面作为中尺度研究的话，那么乡镇及村级研究可以归入农区的小尺度研究范畴。与其他尺度相比，乡村层面不包含县城数据，经济活动主要以农业为主，物质景观也主要表现为农区特征（李小建，2006）。

河南作为中国最大的农业大省，不仅农业人口众多（乡村人口 6499 万，居全国第一位，占河南总人口的 69.35%）、农区面积广大（耕地面积 8110.3 千 hm^2，占全国的 6.24%），而且农业产值（第一产业产值占全国的 8.24%，在 31 个省级单元中排名第二）和许多农产品（粮食产量占全国的 9.47%，排名第一，棉花产量占全国的 11.84%，排名第三；油料产量占全国的 14.6%，排名第一）在全国占有重要地位（河南省统计局，2006）。较低的收入水平和特殊的农村经济结构，使得河南在研究地理环境对农户收入的影响中具有十分重要的意义。

34.2 数据来源及其处理

本章所用的河南省（乡）镇属性数据主要来源于国家统计局河南省调查总队的2005年河南省各乡镇社会经济数据。该数据包括河南省乡镇的四大类33项社会经济指标。经核查，开封县曲兴镇的各指标和济源市克井镇的预算内收入存在明显错误，故在分析时予以剔除。

乡镇名称及其地域范围处于不断变化之中。2005年，河南省进行了撤乡并镇工作，截至2005年年底，全省共有乡镇1907个（镇841个，乡1066个）。但由于河南省2005年的撤乡并镇工作到10月份仍在进行，因此，国家统计局河南省调查总队提供的2005年乡镇数据，只有1856个乡镇能够和河南省民政厅提供的撤乡并镇后的结果相对应。

为了进行地理因素的分析，我们又从国家统计局河南省调查总队其他数据库获取了乡镇地形和地理位置数据。按照乡镇的主体地形（该类地形面积占全镇面积的50%以上），将其分为平原、丘陵和山地。按照乡镇所在地与县城的距离，将其分为1（0～5km），2（5～10km），3（10～30km），4（30～50km），5（50km以上）五类。地理位置数据仅有1736个乡镇与以上2005年社会经济数据相匹配，占总乡镇总数量的91%。且这些缺失的乡镇大致按比例分布在各不同收入组。利用该数据进行量化分析，不会使总体结果产生较大偏差。

本章空间数据源于河南大学秦奋副教授及其研究生对河南省各乡镇地图进行矢量化的结果。在ArcGIS中核对并对一些空间对象进行了合并处理，使乡镇名称具有唯一性。由于上述矢量化数据产生于河南省撤乡并镇工作以前，因此，我们根据河南省民政厅提供的2005年撤乡并镇名单进行对应处理，最终得到2007个空间对象。其中，有100个为县城市区辖区（办事处）、国营或集体农场等，不在河南省统计局所定义的乡镇之列。这样，余下的1907个乡镇的空间数据正好与2005年年底的全省实际情况相对应。

上述处理之后，根据国家统计局河南省调查总队提供的各乡镇行政编码，在ArcGIS软件中进行了编码处理，实现空间数据与属性数据的连接。据此，可以分析河南省乡镇层面的图形分析（图34.1）。图形共包含了2007个空间单元，但根据本研究的需要和数据可获得情况，各图层实际显示的乡镇属性数据有所不同。

34.3 农区经济发展空间差异

农区发展可用多种指标来度量。本章根据数据可获得情况，选取农民人均纯收入作为衡量农区发展的主要指标。从图34.1中可以看出，河南省各乡镇之间的收入水平差别明显。这种差异与地理位置、地形、非农产业等存在不同程度的联系。

1. 中部地区明显高于周围地区

中部地区高，南部、东部平原和西部山地低。河南中部的郑州、焦作、许昌等市的

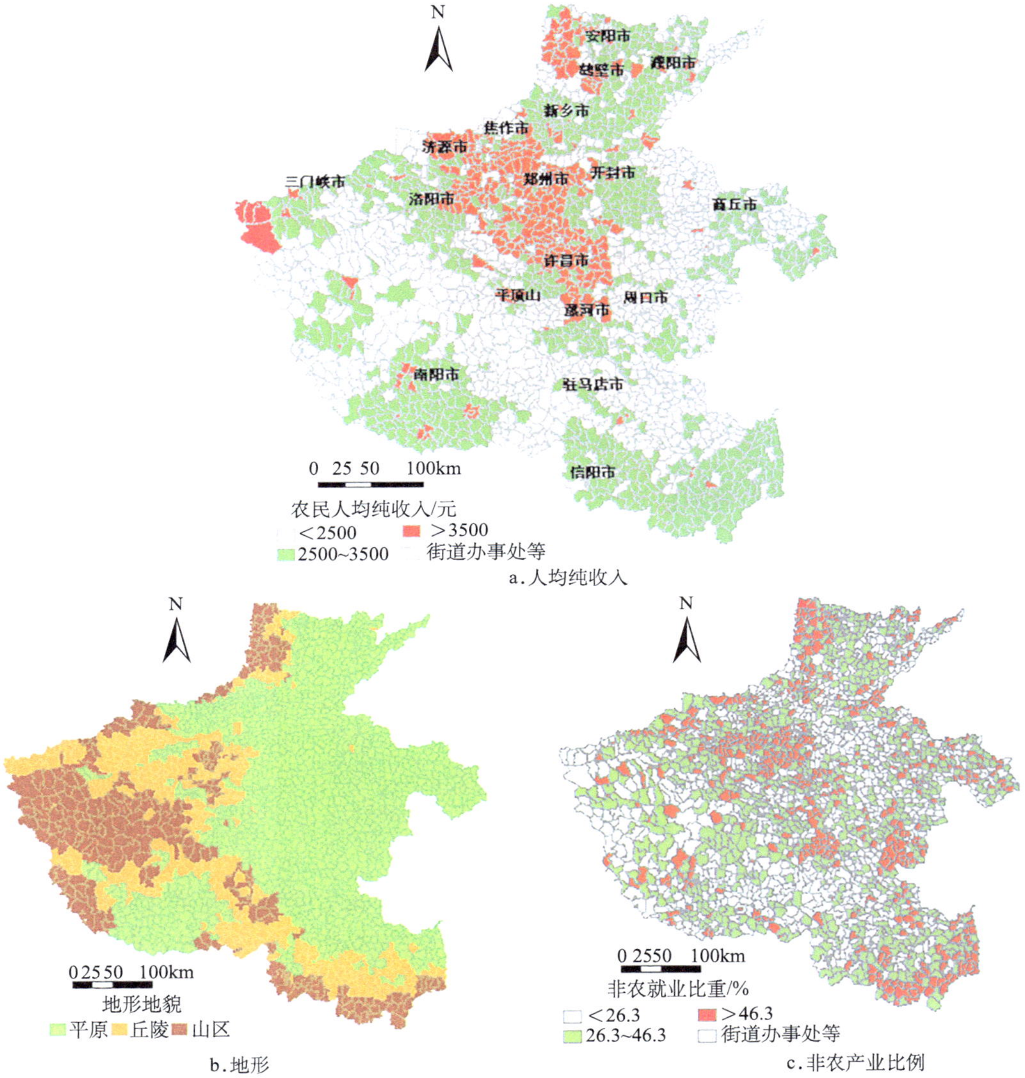

图 34.1　河南农区经济发展与地理环境

大部，洛阳、济源的东部，漯河的北部，开封的西部，形成了高收入乡镇集中区。全省人均收入超过 3500 元的乡镇有 274 个，其中，有 70%位于该区域之内。人均收入位于全省前 10 名和前 100 名的乡镇中，分别有 7 个和 80 个位于该区域。此外，三门峡西部、安阳西部也有小片高收入集中区。

2. 地理位置对高收入乡镇具有明显影响

从空间范围上看，高收入乡镇集中区正好与中原城市群相吻合。中原城市群是河南省近年集中发展的城市集中区域，它包括济源、焦作、新乡、开封、郑州、洛阳、许昌、平顶山、漯河等城市。这里是河南省经济集中区，2005 年这 9 个城市的国内生产总值占全省的 59.4%。它们对区内的辐射带动作用，促进了农村地区的发展。此外，从图 34.1 中还可看出，在中原城市群以外的多数城市的周围地区，也集聚有一些收入水平较高的乡镇。

3. 地形对人均收入分布具有一定影响

这主要表现在两类地区。一类是河南东部和南部平原地区。在商丘、周口、驻马店和南阳 4 个地级市的平原地区，集中分布有一些收入水平较低的乡镇。该地区的平原乡镇共有 606 个，其中，有 351 个农民人均收入在 2500 元以下。第二类是河南西部山区。该地区的栾川、嵩县、洛宁、卢氏、西峡、淅川、南召、汝阳 8 个县共有山区乡镇 84 个，其中，有 62 个农民人均收入在 2500 元以下。

4. 非农产业对农区影响有明显差别

一般来讲，由于农业附加值较低，农区非农产业的发展对农区发展具有明显带动作用（朱玲，1992；Wu and Zhu，2004）。但是，不同条件下，非农产业对农区发展的作用有所不同。对照图 34.1a 和图 34.1c 可以看出，人均收入高的乡镇多具有较高的非农产业比重；而高非农产业比重乡镇，并不一定具有高的人均收入。前者如河南中部地区和安阳西部，后者如东部平原区的一些乡镇。

以上直观的分析，初步表明了地理因素的影响存在。以下通过计量模型，对其影响做进一步分析。

34.4 指标分析与模型建立

为了解释农区发展差异的原因，我们从所获取的河南省乡镇数据的 35 项指标中不断筛选，最终选取了 8 个指标。它们包括 1 个标志农区发展程度的指标：乡镇人均纯收入（Y）；7 个反映影响因素的指标：乡镇离县城的距离（X_1），乡镇人均土地（X_2），乡镇地形（DD），各乡镇肉粮比（X_3），乡镇非农就业比重（X_4），乡镇人均电话（X_5），乡镇人均财政支出（X_6）。7 个影响因素中前 3 个可看作地理环境因素，后 4 个为社会经济影响因素。地形变量只有三个取值，即山区、丘陵和平原，我们选取了两个虚拟变量来表示这些取值。DD_1 对丘陵取 1，对山区和平原取 0；DD_2 对平原取 1，对山区和丘陵取 0；因此，当两个虚拟变量都取值为 0 时表示山区，DD_1 取 1 且 DD_2 取 0 时表示丘陵，DD_1 取 0 且 DD_2 取 1 时表示平原。

不同发展水平的乡镇其影响因素不同，而且相同因素对人均收入的影响程度也可能不同。为此，我们利用最优拟合方法将 1736 个乡镇划分成 3 个组（图 34.1a），人均年收入低于 2500 元的低收入组（有 721 个乡镇），人均年收入在 2500 元（含 2500）至 3500 元（不含 3500）的中等收入组（有 741 个乡镇），人均年收入高于 3500 元（含 3500）的高收入组（有 274 个乡镇）。最优拟合方法就是不断改变临界点以达到最优拟合，利用最优拟合方法可以得到利用统计分析中有序样品聚类方法得到的类似的结果。我们利用两个虚拟变量来刻画 3 个收入组，D_1 对中等收入组取值为 1，对其他 2 个组取值为 0，D_2 对高收入组取值为 1，对其他 2 个组取值为 0。

为了探讨人均土地对人均收入的影响，我们按照非农产业发展程度将 1736 个乡镇划分为 2 个组：非农产业就业比重低于 20%（不含 20%）的低比重组和非农产业就业比重高于 20%的高比重组，低比重组和高比重组由虚拟变量 DDD 取 1 和取 0 加以区分。

在 34.5 节中我们报告的结果包含以上所述的所有变量，表 34.1 列举了这些变量及其定义。

表 34.1　模型分析所涉及的变量及其定义

变量	定义
Y	农民人均纯收入（元/人）
D_1	中等收入属性变量，中等收入取 1，其他取 0
D_2	高收入属性变量，高收入取 1，其他取 0
DD_1	丘陵属性变量，丘陵取 1，其他取 0
DD_2	平原属性变量，平原取 1，其他取 0
DDD	非农产业就业低比重属性变量，低于 20%取 1，其他取 0
X_1	离县城距离（km）
X_2	人均土地（hm^2/人）
X_3	肉粮产量比
X_4	非农产业就业比重
X_5	人均固定电话（部/人）
X_6	人均财政支出（元/人）

我们使用 2005 年河南各乡镇的横断面数据，用普通最小二乘法（OLS），利用人均收入 Y 直接对表 34.1 中列举的其他 11 个变量及其相关交叉变量做线性回归。最初的预估计模型包括的解释变量（表 34.1 中的 11 个变量及相关组合变量）很多，通过不断剔除不显著的解释变量，最终的预估计模型为（省略了表示乡镇的下标 i）

$$\begin{aligned}Y=&\beta_0+\beta_{D_1}D_1+\beta_{D_2}D_2+\beta_{DD_1}DD_1+\beta_{DD_2}DD_2+\beta_{D_1DD_2}D_1DD_2+\beta_{D_2DD_2}D_2DD_2\\&+\beta_{X_3}X_3+\beta_{X_4}X_4+\beta_{D_1X_3}D_1X_3+\beta_{D_1X_4}D_1X_4+\beta_{D_1X_5}D_1X_5\\&+\beta_{D_2X_1}D_2X_1+\beta_{D_2X_3}D_2X_3+\beta_{D_2X_4}D_2X_4+\beta_{D_2X_5}D_2X_5+\beta_{D_2X_6}D_2X_6\\&+\beta_{DD_1X_3}DD_1X_3+\beta_{DDDX_2}DDDX_2+u\end{aligned}\tag{34.1}$$

式中，β_0 为常项；其余各 β 为相应解释变量的系数。

34.5　模型分析结果

34.5.1　模拟结果

我们利用 Eviews 计量软件，对式（34.1）中各参数进行了估计，结果见表 34.2。

将这些结果代入式（34.1），得

$$Y = 1857 + 813D_1 + 1548D_2 + 132\mathrm{DD}_1 + 236\mathrm{DD}_2 - 123D_1\mathrm{DD}_2 - 185D_2\mathrm{DD}_2 - 218X_3 + 249X_4 + 378D_1X_3 - 199D_1X_4 + 754D_1X_5 - 8D_2X_1 + 304D_2X_3 + 442D_2X_4 + 632D_2X_5 + 1.1D_2X_6 - 258\mathrm{DD}_1X_3 + 96\mathrm{DDD}X_2 \quad (34.2)$$

表 34.2　OLS 回归结果（被解释变量为农民人均纯收入 *Y*；观测个数为 1735）

解释变量	*B* 系数	*t* 统计量	*P* 值
常数	1856.594	40.71730	0.0000
中等收入组附加常数 D_1	812.5794	14.89712	0.0000
高收入组附加常数 D_2	1548.137	15.02696	0.0000
丘陵地区附加常数 DD_1	131.7678	3.220746	0.0013
平原地区附加常数 DD_2	236.2591	6.879342	0.0000
中等收入平原地区附加常数 $D_1\mathrm{DD}_2$	−122.5168	−3.016146	0.0026
高收入平原地区附加常数 $D_2\mathrm{DD}_2$	−184.9855	−3.072018	0.0022
肉粮比 X_3	−217.5250	−4.113402	0.0000
非农就业 X_4	249.2684	2.675044	0.0075
中等收入组附加肉粮比 D_1X_3	378.1196	5.050296	0.0000
中等收入组附加非农就业 D_1X_4	−198.6129	−1.735273	0.0829
中等收入组人均电话 D_1X_5	753.8818	3.218529	0.0013
高收入组离县城距离 D_2X_1	−7.911522	−3.755276	0.0002
高收入组附加肉粮比 D_2X_3	304.3060	3.955712	0.0001
高收入组附加非农就业 D_2X_4	441.7412	2.991271	0.0028
高收入组人均电话 D_2X_5	631.9460	2.011307	0.0444
高收入组财政支出 D_2X_6	1.127632	9.665573	0.0000
丘陵地区附加肉粮比 DD_1X_3	−258.0852	−2.176129	0.0297
低比重非农就业地区人均土地 $\mathrm{DDD}X_2$	95.70514	1.857258	0.0634
修正后 $R^2=0.808848$	$F=408.6299$		

注：由于一个山区乡镇的粮食产量统计为 0，在计算肉粮比时无数学意义，故回归时仅考虑了 1735 个观测值。

表 34.2 表明所有变量都是显著的，而且绝大部分解释变量是高度显著的，模型拟合效果较好，修正的判定系数达 0.8 以上。重要的是，表 34.2 或式（34.2）明确给出了地理因素和其他社会经济因素对农民收入的影响。

34.5.2　地理因素对农民收入的影响

三个地理因素，离县城距离、人均土地面积和地形对所有乡镇或部分乡镇的人均收入存在显著影响。

离县城距离显著影响高收入乡镇的人均收入。平均而言，离县城距离每增加 1km，高收入乡镇的人均收入就减少约 8 元。离县城距离只显著影响高收入乡镇的原因是高收入乡镇的非农产业占较大比例，距离通过对市场、交通条件、信息等的影响而影响非农产业的发展。

人均土地面积显著影响非农产业发展水平较低乡镇的人均收入。对非农产业比重低于20%的乡镇而言，人均土地每增加 $1hm^2$，人均收入就增加约 96 元。人均土地面积只显著影响非农产业发展水平低下的乡镇，说明农业资源对不发达农区仍具有十分重要的意义。

地形显著影响所有乡镇的人均收入，而且随着收入的增加，地形影响递减。在低收入组，相对山区而言，丘陵地区的人均收入高出约 132 元（DD_1的系数），平原地区的人均收入高出约 236 元（DD_2的系数）。但是，在中等收入组，平原地区的人均收入只比山区高出 113 元（DD_2的系数与 D_1DD_2的系数之和）；在高收入组，平原地区的人均收入只比山区高出 51 元（DD_2的系数与 D_2DD_2的系数之和）。不同地形的乡镇之间的收入差异随着收入的提高而下降，地形对低收入乡镇的影响最大，对中等收入乡镇的影响次之，对高收入乡镇的影响最小。造成地形影响（随收入）递减的背后原因是，收入越高，对农业乃至对地形的依赖性越小。在平原与山区之间，平原与丘陵之间，这种地形影响递减现象是显著的，但在丘陵与山区之间，这种地形影响递减现象不显著。

34.5.3　社会经济因素对农民收入的影响

肉粮比、非农就业比重、人均电话和人均财政支出 4 个社会经济因素与农民人均收入存在显著的相关关系。与 3 个地理因素不同的是，并非每一个社会经济因素与人均收入之间存在严格的因果关系。

肉粮比与农民收入之间的关系比较复杂，而且它们之间的关系并非简单的因果关系，而是一种复杂的相关关系。例如，在低收入乡镇，肉粮比与收入负相关，主要原因在于，低收入乡镇的粮食生产条件差，一方面，粮食生产条件越差，肉粮比越高，另一方面，农业生产条件越差，农民收入越低。只有在山区与平原的中等收入和高收入乡镇，肉粮比与收入正相关，在其他乡镇，肉粮比与收入负相关。

非农就业比重与农民收入之间的关系主要是因果关系，在低收入和高收入乡镇更为明显。在低收入乡镇，非农就业比重每提高一个百分点，人均收入就增加约 2.49 元（X_4的系数除以 100）；在高收入乡镇，非农就业比重每提高一个百分点，人均收入就增加约 6.91 元（X_4的系数与 D_2X_4的系数之和再除以 100）。然而，在中等收入乡镇，这种积极的因果关系明显较弱，非农就业比重每提高一个百分点，人均收入仅仅增加约 0.51 元（X_4的系数与 D_1X_4的系数之和再除以 100）。据我们调查，造成这种现象的原因主要是中等收入乡镇的农业资源优势。由于这些乡镇有较高的农业收入，人们长期形成对农业的依赖，而非农产业的发展则不活跃，其在经济结构中的比重较低。与中等收入乡镇不同，低收入乡镇的农业收益较差，刺激人们对非农产业发展的关注，由于非农产业回报较高，又反过来激励非农产业发展的积极性。高收入乡镇的非农产业大多是创新型的（否则不可能成为高收入乡镇），因此，非农产业的发展具有很大的积极作用。

人均电话只与中等收入和高收入乡镇的人均收入正相关。在中等收入乡镇，人均电话增加 1 部与人均收入增加 754 元相对应；在高收入乡镇，人均电话增加 1 部与人均收入增加 632 元相对应。这种正相关关系来自生产上的正向因果关系和消费上的逆向因果关系。生产上的正向因果关系是，电话增加，信息获取能力增加，因此收入增加；消费上的逆向因果关系是，收入增加，对电话的需求增加。在低收入乡镇，电话与收入不存在显著相关关系，原因在于生产上的正向因果关系和消费上的逆向因果关系都很弱。低收入乡镇的收入来源主要是农业，传统农业生产对信息的依赖性较低；低收入水平下对电话的需求小，在低收入阶段内的收入变化几乎不引起对电话需求的变化。

人均财政支出只对高收入乡镇的人均收入有显著影响，且具有正的净回报。在高收入乡镇，人均财政支出每增加 1 元，人均收入就增加约 1.13 元，净回报率为 13%。高收入乡镇的财政支出主要用于农业基本建设，因此，财政支出的增加必然引起农民收入的增加。净回报率为 13%说明增加财政支出是值得的。在中等收入和低收入乡镇，财政支出影响不显著的原因尚不十分明确，需要进一步研究。

第一个和第二个社会经济因素是产业结构因素，肉粮比部分反映农业内部的产业结构，非农就业比重部分反映一、二、三产业之间的产业结构。第三个社会经济因素部分反映信息，人均电话的多少反映信息获取能力的高低。第四个社会经济因素是政策环境，在农区的财政支出是农业政策。以上分析表明，产业结构、信息和农业政策与农民收入之间存在显著的相关关系，特别是在很多情况下存在明确的因果关系。

34.6 结论与讨论

基于河南省乡镇数据的分析表明，地理因素对农区经济发展起着重要作用。地理位置影响着相关农区经济的发展，尤其是对收入较高的农区，这种影响十分明显。全省高收入乡镇的 70%集中在河南中部地区，正好与中原城市群的空间范围相吻合。模型分析表明，就单个乡镇而论，离县城的距离，显著影响高收入乡镇的人均收入。平均离县城距离每增加 1km，高收入乡镇的人均收入就减少 8 元。与此相对应，人均土地面积显著影响非农产业发展水平较低乡镇的人均收入。非农产业比重低于 20%的乡镇，人均土地每增加 $1hm^2$，人均收入就增加约 96 元。地形显著影响所有乡镇的人均收入，而且随着收入的增加，地形影响递减。即对低收入乡镇的影响最大，对中等收入乡镇的影响次之，对高收入乡镇的影响最小。以上结论可进一步概括为，地理因素对欠发达农区发展的影响，在较低的经济发展水平上，地形和农业资源条件（如人均土地面积）会产生更为显著的影响；在相对较高的经济发展水平上，地理位置以及与此相伴生的基础设施条件会产生更为显著的影响。

与现有的经济地理学相关讨论相联系，本章研究结果具有以下启迪：①尽管随着技术的发展和经济的全球化，地理在经济发展中的作用被人质疑（李小建等，2006；Morgan，2004），但是在不同地区、不同产业的发展中，地理因素的影响明显不同。欠发达农区发展中地理因素的影响正是这样的例证之一。②地理因素对欠发达农区经济发展的影响处于变动之中。随着经济水平的提高，传统地理因素（如地形、农业资源因素等）的影响有逐渐减弱的趋势。但是，对经济集聚有明显影响的地理临近性和基础设施要素，却更明显地影响着农区的发展。因此，并不能简单地认为地理因素对经济发展的影响在下降。③不同发展水平的国家，应关注不同的农区地理研究问题。与发达国家关注后生产型农区、全球化、农区结构新变化、农区管制等（李小建，2006）研究不同，中国的农区发展研究中，应该侧重中国特色的研究问题。在地域广阔的欠发达农区，应该对地理因素对区域发展的影响，以及不同地理环境条件下的农区发展途径的研究给予关注。

基于乡镇数据的分析，能更准确地反映研究单元的地理条件。一县之内，各乡镇之间的地形、地理位置、农业条件、经济结构等，存在明显差别。由此，基于乡镇单元的研究，比县域单元研究具有明显优势。但是，进一步的细分，村级水平上的研究，更能揭示农区发展的空间差异和地理条件的影响。对村内农户的调研和分析，还可以得出农户对发展环境和影响因素的感知和判定（李小建，2002）。

参考文献

河南省统计局. 2006. 河南统计年鉴 2006. 北京：中国统计出版社

贺梅英. 2003. 广东农村居民收入的变化及影响因素分析. 华南农业大学学报，(S1)：148～152

黄祖辉，王敏，宋瑜. 2005. 农村居民收入差距问题研究：基于村庄微观角度的一个分析框架. 管理世界，(3)：75～84

李小建. 2002. 欠发达农区经济发展中的农户行为研究：以豫西山地丘陵区为例. 地理学报，57 (4)：459～468

李小建. 2006. 农区地理学国际研究进展. 人文地理，21 (6)：1～5

李小建等. 2006. 经济地理学（第二版）. 北京：高等教育出版社

林毅夫. 2001. 增加农民收入需要农村基础设施的牢固. 调研世界，(7)：3～4

刘希凤，王联兵. 2007. 影响宁夏农村经济收入因素的灰色关联分析. 宁夏工程技术，6 (1)：98～100

孟凡胜. 2003. 影响黑龙江省农民收入增长的主要因素. 哈尔滨商业大学学报（社会科学版），(1)：22～25

万广华. 1998. 中国农村区域间居民收入差异及其变化的实证分析. 经济研究，(5)：36～41

王桂荣，孟祥书，石玉芳，等. 2006. 河北省农村居民人均纯收入的影响因素分析. 河北农业科学，10 (4)：76～79

王韧. 2006. 中国农村居民收入决定特征及其影响变动：1952～2003 年. 数量经济技术经济研究，(4)：3～13

张平. 1992. 中国农村区域间居民的收入分配. 经济研究，(2)：62～69

周其仁. 2002. 增加农民收入不能回避产权界定. 发展，(03)：44

朱玲. 1992. 非农产业活动对农户收入分配格局的影响. 经济研究，(3)：23～30

Knight J，Song L. 1993. The spatial contribution to income inequality in rural China. Cambridge Journal of Economics，17 (2)：195～213

Meng X，Wu H. 1998. Household income determination and regional income differential in rural China. Asian Economic Journal，12 (1)：65～88

Morgan K. 2004. The exaggerated death of economic geography：Learning，proximity and territory innovation systems. Journal of Economic Geography，4 (1)：3～21

Wan G，Zhou Z. 2005. Income inequality in rural China：Regression-based decomposition using household data. Review of Development Economics，9 (1)：107～120

Wu Z，Zhu Y. 2004. Income deferential and out-migration：The impacts of between-gap and within-gap. Journal of Chinese Economic and Business Studies，2 (1)：27～37

第35章　中部平原村农业生产区位

农业区位的研究，一直得到地理学家和农业经济学家的关注。100多年前，杜能在德国的研究中，对一些自然条件和社会经济条件进行假设后，抽象出相对简单的“孤立国”，并对“孤立国”内的农业区位进行了系统的研究（杜能，1997）。他提出的环状农业结构被后人广泛引用。在后人的研究中，其假设条件也逐步放宽，研究也逐渐接近实际。中国中部传统农区的实际与杜能研究的条件，以及欧美多数国家的农区实际均有很大不同。例如，数百甚至上千年居民的长期定居和耕作，使村庄周围的不同空间距离上的土地质量发生变化；农业一般围绕规模较小的居民点（村庄），并以这些村庄的农户为运营单元；生产活动只有部分用于商业目的（半商品性农业），等等。在这样的条件下，围绕村庄的农业生产活动区位会出现什么特点？本章通过对河南南阳的一个平原农村的实例分析对此做一探索。

通过对河南南阳黄庄村农户和农业生产调查以及遥感数据分析，发现人口高密度地区的平原村庄在耕作半径极小的情况下，存在以住宅和村庄为中心的带状农业区位。从村边向外，可分为蔬菜带、蔬菜粮食混作带和粮食带。相应地，作物的劳动密集度逐渐降低，村地块的蔬菜种植面积比例，以及农户微地块单位面积的投入和收益随距村庄距离的增加而减少，距离对农户农业生产区位的选择具有重要影响。该结果验证了杜能环在耕作半径较小的中国中部农村的存在，但是造成这种空间分异的根本原因并不是物理交通费用的不同，而是作物劳动密集度和地块肥力的差异，基于一定技术条件下的劳动力耕作能力也有一定影响。

35.1　文献评述与理论分析

35.1.1　文献评述

杜能对农业区位的研究表明，随距中心城市距离的增加，农业生产呈环带状分布，从近到远依次为自由农作带、林业带、轮作农业带、谷草轮作带、三圃农作带、畜牧带（杜能，1997）。这种农业经营方式的差异，在于农业收益的不同，而单位农产品的纯利润等于农产品的销售价格减去生产成本和交通费用的和。例如，假设生产成本固定不变，农业利润便取决于由距离决定的交通费用。距离越远，交通费用越高，单位农产品的价格就越高；距离越近，交通费用越低，应该布局市场需要量大、运费比率大的农产品（Kellerman，1989；Grigg，1995）。杜能之后许多学者认为杜能所揭示的以城市市场为中心的农业区位环带状规律具有一定的普遍性，市场距离被重复地报告为决定土地利用和地租的因素（Griffith，1973；Grigg，1995）。

在杜能理论的影响下，多数国外学者在较大尺度上对杜能理论进行证实、证伪（Blaikie，1971；Griffith，1973；Richard，1976；Hill and Smith，1994），以及修正和扩展（Wolpert，1964；Haggett，1975；Blunden，1977）。但也有人在农场内部和村级水平等微观层面上对农业区位进行了研究。例如，Blaikie（1971）认为，在自给农业的微观水平上，距离村庄的远近是决定土地利用的因素，因为农民不得不克服距离去地里耕作。根据微观水平上的研究，Found（1970）和 McCall（1985）认为，在特定的假设下，净收入随离家距离的增加而减少，最适宜的土地利用类型也随离家距离而变化。Lee（2000）通过对吉林省某村的实证研究，发现从劳动力中心（村）向外，依据劳动力投入的多少可分为 4 个农作物带（蔬菜和甜菜带—玉米和大豆带—向日葵带-草地）。De Lisel 通过对加拿大 Manitoba 地区一个农场的分析，发现距离是影响农场内部作物布局的因素之一（De Lisel，1978）。纳瓦佛等发现中部非洲卢旺达的丘陵地带，以农村聚落为中心，存在同心圆状的土地利用形态（李小建，2006）。

中国学者在这方面的工作主要集中在验证杜能理论在我国的适用性并分析其实践意义，如华熙成（1982）研究发现，20 世纪 80 年代初上海市郊区农业分布具有环带状分布的特点；梁增泰（1995）认为，农业区位论对目前我国的农业发展具有借鉴意义，经营者可以依据当地的具体条件，包括所处的区位条件决定自己的经营方向；马兰和张曦（2003）认为，农业区位论在我国还存在着较大的适用空间，中国农业的布局必须遵循农业区位论的空间法则；叶长卫和李雪松（2002）认为，杜能的农业区位论模式仍在起作用，农业政策的制定必须重视运用区位地租；董晓霞等（2006）通过对北京周边地区农业结构的研究，认为地理区位假说对当前城市周边地区农业生产依然成立，但农村交通基础设施的完善不仅促进了地区种植业结构调整，而且大大削弱了生产地与中心消费地之间的地理距离对农业生产空间选择的影响。但是与国际研究比较，我国学者缺乏微观的研究，在村级水平上的研究还少见成果发表。

基于农户和村级水平的微观农业区位研究有助于我们深入了解中国特殊背景下农业区位特点和形成机制。不仅可以丰富和发展农业区位理论，而且可以弥补宏观农业区位论在实际应用时的局限，对农户农业生产具有一定的指导意义。微观分析的方法对现代高速变化的农业的政策制定、规划和项目发展具有实践价值。同时，也有助于理解农作系统的静态和动态机制（De Lisel，1978；王鹏等，2004）。本研究以农户为农业经营主体，以村地块和农户微地块为农业活动场所，研究自然村（生产小组）级水平上的农业区位问题，主要关注以村和住宅为中心的半自给性农业、随距离的增加所发生的区位变化特点，以及影响这种现象的原因。

35.1.2　制度与地块耕作类型

耕作地块是农户进行农业生产的基本场所。除了少部分农户租用其他农户的土地和承包生产小组的备用地外，绝大多数农户的农业区位选择是在属于自己的地块中种植不同的农作物，因此，耕作地块是农户农业活动区位的基础，耕作地块的面积大小、距离远近、农作属性特征直接影响着农户农业活动的方式和类型。

均田承包制是农户取得耕作地块的基本土地使用制度。所谓均田承包是将生产小组所拥有的土地按人口多少进行均分。这些土地一般位于自然村的周围，但不完全是环绕自然村的形态，可能只集中于某些侧面向外延伸，直到与另一生产小组的耕地交界。

均田承包制的基本操作方法是土地分段、抓阄确定顺序和按人口均分。土地分段是将生产小组所有的供分割的村地块按距离远近、肥力大小和能否灌溉等进行分区，同一地段，地块的远近和肥力大小及灌溉条件基本一致，不同地段则差别较大。土地分段的地段数量由生产小组土地的复杂性决定，如果地形复杂、村地块农作属性差别较大，则分段数量较多；相反，如果地形单一、村地块农作属性差别较小，则分段数量较少。当然，地段数量由村干部决定，有时为了公平，平原地区也可以有许多地段。在具体某一地段内进行土地分割时，先决定分地的方向，然后决定分地的顺序，最后按人口进行均分。

均田承包制带来了土地的细碎化，村地块被农户均分后，就形成了村地块由农户微地块构成的情况。微地块之间通常有界石为分割标志，农户的耕作在微地块之内进行。微地块的宽度一般在不足 1m 到十几米之间，有时，较窄的微地块为耕作带来许多不便。

设 S 代表某村的全部耕地，被分为 n 个地段，该村共有农户 m 户，u 为农户在各个地段内分得的土地面积，则

$$S=S_1+S_2+\cdots+S_n=(u_{11}+u_{12}+\cdots u_{1m})+(u_{21}+u_{22}+\cdots+u_{2m}) +\cdots+(u_{n1}+u_{n2}+\cdots u_{nm}) \tag{35.1}$$

$$S=\sum_{i=1}^{n}S_i=\sum_{j=1}^{m}\sum_{i=1}^{m}u_{ij} \tag{35.2}$$

由此可以看出，村子全部耕地被 n 个地段 m 个农户分割成为 $n\times m$ 个微地块，如果考虑到某地段由若干个村地块组成，那么微地块的面积更小。

35.2 研究村庄选择与数据获取

35.2.1 研究村庄选择

为了研究农户农业生产活动的区位差异，本章选择了紧邻城镇（商品性农业活动较为发达）、土地利用以农业为主且农业耕作多样化（具有多种类型农业活动）的河南省南阳市镇平县的牛王庙行政村黄庄自然村进行实例分析。河南省及其南阳市在农区研究中具有一定的代表性和典型性。河南是全国农业大省，农业人口众多、农区面积广大，而且农业产值和许多农产品在全国占有重要地位。南阳市是河南省的农业大市，农业人口众多，城镇化水平低（农业人口占 70%），农区面积大（耕地面积在河南排名第一），农业产值和主要农产品在河南省占有重要地位（农林牧渔业增加值、油料产量在河南居首位）（河南省统计局，2006）。

南阳市镇平县为典型的农业县，农业人口（占 88.59%）和农区面积（耕地面积 78.66 千 hm^2，在 13 个县级单元中排名第四）较大，城镇化水平较低（23.02%），农业产值在当地的经济结构中占较大比例（第一产业产值占生产总值的 16.55%）。在镇平县内，选择了城关镇牛王庙村黄庄自然村作为研究样本村，主要考虑其典型性、数据可得性和种植结构的复杂性。该村为平原地形，紧邻镇平县城（约 1km），总人口 236

人，总户数 49 户，总土地面积 292.5 亩（1 亩＝0.0667hm^2），全部为农用地。由于该地自然环境优越又紧邻县城，因而人口密度较大，人均耕地仅 0.8979 亩。该自然村经济为以农业为主，除了少部分劳动力出外打工外，多数农户在家种地。因为离县城很近，且灌溉方便，所以蔬菜种植面积较大，除此之外，还种植有粮食作物和经济作物，蔬菜的商品率很高，而粮食作物则较低，主要供农户自己消费。冬小麦平均产量约 400kg/亩，玉米产量平均约 450kg/亩。蔬菜从地里采摘后，运回到村里农户家中进行分选和初步加工，然后用人力三轮车或机动三轮车运送到约 2km 处的县城蔬菜批发市场销售。农业生产资料主要在县城或附近村里的农业生产资料代卖点购买。该村实行一年两熟的耕作制度，夏粮作物主要为冬小麦，秋粮作物主要为玉米、大豆、红薯、绿豆、芝麻等；蔬菜种植在全年均可进行，但是冬季蔬菜种植品种较少，面积也较小，采用塑料大棚技术种植蔬菜的农户很少。除了种植业外，几乎没有农户饲养家畜和家禽，也没有饲养大型役畜。

35.2.2　问卷设计与数据获取

问卷设计的核心是农业生产的区位问题，主要内容包括农户耕作地块的详细情况，各个耕作地块农业种植类型、耕作制度与详细的投入产出情况，2000～2005 年种植类型的变化情况，农业结构调整情况等。对问题的回答根据不同的提问内容设计了如填空、填写表格、选择等方式。另外，为了获取真实信息和判断问卷的有效性，我们还设计了部分隐蔽性重复题，以判断前后回答是否一致。

数据获取主要通过入户问卷调查、个人访谈（对农户和村干部）、地块调查三种方式进行。在国家自然科学基金重点项目的资助下，河南大学环境与规划学院和南阳师范学院环境科学与旅游学院 6 名硕士研究生和优秀本科生，经过严格培训后，于 2006 年 7～8 月，对该村所有农户（除个别不在家的农户外）进行了面对面调查。同时，调查人员还借助高分辨率（0.6m）卫星影像，对村域的大小道路、居住区域、各户住宅、灌溉设施、各个地块的范围、土壤、坡度、海拔高度、种植类型等进行外业测量并绘制地图。

个人访谈对象为农户代表和村干部。我们选择了 5 名有文化、长期在家种地的男性壮年劳动力，另选择小组组长、（行政村）村长、村支书进行访谈。访谈的内容主要是该村种植农作物的类型、投入、产出、结构调整、农民收入、距离对种地的影响等情况。

本次调查共获取农户农业区位调查问卷 45 份，其中有效问卷 44 份。调查问卷回收后，进行甄别，去除无效问卷，对有效问卷进行编号，将数据输入到 EXECL2000 中，形成农户农业区位数据库（44×196）。

35.3　农户农业区位的选择

黄庄村为城市郊区平原村，耕地面积较小，耕作半径很小，最远地块的直线距离仅有 655m，各个地块的自然条件差异很小，其他影响农业生产的外在因素也基本上无什么差别，可以认为是一个均质的区域，因此，本章将主要分析距离对农业区位选择的影响。

35.3.1 农户农业生产区位选择的空间范围

由于黄庄村租地情况很少发生，因此，农户全在属于自己的责任田里耕作。2006年，该村共有耕地 211.91 亩。根据肥力大小、土壤质量高低、灌溉方便程度、交通方便程度和距村的远近，在 1996 年分地时，经村民和村干部讨论，将其分为三个等级，即一等地（即一段地，包括家后一段地、庄西一段地、下洼一段地和庄南一段地 4 块）、二等地（包括庄南二段地、河西二段地和路东二段地 3 块）和三等地（包括庄后三段地、河西三段地和路东三段地 3 块）。其中，一等地 96.25 亩，人均 0.4498 亩（当时全村 214 人）；二等地 82.37 亩，人均 0.3849 亩；三等地 33.29 亩，人均 0.16 亩（图 35.1a）。

黄庄村地块距离较近。以村几何中心到村地块几何中心的交通距离而论，地块最小距离为 125m，最大距离为 581m，平均距离为 316.9m。以农户家庭到微地块几何中心的交通距离而论，最大为 745m，最小为 128m，平均值为 455m。黄庄村地块按每户的人口规模和地块等级被划割为 156 个微地块（图 35.1b），平均每户拥有 3 个微地块（1996 年分地时有 52 户农户）。

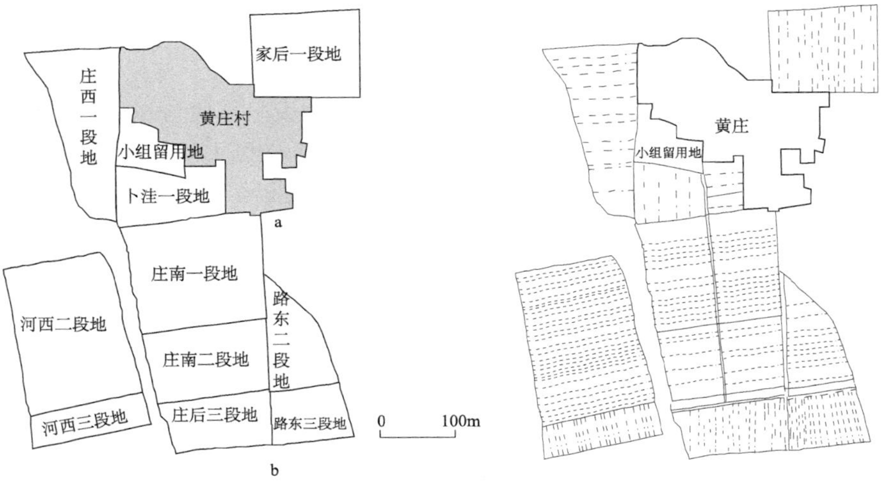

图 35.1 黄庄地块与微地块分布

35.3.2 农户种植作物品种的分布

农业区位的选择问题，具体到该村就是每个微地块和整体村地块的种植作物品种的布局问题。由于地形的原因和长期的农作习惯，本地只发展了种植业，而没有发展林业、渔业、畜牧业。在种植业方面，本村不仅种植粮食作物，而且也大量种植蔬菜，还有少量的其他经济作物。由于蔬菜品种很多，为研究方便，不再将蔬菜品种细分。

随距离的增加，村地块蔬菜种植面积比例逐渐减少，而粮食种植面积比例逐渐增加。据调查和统计，可得到黄庄村各个地块粮食、蔬菜种植面积及其比例。其中，距离的测算以村庄和住宅为中心。农户经营农产品的目标，可分“自用”和“销售”，但不论是“自用”还是“销售”，农产品收获后都要先运输到住宅中进行储存和初步加工。据计算，粮食种植面积比例与交通距离的 Pearson 相关系数为 0.8792（显著性水平均为 0.01）。进一步的回归分析更揭示出粮食种植比例随距离变化的规律：

$$t_g = -0.05 + 0.002d_c \tag{35.3}$$

$R=0.879$，$F=27.246$，sig. $=0.001$。
式中，t_g 为粮食种植比例；d_c 为地块交通距离。式（35.3）表明粮食种植面积比例随距离的增大而增大。

因为没有休闲地，所以蔬菜种植面积比例和粮食种植面积比例是互补关系。蔬菜种植面积比例将与距离呈高度负相关关系，即距离越近，蔬菜种植面积越大，距离越远，蔬菜种植面积越小（图 35.2）。

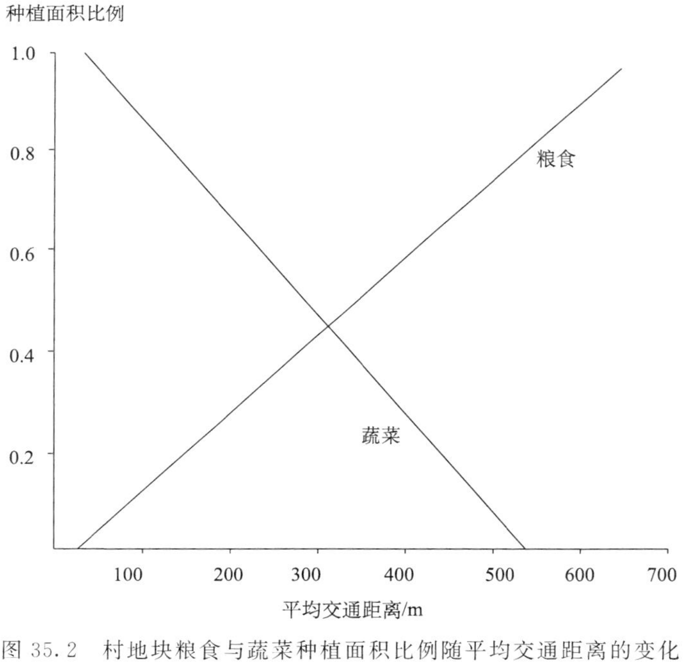

图 35.2　村地块粮食与蔬菜种植面积比例随平均交通距离的变化

35.3.3　农户微地块投入、收益与耕作距离的关系

耕作距离反映了农户实际耕作时所跨越的地理空间。对各农户微地块总投入与耕作距离进行线性回归分析，可得到如下的线性方程：

$$p_t = 1584.938 - 1.833d_c \tag{35.4}$$

$R=0.742$，$F=139.923$，sig. $=0.000$。

式中，p_t为地块的总投入；d_c为微地块耕作距离。式（35.4）表明，随微地块耕作距离的增加，微地块的总投入呈线性减少。

微地块总投入主要由化肥、农药、种子、灌溉、收割、耕地等项目构成。种植蔬菜的化肥、农药和灌溉费用远高于种植粮食作物。根据调查，种植蔬菜的该三项投入分别为600～700元/亩、100～200元/亩、200～300元/亩；而种植粮食作物该三项费用为100～200元/亩、20～50元/亩、30～60元/亩。种植同类作物在各微地块之间其三项投入差别较小。因此不同的粮食蔬菜种植面积比例是造成微地块总投入随距离递减的主要原因。

与微地块总投入随耕作距离增加而减少相对应，微地块收益也随距离增加而减少（图35.3）。对总收益与耕作距离进行线性回归，可得到如下线性方程：

$$P_u=3058.758-3.86d_c \tag{35.5}$$

DW $=1.954$，$R=0.819$，$F=232.506$，sig. $=0.000$。

式中，P_u为地块的总收益；d_c为微地块耕作距离。

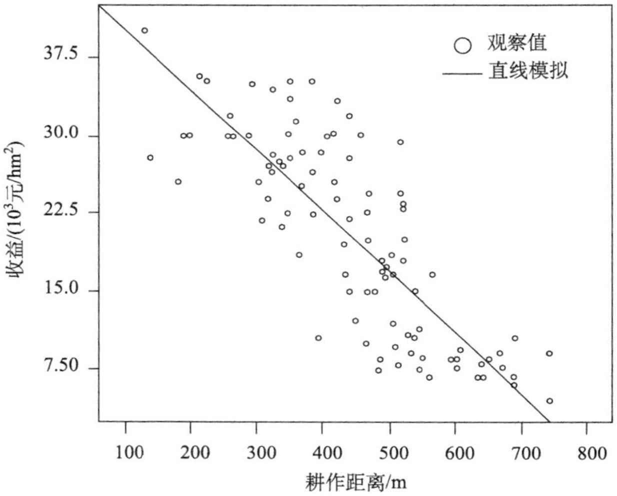

图35.3　农户微地块每亩收益随耕作距离的变化

总收益除了与农业技术和农业内部投入（如农药、化肥、种子等）有关外，还受到土壤类型、土壤肥力、灌溉、排水、坡度、海拔高度、地块交通等条件的影响。对于本案例村而言，土壤类型、灌溉、排水三个因素与总收益无相关关系，其他几个因素中，总收益与肥力等级高度正相关（相关系数为0.9838，显著性水平为0.01）。总收益与坡度、海拔高度和地块交通状况的相关系数不仅较小（分别为0.4397、0.5458和0.2835），且都没有达到显著性水平。

总收益主要由种植蔬菜的收益和种植粮食作物的收益两部分构成。尽管地块之间的蔬菜收益和地块之间的粮食收益有差别，但差别较小，它们对总收益贡献较小。但是种植蔬菜和种植粮食作物之间的收益则差别很大，种植蔬菜一般收益为1500～3000元/

亩，种植粮食为 400～700 元/亩。因此，造成总收益随耕作距离变化的主要原因是不同作物种植面积比例。近地块由于蔬菜种植比例较大，因而地块单位收益较高；而远地块粮食种植比例较大，因而收益较低。

在一定的农业技术水平下，土壤肥力与距离高度相关，黄庄村土壤肥力等级与平均交通距离的 Pearson 相关系数为－0.9133，显著性水平为 0.01（2 尾法）。这可能意味着，历史上，距离村庄较近的地块，投入的有机肥较多，投入的农作劳动力也较多，因而形成较高的肥力（至少在 1996 年分地时如此）。

35.3.4　以村为中心的带状农业格局

无论是在农户微地块尺度上还是在村地块尺度上，农业投入与产出均表现出随距离增加而递减的现象。根据村地块粮食蔬菜作物种植面积比例和农户微地块投入产出随距离变化情况，可以将本案例以村中心为中心的农业布局变化抽象为三个带（图 35.4）。

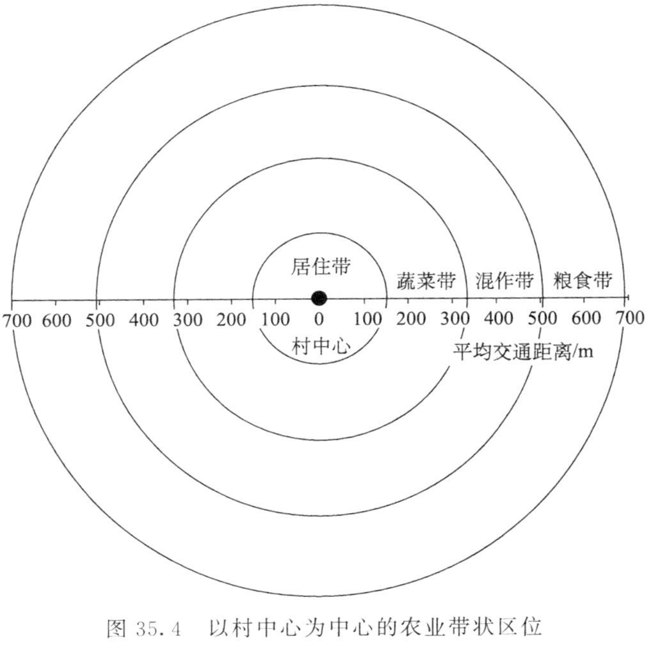

图 35.4　以村中心为中心的农业带状区位

村中心周围直线距离约 150m 的范围内为居住带，由此向外分别如下。

第一带，蔬菜带。该带分布在居住带外侧交通距离 310～350m 内，主要种植蔬菜，蔬菜种植面积比例一般在 80%以上。由于蔬菜种植需要大量的劳动投入，因此，又可称为高劳动密集带。该带农业投入最高，收益也最高。所种植蔬菜主要用作销售，因此，又可称为高商品带。

第二带，混作带。该带范围延伸至交通距离 480～520m，种植蔬菜和粮食及其他经济作物，蔬菜种植面积比例 30%～80%，劳动密集程度中等。该带农业投入中等，收益也较高，商品率中等，为中商品带。

第三带，粮食带。该带范围延伸至交通距离 680～720m，主要种植粮食作物和除了蔬菜外的其他经济作物，很少种植蔬菜，种植作物的劳动密集度最低。该带农业投入最低，收益也最低。所种植的粮食主要供自己消费，又叫做低商品带。

35.4 影响农户农业区位选择的主要因素

粮食蔬菜种植面积比例决定着地块总收益和总投入，那么，又是什么影响着农户选择种植蔬菜还是粮食作物呢？在农户家庭收益最大化的前提下，该案例村农户主要考虑了以下几个因素。

35.4.1 作物劳作的交通成本

不同的农作物具有不同的管理特点和农作强度，因而需要投入的交通成本具有很大差异。粮食作物在当前的农业技术水平下，劳作强度较小，根据对黄庄村的调查，一个劳动力种植一亩玉米或小麦，需要投入的劳动力约为 40～50 个工时（约 4～5 个工作日）。而蔬菜作物的种植则需要非常大的劳动投入，一个劳动力在一年内可种植 2 亩蔬菜，除下雨、下雪外，劳动力几乎全在地里耕作和管理，即种植一亩蔬菜的劳动力投入约为 1500～1700 个工时（约 150～170 个工作日）。以 150 个工作日、每个工作日到地里两个往返计算，一个劳动力种植一亩蔬菜的往返次数约 300 次，而一个劳动力种植一亩粮食的往返次数约 10 次（按 5 个工作日计算），设农户种植蔬菜的耕作距离为 d_{fv}，种植粮食作物的耕作距离为 d_{fg}，每米的交通费用率，客运为 rm（单位：元/m），则一个劳动力种植蔬菜的客运交通成本 c_v 为

$$c_v = 300 \times 2 \times r_m \times d_{fv} = 600 r_m d_{fv} \tag{35.6}$$

种植粮食作物的交通成本 c_g 为

$$c_g = 10 \times 2 \times r_m \times d_{fg} = 20 r_m d_{fg} \tag{35.7}$$

种植蔬菜与种植粮食作物的交通成本比为

$$\frac{c_v}{c_g} = \frac{600 r_m d_{fv}}{20 r_m d_{fg}} = 30 \frac{d_{fv}}{d_{fg}} \tag{35.8}$$

$$c_v = 30 \frac{d_{fv}}{d_{fg}} c_g \tag{35.9}$$

由式（35.8）和式（35.9）可看出，如果 $d_{fv} = d_{fg}$，则种植蔬菜的客运交通成本是种植粮食作物的 30 倍。也就是说，种植蔬菜的客运交通成本远远高于种植粮食。如果采取近距离种植蔬菜远距离种植粮食作物的策略，则可以最大限度地减少交通成本。

另外，种植蔬菜作物的货运成本也远大于种植粮食作物。种植蔬菜的农业生产资料投入远高于种植粮食。例如，化肥在蔬菜种植中的投入为 600～700 元/亩，而在粮食作物中为 100～200 元/亩；农药的蔬菜投入为 100～200 元/亩，粮食为 20～50 元/亩。现在已很少有农户使用农家粪作肥料，即使有也是仅在近距离地块使用。同时收获的成品

蔬菜要经常从地里运送到住宅中进行分选和包装，其运输非常繁琐和不便，而粮食则是一次性的收割（现在多数使用收割机进行），运输量较小。

35.4.2 地块肥力大小

土壤肥力是影响作物产量的基本因素。土壤肥力是土地自然性能的经济体现，它与土壤结构、成分、微地形、水气循环直接相关，同时土壤肥力也受到人类土地利用的影响，人们有意识地培养肥力，如施有机肥、合理的耕作和灌溉等，将会促进土壤肥力的提高。在土地收益上，在其他条件相同或相似的情况下，高肥力土壤将会有较高农业收益。

不同地块的土壤肥力影响到农业种植区位的选择。在高肥力土壤地块，农户一般趋向于种植高投入和高产出的农作物，从而获得较高的报酬；而在低肥力土壤地块，农户一般趋向于种植投入和产出相对较小的农作物，以保持合理的投入产出比。由于该样本村周围近距离地块肥力较高，因此种植蔬菜的比例较大，相反，远距离地块肥力较低，因此主要种植粮食作物。

35.4.3 农业技术条件与劳动力耕作能力

在一定的农业技术水平下，劳动力能够耕作的土地数量是有限的。就目前样本村的情况看，土地耕作及部分作物（如小麦）收割已实现机械化，已经实现机井灌溉，但如施肥（除耕作时施底肥外）、喷洒农药、多数的蔬菜播种、蔬菜收割与采摘等农作过程仍主要以人工为主。运输机械主要有人力三轮车、机动三轮车、二轮摩托车、自行车等。根据调查，平均每个劳动力能够耕作蔬菜的土地面积为 2 亩，粮食作物为 10 亩。在劳动力数量一定的情况下，近距离地块的土地面积已经能够满足这些劳动力的蔬菜种植需求，他们就没有必要在增加交通成本的情况下到较远地块进行蔬菜种植。这也是造成近距离地块种植蔬菜、远距离地块种植粮食作物的重要因素之一。

当然也可能有例外，有些劳动力缺乏的农户，在自己的近距离责任田里仍以种植粮食作物为主，或全部种植粮食。

35.5 结论与讨论

黄庄村为平原城郊近邻村，所有地块均为平地，土壤类型、灌溉条件基本一致，耕作半径很小。农户为基本生产单元，粮食生产以自用为主，蔬菜生产主要为商业目的。对该村的实证研究可以得出以下结论。

距离对农户农业生产区位的选择具有重要影响。围绕平原村庄，存在带状农业区位布局结构。从村边向外，可分为蔬菜带、蔬菜粮食混作带和粮食带。相应地，作物劳动密集度逐渐降低，分为高劳动密集带、中劳动密集带和低劳动密集带。农户微地块的投入和收益表现出随交通距离和耕作距离的增加而减少的现象。本章在耕作半径较小的中国中部农村，进一步验证了杜能带状农业区位的存在。但是，与“杜能环”相比，该村庄的案例表现出如下不同特点：①农业区位变化表现在较小（数十米）的尺度上；②由于当地农业生产和居民消费习惯不同，农业带状类型比较单一（仅表现为蔬菜和粮作）。

引起不同距离农业区位差异的主要原因是作物劳动密集度决定的生产成本差异。和“杜能环”不同的是，环状结构不是由货物从生产地运送到市场的交通费用造成的，而是由劳动密集度造成的。由于蔬菜生产需要投入大量劳动力，村庄又是劳动力的供应中心，农户从村庄到耕地的通勤成本要远远大于从耕地到蔬菜市场的运输成本。由此带来了蔬菜生产近邻村庄的布局。研究农村现在的交通工具状况（多为自行车或步行），又进一步加剧了劳动密集型农业生产的就近布局。此外，近邻村庄耕地的较高肥力，也利于高投入高产出的蔬菜生产。需要进一步指出的是，研究农村的农业完全以农户为经营单元。由于该村户均耕地的分布大致相同（即每户均有不同距离的微地块），加之多数农户经营的农业结构类似（种植蔬菜和粮作），使得这里的农业布局在整体上体现出了距离对农业土地利用的影响。如果不同农户经营行为不同，或农户耕地集中于某些地段，可能会带来不同的结果。此外，如果村子相关农业活动的劳动密集度差别较小，农户农业区位的选择也可能会出现不同情况。因此，本研究所得结论在不同情况下应慎重使用。

参考文献

董晓霞，黄季焜，Scott Rozelle，等. 2006. 地理区位、交通基础设施与种植业结构调整研究. 管理世界，(9)：59～63

河南省统计局. 2006. 河南统计年鉴 2006. 北京：中国统计出版社

华熙成. 1982. 上海市郊区农业区位模式及农业生产问题的探讨. 经济地理，(3)：17～23

李小建. 2006. 经济地理学（第二版）. 北京：高等教育出版社

梁增泰. 1995. 运用农业区位理论调控农业生产布局与生产要素的投入，提高经济效益. 经济改革，(2)：21～23

马兰，张曦. 2003. 农业区位论及其现实意义. 云南农业科技，(3)：3～5

王鹏，黄贤金，张兆干，等. 2004. 江西红壤区农业产业政策改革的农户行为响应与水土保持效果分析——以江西省上饶县村庄及农户调查为例. 地理科学，24 (3)：328～332

叶长卫，李雪松. 2002. 浅谈杜能农业区位论对我国农业发展的作用与启示. 华中农业大学学报（社会科学版），(4)：1～4

约翰·冯·杜能. 1997. 孤立国同农业和国民经济的关系. 北京：商务印书馆

Blaikie P M. 1971. Spatial organization of agriculture in some north Indian villages, Part I. Transactions of the Institute of British Geographers, 52: 1～40

Blunden J. 1977. Rural land use. Fundamentals of human geography: section Ⅱ area patterns. Milton Keynes: Open University Press

De Lisel D de G. 1978. Effects of distance internal to the farm: A challenging subject for North American geographers. The Professional Geographer, 30 (3): 278～288

Found W C. 1970. Towards a general theory relating distance between farm and home to agricultural production. Geographical Analysis, 2: 165～176

Griffith E. 1973. Testing the von Thünen theory in Uruguay. Geographical Review, 63: 500～516

Grigg D. 1995. An introduction to agricultural geography. New York: Routledge

Haggett P. 1975. Geography: A modern synthesis. Harper and Row, New York

Hill R，Smith D L. 1994. Is von Thunen alive and well? A transport-cost surface model for South Australian wheat. Australian Geographical Studies，32：183～190

Kellerman A. 1989. Agricultural location theory：Basic models. Environment and Planning A，21：1381～1396

Lee L. 2000. Labor location and agricultural land use in Jilin，China. Professional Geographer，52（1）：74～83

McCall，M K. 1985. The significance of distance constraints in peasant farming systems with special reference to sub-Saharan Africa. Applied Geography，5：325～345

Richard C J. 1976. Testing macro-Thonen models by linear programming. The Professional Geographer，28（4）：353～361

Wolpert J. 1964. The decision process in the spatial context. Annals of the Association of American Geographers，54：537～558

第 36 章　欠发达区专业村空间分析

专业村是指某农村的大部分农户商品性地从事一种或多种相互关联的生产或服务活动，从而使该活动的经济总量（如产值）构成这个村的经济总量的主体（李小建等，2009a）。中国现阶段的农区发展中，专业村具有重要作用。2010 年年底，全国专业村达到 51486 个，农民人均纯收入高于全国平均值的 15.56%；从事主导产业的农民人均纯收入高出全国的 25.82%（农业部，2011）。已有研究表明，企业家精神是专业村形成与发展的关键因素，在传统小农经济占主导地位的农区，是否拥有企业家精神的农户决定着专业村的有无；正是那些具有企业家精神的农户，通过发现新的商机，促进新型经济活动的出现，形成专业村的先导农户，并通过示范效应和网络联系扩散至其他农户。村庄所在地的资源禀赋、地理区位、经济基础和传统习惯决定着专业村的类型，即决定着专业村发展的方向。同样具有企业家精神的先导农户，在不同类型的环境中，可以形成不同类型的专业村（李小建等，2009a）。但是，从农区经济发展及其相关地理环境角度，在已形成的专业村中，环境对专业村的专业化率是否有显著的影响？环境在多大程度上影响专业村的发展？不同类别的专业村形成中，环境的影响又有什么具体差别？对此，相关文献少有论述。

本章基于经济学和地理学中的“理性小农”“劳动分工与专业化”和“距离衰减与邻里效应”理论，并考虑资源环境条件，建立了解释专业村形成机理和形成类型的理论框架。用数理方法推理了村产业结构的发展变化和专业村的形成。在理论分析的基础上，运用 2010 年河南省的专业村数据，选择地形、区位、土地和劳动力等环境变量和 16 种专业村的虚拟变量，使用最小二乘法进行回归，结果表明村环境资源条件对专业化率有显著影响：①村劳动力资源越多，专业化率越低；②村土地越多越利于专业化生产；③村离县级市距离越近，越有利于形成农产品加工专业村；④具有批发市场可以提高所有专业村的专业化率，对养殖业和加工业专业村更是如此；⑤如果其他环境相同，丘陵地区的专业化率比其他地区低；这主要与丘陵地区交通条件不畅、人均耕地较少等有关。采用定性模型分析表明，环境影响在不同类别的专业村有所不同。土地丰裕程度对茶叶、林业和水果种植等类专业村形成有正面影响，劳动力资源对花卉等专业村的形成产生影响；地域通达性对水果、蔬菜和花卉等时鲜产品专业村的形成产生正面影响。该研究结果的实践引申，在不同环境条件的地区，可以制定相应的适宜专业化发展的引导政策。结合河南省实际，本章的专业村，主要指以农业或农产品加工业为主的专业村。

36.1　理论基础

中国的农区主要是以农户为基本单元的社会。农户家庭担负着人类繁衍发展的职能和农区社会最基层的管理职能，也具有经济组织的基本职能。农村实行联产承包责任制后，这种经济职能更为明显。在对农户行为进行研究时，有人认为农户相当于市场经济中的企业（舒尔茨，2010），小农无论在市场领域还是政治社会生活中，都更倾向于按投资者的原则行事（Popkin，1979），即“舒尔茨—波普金的理性小农”命题。与此不同，一些人认为小农坚守“安全第一”原则，提出“道义小农”命题，即小农宁可选择避免经济灾难，也不愿冒险追求收益最大化（詹姆斯·斯科特，2001）。这可称为“生存理性”，前者也称为“经济理性”。还有人从家庭内部分配角度认为农户不是一个厂商，它很少“按劳”分配，更多是“按需”分配；但这种利他主义主要反映在内部，其对外经济上仍偏向厂商原则（史清华，2005）。改革开放以来，农民基本生存得以满足以及农民义利观的变化，中国农户经济行为呈现出由生存理性向经济理性转变（李红涛和付少平，2002）。同时，单一农户与农户整体行为也存在差别。就单一农户而论，不同的家庭人员素质和决策能力影响着农户对自然资源和环境条件的利用（李小建等，2009）。农户整体行为更符合理性原则。舒尔茨通过对处于贫穷农村社会的印度和危地马拉的农民考察，认为“在传统农业中，生产要素配置效率低下的情况是比较少见的”（舒尔茨，2010）。

古典经济学强调经济增长与生产专业化的相互作用。认为，经济增长、资本积累会推动生产专业化和劳动分工的发展，而生产专业化和劳动分工会进一步让资本流向更具效率的生产领域，实现规模经济，进而带来更快的经济增长（亚当·斯密，2011）。由此导致经济发展的良性循环。新古典经济学认为，企业按利润最大化方式使用其购买或雇佣的生产要素（土地、劳动力、资本等）；家庭出售他们拥有的生产要素，否则就只有劳动；消费者在收入和价格约束下，在多种“商品束”间配置支出以最大化效用。这样，生产要素按照边际效用原则分配，农户从生产角度趋向于向边际生产率最高的部门发展，从消费的角度趋向于采纳边际效用最高的分配方案（Johnston et al.，2000）。20世纪80年代，杨小凯等经济学家重新强调分工和专业化的思想，认为作为经济增长动力的分工与专业化是内生的，即使外部环境、技术、制度不变，在社会生产条件下，分工和专业化水平也会自发地提高，从而推动经济持续增长（杨小凯和黄有光，1999）。尽管这些理论所论及的主要是工业，但现代农业的发展在原理上与此并无原则区别，尤其是在农户的理性原则假设及其农户经营并不限于农业种植的前提下，作为经济单元的农户与企业基本类似。

基于以上分析，在接近自由竞争的环境中，农户家庭经济的发展会逐步显现出专业化趋势。如果这种专业化的农户集中在一个较小地域（如村庄），即形成专业村；如果在较大的地域拓展，即形成专业化区域。从理论上说，如果某村有农户出现专业化发展，村内的邻近农户最易受到影响。瑞典学者哈格斯特朗在20世纪中叶通过研究创新扩散，发现社会经济现象的扩散存在距离衰减和邻里效应（Hagerstrand，1968）。距离衰减被认为是地理学第一定律，它强调所有事物都相互关联，事物之间的关系随着它们之间的距离增大而逐渐疏远（Tobler，2004）。与此相关，近距离的邻里在长期频繁的相互作用之中，形成相同或相似的行为方式，增强了个体之间的一致性（Johnston，2009）。将这些理论用于村庄内农户之间的关系，可以推理专业化的农户只要能够成功运作，很易于带来一定程度的村庄专业化发展。尤其是在中国传统文化下，亲缘网络、邻里关系均比较浓厚，更会促进村内新的经济活动的扩散（罗庆和李小建，2010；Li et al.，2011）。

以上三种理论可以共同解释专业村的形成（图 36.1）。其中，“理性小农”理论决定了农村决策者的基本行为准则。农户只要按照“经济理性”决策，其结果一定会综合考虑各种环境和资源条件，尽最大可能配置要素以取得最大效益。只有“理性小农”的环境，才会出现企业家精神的先导农户（郑风田和程郁，2006）。因此，“理性小农”是专业村形成的先导条件。“劳动分工和专业化”理论解释了资源流动的方向。各地环境和资源条件的差异，形成了边际生产率的差异。分工和专业化会进一步促进资本流向最具效益的部门，带来规模经济。“分工与专业化”是专业村形成的重要动力。“距离衰减和邻里效应”理论解释了专业化在空间上近距离集中分布，这对于专业村的形成十分必要。但形成什么样的专业村又与各地的资源环境条件相关联。村资源禀赋形成经济活动的基础；村地理区位是各种资源有效利用和新的要素注入的重要条件。尤其在欠发达农区发展中，区位及交通条件起着重要作用（李小建等，2008）。此外，传统基础和文化条件也有一定作用（李小建等，2010）。

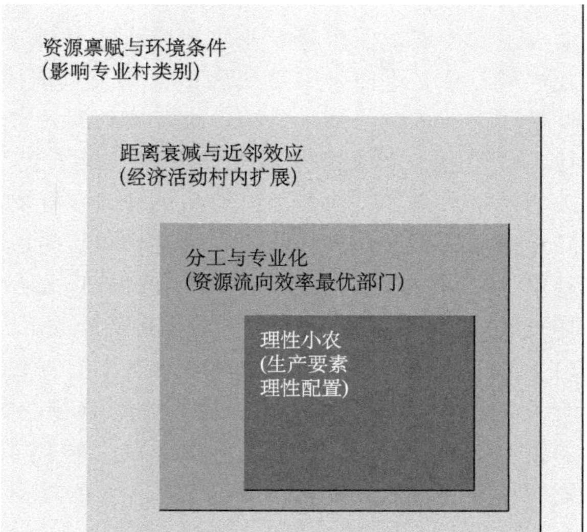

图 36.1 专业村形成理论

36.2 专业村与环境关系的数理分析

36.2.1 村经济结构与环境

1980 年实行联产承包责任制后，农户成为生产和消费的基本经济单元。农户是产品的生产者和生产要素价格的接受者，生产和消费行为属竞争性行为，在这种情况下，学者们往往使用代表性农户模型（哈尔·瓦里安，1997）来研究村经济活动，用村集中行为来代表农户分散行为的总和。由此，我们假定一个村为一个代表性农户，在地理环境、市场环境和资源禀赋约束下，安排生产和消费，最大化效用。假定村效用函数为 $U(X^D, Z)$，即效用水平取决于村自产物品 X^D 和村非自产物品 Z 的消费量（X^D 和 Z 均为向量）。村面临的预算约束为 $p'X^D + qZ = M$，其中，p' 和 q 分别为自产品和非自产品的价格向量；M 为村收入。收入来自三个方面，自产品销售收入、打工收入和地租收入，即 $M = p'X^S + wL_w + rA_r$，其中，p' 和 X^S 为自产品价格和产量向量；w 和 L_w 为打工工资和打工劳动力数量；r 和 A_r 为单位土地面积地租和出租的土地。假定 i 产品产量取决于劳动投入 L_i 和土地投入 A_i，以及地形 T，则生产函数为 $X_i^S = F_i(L_i, A_i, T)$。一个村的资源是有限的，投入各产业的生产资源之和必须等于固定的资源禀赋，因此，村资源约束为 $\sum_{i=1}^{I} L_i + L_w = L$ 和 $\sum_{i=1}^{I} A_i + A_r = A$，即各产业的劳动投入之和等于劳动供给，土地投入之和等于土地供给。

在村预算约束中出现的自产品价格 p' 是净价格，它等于市场价格与单位产品交易费用之差，即 $p_i' = p_i - c_i$。单位产品交易费用取决于交易数量和运输距离，且交易数量越大，单位产品交易费用越低；运输距离越大，单位产品交易费用越高。单位产品交易费用函数可设定为 $c_i = G_i(|X_i^S - X_i^D|, D_i)$，且 $\partial G_i(|X_i^S - X_i^D|, D_i)/\partial|X_i^S - X_i^D| < 0$，$\partial G_i(|X_i^S - X_i^D|, D_i)/\partial D_i > 0$，其中，$D_i$ 为运输距离，$X_i^S - X_i^D$ 为产品 i 的净供给。净供给可以大于零，等于零，也可小于零，无论净供给大于零还是小于零都存在交易费用，因此，交易费用是净供给绝对值 $|X_i^S - X_i^D|$ 的函数。

村作为代表性消费者其目标是最大化全村居民效用水平，即最大化代表性效用函数，所面临的约束如上所述，综合起来村经济的最优规划为

$$\max U(X^D, Z) \tag{36.1}$$

$$s.t.\ p'X^D + qZ = M \tag{36.2}$$

$$M = p'X^S + wL_w + rA_r \tag{36.3}$$

$$X_i^S = F_i(L_i, A_i, T) \tag{36.4}$$

$$\sum_{i=1}^{I} L_i + L_w = L \tag{36.5}$$

$$\sum_{i=1}^{I} A_i + A_r = A \tag{36.6}$$

$$p_i' = p_i - c_i \tag{36.7}$$

$$c_i = G_i(|X_i^S - X_i^D|, D_i) \tag{36.8}$$

求解这一最优问题能够得到一个我们关心的一阶条件 $p_i \partial F_i(a_i, L_i, M_i)/\partial L_i = w$，其含义是各产业劳动的边际产值相等，都等于打工的边际产值（打工工资），这就是著名的戈森定理或等边际分配原则在劳动资源分配问题上的具体体现。等边际产值分配劳动原则决定了全村的产业结构（图 36.2）。

环境和资源不同导致生产的边际生产率不同，处于不同环境下的村落具有不同的产业结构。村环境变量在最优规划问题中已经涉及，它包括地形和离城镇距离等自然和区

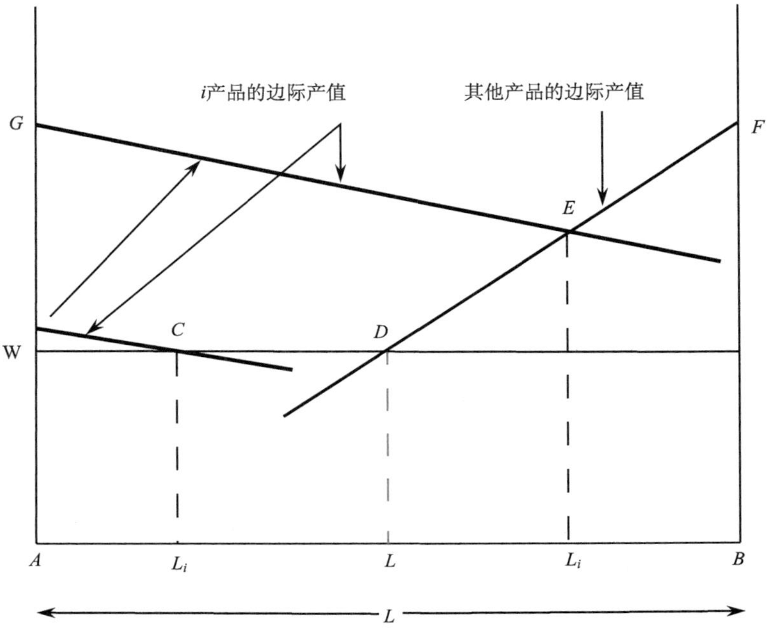

图 36.2　专业村的形成

位环境、产品价格和要素价格等市场环境、土地和劳动力资源禀赋等。

36.2.2　专业村形成与环境

图 36.2 中线段$\overline{AB}$表示全村既定的劳动力资源 L，纵轴表示劳动的边际产值，向右下方倾斜的两条线表示两种环境下 i 产品生产的劳动边际产值线，向左下方倾斜的为其他产品的劳动边际产值线，它等于其他产品的劳动边际产值线在水平方向上相加，高度为 w 的水平线表示打工的劳动边际产值线。等边际分配原则要求各产业的劳动边际产值相等，都等于工资 w。在 i 产品生产不利的环境下，两个交点 C 和 D 决定了 i 产品劳动投入为$\overline{AL_i}$，打工投入为$\overline{L_iL_{iw}}$，其他产品生产的劳动投入为$\overline{L_{iw}B}$。在有利于 i 产品生产的环境下，i 产品劳动边际产值线位于较高的位置，新的交点 E 决定了不同的劳动力配置，i 产品劳动投入为$\overline{AL_i'}$，打工消失，其他产品生产的劳动投入为$\overline{L_i'B}$，这时 i 产品劳动投入占劳动资源的大部分，从而形成集中生产 i 产品的专业村。

36.3　数据讨论

本章所使用的河南省专业村属性数据主要来源于河南省农业厅 2010 年统计调查数据。该数据包括河南省专业村调查的产业类别、龙头企业情况、主导产品、经济收入和农产品基地状况五大类 39 项社会经济指标。2010 年河南省专业村调查中具备所有 39 项经济指标数据的专业村共有 2276 个，对所有专业村数据进行核对后，发现有 68 个专业村数据可能存在异常。经电话联系及部分实地核实后，确认共有 51 个专业村的部分指标存在不确定性，剔除后，共剩余 2225 个专业村。

为了从多角度探究专业村形成原因，我们加入了空间数据。主要包括专业村地形和专业村到所属市、县、乡的距离。地形数据来自于国家统计局河南省调查总队。距离数据通过利用 ArcGIS 软件计算得到；空间背景数据来源于河南省 1：25 万地图数据。计算方法如下：①采用专业村到所属市、县、乡政府的直线距离代表其相应的真实距离；②在 ArcGIS 软件中标出各个专业村和其所属市、县、乡政府所在地的空间位置；③量测各个专业村到其所属市、县、乡政府所在地的直线空间距离。

由于河南省专业村属性数据和空间数据来源的差异性，在进行数据检验时发现有部分数据不能匹配，或存在明显错误，进行剔除后最终得到 2007 个专业村的空间数据和属性数据，占 2225 个专业村的 90.2%，且所剔除的专业村在各类产业中均有分布。因此，利用该数据进行分析，不会使总体结果产生较大偏差。

图 36.3 为河南省 2010 年分县域的专业村总数、七个代表性类别的专业村分布及河南省的地形分布。之所以选择此七个类别，主要考虑了它们的数量和特色方向。从图中可以直观看出，专业村分布与地形、区位等地理因素有着一定的关系。①平原与山区专业村较多。图 36.3 显示，河南省东部平原地区和西南部山区的专业村较多，其中，平原地区有专业村 1470 个，山区有专业村 280 个。平原地区和山区专业村数量占总数量的 87.19%。②地理区位与专业村类型相关度较大。河南省茶叶种植专业村集中分布于河南南部亚热带地区，此类专业村共有 9 个，其中，8 个分布于信阳市辖县；加工业专业村主要分布于北部和中部经济较发达的城市周边，如加工业专业村共有 51 个，其中，郑州市周边 100km 内有 26 个，占 51%。③不同类别的专业村集中度不同。蔬菜种植和养殖业专业村较为普遍地分散分布于各地；茶叶、花卉、林业等专业村对自然条件有着特殊要求，主要集中于少数县域。

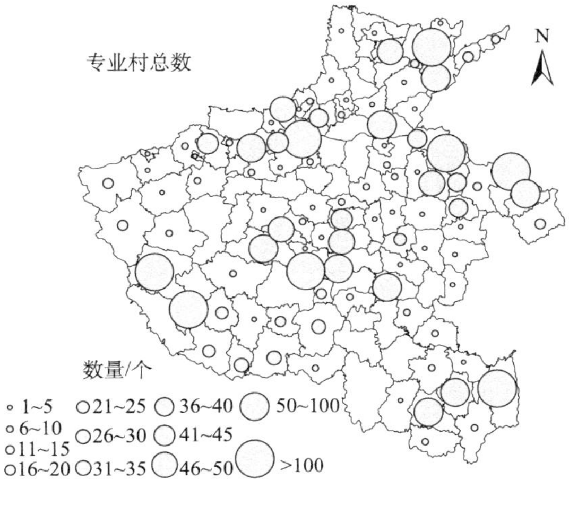

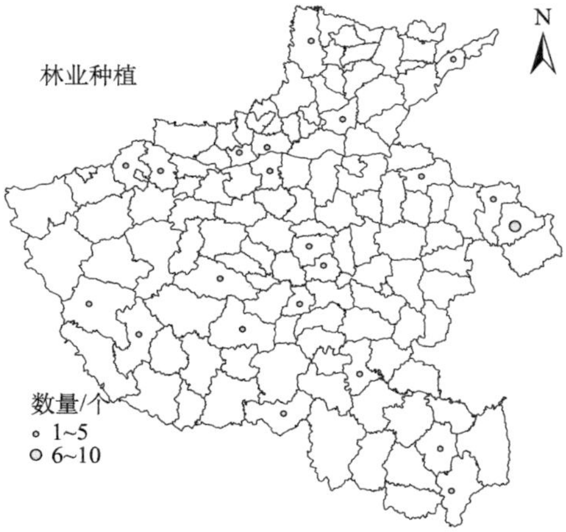
林业种植
N
数量/个
1~5
6~10

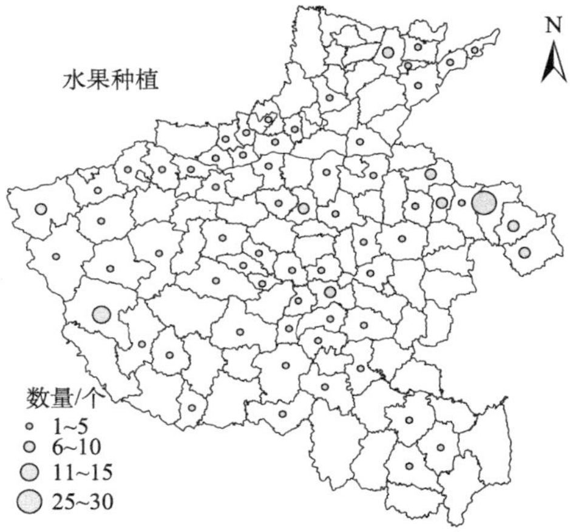
水果种植
N
数量/个
1~5
6~10
11~15
25~30

花卉种植
N
数量/个
1~5
6~10

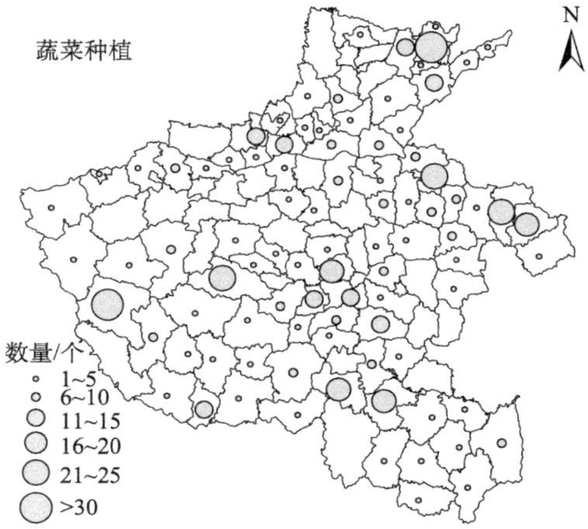
蔬菜种植
N
数量/个
1~5
6~10
11~15
16~20
21~25
>30

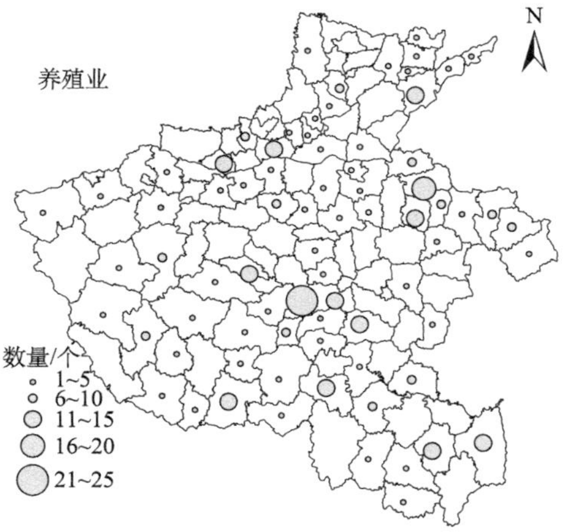
养殖业
N
数量/个
1~5
6~10
11~15
16~20
21~25

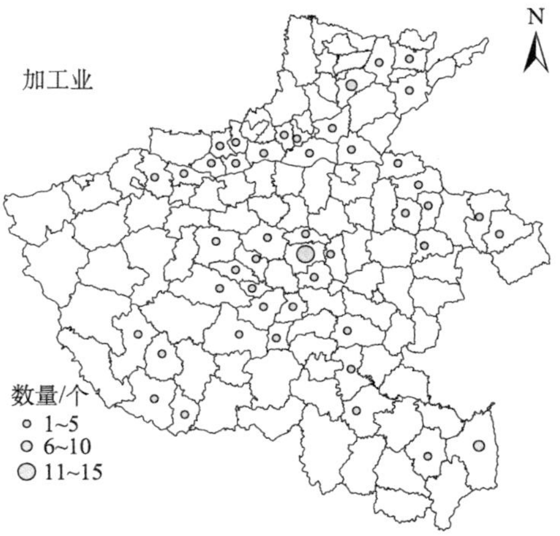
加工业
N
数量/个
1~5
6~10
11~15

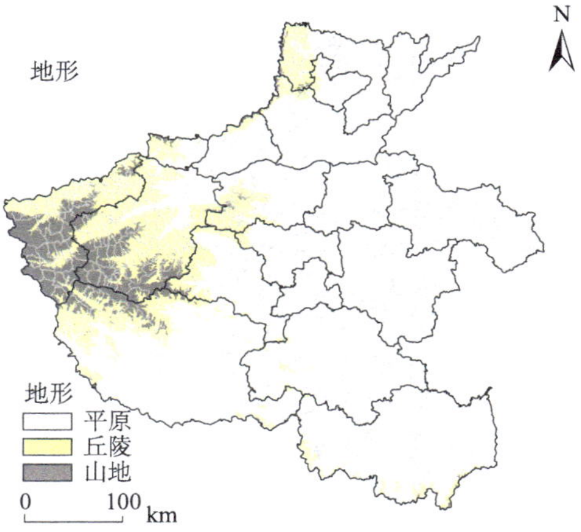

图 36.3　2010 年河南省专业村分类分布

36.4　专业村与环境关系的经验分析

在分析中，我们定义一个村的主导产业从业人数与全村劳动力资源的比率为专业化率。如果一个村的专业化率达到一定标准，就认为已成为专业化村。这样，影响专业化率的环境因素就是影响专业村形成的因素。环境因素是在专业村未形成之前就已经存在的客观因素，根据获得的数据情况，我们选取了反映劳动力资源禀赋的劳动力资源变量，反映土地相对丰裕程度的主导产业投入土地和劳动之比变量，反映地域通达性的“距不同城镇中心的距离”变量，反映市场环境的“是否有批发市场”的虚拟变量，反映自然环境的地形虚拟变量作为环境变量，同时选择了 16 种专业村的虚拟变量（表 36.1）。使用最小二乘法回归的结果表明，村域环境对专业化率，乃至专业村的形成的确有显著影响，且不同类型专业村对环境的要求是不相同的。

表 36.1　变量及定义

变量	定义
L_i	主导产业从业人数
L	劳动力资源数
K	主导产业土地/劳动投入之比
D_1	离地级市距离
D_2	离县城或县级市距离
D_3	离乡镇距离
W	批发市场属性变量，有批发市场取 1，否则取 0
T_1	平原属性变量，平原取 1，其他地形取 0

续表

变量	定义
T_2	丘陵属性变量，丘陵取 1，其他地形取 0
T_3	山区属性变量，山区取 1，其他地形取 0
I_1	茶叶种植业属性变量，茶叶种植业取 1，其他产业取 0
I_2	干果种植业属性变量，干果种植业取 1，其他产业取 0
I_3	药材种植业属性变量，药材种植业取 1，其他产业取 0
I_4	林业属性变量，林业取 1，其他产业取 0
I_5	油料种植业属性变量，油料种植业取 1，其他产业取 0
I_6	粮食种植业属性变量，粮食种植业取 1，其他产业取 0
I_7	水果种植业属性变量，水果种植业取 1，其他产业取 0
I_8	棉麻种植业属性变量，棉麻种植业取 1，其他产业取 0
I_9	花卉种植业属性变量，花卉种植业取 1，其他产业取 0
I_{10}	烟叶种植业属性变量，烟叶种植业取 1，其他产业取 0
I_{11}	蔬菜种植业属性变量，蔬菜种植业取 1，其他产业取 0
I_{12}	养殖业属性变量，养殖业取 1，其他产业取 0
I_{13}	加工业属性变量，加工业取 1，其他产业取 0
I_{14}	建材业属性变量，建材业取 1，其他产业取 0
I_{15}	服务业属性变量，服务业取 1，其他产业取 0
I_{16}	其他非农产业属性变量，其他非农产业取 1，否则取 0

注：表中的三个地形虚拟变量（T_1，T_2，T_3）没有在一个模型中同时使用。

对表 36.2 的分析可得到如下结果：①劳动力资源越多，专业化率越低：实际回归表明，每增加一个劳动力专业化率就降低 0.000036。这是因为，劳动力资源丰富，则村庄人口多，人均耕地少。这样的情况下，土地主要用于维持生计，用于商业生产的比例很低，不利于专业化。②土地密集型产品行业的专业化率较低：回归结果表明，土地/劳动投入比增加一单位，专业化率就降低 0.01。土地越多越利于专业化生产。③离县级市距离越近，越有利于形成农产品加工专业村。回归结果表明，离县城或县级市距离每减少 1km，农产品加工村的专业化率就提高约 0.00001。城镇中心提供了市场和信息，这对专业化具有重要作用。④具有批发市场可以提高所有专业村的专业化率，对养殖业和加工业专业村更是如此。回归结果表明，对其他专业村而言，具有批发市场时专业化率会提高约 0.08，对养殖专业村而言会提高约 0.25，对加工专业村而言会提高 0.33。⑤如果其他环境相同，丘陵地区的专业化率比其他地区低大约 0.05。丘陵地区专业化率低于山区，是因为丘陵资源条件较差；而低于平原则是因为交通条件较差。

表 36.2　专业化率 OLS 回归结果（被解释变量：专业化率 L_i/L；有效观测个数为 2007）

解释变量	B 系数	t 统计量	P 值
C	0.769230	38.98746	0.0000
L	−3.60E−05	−3.060082	0.0022
K	−0.010253	−4.594774	0.0000
$I_{13}\times D_2$	−9.88E−06	−3.169145	0.0016
W	0.077522	3.399308	0.0007
$I_{12}\times W$	0.177702	2.699341	0.0070
$I_{13}\times W$	0.254196	2.983513	0.0029
T_2	−0.058460	−2.518279	0.0119
I_{11}	−0.045142	−2.442569	0.0147
I_{12}	−0.116278	−5.094755	0.0000
I_{13}	0.112042	1.900470	0.0575
F 统计量＝10.10075		P 值＝ 0.000000	

注：表中只给出了有显著影响的解释变量，同时给出了有显著影响的交互项。交互项 $I_{13}\times D_2$ 的作用在于说明离县城距离对加工业专业化率的影响不同于其他产业；交互项 $I_{12}\times W$ 和 $I_{13}\times W$ 的作用在于说明与其他产业相比，批发市场对养殖业和加工业存在更大的正面影响。

36.5　专业村类型与环境关系模拟

以上使用 OLS 模型直接解释的是专业村的专业化率，对专业村类型的解释并不充分。专业村类型是一个“是”与“否”的问题，例如，是否为水果专业村，是一个定性问题。这里我们采用定性响应模型分析村域环境对不同类型专业村形成的影响，所用的是定性响应模型中 ML-Binary Logit 模型，在 16 个产业中选择 7 个产业（茶叶、林业、水果业、花卉业、蔬菜业、养殖业、农产品加工业）的回归结果做一分析。

表 36.3 中 Z 统计量或 P 值表明，显著影响专业村类型的因素有劳动力资源、土地相对丰裕程度、离城市距离、是否有批发市场和地形。表中的 β 系数的大小没有太多意义，但系数的符号表示对专业村的影响方向，正号表示提高形成某种专业村的概率，负号表示降低形成某种专业村的概率。鉴于此，我们把各种因素对七种类型专业村的影响方向归纳在表 36.4 中。

表 36.3　主要产业专业村的回归结果

产业	解释变量	β 系数	Z 统计量	P 值	Probability（LR stat）
茶叶	C	−8.306503	−11.29755	0.0000	0.000000
	K	0.055699	2.445053	0.0145	
	D_1	2.67E−05	5.079006	0.0000	
	D_2	5.54E−05	2.817967	0.0048	
	T_2	2.026622	4.469687	0.0000	

续表

产业	解释变量	β 系数	Z 统计量	P 值	Probability (LR stat)
林业	C	−5.698801	−9.062818	0.0000	0.000000
	K	0.053013	2.609554	0.0091	
	D_1	1.09E−05	2.313369	0.0207	
	T_1	1.295145	2.496868	0.0125	
水果	C	−1.839102	−12.26013	0.0000	0.000072
	K	0.050143	2.810887	0.0049	
	D_1	−1.05E−05	−3.516604	0.0004	
	W	0.295596	1.655381	0.0978	
	T_3	0.419428	1.686963	0.0916	
花卉	C	−3.797910	−10.00634	0.0000	0.001232
	L	0.000507	2.964706	0.0030	
	D_2	−3.74E−05	−2.158742	0.0309	
蔬菜	C	−0.664145	−6.689597	0.0000	0.000000
	D_2	−1.34E−05	−2.666373	0.0077	
	W	1.035929	8.546508	0.0000	
	T_2	−0.949708	−5.230769	0.0000	
养殖	C	−2.542629	−10.67397	0.0000	0.000000
	W	−0.935605	−4.880739	0.0000	
	T_1	1.307841	5.291630	0.0000	
	T_2	1.360484	4.828995	0.0000	
加工	C	−3.201584	−14.38177	0.0000	0.011941
	T_1	0.584188	2.379257	0.0173	

表 36.4　主要产业专业村环境影响方向分析

产业	L	K	D_1	D_2	D_3	W	T_1	T_2	T_3
茶叶		+	+	+				+	
林业		+	+				+		
水果		+	−			+			+
花卉	+			−					
蔬菜				−		+		−	
养殖						−	+	+	
加工							+		

注："+"表示具有增加专业村形成的概率；"−"表示具有降低专业村形成的概率。

定性模型的分析按产业可得如下结果：①茶叶生产有特殊的环境要求。在河南主要集中于信阳市的亚热带地区，这里地形以丘陵和低山为主。在这些特定的地区中，土地资源丰富、离地级和县城（县级市）较远、丘陵地形等环境变量，对茶叶专业村的形成有重要的作用。②林业专业村形成中，土地资源越丰裕，离地级市越远，形成的概率越高；平原地区形成林业专业村的概率比丘陵和山区高。③水果专业村形成中，土地资源越丰裕、离地级市越近，形成该专业村的概率越高；山区地形、附近有批发市场的环境也可以提高形成水果专业村的概率。④劳动力资源越丰富、离县城（县级市）越近，形成花卉专业村的概率越高。⑤离县城（县级市）越近形成蔬菜专业村的概率越高，附近有批发市场可以提高形成蔬菜专业村的概率，丘陵地区形成蔬菜专业村的概率比平原和山区低。⑥由于交通的影响，平原和丘陵地区比山区更有利于形成养殖专业村。附近有批发市场妨碍形成养殖专业村，这主要是因为批发市场附近土地成本较高，不利于建立养殖基地。⑦便利的交通，使得平原地区更有利于形成加工专业村。

环境对不同专业村的影响可以归纳如下结论：①劳动力资源：丰富的劳动力资源对形成花卉专业村有正面影响，因为种植花卉耗费人工最多。②土地资源：丰富的土地资源对茶叶、林业和水果专业村形成有正面影响，因为茶叶、树木和水果的规模生产都需要大量的土地。③交通位置：离城市距离越远，越有利于形成茶叶和林业专业村，因为边远地区更适合生产茶叶和木材。离城市越近越有于形成水果、花卉和蔬菜专业村，因为近距离销售可以大大节约交易成本。离乡镇距离的大小对任何专业村的形成都没有影响，因为乡镇的位置所在可能不影响任何产品的生产和销售。④批发市场：水果和蔬菜都是时鲜物品，对市场依赖程度强，所以有批发市场对形成这两类专业村有正面影响，但批发市场附近土地相对较为紧张，故对养殖业专业村形成有负面影响。⑤地形：平原地区有利于形成林业、养殖业和加工业专业村的形成。丘陵地区有利于茶叶和养殖业专业村的形成，但不利于蔬菜专业村的形成。山区有利于水果专业村的形成。

36.6　结论与讨论

本章认为“理性小农”、“劳动分工和专业化”和“距离衰减和邻里效应”理论，是解释专业村形成机理的主要经济学和地理学理论。农户只要按照“经济理性”决策，其结果一定会综合考虑各种环境和资源条件，尽最大可能配置要素以取得最大效益。各地环境和资源条件的差异形成了边际生产率的差异。分工和专业化，会进一步促进资本流向最具效益的部门，通过规模经济带来更快的经济增长。“距离衰减和邻里效应”解释了专业化部门在空间上近距离集中分布，这对于专业村的形成十分必要。河南农村虽然仍处于工业化进程中，农户个体不一定完全具有经济理性，但总体上或长期来看，仍趋于理性决策。

基于这些理论，本章用数理方法对村产业结构的发展变化进行了推理，认为村产业结构与村环境有关。环境不同将导致不同村落的边际生产率不同，从而处于不同环境下的村落将形成不同的产业结构。如果村环境非常有利于某种生产或服务的形成，其劳动和资本的边际收益远大于其他部门，就存在专业村形成的适宜环境。

村环境变量包括多个方面。本章选择具有代表意义的地形、区位、土地和劳动力等。通过 2010 年河南省 2007 个专业村的实例研究表明，村环境因素对专业村的专业化率以及专业村的形成的确有显著影响。显著影响专业村的因素有劳动和土地资源、地域通达性、地形和市场环境。回归结果表明：①劳动力资源越多，专业化率越低：每增加一个劳动力，专业化率就降低 0.000036；②村子土地越多，越利于专业化生产，土地/劳动投入比增加一单位，专业化率就降低 0.01；③离县级市距离越近，越有利于形成农产品加工专业村，离县城或县级市距离每减少 1km，农产品加工村的专业化率就提高约 0.00001；④具有批发市场可以提高所有专业村的专业化率，对养殖业和加工业专业村更是如此，对其他专业村而言，具有批发市场时专业化率会提高约 0.08，对养殖专业村而言会提高约 0.25，对加工专业村而言会提高 0.33；⑤如果其他环境相同，丘陵地区的专业化率比其他地区低大约 0.05。这主要与丘陵地区交通条件不畅、人均耕地较少等有关。山区反而有一定的资源优势，为专业村的发展提供了可能。

环境的影响在不同产业的专业村有所不同：土地丰裕程度对茶叶、林业和水果种植等要求较为广阔种植面积的专业村形成有正面影响；劳动力资源对花卉等劳动密集型专业村的形成产生影响；地域通达性对水果、蔬菜和花卉等时鲜产品专业村的形成产生正面影响，对茶叶和林业专业村的形成产生负面影响；临近市场促进水果和蔬菜专业村的形成；不同的地势影响不同类型专业村形成的概率。

本章的经验研究可以进一步联系到环境与专业化关系的理论层面。由于农业生产与自然条件关系很密切，所以在天然农产品的专业化生产或相关专业村的形成中，地形、土地等自然环境条件及其生产的主体——劳动力资源，起着十分重要的作用。而农产品加工专业村的形成，则与区位和市场条件有关。这种结论的政策含义是，不同环境条件的地区，可以选择相关的专业化发展导向。

本章以河南为例的研究有一定的局限性。河南与其他地区，尤其是与沿海地区相比，在专业村类别、发展水平和发展条件上会有所不同。同时，基于调查数据的局限，在本章分析因素之外，还有一些因素对专业村形成具有重要影响。例如，村的传统文化、经济基础等也在一定程度上影响专业村形成，但由于资料所限未被包括。此外，专业村中除农产品之外，还有工业、矿产、旅游、文化等类别。但是，与城镇相比，农村不具有发展工业和商业专业村的优势。在中国由计划经济向市场经济转型中，由于特殊的市场需求，出现了一些工商业专业村。但其发展的潜力及其前景并不乐观。其中一些会做大做强，脱离农村成为工业专业园区或发展成为镇，不再以专业村存在；另一些会逐渐消亡。

中国农村聚落的原始功能与专业村生产之间并不一致。中国早期的农村居民点主要是居住和为居民提供基本生存条件，以后，其功能逐渐扩展，但并不是为了专业化商品生产需要。而专业村则主要从生产和提供服务的角度来考虑。这种从居住到专业生产的演变，是否隐含着村落性质的转变，这种演变是否具有必然的趋势，都需要理论和实践的深入研究。发达国家的农庄，尤其是和我国环境比较类似的日本农村，也有一些专业化的农业生产，但中国的规模和数量在世界上非常独特，对此研究具有十分重要的意义。

参考文献

哈尔·瓦里安. 1997. 微观经济学（高级教程）. 北京：经济科学出版社

李红涛，付少平. 2002. 理性小农抑或道义小农，重读农民学经典论题. 读书，(2)：104～111

李小建等. 2010. 中国中部农区发展研究. 北京：科学出版社

李小建，罗庆，樊新生. 2009a. 农区专业村的形成与演化机理研究. 中国软科学，(2)：71～80

李小建，周雄飞，乔家君，等. 2009b. 不同环境下农户自主发展能力对收入增长的影响. 地理学报，4（6）：643～653

李小建，周雄飞，郑纯辉. 2008. 河南农区经济发展差异地理影响的小尺度分析. 地理学报，63（2）：147～155

罗庆，李小建. 2010. 农村社区农户互动效应的定量评估. 地理研究，29（10）：1757～1766

农业部. 2011. 全国一村一品平稳较快发展. 农业工程技术（农产品加工），(9)：4～5

史清华. 2005. 农户经济可持续发展研究—浙江十村千户变迁（1986～2002). 北京：中国农业出版社

舒尔茨. 2010. 改造传统农业. 梁小民译. 北京：商务印书馆

亚当·斯密. 2011. 国民财富的性质和原因的研究. 郭大力，王亚南译. 北京：商务印书馆

杨小凯，黄有光. 1999. 专业化与经济组织：一种新兴古典经济学框架. 张玉刚译. 北京：经济科学出版社

詹姆斯·斯科特. 2001. 农民的道义经济学：东南亚的反叛与生存. 程立显，刘建等译. 南京：译林出版社

郑风田，程郁. 2006. 创业家与我国农村产业集群的形成与演进机理——基于云南斗南花卉个案的实证分析. 中国软科学，(1)：100～107

Hagerstrand T. 1968. Innovation diffusion as a spatial process，trans. A. Pred. Chicago：University of Chicago Press

Johnston R J. 2009. Neibourhood effect. In Gregory D，Johnston R J，Pratt G. The Dictionary of Human Geography. Chichester：Wiley-Blackwell

Johnston R J，Gregory D，Pratt G， et al. 2000. The Dictionary of Human Geography. Oxford：Blackwell Publishers Ltd

Li E L，Li X J， Liu Z G. 2011. Relationships and evolving networks of rural manufacturing clusters：A case study in Yucheng county，Henan province of China. Chinese Geographical Science，21（3）：364～376

Popkin S L. 1979. The rational peasant：The political economy of rural society in Vietnam. Berkeley：University of California Press

Tobler W. 2004. On the first law of geography：A reply. Annals of Association of American Geographers，94（2）：304～310

第 37 章　山区农田系统投入产出分析

地理学对人地关系的关注由来已久（吴传钧，1981，1991）。随着人们对可持续发展问题的关注，相关研究上不断有重要成果问世（郑度，2002；陆大道，2002；樊杰等，2003）。人们已从哲学层面的定性研究逐渐走向不同层面的量化探索（Mohan and Jeffret，1996；Li et al.，2001；王爱民等，1999）。其中，微观尺度的精细解剖，对深入认识和解释其内部机理，具有十分重要的作用（Haraldsson，1998；鲁礼新等，2004）。有关人地关系地域系统的重要研究内容之一为人与地两大系统间相互作用和物质、能量传递与转换问题（陆大道和郭来喜，1998）。通过该研究，可剖析人类活动对物质和能量传递与转换自然过程的影响，以及人类活动在自然平台上的物质或能量转换方向和效率。

农田人地系统是指以地球表层耕地农田为基础构成的人地关系系统。在农区，农田系统可为农民提供 60%左右的收入和 70%左右的生活必需品（郜庆炉，2000）。在山地农区，农田系统对人类生存意义更大（Ekins，1986）。农田系统状况在更大程度上表征了该地区人地关系状况。有不少学者关注农业系统的相关研究，发表了一系列有价值的研究成果（郜庆炉，2000；Ma and Edwards，1997；Fluck，1979）。但这些研究大多侧重于宏观层面。在另一侧面，地理学家将土地利用作为人地关系地域系统研究的核心领域（樊杰等，2003），高度重视相关研究。但目前成果多集中于土地利用类型的变化和其原因的解释，在精细到微小系统——农田地块方面的研究尚不够深入。从更细微的角度，进行特定农田地块上的物质、能量传递和转换问题的成果还十分少见。本章尝试从山区农田系统的能量转换角度弥补这一不足。

影响农田系统能量转换的因素很多。在山区，地形条件起着至关重要的作用。故本章研究中主要集中于地形因素；并从高程、坡度、坡向、坡位、坡型诸方面作以分析。由于山区农田地块面积较小，可暂时忽略地块内不同点位的差异。为此，本章选取河南省吴沟村 81 户的 482 块农田进行了相关调查，调查内容包括农田的基本属性、类型、分布及农户对每一地块的物质、能量、价值的投入产出等。并从生产函数角度进行山区农田地块（平均 350m^2/块）的投入产出分析，尤其侧重于不同地形条件下，人地相关作用的差异，在山区农村人地关系的微观定量研究上做一探索。

37.1　分析模型

在农田系统中，其能量来源为太阳辐射能及辅助能，后者包括自然辅助能和人工辅助能，其中，人工辅助能投入可由人类直接调控。这些辅助能不但对农作物转化太阳能效率产生决定性影响，同时也控制着这些化学能的进一步转化和有效分配（陈阜，2002）。本章着重于分析人工辅助能的投入产出及其转化效率。

对农田人地关系的能量流研究，可采用多种方法。受相关成果启迪（千怀遂和秦耀辰，1990），本章借用经济学中生产函数的概念，把多种可变农业投入（X_1，X_2，…）与产出（Y）之间的关系以科布-道格拉斯生产函数表示为

$$Y=Y(X_1, X_2, \cdots)=AX_1^{\alpha1}X_2^{\alpha2}\cdots \tag{37.1}$$

式中，A 为反映生产条件的综合系数，主要与农田其他天然能量投入（如天然肥力、光热条件等）有关；α 为投入的弹性系数。当 $\alpha=1$ 时，生产为等比收益，即投入以相同幅度扩大的话，产出也以相同幅度扩大；当 $\alpha<1$ 时为减比收益；$\alpha>1$ 时为增比收益。

从理论上分析，生产函数反映了一定条件下的农田人地相互关系状况。α 值可视为能量转换效率，当 α 值大于 1 时，表明人们较好地利用农田自然条件，人工投入能量与自然能量有效结合，在农田系统中获取增比能量转换；反之，当 α 值小于 1 时，表明了人工投入能量转换为产出时，具减比收益，在这种情况下，人们应该反思利用自然的方式是否正确。

37.2　研究区概况与数据处理

37.2.1　研究区域概况

巩义市位于河南省中西部，介于河南省最大的两个城市郑州市和洛阳市之间，位于东经 112°49′～113°17′、北纬 34°31′～34°52′。为暖温带大陆性季风气候，雨热同期。2002 年名列全国县域经济基本竞争力百强县第 55 名，是中西部地区最强的三个县市之一。2001 年巩义市有常住人口 79.32 万，外来人口 11 万，人口密度达 866 人/km^2，人均耕地 0.043hm^2。

吴沟村位于巩义市南部，是一个较为闭塞的山村。该村属嵩山山地的北延部分，绝大部分为山地，地形起伏很大（图 37.1），起伏度达 0.241。面积为 1.41km^2，平均海拔为 725m。该村干旱少雨，生存条件相对较差，但拥有较丰富的石质资源。全村现有人口 313 人，耕地 17.26hm^2，且比较贫瘠。在 1990～2000 年，吴沟村人口年均下降 5.57‰；因为农民陡坡开荒，10 年内全村耕地增加 1.04hm^2；受降雨影响，该村粮食产量波动较大（表 37.1）。吴沟村近 10 年来的发展状况有所改善，在巩义市各村中的位次由 1990 年的倒数第二位，抬升到 1995 年的倒数第四位，2000 年的倒数第八位。

表 37.1　吴沟村社会经济基本情况

年份	人均纯收入/元	人口数/人	人均耕地/hm^2	工农业产值比	平均粮食产量/(kg/ hm^2)
2000	961（284）	313	0.055	1.57	1 086
1995	315（289）	330	0.048	2.00	3 977
1990	133（295）	331	0.049	6.13	2 421

注：括号内的数字为吴沟村在巩义市各村中的位次（巩义市 1990 年有行政村 296 个，1995 年 293 个，2000 年 292 个）。

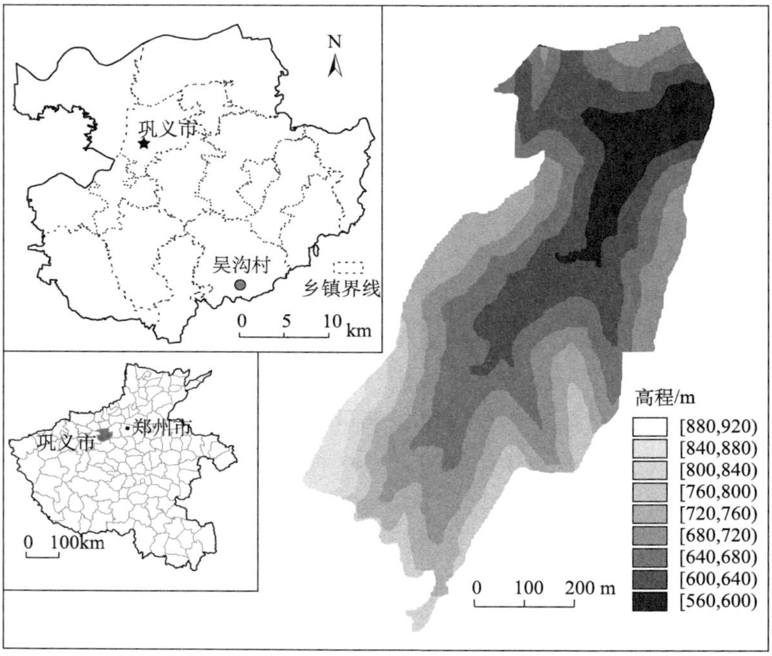

图 37.1　吴沟村地形图

选择吴沟村进行农田人地关系研究主要有以下原因：①该村处于小山谷上部，为一个相对封闭的人地关系系统；②全村经济活动以农业为主，农田是人地关系相互作用较为集中的场所；③该村位于经济相对比较发达的巩义市，既具有山区特征，又具有相对较好的外部信息来源。

为获取该村农田相关数据，作者于 2002～2003 年两次到巩义市统计局、土地局、计委访问。在此基础上，2003 年 4 月带领 10 名研究生和本科生到吴沟村进行了 5 天的实地调查。在调查中，访问了村子中的 81 户农户，填写了 482 块农田的投入产出实物资料。每块农田收集了 50 个数据。

37.2.2　数据库建立与数据处理

1. 数据库建立

根据研究需要，我们运用 Arcview 3.2 和 EXCEL2000 软件作为研究区数据库建立的运行环境，以此完成空间及属性数据库的建立、分析模型构建及数据应用分析。入库的空间信息包括 1∶1 万吴沟村行政区划图、1∶1 万吴沟村地形图、1∶1 万吴沟村土地利用现状图及 1∶1000 农户耕地分布图（调查清绘）；属性信息包括吴沟村各类地块投入产出的各项物质、能量和价值，以及地块的类型和面积等数据。在数据编码设计中，根据系统性、唯一性、简易性等原则，对各类地块均采用 5 位数字（ABCDE）进行编码。其中，A=1、2、3，分别代表吴沟村一队、二队、三队；BC=01、02、03、…，分别代表该队的第一户、第二户、第三户，…；DE＝01、02、03、…，代表该户第一、第二、第三块地，依次类推。

2. 数据处理

由于耕地物质投入原始数据量纲的差异，在进行地块比较时，存在一定难度，故我们利用有关学者的研究成果（陈阜，2002）确定折能系数，进行农田地块能量投入产出及效率的有关折算。当然价值也可作为该文分析的基础，但通过分析发现，采用能量进行分析与采用价值进行分析的结果具有很强的相似性，为了集中说明地形对农田地块投入产出的影响，我们采用地块能量的投入产出作为数据分析的基础。为了进行不同面积地块的对比分析，我们采用以公顷为分析单位的处理，以便更好地展示农田地块的投入产出特征及其效率。由于部分地块面积较小，调查过程中做了适当处理，即把具有同类性质的地块进行一定的归并，此处理基本不影响地块的投入产出特征。

37.2.3　相关能量折算

参照有关学者的研究思路（刘绍明和吴文良，2003），对吴沟村农田系统的 2002 年有关能量投入、产出及产投比进行了调查，并进行相关折算。其中，种子、有机肥、劳力和畜力被称为有机能，化肥、农药、农机具、水电为无机能，吴沟村的农机具/畜力主要指牛耕，数据均以公顷为基础来计算所投物质量，并进行折算能量。在能量换算中，折能系数参照有关学者（陈阜，2002；尹钧等，1999）的研究成果。

37.2.4　吴沟村农田概况

参照有关文献（杨瑞珍，1994），可将吴沟村耕地划分为旱平地（坡度＜8°）、缓旱坡地（8°＜坡度＜25°）和陡旱坡地（坡度＞25°）。其中，旱平地主要分布在沟谷低部及居民点周围，面积为 4.98hm^2；缓旱坡地分布在旱平地的外侧，位于山坡下部，面积为 2.95hm^2；陡旱坡地分布在山坡中部、中上部，面积为 9.33hm^2，耕地坡度较大，位置较高（图 37.2）。

吴沟村农田面积为 17.26hm^2，因为地形较为复杂，同时，农户陡坡开荒进一步导致地块面积较小，分布零碎，全村农田地块数达 279 块。此外，在农户承包责任田时，常根据地形、单产、距居民点距离等因素，将全村农田地块进一步划分，从而使得每户地块更为零散，地块总数达 482 块，平均每户地块数为 5.95 块/户（表 37.2），个别农户的地块数达 18 块。旱平地由于地形相对单一，地块数相对较少（全村仅 42 块），使

表 37.2　吴沟村耕地属性

类型	平均高程/m	地块数/块	总面积/hm^2	户均地块数/(块/户)	户均面积/(hm^2/户)
旱平地	623	42	4.98	1.35	0.061
缓旱坡地	626	51	2.95	0.95	0.036
陡旱坡地	666	186	9.33	3.65	0.115
全村合计（平均）	638	279	17.26	5.95	0.213

注：地块数为集中连片的耕地块数，户均地块数为每户耕地块数（不等于地块数/户数）。

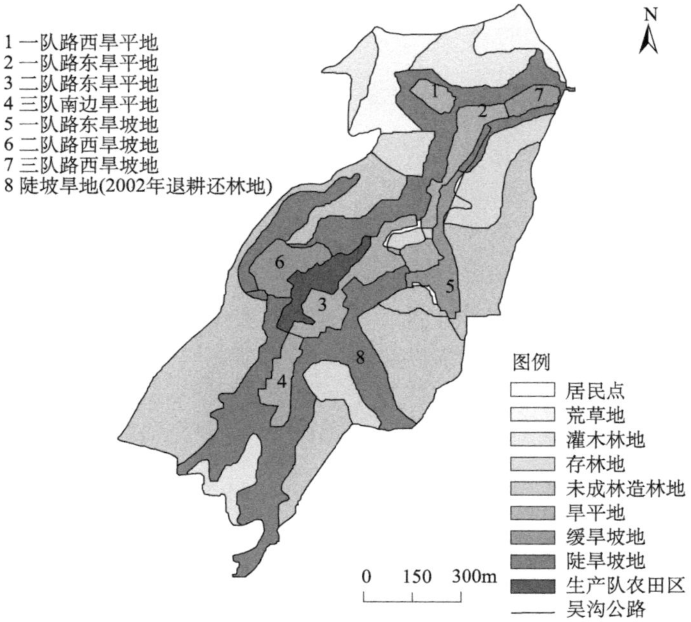

图 37.2　吴沟村土地类型及农田分布

得农户分得的田地相对集中，随着高程的增加及其他各种因素的附加，地块条件差异显著，农户的地块也随之更加零散、破碎。户均地块数由旱平地的 1.35 块增加到陡旱坡地的 3.65 块（表 37.2）。

37.3　地形对农田投入产出的影响

37.3.1　高程对农田投入产出的影响

在影响农田的投入产出效率中，高程是一个重要因素。随着农田地块海拔高度的增加，大气温度、湿度会有明显变化，进而导致人工能量投入具有不同的转换效率。就一般山区而论，农田的人工能量转换效率应随着高程增大而逐渐降低。但又有诸多因素影响这种趋势，如在较高高程的山坡修筑梯田，利用科学方式选择适宜种植的农作，也可以带来较大的能量转换效率。反之，如果在某一高程地区选择与当地环境不相适宜的农业生产活动，或过度利用自然资源，也可带来相应的负面影响。

根据对 482 块农田的人工能量投入和产出的生产函数计算表明，总体而论，在研究区域可粗略看出人工能量转换效率随高程增加而减少的特征。表征这种转换效率的 α 值从 570m 以下的 2.02 减到 660～675m 的 1.75（表 37.3）。但是在研究区居民居住地高程（630～645m）范围内，α 值很低（0.83）。对当地实际情况的进一步调查，发现在该高程范围内的农田耕作有两个特征：一是年内两季轮作现象普遍；二是农田平均投入较多。这说明村民已经最大限度地利用这些农田，天然能量的潜力已得到充分挖掘。由

于 α 值小于 1，显示了能量转换中的减比收益特征。这种减比收益还出现在 675m 高程以上地段，这里的农田坡度较大，土壤肥力较低，故人工能量投入并不能带来相应规模的产出。也可以说，从农田系统看，这两个高程段的人地关系处于最不协调状态，应采取相应措施加以调整。

表 37.3　按高程划分的吴沟村农田及其生产函数

地块高程	生产函数	R^2	F 值
所有地块	$Y=0.0092x^{1.4020}$	0.7656	597.687**
＜570m	$Y=0.00001x^{2.0217}$	0.8616	87.160**
[570m，585m)	$Y=0.0010x^{1.5880}$	0.8043	61.630**
[585m，600m)	$Y=0.0843x^{1.2187}$	0.8648	140.768**
[600m，615m)	$Y=0.0064x^{1.4367}$	0.7846	619.24**
[615m，630m)	$Y=0.2979x^{1.1117}$	0.6199	32.614**
[630m，645m)	$Y=8.1076x^{0.8319}$	0.4625	24.093**
[645m，660m)	$Y=0.0058x^{1.4498}$	0.8107	111.335**
[660m，675m)	$Y=0.0002x^{1.7472}$	0.8071	62.775**
≥675m	$Y=11923.9x^{0.1252}$	0.0595	0.696

** 显著性水平为 0.01。

37.3.2　坡度对农田投入产出的影响

我们首先根据前述农田坡度的三分法（＜8°、8°～25°、＞25°）进行生产函数分析，结果发现＞25°的农田生产函数模型回归效果不显著（未通过 0.1 水平显著性检验）。之后，我们又根据吴沟村农田的特性将其划分为＜8°、8°～15°、＞15°三类。三种类型农田中，大坡度农田占重大比例。该村农田主要集中于 8°以上，农田地块数占全村总地块数的 78.42%，面积占全村耕地面积的 71.15%。总体来说，就农田地块的投入产出比而论，明显呈现出随坡度增加而下降的特点（图 37.3）。把吴沟村 482 块农田的坡度与其能量产投比做相关分析，得出，坡度与农田能量投入的相关系数为－0.723，与其产出的相关系数为－0.766，与其产投比的相关系数为－0.604。均说明农田的坡度越大，其投入、产出和产投比越小的变化特征。

对三种类型农田的生产函数分析表明（表 37.4），坡度为 8°～15°的农田的能量转换效率最高（$\alpha=1.63$），而 8°以下和 15°以上的坡度的农田均显示出减比收益特征。大坡度农田的减比收益较易于理解，而平坡农田的减比收益则与农田过度利用有关。平坡农田多数集中于村子居民居住地附近，少数集中于较低高程上。从农田地块的坡度角度分析，研究区域人类进一步扩展农田生产的空间应集中于中低坡度的农田。

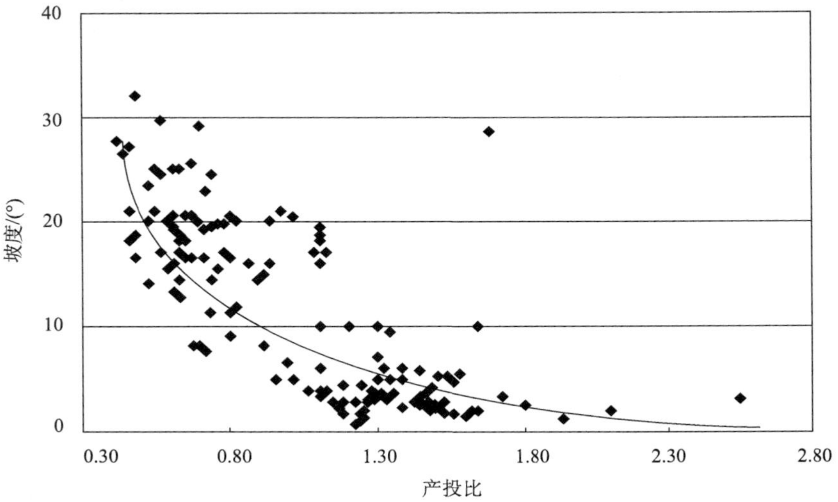

图 37.3 农田坡度与其能量产投比的关系

表 37.4 按坡度划分的吴沟村农田及其生产函数

地块坡度	生产函数	R^2	F 值
所有地块	$Y=0.0092x^{1.4020}$	0.7656	607.367**
＜8°	$Y=1.9907x^{0.9567}$	0.4938	99.505**
[8°, 15°]	$Y=0.0006x^{1.6322}$	0.7841	76.249**
＞15°	$Y=4.5635x^{0.8436}$	0.4848	52.282**

** 显著性水平为 0.01。

37.3.3 坡向对农田投入产出的影响

坡向直接影响光照强度，进而影响农田能量转换效率。将吴沟村 482 块农田的坡向与其能量产投比两变量做散点图可以发现，农田能量产投比与坡向的相关程度不高。我们以正北方向定为 0，则全村农田地块大多分布于 0°～150°、300°～360°。而 150°～300°坡向的地块则分布较少。对八个方位农田的生产函数分析表明（表 37.5），在 [135°, 180°）坡向的农田能量转换效率最高（$\alpha=1.78$），其次为 [90°, 135°）坡向的农田。而 [180°, 270°)、[315°, 360°）坡向的农田均表现出减比收益特征。这与吴沟村农田分布及自然条件影响密切相关。能量转换效率较高的两组农田分别为早晚向阳区位。

表 37.5 按坡向划分的吴沟村农田及其生产函数

地块坡向	生产函数	R^2	F 值
所有地块	$Y=0.0092x^{1.4020}$	0.7656	584.312**
[0°, 45°)	$Y=0.0383x^{1.2841}$	0.6849	71.685**

续表

地块坡向	生产函数	R^2	F 值
[45°，90°)	$Y=0.0572x^{1.2503}$	0.7251	113.221**
[90°，135°)	$Y=0.0023x^{1.5158}$	0.7868	99.862**
[135°，180°)	$Y=0.0001x^{1.7812}$	0.8972	207.947**
[180°，225°)	$Y=2337.9x^{03729}$	0.6947	6.825
[225°，270°)	$Y=15587814x^{-0.4800}$	0.0560	0.118
[270°，315°)	$Y=0.0149x^{1.3601}$	0.8606	86.995**
[315°，360°)	$Y=42.7342x^{0.6877}$	0.3244	11.525**

** 显著性水平为 0.01。

37.3.4 坡位对农田投入产出影响

坡位指农田地块在山坡中的位置。我们设 dv 为某农田距最近坡底的欧氏距离，dr 为该农田距最近坡顶的欧氏距离，则该地块农田的坡位 $s=\mathrm{d}v/(\mathrm{d}v+\mathrm{d}r)\times 100$。坡位影响土壤湿度（Li et al.，2001），进而影响农田的能量产出。通过对吴沟村 482 块农田与其坡位的分析，得如下结论：农田地块的坡位与其能量产投比呈反比例关系，基本趋势是随着农田地块坡位的升高，其能量产投效率呈降低态势（图 37.4）。对不同坡位组进行的生产函数分析表明，在坡位较低的农田中，其能量转换效率较高（表 37.6）。坡位小于 25 的农田具有增比收益。这说明在研究区域，由于降水量相对较少，且农作主要依赖自然降水。较低坡位土壤易于保墒，带来较高产出。

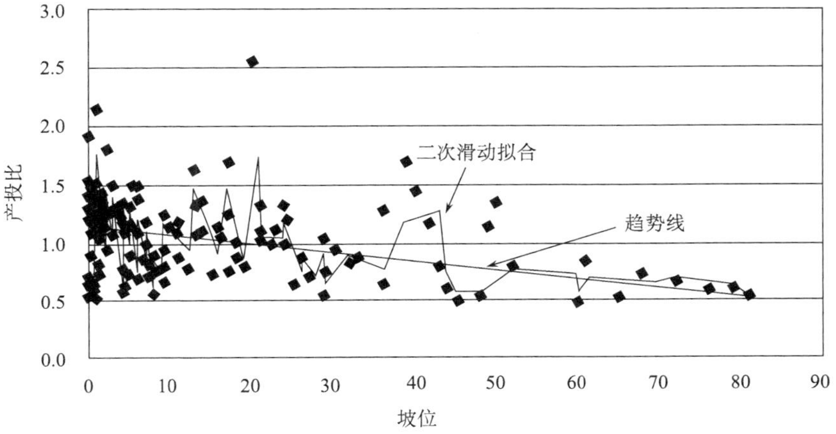

图 37.4 农田坡位与其能量产投比

表 37.6 按坡位划分的吴沟村农田及其生产函数

地块坡位	生产函数	R^2	F 值
所有地块	$Y=0.0092x^{1.4020}$	0.7656	600.942**
≤5	$Y=0.0048x^{1.4617}$	0.7805	359.135**

续表

地块坡位	生产函数	R^2	F 值
(5, 25]	$Y=0.0883x^{1.2072}$	0.6848	115.161**
(25, 50]	$Y=2539.5x^{0.2750}$	0.1371	2.384
> 50	$Y=26.068x^{0.6723}$	0.5012	9.045*

* 显著性水平为 0.05；** 显著性水平为 0.01。

37.3.5 坡型对农田投入产出影响

坡型指坡度之坡度，有平坡、凸坡、凹坡三种类型。吴沟村农户虽无高深的理论知识，但数百年的农业生产实践形成了全村农田分布主要位于凹坡的发展特点（凹坡中农田数占全村总数的 62.37%）。一般而论，在其他农业条件相等的情况下，凹坡和平坡的农田比凸坡更易于农作物生长。在该类型农田的生产中，人工能量投入与产出的转换效率较高（表 37.7）。从人地关系的角度，在这类农田上人们仍有继续利用自然发展的空间。但是，吴沟村的凸坡中，仍有一定数量的农田（其地块数为 49 块）能量产投比均低于 1，且不说其环境成本（水土流失等），仅从农田能量产投效率来看，这些农田也是不经济的。

表 37.7 按坡型划分的吴沟村农田及其生产函数

地块坡型	生产函数	R^2	F 值
所有地块	$Y=0.0092x^{1.4020}$	0.7656	601.327**
平坡	$Y=0.0070x^{1.4229}$	0.8070	83.707**
凸坡	$Y=0.0979x^{1.1951}$	0.6762	100.321**
凹坡	$Y=0.0030x^{1.5004}$	0.8007	448.204**

** 显著性水平为 0.01。

37.4 结论与讨论

农田系统属半人工生态系统，具有很强的自然、人工特征，有助于我们在微观层面上研究人与地的关系。基于对河南省巩义市吴沟村 482 块农田的调查表明，地形因子对山区农田人地系统投入产出特征具有重要影响。其中，高程的影响最为明显。农田人工能量的投入与产出能量转换效率，具有随地块的高程增加而逐渐降低的特征。但农田的轮作特点和潜力的挖掘程度又影响这种变化趋势。在坡度的影响中，人工能量投入的转换效率具有随着农田的坡度增大而下降的态势。其中，坡度位于 8°～15°区间的农田转换效率最高。农田地块的坡位与其能量转换效率呈反比例关系，基本趋势是随着农田地块坡位的升高，其农田能量转换效率逐渐降低。坡型也是影响农田投入产出效率的重要因素，凹坡、平坡产投比明显大于凸坡。

以农田人工能量投入产出关系衡量山区农民对自然条件利用的过程，表现出明显的经验型利用特征。例如，在高程和坡度等条件适宜的农田中，村民已最大限度地开发了农田潜力。此类农田成为经济活动十分频繁的场所。同时，从提高农田投入产出效益角度，村民对农田的利用仍有一定的盲目性。

有关农田人地系统的研究内容颇多，本章仅侧重于地形因子的有关影响，且偏向于农田地块的能量投入产出，其他更为精细的研究（如地形对不同农田地块物质、能量、价值的投入、产出及投入产出转换效率的总体影响，对不同种植作物物质、能量、价值的投入、产出及其转换效率的影响，对不同地块类型的物质、能量、价值的投入、产出及其转换效率的影响等）将是很有意义的工作。

致谢：熊剑同学进行了调研数据的整理工作，特表谢忱！

参考文献

陈阜. 2002. 农业生态学. 北京：中国农业大学出版社

樊杰，许豫东，邵阳. 2003. 土地利用变化研究的人文地理视角与新命题. 地理科学进展，22（1）：1～10

郜庆炉. 2000. 我国耕地资源可持续利用的内在机制及对策. 农业现代化研究，21（2）：96～99

刘绍明，吴文良. 2003. 县域农业生态经济系统的分析（Ⅱ）——功能和效率. 农业环境科学学报，22（1）：78～81

鲁礼新，马昌河，鲁奇. 2004. 水城县沙坡村农户经济行为调查研究. 地理研究，23（2）：218～226

陆大道，郭来喜. 1998. 地理学的研究核心：人地关系地域系统——论吴传钧院士的地理学思想与学术贡献. 地理学报，53（2）：100～105

陆大道. 2002. 关于地理学的"人-地系统"理论研究. 地理研究，21（2）：135～145

千怀遂，秦耀辰. 1990. 河南省山区农业生产潜力与增产途径. 载：孙九林. 黄土高原地区综合开发治理模型研究. 北京：科学出版社

王爱民，刘加林，缪磊磊，等. 1999. 人地关系研究中的土地利用特征指标分析～以兰州市为例. 经济地理，19（1）：62～66

吴传钧. 1981. 地理学的特殊研究领域和今后任务. 经济地理，创刊号（1）：5～10，21

吴传钧. 1991. 论地理学的研究核心——人地关系地域系统. 经济地理，11（1）：1～6

杨瑞珍. 1994. 我国坡耕地资源及其利用模式. 资源科学，（1）：1～7

尹钧，曹卫星，周乃健，等. 1999. 农田能量投入产出规律的研究. 干旱地区农业研究，（3）：97～102

郑度. 2002. 21 世纪人地关系前瞻. 地理研究，21（1）：9～13

Ekins P. 1986. The living economy. London：Routledge

Fluck R C. 1979. Energy productivity：A measure of energy utilization in agricultural systems. Agricultural systems，4（1）：29～37

Haraldsson H V. 1998. Is ecological living in Sweden different from conventional living? Lund University master's thesis

Li X J，Peterson J，Liu G J，et al. 2001. Assessing regional sustainability：The case of land use and land cover change in the Middle Yiluo catchment of the Yellow River basin，China. Applied Geography，21：87～106

Ma Z Y，Edwards～Jones G. 1997. Optimizing the external energy input into farmland ecosystems：A case study from Ningxia，China. Agricultural systems，53（2～3）：269～283

Mohan M，Jeffret M. 1996. Key concepts and terminology of sustainable development，defining and measuring sustainability. New York：The Biogeophysical Foundations

第 38 章　中尺度流域土地利用/土地覆盖变化评估

流域是人口、资源、环境相互作用较强、整体性相对突出的区域。土地利用/土地覆盖变化作为人类活动对地球表层重建的重要标志之一，曾被不少学者用于可持续发展研究之中［Turner and William，1990；International Geosphere-Biosphere Programme（IGBP），1993；Gaoutzi and Nijkamp，1993；Selman，1996；傅伯杰等，1999］。本章从可持续发展的角度探索中尺度流域土地利用/土地覆盖变化的研究方法。注重利用地理信息系统和遥感技术，强调区域可持续发展研究应从点位角度和演化方向角度着手。

38.1　研究思路与方法

特定区域的土地可持续利用研究有两个重要问题值得讨论（Li et al.，2001）：①思维方法上，现行的研究多遵从规范方法（normative approach），即用某些被认为是通用的原则来评估研究区域的状况［World Commission on Environment and Development（WCED），1987；中国科学院可持续发展研究组，1999；Costanza，1994；Gale and Cordray，1994；Bowers，1995；Institute of Geography et al.，1994］。这种分析在一定条件下是正确的，但却忽略了区域生态环境条件与社会经济关系的区域差异。例如，在地广人稀的澳大利亚，有一些适宜农耕的土地被用作放牧；而在人口稠密的中国，不少地区却开垦了不宜耕作的土地。衡量土地可持续利用的标准在这两种类型的地区应该有所不同。因此，强调实际上“是什么”，而不是“应该是什么”的实证主义方法（Keynes，1965），可以更好地适应区域可持续发展评估的需要。②研究尺度上，一些研究将区域（或区域中的一部分）作为一个整体，忽略了环境条件上的点位（site）差异性。而这种点位差异在生态环境与社会经济发展的关系中具有重要作用。大比例尺的地形高程模型以及基于此建立起的地理信息系统，与遥感数据的结合使用，提供了在点位尺度分析区域可持续发展的可能性。

基于以上讨论，本章提出以下研究区域土地利用/土地覆盖变化的基本原则：①区域土地利用/土地覆盖变化的评估应采用相对原则，即观察所研究时段内的变化方向；②判定准则为这种变化是否更趋于适应当地环境，所采用的定量指标完全取之于当地实际；③空间上，所研究的尺度应细至点位，以展示区域内的差异。

遵循这三条原则，本章的研究方法可直观表示为图 38.1。为建立判定基准和评估，我们选取了 10 个变量（表 38.1）。这些变量中，有一部分直接构成点位的生境条件（如降水、土壤湿度、气温等），另一部分通过其他变量影响点位生境条件。

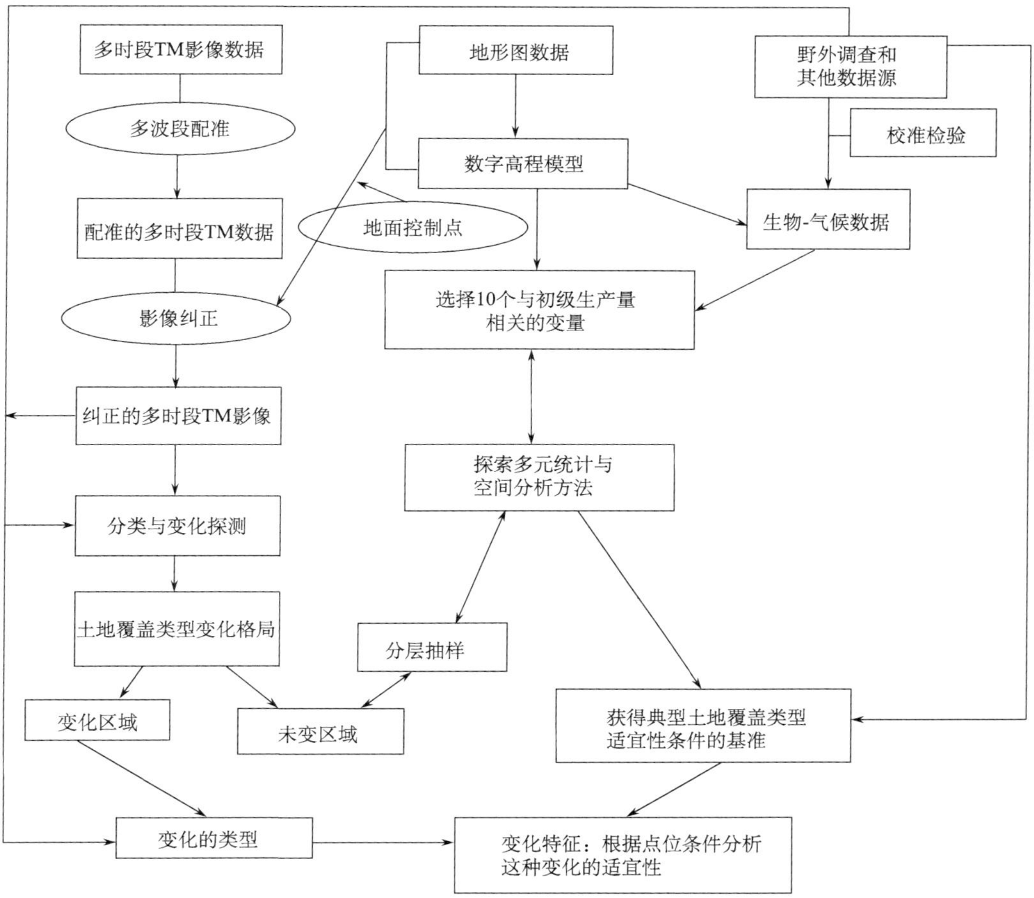

图 38.1　研究方法框图

表 38.1　伊洛河流中部地区土地利用/土地覆盖分析变量

变量	取值范围	定义及对土地利用的主要影响
高程（x_1）	100～2500m	海拔高度：通过影响气温、降水、土壤等影响土地利用
坡度（x_2）	0～45°	坡面与水平面夹角：影响水分及其他物质流动及点位上的太阳辐射
坡向（x_3）	0～360°（平地定义为－1）	以正北为 0，顺时针方向量度：影响点位的湿度和太阳辐射
坡型（x_4）		坡度之坡度，以凸坡（＋）或凹坡（－）表示之：影响土壤湿度
坡位（x_5）	0（坡底）～100（坡顶）	$x_5=dv/(dv+dr)$，其中，dv 为距最近坡底的欧氏距离，dr 为距最近坡顶的欧氏距离：影响土壤湿度
太阳辐射（x_6）		地面单位面积每年接受到的短坡辐射（kJ/m^2）：影响植物生长
土壤湿度（x_7）		潜在的土壤湿度含量：影响植物生长
土层厚度（x_8）	1～100cm	地面壤土厚度：影响植物生产所需的营养量
积温（x_9）	3000～5000	日平均气温≥10℃的年积温：强烈影响植物生长
降水（x_{10}）	500～1000mm	年均降水量：强烈影响植物生长

为了建立判别基准，我们首先借助遥感和实地调查数据，在研究区域、研究时段内确定未变化的土地利用/覆盖区。接着在每种未变化的土地利用/覆盖类型中，随机抽取20%的点位（每个点位 30m×30m）。每种类型相应点位上各个变量的样本均值被用做研究区域内、研究时段间该类土地利用的典型生境标志。

以每种土地利用的典型生境条件为参照基准，可对研究区域内、研究时段间相应的各类土地利用/土地覆盖变化点位的变化合理与否进行判别。判别中应用多变量分析中的 M 距离（或称马氏距离）（Huberty，1994），其计算式如下：

$$D = [X_i - X]' \sum^{-1} [X_i - X] \tag{38.1}$$

式中，D 即 M 距离，用来量度某一点位上某一类型土地利用/土地覆盖的生境条件与该类型典型生境条件的差距状况；X_i 为该点位上各变量值（矩阵）；X 为该类土地利用/土地覆盖的各变量均值（即典型生境条件矩阵）；Σ 为研究中未变化区各变量的协方差矩阵。

根据式（38.1），研究区域内每个点位上可计算出多个值，分别表示该点位与各类土地利用/土地覆盖的典型生境条件的距离。为了评估相应的变化合理性，本章采用以下判别式：

$$P_{i\to j} = \begin{cases} \text{合理}, & \text{if } D_i > D_j \quad (i \neq j) \\ \text{不合理}, & \text{if } D_i < D_j \end{cases} \tag{38.2}$$

式中，$P_{i\to j}$ 为研究点位上的土地利用/土地覆盖由研究时段初 i 类型变为研究时段末的 j 类；D_i、D_j 分别表示该点位的生境条件与 i 类型和 j 类型土地利用/土地覆盖典型生境条件的 M 距离。

显然，本章以上分析思路兼顾了规范和实证两种方法。土地利用/覆盖的生境变量选择反映了规范分析思路，而变量取值、典型生境条件的确定和点位生境与各类典型生境的差距，则完全基于实证分析方法。

38.2 研究区概况

伊洛河是三门峡大坝以下黄河最大的支流。它发源于陕西省华山南麓蓝田县境，北以华山、崤山与黄河干流为界，南以伏牛山与长江水系分水，东以外方山与淮河为邻，流域面积为 18881km^2。流域内山地占 52.4%，黄土丘陵占 39.7%，冲积平原（谷地）占 7.9%，属山地景观。年降水量为 600（东北部）～900mm（西南部）。降水集中于夏季，常出现暴雨，造成下游洪涝灾害。年均气温为 12～14℃。土壤以褐土、棕壤、黄垆土为主。

自然植被群落以华北区系的壳斗科、华木科（Betulaceae）、杨柳科（Salicaceae）、胡桃科（Juglandaceae）、槭树科等科的一些树种组成的暖温带落叶阔叶林为主，亚热带区系的植物成分，如黄连木、黄栌、山胡椒、牛鼻栓（*Fortunearia sinensis*）、美丽胡枝子（*Lespedeza formosa*）等也有出现。

本研究选择伊洛河的中部地区：北以洛河流域北缘、南以伊河主干道、西以故县水库上端、东以伊洛河交汇处为界，面积为 9276.18km^2（图 38.2）。这种选择主要考虑：①陆地卫星 TM 的一景数据（125/36）正好覆盖该区，作为案例研究，无拼接之繁；②该区域包括重要工业城市洛阳，精耕细作农业区（河谷地）和大面积林地，土地利用类型多样；③作者曾在该区域进行过多次实地调查，便于卫星数据解译。

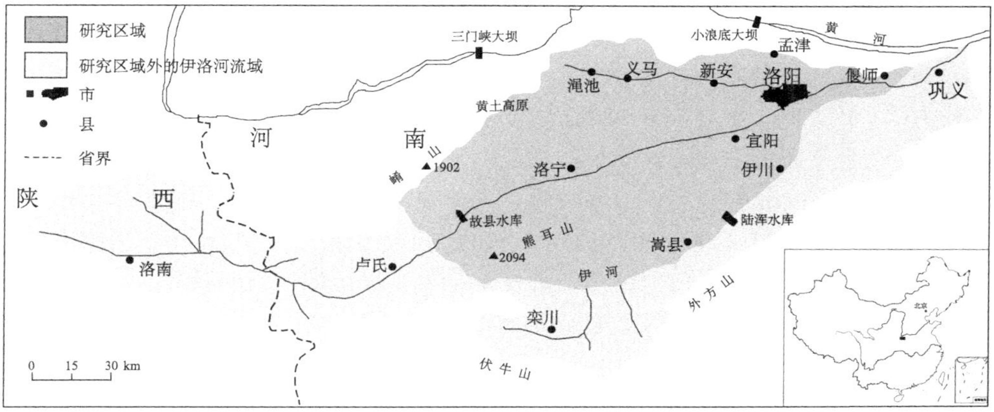

图 38.2　位于黄河中游的研究地区

研究区域约有 600 万人口，其中，农业人口占 70%以上。第二、三产业在多数地区并不发达。多数县（市）农矿业占国民生产总值的 20%以上；一些县（如嵩县、宜阳、洛宁）该数值高达 30%以上。农村工业中，2/3 以上为农矿资源加工型（李小建，1993）。在这样的区域中，社会和经济的发展，更密切地与土地利用变化相联系。

38.3　数据来源与数据库开发

38.3.1　研究数据

本章的研究数据来自三方面。第一，两个时段点（1996.5.11 和 1999.5.4）的 Landsat-5 TM 遥感数据①。该数据的选取，除了其云量稀小、数据真实度较高外，还由于此时当地正好位于初夏，区域内的主要粮食作物（小麦）正处于茁壮生长期，主要树种落叶林已经叶绿，草地也已返青，土地利用/土地覆盖情况较易于判别。

第二种数据来源为 1∶5 万地形数据。数字化的地形数据被用做建立地形高程模型(DEM)，利用该模型，可以获取表 38.1 中的 9 个变量（1～7，9，10）值。

第三种数据来源为我们的野外工作记录，以及河南大学环境与规划学院在此区域数十年的工作积累。这些数据用于控制点选择、土地利用/土地覆盖的分类校正，以及表 38.1 中一些变量值的获取。

① 由中国科学院遥感卫星地面站提供。

38.3.2 数据库开发

空间数据库由根据地形图、野外考察资料和卫星图像绘制的土地利用/土地覆盖图组成。在研究地区使用了1975年（1∶5万）的地形图，结合得到的研究地区1996年5月和1999年5月的TM影像。这些数据的复合处理产生了各种土地覆盖两个时段的分类和图解描述。虽然在野外制图工作中提供了训练地以帮助分类，但未进行地面校核以确定分类精度。

我们还搜集了耕地作物种类和耕作制度的数据。通过分析这些数据确定了农事活动中种植粮食作物及商品作物的比例。

利用Erdas Imagine和Arc/info软件，对遥感数据进行处理。处理分以下四个步骤：①选取20个控制点进行多时段数据之间的校正（影像对影像校正），精确度保持在亚像元水平上；②影像与地形数据之间的校正，由于该区域地形起伏较大，选取了115个控制点；③几何校正后的影像数据先进行非监督分类（150类），再按照地形、光谱特征和实地工作经验进行监督分类。结果为六大类：林地、水面、河谷耕地、山坡丘陵区耕地、草地、建成区；④利用NDVI变化图，为确定各点位1996～1999年各类土地利用/土地覆盖的变化提供参考。

地形图和野外考察得到的土地覆盖类型被数字化并输入地理信息系统（GIS）的数据库中。从陆地卫星影像得到的分类及从研究地区1∶5万地形图数字化后得到的数字化高程模型也包括在地理信息系统的数据库里。地理信息系统为连接不同空间尺度和不同时间采集的、在不同投影下制图的光栅和矢量数据提供了一种方法。

38.4 土地利用/土地覆盖变化：1996～1999年

利用NDVI变化图、野外工作经验和两景纠正后卫星影像的假彩色（RGB）合成信息，可对研究区域的土地利用/土地覆盖变化做以下分析。需要提出，在处理过程中，为减少工作量，忽视了较小的变化区（<6个像元）。这种所忽略的变化区总计占1996～1999年总变化区域面积的12.87%。

38.4.1 建成区

尽管小块变化区未能反映出来，研究区域内建成区的面积从1996～1999年增长了7.48km²（表38.2）。空间上，这些变化集中于涧河、洛河和伊河河谷，尤其是洛阳市周围地区（图38.3）。该区域之外，建成区扩充常出现在铁路和公路沿线。这种格局主要与这些地区经济增长和人们生活需求提高有关。

表38.2 伊洛河中部地区土地利用/土地覆盖变化（1996～1999年）

变化类型	变化面积/km^2
河谷耕地变为建成区	3.7863
山坡丘陵区耕地变为建成区	3.6972

续表

变化类型	变化面积/km²
林地变为草地	2.6972
草地变为林地	8.0487
草地变为水面	3.6549
河谷地区休闲地变为农作（绿地）	24.7842
河谷地区农作（绿地）变为休闲地	5.8743
山坡丘陵区休闲地变为农作（绿地）	35.8488
山坡丘陵区农作（绿地）变为休闲地	73.0746

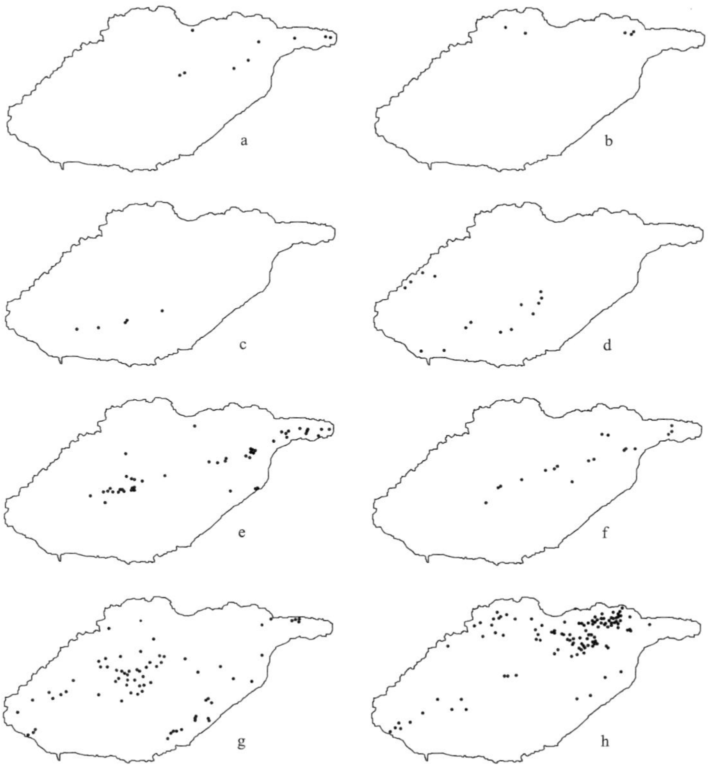

图 38.3　土地利用/土地覆盖点位变化特征示意图（1996～1999 年）

38.4.2　林地覆盖

研究区有三大片林地集中区：南部的熊耳山区、西部崤山林区和北部义马以北的林区。通过对 TM 数据分析，研究时段内有两类林地变化发生。一类是林场伐木和植树引起的变化，它多发生在高程 1200m 以上地区。1200～1800m 生长着落叶阔叶林。优势树种为油松、辽东栎、栓皮栎；1800m 以上为针叶林，优势树种为华山松。为了管理和利用这些森林，林区建立了数个林场。林场的砍伐和植树，空间尺度较大，可从卫星影像数据中判断（图 38.3c，38.3d）。

另一类变化发生于林地与耕地间的过渡带。该地带中，长期人多地少的矛盾促使林地砍伐后逐渐代之以灌木和草地，少数地方变为耕地。近年来，政府提倡退耕还草、退耕还林。研究区域的实践提供了相应的证据；研究时段内，8km^{2}以上的草地返为林地（表 38.2）。

38.4.3 农作覆盖

前已述及，研究区域内最重要的夏季作物是小麦。统计数据表明，1998 年小麦播种占夏作播种面积的 80%以上。TM 数据分析显示，在河谷地区，1999 年的播种面积远大于 1996 年；而在山坡丘陵区，则出现相反的情况（表 38.2）。

根据经验对这些变化做进一步分析，揭示出河谷地区绿地的增加有三类：①由休闲地变为麦田；②由河间沙洲或荒地变为季节性草地；③麦田本身生长状况的变化（1999 年较多的降水导致小麦长势较好，故 NDVI 明显增加）。而在山坡丘陵区，尤其是东北部的丘陵区（如新安和孟津），1999 年的小麦种植面积明显减少，代之以经济作物（如烟叶等）。

38.4.4 水面

三年间，研究区域内较大的水面变化主要发生于陆浑水库（表 38.2 和图 38.2）。1999 年春季相对较多的降水，使该水库水面扩大约 8km^2。其他水面的微小变化，由于研究精度所限，难以显现出来。

38.5 结果讨论

根据以上分析，研究区域内土地利用/土地覆盖变化可分为三个变化类型：从耕地到建成区，从草地到林地，从林地到草地。相应地，通过在未变化区随机抽样，河谷耕地、山坡丘陵区耕地、建成区、草地、林地的典型生境条件也计算出来。通过 M 距离计算，每一点位与各类典型生境相应的差异可表示为图 38.4。

比较图 38.4 中的 5 幅 M 距离图，可以看出高程在决定各点位的适宜性方面起着重要作用。这一点，与早期对该区的一项专题研究相一致（河南大学地理系，1983）。

对各种土地利用类型的 M 距离图（图 38.4）与各点位的土地利用/土地覆盖变化（图 38.3）进行叠加，可以对各类变化方向进行评估（图 38.5 和图 38.6）。结果表明，每种土地利用/土地覆盖类型中，均有合理变化和不合理变化（图 38.5）。十分清楚，在河谷地区，耕地变为建成区不利于区域的可持续发展。但是，在山坡丘陵区，这种变化中多数被认为是合理的。

林地和草地之间的变化分析，与一般经验基本一致；多数草地变为林地被评估为合理，而林地变为草地的多数点位被评估为不合理（图 38.6c，图 38.6d）。值得指出，并非所有草地向林地的变化是合理的，因为一些点位上更适宜草被生长（图 38.5，图 38.6c）。

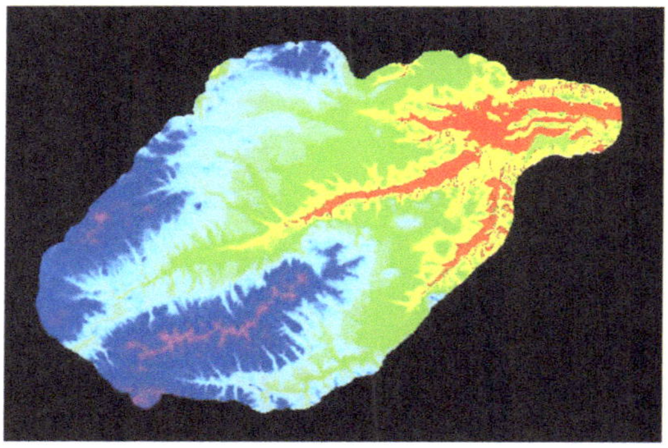

a. 河谷耕地

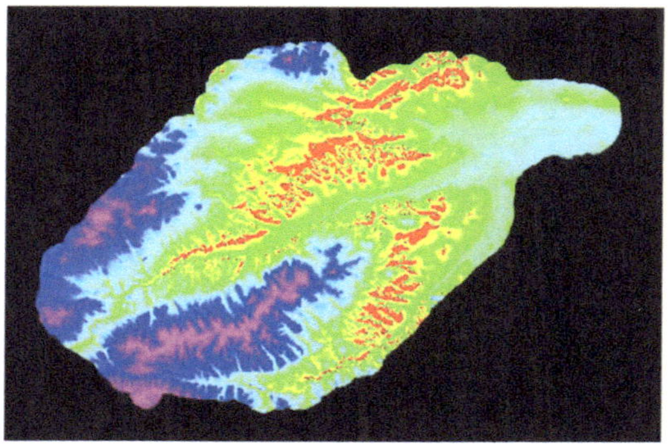

b. 坡耕地

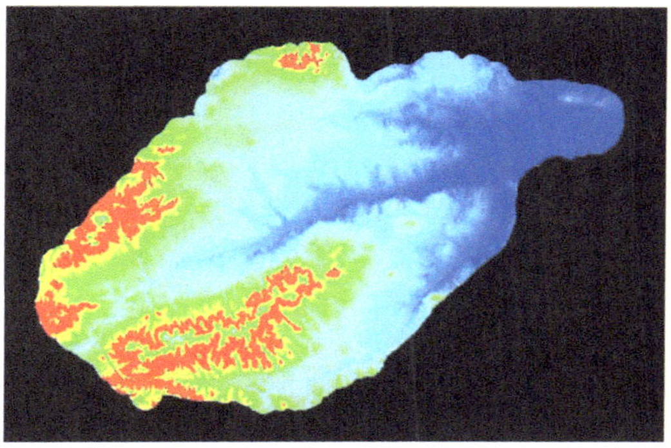

c. 林地

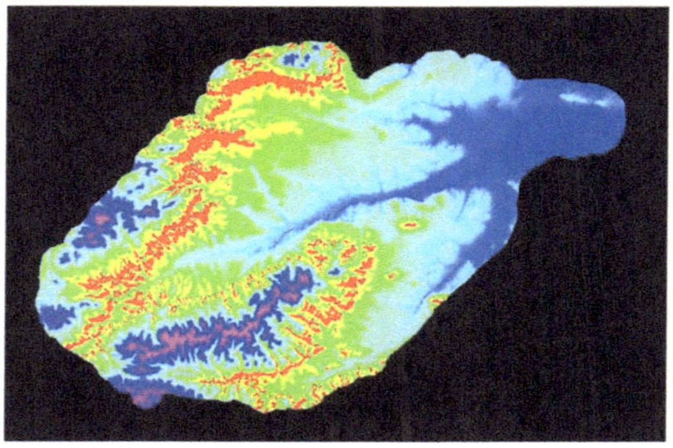

d. 草地

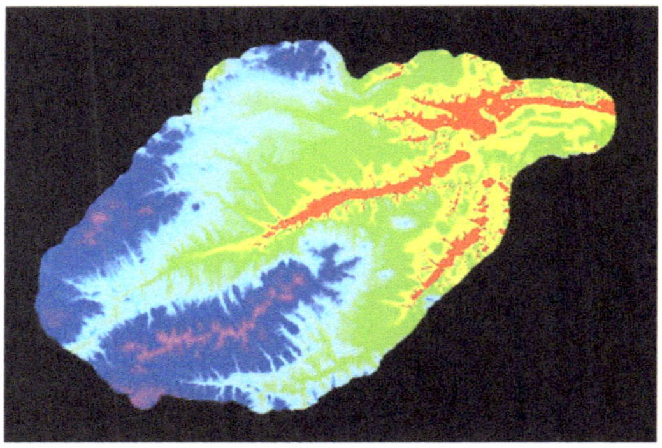

e. 建成区

图 38.4　5 种土地利用类型的 M 距离

对伊洛河中部地区 1996～1999 年的土地利用/土地覆盖变化的可持续性评估结果，喜忧皆存。一方面，从总体上看，草地和林地之间的互相变化表明政府的植树造林政策呈现出可喜的局面。不仅造林的面积远大于伐木的面积，而且变化点位中多数被评估为合理的（可持续的）（图 38.5）。另一方面，建成区的不断扩大带来了河谷地区大片良田的丧失。如果考虑所删去的 TM 影像中所显示出的小片变化，那么河谷地区建成区

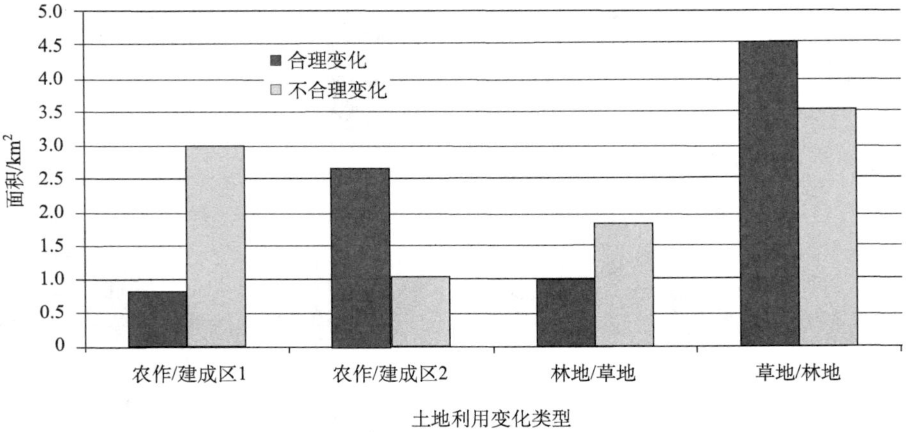

图 38.5　土地利用四种变化类型（1996～1999 年）

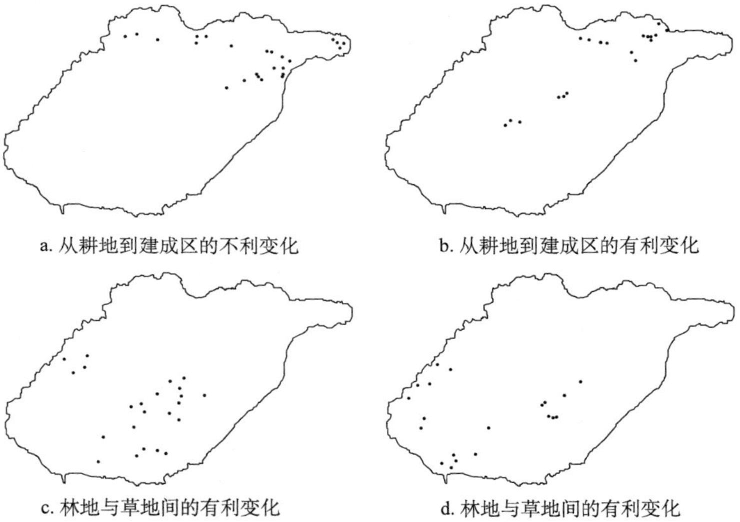

图 38.6　土地利用变化评估（1996～1999 年）

对良田的侵占面积可能还会更大。

我们野外工作发现每个村镇的外围均有新建房屋出现。由于当地人们非常重视住宅状况，尽管有土地法的约束，完全抑制这种耕地流失现象是非常困难的。

38.6　结论与讨论

多数可持续发展研究侧重于规范方法［见 Meppem 和 Gill 的评述（Meppem and Gill，1998)］。它们多使用既定的公共价值观来评估人地相互作用的状态，并制定未来发展政策（WCED，1987；Costanza，1994；Gale and Cordray，1994；Bowers，

1995)。毋庸置疑，这种价值原则是人类经验和科学研究的总结，它在引导经济和社会发展总体方向上起有十分重要的作用。但是，在实施这些原则时必须考虑各地地理条件的差异和社会经济实践的差异。经济增长与环境保护之间的矛盾在人口稠密的不发达地区与人口密度较低的经济发达地区会面临不同的处理方法（Wilbanks，1994)。甚至同一区域的不同点位上，可展示不同的人地相互作用特点。

考虑规范分析方法的缺陷，本章采用规范和实证相结合的方法。该方法基于以下四个原则：①一区域的可持续发展效果应该通过评估一个时段内相关指标的变化方向来判定；②判定的准则着重于这种变化是否更加适应于当地的环境条件；③就土地利用/土地覆盖而论，可以通过物理模型和统计模型的嫁接确定研究区域的典型生境条件，以此作为各相应土地利用类型的适宜性参照基准；④利用多变量分析技术量度任一点位上实际变化情况与参照基准的差异。在使用这种研究方法时，GIS和遥感技术起着关键作用。通过这些技术，本章对伊洛河中部地区的土地利用/土地覆盖变化的研究，可以精细到较小的点位上。与常规的区域研究相比，这种研究结果更易于反映各地（点位）的实际情况，相应地，也更易于被研究区域政府采用。

本研究中也提出了一些值得进一步关注的问题。第一，高质量数据对研究有十分重要的作用。在30m×30m空间解析度情况下，为获取生境条件的各变量值，纠正卫星影像，需要高质量的大比例尺的地形数据。一开始，我们曾试用1∶25万地形数据，不成功后改为1∶5万数据。当然地形数据越精细（比例尺越大），越需要详细的地面真实情况经验。中国县级地籍数据，可在以后的相关研究中发挥作用。

第二，研究区域范围对结果有一定影响：①由于本章中的典型生境条件受制于土地利用/土地覆盖未变化点位的平均状况，这样，研究区域越大，所得结果与各点位的实际情况的差距的就越大；换句话说，也就越忽视了区域的差异性。本研究区域已超9000km^2，同用样方法对更小区域的研究，可望获取更理想的结果。②在本章中，地形高程在生境条件中起着控制作用。在更精细的解析度（15m×15m）情况下，坡位和土壤湿度对生境的影响趋于明显（Liu and White，1999)，这是否有规律可循，有待进一步研究所证实。

本项研究也存在一定局限。例如，由于篇幅所限和本章的侧重点不同，在土地利用变化方向的评估中，没有考虑区域内社会经济条件（如人口增长、经济结构等）指标，而这些指标的作用有时还是较为重要的。因此，本章的研究模式在工商业发展迅速的地区应用时，应有所修正。本章的研究结论也只能适应于该地区，以及环境条件和社会经济发展与此相类似的地区。

致谢：马建华，千怀遂，管华，秦奋，张晓平提供了诸多帮助，特表谢意。

参考文献

傅伯杰，陈利顶，马克明. 1999. 黄土丘陵区小流域土地利用变化对生态环境的影响. 地理学报，54（3)：241～246

河南大学地理系. 1983. 豫西中部山地区自然条件与自然资源（专题研究). 河南大学学报丛书

李小建. 1993. 河南农村工业发展环境研究. 北京：中国科学技术出版社

中国科学院可持续发展研究组. 1999. 中国可持续发展战略报告. 北京：科学出版社

Bowers J. 1995. Sustainability, agriculture, and agricultural policy. Environment and Planning A, 27: 1231～1243

Costanza R. 1994. Three general polices to achieve sustainability. In. Investing in Natural Capital. A. Jansson M, Hammer C. Folke and R. Costanza. Washington D C: Island Press

Gale RP, Cordray S M. 1994. Making sense of sustainability: nine answers to "what should be sustained?". Rural Sociology, 59 (2): 311～332

Giaoutzi M, Nijkamp P. 1993. Decision Support Models for Regional Sustainable Development. Aldershot: Avebury

Huberty C J. 1994. Applied Discriminant Analysis. NewYork: John Wiley &Sons

Institute of Geography, Chinese Academy ofScience, The State Economic Information Centre, et al. 1994. The National Economic Atlas of China. Hong Kong: Oxford University Press

International Geosphere-Biosphere Programme (IGBP). 1993. Landuse and Landcover Change Science/Research Plan (IGBP Report No. 35). IGBP

Keynes J. 1965. Thescope and method of political economy. New York: Augustus M. Kelley, 1890, 1965 reprint

Li X J, Peterson J, Liu G, et al. 2001. Assessing regional sustainability: The case of land use and land cover change in the Middle Yiluo Catchment of the Yellow River Basin, China. Applied Geography, 21 (1) : 87～106

Liu G, White J. 1999. DEM-Based Habitat modelling for the baw bawfrog. Melbourne, Australia: Natural Resource System

Meppem T, Gill R. 1998. Planning for sustainability as a learning concept. Ecological Economics, 26: 121～137.

Selman P. 1996. Localsustainability: Managing and planning ecological sound places. New York: St. Martin Press

Turner II BL, William C C. 1990. The earth as transformed by human action: Global and regional changes in the biosphere over the past 300 years. London: Cambridge University Press

Wilbanks T J. 1994. Presidential address : "Sustainable development" in geographic perspective. Annals of the Association of American Geographers, 84 (4): 541～556

World Commission on Environment and Development (WCED). 1987. Ourcommon future. Oxford: Oxford University Press

第五篇　区域研究

第39章　社会不公平问题的地理研究

经济地理学的研究主题与社会现实密切相关。在发展中国家，经济增长缓慢是社会的主要矛盾，众多地理学家多侧重于依据相关理论（如增长极等）从空间视角为经济增长提供理论支持。而在经济发展达到一定水平之后，由于经济发展中的一些问题凸显出来，学者们可能更多地从地理角度揭示经济增长带来的弊端，并研究缓和解决社会相关问题的途径。这两种研究视角在一定程度上反映了正在工业化的发展中国家和后工业化的发达国家地理学的立场分异（李小建，2004）。然而，这种差别并非水火不相容，发展中国家在经济发展过程中，也会不断出现一些严重的社会问题。学者们不仅要关注发展，也应该关注发展问题。在某些情况下，这些发展问题也许更应引起关注。目前，中国经济社会发展中，便有一些社会不公平问题，需要从地理视角加以关注。例如，区域发展中的不公平问题，城市内部的不公平问题，农民与农区问题，特殊社会问题的地理研究。本章力图对此加以探索，揭示经济地理学研究中对社会不公平问题的忽视，以望引起学界同行的关注。

39.1　区域发展中的不公平

中国经济发展的区域差异，吸引众多学者从不同角度进行研究，发表了一批很有影响的成果。这些成果帮助我们深入了解中国近几十年的区域经济发展差异变化及其形成原因，并在此基础上为相关政策提供参考建议。但是，区域经济差异与区域发展中的不公平并非等同。由于各地资源禀赋、发展条件、居住人口等不同，从某些视角观察，区域经济差异完全可以是一种公平现象。尽管地理学家在中国区域差异研究中，多少涉及了区域间的公平问题，但专门研究该问题的成果还很少。比较而言，经济学家则有所不同。王绍光等从政治经济学角度专门研究了中国区域发展中效率与公平关系问题，指出20世纪80年代后期以来，中国区域之间的不公平现象越来越严重，应该引起政府高度关注（王绍光和胡鞍钢，1999）。在经济发展和市场经济转型过程中，存在使社会相对公平的市场改革之路。

中国地理学家的研究视角，根植于20世纪50年代以来以服务于国家宏观区域经济布局战略为主的思维范式。这些研究中，尽管也有对国家大型项目布局不合理提出批评性的观点（多为事后的批评），但多数以阐释和正面论证为主。在以经济快速增长为国家和区域主要目标的工业化进程中，地理学家无疑扮演的是正确的角色。但是，至今经过几十年的改革，中国的区域冲突与其他社会矛盾一样，也逐渐凸显出来。在这种情况下，地理学家应该关注区域发展中的不公平问题。

区域发展的不公平包括诸多研究内容。例如：①国家政策造成的区域发展机会不平等。例如，相当一段时间内，国家区域政策侧重于“锦上添花”，而不是“雪中送炭”，致使一些相对不发达地区的发展受到抑制；迅速的政策变动也带来“事实上的不公平”，当一些欠发达地区认识到可以利用政府的某些有利政策时，这个政策却发生了变化。②区域分割带来的社会不公。最为典型的是高考录取上的省（市）际差异，有悖于宪法赋予公民的平等受教育权。③经济增长与区域贫困化。中国改革开放以来，区域经济差异的变化已有不少学者研究。但地理学家对空间数据的处理，还可发现伴随着经济的快速增长，中国有更多的区域在相对贫困化。例如，1990 年全国有 531 个县的人均 GDP 低于全国平均值的 50%（李小建和乔家君，2001），而到 2013 年，这个数字增加到 858 个。在经济欠发达的河南省，这种情况更为突出，全省 127 个县域（含县级市）中，人均 GDP 低于全国平均值 50%的县由 1990 年的 7 个，增至 2013 年的 35 个（表 39.1）。

表 39.1　河南省内人均 GDP 低于全国平均水平 50%以上的县域（1980～2013 年）

项目	1980 年	1990 年	2000 年	2013 年
县域/个	7	7	15	35
占全省/%	5.5	5.5	11.8	32.4

资料来源：河南省统计年鉴 1981，1991，2001，2014。

39.2　城市内部的不公平

伴随着市场经济发展和城市内部的阶层分化，反映不同阶层的社会空间逐渐形成。从就业的角度，一方面是白领集中的金融业和公司总部区，另一方面是加工组装、小商小贩聚集区。前者环境优雅，后者拥挤并伴随着污染。同样的时间付出，却有很大的收益差别。不仅如此，不同区域的工作环境对人们的影响也有很大不同。从居住角度，不同等级的居住区逐渐发展起来（图 39.1）。一方面是空间狭小的低收入家庭居住区，另一方面是可与世界级富商豪宅相媲美的高档花园别墅。在市场经济“公平”的竞争条件下，形成的这种区域分异是否隐含着诸多不公的问题，也颇值得探讨。例如，在有限资源的占用上，是否金钱就能剥夺低收入者的共有权？以弱势地位居民为主的城市区，在公共利益上是否可以得到公平的待遇？在处理不同居住区的利益冲突时，政府或非政府组织应持何种立场，等等。

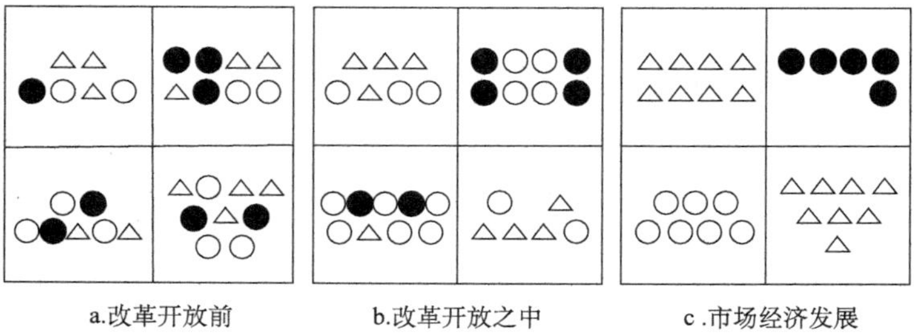

图 39.1　改革开放以来城市居住空间分化

●高收入家庭　○ 中等收入家庭　△低收入家庭

城市空间拓展中的不公平问题更应引起关注。由于征地制度非市场化和用地制度中扭曲的市场化，伴随着中国的快速城市化，出现了诸多不合理现象。例如，在供地方面，通过 20 世纪 90 年代的改革政策，政府可以通过出让国有土地收取土地出让金；在征地方面，各级政府仍沿用计划经济办法低价甚至强行征地。低价征地与以“市场化”方式出让土地之间，是一个相当可观的政府收入和权力寻租空间。其收益分配首先流向地方政府和房地产开发企业，其次才是村级组织和农民（柏晶伟，2004）。例如，2014 年土地财政收入 64995 亿元，占地方财政收入的比例达 54.9%（亢亚娟，2015）。土地所有者的国家和土地使用者的农民在城市化过程中承担着巨大的变革成本。

39.3　农民与农区问题

除了城市边缘区的农民之外，全中国的农民均承担了很大的改革成本。例如，在生产过程中，农民只能参与农业生产链中增加值最低部分的活动——农田生产，而产前和产后增加值较高部分，却被权力部门垄断。农业生产资料价格再高，农民也得买；农产品价格再低，农民也得卖，因为供应渠道和收购渠道均单一。而且，农民只有生产自主权，没有不生产自主权。即使在无利或微利时，也不能选择不生产以规避风险。一些人进城务工，也不能得到城里人同样的待遇。除了生产过程中农民需承担制度变革的成本之外，在社会再分配中，农民处于边缘地位。长时期农民是中国主要的纳税群体，却难以享受纳税人的待遇。没有公费医疗，没有养老保险，更没有城里人那些名目繁多的社会福利待遇（刘亚洲，2005）。

农民的不公平反映在区域上便是农区的不公平。以上问题均在农区层面显现出来，并在很大程度上制约着农区的发展。然而，农区发展问题在改革开放之初的一些年代曾被政府关注，之后便慢慢被置于次要地位。21 世纪初以来，围绕“三农”（农民、农村和农业）出现了不少问题，农区的综合发展再次引起决策者的重视。中央出台了一系列文件，重点解决“三农”问题，从而为农区发展提供了新的机遇。

然而，长期以来，地理学并不十分重视农村地区的发展问题。例如，在区域发展理论中，通用理论的基本思想是假设区域存在着以农业为主导产业、以工业为主导产业、以第三产业为主导产业的演化过程。农业只是在区域发展的早期阶段起重要作用。与此相对应，以农业为主的区域也只是区域发展的早期阶段的产物。随着经济的发展，以农业为主的区域逐渐被以工业为主的区域、以第三产业为主的区域所取代。

与这样的假设相联系，主体的区域发展理论基于不平衡发展思想，将农业地区的发展置于其他产业的外围地位。例如，杜能农业区位理论中，城市是控制区域发展的重要因素，农业的发展和类型结构，由距城市的远近来确定（杜能，1997）。同样，在增长极理论中，增长极是推进型产业及其相关产业的聚集。尽管在不同的工业化阶段，推进型产业会有所不同，但由于其较强的创新能力、较广的产业关联性、较高的需求收入弹性等特性（李小建和苗长虹，1993），主要是非农业部门。因而，增长极实际上与城镇密切关联，“增长极就是城市增长中心，该增长中心的增长可以向周围地区扩散”（Brookfield，1995）。农业为主的地区只能是接受增长极扩散的地区。

农业地理学作为研究农业生产结构与地域分异规律的科学，在从空间的角度研究农业发展的过程中，不可避免地会关注农业所在区域的发展（吴传钧，2001）。相关研究成果除强调合理利用资源条件发展农业之外，在农区发展上则进一步强调农业产业化、农村工业化和城镇化等发展战略（刘彦随等，2004）。对这些发展思路的理论追溯，很容易看出它们与产业演化的规律和区域不平衡发展等理论的密切关联。

中国作为一个农业大国，目前仍有半数人口生活在农村，农村地区的发展成为中国区域发展中最令人关注的大问题。尤其从“人文关怀”的角度，全面建设小康社会的重点和难点均在农村地区。地理学家应当重视农村地区的研究，为揭示和解决农区发展中的不公平问题做出贡献。

39.4 特殊社会问题的地理研究

任何社会均不可能避免社会问题的出现。中国作为社会主义市场经济国家，十分重视不同群体在社会中的作用，不断解决影响稳定和发展的社会问题。但是由于中国改革涉及诸多领域，且很多制度均在探索中建立，因而在改革中一些群体的利益难免会受到较大冲击，引起系列社会问题。地理学家可以发挥专业特长，分析引起社会问题的环境条件，以及它们对区域发展的综合影响。

在众多的社会问题中，城市下岗职工问题曾颇为引人关注。国有企业改革是中国经济改革的重点之一。在“效率优先”的执政理念下，各级政府并未很好地考虑国企改革的成本及成本分摊机制。由此导致其成本的很大一部分被下岗职工所承担。据估计，1996～2002年，国有和集体单位在岗人员累计减少了5500万人（胡鞍钢，2005）。这批规模庞大的下岗群体对所在地区的经济和社会均产生着重要的影响。以河南省郑州市为例，截至2005年3月有累计下岗失业人员84231人，其中，有近3万人集中于中原区。这里过去曾是郑州市经济最有生机的区域之一，区内的六大国有棉纺织厂奠定了郑州在全国的工业地位。但在产业结构调整和国有企业改制中，企业职工利益受到了很大的影响。该区所要支付下岗职工的生活保障、养老、失业、医疗保险金达2亿多元，从而影响政府对基础设施的投资，也影响相关企业的再生产投资能力。这些下岗工人中年龄在40～50岁的占1/3以上，他们家庭负担很重，再就业十分困难。诸多问题影响区域经济发展和社会稳定，影响和谐社会的构建。

民工流是另一个值得关注的社会现象。从20世纪90年代开始，大批农民涌入城市，从事组装、建筑、家庭服务等，为城市建设做出了特殊贡献。根据国家统计局公布的《2013年全国农民工监测调查报告》，我国进城农民工数量已达1.61亿。但是，农民工们并未得到公平的待遇。不仅他们的工资标准远远低于正常状态，他们在包括子女教育在内的诸多方面也都受到一定的歧视。根据抽样调查研究，近半数的进城务工人员能够享受基本生活和社会保障，30％左右的务工人员能够享受礼品或带薪休假等额外福利，但依然有较高比例的进城务工人员没有基本的生活或社会保障，福利待遇水平较低（李宝元，2013）。这种社会不公平在一些民工集中的区域表现更为突出。它对城市基础设施、社区管理，甚至人们的心理均造成了明显负面影响。而在民工流的来源地，由于大量成年劳动力外流，形成所谓的“空心村”现象，在很大程度上影响着当地农业的发展。

39.5　结　　语

对中国日益严重的社会不公平问题，地理学家理应给予关注。不公平问题十分有悖于社会主义的基本原则。中国地理学家应对这些问题有足够的敏感。应通过研究揭示这些不公平的严重性，分析其形成原因，提出解决这些不公平的参考建议。然而，正如香港中文大学郎咸平教授对中国大陆主流经济学家立场（与新兴既得利益者具共谋关系）的批评一样，中国的地理学家在另外一种层面上，忽略着弱势群体的地理问题。在研究主题和研究方法上逐渐出现了一些偏见，诸如，学者的研究选题重城市而轻农村，重城市宏伟规划而轻弱势群体区域环境，重自上而下的政策论证而轻自下而上的民意反馈，重宏观研究而轻微观（城镇居民、农户）研究，重科技进步知识创新而轻中国特色优势（丰富劳动力）的发挥，等等。认识到这一点，人文地理学家应该以一种学者的良知，做好面向广泛社会大众的研究工作。

参 考 文 献

柏晶伟. 2004. 警惕政府部门滑向“新双轨制”. 中国经济时报，12～24
杜能. 1997. 孤立国同农业和国民经济的关系. 吴衡康译. 北京：商务印书馆
胡鞍钢. 2005. 我们需要对改革进行反思. 读书，(1)：3～9
亢亚娟. 2015. 2014 年土地财政略有弱化 财税体制亟须改革. 上海房地，(6)：37～38
李宝元. 2013. 2013 中国人本发展报告：民工生态. 北京：经济科学出版社
李小建. 2004. 国际背景与中国特色经济地理学. 人文地理，19 (1)：27～31
李小建，苗长虹. 1993. 增长极理论分析及选择研究. 地理研究，12 (3)：45～55
李小建，乔家君. 2001. 20 世纪 90 年代中国县际经济差异的空间分析. 地理学报，56 (2)：136～145
刘亚洲. 2005. 把八亿农民纳入政治体制改革的轨道. 思想理论动态参阅，(9)：9～11
刘彦随，王大伟，彭留英. 2004. 中国农业地理学研究的进展与趋势. 地理学报，59 (5)：175～182
王绍光，胡鞍钢. 1999. 中国：不平衡发展的政治经济学. 北京：中国计划出版社
吴传钧. 2001. 中国农业与农村经济可持续发展问题. 北京：中国环境科学出版社
Brookfield H. 1995. Interdependent Development. London：Methuen

第 40 章　中部地区经济发展与社会福利分析

经济发展水平与社会福利水平之间的关系，一直是学者们关注的焦点之一。庇古(2007) 根据边际效应基数理论，提出两个关于福利的基本命题，一是国民收入越大，社会福利越大；另一个是国民收入分配越平均，社会福利越大。邓泽宏和熊丁 (2006) 对战后“亚洲四小龙”低福利政策做了分析，认为经济赶超意识、高储蓄、出口导向发展战略等经济因素是这些地区形成低福利的重要原因之一，并认为中国现阶段情况与此类似。赵海霞等 (2008) 通过对中国 1985～2004 年的时序数据与面板数据的分析，认为诸如中国这样处于经济快速增长阶段的发展中国家，环境污染问题突出，从而造成了社会的福利损失。谢思全等 (2009) 认为一个社会的工业化进程与经济发展不能简单地以 GDP 总量与增长幅度来衡量，还应考虑由于“反哺农业”而导致的财富支出与社会福利总量损失。聂正彦 (2009) 认为经济增长的高速度并不意味着社会福利水平的最优，较大的收入差距对于社会福利水平具有较大的影响。杨开忠等计算了全国各省区市的 GDP“含金量”，又称为居民收入幸福指数，结果表明，GDP 高的省份，居民收入幸福指数的排名并不靠前，很多省区市排名很靠后 (汪孝宗，2011)。

以上学者对经济水平与福利水平做了很有价值的研究，但对“空间”因素考虑不够，或者考虑了“空间”因素，但没有对经济发展水平与社会福利水平之间的关系做分析。本章旨在县域区域尺度上，通过计算人均 GDP 指数及人均福利指数，探讨中部六省 (山西、河南、湖北、湖南、安徽、江西) 经济发展水平与社会福利水平之间的关系。

40.1　指标及数据来源

用县域人均 GDP 与全国或省域人均 GDP 的比值，表示县域经济发展水平，是较常用的方法 (李小建和乔家君，2001；李小建和樊新生，2006)。本章提出了人均 GDP 指数与人均福利指数。人均 GDP 指数是指某一县域的人均 GDP 与中部六省人均 GDP 的比值。国民社会福利不仅包括经济福利，还包括无法用货币表示的与人类幸福感密切相关的非经济福利 (杨缅昆，2009)。由于非经济福利数据极难得到，这里主要考虑经济福利。社会福利涉及社会总产品等的分配，可以将其分为两类，一是个人所得，即私人福利；二是社会的公共支出，即公共福利 (顾金土，2009)。国内外学者构建了一些社会福利指数表示形式 (Sen，1974；余谦和高萍，2011；朱荣科，1992；屈锡华和王海忠，1995；刘长生等，2008)。这些福利指数共同点是除了考虑经济指标外，还尽可能考虑更多的指标，如健康、教育、环境污染、分配公平程度等，不同点主要是考虑的具体指标及其权数不同，因而形成的数学表达式不同。阿玛蒂亚·森 (Amartya Sen) 提出的福利水平指数 (welfare index) 所包含的表示收入分配状况的基尼系数在学术界有争议（蔡增正，1999），并且县域基尼系数极难获得，因此，不考虑基尼系数这个指标。为了简化研究，本研究用平均量表达福利水平，用相对平均量进行不同县域在某区域尺度上相互比较。

本章利用城镇人均在岗职工工资、农民人均纯收入、城镇在岗职工数、乡村总人口、总人口、财政总支出等指标表示福利指数。选择这些指标基于以下考虑：一是用前四个指标的简单运算得到个人总收入，即私人福利，这包括城市职工总收入与农民总纯收入。二是《中国城市统计年鉴 2009》中的财政支出，包括一般公共服务、外交、国防、公共安全、教育、科学技术、文化体育与传媒、社会保障与就业、社会保险基金支出、医疗卫生、环境保护、城乡社区事务、农林水事务、交通运输、工业商业金融等事务、其他支出、转移性支出。这些内容较好地反映了公共福利情况。其他统计年鉴虽然财政支出与这不完全相同，但大同小异，为了简化研究，本研究认为财政支出的各项目一样。三是这些指标能较好地反映经济、社会、文化、生态环境等方面，体现了私人福利与公共福利的基本情况。用人均福利指数表示中部六省各县市的福利水平，计算公式如下：

人均福利指数＝县域人均福利/中部六省人均福利

社会福利＝私人福利＋公共福利

公共福利＝财政支出

私人福利＝城镇在岗职工总工资＋农民总收入

人均福利＝社会福利/县域总人口

＝(城镇在岗职工总工资＋农民总收入＋财政支出)/县域总人口

城镇在岗职工总工资＝在岗职工人均工资×在岗职工人数

农民总收入＝农民人均纯收入×农业人口

将县域及中部六省相关指标数据代入上述公式，则得到县域人均福利与中部六省人均福利。

数据绝大多数来源于《中国城市统计年鉴 2009》，《中国区域统计年鉴 2009》，并参照六省 2009 年的统计年鉴和《武汉市统计年鉴 2009》。中部六省共 581 个县市，去除没有数据的三个县区（湖南省靖州苗族自治县、玉屏侗族自治县、湖北省神农架林区），共有 578 个样本。

在研究中，人均 GDP 指数的比例参照联合国划分（只是更细化）地区经济水平的比例，0～0.50 属于很贫困地区，0.50～0.75 属于比较贫困地区，0.75～1.00 属于稍贫困地区，这些类型地区统称为贫困地区；1.00～1.50 属于稍发达地区，1.50～3.00 属于比较发达地区，3.00 以上属于很发达地区，这些类型地区统称为发达地区。福利指数比例还没有参照标准，为了便于将社会福利水平和经济发展水平对照分析，这里采用与人均 GDP 完全相同的比例来划分社会福利水平。0～0.50 属于很落后地区，0.50～0.75 属于比较落后地区，0.75～1.00 属于稍落后地区，1.00～1.50 属于稍富裕地区，1.50～3.00 属于比较富裕地区，3.00 以上属于很富裕地区（表 40.1 和表 40.2）。

表 40.1　中部六省县（市）不同发达程度的地区数量及所占比例

发达程度	地区数量/个	所占比例/%
很发达地区	14	2.4
比较发达地区	81	14.1
稍发达地区	89	15.4
稍贫困地区	99	17.1
比较贫困地区	159	27.5
很贫困地区	136	23.5

表 40.2　中部六省县（市）不同富裕程度的地区数量及所占比例

富裕程度	地区数量/个	所占比例/%
很富裕地区	3	0.5
比较富裕地区	36	6.3
稍富裕地区	181	31.3
稍落后地区	229	39.6
比较落后地区	123	21.3
很落后地区	6	1.0

40.2　中部地区经济与福利水平空间差异

40.2.1　经济发展空间差异

在578个县市中，394个县市属于贫困地区，184个县市属于发达地区，分别占68.17%和31.83%，发达地区数量由北到南递减，主要分布于晋中、晋南、豫西北、豫东北、豫中地区，大约近一半发达地区集中在此，其他则分布于各省的城市圈（群、带）（图40.1）。从交通角度看，发达地区连片区在山西主要分布于石太铁路、同蒲线两侧；河南省主要位于陇海线、京广线两侧；湖北、安徽两省主要集中在长江两岸；湖南省的发达地区连片区主要位于京广线两侧；江西省的发达连片区位于连接南昌与新余两市铁路两侧。贫困地区基本上是大面积连片分布，只是在山西、河南两省有小面积零星分布。山西省贫困地区主要分布在吕梁山、太行山与黄河东岸地区；河南省贫困地区主要位于豫西南、豫东及豫东南；湖北省的贫困地区主要分布在与河南省、重庆市、湖南省、江西省、安徽省交界的山区；湖南省则是京广线西侧广大地区，以及与江西省交界地带；江西省除了南昌市、一些市辖区、个别县级市，其他都是贫困区；安徽省与江西省相似，只是在铜陵到马鞍山沿江地带被发达地区明显分割。

发达地区主要位于自然条件优越、交通便利和矿产丰富，特别是煤矿丰富地区。贫困地区主要分布于山区、皖北、豫东平原等地区。整个中部六省则是发达地区被贫困地区包围，但局部贫困地区也被发达地区包围或分割，山西、河南两省的一些块状贫困地区被发达地区包围，湖北、安徽两省的沿江发达地区各自将两省的贫困地区分割。

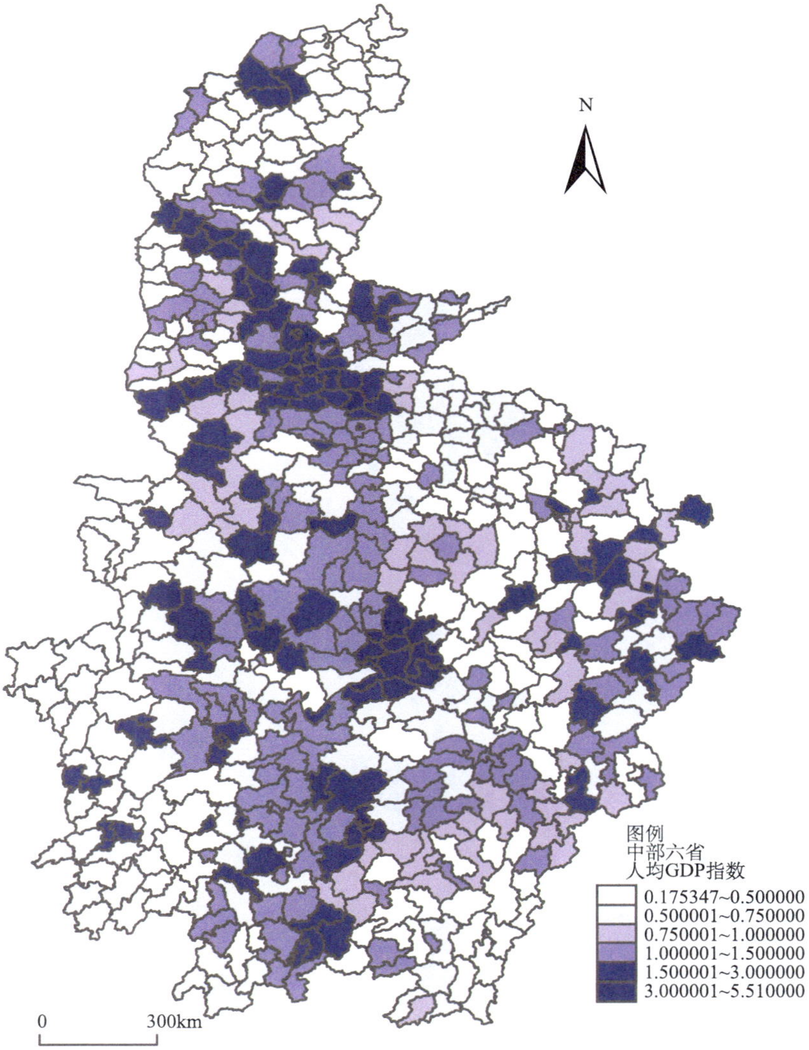

图 40.1　中部六省县域人均 GDP 指数分布图

40.2.2　福利水平空间差异

中部六省 578 个县市中，富裕地区 220 个，落后地区 358 个，分别占整个地区的 38.1%与 61.9%。富裕地区包括很富裕地区 3 个，比较富裕地区 36 个，稍富裕地区 181 个；落后地区中稍落后地区有 229 个，比较落后地区有 123 个，很落后地区有 6 个。稍富裕地区与稍落后地区是主体，共有 410 个，约占县市总数的 70.9%，这是两个富裕程度相互过渡的地区，表明富裕程度的相互转化有很大的空间；比较落后地区远远多于比较富裕地区；很富裕地区与很落后地区数量极少（图 40.2）。

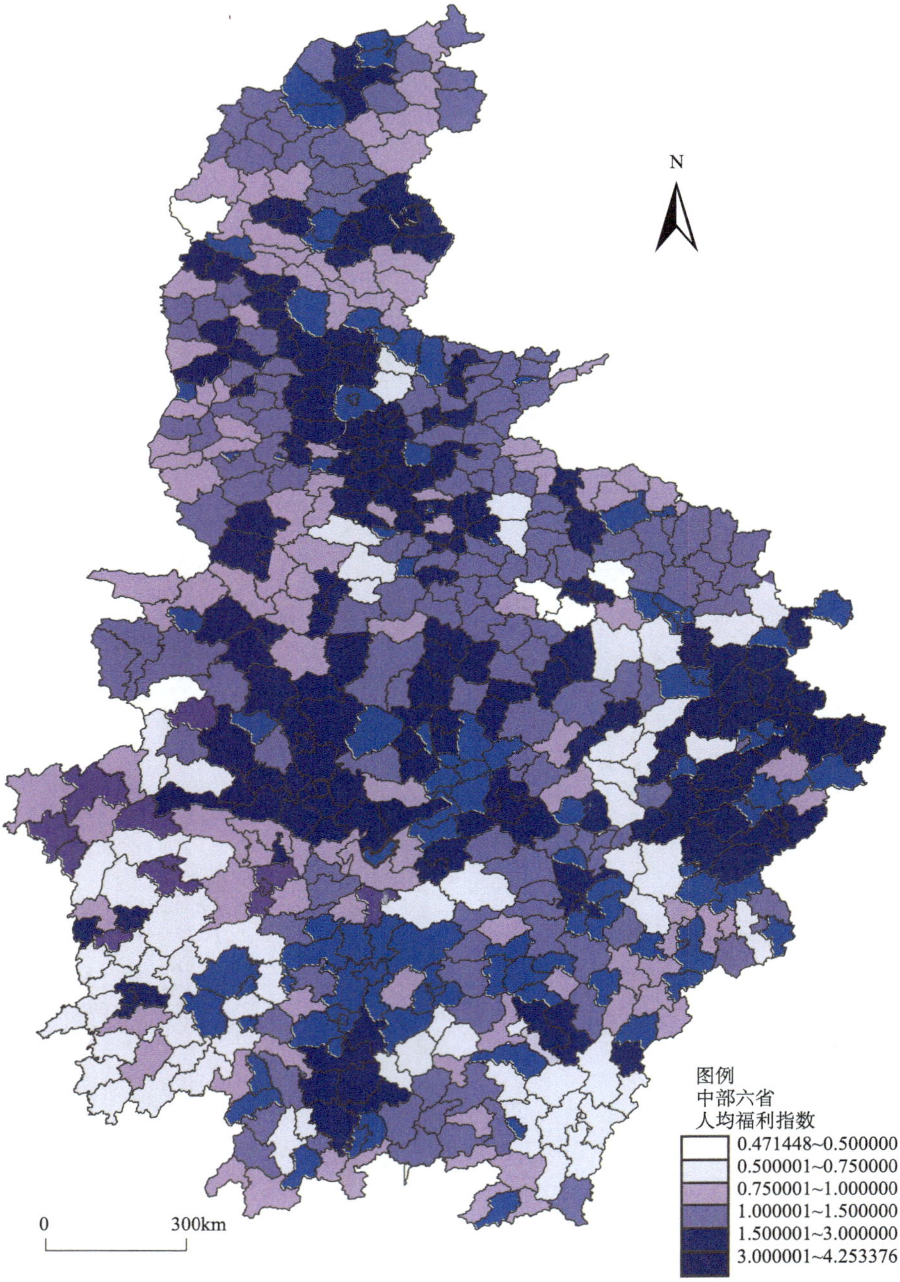

图 40.2 中部六省县域人均福利指数分布图

总的来说，富裕地区与落后地区相互分割相互包围，富裕地区分布于中部六省的六大城市群（圈、带）、一些市辖区和少数县市；落后地区主要位于六大城市群的腹地。稍富裕地区与稍落后地区是两种不同的过渡地区，如果把这两者合起来考虑，则几乎连成一片，其他类型的地区只是零星分布其中，表明中部六省大多数县市处于落后地区与富裕地区相互过渡的状态。

40.3　经济与福利水平之间关系分析

40.3.1　经济与福利水平的“差距”及“伸缩性”

中部各县市人均GDP指数最大值是5.5072，最小值是0.1753，最大值是最小值的31.42倍；人均福利指数最大值是4.2534，最小值是0.4714，前者是后者的9.02倍，31.42是9.02的三倍多，表明人均GDP指数的差距比人均福利指数的差距大得多。很发达地区与比较发达地区共有95个，很富裕地区与比较富裕地区共有39个，前者是后者的2.44倍；很发达地区14个，很富裕地区3个，很发达地区个数是很富裕地区的4.67倍。稍发达地区与稍贫困地区共188个，稍富裕地区与稍落后地区共有410个，前者只有后者的0.46倍。比较贫困地区多于比较落后地区36个，很贫困地区136个，远远多于很落后地区的6个。人均GDP指数的“伸缩性”明显大于人均福利指数的“伸缩性”。

40.3.2　发达程度与富裕程度类型地区转化分析

（1）上行与下行及其衍生概念。A_i表示发达程度类型，$i=1$，2，3，4，5，6。A_1，A_2，A_3，A_4，A_5，A_6分别表示很贫困地区、比较贫困地区、稍贫困地区、稍发达地区、比较发达地区、很发达地区。i值逐渐增大，发达程度递增。B_j表示富裕程度类型，$j=1$，2，3，4，5，6。B_1，B_2，B_3，B_4，B_5，B_6分别表示很落后地区、比较落后地区、稍落后地区、稍富裕地区、比较富裕地区、很富裕地区。j值逐渐增大，富裕程度递增。由于同一区域存在发达程度（A_i）与富裕程度（B_j），所以同一区域的发达程度类型与富裕程度类型有对应关系，即一个区域的A_i对应一个B_j。

如果$i>j$，那么地区下行；如果$i=j$，那么地区既不上行也不下行；如果$i<j$，那么地区上行。例如，如果一个很发达地区是很富裕地区，就认为这个地区既不上行也不下行；如果很发达地区是比较富裕地区，就认为其下行；如果比较贫困地区是稍富裕地区，就认为其上行。如果某发达程度类型地区出现上行或下行，那么该地区类型已转化。

应用上行比例或下行比例来分析发达程度类型地区与富裕程度类型地区的相互转化。上（下）行比例=发达程度类型已变化为某个较高（低）富裕类型数量/该发达程度类型数量。

（2）经济水平高的地区，福利水平有下行趋势。经济水平高的地区指很发达地区与比较发达地区。很发达地区有14个，只有两个是很富裕地区，10个是比较富裕地区，两个是稍富裕地区，很发达地区与很富裕地区数量上不相等，而是大多数很发达地区下行到比较富裕地区或稍富裕地区。应用上行比例或下行比例来论证发达程度类型地区与富裕程度类型地区的相互转化。很发达地区有两个下行比例，一个是很发达地区转化为比较富裕地区下行比例 10/14，即 0.7142，另一个是很发达地区转化为稍富裕地区比例为 0.1429。由此可见，很发达地区不一定就是很富裕地区，而是大多数转化为比较富裕地区，甚至是稍富裕地区，表明经济发展水平高只是影响福利水平的一个因素。

比较发达地区有 81 个，有 18 个比较富裕地区，1 个很富裕地区，54 个稍富裕地区，8 个稍落后地区，上行比例为 1/81，即 0.0123，两个下行比例，一个是 54/81，即 0.6667，另一个是 8/81，即 0.0988。由此可见，比较发达地区转化为很富裕地区比例极小，这说明比较发达地区转化为很富裕地区需要经济实力作为后盾；比较发达地区转化为稍富裕地区比例很大；比较发达地区转化为稍落后地区较少，这些地区福利水平相对于经济实力而言，社会福利很差。

（3）经济水平一般地区福利水平比较稳定。经济水平一般的地区指稍发达地区与稍贫困地区。稍发达地区有 89 个，其中，稍富裕地区有 57 个，比较富裕地区有 6 个，稍落后地区有 27 个。上行比例为 6/89，即 0.0674，下行比例为 27/89，即 0.3034。稍发达地区以稍富裕地区为主，转化则以下行为主，上行很少。由此可见，稍发达地区的福利水平比较稳定。

稍贫困地区有 99 个，包括稍落后地区 65 个，稍富裕地区 30 个，比较富裕地区两个，比较落后地区两个。上行比例有两个，上行比例分别为 30/99，即 0.3031，2/99，即 0.0202；下行比例为 2/99，即 0.0202。稍贫困地区仍以稍落后地区为主，转化则以上行为主，并且上行两个富裕类型，下行很少。由此可见，稍贫困地区福利水平比较稳定，而转化以福利水平上行较多。

（4）经济水平低的地区，福利水平有上行趋势。经济水平低的地区指比较贫困地区与很贫困地区。比较贫困地区有 159 个，其中，比较落后地区有 34 个，稍落后地区有 92 个，稍富裕地区有 32 个，比较富裕地区有 1 个。有三个上行比例，分别为 92/159，即 0.5786，32/159，即 0.2013，1/159，即 0.0063。比较贫困地区上行三个富裕类型，上行比例依次锐减，贫困地区以上行为稍落后地区为主，比较落后地区与稍富裕地区数量差不多，比较贫困地区没有很落后地区类型。

很贫困地区有 136 个，其中很落后地区有 6 个，比较落后地区有 83 个，稍落后地区有 38 个，稍富裕地区有 9 个。有三个上行比例，第一个是 83/136，即 0.6103，第二个是 38/136，即 0.2794，第三个是 9/136，即 0.0662，三个上行比例依次锐减，很贫困地区以上行为比较落后地区为主。

（5）发达程度类型所相应的富裕程度类型。①发达程度的两个极端类型，即很发达地区与很贫困地区，分别有下行与上行的趋势，但以相邻的富裕程度类型为主，保持在很富裕地区与很落后地区很少。很发达地区下行两个富裕程度类型，以比较富裕地区为主。很贫困地区上行三个富裕程度类型，以比较落后地区为主。很发达地区保持很高的福利水平，“阻力”很大，而很贫困地区维持很低的福利水平，“阻力”也很大。②比较发达地区上行到很富裕地区与比较贫困地区下行到很落后地区的“阻力”大，表明比较发达地区提高福利水平与比较贫困地区降低福利水平，除了受制于经济因素外，还受到发展理念与扶贫政策等更重要因素的制约。发达地区与贫困地区的富裕类型转化多，但后者较前者更复杂。③稍发达地区与稍贫困地区福利水平比较稳定，各自主要保持对应的富裕程度类型，即稍发达地区、稍贫困地区分别以稍富裕地区、稍落后地区为主。两者富裕类型转化都有三个，不过转化的稍发达地区主要以下行为主，转化的稍贫困地区以上行为主。

40.3.3　经济水平对福利水平影响的机理分析

经济水平是影响福利水平的重要因素。经济基础较好，用于社会福利投入比较多，但受到经济赶超意识、高储蓄、出口导向发展战略等因素影响，特别是 GDP 至上意识，福利水平并没有与经济水平同等提高；按要素分配进一步拉开了生产要素所有者与无生产要素所有者之间的收入差距，同时，按劳分配内部也存在收入差别较大问题；工业化与城市化进程加快，使得乡村与城市的“二元”结构越发凸显，而社会协调发展须以农村发展为前提，造成倒逼工业反哺农业，导致财富支出与社会福利总量损失；经济发展往往伴随着环境污染与生态破坏，在环境不公平条件下，社会净收益的分配有利于环境污染者及生态破坏者，从而导致社会福利损失；国家财政、产业与扶贫政策对县市的支持，提高了福利水平，同时，福利提高的程度还取决于当地利用这些政策的效率。这些主观或客观原因，不同程度地影响着不同经济水平的县市，从而形成了福利水平不同的变化趋势。

40.4　结论与讨论

本章通过对中部六省各县域的经济发展与社会福利的定量分析表明：2008 年，31.8%的县域为经济发达区，68.2%为较为贫困。发达地区主要位于自然条件优越、交通便利和矿产丰富，特别是煤矿丰富地区。贫困地区主要分布于山区、皖北、豫东平原等地区。从社会福利角度考虑，富裕地区县域占 38.1%，落后地区占 61.9%。富裕地区分布于中部六省的六大城市群（圈、带）、一些市辖区，以及少数县市；落后地区主要处于六大城市群的腹地。稍富裕地区与稍落后地区则连片分布。

人均 GDP 指数的“伸缩性”明显大于人均福利指数的“伸缩性”。经济水平高的地区，福利水平有下行趋势；经济水平一般的地区，福利水平比较稳定；经济水平低的地区，福利水平有上行趋势。

后续研究还可以从以下方面继续探索，一是选取多年数据，作动态趋势研究；二是结合 GIS 图，对经济发展水平与社会福利水平空间差异进行对比，研究两者之间的空间关系。经济发展水平与社会福利水平之间的关系错综复杂，研究只是对其做尝试性研究，有待进一步改进。

参 考 文 献

庇古. 2007. 福利经济学. 金镝译. 华夏出版社

蔡增正. 1999. 吉尼系数在衡量经济发展水平中的地位. 经济科学，(3)：99～101

邓泽宏，熊丁. 2006. 二战后“亚洲四小龙”福利政策反思. 武汉大学学报（人文科学版），59 (3)：343～348

顾金土. 2009. 公共福利的内涵辨析. 学习与实践，(9)：109～116

李小建，樊新生. 2006. 欠发达地区经济空间结构及其经济溢出效应的实证研究——以河南省为例. 地理科学，26 (1)：1～5

李小建，乔家君. 2001. 20 世纪 90 年代中国县际经济差异的空间分析. 地理学报，56 (3)：136～145

刘长生，郭小东，简玉峰. 2008. 社会福利指数、政府支出规模及其结构优化. 公共管理学报，(3)：92～96

聂正彦. 2009. 收入差距与中国经济增长——福利分析的视角. 生产力研究，(22)：85～86

屈锡华，王海忠. 1995. 经济增长中的社会福利指数模型. 经济研究，(5)：70～73

汪孝宗. 2011. 哪个省的 GDP 含金量更高？中国经济周刊，(8)：26～31

谢思全，刘茜，李博. 2009. 关于城乡二元转化成本问题的思考——一个福利分析的视角. 南开学报（哲学社会科学版），(1)：86～89

杨缅昆. 2009. 社会福利指数构造的理论和方法初探. 统计研究，26 (7)：38～42

余谦，高萍. 2011. 中国农村社会福利指数的构造及实测分析. 中国农村经济，(7)：64～65

赵海霞，曲福田，朱德明. 2008. 经济快速增长阶段环境污染的特点及福利损失. 干旱区资源与环境，22 (1)：97～101

朱荣科. 1992. 福利指数及确定方法. 数量经济技术经济研究，(7)：45～47

Sen A. 1974. Informational bases of alternative welfare approaches: Aggregation and income distribution. Journal of Public Economics，31 (2)：387～403

第 41 章　经济地理学研究中的区域关怀

经济地理学研究中，要进行思维转换和研究重点的转换，特别应关注不同发展阶段的区域特点，关注欠发达区域、弱势区域和问题突出区域的研究。通过贯彻尊重原则，机会平等原则和合理补偿原则，实现区域间的和谐发展，体现区域关怀。所谓区域关怀，就是把人文关怀的理念落实到区域，尊重区域主体地位，发挥区域优势，保障区域权益，促进区域间和谐发展，从而走向区域共同富裕；做到整个国家的发展是为了区域，整个国家的发展依靠区域，使发展成果为各个区域所共享。区域关怀有两个基本要求：一是以各地的自然、人文和制度资源的最有效利用为基础，使区域特点得到发挥，区域优势得以体现；二是区域的发展不应该以牺牲其他区域的发展为代价。

之所以提出区域关怀的概念，主要基于以下当前中国的背景。一是区域社会经济差异不断扩大。从每千人所拥有有卫生技术人员数来看，2007 年最高的省份北京（8.56 人）是最低省份贵州（2.27 人）的 3.77 倍，而 2013 年最高的省份北京（15.46 人）是最低的省份贵州（3.64 人）的 4.25 倍。从人均 GDP 来看，2007 年最高的省份上海达 66367 元，高出最低省份贵州（6915 元）59452 元，而 2013 年最高的省份天津达 99607 元，高出最低省份贵州（22922 元）76685 元。在县级尺度上，1990 年全国有 531 个县的人均 GDP 低于全国平均值的 50%（李小建和乔家君，2001），而到 2013 年这个数字增加到 858 个。二是区域之间的矛盾日益显现。这种矛盾表现在经济、社会、资源、环境等多个层面，如区域经济发展所带来的诸如水资源冲突、原燃料冲突和区域经济活动的区际外部性等在一些区域表现突出。例如，随着淮河流域经济社会的发展，淮河流域上游所产生的污染对下游区域人们的健康造成的严重危害，在一些地区出现“癌症村”。还有，国家政策的不公平也可导致区域间的冲突。由于区域发展条件差异明显，中国各地的经济发展进程明显不同。在这样的背景下，同样的国家政策可带来不同的区域实施效果。例如，在过去 30 多年里，沿海地区在相对宽松的政策下大量占用耕地资源，实现了经济的快速发展。目前，中西部地区进入快速工业化时，国家出于粮食安全和可持续发展的考虑，实行了较严格的耕地保护政策。发达区域很难对欠发达区域的牺牲给予完全的补偿，而欠发达区域则会认为自己在某种程度上受到了发达区域的“剥削”。三是中央政府经济实力不断增强且关注区域问题。经过改革开放 30 多年的发展，我国已达到中等偏上收入国家水平。2014 年，人均 GDP 达 46652 元（约合 7600 美元），超过了世界银行公布的中等偏上收入国家标准的下限收入。中央政府的财政收入达 64490 亿元，是 1978 年的 367 倍。中央政府财政收入的增强使其具备解决区域问题的能力。党的十七届三中全会提出把建设社会主义新农村作为战略任务，把加强农业基础、增加农民收入、促进农村和谐作为工作重点。这表明中央政府已开始关注弱势区域和弱势群体，特别是农业区域和农民。因此，只有适应这些新的变化和处理好这些变化所带来的一系列矛盾和问题，才能形成各个区域各尽所能、各得其所而又和谐相处的社会。

41.1 区域经济研究的“重富”传统

41.1.1 忽视弱势群体的区域发展理论

在区域发展理论中，相当一部分忽略弱势区域或弱势产业。例如，在著名的杜能农业区位理论中，城市是控制区域发展的重要因素，农业的发展和类型结构，视距城市的距离而定（杜能，1997）。相应地，以农业为主的地区的发展只有依赖于城市地区。同样，在区域增长极理论中，增长极是推进型产业及其相关产业的聚集。尽管在不同的工业化阶段，推进型产业会有所不同，但由于其较强的创新能力、较广的产业关联性、较高的需求收入弹性等特性（李小建和苗长虹，1993），农业部门很难包含其中。因而，增长极实际上与城镇密切关联，“增长极就是城市增长中心，该增长中心的增长可以向周围地区扩散”（李小建和苗长虹，1993）。农业部门所在地区只能是接受扩散地区。

弱势地区的从属地位在区域之间关系理论中也明显体现出来。在赫希曼的“极化-涓滴效应学说”中，以农业为主的“南方”与经济发达的“北方”之间存在着极化效应和涓滴效应。极化效应导致“南方”的发展受到抑制，涓滴效应推动“南方”的发展，但“北方”则是这种推进作用的主导方（Hirschman，1958）。同样，在弗里德曼的中心-外围理论中，以农业为主的不发达地区在发展中也处于不利地区（李小建，2006）。

弗里德曼认为，因为多种原因，会有个别区域率先发展起来而成为“中心”，而其他区域因发展滞后而成为“外围”。中心和外围之间存在着不平等的发展关系，中心处于控制地位，外围则在发展上依赖于中心。这主要是由于经济权力、技术进步、创新活动等集中于中心，从而带来生产活动效率和贸易的不平等。这就产生了空间二元性，它随时间而不断强化。尽管以后的研究涉及创新的扩散、国家干预等对外围区域有利的影响，但总的来说，外围区域发展的从属地位以及外围区的贫困问题并没有在理论上引起足够的重视。核心-外围理论包含了政治和经济权力不平衡，以及区域间文化变迁速率的不对称性（Firedman，1966）。

缪尔达尔的循环累积因果原理则强调工业在空间上的累积增长过程。根据他的观点，不管是什么原因，一旦一种新工业配置于一个地区就会发生连锁效应，从而进一步吸引新的工业，从而使这个地区成为增长中心。这个中心的增长动量将会对其他地区产生扩散效应。例如，通过不断购买其他地区的农产品和矿产原料，或到其他地区进行旅游等活动，使资金流向那些地区。然而，由于生产要素的流动和贸易的发展，增长中心对边缘贫困地区存在着一种不良效应，即回波效应，它使贫困地区的发展减慢，因而地区差异加大。例如，贫困地区的劳动力，尤其是有事业心的年轻人迁移到增长中心；银行系统把边缘地区的储蓄吸走而投资到中心地区；竞争使边缘地区传统的弱小工业破产等（Myrdal，1957）。

克鲁格曼的中心-外围模型通过在新贸易理论中加入要素地区间流动的可能性，阐述了基本条件原本相同的两个区域是如何在规模收益递增、运输成本和劳动流动的相互作用下最终分别演变成以制造业为中心的核心区和以农业为核心的外围区。克氏的中心-外围模型认为，较低的运输成本和较大的制造业份额是集聚可持续的必要条件。若一个区域的制造业份额比另一个区域大，该区域的价格指数就较低，由于紧密的前、后向联系，厂商就能以较低的生产成本生产，从而能支付工人较高的工资，这样，该区域就能吸引更多的制造业工人。从而在空间上出现中心-外围结构。并且这种中心-外围模式一旦建立，就能持续下去（李小建，2006）。显然，克氏的研究焦点仍然放在制造业和制造业集聚的中心上，而忽略了农业和以农业为主导产业的外围区域的发展问题。

从以上简要讨论中可以看出，佩鲁的增长极理论、缪尔达尔的累积因果关系理论、弗里德曼和克鲁格曼的中心-外围理论和赫希曼的极化-涓滴效应学说，都强调了区域经济增长的不平衡规律，强调了城乡联系中城市的主导作用（安虎森，2004），以及发达地区、工商业、大型企业或创新企业、创新性企业家、经济能人等的重要作用。与此相对应，不发达地区、农业、中小企业、一般民众等弱势群体则被忽视。

41.1.2　中国区域发展研究的“重富”传统

作为发展中国家，经济增长问题是中国政府和民众最为关注的议题。长期以来，中央政府的政策主要以经济增长为中心，为此十分强调培育和加强经济增长点。①重点支持城市增长。新中国成立以来，为了促进以工业为主导产业的城市区域的快速增长，国家实行了“以农补工”的政策，财政支出结构具有明显的“城市偏向”特征：财政支出的大头在城市，保障的对象主要是非农业人口。1952～1990年我国农业为工业化提供资金积累的总额达11594亿元，农业提供的积累在国民收入积累额中所占的比重在工业化初期达40%以上，20世纪整个60年代也都维持在较高水平，进入80年代才有所减小（冯海发和李溦，1993）。②重点支持发达地区。在20世纪80年代，为促进国民经济的快速增长，增强国家经济实力，尽快缩小与发达国家的差距，国家采取了优先支持区位和经济条件较好的沿海地区的经济发展的相关政策。包括支持经济特区、沿海开放城市、经济开放区和保税区、沿海开放地区等（魏后凯，2006）。国家的投资布局也向沿海倾斜。截至1990年，在全国基本建设投资的地区分配中，沿海地区已经提高到50.9%。

与此相应，中国区域经济研究十分重视对区域经济增长相关侧面的研究。从20世纪50至90年代，先后进行了待开发地区的自然和经济综合考察，工业基地规划、铁路沿线调查，重点地区区域规划、农业区划、各省市区地域开发规划；20世纪90年代至21世纪初，进行了大区域发展战略研究，包括东部沿海地区发展、西部大开发、东北老工业基地振兴等；21世纪以来，进一步参与国家和各地区政府决策，在国家以及大区域的区域规划、产业集群、外资区域影响等方面进行系统的理论和实践研究（陆大道，2007）。不可否认，这些研究对国家的经济发展做出了巨大的贡献。然而，这些研究都主要以区域经济增长，尤其是发达区域的经济增长为主线，其核心都是围绕促使具备特定发展条件的地区先行发展起来，优势区域先富起来，其结果是在国家政策视野和学者研究视野中农村区域和以农业为主导产业的落后区域逐渐被边缘化。

然而，中国是一个农业大国，根据第六次人口普查数据，仍有过半数的人口生活在农村。这与西方发达国的后工业化社会有很大不同，中国区域经济研究者不应该盲目跟从西方学者的研究，应该基于中国实际，发掘具有中国特色的研究问题。从区域关怀的角度来看，全面建设小康社会的重点和难点均在农村地区和弱势地区。区域经济研究者为了服务国家需求，应该关注对这些地区的研究。

41.2 区域关怀研究的内容

41.2.1 关注区域发展阶段的差异

对于中国这样的发展中大国，各区域之间的发展基础、发展条件存在很大差异。这些发展条件的差异，在发展速度、发展进程上也有明确反映。其中，主要表现之一就是在同一时刻，不同区域往往处于不同发展阶段。正如图 41.1 所示，在 t_1时刻，区域 1 已经进入快速发展阶段时，区域 2 才刚刚起步，而区域 3 的经济发展还没有进入起步阶段；到 t_2时刻，区域 1 进入发展的后期阶段时，区域 2 才进入快速发展阶段，而区域 3 的经济发展才刚刚进入起步阶段。处于不同发展阶段的区域有不同发展特点，有不同的政策需求及其他环境需求。在全国统一的格局下，应考虑不同发展阶段区域的要求。以经济增长与资源消耗的关系而论，一般来说，处于发展初期阶段的区域由于快速的工业化进程，经济增长方式相对比较粗放，对土地、能源等资源的需求大，对环境污染也比较严重；而已经进入发达阶段的区域，由于技术进步和经济结构的调整，开始逐步由粗放型经济向集约型经济转型，对资源的消耗降低，同时污染物的排放量也开始逐渐减少（图 41.1）。如果全国实施完全一致的资源政策，可能会带来十分矛盾的结果：如对发达地区有利，便对欠发达地区不利；若照顾欠发达地区，则对整个社会带来资源过度消耗的威胁。因此，从区域关怀的角度来看，应该关注区域发展阶段的差异，区别对待。当然，从全国宏观调控角度，也可为了资源持续利用和环境保护，采取相对严厉的政策。但必须配以公平的资源环境补偿机制，使为保护资源环境做出贡献的区域得到较好的回报。

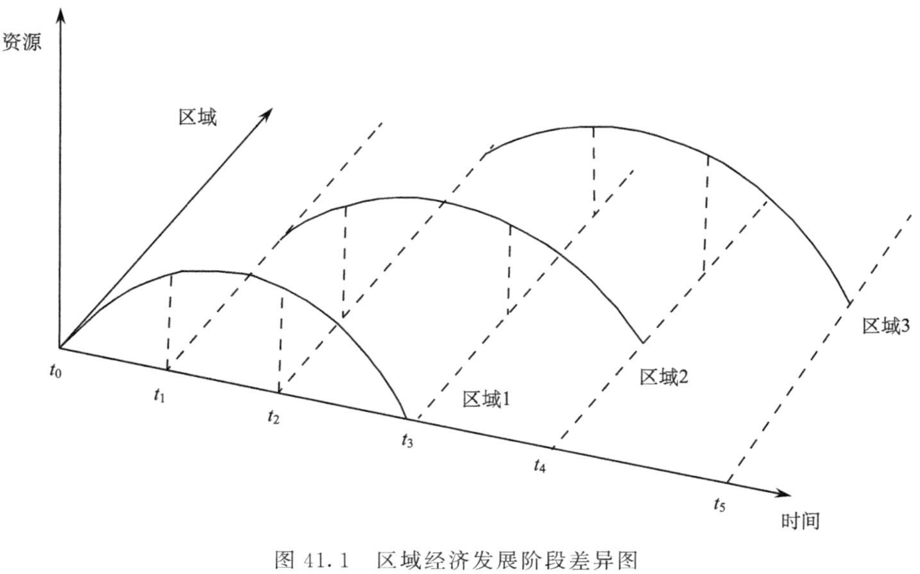

图 41.1 区域经济发展阶段差异图

41.2.2　关注区域优势的发挥

不同区域有着不同的优势。基于国家优势的发展设计，并不一定是区域层面的最优设计。从区域关怀的角度研究区域，应注重充分发挥每一个区域的优势，针对每一个区域的优势，设计相应的发展战略、发展途径和举措，进而建立不同类型区域的发展理论。例如，城市地区具有基础设施好、人才密集的优势，在研究中，应关注其集聚经济效应的进一步发挥；同时，还应考虑对周围地区的辐射带动及其负向外部性问题。相反，农村地区具有自然资源丰富、环境优美等优势，在促进农村地区这些优势发挥中，应该兼顾区域经济发展与资源持续利用和生态环境的保护。不仅如此，同样的城市地区，同样的农村地区，也可具有不同的优势特点，相关研究更应关注这些具体差异，以充分调动区域的发展积极性。

41.2.3　关注落后地区的发展

尽管区域关怀不应该有区域歧视，但由于落后地区长期被人忽视，故应该给予特殊关怀。从区域经济研究的角度对落后地区进行关怀时，可从明确落后地区的发展条件和所处发展阶段的特点入手，根据这些发展条件和阶段特点思考落后地区的发展机理、发展路径。例如，思考如何激发落后地区各种行为主体的积极性，使他们参与到区域的发展中来。例如，在农村地区，如何调动农户的积极性，促进农区发展，进而建立基于农户的农区发展理论。还可研究如何通过区际联系促进落后地区借助发达地区的力量实现发展等。

41.2.4　关注特殊问题地区的发展

特殊问题地区包括资源枯竭地区、老工业基地地区、农民工集聚地区、农民工流出区等。从区域关怀角度，应该针对这些地区所存在的主要矛盾，研究其形成原因和解决途径，并进而在理论层面进行凝练，为相关决策提供支持。事实上，有些特殊问题是社会不公造成的，这些区域实际上承担了应该有更多的区域承担的负担。例如，长期以来，资源型区域为国家的经济建设做出了巨大的贡献。然而，伴随着资源枯竭，这些地区原有产业萎缩，职工下岗，并可能出现诸如矿区沉陷、环境污染、生态恶化等问题。类似的，国家所进行的国有企业改革，把原来缺乏生机的国有企业改变成为一个充满活力的崭新企业。在为企业拥有者带来巨大利益的同时，也带来了原有工人下岗失业，导致一些国有企业集聚地区成为了低收入人群集中区。最近，由于受全球金融危机的影响，大量农民工返乡也带来了一系列问题。以河南为例，2008 年 9 月～11 月，共有 120 万农民工返乡，主要集中于河南东南部地区，这些返乡的农民工已难适应农村生活和农业生产，给所在区域带来了就业压力和社会问题，有些地区已出现社会治安恶化的苗头。区域问题的背后隐含着一些深层次的机理。例如，有些问题的形成便与受益者和实际成本支付者错位有关。从区域关怀的角度，研究者应该更深层次挖掘，从更全面的角度分析，为更好地解决问题、改变区域状况服务。

41.3 区域关怀研究中的思维转换

41.3.1 研究立足点的转变

前面对传统区域发展理论的分析表明，区域经济发展研究在立足点上存在一些偏向。从区域关怀的角度，这些偏向应该给予纠正（表 41.1）。①从工业偏向转变。前已述及，区域发展理论和中国的区域发展实践均十分注重工业，尤其是具有特殊意义的创新性产业的特殊作用。然而，农业在中国具有十分重要的战略意义。在中国的广大农区，工业很难在短期内取代农业而成为区域的主导产业。因此，在相当长的时间内，农业在农区发展中的特殊作用必须给予足够的关注。甚至在某些农区，农业应该成为区域研究的核心。②从城市和核心区域偏向转变。为促进经济增长，长期以来城市或经济核心区被放在区域发展的首要地位。但是，这些区域仅仅是众多区域的一部分。从区域关怀的角度，在这些区域之外有更多的区域需要我们的关注。与此相关联，一些非区域性政策也具有明显的（或潜在的）空间影响。例如，对于特定产业部门的激励，基础设施领域的投资，以及标准价格政策和税收政策等，也会对不同区域产生不同的影响。在诸多情况下，这些影响严重偏向于繁荣的核心区和首位城市（哈里和彼特，2001）。③从强势个体（大型企业、人才等）偏向转变。长期以来，在中央政府和许多地方政府眼里，大型企业是区域经济增长的核心，通过促进大型企业的发展，可以直接或间接地带动整个区域的发展。这种认识上的偏见导致政府在政策制定和资源分配过程中对强势个体的偏向。因此，为了做好区域关怀研究，区域研究在研究立足点上应该由过去关注强势群体（城市、工业和发达地区）为主的格局向两者兼顾或关注弱势群体的格局转变。

表 41.1 研究立足点的转变

过去研究的立足点	区域关怀研究的立足点
增长极理论中的极化	关注集聚外部性以及集聚扩散效应
中心地区或发达地区	发达、欠发达兼顾
城市	农村、城市兼顾
沿海	沿海、内陆兼顾
工业	工业、其他产业兼顾
大型企业	大型企业、中小企业兼顾
人才	特别关心弱势群体

41.3.2 研究思维的转变

1. 内外理论嫁接

中国本土的区域研究侧重于问题导向，并不注重科学规范基础上的科学问题提炼。与此相对应，近年来一些学者引入西方区域经济或区域科学的研究范式，强调区域研究的科学化；还有一些学者关注西方新近兴起的人本主义、结构主义、后现代主义等区域研究新思潮（刘云刚和许学强，2008）。从区域关怀角度看，这些中外研究范式各有侧重，各有使用的区域背景。为此，在区域研究中，应注重内外理论的嫁接，不同方法的融合。一方面要结合区域的实际情况，选择适宜的研究思路；另一方面要将西方范式中的精华与本土实际相结合，创新思维，发展富有中国特色的区域经济研究模式。

2. 经济、社会和环境统筹

中国的经济、社会和环境之间的矛盾十分突出。资源、生态环境在很大程度上制约着经济和社会的发展。在区域关怀研究的过程中，应该将经济发展、社会进步和环境保护统筹起来。不仅要注重经济发展对社会的贡献，更要注重区域资源环境保护对社会的贡献，并对这种贡献给予相应的经济补偿。

3. 区域导向性理论选择

不同区域应该有不同的理论。已有的区域发展理论，都出自一定的区域背景，并且有一定的适应条件。在具体的区域发展研究中，应根据不同类型地区的资源环境和社会经济状况，选择相应的理论支撑框架。注意通过特殊环境条件下的区域发展特殊机理的研究，构建相应的区域发展理论。

4. 弱势区域理论构建

从区域关怀角度构建弱势区域的发展理论，应着眼于发挥区域优势，考虑如何最大限度地调动区域内行为主体（如农区中的农户、农民等）的积极性，创造适合弱势行为主体优势发挥的环境，建立不同行为群体之间或它们与环境之间的良性互动。此外，研究区域之间的联系，尤其是与强势区域之间的联系，将外生力量转变为区域发展的驱动力，构建内外因素融合、利于弱势区域发展的理论。

41.4 结　　语

基于区域经济社会差异在不断扩大、区域之间的矛盾日益显现、区域不公平有所增加，以及区域研究者的“重富”状况，在中央政府经济实力不断增强且关注区域问题的背景下，笔者将人文关怀理念用于区域经济研究，提出了区域关怀概念。区域关怀的关键，是始终贯彻尊重原则，机会平等原则和合理补偿原则。尊重、平等和自由是现代意义上的公正的最基本理念（王小文，2008）。区域关怀的核心是区域之间的公平待遇。中央与地方以及各地方之间的关系，应该是一种和谐式的家庭关系，是一种互相尊重的关系。区域的机会平等指每个区域有大致相等的发展机会，即各区域发展机会起点应该平等，发展机会的实现过程也应该平等。承认不同区域发展条件的差异和发展阶段的不一致，给予适应其发展条件和发展阶段的发展理论支持，给予相应的政策关怀。补偿原则是指国家或大区域为了某些整体利益的实现，可能要危及某些小区域发展机会时，应当给予这些小区域应有的机会或利益补偿。

长期以来，中国区域经济研究在立足点和思维上都存在一些偏见，如学者的研究重城市而轻农村，重城市宏伟发展而轻其中的弱势群体，重自上而下的政策论证而轻自下而上的民意反馈（李小建，2005）。国家利益是各个区域利益的集合。忽视具体地区发展的区域经济研究是有缺陷的。中国正进入全面建设小康社会阶段，全面建设小康社会是一个系统工程。它既包括城乡之间的和谐发展，也包括发达地区与落后地区之间的和谐发展、工业和农业之间的和谐发展、大型企业和中小企业的和谐发展，以及不同类型民众（如人才、普通民众、弱势群体等）之间的和谐发展。在这种背景下，区域经济与发展研究者应从区域关怀的角度来注重对各种类型区域的发展问题研究。在研究中，应进行相应的思维转换，注重不同的理论融合、经济社会和环境的协调，尤其是区域对资源环境的贡献；善于基于区域特殊性构建相关理论，特别关注欠发达区域、弱势区域和问题突出区域的发展机理研究。

参考文献

安虎森. 2004. 区域经济学通论. 北京：经济科学出版社

冯海发，李溦. 1993. 我国农业为工业化提供资金积累的数量研究. 经济研究，(8)：60～64

哈里·W·理查森，彼得·M·汤罗. 2001. 发展中国家的区域政策. 区域和城市经济学手册第 1 卷（区域经济学）. 北京：经济科学出版社

李小建. 2005. 社会不公平问题的地理研究. 地域研究与开发，24（5）：1～4

李小建. 2006. 经济地理学（第二版）. 北京：高等教育出版社

李小建，苗长虹. 1993. 增长极理论分析及选择研究. 地理研究，12（3）：45～55

李小建，乔家君. 2001. 20 世纪 90 的代中国县际经济差异的空间分析. 地理学报，56（2）：136～145

刘云刚，许学强. 2008. 中国地理学的二元结构. 地理科学，28（5）：588～593

陆大道. 2007. 中国经济地理学的发展历程. 世界地理研究，16（4）：1～4

王小文. 2008. 环境正义研究需要关注. 科学时报，12～31

魏后凯. 2006. 现代区域经济学. 北京：经济管理出版社

约翰·冯·杜能. 1997. 孤立国同农业和国民经济的关系. 北京：商务印书馆

Friedmann J. 1966. Regional Development Policy：A Case-study of Venezuela. Mass：MIT Press

Hirschman A O. 1958. The Strategy of Economic Development. New Haven：Yale University

Myrdal G. 1957. Economic Theory and Underdeveloped Regions. London：Duckworth

第 42 章　增长极理论分析及选择研究

增长极和由此引出的增长中心、中心-外围理论，曾被不少国家在区域规划政策中加以应用。我国也有学者对此进行了理论介绍分析及案例研究（李仁贵，1988；曹勇，1990；朱翔，1991；曾艳红，1992）。国外学者在增长极研究和应用中的概念混乱，也同样在我国学者中反映了出来。为此，本章根据较为广泛的文献阅读和研究，以及作者与国外有关专家的讨论，分析了佩鲁式增长极与修改式增长极的区别，指出了修改式增长极概念的不足，肯定了佩鲁式增长极在区域发展规划中的实用性，提出了从宏观到微观，从推进型产业到推进型企业区位及发展环境的增长极选择方法。并针对推进型产业及其区位的性质和有关影响因素提出了相应的选择指标与方法。最后以河南省郑州市为例，验证了选择方法的实际可操作性与实用性。

42.1　增长极理论及实践

42.1.1　佩鲁本人的增长极理论

增长极概念源于法国经济学家 F. 佩鲁。1950 年，他认为“经济空间是由中心（或极、或焦点）组成的，这些中心是离心力的发散地和向心力的收敛点（Perroux，1950）”。这里“极”或“中心”概念，与力场密切关联（即吸引力和排斥力的集中地），与一般地理意义上的工厂和人口的集聚地是有本质区别的。

1955 年，佩鲁通过对经济空间进一步分析，首先提出了增长极概念。其主要观点是：“增长并非在各个地方同时出现，它首先出现于不同强度的增长点或增长极上，并通过不同渠道向外扩散，对整个经济产生不同的终端效应”（Perroux，1971）。20 世纪 60 年代，佩鲁在一部著作中用相当篇幅对增长极理论作了进一步阐述（Perroux，1961）。他的理论的基本思路和要点可概括如下：①市场经济下的经济增长是不均衡的，存在着极化（polarization）发展趋势；②由于技术创新，才带来经济发展，而技术创新是由推进型企业（propulsive enterprise）来实现的；③具有创新技术的推进型企业的形成需要特定的环境，这些推进型企业的集中地即为增长极；④推进型企业与其前后生产关联的企业之间存在着相互作用的“力场”（field of forces），并由这种力场形成该企业的经济空间；⑤在推进型企业的经济空间中，相关企业之间的关系是不对等的，即推进型企业支配其他企业（企业间的支配依赖关系），由此引出推进型企业所存的增长极对其他企业所在地区起着支配作用（空间上的支配依赖关系）；⑥增长极通过推进型企业的力场，来实现其在经济空间中的扩散效心（即增长极的增长向其他企业所在地区扩散），从而带动整个经济的增长。

关于佩鲁的增长极理论，需要强调以下三点：①理论的出发点和最终结果是宏观的经济整体增长，即经济整体增长中有极化现象，通过极化和扩散最终带动经济整体增长，并无区域发展之意。尽管推进型企业的存在与发展脱离不开空间，但该理论所提及的仅为抽象的经济空间，与一般地理空间的含义有明显迥异。②扩散效应的形成，与推进型企业的关联强度有关，较高的关联强度带来较大的扩散效应。③扩散效应并不一定产生于与增长极直接邻近的地区，即不一定在佩鲁所称的一般地理空间（banal space）中扩散。

增长极概念提出以后一段时间，经济发展问题日益受到经济学家的重视，学术界开始把经济发展与经济增长区别开来。与此相应，佩鲁也提出了发展极（development pole）概念（Perroux，1957），与增长极的经济整体增长思路一致，发展极是整体发展理论研究的一部分。即“发展极是有能力导致经济和社会结构相关发展的一种经济组合，通过其扩散效用，可增加整体发展的复杂性，扩大多元收益”（Perroux，1988）。十分明显，用“发展”概念取代增长极中的“增长”概念，可以从发展角度全面讨论社会经济水平和结构的变化，使其研究更加切合实际。

42.1.2 其他学者的有关理论及应用

佩鲁的增长极思想在区域发展领域引起密切关注，不少学者对其进行研究并将其应用于实践之中。其中，法国经济学家 J. R. 布代维尔在解释和修改增长极理论方面影响最大。由于他的研究出发点是区域经济规划，故首先将佩鲁抽象经济空间转换成地理空间。他认为，经济空间是经济变量在地理空间上的运用。由于外部经济和集聚效益，形成增长极的工业在空间上集中分布，并与现存城市结合在一起（Boudeville，1966）。经过这种转换，增长极概念便同城镇体系联系起来，增长极的层次性便对应于城镇体系的等级性，并且将这种结构发展成为具有可操作性的区域模式。其他一些学者，如 R. K. 塞姆普尔等，也作了类似的阐述（Semple，1972）。由此便形成了一种新的增长极概念，即“增长极就是城市增长中心，该增长中心的增长可以向周围地区扩散”（Brookfield，1975）。

显然，这种经修改而形成的修改式增长极是以城市中心作为增长极，其扩散效应十分便于区域规划政策制定者所理解和接受，以解决不发达区、衰退区的增长问题，以及发达区的过度集中问题。20 世纪 60～70 年代，处于各种发展水平的数 10 个国家曾声称它们按增长极策略制定过城市和区域发展政策（Higgins，1981）。其政策要点可概括为，通过各种激励措施在不发达区域或衰退区域的城镇增长中心建立新企业，并通过增长中心的扩散，带动不发达区或衰退区的经济增长。

随着多数国家该项政策的失败（澳大利亚等），一些人开始怀疑增长极理论的正确性。然而实际情况是，各国所实施的政策很少依据佩鲁理论。它们不是加强和鼓励现存增长极的发展，而是人为地在不发达地区创造增长极，并期望通过其发展来带动周围区。正如，B. 希根斯所说的：“增长中心策略的失败，并不是佩鲁理论的失败，而是主要由布代维尔修正的理论的失败”（Polenske，1988）。

42.1.3 佩鲁式增长极理论的实用性

正是由于佩鲁式增长极抽象复杂，难以操作运用，才有人对其加以修改，以加强其可操作性。修改式增长极在多数国家实践的失败，不得不使我们回头重新审视佩鲁式增长极在区域发展规划中的应用问题。

首先，佩鲁关于发展存在极化的思想，在区域发展规划中是有实际应用价值的。实践证明，市场经济的自然发展和国家有关政策的规定都必须适应这种趋势。事实上我国各区域目前的经济政策总方针便是不平衡发展，极化的趋势已经出现。其次，极化必然导致增长极出现，它是经济增长推动力的发源地，将在一定地区（并非一定是邻近地区）产生扩散效应。这一观点，真正怀疑者也不多（Higgins，1981）。作者对河南城乡工业联系的近 290 家企业调查也证实城市工业扩散效应的非地理确定性。修改式增长极理论对扩散效应范围的修改，是出自对特定区域的发展考虑。基于对国外按此理论发展的增长极的调查分析（李小建，1992），我们认为，这种增长极主要是由于增长极本身增长缓慢，并不在于其对周围扩散效应不足。所以，完全可以按佩鲁式增长极理论来制定区域政策，促使增长极发展并产生其扩散效应。再次，佩鲁式增长极强调其形成的环境条件，即适应推进型产业出现并发展的条件。修改式增长极理论最大的修改之处，便是增长极的人为创造性。有关规划者期望通过政府努力，将一些企业“推”“拉”到发展迟缓区域的增长极，并通过扩散效应以带动区域发展。由于这种修改忽视了增长极形成的环境条件，才导致了其区域规划政策的失败。各国的实践也证实了这一点。最后，佩鲁式增长极理论十分强调推进型产业。由于推进型产业以关联度高、技术先进和增长快为特点，它的增长无疑会带来较大的扩散效应。

如果通过以上分析已说明佩鲁式增长极存在着区域实用性，那么新的问题是，如何应用这种理论？这种理论能否和政府重点资助政策统一起来？应用佩鲁式增长极理论，关键是要确定（实际上是认识）增长极。我们认为增长极的确定，应从宏观经济整体考虑，从上到下逐层次弄清各范围的推进型产业，然后根据推进型产业形成与发展所需的环境条件，分析推进型产业的理想区位，推进型产业的集中地或潜在集中地就是增长极。应用这种方法确定的增长极，是可以和政府的选择性资助政策协调起来的。但关键是后者应服从前者，即政府只能在本身是增长极的区位进行重点投资或重点资助他人投资，而不是在不是增长极的区位花费巨资创造增长极。

42.2 增长极选择的指标与方法

增长极的认识与选择包括以下三个步骤：①从国民经济发展的整体出发，针对区域性质的作用确定什么产业为推进型产业；②从促进推进型产业迅速发展的环境条件和其最大区域带动作用出发，确定把推进型产业中的推进型单元（企业）配置在什么样的区位；③根据推进型产业的区位确定增长极。推进型产业的集中地或具有发展这种产业的优越条件地区便是增长极。

42.2.1 推进型产业选择

1. 推进型产业的性质

推进型产业又称关键产业、主导产业，它在区域发展中起着“动力源”式的支配推进作用，这种产业一般应具有以下性质：①较强的创新能力，尤其是技术创新能力；②较强的产业关联度，能促进产业综合体的形成，并能产生“列昂捷夫”和缪尔达尔循环累积效应；③较高的需求收入弹性，产品市场广阔，市场扩张和生产发展速度较快；④较高的发展速度或潜在发展速度，能带动经济整体的快速发展；⑤较高的比较利益或预期利益，能充分利用区域的比较优势，有较大的发展潜力；⑥动态更替性。不同的工业化阶段，不同的发展时期，其主导产业不同。按动态比较费用的观点，幼小的产业也可能发展成为主导优势产业。

2. 推进型产业选择的指标

根据推进型产业的性质，本章提供以下 7 个方面的指标。

（1）产业关联度

产业关联度分析一般常基于列昂捷夫逆阵，据此可求得各产业的扩散能力和感应能力。由于在市场机制下前向关联对区域发展的诱导影响较小，在选择推进型产业时仅考虑由后向关联导出的扩散能力指标。令列昂捷夫逆阵为

$$B=(I-A)^{-1}=[b_{ij}]_{n\times n} \tag{42.1}$$

式中，b_{ij} 为列昂捷夫逆矩阵中的元素；n 为投入产出表中的部门个数；A 为中间消费矩阵。

则扩散能力为

$$B._j=\sum_{i=1}^{n} b_{ij} \tag{42.2}$$

依据赫希曼（Hirschman，1958）的方法，将该指标进行标准化，即将每一列的均值与整个逆矩阵各元素的均值相比；经推导，产业的产出扩散能力（x_1）为

$$x_1=n\cdot\sum_{i=1}^{n} b_{ij}\Big/\sum_{i=1}^{n}\sum_{j=1}^{n} b_{ij} \tag{42.3}$$

同理，可求得就业关联系数：

$$x_2=n\cdot\sum_{i=1}^{n} l_i b_{ij}\Big/\sum_{i=1}^{n}\sum_{j=1}^{n} l_i b_{ij} \tag{42.4}$$

式中，l_i 为某产业单位产出的就业人数。

（2）技术创新能力

由于技术创新能力的直接指标难以获取，选用了全要素生产率指标，经标准化处理，技术创新能力（x_3）的计算公式为

$$x_3=w_a l_{i2}(\mathrm{TFP}_{i2}/\mathrm{TFP}_{i1})/l_2(\mathrm{TFP}_2/\mathrm{TFP}_1)+w_b.\mathrm{TFP}_{i2}/\mathrm{TFP}_2 \tag{42.5}$$

式中，TFP_i 和 TFP 分别为 i 产业全要素生产率和区域有关产业总体的全要素生产率，1 和 2 分别为基期和对比期，w_a 和 w_b 分别为相对技术进步速度和相对技术水平的权重。全要素生产率 TFP 的计算可采用公式：

$$TFP=(Y/L)^{1-K/Y}(K/Y)^{-K/Y} \tag{42.6}$$

式中，Y 为产出量；K、L 分别为资金和劳动的投入量。

(3) 比较优势

以资金利税率作为基本指标，综合考虑区域内部不同部门间的比较利益和同一部门不同区域间的比较利益，所采用的比较优势系数（x_4）为

$$x_4=\frac{1}{2}\left(\frac{R_i}{\bar{R}}+\frac{\bar{R}_i}{\bar{R}}\right) \tag{42.7}$$

式中，R_i、$\bar{R}$ 和 $\bar{R}_i$ 别为某区域中 i 产业资金利润率、某区域中所有产业平均资金利润率和全国 i 产业的资金利税率。

(4) 收入弹性

经标准化处理后的相对收入弹性指标（x_5）为

$$x_5=\left(\left|\frac{\mathrm{d}\theta_i}{\theta_i}\Big/\frac{\mathrm{d}p}{p}\right|\right)\Big/\left(\left|\frac{\mathrm{d}\theta}{\theta}\Big/\frac{\mathrm{d}p}{p}\right|\right)=\frac{\mathrm{d}\theta_i}{\theta_i}\Big/\frac{\mathrm{d}\theta}{\theta}\approx\frac{\Delta\theta_i}{\theta_i}\Big/\frac{\Delta\theta}{\theta} \tag{42.8}$$

式中，$\Delta\theta_i/\theta_i$ 和 $\Delta\theta/\theta$ 分别为同一时段内 i 产业生产产品的需求增长率和研究区域的总产品的需求增长率。由于在实际计算时，难以取得产品需求量的数据，故可用产出增量近似代替需求增量。

(5) 发展战略及政策（P_1）

依据各产业对区域发展战略的贡献大小和地方发展政策之倾斜状况，分别给予逻辑数值。即若政策鼓励某产业发展，则 $P_1=1$；反之，若某产业无明显鼓励政策，则 $P_1=0$。

(6) 产业协调（P_2）

考虑区域产业结构的现状，根据各产业对与区域产业结构协调作用大小，分别给予逻辑数值。即对明显利于产业结构协调的产业，令 $P_2=1$；反之，则令 $P_2=0$。

(7) 工业化阶段（U_1）

根据研究区域内工业发展水平和各产业区域工业进一步发展和结构转换的关系，分别对各产业赋予逻辑数值，若某产业为区域新兴部门，对区域工业化程度提高有明显促进作用，则 $U_1=1$；反之，则令 $U_1=0$。

42.2.2　推进型产业选择的方法

推进型产业的选择，应综合考虑反映产业现状及潜力特性的特性变量（x_i）、反映决策者价值取向的政策变量（P_j）和反映其他重要经济参数的参数变量（u_k）。据此，可以采用给定权重的方法对这些变量加权，求出推进型指数。其表达式为

$$V_i=a_1x_1+a_2x_2+a_3x_3+a_4x_4+a_5x_5+a_6P_1+a_7P_2+a_8u_1 \tag{42.9}$$

式中，V_i 为 i 产业的推进型指数；$a_1 \cdots a_8$ 为根据各变量对推进型产业选择的重要程度所给定的权数；$x_1 \cdots x_5$ 同前。由于关联系数是推进型产业选定的主要指标，故应给予较高权重。

42.2.3 推进型企业区位的选择

1. 推进型企业区位的性质

任何产业都是由大大小小的企业组成的。在推进型产业确定之后，组成该产业的若干关键企业或潜在关键企业便是该产业的推进型企业，一个或若干个推进型企业的区位集中地便是增长极。在多数情况下，城市特别是大中城市往往就是这样的集中地，但不能由此把任何一个城镇都作为增长极来对待。增长极有其内在的区位特性：①从费用-效益分析的观点来看，推进型企业是一个投资项目，在不同的经济尺度和建设区位，其投资效果是不同的。某些项目投资对所在区域可能是有益的，但由于它占用了稀缺的生产要素，失去了布局在区位条件更优区域而获得更多经济和社会利益的机会，因而可能会对国民经济整体产生不良影响。因此，推进型企业的区位必须是国家利益和区域利益相对一致的区位。②从推进型企业发展的环境来看，虽然不同产业性质的企业对其环境条件的要求各异，但均需要有良好的资源（包括自然与人文）基础和基础设施条件，交通与信息传输便捷性，能为居民提供适当的收入和较好的发展机会。因此，推进型产业的区位必须区位优势突出。③从推进型企业发展的内部条件来看，企业的增长潜力深受区位企业家阶层（经济能人）及其他生产要素供给状况的影响，若区位能够吸收稀缺的资源，能在其相应的社会经济基础上实现自我积累和自我发展，该区位才有可能成为区域增长的动力源。因此，推进型产业的区位必须增长潜力较大。④从推进型企业的区位功能来看，企业在此区位布局要么能获得令决策者满意的利润，要么能为区域带来尽可能大的福利（如增加就业机会、缩小区域间发展的差距等）。必须能为区域发展起支配带动作用。

2. 推进型企业区位选择的基准与因素

根据区位的性质，可以提出 4 个方面的选择基准与因素。

（1）功能基准

依区域问题对推进型企业区位功能的要求而选择。落后地区面对的突出问题是人口增长过快、贫穷、缺少带动区域自我发展的现代产业，因而推进型企业的主要功能是为区域带来福利，促进区域经济的“起飞”，其区位倾向于区域城镇体系的高级中心；衰退地区面对的突出问题是经济发展停滞、就业严重不足，因而推进型产业的主要功能在于增强区域结构的转换能力，其区位倾向于区域城镇体系中的中高级中心；过度集中地区面对的突出问题是过度拥挤、环境及生活质量下降，因而推进型产业的主要功能在于分散增长压力，其区位倾向于区域城镇体系中的低级中心。

（2）利益一致性基准

依国家有关的产业政策、区域政策和区域发展的内在要求而选择。所在区域应符合国民经济整体利益提高的需要，有利于全国经济的统一性和地区经济特色的有机结合；区域自身的优惠政策和国家实施的区域政策和资助政策应具有一致性。

（3）增长潜力因素

增长潜力的大小可借助增长潜力指数来测度，其公式为

$$y_1=(k_1\times k_2\times\cdots\times k_n)^{\frac{1}{n}} \tag{42.10}$$

式中，y_1 为某区位的增长潜力指数；$k_1\cdots k_n$ 分别为反映增长潜力特性的可比指标，如就业增长率、产业增长率、职能多样化指数、固定资产投资增长率、社会商品零售总额增长率等。

（4）资源与基础设施因素

在应用中可借助增长环境指数来测度，其公式为

$$y_2=(b_1\times b_2\times\cdots\times b_m)^{\frac{1}{m}} \tag{42.11}$$

式中，y_2 为某区位的增长环境指数；$b_1\cdots b_n$ 分别为反映增长环境的可比指标，如资源丰度指数、能源供给指数、交通可达性指数、交通运输指数、信息业务量指数、自然障碍指数等。

3. 推进型企业区位选择的方法

可分两步来进行：在推进型项目确定之后，首先可依功能基准和利益一致性基准选出其可能的若干区位，然后可以根据 y_1 和 y_2 标准化值计算区位优势指数（$y_1\cdot y_2$），选择得分值最高的前几个区位作为项目评估方案，在问题不太复杂的情况下，对这几个区位进行详尽考察与判断就能得出最理想区位；在问题较为复杂的情况下，可借助费用-效益分析技术来评估。

42.3　增长极选择案例

郑州市作为河南省省会，位于河南省中部，辖 6 区 4 市 1 县：中原区、二七区、金水区、管城区、惠济区、上街区、中牟县、新郑市、新密市、荥阳市、登封市，另有高新技术开发区（简称“高新区”）、经济技术开发区（简称“经开区”）、航空港经济综合实验区（简称“航空港区”）3 个国家级开发区。总面积为 7446km^2，总人口为 911 万，其中，人均生产总值为 68073 元。郑州交通条件优越，处于中国交通大十字架的中心位置，是全国重要的综合交通枢纽、中部地区最大的物流集散地。但作为省会城市，对全省的带动作用还未充分发挥出来，在全国省会城市中相对落后。具体表现在经济规模相对较小、外向度低、产业层次低等方面。本章主要分析在工业发展方面，郑州如何选择增长极，加快发展。

在郑州市工业增长极选择中，我们首先针对郑州市计算了以上讨论的推进型产业选择指标。其中，产业关联度计算所需数据来自河南省 2010 年及 2005 年的投入产出表，其他指标的计算所需数据来自于《2014 年郑州市统计年鉴》、《2014 河南省统计年鉴》。在计算中根据情况合并和删除了少数部门，最后将 35 个部门的有关指标列入表 42.1

中。在此基础上，采用加权平均法，将扩散能力和就业关联给予最高权重（0.18），技术创新能力给予较高权重（0.14），剩余其他四个指标的权重为0.1，计算出各部门的推进型指数（表42.1）。据此，在0.5的水平上，选择出中近期内郑州市的推进型工业行业为，以交通运输设备、通用专用设备、电气机械及通信计算机设备为主的机械设备制造业，以化学原料、纤维、医药、橡胶为主的化学工业。

表 42.1 郑州市推进产业指标

部门	扩散能力 X_1	就业关联 X_2	技术创新能力 X_3	比较优势 X_4	收入需求弹性 X_5	政策 P_1	产业协调阶段 P_2	工业发展 U_1	推进型指数 V
农林牧渔业	0.188	0.000	0.035	0.006	0.215	1	1	0	0.261
采矿业	0.621	0.028	0.015	0.002	0.429	1	1	0	0.362
食品制造及烟草加工业	0.605	0.009	0.213	0.035	0.427	1	1	1	0.486
纺织业	0.688	0.007	0.089	0.015	0.684	1	1	0	0.407
服装皮革	0.697	0.018	0.162	0.027	0.432	1	1	0	0.397
木材加工及家具	0.660	0.008	0.227	0.038	0.469	1	1	0	0.403
造纸印刷及文教	0.736	0.033	0.043	0.007	0.419	1	1	1	0.487
石油加工、炼焦及核燃料加工业	0.748	0.019	0.461	0.077	0.507	1	1	0	0.461
化学工业	0.886	0.021	0.092	0.015	0.564	1	1	1	0.534
非金属矿物制品业	0.811	0.036	0.174	0.029	0.596	1	1	0	0.439
金属冶炼及压延加工业	0.950	0.027	0.023	0.004	0.491	1	1	0	0.429
金属制品业	0.933	0.030	0.241	0.040	0.583	1	1	0	0.469
通用、专用设备制造业	0.885	0.043	0.077	0.013	0.778	1	1	1	0.557
交通运输设备制造业	0.882	0.049	0.089	0.015	0.904	1	1	1	0.572
电气机械及器材制造业	0.852	0.055	0.129	0.021	0.675	1	1	1	0.551
通信设备、计算机及其他电子设备制造业	0.749	1.000	0.062	0.010	0.224	1	0	1	0.547
仪器仪表及文化办公用机械制造业	0.811	0.160	0.027	0.004	0.814	1	0	1	0.460
工艺品及其他制造业	0.840	0.010	0.227	0.038	0.106	1	0	1	0.399
废品废料	0.963	0.025	1.000	0.000	0.098	1	0	1	0.528
电力、热力、燃气及水生产和供应	1.000	0.033	0.004	0.001	0.010	1	0	0	0.288
建筑业	0.719	0.060	0.034	0.006	0.341	1	0	0	0.280
批发和零售业	0.329	0.040	0.049	0.008	0.093	1	0	0	0.183
交通运输、仓储和邮政业	0.013	0.095	0.055	0.009	0.257	1	0	0	0.154
住宿和餐饮业	0.075	0.020	0.037	0.006	0.354	1	0	0	0.158
信息传输、软件和信息技术业	0.467	0.010	0.051	0.008	0.319	1	0	1	0.326
金融业	0.000	0.031	0.167	0.028	1.000	1	0	1	0.332
房地产业	0.069	0.078	0.000	0.000	0.538	1	0	0	0.180
租赁和商务服务业	0.499	0.142	0.061	0.010	0.448	1	0	1	0.370

续表

部门	扩散能力 X_1	就业关联 X_2	技术创新能力 X_3	比较优势 X_4	收入需求弹性 X_5	政策 P_1	产业协调阶段 P_2	工业发展 U_1	推进型指数 V
科学研究和技术服务业	0.457	0.092	0.074	0.012	0.161	1	0	1	0.327
水利、环境和公共设施管理	0.295	0.083	0.000	0.000	0.331	1	0	0	0.201
居民服务、修理和其他服务	0.498	0.019	0.029	0.005	0.000	1	0	0	0.197
教育	0.164	0.076	0.069	0.011	0.490	1	0	0	0.203
卫生、社会保障和社会福利业	0.607	0.072	0.048	0.008	0.243	1	0	0	0.254
文化、体育和娱乐业	0.211	0.159	0.002	0.000	0.296	1	0	1	0.297

对这两组产业的推进型行业及其区位可做以下分析：①机械设备制造业。郑州市的机械设备制造业主要集中在高新区、经开区、航空港区，以及上街区、荥阳市等老工业区。但根据发展势头，以及交通条件和区域发展政策，经开区、高新区、航空港区可以作为机械设备制造业的主要布局区位。航空港区以上升国家发展战略为契机，可以重点发展航空设备制造、电子信息、精密机械、新材料等产业。经开区继续发展基础优势，重点发展汽车、工程机械等装备制造业。高新区重点发展软件、电子信息、光机电一体化、新材料等高科技制造业。荥阳利用已有的工业基础，重点发展阀门、建筑机械、客车。上街以通用航空基地为依托，重点发展通航飞行器组装制造等新兴的通航核心产业。②化学工业。化学工业包括化学原料及化学制品制造、医药制造、化学纤维制造、橡胶和塑料制造业等。高新区集中了全市 80%以上的通过 GMP 认证的制药企业，医药产业作为其支柱产业之一。新密和荥阳也有发展医药产业的基础，也可以作为产业发展方向之一。郑州市的化纤及化学原料、化学制品制造、橡胶和塑料制造业等化工产业主要集中在周边的辖区市，化纤和化学制品主要集中在新密，橡胶塑料制造业主要集中在中牟、登封、新密和郑州化工物流园。因此，中牟、登封、新密等可作为郑州市化学工业的增长极。

综合以上分析，经开区、高新区、航空港区作为郑州市重要的产业集聚区应作为首位增长极，重点发展电子信息、医药、汽车和高端装备制造业。周边的县市区可作为二级增长极，重点发展化学工业和基础好的制造业。

42.4　结论与讨论

第一，本章的分析认为，佩鲁式增长极长期以来被修改式增长极所取代并被应用于区域政策的实践中去，经多次修改后的增长极（增长中心）理论已与佩鲁本人的思想差别甚远。从一些国家根据修改后的增长极理论制定政策并证实不成功之后的实践中，作者认为有必要重新认识佩鲁式增长极理论。佩鲁式增长极理论的核心是增长极的客观性、推进型产业（企业）和经济空间。即客观存在的增长极是推进型产业的集聚地，推进型产业通过其关联作用使经济增长在经济空间中扩散。

第二，根据对佩鲁式增长极的分析，作者认为在增长极选择中，应强调整体原则、层次原则和认识原则。所谓整体原则，即增长极选择应从经济总体发展考虑，增长极只是一定经济发展阶段中推进型产业的空间存在侧面。选择增长极应从宏观经济着手，采用从宏观（经济整体）、中观（产业）到微观（企业区位）的方法。所谓层次原则，即在不同的宏观尺度上有不同层次的增长极。从国家整体分析，可以选择全国性增长极；从一个地区经济考虑，可以选择一个区域的增长极。所谓认识原则，即增长极的选择只是认识客观存在的增长极（或未来增长极），并非人为创造增长极。基于以上原则，增长极选择的核心是推进型产业（企业）选择。而推进型产业（企业）选择是可以通过对扩散能力、就业能力、技术创新能力、收入需求弹性、比较优势等定量指标和其他有关定性指标的综合分析来实现的。

第三，根据本章设计的 8 个定量和定性指标，对河南省郑州市的统计资料和有关政府文献进行了计算和分析，从而求得郑州市的推进型产业。继而通过对这些产业及企业区位环境的研究，分析了郑州市的增长极。实例研究表明，这种从宏观到微观，从推进型产业着手选择增长极的方法是可行的。

第四，在确定了增长极之后，为了促进推进型产业发展，吸引有关企业在增长极投资，政府应给予一定的经济补贴和政策优惠。一旦这些工业形成一定规模，这种补贴和优惠政策应逐步取消。失去扶植便不能自我发展的推进型产业，要么不是真正的推进型产业，要么区位环境（即增长极）本身存在缺陷。

参考文献

曹勇. 1990. 增长极与增长中心研究综述. 地理研究，9（3）：87～93

李仁贵. 1988. 区域经济发展中的增长极理论与政策研究. 经济研究，(9)：63～70

李小建. 1992. 澳大利亚增长中心政策及实践分析. 人文地理，(1)：56～62

曾艳红. 1992. 区域开发研究中的增长理论及其应用：以十堰二汽为例. 经济地理，(2)：4～8

朱翱. 1991. 湖南省经济增长极研究. 地理研究，10（3）：11～21

Boudeville J R. 1966. Problems of Regional Development. Edinburgh：Edinburgh University Press

Brookfield H. 1975. Interdependent Development. London：Methuen & Co Ltd

Higgins B. 1981. Francois Perroux. In Higgins B and Savoie D J. Regional Economic Development. Boston：Unwin Hyman. 31～47

Hirschman A O. 1958. The Strategy of Economic Development. New Heaven：Yale University Press

Perroux F. 1950. Economic space：Theory and applications. Quarterly Journal of Economics，64（2）：89～104

Perroux F. 1957. The development poles and international economy. Jerusalem：The Challenge of Development（symposium）

Perroux F. 1961. The Economy of the 20th Century. Paris：PUF

Perroux F. 1971. Note on the concept of "growth poles". In：Livingstone L. Economic Policy for Development：Selected Reading. Harmondsworth：Penguin Books Ltd. 278～289

Perroux F. 1988. The pole of development's new place in a general theory of economic activity. In：Higgins B and Savoie D. Regional Economy development. Boston：Unwin Hyman

Polenske K. 1988. Growth pole theory and strategy reconsidered：Domination，link ages and distribution. In：Higgins B and Savoie D J. Regional Economic Development. Boston：Unwin Hyman. 91～108

Semple R K，et al. 1972. Growth ploes in San Paulo，Brazil. A. A. A. G. 62：591～598

第43章　黄河沿岸人地关系与发展

进入21世纪，区域关怀逐渐得以重视，区域关怀的核心是区域之间的公平待遇，通过贯彻尊重原则、机会平等原则和合理补偿原则，实现区域间和谐发展（李小建，2009）。2011年中央一号文件《中共中央国务院关于加快水利改革发展的决定》，是新中国成立以来中央首个关于水利的综合性政策文件，明确了新时期水利发展战略定位，为推进沿河（江）区域和全国经济、社会、生态的可持续发展提供支持。加快黄河沿岸地区的发展，无论是对黄河流域及沿黄地区还是对全国经济社会发展都具有重大的意义。在黄河沿岸地区的发展考虑中，人地相互协调应成为一个重要原则。人地关系包括人类活动对环境的冲击及其引起的自然环境的变化和产生的影响，被改变了的自然环境对人类活动的反作用（吴传钧，1981）。中国学者强调"人地关系"为地理学研究的主要对象。中国历史传统奉行"天人合一"，但有一段时间支配思想以"人定胜天"占上风。西方地理学中，强调地理环境对人类的影响，形成了法国维达尔（Vida de la Blache）"人生地理学"（维达尔，1921），美国亨廷顿（Huntington）的气候对文明影响学说（Huntington，1915），森普尔（Semple）的地理环境对人类活动影响的观点（Semple，1911），澳大利亚泰勒（G. Taylor）的环境"决定行至论"（Taylor，1942）等，但是在西方相关辞书中人地关系（man-land relationship）并未被突出强调（Gregory，2009）。在中国政界、学界，环境对人类活动的影响也未得到应有的强调。基于此，本章从强调地理环境的影响基点出发，分析了黄河文明的起源、扩散与地理环境的关系，黄河特殊的"曲流"形式，以及中国特殊的地形阶梯及气候带与晋商的形成，黄河沿岸东西、南北经济的相互作用及其现代发展滞后的地理因素的影响，得出了一些新的观点。在此观点的基础上，认为黄河沿岸的现代发展应该考虑：由河流治理为主转变为发展为主，重新认识黄河流域特殊的地理要素和社会文化要素的优势，充分利用黄河沿岸的上下互动、两岸腹地的左右互动，系统地考虑和反思黄河对国家和沿岸地区发展的综合作用，综合谋划黄河沿岸地区的发展。力图重新认识产生古文明的环境，重新审视黄河沿岸地区的发展思路。

43.1　黄河文明起源与扩散

43.1.1　黄河文明起源

文明产生于挑战（汤因比，2005），黄河文明的产生和发展同样来自对大自然的挑战，尤其是洪涝和干旱的挑战。随着最后一个冰期的结束，全球的气候开始转暖。中国农耕发轫于距今7000～5000年，为全新世的仰韶温暖期。当时黄河中游的气温比现在要高2～3℃，降水量也比现在要多，植被茂盛，土壤肥沃，黄土又易于开挖成窑洞供人类居住。从旧石器时代至新石器时代，黄河流域的地理环境比较适宜古人类的生存和原始农耕文明的产生（李玉洁，2010）。黄河中下游地区产生了裴李岗文化、磁山文化、后李文化、仰韶文化、北辛文化、大汶口文化和龙山文化。而中国东部地区地势低下卑湿，湖泽密布，河、济之外，又有淮、汉、洒、沂、汁、唯、涡、颖、汝等水流，大泽如巨鹿、巨野、菏泽、雷夏、孟诸、圃田、海隅等散布其中，居民主要从事渔猎。

气候突变导致自然环境的变化，人类活动也必然出现相应的调整。以人地相互作用的重要表现形式之一的聚落为例。依据《中国历史地图集》（谭其骧，1982）中《原始社会遗址图》、《原始社会早期遗址图》（旧石器时代），以及《黄河流域原始社会晚期遗址图》（新石器时代）三幅地图综合来看，在旧石器时代早期，聚落集中在黄河与渭河的交汇处，以及黄河向南流动及外延区域，其他区域只有零星分布；在旧石器中期，聚落向北迁移至黄河南北流动和邻近区域，其他区域基本上是一片空白；到了旧石器晚期，聚落增多并向上下游扩展，向上至甘肃、内蒙古和宁夏地区，向下至古黄河的下游（今北京、天津、河北）。距今4000年前后，自青海经甘肃、山西到内蒙古东部，发生了由洪水到干旱的气候突变，山东、江苏地区发生了较大的洪水（王绍武和黄建斌，2006），致使当地文化没有延续。而地处第二阶梯与第三阶梯交接部位的中原地区仰韶文化和龙山文化密集分布，时间上具有继承关系。经史前晚期的发展，在郑洛地区已产生中心聚落，大部分中心聚落位于山体南坡、坡度小于3°的地点（毕硕本等，2010）。中心聚落势力强大，最终影响、合并其他聚落群，逐渐形成了更大的政治同盟，征服了整个黄河中下游地区。

黄河流域，特别是中游和下游的上段地区成为文明源地有以下三个原因：第一，地处中央。人类交往便利，为文明起源和发展创造了有利的区位条件。第二，适宜农业。黄土高原地区土地生产力等级最高（《禹贡》评定为“厥田惟上上”）。第三，氏族部落经受住了气候变化带来的水灾挑战。正是在治理洪水中，夏王朝得以建立。黄河泛滥的逆境加速了其文明进程的发展，使它的政治、军事和经济力量远远超过了其他局部文明。

43.1.2　黄河文明扩散

气候变化引起文明中心的迁移，而文明中心的转移促使文明的扩散。古代文明中心一般是复合型的，兼具政治中心、经济中心和文化中心。全新世中期因气候的冷暖交替，尧舜部落和以尧舜为主体的部落联盟中心在晋南。禹夏部落、先商部落和先周部落均参加了部落联盟，然后迁徙四方：夏人南下渡过黄河，与豫西的氏族融合；商人先祖东迁至豫北；周人先祖则由晋南西渡黄河进入关中平原（李民和王健，1990）。禹都阳城（登封），之后夏都多次迁移，但一直在河洛平原（陈淳和龚辛，2004）。商人虽屡次迁都，但其政治中心皆在黄河和济水所在的华北平原（王星光，2008）。至晚商盘庚时，旧都生态环境的破坏导致迁都于殷（杨升南，1986）。而甚至古人有观点认为，气候的干旱导致了周人克商的牧野之战，即“河竭而商亡”（《国语·周语上》）。

尧舜部落联盟的形成和夏商周三代先祖的迁徙，是在炎黄集团东迁和东西两大部落集团融合的基础上完成的，他们的活动和迁徙是黄河流域东西文化交往的新发展，这一发展直接推动了文明国家的产生和发展。夏商周奠定了黄河文明的根基之后，几次气候变冷干，使发端于黄河中游的古代文化向南传播，并与长江流域的文化结合而得到发展。北方少数民族南下中原，各族人民在与汉族人民长期共同生活中与汉族文化相互吸收、融合，逐渐形成了中华民族的文化。这种文化的形成和扩散与我国幅员广阔、地理地形条件的多样性相关联。当气候变暖，降水量增大时，黄河下游频繁泛滥，黄河文明中心转移至中游地区的西安；当气候变冷、降水量减少时，黄河下游泛滥大大减少，黄河文明中心转移至中下游地区的洛阳。宋代是中国古文明，也即黄河文明的巅峰，当时的文明中心处于黄河沿岸的开封，也是在夏商周文明模式的基础上延伸和发展。

43.2　历史经济发展与黄河

43.2.1　东西联系

中国早期的城市发展是沿黄河出现和发展的，文明中心在黄河流域东西迁移促使了东西联系的加强。黄河下游最早的河道主要有两条：山经河和禹贡河，两者都沿太行山与华北平原交接处向北流（谭其骧，1981）。战国中期（公元前 4 世纪 40 年代左右），齐与赵、魏各在当时河道的东西两岸修筑了堤防，此后，山经河和禹贡河断流，使黄河下游逐渐转变为东西流向并成为地上河（许炯心，2001）。河道的变动改变了河流地貌演变方向，并对区域地理环境产生重大影响，以东西向为主的漕运、驰道和丝绸之路是黄河沿岸东西联系繁荣的明证。战国至秦汉时期黄河沿岸发展达到空前繁荣，交通枢纽城市或者被择为列国中心都邑，或者为商人会聚之所，成为有名的商业都会。秦统一全国后，大力修建直道、驰道、驿站、运河等，五大交通干道中的两条围绕黄河流域而修建。其中，咸阳到琅琊的驰道，以及与此驰道有联系的黄河和济水，在加强东西交往方面发挥了巨大作用（曹尔琴，1975）。之后在黄河中游及支流相继开凿了漕渠、六辅渠、龙首渠、白渠、成国渠、汴渠等大型水利工程。这些水利设施一方面使沿途的土地得以灌溉，同时又可作为运输的水道。有“河渭漕挽天下”（《史记·留侯世家》）之称。丝绸之路通过连接漕运和驰道，把黄河沿岸东西贯穿起来并与世界交往，直接造就了北宋汴京（今开封）的繁荣（周建明，2000）。文明是人的最高文化归属，是人必不可少的文化认同的最大层面，统一的文化内涵是人的联系，也是区域联系的最高形式。在东西联系的强化及不同的自然地理条件，黄河流域衍生出具有鲜明地方文化特征的晋商文化、中原文化和齐鲁文化，但本质都是传统儒家文化，也即黄河文明。

43.2.2　南北联系

南北曲流形式使黄河没有完全东西直下，由北向南建立了南北联系的通道，黄河渡口是其主要表现形式。三门峡、风陵渡和蒲津渡一线的黄河渡口早在春秋时期就有“秦粟输晋，泛舟之役”的记载，之后一直作为历代漕运的重要码头。禹门渡、蒲津渡、吴王渡、风陵渡、大禹渡、茅津渡等本身就是中华文明不可或缺的重要角色（鲁顺民，2004）。而晋商的兴起与沟通东西南北大动脉的黄河渡口有密切关系，其在黄河沿岸的活动打通了黄河沿岸及其腹地之间的联系，造就了晋商渡口、渡口商业的繁荣。明代晋商主要集中于晋西南、晋东南地区，清代主要集中于晋中地区。在晋商由晋西南到晋东南，由晋南到晋中的发展脉络中，黄河南北流向和相关渡口起到了独特的影响作用。从大尺度来考察，这种黄河南北流向，联系了北部的牧业文明和南部的农业文明。两文明的互补和交换需要进一步促进了晋商的形成和发展。

综观黄河流域的发展，可以得到如下结论（图 43.1）：早期的黄河沿岸城市 A、B、C(a、b、c)之间的联系大于其与两边腹地之间的联系，即联系程度 AB 或 BC(ab 或 bc)$>AA'$(aa')或 BB'(bb')或 CC'(cc')。随着黄河流域环境的变化，伴随而来的政治、经济重心的转移，沿岸城市之间的联系逐渐被分割成相对独立的区域，沿河城市间的联系被城市及其腹地之间的联系取代，出现了 AB 或 BC（ab 或 bc）$<AA'$（aa'）或 BB'(bb')或 CC'(cc')。这对于一个流域的整体发展产生了一定的不利影响，黄河流域难以整合成为一个完整的经济流域。特别是进入近现代，黄河流域被严重分割，成为东、中、西梯度经济差异的典型区域。

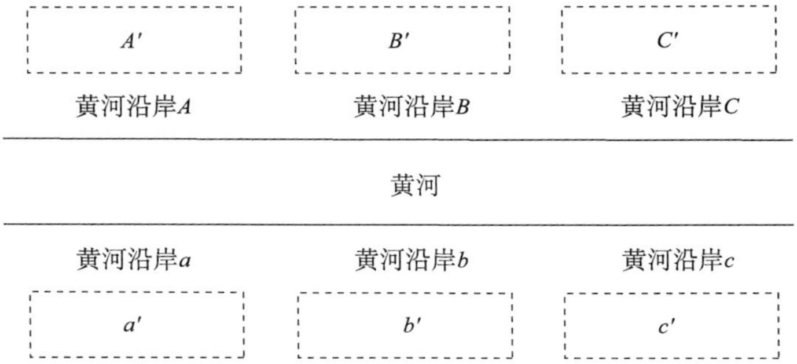

图 43.1　黄河流域联系强度示意图

43.3　黄河沿岸现代发展

43.3.1　沿河经济带缺失

黄河沿岸地区发展速度较慢，发展水平较低，很多标志性的发展在全国处于后序的地位。改革开放以来，以 20 世纪 80 年代建立深圳特区为标志的珠江三角洲和 90 年代以上海浦东开发为标志的长江三角洲的开放与开发，推动了沿海地区经济的发展。2013 年全国国内生产总值为 588018.8 亿元，长三角地区 GDP 逼近 10 万亿元，占全国的 17.2%；珠三角地区（广东省）GDP 达 53060.48 亿元，占全国的 9%；而黄河三角洲地区的 GDP 仅 7985.2 亿元，仅占全国的 1.4%。从整个流域来讲，黄河流经的 9 省（山东、河南、山西、陕西、内蒙古、宁夏、甘肃、四川、青海）GDP 共 170631.21 亿元，占全国国内生产总值的 29%，如果除去位于沿海地区的山东（9.4%）和黄河流域面积极小的四川（4.5%），更甚之，如果只考虑黄河沿岸地区的话，所占比重会更小。

黄河沿岸各地区滞后的原因主要有：第一，治理大于发展。自有文献记载以来，黄河决口泛滥和改道相当频繁。长期以来，对黄河以治理为主，黄河下游不稳，难以进行大规模开发。第二，三角洲发展滞后。黄河的下游改道，造成三角洲来回变动，黄河下游河道经历了从北到南，又从南再到北的大循环摆动，大体上以孟津为顶点，在北抵天津、南界淮河的大三角洲上，不能形成一个稳定的三角洲，而现代的黄河三角洲又是有海无港，有港无航，一直缺乏通航功能，傍河靠海的优势一直未能发挥。第三，上下游分割。黄河因其含沙量大，水流较缓，丧失了大河所拥有的通航能力，流域的天然联系被阻隔，黄河沿岸只能通过纵向联系替代河道联系，致使黄河流域难以一体发展。第四，资源要素并未发挥优势。虽然黄河流域沿岸自然资源丰富，人文景观雄厚，但在新时期并未发挥其资源优势谋求发展。

43.3.2　重新认识资源环境优势

不同时期的文明是特殊的人地关系相互作用的结果，资源环境所起的作用不同。在新的时期复兴黄河文明，重新认识形成文明的资源环境因素非常重要。首先，环境要素。古文明一般形成于中纬度地区的大河沿岸的内陆地区，适宜的气候、肥沃的土壤条件较适宜人类活动。而随着科学技术的发展，这些要素逐渐被弱化，人类活动已经从内陆转向海洋，出现了沿海向内陆的经济梯度。对比古文明与沿海文明的环境差异，其中，最核心的是交通和可接近性对相关环境要求的改变。但高速公路和铁路等陆上交通的发展，又使内陆地区发展进入新机遇。其次，资源要素。黄河流域农业资源丰富，为粮食主产区，对国家的战略安全至关重要。黄河流域煤炭储量占全国的 40.5%，石油储量占 26.6%，稀土资源占 98%。同时，黄河流域独特的自然、经济、社会、历史形成众多饶有价值的风景点和风景区，构成了独具特色的、富有吸引力的旅游资源。这些资源对现代发展仍具有重要意义。因此，黄河沿岸地区可发挥资源环境的综合优势，构建大范围线状分布和小范围点状集中相结合的点轴系统，逐渐形成我国沿黄经济开发轴线（魏心镇和韩百中，1992）。

43.3.3　治理转向发展

在中华民族生存发展史中，有很大的篇幅与黄河治理有关。黄河一方面是中国文化的摇篮，另一方面又是中国的忧患。目前我们基本上已经掌握了黄河洪水、固定河口和稳定河势的主动权，黄河的主要矛盾应由防洪减灾为主转化为增水兴利为主（李殿魁，1996）。过分宣扬黄河历史灾害，客观导致黄河在国家发展中的地位大大下降，十分不利于沿黄各省的经济发展，甚至国家经济格局的合理构建。应该逐渐把黄河作为一种“资源”，而不是一个“灾害之源”。任美锷院士较早提出黄河建设地理的概念（任美锷，2002）。把黄河从治理转向发展或建设已经具备了现实条件。小浪底水库总库容为 126.5 亿 m^3，控制黄河流域面积的 92.3%，控制黄河径流量的 91.2%，下游防洪标准由 60 年一遇提高到千年一遇（罗盘和陈仁泽，2009）。我们应在科学发展观的指导下，把黄河治理转变为“沿黄发展”，把黄河沿岸地带承载力及其社会经济自然系统之间的协调作为考察基点，充分评估黄河在当代中国经济发展中的重大意义，勾画和实施黄河发展战略。

43.3.4 加强纵横互动

大江大河皆源于山、行于地，而归于海，人类进入近现代社会也是由封闭的内陆文明奔向开放的海洋文明的历程。在这一历程中，天然的流域可以发展为现代经济区域（杨玉珍，1990）。区域内沿河经济联系及其河流与腹地其他区域的联系不断发生变化。黄河流域及沿黄地区特殊的地理环境决定了其经济发展的特殊区域组合。既强调沿黄区域的纵向联系，又要加强各沿黄地区的横向联系，形成各具特色的发展模式。目前，既然黄河三角洲还担当不起引领黄河发展流域发展的作用，黄河流域广大的区域更不能等待黄河三角洲溯流而上的辐射带动，而应采取更加主动的方式重构现代黄河经济区域。黄河流域已经出现黄河三角洲高效生态经济区、中原经济区、国家资源型经济转型综合配套改革试验区、关中-天水经济区、循环经济示范区 5 个国家级发展规划战略。这些战略区域内和之间的互动理应成为构建黄河沿岸经济区的重要内容。

43.3.5 黄河沿岸发展伦理

黄河对现代中国的重要意义更多地体现在发展伦理上，不仅关系到防洪安全、供水安全、粮食安全，而且关系到经济安全、生态安全和国家安全，尤其是她承载了炎黄子孙的精神凝聚力。作为海内外华人情系黄河的精神纽带，“黄河母亲”雕塑于 2010 年被国家文物局列为新品类文物。黄河沿岸的发展，第一，影响国家现代化。中国逐渐迈向现代化，但黄河流域农业仍占较大比重，工业化滞后，成为制约国家进一步推进现代化的问题区域。没有黄河流域的现代化就没有中国的现代化。第二，生态贡献。黄河流经干旱、半干旱等生态脆弱区，对维持这些地区的生态平衡有重要作用。通过引黄灌溉，对干旱地区的河套平原、半干旱地区的关中平原，以及下游的天津、青岛等重要城市的经济发展提供了保障，改善了当地的生态系统。第三，文明贡献。黄河流域是中华民族的摇篮和中国文明的发祥地。黄河文明是唯一没有中断的古文明，这里几千年前出现的东西，现在同样产生影响。虽然，从物质文明观察，黄河地区的经济地位已经不是国家的中心，但从精神文明来看，黄河作为国家和民族的象征，其地位无可取代。黄河流域所拥有的人文资源、历史遗迹、文化精华，是长江流域或者其他流域不能替代的，在文化传承中所起的作用也是任何其他文明所不能替代的（葛剑雄，2009）。因此，黄河沿岸地区的发展具有十分特殊的精神意义。

43.4 结论与讨论

基于黄河沿岸人地关系与发展的研究表明：黄河文明起源与扩散与其历史时期的地形地貌、气候水文密切相关。黄河文明之所以成为中华文明的直根系，成为中国古代文明发展的中心地区，与人类进入文明时期时的黄河中下游地区特殊的地理环境条件——气候温暖湿润、水量充沛、黄土冲积平原最适合早期的居住和农耕有着直接的关系。黄河文明的扩散与黄河特殊的南北、东西交汇的流向形态密切相关。在夏商周文明模式的基础上，随着气候的寒暖交替，黄河文明中心在流域上下来回变动，扩大了黄河文明的影响范围，丰富了黄河文明的内容。环境变化和黄河泛滥，导致中国文明重心移出了黄河流域。黄河沿岸落后于其他地区的现状，要求重新认识黄河流域特殊的地理要素和社会文化要素的优势，转变河流治理为发展的观念，利用黄河沿岸的上下互动、两岸腹地的左右互动，系统地考虑和反思黄河对国家和沿岸地区发展的综合作用，综合谋划黄河沿岸地区的发展。

不同的地理环境要素在人类的利用下会导致不同文明形式的出现。在人类的早期，地理因素一定程度上对文明拥有决定性的作用，古文明产生于中纬度地区的大河两岸，形成大河文明，而气候的变化往往导致文明的中断和消亡。随着人类在人地关系中的作用不断增强，人类扩大了活动区域，在新的环境中形成新的文明。因此，从历史视角来看，在文明早期，地理环境在人地关系中起着主导作用。而随着人类利用环境能力的增强，人类在人地关系中的作用越来越大。但是，在反对“地理环境决定论”观点的同时，应当明确人类再强大，也属于自然的一部分。地理环境对人类文明发展的影响仍然要给予足够的重视。

相对优越的地理环境可使一个文明形成相对于其他文明的优势。文明的扩张带来对其他文明的冲击，在相对隔离的时代，这种冲击导致了一些落后文明消亡。四大古文明都遭受过其他文明的冲击，只有黄河文明在漫长的发展中延续了下来，但又面临着海洋文明的冲击。海洋文明是以科技、商业为表征的文明，在现代发展中，具有黄河文明不具有的优势。但以科学发展观来衡量，黄河文明更具有生态文明的内涵，海洋文明中的科技、商业的发展并不能完全替代黄河文明所体现的人地协调。两大文明应该在更高水平上融合共存。

历久 105 万年的古老黄河，孕育了伟大的中华民族。黄河流域产生了中华民族灿烂的精神文明和物质文明。然而，黄河的璀璨，似乎已终归历史。在现代中国改革成就惊天动地带来的繁荣包围之中，这片土地却成了例外（茅于轼，2006）。21 世纪，中国区域经济发展格局加快北移西进的步伐，建设黄河经济带是必然趋势。从敬畏黄河到亲近黄河，人们的观念因时代进步而改变。应以全新的视角重新审视着这条交织着中华民族千年爱恨的大河，恢复和巩固黄河在国家的传统重要地位。在文明冲突和融合的时代背景下，我们期待黄河文明复兴和发展，再现光辉。

参考文献

阿诺德·汤因比. 2005. 历史研究. 刘北成，郭小凌译. 上海：上海人民出版社

毕硕本，郭文政，闾国年. 2010 郑洛地区史前聚落遗址坡向坡度分析. 测绘科学，35（6）：139～141

曹尔琴. 1975. 秦始皇的驰道和法家路线. 西北大学学报（自然科学版），（1）：20～29

陈淳，龚辛. 2004. 二里头，夏与中国早期国家研究. 复旦学报（社会科学版），（4）：82～91

葛剑雄. 2009. 黄河：河流伦理与人类文明的延续. 中国三峡，（6）：5～11

李殿魁. 1996. 黄河治理论. 发展论坛，（2）：7～10

李民，王健. 1990. 略论黄河流域东西部落集团融合及其意义. 中州学刊，（2）：102～107

李小建. 2009. 中国区域经济研究的新思考. 经济学动态，（3）：64～67

李玉洁. 2010. 黄河流域的农耕文明. 北京：科学出版社

鲁顺民. 2004. 山西古渡口：黄河的另一种陈述. 沈阳：辽宁人民出版社

罗盘，陈仁泽. 2009. 黄河小浪底工程通过验收 下游防洪标准变千年一遇. 大河网. 2009-04-08. http：//news. 163. com/09/0408/09/56CAQLPN000120GR. html. 2011-11-18
茅于轼. 2006. 中国黄河调查（序）. 张华侨，王健. 中国黄河调查. 武汉：湖北人民出版社
任美锷. 2002. 黄河地理研究的若干问题. 科技导报，(9)：3～7
谭其骧. 1981. 以前的黄河下游河道. 中国地理学会历史地理专业委员会《历史地理》编辑委员会. 历史地理（创刊号）. 上海：上海人民出版社. 48～64
谭其骧. 1982. 中国历史地图集. 北京：中国地图出版社
王绍武，黄建斌. 2006 . 全新世中期的旱涝变化与中华古文明的进程. 自然科学进展，16（10）：1238～1244
王星光. 2008. 商代的生态环境与农业发展. 中原文物，(5)：57～62
维达尔. 1921. 人生地理学原理. 亨丁敦，克兴，王诲初，等译. 上海：商务印书馆
魏心镇，韩百中. 1992. 沿黄河地带——我国国土开发布局轴线. 地理学报，47（1)：12～21
吴传钧. 1981. 地理学的特殊研究领域和今后任务. 经济地理，(1)：5～10
许炯心. 2001. 论黄河下游河道两次历史性大转折及其意义. 水利学报，(7)：1～7
杨升南. 1986. “殷人屡迁”辨析. 甲骨文与殷商史：第二集. 上海：上海古籍出版社
杨玉珍. 1990. 流域·经济域·辐射域——黄河流域经济发展断想. 经济地理，10（3)：27～29
周建明. 2000. 论北宋漕运. 中国社会经济史研究，(2)：57～65
Gregory D, et al. 2009. The Dictionary of Human Geography（5th Edition）. West Sussex：Wiley-Blackwell
Huntington E. 1915. Civilization and Climate. New Haven：Yale University Press
Semple E C. 1911. Influences of Geographic Environment on the Basis of Ratzel's System of Anthropogeography. New York：Henry Holt
Taylor G. 1942. Environment，village and city：A genetic approach to urban geography：With some reference to possiblism. Annals of the Association of American Geographers，32（1)：1～67

第 44 章　农区地理学研究进展与发展思路

农区地理学（Rural Geography）侧重于农村区域的地理综合研究，它在20世纪50年代成为一个独立的经济地理学分支（Woods，2005）。传统上，农区地理包括农业地理、农区空间上的人类活动组织及其对环境的影响、农区景观和土地利用等。之后，受农区社会学、人类学等相关学科的影响，并在政治经济和文化转向中，形成了一些新的研究领域（Cloke，1997；Moris and Enans，2004；Little and Leyshon，2003）。首先基于国际文献，本章总结了农区地理学的发展特点和新近研究动向。认为社会学、人类学和政治经济学对农区研究的关注，从不同角度影响着农区地理学的研究内容和思维变化。人文地理学的文化转向，也带来了农区地理学的相应转向。西方发达国家农区地理学的新近研究方向包括后生产型农区发展、全球化与农区发展、农区结构变化、农区基础设施、农区管制等。其次，结合中国实际，本章对中国农区地理学的研究思路进行了思考。

44.1　农区地理学发展特点

在20世纪50年代之前，农区研究归于区域地理。一段时间内，区域地理学以农区的人及其环境为主要研究对象。随着城市和非农产业的兴起，农区逐步被边缘化。70年代之后，农区地理学开始复兴，并逐渐形成3个研究领域：农区产业（如农业、林业、矿业等）、人类活动对农区空间的影响、农区景观与土地利用（Woods，2005）。在研究中，地理学家十分关注空间和空间差异，关注景观，关注人地相互作用。

这种地理学传统在农区研究中仍具有强大生命力。但近些年来，社会学、人类学和政治经济学对农区的研究不断得到关注，并影响农区地理学的研究。社会学研究强调通过城乡差异的感知来建立农区理论，强调关注社会关系和社会结构、关注社会服务设施，强调农户应作为农区研究的重要分析单元（Mormont，1990）。

人类学研究采用人种志学的技术，研究者常常要在农村社区生活一段时间。这类研究常采用综合方法，研究农村社区的社会结构、经济活动、家庭、宗教、政治和文化活动。从人类学角度对农区的研究，在多数国家没有地理学和社会学活跃，但澳大利亚则为例外。在这个国家，农区研究主要在大学的人类学系进行。人类学研究对农区地理的影响，主要表现为对农村社区、农区认同的关注，以及人种志学农区研究方法（在各种人类文化的科学性描述中，强调观察、描述和实地调查等）的应用（Woods，2005）。

农区研究中的政治经济学观点，强调政治经济因素在农区研究中的重要作用。通过建立研究框架，将农区变化与更宽泛的社会经济进程联系起来。该方向的研究不仅开创了一个新的思维方式，而且还带来了一些新的研究领域。例如，西方国家的一些学者从工商业企业角度进行农业研究、农区社区内部阶级（阶层）差异的研究，从更广泛的角度（如城乡关系）对农区经济变化的研究、政府的农业政策和农区规划的研究等（Buttel and Newby，1980）。

20世纪后期的人文地理学的文化转向也影响着农区研究。农区地理学家借用认同和代表性概念，审视农区特点的构成方式。主要关注的问题包括（Cloke，1997）：①自然-社会关系，认为自然在农区特点形成中起重要作用，农村空间与人地相互作用密切相关；②农区过去经历与未来发展讨论，旨在揭示农区不同的生活方式和经历、农区特点的社会构成等；③农区文化的标志性特点，如农区特点的不同外在表现形式、农区标志与历史遗产等；④农区空间中的运移研究包括旅游活动、就业通勤、游牧等。

44.2 农区范围界定

农区是个十分难以定义的概念。尽管人们对这一名字十分熟悉，但目前并无公认的科学定义。比较常用的农区概念基于以下假设：根据统计指标所量度的一些农区社会空间特征来进行农村地区和城市地区的地理划分。例如，以人口数量计，城镇比农村具有较大的人口规模。故诸多国家官方以此来定义农区。但是，不同国家由于社会经济状况不同，所用的农区人口规模的上限也不同。例如，爱尔兰为300人，英国为10000人，日本为30000人（Woods，2005）。以人口规模来定义农区存在以下问题：①人口规模与居民点的边界有关。不同的边界划分会有不同结果。②仅用人口规模难以衡量不同区域环境中居民点的功能及其同周围地区的关系。例如，有些地区居民点人口规模不大，但主要为城镇职能，而另一些地区则相反。③量化的人口规模难以准确区分渐变与质变。如把30000人定义为城镇，那么29999人的农村与此有多大区别？为此，一些国家采用了综合性指标，除了人口规模之外，还包括人口密度、土地利用和距离城市中心的距离等。中国特殊国情下，还考虑非农业人口比例、经济水平等指标。

但是，这种观点受到另一些人的质疑。例如，联合国人口年鉴认为，在聚落类型上，从大型集聚到小集群再到零散居民点，并没有一个清楚的区分城市性失去或农区性开始的标志。城市和农村人口划分只是一个人为行为（Hill，2003）。由此，一些学者提出以农村性指数（index of rurality）的概念来定义农村性的程度（Cloke and Edwards，1986）。该指数包括人口状况（如人口规模、人口密度、人口变化、移入人口、移出人口、年龄状况），家庭状况（如供应热水户、家庭洗澡设备、家庭厕所等的比例），职业状况（如农业劳动力比例），通勤状况，离城市中心的距离等。根据这些指数的计算结果，可将研究地区分为5个等级：农区、过渡农区、过渡非农区、非农区、城区。

还有一些学者从社会文化角度定义农村社会。认为，城市和农村的居民在价值和行为方面、城市和农村社区在社会和文化特点方面会有明显的区分。例如，有学者认为，城市生活是有生机的、不稳定的和缺乏人情味的（impersonal），农村生活则相对稳定、综合和有层次（stratified）；城市居民在工作、家庭和休闲方面接触不同的人群，而农村居民在诸多社会活动方面接触同一人群（Woods，2005）。

中国在相当长的时期内，侧重于以户籍关系和产业类别来定义农区。随着户籍约束的淡化，产业类别起着重要作用。但是，由于农村工业化的发展，在一些农村已经逐步转变为以非农产业为主。但是这些村庄又不具备城镇特征。因此，中国农区的划分需要借鉴国际研究，并结合中国特点，进行多指标的综合考虑。其中，人口规模和密度、农业地位、基础设施和商业服务业状况等，应该给予特殊关注。

44.3　农区地理学的新近研究方向

传统的农区地理学关注农牧业格局和农区定居格局，现在这种传统仍有市场。但20世纪末以来，在新的环境条件下，国际上农区地理学的研究出现了一些新的方向。这些方向包括后生产性农区发展、农业食品研究（Roche，2002）、农区问题的政治经济研究（Buttel，2001）、自然-社会关系（如自然在农区特性形成中的重要作用，以及农区空间与人地关系）、农区经验及其理论分析（不同农区生活方式经验及其理论分析）、农区文化的氛围（不同的农业类型形成不同的文化）、农区空间中的运移特点（如旅游、旅行、游牧部落等）（Cloke，1997）、食品地理研究、耕作文化等。还有学者认为应进一步重视全球化影响（如在WTO新的条件下的农业社会和产品结构的经验和理论研究等）、加强理论问题研究、农产品系统与农业结构变化的实践研究相结合等（Roche，2002）。一些学者根据对20世纪80年代以后美国的实际研究将农区和食品研究归为4个理论侧面：食品体制研究（food regime studies）、农业产品链、农业食品系统规制和行动者-网络研究（Buttel，2001）。除此之外，还有一些学者研究了一些地区的逆城市化问题，发现一些新型中产阶级由城区移向农区（如西班牙）。许多学者进行了关于农业产业的发展研究（Roche，2003）。传统农业地理学的另一些研究领域，如农业土地利用格局、文化景观和城市外扩问题等，也被众多学者关注（Roche，2005）。来自美国加利福尼亚和澳大利亚悉尼的土地利用长期变化研究揭示了城市周围地区土地变化的不同特点。以下对若干重要方面做一评述。

44.3.1　后生产型农区发展

尽管基于农产品的农区是研究的重点，但近期开始关注后生产型农村的相关研究。一些文献研究了后生产型转型（postproductivist transition）问题。强调农区发展从农业生产目标转向环境和社会目标（Woods，2005）。在生产型农业时代的农业集约化、集中化和专业化逐渐被后生产型农业时代的农业粗放化（extensification）、农场多元化、乡村管家化（countryside stewardship）和农产品增值等所取代。例如，在一些发达国家，伴随着支持精细农业的补贴的取消及对休耕的鼓励（如欧盟对20%以上农田休耕的农场给予一定的补偿），出现了农田化肥及其他人为投入减少现象，并出现休耕面积的增加。农场多元化指农户作为经济组织逐渐增加农业之外的经济活动（如农场旅游、位于现场的农场商店、骑马、现场食品加工、自采水果、小工艺等），以减少对农业生产的依赖。例如，1997年美国农业家庭的收入中，有88%来自农业之外（Johnson，2000）。乡村管家化强调农业活动在创造和保持农区景观中的作用。农业劳动者通过支付报酬从事各种各样的管理乡间的活动。农产品增值是指农民通过降低产量、提高质量，尤其是发展特定区域的品牌产品，以稀缺来提高农产品的价值。如意大利北部的帕尔玛火腿、比利时的贝尔福奶酪、英国的泽西皇家马铃薯（Jersey Royal potatoes）等。

文化转向也体现在后生产型农区研究上，如一些英国学者还在相关研究中关注农区无家可归人群、儿童问题、女性问题等，这些均有明显的政策取向（Evans et al.，2002）。

44.3.2 全球化与农区研究

随着日益加速的全球化进程，全球化对农区发展的影响逐渐突出。一些西方学者研究了不同类型的全球化对农区的影响（Woods，2005）。首先是经济全球化的影响：①带来农产品消费的全球化。农产品贸易在世界消费品贸易中的比重逐渐上升。例如，牛肉产品、猪肉产品、禽肉产品和奶类产品在世界总消费品出口中的比重分别从1964～1966年的9.4%、5.7%、4.0%和6.0%上升到1997～1999年的16.4%、9.6%、13.9%和12.8%（Bruinsma，2003）。与此相应，农业生产实践也发生着重大变化，他国的生产实践、生产技术也不断引入本土。农场主变得更加专业化，以便通过向食品加工公司或大型超市销售获取较大利润。农业生产与当地社区生活的联系在减弱。受全球性因素影响，农业变得更加脆弱。②带来全球性公司的兴起。一些国家的食品加工业的公司规模不断增大。世界的农产品贸易主要集中于少数大公司的控制之中。③加强了全球性调节的重要意义。随着农产品贸易的全球化，国家在农区经济发展中的干预能力逐渐减弱，而世界性组织（如世界贸易组织）的作用逐步增强。其次是空间运移全球化的影响：包括移民对农区社会的影响。与发展中国家不同，发达国家逆城市化过程中出现了人口向农区的移入，尤其是来自其他国家的移民向农区的移入（Bruinsma，2003），由此改变了人们心中关于农区人口固守本土的观点。而来自世界各地的游客，也促进了一些国家农区经济的发展（如新西兰的农区探险旅游享誉世界）。最后是价值全球化的影响：以电影、电视和其他媒介所带来的文化全球化逐渐弱化了人们对乡村感知的区域差异。西方价值不断在一些国际条约和经济实践中反映出来。这影响着居住在农区的人们对农区资源和自然条件的利用。

44.3.3 农区结构变化

与整个经济的发展趋势相类似，农区的经济结构变化也以农业的下降和其他产业的上升为特点。以发达国家为例，近几十年来，传统的农业、林业、渔业、矿业和采石业的生产与就业不断下降，而制造业、旅游业和服务业的比例则不断上升。例如，1969～1997年，美国农区县的农业就业下降了75万人，制造业上升了82万人。当今的加拿大、法国和英国农区中，每10个就业者中分别有6人、5人和7人位于服务业（Woods，2005）。对这种变化，学者们从不同角度进行了分析，提出了一些观点。包括：①区位限制论：认为城市可利用空间的数量和质量限制了企业的发展，促使其向农区发展（Fothergill and Gudgin，1982）。②生产成本论：认为企业移向农区，可以获取生产成本差异（如农区工资和土地价格较低）的优势，提高利润（Tyler et al.，1988）。

③产品周期论：将工业区位与产品周期相联系，认为在产品发展的早期阶段，城市区位提供了便于工业布局的熟练劳动力和专业知识投入，后来，生产变得程序化，工业可以到农区布局以降低成本（Markusen，1985）。④资本结构调整理论：认为不同的资本积累阶段存在不同的劳动力和区位需求。技术和生产过程的现代化减轻了制造业对熟练劳动力集中地的依赖，从而促使企业由城市移向农区以利用其低工资成本和低地价等优势（Massey，1984）。⑤居住偏好理论：主要是关于新企业区位的理论。认为企业家采取在农区建立工厂，是由于他们可以在这里享受高质量的生活（Gould and Keeble，1984）。

关于农区的制造业发展，在发达国家出现以下特点。一是产业部门发生了变化。传统的农区工业，如食品加工业、木材和造纸业、纺织业等逐渐下降，而轻型工程、高技术产业、特定区域的高质量食品生产等不断增长。二是这种变化仅出现在特定的空间。例如，研究表明，美国农村工业的增长集中在临近都市的县域，英国的东南英格兰地区的农区工业增长最为明显（North，1998）。三是城乡转移改变了农区制造业的特点。工厂与农区社区的联系在减弱。它们较少利用当地资源，当地人所拥有的比例也较低。

44.3.4　农区基础设施

在一些发达国家，受全球社会和经济进程，以及国家和区域性因素的影响，人们开始关注农村社区的基础设施和服务设施的不足。例如，在 2000 年，英国英格兰仅有 29%的乡镇具有百货商店，54%具有邮局，52%具有小学。20 世纪以来，三次集中化对农区基础设施状况带来了严重的不利影响。第一次是 20 世纪早期，农区公共交通的发展和农区人口的下降带来了基础设施由农区向小城镇转移；第二次是二次世界大战后，个人汽车拥有量的上升带来了对公共设施的合理化调整；第三次是 21 世纪初，正在发展的大型超市和城外商业中心，影响了相邻农区的商业设施的建立（Woods，2005）。美国农区基础设施的下降主要与农区人口的减少有关。而公共部门的成本最小化和私营部门的利润最大化策略，也带来了农区社区的服务设施的合理化调整。总的来说，发达国家的农区设施变化可归纳为三个原因，一是经济因素。随着农区当地公司被大公司购买，并逐步调整其生产和贸易网络，一些非营利的企业逐渐被关闭。二是社会因素。人们的消费习惯在发生变化。汽车的普及使人们越来越少地依赖在其居住地的商店购物。三是国家和区域因素。不同国家和区域的文化和农区居住地理的差异，对各地的农区基础设施也会产生重要影响（Woods，2005）。

与以上发达国家相比较，发展中国家的情形应有不同。但随着经济社会的发展，农区基础设施也在发生较大变化。例如，伴随计划生育人口下降，中国农区出现中小学的数量减少和区位调整。交通、卫生等设施也随着经济发展而发生较大变化。这些不同的变化特征背后，具有不同的影响因素。

44.3.5　农区管治

各国不同的政治制度带来了不同的农区管治特点。例如，美国和法国农区社区的政府机构较为完善，且具有较大权力；而英国和新西兰农区政府机构则明显松散。尽管管理结构不同，近几十年来多数国家农区地方政府均发生了重要变化。发达国家的变化主要表现在，从20世纪早期的家长式管理时代，变化到20世纪中期的中央经济式管理时代，以及20世纪末21世纪初的管治时代（Woods，2005）。管治与政府管理的区别在于，除政府机构外，还有一系列相互作用的组织、机构、合作者等参与其中。公共部门、私人部门和自愿者之间的边界变得十分模糊。从政府到管治，不仅相关组织机构的变化，而且治理的风格、语言和对话方式均发生了变化。

来自发达国家的实例表明，农区管治主要表现在合作共事和社区介入。合作共事是农区管治的一个中心概念。合作共事指相关组织之间通过联络会议或者相关咨询论坛，为了一个特殊目标而一起工作。在一些特殊情况下，几个相关组织可以形成正式或半正式的合作型组织（Edwards et al.，2000）。农区管治中的合作共事包括3种类型：①战略合伙。农区的不同政府机构（有时也包括农户联合体、工商业协会和自愿组织的代表等）为了协调政策和激励措施而形成战略伙伴。②实施合作。当地一些机构为了实施某项特殊政策和激励而形成的合作。一般来说，当地政府扮演重要角色，而基金组织、商会、当地开发机构和企业界等也起着重要作用。③咨询合作。指在管治过程中农区社区形成的咨询机制。社区介入在农区管治中也起着十分重要的作用。社区介入加强了当地人在相关事务中的影响力量，将国家的责任分散到公民身上。在英国，20世纪末通过英国农区白皮书（British Rural White Paper）使地方社区介入成为农区管理的一个重要原则（Edwards，1998）。在这方面，多种居民群体（如居民协会、康乐设施协会、合作组织等）发挥着重要作用。

20世纪末以来，农业（区）地理学家开始重视农区管治尤其是新农区管治的研究。农业研究杂志（Journal of Rural Studies）1998年出版专刊讨论农区管治问题。这些研究表明，管治理论用于理解农区的经济、社会和政治变化是十分有价值的（Little，2001）。新农区管治指20世纪末社会规制方式的变化带来政府机制和文化的变化。马斯登在他人研究的基础上，根据地方和区域权利关系，以及农业、商业和其他居住用地的类型，提出4种类型的农区。进而，他提出了4个圈层（sphere）的土地发展过程：大宗食品市场、高质量食品市场、农业相关联的发展、农区重构（非农业的发展）。对于农区管治来说，关键是理解在不同农区空间上，这些圈层产生不同的“权力构架（power geometries）”（Marston and Smith，2001）。

44.4　中国农区地理学的研究思考

44.4.1　全面发展中国农区地理学

农区地理学的研究应包括农业、农村、农民（农户）等研究主体。这些主体中，有些在中国地理学中得到了较多关注，有些则被人忽视。例如，由于农业在经济活动中处于十分特殊的地位，农业地理学一直是中国经济地理学的重要分支之一。除了结合国家需要，中国地理学家在农业区划、农业资源调查、土地利用等方面做了许多实际工作之外，关于农业地理学的理论研究也有诸多成果问世（刘彦随等，2004）。关于农村的地理学研究，主要在聚落地理中有所涉及，但仍有众多侧面被忽视。例如，农村社区内的居住格局、农村基础设施建设、农村社区组织与乡村发展、农村社会结构等。而中国地理学关注最少的是农民及农户的地理研究。农户作为目前农村的一个最为基础的经济组织、社会组织和消费单元，并没有引起地理学家的关注（李小建，2005）。因此，在全面发展中国农区地理学的进程中，尤其要注意对农户地理学的研究。中国独到的农户组织形式和社会经济背景，为农户地理学的建立奠定了良好的基础。基于中国实例的实证研究和理论凝练，可望推出国际上有影响的创新成果。

44.4.2　注重中国特色理论的建设

与发达国家和其他发展中国家相比，中国农区发展环境具有一些独特之处。例如，农业在国民经济中占有重要地位，农民是国民的主体，农区发展对国家整体的稳定与发展至关重要，农民身份对空间迁移的限制，农业土地资源对农业发展的约束，农业经营体制的重大变化，传统文化对农户家庭的深远影响，区域差异巨大，等等。在这种背景下，中国农区地理学研究，一方面应当借鉴国际研究前沿的学术思想，开拓研究思路；另一方面更应立足中国特色，研究与中国发展背景相关联的中国农区地理学的特殊实际问题，并揭示其背后的相关理论。例如，兼顾生产型和后生产型特点的农区产业地理，全球化对长期相对封闭的农区发展的影响，农村工业化与农区非农产业发展，农区基础设施的快速改善及其相关影响，农村基层组织、农户与农户合作组织为主体的农区管制，基于血缘或宗族关系的农村聚落，日益扩大的农村内部的贫富差距问题等，均是颇有特色的研究领域。此外，新近中国政府倡导的社会主义新农村建设以及和谐社会构建，也对中国的农区地理学研究提出了新的实践问题。

44.4.3　农区地理学与新农村建设

将农区地理学的理论研究与新农村建设的实践相结合，可为新农村建设提出一些新的思路。这些思路包括：①新的资源观。农区资源不仅是传统的农业资源，还包括其他种类的资源。例如，旅游和休闲资源、房地产开发、特色农产品资源等。这种资源具有较高的开发利用价值。尤其是随着居民收入水平的提高，这种资源显得更为重要。②新的发展观。农区的发展不只限于经济水平的提高。社会文化与经济的协调，以及人类活动与自然的协调均十分重要。与此相关联，农民教育水平的提高、医疗水平的提高、各种社会保障的完善、农区基础设施的改善、人们绿色发展观念的建立均应引起重视。③新的统筹观。农区发展应该统筹考虑农村产业、农村居住环境、农民与农户等重要方面。农村产业应关注农业与其他产业的关联和相互促进；农村居住环境应注重人文和谐和自然和谐；而农民及农村的基本经济单元农户则为实现前两项统筹的关键。④新的尺度观。新农村建设可以具体到某一村子，这是微观层面的问题。但是，某一农村的发展又与区域环境密切相关。区域经济社会状况为新农村建设提供了重要的中观尺度的环境。而全国层面和全球化等宏观层面问题，也对农区发展至关重要。多尺度问题的综合考察，当为新农村建设的重要问题之一。

参 考 文 献

李小建. 2005. 经济地理学中的农户研究. 人文地理，20（3）：1～5

刘彦随，王大伟，彭留英. 2004. 中国农业地理学研究的进展与趋势. 地理学报，59（s）：175～182

Bruinsma J. 2003. World Agriculture：Towards 2015/2030 – an FAO Perspective. London：Earthscan

Buttel F. 2001. Some reflections on late twentieth century agrarian political economy. Sociologia Ruralis，41：165～181

Buttel F，Newby H. 1980. The Rural Sociology of Advanced Societies：Critical Perspectives. Montclair N J：Croom Held

Cloke P. 1997. Country backwater to virtual village? Rural studies and "the cultural turn". Journal of Rural Studies，13：367～375

Cloke P，Edwards G. 1986. Rurality in England and Wales 1981：A replication of the 1971 index. Journal of Rural Studies，20：289～306

Edwards B. 1998. Charting the discourse of community action：Perspectives from practice in rural Wales. Journal of Rural Studies，14：63～78.

Edwards B，Goodwin M，Pemberton S，et al. 2000. Partnership Working in Rural Regeneration. Bristol：Policy Press

Evans N，Morris C，Winter M. 2002. Conceptualizing agriculture：A critique of post-productivism as the new orthodoxy. Progress in Human Geography，26（3）：313～332

Fothergill S，Gudgin G. 1982. Unequal Growth：Urban and Regional Employment Change in the UK. London：Heinemann

Gould A，Keeble D. 1984. New firms and rural industrialization in East Anglia. Regional Studies，18：189～202

Hill M. 2003. Rural Settlement and the Urban Impact on the Countryside. London：Hodder & Stoughton

Johnson T G. 2000. The rural economy in a new century. In：Center for the Study of Rural America. Beyond Agriculture：New Policies for Rural America. Kansas City：The Federal Reserve Bank of Kansas City. 7～20

Little J. 2001. New rural governance. Progress in Human Geography，25（1）：97～102

Little J，Leyshon M. 2003. Embodied rural geographies：developing research agendas. Progress in Human Geography，27（3）：257～272

Markusen A. 1985. Profit Cycles，Oligopoly and Regional Development. Cambridge，MA：MIT Press

Marston S A，Smith N. 2001. States，scales and households：limits to scale thinking? A response to Brenner. Progress in Human Geography，25（4）：615～619

Massey D. 1984. Spatial Division of Labour. London：Macmillan

Moris C，Enans N. 2004. Agricultural turns，geographical turns：Retrospect and prospect. Journal of Rural Studies，20：95～111

Mormont M. 1990. Who is rural? Or，How to be rural：Towards a sociology of the rural. In：Marsden T，Lowe P，Whatmore. Rural Restructuring：Global Processes and Their Responese. London：David Fulton. 21～44

North D. 1998. Rural industrialization. In：Ilbery B（ed）. The Geography of Rural Change. Harlow：Addison Wesley Longman. 161～188

Roche M. 2002. Rural geography：Searching rural geographies. Progress in Human Geography，26（6）：823～829

Roche M. 2003. Rural geography：A stock tally of 2002. Progress in Human Geography，27（6）：779～786

Roche M. 2005. Rural geography：A borderland revisited. Progress in Human Geography，29（3）：299～303

Tyler P，Moore B，Rhodes J. 1988. Geographical variation in industrial costs. Scottish Journal of Political Economy，35：22～50

Woods M. 2005. Rural Geography. London：Sage Publications. 1～170

第 45 章　新型城镇化概念分析

城镇化是英美发达国家较早出现的现象，20 世纪这些国家已经完成了城镇化过程，甚至出现了逆城镇化现象。作为全球最大的发展中国家，伴随工业化和农业现代化，中国在快速城镇化一段时间后，总结国内外城镇化的发展经验和教训，提出了新型城镇化的发展思路并按此规划、实施。对此，发达国家的一些官员和学者不以为然。甚至一些学者持质疑态度，认为城镇化本身可分为不同阶段，各阶段有不同特点，为什么要提新型城镇化?

我个人的观点是，不同国家由于国情不同，可以有不同的城镇化发展路径和外在表现，中国提出的“新型城镇化”有着实实在在的新内容。中国实现“新型城镇化”是对中国国情下城镇化发展路径和实现方式的创新探索，也是对世界新形势下后城镇化发展道路的重大贡献。

新型城镇化至少包括“三新”：一是对中国过去一段时间的“老”城镇化道路的反思和革新；二是对西方发达国家“旧”城镇化过程中出现的问题的思考和规避；三是对世界新技术、新生产方式、新规划理念下的未来城镇化前景的新设想。下面分别阐述这三点。

45.1　新型城镇化是对中国过去城镇化的反思

中国城镇化的发展，改革开放以来进入快速时期，据统计，1949～1978 年，我国城镇化率由 10%上升到 16%，而 1979～2013 年，城镇化率则由 16%迅速增加到 53%。与此相对应，也形成了中国特色的发展道路。第一，政府在城镇化推动中起主导作用。一方面，政府通过城镇规划和促进城镇发展政策，运用行政力量影响城镇化进程；另一方面，政府直接介入城镇化具体实践过程，干预城镇化的微观运行。本来，有多少城镇，各城镇有多大规模，在什么地方建设，发展速度怎样，应该由市场决定，但中国政府决策起了十分重要的作用。政府主导的城镇化可以带来城镇化的快速发展，但却导致了资源配置的低效，造成土地资源的浪费。在某种程度上也造成了我国投资结构失衡、地方债务负担沉重。第二，土地城镇化快于人口城镇化。中国长期实行城乡分割的户籍制度，限制了农村人口向城镇的转移。改革开放以来，农村剩余劳动力到城镇寻找新的就业机会，一定程度上突破了过去对人口流动的限制，但这些人并没有真正成为市民，不能享受到和城镇居民一样的公共服务。2013 年尽管按常住人口统计的中国城镇化率达到 53%，但其中有 2 亿多为农民工。因此，如果排除未被城镇完全认同的农民工，我国真正的城镇化率在 40%以下。与此相对应，在政府主导下，中国的土地城镇化或景观的城镇化却发展很快。城镇征地在快速增加，城镇新区、开发区、工业区、产业集聚区遍地涌现。有人估计，我国城镇建设用地总规模已达 8 万 km^2，可容纳的人口远大于现已城镇化的人口。第三，人为限制大城市的发展。我国在 20 世纪 80 年代制定并实行“大力发展小城镇、合理发展中等城市、限制发展大城市”的政策。小城镇的发展对带动地方经济、吸引农村劳动力就业、增加当地居民收入起了一定作用，但也存在资源浪费、基础设施薄弱、环境污染等问题。限制大城市发展，难以提高土地利用效率、实现规模经济，难以形成强大的经济增长中心并辐射带动较大区域的发展。与此不同，20 世纪发达国家城镇化中，大城市、特大城市、城市群等，在国家经济甚至世界经济发展中均产生过重要引领作用。

反思以上中国城镇化道路中的不足，新型城镇化就是要立足市场在资源配置中的决定作用，政府恰当助推城镇的发展；立足经济发展是城镇的原动力，通过发展二、三产业经济活动，吸引就业，带动人口的聚集；立足大中小城市和小城镇协调发展，既通过发展大中城市以实现其聚集功能，又通过发展小城市和城镇以发挥其在城乡生产要素流动方面的桥梁和纽带作用。

45.2　新型城镇化是对发达国家“城市问题”的规避

发达国家城镇化在促进经济社会变革的同时，也产生了一些负面后果，所伴生的“城市问题”困扰着政府和社会，产生了不少矛盾，引起了学者和政界的关注。第一，交通拥堵。交通拥堵是个世界性的城市难题，面对城市扩张所带来的交通问题，不少城市或通过拓宽道路、建设高架、修轻轨、铺地铁等技术及设施改善的方法增加容量，或通过限行、控制个体交通等方式实施交通管制，或采取组团式发展减少交通压力，但大部分城市未能彻底有效解决此问题。第二，环境污染。发达国家的城市化都经历过严重的环境恶化，其中，大气污染最为突出。洛杉矶是美国臭氧污染最严重的城市，1990～1993 年，该市分别有 118 天、111 天、130 天和 102 天臭氧浓度超过全美警戒标准，生活在洛杉矶的居民每年死于由地表臭氧引起的呼吸道疾病的风险要高出 25%～30%。根据美国肺病研究会 2011 年的全美空气质量报告，洛杉矶约有 100 万成人和 30 万儿童患有哮喘病。其他发达国家城市也面临此问题，如全英国大气污染最严重的 50 个监测点全都位于伦敦，德国也于 2013 年因为 33 个城市氮氧化物排放超标而遭到了欧盟的警告。此外，河流污染也很严重，英国泰晤士河在产业革命后是一条排污明沟，由于饮水污染和有毒气体弥漫，滨河地区多次爆发霍乱大流行，直到 20 世纪 80 年代才得到有效治理，足足死寂 150 年之久；欧洲莱茵河曾有“欧洲下水道”和“欧洲公共厕所”之称，鱼类一度绝迹。人口和经济活动密集，细菌、病毒和微生物容易通过大气、水体、土壤、食品、人类交往等途径，危害人类健康、破坏经济发展、危害生物多样性，引起生物污染。城镇固体废弃物污染问题在发达国家日渐突出，城市生活垃圾处理已成为世界难题。第三，地价上涨过快。城市化进程中，土地因人口、经济活动的集聚带来增值，若管控不当，容易导致地价快速增长，发达国家就有先例。例如，日本六大城市的地价从 1960～1990 年上涨了 56.1 倍，年平均增长 14%以上，而其国民生产总值只上升了 17.4 倍，每年增长 6%～10%，与地价的增幅形成了惊人的差距，由此导致了严重的房地产泡沫经济。第四，城市贫困。城市提供大量就业岗位的同时，因发展过程中充满不确定性，也带来严重的失业问题，并导致贫困，这一问题在多数发达国家城镇化过程中均出现过，现在一些国家仍较为突出。一些发达国家的贫困人口主要分布在都市区，形成与现代文明截然相反的贫民窟。据《欧洲时报》报道，过去数年里，德国大城市里的贫困问题出现恶化，原因在于大城市居民的消费能力平均比乡村地区人口逐渐降低，而后者的购买力相对稳定。据美国人口普查局的统计，2012 年美国仍有 15%的人口，即将近 5 千万人生活在贫困线下，美国最贫困城市新泽西州卡姆登市 7.7 万居民中，有 3.2 万人生活在贫困线以下，城市失业率高达 19%。2011 年，美国低于贫困线 50%的极贫人口达 2050 万人，占总人口的 6.7%，首都华盛顿最贫困人口占城市总人口的 10.7%，比例最高。美国城市贫困人口集中在城市中心，但 20 世纪以来有向郊区扩散的趋势，据布鲁金斯学会研究报告，生活在大都会地区的贫困人口从 2000 年的 11.2%增加到 2011 年的 15%。

发达国家历史时期面临的城市问题，虽然经过治理有所好转，但仍没得到有效解决，拉美、南亚等欠发达国家正在经历“城市病”之痛，其严重程度并不亚于发达国家历史时期。中国新型城镇化应该直面这些问题，妥善解决，有效规避，通过更具前瞻性的规划来分散拥堵压力，以可持续发展理念提高城市承载能力，以产业支撑和有效就业为基础预防失业和贫困增加，通过土地制度改革、改变传统的城市治理方式来遏制土地和房价过快上涨势头，以增加基础设施、环境卫生、教育、社会保障等公共服务供给来提高城市综合保障能力。

45.3　新型城镇化是对中国理想城镇化模式的新构思

新型城镇化是中国抱着对世界负责、对历史负责的态度，立足中国国情，借鉴西方经验，吸收中国传统文化精髓，借助新技术发展趋势，对中国如何积极、稳妥、扎实、有序推进城镇化的重大探索，是对中国理想城镇化模式的新构思，其内涵十分丰富，其中，以人为本、低碳节约、格局优化、新技术引领可产生重要影响。

45.3.1　以人为本

以人为本在哲学层面是对传统城镇化的反思和扬弃，传统城镇化把物质财富的增加作为其实现手段和追求目标，带有资本拜物教性质。新型城镇化以人的城镇化为核心，推进人的全面自由发展和社会公平、正义、和谐，人是城镇化的主体和价值取向。以人为本在理论层面是对传统城乡二元发展的突破，新型城镇化突出城乡统筹、城乡一体、工农互惠，强调城乡要素平等交换和公共资源均衡配置，大中小城市和小城镇协调发展，城镇化和新农村建设协调推进，摈弃了“城市偏向”和“歧视乡村”的发展逻辑。以人为本在实践层面是在对中国城市化客观条件慎重考量的基础上，最大限度地实现人的城镇化、最大限度地保障人权的有效途径。在人多地少、农村人口数量庞大的特殊国情下，合理引导人口流动，有序推进农业转移人口市民化，稳步推进城镇基本公共服务常住人口全覆盖。保障农民集体经济组织成员权利，赋予农民更多财产权利，消除城乡二元结构的体制机制障碍，让农民平等参与城市化进程，充分尊重农民在城乡居住上的自主选择权，宜城则城、宜乡则乡。

45.3.2　低碳节约

新型城镇化将生态文明理念全面融入城市发展过程，构建低碳节约的生产、生活和消费方式。首先，经济活动要节约集约，产业发展和城市建设要节约集约利用土地、水和能源等资源，强化资源循环利用，发展环境友好型产业，推动环境友好型生产改造，降低污染排放；其次，要发展绿色交通，加快发展新能源、低排量交通工具，完善公共交通体系，提高公共交通出行比例；再次，要推广绿色建筑，提高新建筑能效水平；最后，要推崇简约适度、文明和谐的生活方式，慢生活、简出行，培育绿色低碳的生态文化。

45.3.3　格局优化

新型城镇化以城镇体系和城市内部空间结构、格局和形态优化为基础。根据资源环境承载能力，实施主体功能区规划，优化城镇空间布局，构建科学合理的城镇体系，促进各类城市和小城镇协调发展；依据城市化发展阶段，优化城市内部空间结构，实施组团式发展，合理定位组团功能，根据组团配置商业、医疗、教育等公共资源，增加组团内部联系，减少组团间的通勤，以多中心组团为节点，构建城市综合交通体系；顺应城市规划和发展趋势与生态文明新要求，推动产城融合，实现产业和城市良性互动、融合发展。通过规划引导、市场运作，培育各具特色的卫星城、卫星镇，疏散中心城区功能，提高城市生产和生活效率，提升城市综合承载能力和可持续发展能力。

45.3.4　技术引领

城市发展周期与经济技术周期紧密相连，城市化过程必然留下当时产业和技术进步的烙印。蒸汽革命及之后的电力、化学革命，引起了大量产业和向人口城市集聚，城市数量和规模迅速增加，形成“生产型城市”发展阶段。20 世纪后，以分工和专业化为基础的福特主义出现，实现了大批量生产和快速运输网络的形成，促进了城市扩散和逆城市化过程，城市从重生产逐渐向生产和服务并重转变。之后，信息技术、微电子技术广泛应用，以弹性专业化和精益生产为特征的后福特主义出现，城市发展完成了从“生产型城市”到“服务消费型城市”的跨越。当前，基于物联网、大数据、云计算、移动互联等新一代信息技术正在深刻改变城市的生产和生活方式，产生诸多与此相应的城市发展模式，智慧城市就是其一。新型城镇化应当应用智慧城市理念进行城市规划和建设，把技术和人有机结合，建立城市智慧管理系统，提升城市建设和管理的智能化、精准化，促进城市生产、流通高效运作、智慧运营，增加城市发展红利，促进城市健康可持续发展。同时，通过信息化与城市化的高度融合，顺应知识社会发展潮流，培育更多创新形态，引导城市向更高阶段跨越。

第 46 章　新型城镇化中的协调思想

党的十八大提出中国要走新型城镇化道路，并将城乡一体化作为解决“三农”问题的根本途径（胡锦涛，2012）。与此同时，2013 年 1 月《中共中央国务院关于加快发展现代农业进一步增强农村发展活力的若干意见》中提出，深入推进社会主义新农村建设（中共中央国务院，2013）。在此政策背景下，各地把城镇化作为拉动经济增长的重要引擎（李小建，2013）。国家发展和改革委员会主导的《全国促进城镇化健康发展规划（2011～2020 年）》预测，城镇化将在未来 10 年拉动 40 万亿投资（杨仕省，2012）。在新型城镇化的引导下，不少地区推行新农村建设。据我们在山东、河南等省的一些地区调查，相当一些县进行了新型农村社区的定点规划，并按照规划逐步实施。

无疑，这种政府主推的新型城镇化建设对农村经济社会发展具有一定的促进作用。但这种政策实施涉及农区社会经济，尤其是中国几千年聚落传承的巨大改变，学术界对其在操作过程中出现的问题比较关注（党国英，2013；吴良镛，2013）。例如：①改革开放以来中国城市化速度已经很快，一些地区把新农村建设列入新型城镇化后，会进一步加快城镇化进程。过快的城镇化可带来更为严重的环境、资源等诸多问题（吴良镛，2013）。②前瞻性缺乏。中国农村未来的聚落格局发展趋势怎样？聚落大小及空间格局会呈现什么形态？在没有科学研究并有令人信服的结论之前，如果按照统一模式规划和建设，可能会带来不可挽回的损失。③对传统聚落利用不够。一些新农村建设以新建村镇为主，在建设过程中常伴随“大拆大建”，而中国乡村聚落是当地居民长时期人地相互作用的结果，反映了人们适应和利用环境的智慧。不考虑原有聚落格局的新农村建设，将不利于中华民族几千年传统的人居环境中的延续。④用地问题。新建聚落多选择在多聚落区域的中心区或交通便利区，这些区域多为良田成片区。在这里建立较大聚落会占用本已稀缺的基本农田。虽然理论上原有村子搬迁后会整理出农田，但多数地区把原有村庄用地作为建设用地指标做有偿转让。其结果是农田面积不会增加，农用地质量会有所下降。此外，新农村建设多按当地户籍人口分配居住用地，随着人口城市化进程，不少居民会进入城市居住，由此带来建设用地的空间错位，等等。

这些问题主要形成于实际操作过程中。但之所以产生这些问题，主要在于其指导理论薄弱。乡村聚落的发展虽然与多个学科有关，但其体系和空间格局本质上属于人文地理学研究范畴，聚落是人们利用自然的一种反映。其指导理论应该是“人地关系”理论（吴传钧，1998，2008）：“一定的地理环境只能容纳一定数量和质量的人及其一定形式的活动”“人必须依赖所处的地为生活的基础，要主动地认识并自觉地在地的规律下去利用和改变地”（吴传钧，1998）。以“人地关系”理论为指导，地理学家在乡村聚落研究上做了许多工作（金其铭，1988；张小林，1999；刘彦随和杨忍，2012；龙花楼，2006；石忆邵，1992）。这些成果对聚落差异、乡村转型、土地利用、空心村整治、县域城镇化等做了很好的研究总结，对城镇化过程中的村镇建设具有很好的借鉴作用。但是，新型村镇建设及新农村建设中，还有一些亟待解决的理论问题。从“人地协调”理论出发，可以对新型城镇化及新农村建设做以下梳理。

46.1　新型城镇化本质是城乡协调

依据规模大小和功能差异，聚落可以分为若干等级，如特大城市、大城市、中等城市、小城市、县城、建制镇、中心集镇、一般集镇、中心村、基层村等（王雨村和杨新海，2002）。一般意义上，城镇化是指人口由农村向城或镇转移的过程。由此，把聚落的诸多等级差别概括为城镇与乡村两类。在城镇与农村的基础设施和公共服务差别明显的情况下，此概念可用来表征人民生活水平的提高和社会进步。但也带有重城镇、轻农村的价值判断。随着社会的发展和技术的进步，农村聚落的基础设施不断完善，而城市的拥挤和环境问题使一些居民向往农村居住环境。在有些发达国家，已经出现了逆城市化现象。所以，从本质上讲，新型城镇化并不单单是农村人口向城镇转移，而应该是全面整合城乡聚落体系，使大小不同、功能差别、环境各异的各类聚落形成统一和谐的整体。

把新型城镇化理解为城乡聚落体系结构合理化的调整过程，对于中国这个农村居民占主体的国家具有特殊意义。我国人口众多，土地资源有限，农业文明根基深厚，不可能像日本、澳大利亚、墨西哥等国那样，将人口集中在少数几个大都市。将大、中、小城市与小城镇、村镇协调发展，尤其是加强中小城市和村镇的建设，使不同等级的城乡聚落充分发挥作用，成为吸纳农村人口的重要平台，可成为中国城镇化路径的重要选择。

将城乡聚落看作一个体系，要用系统观点考虑其发展变化。系统论强调整体性、关联性、等级结构性、动态平衡性和时序性（高隆昌，2010）。在新型城镇化建设中，要考虑不同等级、不同类别聚落与城乡聚落整体的关系。各等级城乡聚落在人居聚落系统中都起着特定作用，它们之间相互关联，构成了一个不可分割的整体。以此理论为指导，各地就会在新型城镇化中注重科学的顶层设计，省、市、县、镇等不同层次的规划相互衔接，发挥不同的作用；以此理论为指导，各地就会在新型城镇化中统筹考虑大小不同的聚落相互协调，在新农村建设中考虑几千年来形成的农村聚落体系的承继。

46.2　新型城镇化核心是内部协调

其一，大、中、小城市和村镇协调发展。新型城镇化不仅包括城市地区的建成区扩展进程，更主要是广大农村地区人文景观的变化，尤其是小城镇和村镇的发展。在发展中，要注意大中城市的土地集约利用，村镇的相对开敞（李兵第，2013）。党的十八大报告提出的“生产空间集约高效、生活空间宜居适度、生态空间山清水秀”（胡锦涛，2012），是我们发展不同规模、不同类型城镇的指导原则。事实上，我国城镇空间利用上，一方面存在土地资源利用效率低下，如我国十大城市群（京津冀、长三角、珠三角、辽中南、山东半岛、海峡西岸、中原、长江中游、关中和川渝）占全国经济总量的

2/3，但只承载了全国人口的1/3（南方都市报，2013）。我国城镇建设用地总规模已近8万km^2，如果按世界园林城市标准每平方千米居住1万人，现有建设用地可容纳8亿人，而实际上我国按城市化率52%计算，城镇人口只有6亿多，其中，还有2.6亿为农民工，非本地农民工为1.6亿（国家统计局，2012）。另一方面，村镇不够开敞，生态环境不够秀美。有些小城镇建设跟大中城市一样密集，一样高大，甚至一些农村社区也建起了高楼。大、中、小城市及村镇协调，尤其是小城镇健康发展方面应给予特别关注。

其二，土地城镇化与人口城镇化相协调。20世纪90年代以来，尤其是2000年以来的快速城市化进程中，全国各地掀起了以开发区、工业区、新城区为主的城市建设热潮，城市用地迅速扩张（方创琳和马海涛，2013），而这些地区仅仅是在土地上或是景观上实现了城市化，缺乏相应的产业和人口支撑，少数新区甚至成为“空城”。城市建设用地大幅扩张、农村建设用地没有减少甚至增加，并没有带来等效的农村人口的有效转移。而新型的城镇化强调工业化和城镇化良性互动，将城市建设用地增加与农村建设用地减少相结合，城镇建设用地增加与人口有效转移相协调，实现城乡土地要素平等交换，促进土地城镇化和人口城镇化的协调推进。

其三，居住城镇化与公共服务城镇化相协调。目前，我国城市化率已经超过50%，统计口径上是将诸如农村进城务工人员等城市常住人口纳入城市人口范围，但这些人员仅仅是在城市中就业和居住，缺乏同城市户籍人口同等的教育、医疗、就业、社会保障等公共服务。按照享受城市公共服务的人口统计，中国城市化率只有35%～36%。新型城镇化强调公共服务均等化和公共资源的均衡配置，使居住城市化同社会保障城市化相协调。

其四，有型的城镇化与无形的城镇文化相协调。城市是人类社会的一种文明形态，城市文明除了完全不同于农业文明的物质文明、完全不同于农业文明的生活方式之外，还包括引领现代城市发展的文化和隐含在现代城市中的居民习惯。与农民居住城镇化、就业城镇化、公共服务城镇化相比，文化和习惯的城镇化更是比较缓慢的过程。新型城镇化应该强调这种无形的文化和习惯的改变，强调人们的行为与城市文明的要求相协调。

46.3 新型城镇化机制强调市场协调

城镇化是工业化和农业现代化在人们居住空间格局上的反映，是社会经济发展的一种自然结果。经济社会的现代化，表现在人口结构上是城镇化，农村人口转为城市人口；从产业结构来看是工业化，产业主体从以农业为主转向以工业及其相关产业为主；从人类发展长期依赖的农业本身来看，经济技术的发展使农业采用现代理念、现代技术、现代管理方式从而带来农业生产效率的大幅提高。比较成熟的经济应该是工业化、城市化和农业现代化协调发展，互相促进互相融合。因为只有实现工业化以后，通过积累才有经济实力反哺农业，促进农业现代化；实现工业化后，就业主要是在第二、第三产业，居住地也主要是在城市。

从比较成熟的发达国家的发展历程看，工业化、城镇化和农业现代化的发展是大致同步的，也是协调的。在英国、美国或其他西欧国家并不存在“三化”发展不协调的明显问题，也没有看到它们就“三化”不协调发展问题提出过什么理论和如何解决“三化”不协调，因为它们的“三化”发展是在自然地、稳步地进行，工业化的同时促进了农业现代化，农业在国民经济中的比例逐渐减少，农业人口的比例也在逐渐减少，人均的农业资源在逐渐增加，农业技术的投入和进步在逐渐加强，自然就逐渐实现了农业的现代化。同时，随着工业和第三产业的发展，城市提供更多就业机会，吸引剩余劳动力由农村向城市转移，城市化也在自然稳步地推进。

在建设有中国特色的社会主义道路上，为什么我们的工业化、城镇化和农业现代化发展呈现不同步现象？这与中国经济社会发展的特殊背景密切相关。一是中国的多数人口生活在农村，农民是中国社会的主体；二是中国实行特殊的工业化，1978 年以后，随着改革开放的实行，工业化在中国铺天盖地地进行，尤其是在中国的农村，工业化发展迅速，从而使得中国的城镇化水平远远落后于工业化，如 2000 年中国的国内生产总值（GDP）首次达到 1 万亿美元的时候，城镇化率仅为 36.2%，同样的，美国在 20 世纪 60 年代 GDP 达到 1 万亿美元的时候，其城市化水平为 80%；日本在 20 世纪 80 年代 GDP 达到 1 万亿美元的时候，其城镇化率为 65%（中国市长协会，2013）。在这种背景下，强调城镇化，通过加快城镇化改变城市化与工业化不相协调的局面，具有十分重要的意义。正如有 3 人体形相当，同步前行，若外力助推一个超前，这时要改变前后错落的局面，最直接的方法是外力助推其他人加速前行。

这是我们理解我国政府推动城镇化的理论基础，但是肯定政府的能动作用的同时，决不能忽视城镇化应该与经济发展相协调的本质。与自给自足的农村经济状态相比，城镇是一个交易成本较高的人口居住形式。所以一地的城镇发展应与当地的专业化社会分工和劳动生产率增长相匹配。在“城”与“市”的关系上，“城”只是形式，“市”才是内容，才是城市持续发展的原动力。“市”主要是经济活动，尤其是专业化的经济活动，并由此带来大量的交易。从这个基点出发，城镇化的进程应该更多依靠市场机制的作用。在本质上，市场机制可以引导经济活动中的资源配置优化，同样可以促进居民的就业和居住优化。政府所做的，只能是逐步认识市场规律，顺势而为，恰当地助推城镇化的发展。这种助推方向要正确，用力也要适当。否则，就会导致出现有些人特别愿意去的城市，却投资不足，设施不足；有些人不愿去的地方，路却修得很好，楼盖得很高。

从市场发展角度考虑，城市化是生产力发展的客观结果。城镇化的直接原因是居住的集聚，而居住集聚又主要受就业机会集聚的影响，就业又与经济发展密切关联。一地的经济发展，又是各种区位优势综合利用和制度、科技相互作用的结果（图 46.1）。

46.4　新型城镇化实施强调上下协调

从聚落空间结构调整角度实施城镇化，可以沿着区域人口变化、转入城市人口、聚落等级规模、聚落空间结构、聚落调整的阶段划分、聚落区位选择的路线进行分析论证。以下简述其中的 5 个问题。

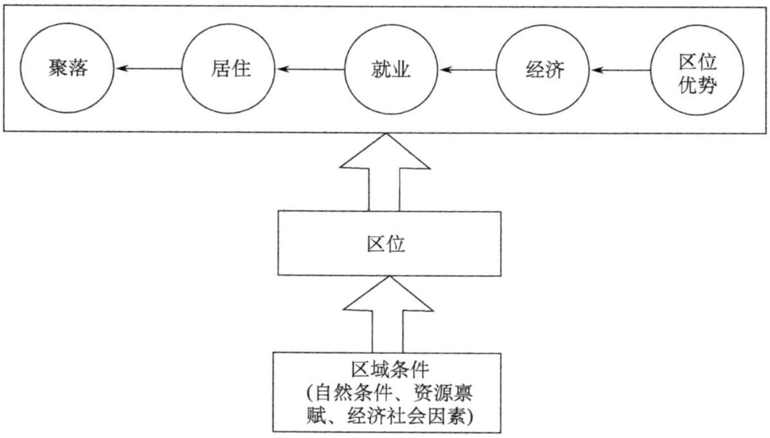

图 46.1　新型城镇化的发展机理

第一，区域城镇与乡村人口变化。发达国家的经历表明，城镇化过程将驱动乡村人口的变化（Cloke，1983）。据中国现代化战略研究课题组研究，中国在 2030 年前后有可能完成第一次农业现代化，农业增加值占 GDP 的比重将低于 15%，农业劳动力占所有劳动力的比重将低于 30%；到 2050 年基本实现农业现代化，农业现代化程度达到世界农业中等水平，农业增加值占 GDP 的比重将低于 5%，农业劳动力占所有劳动力的比重将低于 10%（何传启，2012）。另有学者通过建立模型对中国城市化率进行预测，到 2030 年中国城市化率将达到 70%左右（曹飞，2012）。国家统计局 2012 年农民工调查监测报告显示，中国农民工达 2.62 亿，其中有 3375 万人举家外出务工（国家统计局，2012）。如果这些农民工不再回农村，并将其家属带到城里，必将带来乡村人口的大幅减少。显然，必须首先对区域的总人口和转入城市的人口作出预测。在一定时期居住在乡村的人口是村镇规划的重要人口依据，是考虑一区域的城镇化及乡村聚落结构调整的重要前提。

第二，城乡聚落的等级规模。聚落规模大小服从某种随机分布，这种分布是区域发展过程中空间、人口竞争的平衡点（Simon，1955）。作为随机模型的一种实现，聚落规模在量上遵从 Zipf 规则。然而，有学者认为，乡村聚落的规模-位序分布是一个动态、自组织的多尺度分形现象，并遵循新的规模-位序规律（Sinos and Grossman，1984）。基于英国和以色列典型区域的研究表明，乡村聚落规模-位序曲线的具体形状与区域发挥作用的内在力量（如资源禀赋、非农就业机会、对外贸易和交通通信等）有关（Grossman and Sinos，1989）。虽然乡村聚落的相对规模可以部分由区位特征来解释，但随着运输成本的下降，其解释力有所下降（Ploeckl，2012）。区域农业资源禀赋对不同规模聚落的影响也存在着差异，即对门槛人数以上的聚落影响较小，门槛人数以下的聚落影响较大（Duranton，1999）。此外，基于美国的研究表明，大都市特征对远郊不同类型乡村聚落的规模影响有所差异（Clark et al.，2009）。根据以上理论分析，可以通过对中国聚落长时间的等级分布演化分析，并参考高度城市化国家的聚落等级规模关系，确定相关区域各种不同规模聚落的数量范围，为聚落空间规划提供依据。

第三，城乡聚落的空间格局。基于德国南部聚落的研究，克里斯泰勒发现聚落的空间结构，以及城镇和农村聚落之间存在一定的规律性（克里斯泰勒，2010）。随后，其他学者通过引入随机的或者非规则的因素，产生更接近实际的模型（Mulligan et al.，2012）。但这些模型仍保持有克里斯泰勒所强调的规则性（Kuby，1989）。例如，基于成都平原乡村市场的分布研究，发现中国文化背景下村庄市集空间分布具有六边形的特征（施坚雅，1998）。然而，以中心地理论为基础的聚落模型主要关注静态的聚落空间模式，对聚落空间分布的动态过程（如生物物理、社会和人类决策）重视不够（Pumain，2000），而它们内在地驱动聚落区位的选择。鉴于此，一些学者以持续时间模拟方法构建微分方程模型来对聚落动态进行研究，如基于人口空间分布和就业机会的相互作用，提出动态的中心地模型（Allen and Sanglier，1979）；基于人口迁移和经济活动间的相互作用以及其在聚落空间结构的自组织过程的作用，构建聚落形成的动态模型（Popkov et al.，1998）。另一些学者采取离散时间和离散空间相结合的方法对聚落动态进行建模（如元胞自动机模型、基于主体的模型）。例如，Tang 等（2009）在考虑空间模式和过程的整合、层级关系的表现，以及处理复杂的非稳态聚落动态的非线性关系等基础上，通过构建一个层级的模拟模型，对复杂的聚落动态进行研究。虽然各地的自然条件不同会影响其六边形形状，但这种思想仍可作为区域聚落空间格局的规划指导。

第四，聚落发展的阶段性。乡村聚落的演变会受自然、社会、经济等多种因素的影响。在不同区域和同一区域的不同发展阶段，各影响因素的耦合关系及主导因素不尽相同，从而使乡村聚落的演变具有明显的区域性与阶段性特征（Evans，1980）。人类社会的早期阶段，自然环境对聚落选址起着决定性影响。例如，气候会对人类居住环境、食物可利用率和生产力产生影响，进而影响聚落的区位（Tian et al.，2012）；地形会通过影响区域土地利用方式，进而对聚落形态产生作用（Sevenant and Antrop，2007）；土地的富饶程度和先前居民点的类型也影响村庄现有的空间分布状态（Hoskins，1991）。但是，随着人类改造自然和利用自然能力的增强，聚落选址已超出传统意义上的自然资源禀赋。乡村城市化和农业工业化（Brebner and Briggs，1982）、服务设施的空间集中（Knapp and Dongqi，1991）、交通设施的建设（Antrop，2004）、政府的政策和规划（Palmer，1988）等都导致人口居住集中，新村落规模扩大，与此同时，成千上万的小村落废弃并逐渐消失，造成乡村聚落结构的根本改变（Rey and Bachvarov，1998）。总体取向是人类逐渐向经济发展水平较高、交通便利、环境更宜居区位迁移（图 9.2）。根据效用分析，在生产力较低的条件下，农户选择农业生产条件较好且距水源较近的区位，这时的效用水平 N_1 与当时的农户需求相一致。随着经济水平提高，农户空间需求会逐渐超越原区位所提供的效用水平（如交通不畅、空间狭小等），即通过区位迁移，实现居住区位效用水平与需求新的均衡 N_2。依此类推，只要农户居住区位在原居住区位没得到满足，就存在向新的区位［N_3（l_3，a_3）］迁移的动力。在居民点区位迁移的过程中，经济水平对效用水平的影响逐渐加大，地理环境的影响逐渐变小，表现为效用线与横轴经济发展水平的夹角逐渐变小（李小建，2010）。由此便形成聚落不同发展阶段的不同区位选择。

第五，聚落的区位选择。在城乡聚落的分阶段规划基础上，可以进行聚落的区位选择及发展论证。区位选择要综合考虑某区位作为人居聚落所具有的优势，该区位周围地区的自然条件、资源禀赋、社会经济基础，以及对周边居民的吸引力。同时考虑本区位与周围相邻聚落的关系，从而论证当地经济发展潜力，经济活动可能提供的就业岗位数量。根据经济活动所承载的人口和居住环境对周围地区人口的吸引，预测该区域聚落的大致人口发展规模。以此为基础，与自然环境相协调进行聚落总体格局、空间结构、建筑风格、文化特色等总体规划。聚落区位选择中，要尽可能考虑地区聚落的现状，处理好历史承继与未来发展的关系。根据各地已有城市体系的发展情况，在聚落发展中不仅要注意小城镇、专业集镇、特色村与已有城市的联系，还要注意在快速城市化地区未来城市体系变化，避免所选区位在若干年后又面临拆迁的局面。

46.5　结论与讨论

在人类社会发展的一定阶段上，城市化是社会进步的标志。但本质上，城市化是在市场经济的利益驱动下，生产要素集中、社会分工、资源利用效率提高的产物。所以从社会和谐、人民生活舒适的角度，资本导向资源的过度集中也使得城市人感到诸多不便。欧洲一些国家已经出现了“逆城市化”现象。在这样的背景下，全面审视新型城镇化，就应该：①强调城乡协调，强调聚落本身的多样化，大小不同、功能不同的城乡聚落各有其存在的必要。新型城镇化就是要注意调整各类聚落的关系，使其更好地满足社会经济发展和人类居住的需要。②强调城市与农村聚落的景观多样性，强调景观的城镇化与人口城镇化相协调，居住的城镇化与公共服务的城镇化相协调，有型的城镇化与无形的城镇化相协调。③强调城镇化发展中的市场推动。在“城”与“市”的关系上，“市”（主要是经济活动）才是城市持续发展的动力。城镇化的进程应该主要依靠市场机制的作用，政府所做的，只能是顺势而为，恰当助推。④强调实施中的上下协调。尤其是规划论证中，一定要注意在宏观发展趋势下的村镇格局规划。例如，根据人口发展趋势和城市人口变化趋势，预测一区域未来的人口发展；根据聚落等级——规模变化趋势测度未来各规模的村镇数量；根据聚落空间格局模型规划不同等级聚落的空间关系；根据各区位条件规划每个聚落的区位及发展阶段、发展规模。

和谐发展是新型城镇化的主题。党的十八大报告强调“工业化与城镇化的良性互动、城镇化与农业现代化相互协调”，强调把生态文明建设融入经济建设、政治建设、文化建设、社会建设各方面和全过程中，努力建设美丽中国（胡锦涛，2012）。把这种思想落实到新型城镇化之中，就是要注意人们居住环境、城镇建设、经济发展与地理环境之间的相互协调，从人地和谐的思路考虑，居住与就业关联，就业与经济发展关联，经济发展与区域条件关联，城乡聚落格局与其发展实质上是人们对各种地理环境条件的综合利用的结果。

参 考 文 献

曹飞. 2012. 中国人口城市化 Logistic 模型及其应用——基于结构突变的理论分析. 西北人口，33 (6)：18～22
党国英. 2013. 在高度城镇化基础上实现城乡一体化. 农村工作通讯，(2)：22～26
方创琳，马海涛. 2013. 新型城镇化背景下中国的新区建设与土地集约利用. 中国土地科学，27 (7)：4～9
高隆昌. 2010. 系统学原理（第二版）. 北京：科学出版社
国家统计局. 2012 年农民工调查监测报告. http：//www. stats. gov. cn/tjfx/jdfx/t20130527_402899251. htm
何传启. 2012. 中国现代化报告 2012：农业现代化研究. 北京：北京大学出版社
胡锦涛. 2012. 坚定不移沿着中国特色社会主义道路前进，为全面建成小康社会而奋斗. 北京：人民出版社
金其铭. 1988. 我国农村聚落地理研究历史及近今趋向. 地理学报，43 (4)：311～317
李兵第. 2013. 务实推动小城镇健康发展. 中国科学报，04～22
李小建. 2010. 还原论与农户地理研究. 地理研究，29 (5)：767～777
李小建. 2013. 新型城镇化：经济社会发展的重要引擎. 人民日报，02～22
刘彦随，杨忍. 2012. 中国县域城镇化的空间特征与形成机理. 地理学报，67 (8)：1011～1020
龙花楼. 2006. 中国农村宅基地转型的理论与证实. 地理学报，61 (10)：1093～1100
南方都市报. 2013. "以大带小"：中国将再打造 10 个区域性城市群. 06～02
施坚雅. 1998. 中国农村的市场和社会结构. 史建云，徐景丽译. 北京：中国社会科学出版社
石忆邵. 1992. 乡村地理学发展的回顾与展望. 地理学报，47 (1)：80～88
王雨村，杨新海. 2002. 小城镇总体规划. 南京：东南大学出版社
沃尔特·克里斯泰勒. 2010. 德国南部中心地原理. 常正文，王兴中译. 北京：商务印书馆
吴传钧. 1998. 人地关系与经济布局. 北京：学苑出版社
吴传钧. 2008. 发展中的中国现代人文地理学. 北京：商务印书馆
吴良镛. 2013. 明日之人居. 中国科学报，02-18
杨仕省. 2012. 城镇化拉动投资 40 万亿. 华夏时报，12-22
张小林. 1999. 乡村空间系统及其演变研究：以苏南为例. 南京：南京师范大学出版社
中共中央国务院. 2013. 中共中央国务院关于加快发展农业 进一步增强农村发展活力的若干意见. 人民日报，02-01
中国市长协会. 2013. 2001-2002 中国城市发展报告. 北京：西苑出版社
Allen P M, Sanglier M. 1979. A dynamic model of growth in a central place system. Geographical Analysis, 11 (3)：256～272
Antrop M. 2004. Landscape change and the urbanization process in Europe. Landscape and Urban Planning, 67 (1)：9～26
Brebner P, Briggs J. 1982. Rural settlement planning in Algeria and Tanzania：A comparative study. Habitat International, 6 (5)：621～628
Clark J K, Mcchesney R, Munroe D K et al. 2009. Spatial characteristics of exurban settlement pattern in the united states. Landscape and Urban Planning, 90 (3)：178～188
Cloke P J. 1983. An Introduction to Rural Settlement Planning. London：Methuen & Co, Ltd

Duranton G. 1999. Distance, land, and proximity: economic analysis and the evolution of cities. Environment and Planning A, 31 (12): 2169～2188

Evans S T. 1980. Spatial analysis of Basin of Mexico settlement: problems with the use of the central place model. American Antiquity, 45 (4): 866～875

Grossman D, Sonis M. 1989. Reinterpretation of the rank-size rule: examples from England and the land of Israel. Geography Research Forum, (9): 67～107

Hoskins W. 1991. Making of the English Landscape. London: Hodder & Stoughton

Knapp R G, Dongqi S. 1991. Politics and Planning: Rural Settlements in Contemporary China. Berkeley: Center for Environment Design Research, University of California at Berkeley

Kuby M A. 1989. Location-allocation model of Lösch's central place theory: Testing on a uniform lattice network. Geographical Analysis, 21 (4): 316～337

Mulligan G, Partridge M, Carruthers J. 2012. Central place theory and its reemergence in regional science. The Annals of Regional Science, 48 (2): 405～431

Palmer E. 1988. Planned relocation of severely depopulated rural settlements: Acase study from Japan. Journal of Rural Studies, 4 (1): 21～34

Ploeckl F. 2012. Endowments andmarket access; the size of towns in historical perspective: Saxony, 1550～1834. Regional Science and Urban Economics, 42 (4): 607～618

Popkov Y S, Shvetsov V I, Weidlich W. 1998. Settlement formation models with entropy operator. The Annals of Regional Science, 32 (2): 267～294

Pumain D. 2000. Settlement systems in the evolution. Geografiska Annaler: Series B, Human Geography, 82 (2): 73～87

Rey V, Bachvarov M. 1998. Rural settlements in transition-agricultural and countryside crisis in the central-eastern Europe. Geojournal, 44 (4): 345～353

Sevenant M, Antrop M. 2007. Settlement models, land use and visibility in rural landscapes: Two case studies in Greece. Landscape and Urban Planning, 80 (4): 362～374

Simon H A. 1955. On a class of skew distribution functions. Biometrika, 42 (314): 425～440

Sonis M, Grossman D. 1984. Rank-size rule for rural settlements. Socio-economic Planning Sciences, 18 (6): 373～380

Tang W, Malanson G, Entwisle B. 2009. Simulated village locations in Thailand: A multi-scale model including a neural network approach. Landscape Ecology, 24 (4): 557～575

Tian G, Qiao Z, Zhang Y. 2012. The investigation of relationship between rural settlement density, size, spatial distribution and its geophysical parameters of China using landsatTM images. Ecological Modeling, 231: 25～36

第 47 章　新农村建设中新村镇规模探讨

中国是一个农业大国，目前仍有半数人口生活在农村，农村的经济发展已经成为建设小康社会的重点和难点。农村地区要实现发展可以借助外力推动，但也离不开自身内力的驱动。有人认为中部农村地区的发展需要依靠工商业和城市发展，即工业化和城镇化使农村人口减少到足够少，农村人均资源足够多，农村地区就会走上富裕；而另一些人则认为只有充分利用区域发展的环境条件，充分发挥区域的比较优势和区域自主创新能力，充分利用区域制度创新调动各方面积极性，才能促进区域发展（李小建，2010）。在广大的中部农村地区，应当结合我国国情和其自身特征，兼顾内力与外力，寻求和谐发展。实现农区发展的具体途径有很多，如发展现代农业、非农产业，加快农村工业化进程、发展规模农业，实现规模经济等。实现规模农业的途径也有很多，如实行有偿土地转让，使土地相对集中，发展规模农业；农村聚落迁移合并成为新型村镇，扩大人均耕地面积，也可实现规模农业。

农村聚落合并涉及农村聚落空间分布问题，农村聚落的空间分布在农户的居住空间需求和居住空间偏好不断改变的过程中演变。农户的居住区位选择来自于农户与其所在的空间系统要素之间的空间博弈。当迁入地居住环境、经济条件、社会条件构成足够的吸引力，并且这种吸引力大于迁移成本，农户会向着迁入地进行集聚，这就是新型村镇形成的理论基础（李小建，2009）。同时聚居规模的问题也随之而来，建设规模过大的新型村镇，会造成长距离大规模的农村聚落迁移，耕作半径过大等问题；而规模过小，又会出现规模不经济、基础设施建设不能充分利用等问题，所以本章将对如何通过农村聚落迁移合并，实现农业规模经营，哪种规模为新型村镇的适宜规模等问题进行探讨。

本章所探讨的新型村镇是为了一定目的迁移形成的具有一定人口规模和较为齐全的公共设施的农村社区，是城乡居民点最基层的完整的规划单元。它是一种高级的村庄形态，是农村现代化的载体，是今后新农村发展的典型模式之一。21 世纪初以来，关于中心村与集镇的研究逐渐增多，主要集中在探讨中心村建设相关理论，并论证了沿海地区建设新型村镇的现实性，研究了中心村、集镇的规划布局、空间扩展、建设政策建议等（杨山，2002；范德种，2009；顾军和忻隽，2008），其中规划布局又包括了空间规划、选址、规模定位和具体案例设计（冯健和刘玉，2008；徐全勇，2000，2005；吴九兴，2009；伍玥融，2009）等相关问题。纵观已有研究，仍有问题：①实证研究和定量分析较少。②研究区域多集中于东部沿海地区，对中部和西部地区研究相对薄弱。③多数研究是基于上一级行政规划所确定的中心村进行研究，对适宜的中心村规模研究较少。本章研究的新型村镇，与中心村和集镇这两种组织形式既有区别又有联系，职能类似于中心村，但规模基本与集镇相仿，对这种新型村庄形式还没有直接的研究成果。本章选取位于中部农村地区的河南省封丘县鲁岗乡为研究区，对我国中部农村地区新型村镇建设适宜规模做初步探讨。

47.1　建设新型村镇的意义

促进土地的节约集约利用。2009 年 4 月，国土资源部发布 2008 年国土资源公报，指出 2008 年耕地面积为 12172 亿 hm^2，净减少 1.93 万 hm^2（国土资源部，2009）。如何在促进经济增长的前提下保持耕地的占补平衡已经成为政府关注的重点问题。目前，我国农村中存在大量的闲置土地，农村居民点的建设普遍存在无序、混乱和多占等问题，“空心村”问题，都造成一定的土地浪费。如果经过合理规划新型村镇，对各类“空心村”进行合理改造，置换其中“有效用地”（李君和李小建，2008），就能节省大量土地，缓解人地矛盾。

有利于农业规模经济的实现。发展规模农业，提高农业生产效率，增加农民收益，是当下农村倡导的一种农业生产方式。当前我国的人均耕地为 0.09 hm^2，以家庭为单位，无法实现适度的规模农业。建设新型村镇，人口规模的增加可以带来相应的非农就业岗位的增加，引导农村剩余劳动力就地转移，减少农业人口规模，增加农民的人均耕地面积，取得农业的规模效益。

有利于农村基础设施的建设。各种基础设施都有其服务门槛和最佳规模，低于服务门槛该设施就不能被充分利用。因此小的村庄根本无法充分利用教育、医疗、交通、通信等公共基础设施，造成资源浪费。将小村庄迁并为新型村镇，具有一定的人口规模，就能够合理地配置各项基础设施，改善农民的生活质量。

有利于取得集聚经济效益和农村产业结构调整。人口规模的增加，能为各种经济活动提供充足的劳动力和活动空间，有利于经济活动的集聚。有学者研究表明经济增长与经济活动的集聚之间存在很强的正相关，所以建设新型村镇有利于取得经济活动的集聚效益。当下农村的能源问题与清洁生产也备受关注，在具有一定规模的新型村镇中，能源能够作为一种新型产业大力发展，如发展沼气产业、乙醇产业，这样不仅能够增加农村收入，亦能在农村实现低碳经济。

有利于农村现代化进程。农村现代化是衡量农村经济社会发展水平的一个重要尺度，也是决定农村经济能否持续健康发展的关键（郑晔和佘欢，2009）。农村现代化不仅仅指经济发展，还包括农村生态、社会、农业技术等方面的发展。新型村镇的建设有利于农村产业结构调整，有利于三次产业规模效益的实现以及科学技术的普及，有利于发展新型的能源经济促进农村清洁生产，有利于农村基础设施建设提高农民生活质量，有利于生态环境保护和凸显农村的自然及人文风貌，也就有利于农村的现代化。

47.2　研究区概况

河南省封丘县位于黄河下游北岸（图 47.1），东经 113°23′～114°59′，北纬 34°53′～35°50′，地处黄淮海平原中部，属半干旱暖温带大陆性气候，境内河系分属海河、黄河两大流域，由于历史原因，黄河多次泛滥和改道，在此地区留下了低洼浅滩及盐碱地。

该县总人口 75 万，农业人口约 47 万，是全国优质小麦基地县和 100 个重要的商品粮生产县之一。该县农业结构、人口结构等在中部农区，尤其是黄泛区诸县中有一定代表性。

为了进行区域内各种指标的详细规划计算，选择封丘县鲁岗乡为研究小区。鲁岗乡位于封丘县城东 10km 处，地势平坦，交通便利，属于暖温带大陆性气候。鲁岗乡是典型的农业大乡，是省小麦、花生、红薯良种繁育生产基地，省级节水灌溉示范项目区，黄淮海农业综合开发区，并且乡镇企业的发展也有一定的基础。

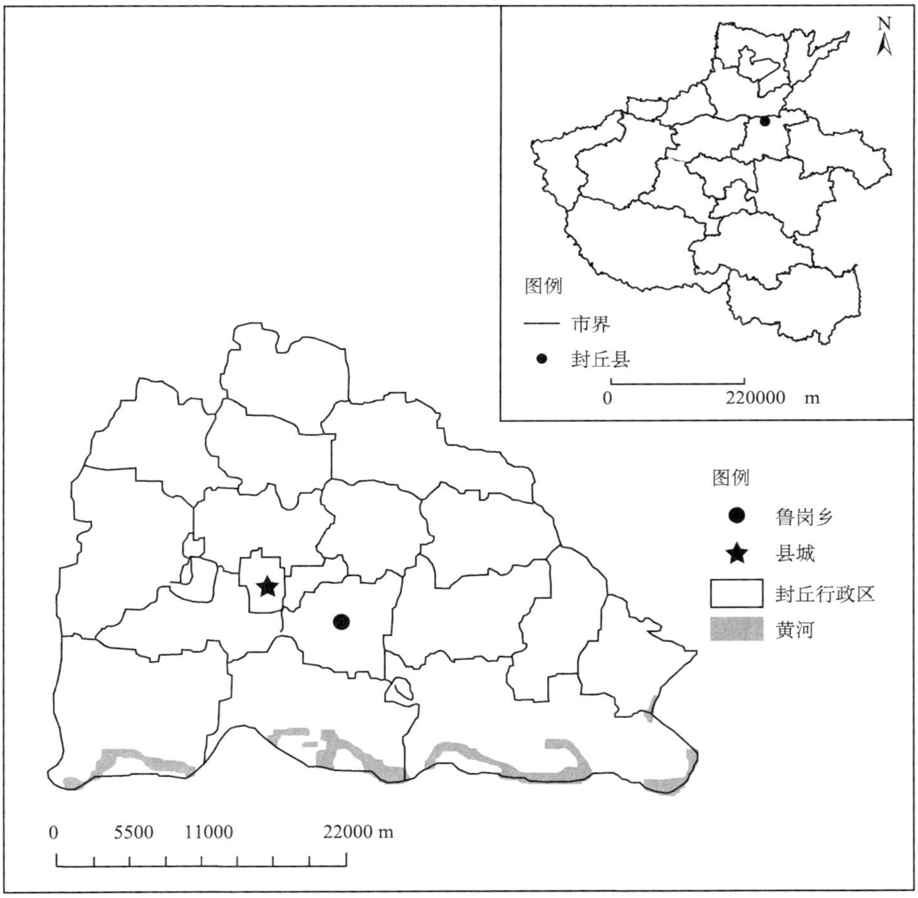

图 47.1　研究区区位

封丘县有着良好的农业生产传统和耕作条件，有利于发展规模农业，进行农村改革，另外地处平原，地势平坦，交通便利，因此，迁并新型村镇的自然阻力不大，适宜作为新型村镇相关问题的研究区。

47.3　数据标准与方法

村庄的规模可以简单分为人口规模和用地规模，本章中涉及的主要指标均是按人口规模计算，处理数据的标准为《河南省社会主义新农村村庄规划建设导则（最终稿-2006）》，《中华人民共和国国家标准镇规划标准（GB 50188—2007）》，计算中所涉及的数据来源于封丘县国土资源局、统计局和乡村实地调查数据。

47.3.1　人口数据处理

人口数据的计算重点在于确定三个产业的人口比例。主要是以农业人口的规模确定为主，剩余劳动力转向第二、三产业，并将转移的劳动力规划为非农业人口。在西方发达国家的工业化进程中，人口比例从以农业为主转向以城市人口为主，以美国为例，19世纪初，农业人口占全国人口的92.7%，20世纪50年代下降到15.3%，2007年又进一步下降到1.8%（彭卫兵和张晓敏，2010）。在我国经济发达的珠江三角洲地区，实际从事农业的劳动力比重逐年下降，由1979年的82%降至1995的25%（张敏和顾朝林，2002）。而在经济较为发达的苏中地区，2005年的农业从业人员年比重为34.44%（王丽娟等，2007）。2005年河南省的农业劳动力比例为66%；封丘县2005年农业从业人员占农村从业人员的72%。依照目前的生产力发展水平，将从业人口的30%作为农业从业人口足以完成各项农业生产，因此，在接下来的计算中，将鲁岗乡的农业劳动力比重定为30%，其余人口从事第二、第三产业。

47.3.2　民居问题处理

民居改造是新农村建设中的重点问题，由于传统的观念，新农村建设中农民最关注的就是民居的改造问题。现行新农村规划中，部分是以独院式住宅规划设计的，包括单排或是联排的别墅式民居，少数是多层或是高层的公寓式民居。前者是最理想的农村居住方式，也是农民最习惯的居住方式，但是不能最大可能地节约土地。公寓民居虽然能够节约更多土地，然而这种方式不符合我国农村几千年来的居住习惯，不仅会造成农民生活生产的不方便，还会造成农民的抵触情绪。新农村建设中实行合并新型村镇就是为了节约更多的土地资源，合理配置各种基础设施，鉴于这种情况，本章规划中宅民居和公寓民居结合的方式。

47.4　不同人口规模下新型村镇的指标对比

选取鲁岗乡为试点进行村庄合并，探讨适宜的新型村镇规模。计算标准采用《中华人民共和国国家标准镇规划标准（GB50188—2007）》、《河南省社会主义新农村村庄规划建设导则（豫建村镇［2006］3号）》的标准进行相关计算。另外本章在计算各项指标时未考虑人口增长因素，并且假设所有节约土地均能够整理为耕地。

47.4.1　规划方案

本章对新型村镇进行规划按照人口规模分为 4 种方案，方案一为 5000 人以下，方案二为 5000～10000 人，方案三为 10000～15000 人，方案四为 15000 人以上（表 47.1）。

表 47.1　规划方案

规划指标	规划方案			
	方案一	方案二	方案三	方案四
N 村庄个数/个	8	4	3	2
P 各种方案下现有新型村镇平均人数/人	4506	9010	12014	18020
P_l 各种方案下现有新型村镇从业人员/人	3028	6054	8072	12108
P_w 各种方案下现有新型村镇二、三产业从业人员/人	1142	2284	3046	4568
A_c 各种方案村庄面积/hm^2	8782	175.635	234.18	351.27
A_f 各种方案耕地面积/hm^2	573.19	1146.38	1528.51	2292.76
P_o 规划非农业人口/人	3596	7192	9592	14386
P_f 规划农业从业人员/人	910	1818	2422	3634
c_f 农业人口村庄面积/hm^2	10.91	21.81	29.05	43.59
h_o 规划非农人口住宅面积/hm^2	4.00	6.78	6.16	7.19
l_o 规划非农人口其他用地面积/hm^2	15.10	38.82	52.73	93.46
A_p 各种方案人均耕地面积/hm^2	0.13	0.13	0.13	0.13
a_c 规划后村庄面积/hm^2	30.02	67.4	87.94	144.24
a_s 节省面积/hm^2	57.80	108.23	146.24	207.03
a_f 规划后耕地面积/hm^2	630.99	1254.61	1674.74	2499.79
a_p 规划后人均耕地面积/hm^2	0.693	0.690	0.691	0.688

注：表中各个指标的计算方法如下，P＝总人口/N，P_l，P_w，A_c，A_f，A_p 数据来源于封丘县统计局调查数据；$P_f=P_l\times 30\%$；$P_o=P_l-P_f$；$c_f=P_f\times 120\text{m}^2$，其中，120m^2 为上文所述标准中的人均用地面积上限；$h_o=P_o\times 120\times l\div 7$，其中 l 为住宅占人均用地面积的百分比，本章按以上 4 种方案依次使用 65%，55%，45%，35%，非农人口住宅建设为 7 层多层住宅；$l_o=P_o\times 120\times(1-l)$；$a_c=c_f+h_o+l_o$，$a_s=A_c-a_c$；$a_f=A_f+a_s$；$a_p=a_f\div P_f$。

以家庭为单位实现农业的规模发展，一个重要的因素就是增加人均耕地面积，上述几种规划方案人均耕地面积均超过了 0.67hm^2，户均耕地将达 2～3.33hm^2，已经能达到实现农业规模发展的要求。此外，对于不再从事农业劳动的村民将统一作为非农人口，一方面为工业的发展提供充足的劳动力，另一方面也能加快我国的农村城镇化进程。

由于以上 4 种方案得出的人均耕地面积十分接近，仅从这个指标无法得出哪种规划方案更加适宜。因此，笔者从合并村村民意愿、农业的耕作半径、行政单元的适宜个数探讨较为合适的规划方案。由于农村的传统思想，多个行政村迁并为一个新型村镇不可避免会使村民产生抵触情绪，从生活在一个只有几百人的村庄变为几万人的村庄，这样的巨大差异会使农民产生较大的心理落差，也会增加新型村镇迁并的社会阻力。经过实地调查，村民对1万人左右或1万以下的新型村镇可以接受；就耕作半径来说，根据耕作半径的圆周模型：$NM=K\pi R^2$，式中，R 为耕作半径；N 为人口数；M 为人均耕地面积；K 为垦殖指数（金其铭，1989）。按照这一公式，上述4种方案的耕作半径如：①1.4km；②2.0km；③2.4km；④3km。实际调查中村民认为理想的耕作半径为出行时间小于20min，步行的一般速度为5km/h，所以耕作半径为1.7km最为理想，然而现在农村出行方式多种多样，所以综合多重因素，2.0 km的耕作半径亦在可以被接受的范围内。从行政单位的个数来看，封丘县总人口为74.5万，如果县城规划为20万人左右，其余人口合并为50个村镇左右基本就可以省去乡一级的行政机构，从而达到精简行政机构的目的。综合以上几个方面的原因，笔者认为1万人左右的新型村镇规模是较为适宜的。

47.4.2　规划结果

根据以上4种规划方案，对封丘县鲁岗乡进行规划，四种方案得出的各种指标见表47.2。

表 47.2　各种规划方案实际指标

规划指标	规划方案			
	方案一	方案二	方案三	方案四
村庄节省总面积/hm^2	559.59	530.01	505.62	470.87
规划后耕地总面积/hm^2	4380.64	4350.76	4322.59	4387.55
平均人均耕地面积/hm^2	0.61	0.60	0.60	0.61
平均耕作半径/km	1.60	2.05	2.40	2.91

实际规划结果与规划方案十分接近，只在平均耕地面积指标中比规划方案少了0.067hm^2左右，已经基本上能以农户为单位实行农业的规模经营。此外，考虑到村民意愿、耕作半径和行政单位个数等原因，得出1万人左右是新型村镇的适宜规模。表47.3给出了方案二中的各项指标，图47.2是按照方案进行规划后新建新型村镇布点情况。

表 47.3　方案二新型村镇各项指标

项目		新型村镇一	新型村镇二	新型村镇三	新型村镇四
现状指标	总人口/人	8377	8954	9734	7973
	总面积/hm^2	1235.91	1422.97	1404.16	1213.35
	耕地面积/hm^2	923.81	1031.18	1015.77	849.99
	村庄占地面积/hm^2	210.53	190.13	232.89	166.01

续表

项目		新型村镇一	新型村镇二	新型村镇三	新型村镇四
规划指标	人均耕地面积/hm^2	0.100	0.115	0.100	0.110
	规划村庄用地面积/hm^2	69.74	67.05	72.99	59.77
	规划村庄耕地面积/hm^2	1064.60	1154.26	1175.67	956.23
	规划人均耕地面积/hm^2	0.585	0.634	0.589	0.586

注：新型村镇一合并村庄为鲁岗、孙寨、后高士、祝店、白店、康寨、前鲁岗、东岗；新型村镇二合并村庄为朱村铺、黄寨、任寨、兴隆庄、邓寨、苌寨、东蒋寨、西蒋寨、东马庄、卷子箱、前高士庄、赵留横；新型村镇三合并村庄为和寨、齐寨、闫产角、西黄村营、郭产角、苌留横、刘留横；新型村镇四合并村庄为东黄村营、李四河、刘产角、罗罗文、陈罗文、徐罗文、周罗文、焦罗文、官庄。

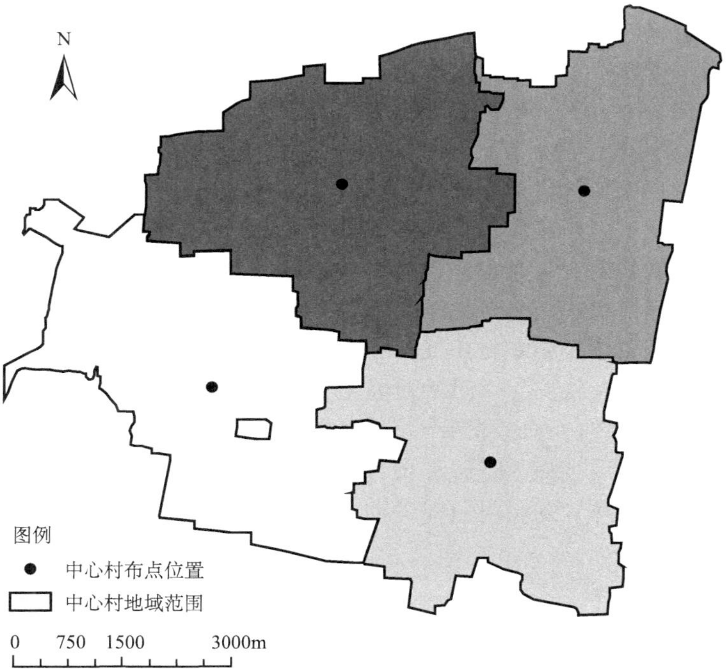

图 47.2　新建新型村镇村庄布点

47.5　结论与讨论

我国中部农村地区的发展既要借助工业化和城镇化的外部推力，又要发挥农村内部的力量，而新型村镇的建设一方面能够为乡村工业化和城镇化提供良好的环境，又能提高农民的生活质量，调动农民参与家园建设的积极性和主动性，是农区发展中内外力耦合的体现形式。

本章以确定新型村镇人口规模为主要研究对象，阐述了新型村镇的建设能够促进土地的节约集约利用，完善农村基础设施，实现规模农业，促进非农产业发展，推动农业产业结构调整，促进农业剩余劳动力就地转移，并且伴随着由农业人口转变为非农人口的过程，最终使得新型村镇人口人均资源增加，加快农村现代化进程。由前文分析可见，综合考虑人均耕地面积、基础设施利用效率、耕作半径、村民意愿、行政单元个数等因素，在我国中部农村地区，1 万人左右的人口规模是较为适宜的新型村镇规模。

处于自然条件较好的平原地区的村落，都有村庄规模小、数量多的特点，农村聚落合并的自然阻力小，由于自然条件的相似性，本章所得结论能在这些地区得到应用，尤其是在农户家庭经济在村域中占主要地位的农村地区，更容易得到实现。但是在自然条件与本章研究区不同的地区，本章结论未必能够直接使用，但是本章涉及的因素、原则和计算方法是具有一定的参考价值的，即依据村庄迁并的原则，在适宜的耕作半径、便于行政管理、满足农民意愿的前提下，尽可能地增加人均耕地面积，当这些因素处于平衡时，就是该地适宜的新型村镇人口规模。

从上述表格中可以看出，按照 1 万人规模建设新兴村镇能节约出 60%左右的土地。土地的节约主要就是来自于农村民居的统一规划、合理布局。从已经实施了农村聚落迁并的试点来看，节约的土地也都在 50%左右。因此，建设新型村镇要将民居土地整理作为重点对象，并且应当对居民点的布局问题进行深入研究。

本研究初步研究了新型村镇适宜规模问题，文中存在以下局限性，首先人口数据的计算中未考虑人口增长因素；其次假设在所有节省的土地都能作为耕地使用的前提下进行计算，但是在实际情况中由于自然条件等各方面因素，很难做到这一点。在新建村镇的选址问题上，只是选取了合并村庄几何中心为新建村镇的位置，没有考虑自然条件因素和现有村庄布点的实际情况。本章的研究主要基于耕地展开，对于土地整理综合指标没有多做考虑。深入研究的方向有两个：一是完善规划设计因素，使规划结果与实际更为接近；二是不同地形（平原、丘陵、山区、湖区等）、不同经济发展水平、不同城镇化水平下的新型村镇选择和新型村镇建设模式研究；三是进行新型村镇建设的具体措施研究。

参考文献

范德种. 2009. 新农村建设中中心村建设存在问题、模式及对策. 小城镇建设，(11)：68～72

冯健，刘玉. 2008. 江苏中小型集镇空间规划与乡村景观重构. 资源科学，30（5）：737～743

顾军，忻隽. 2008. 上海市中心村规划建设的实施难点与对策探讨. 小城镇建设，(zl)：91～93

国土资源部. 2009. 2008 年国土资源公报. 国土资源通讯，(7)：22～31

金其铭. 1989. 中国农村聚落地理. 南京：江苏科学技术出版社

李君，李小建. 2008. 河南中收入丘陵区村庄空心化微观分析. 中国人口·资源与环境，18（1）：170～175

李小建. 2009. 农户地理论. 北京：科学出版社

李小建. 2010. 中国中部农区发展研究. 北京：科学出版社

彭卫兵，张晓敏. 2010. 农村土地流转的再审视——以农村人多地少的基本矛盾为视角. 中国土地科学，24（1）：22～26

王丽娟，刘彦随，翟荣新. 2007. 苏中地区农村就业结构转换态势与机制分析. 中国人口·资源与环境，

17 (6)：135～138
吴九兴. 2009. 平原地区中心村选择的理论与实证研究——以孝感市孝南区为例. 武汉：华中农业大学
伍玥蓉. 2009. 基于可持续发展理念的中心村建设探析——以江苏省淮安市蒋桥中心村为例. 中国市场，(22)：70～71
徐全勇. 2000. 国外乡村中心村建设探讨. 小城镇建设，(2)：69～70
徐全勇. 2005. 上海浦东新区中心村的发展模式研究. 农村经济，(6)：77～80
杨山. 2002. 发达地区的乡村集镇空间扩展差异与模型研究——以锡山市为例. 人文地理，17 (1)：89～92
张敏，顾朝林. 2002. 农村城市化："苏南模式"与"珠江模式"比较研究. 经济地理，22 (4)：482～486
郑晔，佘欢. 2009. 农村现代化的发展趋势及其现实选择. 社会科学研究，(6)：28～33

第 48 章　近百年农村聚落空间格局演变

21 世纪是城镇化的世纪（UN-Habitat，2008）。城镇化是伴随工业化发展，非农产业在城镇集聚、农村人口向城镇集中的自然历史过程，是人类社会发展的客观趋势，是国家现代化的标志（新华社，2014）。中国在快速城镇化进程中，提出新型城镇化构想。新型城镇化摒弃“城市偏向”和“忽视乡村”的发展思维，既包含对中国过去城镇化道路经验教训的总结，也包含对西方城镇化过程中出现问题的思考和规避，更包含对未来城镇化前景的新设想，是对我国城镇化模式的新构思（李小建，2014）。本质上，新型城镇化并不单单是农村人口向城镇的转移，而应该是全面整合城乡聚落体系，使大小不同、功能差别、环境各异的各类聚落，形成统一和谐的整体（李小建和罗庆，2014）。在全球化和新型城镇化大背景下，科学合理的城市发展格局是建设美丽中国和美丽城乡的空间载体（方创琳，2013）。

当今中国社会正由城乡二元结构转变为由城乡之间、城镇之间、城市内部三重二元结构相互叠加的多元结构（魏后凯，2014）。政府主导的城镇化推进模式充分体现了中国的制度创新和制度灵活性（李强等，2012）。政府主导推进城镇化快速发展的过程中，尊重自然、延续历史，充分考虑对几千年来形成的人居环境和农村聚落格局的承继非常重要。在此背景下，研究具有长期居住历史地区的聚落演变特征，弄清不同经济条件、不同地形环境对这种聚落格局演变的影响具有特殊意义。河南省巩义市是中华文明的发源地之一，具有长期的居民居住及生活历史，又经历近几十年的快速城镇化发展。本章选取该市（县级市）为案例，利用 1929～2013 年的聚落数据对聚落规模变化进行实证，以为未来县域聚落演变提供参考。

48.1　文献评述

乡村聚落是乡村地区人类各种形式的居住场所，指除城市以外所有村庄和自然集镇，本章中包含县域内所有类型居民点，即县城、镇、集市、行政村、自然村等。

48.1.1　聚落等级规模

齐夫（Zipf）较早地提出了城市体系中城市位序与人口规模之间服从幂律指数为 1 的关系（Zipf，1949），并成为刻画城市规模分布的著名经验定律。之后，引发大量学者对城市位序-规模进行理论和实证探索。一些研究表明，跨国家（Soo，2005，2014）、国家和地区（Giesen and Suedekum，2011；Rozenfeld et al.，2011）的城镇等级规模均不同程度地服从齐夫定律。具有长时段居住历史中国的城镇在国家和区域尺度上（Ye and Xie，2012）服从齐夫定律。也有研究认为，齐夫定律只是一种特殊形式（Berry and Kozaryn，2012）。在更大的样本上城镇分布则不遵循齐夫定律（Val，

2010)。甚至有学者认为，实际的城市规模分布应该服从“双帕累托对数正态分布”，而非齐夫定律反映简单对数正态分布（Giesen et al.，2010)。总的来说，齐夫指数和分形维数具有重要的实践意义，相关研究有利于正确把握城市规模（人口或用地规模）分布的规律和预测城市的发展规模（谈明洪和范存会，2004)。

48.1.2　聚落空间结构

20 世纪 30 年代克里斯泰勒在研究聚落空间分布时提出中心地理论，用以解释德国南部的聚落空间格局（克里斯泰勒，1998)。但主要用于解释零售业、服务业等的空间分布，而不能对工业主导城市的规模分布给出合理的解释（沈体雁和劳昕，2012)。基于对成都平原的研究，进一步表明乡村聚落是“基层市场共同体”（施坚雅，1998)。在众多研究的基础上，陆大道认为农业经济占绝对优势阶段符合杜能农业区位论中的空间结构，由农业经济向工业化的过渡阶段符合克里斯泰勒的中心地等级体系结构，工业化中期阶段以发展轴线和城镇居民点形成“点-轴”空间结构，工业化后期及后工业化阶段集聚降低和均衡化作用明显，等级-规模曲线重新平缓（陆大道，1998)。

48.1.3　聚落区位环境

近代之前，自然环境对聚落选址和规模起决定作用，随着社会发展，经济结构改变聚落结构（Elvin and Skinner，1974)。中国经济改革促使乡村居民点的转变（Long et al.，2009)，外部环境和聚落内居民居住偏好的改变形成“空心村”（刘彦随等，2009)。不同村庄“居住场势”的非均衡性是推动农户搬迁的基本背景。随着农户由低“居住场势”村庄向高“居住场势”村庄移动，农户在迁入村庄获取了更多的居住空间效用，空间扩展表现出较为明显的区位集中指向（李小建，2009；李君和陈长瑶，2010)。

综上所述，第一，城市等级规模在理论和实证上均做了大量的工作，但对农区聚落长时期的演变及特点研究成果不多。第二，聚落空间结构在不同的发展阶段有不同表现，中国快速城镇化过程中这种变化也会有特殊表现。第三，聚落区位演变研究多关注短期变化，而对长时段和快速城镇化发展期的规律挖掘不够。长期历史发展形成的聚落格局，有着深刻的历史继承性，是未来城市发展不可忽视的历史基础（郑衡泌，2010)。城镇是聚落的形式之一，如果将视野扩大到所有聚落，其等级规模演变过程如何？相关的研究成果较少。鉴于此，本章侧重研究在快速城镇化过程中，乡村聚落等级规模是否遵从 Zipf 规则？或者本身就是动态、自组织的多尺度分形，并遵循新的位序-规模规律？长时段来看，其演变趋势如何？在空间上，应体现何种格局？聚落调整中，如何关注传统聚落中人地关系的承继？

48.2　研究区及数据处理

48.2.1　研究区概况

巩义市（原巩县）隶属于河南省郑州市，位于东经 112°49′～113°17′，北纬 34°31′～

34°52′，西距洛阳市 76km，东距郑州市 82km（图 48.1）。总面积为 $1041km^2$，其中，山地占 25%，丘陵占 60%，平原占 15%。从南部的嵩山高地逐渐向北部的伊洛河冲积平原过渡，许多河流自东南流向西北的冲积平原，最后汇入伊洛河。现辖 15 个镇、5 个街道办事处、2 个园区管委会、290 个行政村、33 个社区居民委员会、2843 个村民小组。2010 年被确立为河南 10 个省直管试点县市之一，是综合改革试点县市、乡村城市化试点县市。2013 年，巩义市生产总值为 581.2 亿元，户籍总人口为 827721 人，城镇化率为 49.06%，城镇居民人均可支配收入为 22516 元，农民人均纯收入为 13951 元。

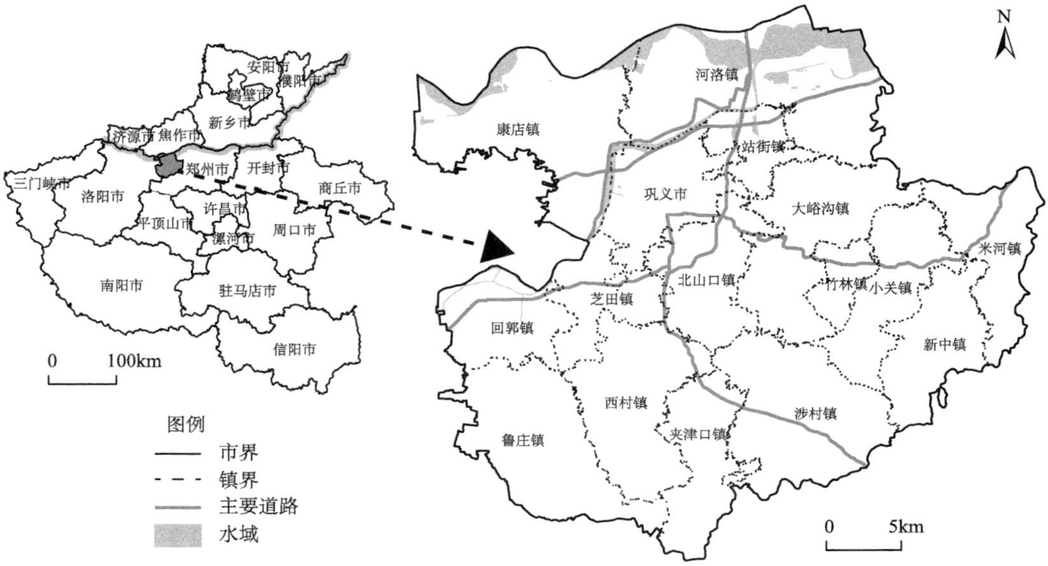

图 48.1　巩义市的区位

巩义作为中国乡镇工业的发源地之一，半个世纪乡镇企业的蓬勃发展深刻地改变了聚落的传统特征（海贝贝等，2013）。选取巩义市研究聚落具有如下意义：①巩义是华夏文明发祥地之一，聚落产生历史悠久，长期的发展过程使其有时间逐渐减缓“偶然因素”的影响。②巩义地处第二阶梯与第三阶梯过渡地带，具有山地、丘陵、平原地形，适宜考察地理环境对聚落的影响。③巩义是京广线以西地区经济实力强县之一，近代以来工业化带动城镇化，对农村聚落影响较大。④巩义资料数据较为齐全，历史上巩义曾八次修志，成书七部。如果把它与现代数据相衔接，可构成中国县域范围历史延续较长、质量较高的历史数据序列。

48.2.2　数据来源及处理

本章数据来源于以下几个部分：①1929 年人口数据来源于《民国二十六年巩县志》（河南省巩县志编纂委员会，1989）。②1990 年、2000 年、2010 年与 2013 年的人口数据均来源于对应年份的统计年鉴。③其余统计数据主要参考《1991 年巩县志》，以及各乡镇志和村志。④空间数据主要来自于巩义市 1990 年、2010 年、2013 年土地利用类型矢量化地图。⑤1975 年聚落面积数据由 1975 年 1∶5 万地形图提取。在研究中对空间数据进行预处理，实现村名与空间位置的对接，将所有数据进行空间配准。需要说明的是，鉴于 1975 年人口数据的缺失，分析中以聚落面积代替，经同一年份数据验证，这种代替不会产生太大偏差。需要指出的是，除非特别指明，本章未对村庄规模进行限制，以巩县志和巩义市统计年鉴中的村庄为分析单元。另外，2010 年与 2013 年巩义市城区的人口为 5 个街道办事处数据的加总。

48.3　聚落规模变化

城市规模一直是经济学家和各级政府关注的焦点（魏后凯，2014）。齐夫指数可以较好地刻画城市规模分布，分形维数可以用来解释其分布规律（谈明洪和范存会，2004），基尼系数也可描述其规模差异（陈彦光和刘继生，1999）。

48.3.1　齐夫指数偏小但增长加快

齐夫提出了城市位序与人口规模之间服从的经验关系（Zipf，1949），经过不断地完善，形成如下城市规模与其位序的关系表达式：

$$P_i = P_1 r^{-q} \tag{48.1}$$

式中，P_1 为城市体系中城市规模由高到低逆序排列的首位城市人口规模；P_i 为 i 位城市的人口规模；r 为城市 i 的位序；q 为幂指数。

通过对位序-规模两边均取对数，表达式转化为

$$\ln P_i = \ln P_1 - q\ln r \tag{48.2}$$

式中，r 表示某城市在城市系统中的位序；P_i 表示位序为 i 的城市人口规模；P_1 在理论上为首位城市人口；q 为齐夫指数，其大小用以衡量城市规模分布的均衡程度。$q=1$，符合位序-规模的齐夫定律；$q>1$，直线斜率较大，表示大聚落在体系中占优势；$0<q<1$，直线斜率平缓，表示城市规模分布较为均匀，即较低位次的中小城市较多，较高位次的大城市不很突出。

对于聚落发展历史较长的区域，城镇聚落体系的规模分布基本上符合位序-规模规律（王法辉，1989）。由于城镇是聚落的特殊形式，本章将齐夫指数引申，用以表示城镇化过程中县域聚落的位序-规模变化。根据式（48.2），对巩义市相关数据进行处理，利用 OLS 线性方程分别拟合各年份数据得出图 48.2～图 48.7。

从总体上看：①齐夫指数偏小。各年份齐夫指数均<1，最大值仅为 0.7206，均小于城市和城市群的齐夫指数（Soo，2014；Giesen and Suedekum，2011；Rozenfeld et al.，2011），也小于中国城市规模的齐夫指数（Ye and Xie，2012）。反映了农区聚落中较低位次的中小聚落较多，大聚落发育不突出。②齐夫指数增长率加快。84 年间齐夫指数整体上呈增长趋势，且逐渐趋近于 1，而且，1990 年后的齐夫指数增长明显加快（表 48.1）。齐夫指数 2010 年达到最大，1990 年齐夫指数比 1929 年增加 0.0251，增加

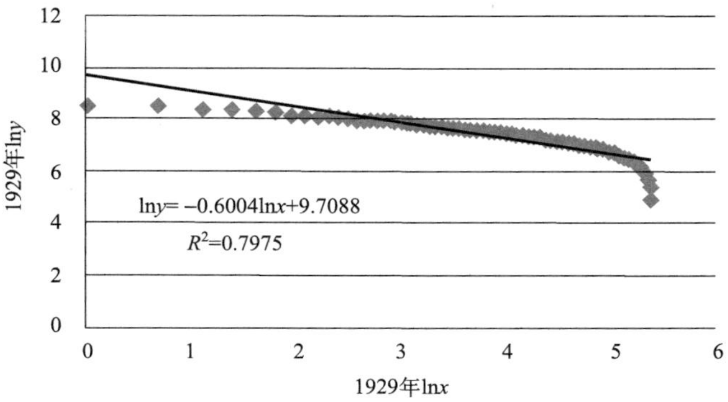

图 48.2　1929 年聚落位序-规模模型

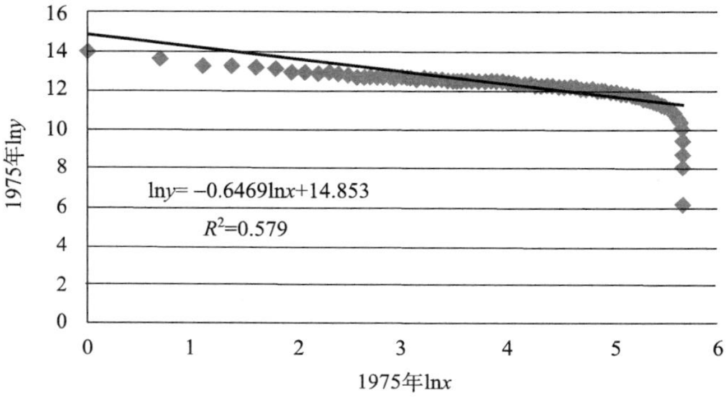

图 48.3　1975 年聚落位序-规模模型

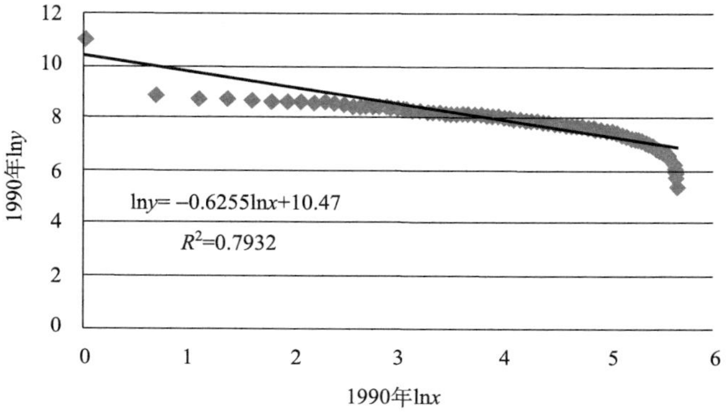

图 48.4　1990 年聚落位序-规模模型

率为 0.411‰/年；而 2010 年比 1990 年增加 0.0951，增加率为 9.51‰/年。后者的增加率是前者的 23.14 倍，说明 20 世纪 90 年代后城镇化速度大大加快，聚落排序越靠前，聚落规模增加的速度越快。③实际值小于理论值。除首位聚落之外，前几位聚落的分布

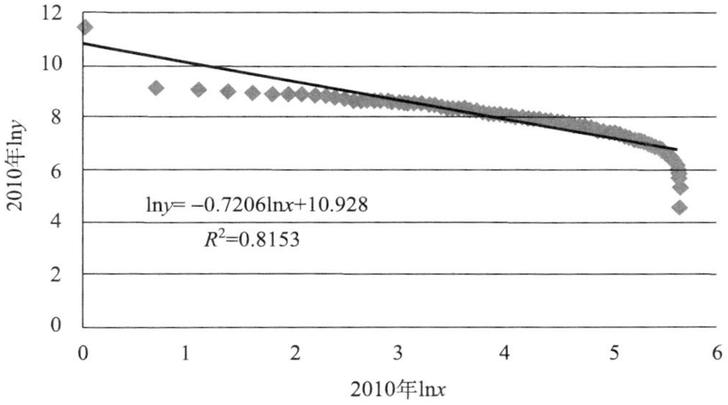

图 48.5　2010 年聚落位序-规模模型

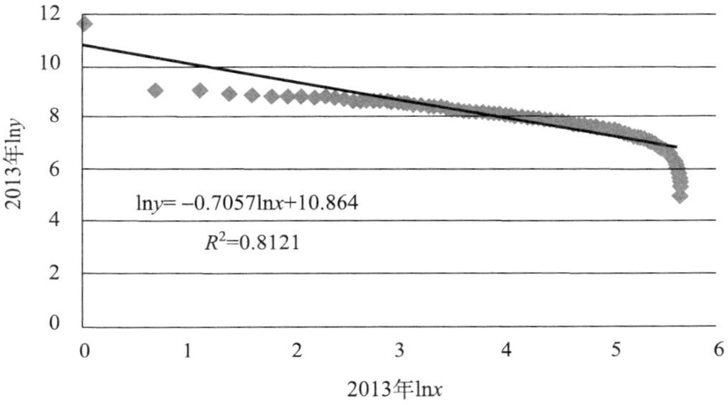

图 48.6　2013 年聚落位序-规模模型

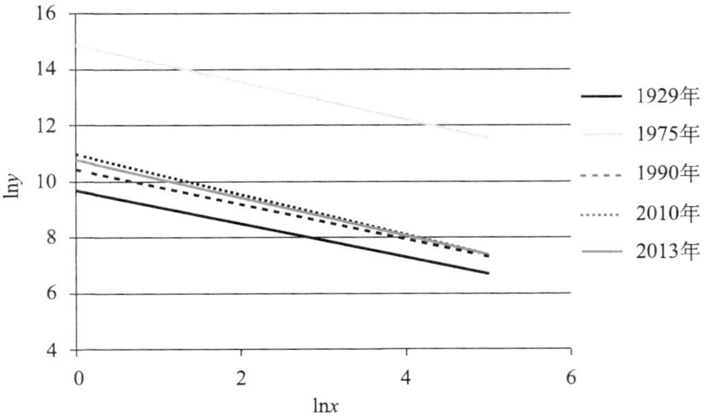

图 48.7　各年的齐夫指数函数

均位于拟合曲线下方，与拟合的理论值相比偏小，说明高位序聚落的人口规模还有增长的空间。而首位聚落实际值大于理论值，在农区城镇化中值得进一步关注研究。④聚落位序-规模曲线随时间而向外推移（图 48.7），这与城市位序-规模演化趋势相一致（Val，2010）。从各年份来看：①1929 年的高位序聚落与之后的聚落之间规模差别不大，具有平稳过渡关系，表明整个聚落系统具有农村聚落的特征。②1975 年位序-规模曲线斜率远远在 2010 年与 2013 年之上，隐含着“土地城镇化”快于“人口城镇化”，建设用地粗放低效，建成区人口密度偏低。③1975 年聚落的实际值小于模型的拟合值，而 1990 年实际值均大于拟合值。而之后拟合值与实际值差距越来越大，更说明了城镇化正处于加速阶段，这与其他关于中国县域城镇化的研究相吻合（刘彦随和杨忍，2012）。④2013 年模型曲线分布在 2010 年之下，齐夫指数有所降低，位序-规模曲线有所下移（表 48.1）。这与在聚落规模分布的演化过程中，聚落规模不均匀程度先增后减的趋势一致（Li and Sui，2013）。分析发现，除了市政府所在城区人口增加之外，其他高等级聚落的人口均有所下降。中等级聚落人口增加，低等级聚落的人口越过中高等级聚落直接向首位的市城区“跃迁”，同时也出现高等级聚落的人口向最高等级的市城区外流的现象。

表 48.1　线性模型中不同年份的齐夫指数

项目	1929 年	1975 年	1990 年	2010 年	2013 年
样本量	218	288	297	295	290
齐夫指数	0.6004	0.6469	0.6255	0.7206	0.7057

需要注意的是，已有研究认为，双对数线性函数的齐夫指数对样本选择极度敏感（Guerin-Pace，1995），用以拟合聚落位序-规模是有偏差的，具有截尾效应（Li and Sui，2013）。大量的聚落处于曲线的右端，而左端的聚落稀疏且形成明显的点状不连续分布，存在明显的“翘尾”现象。仅线性模型不能深刻揭示位序与规模之间的关系，本质上应存在非线性关系，可以加入二次项解决（Rosen and Resnick，1980）。引入双对数变换后的二次项函数为

$$\ln y = c + a\ln x + b(\ln x)^2 + u \tag{48.3}$$

式中，y 为聚落由大到小排列的规模；x 为聚落由高到低排列的次序；a、b 分别为 $\ln x$ 的一次项与二次项的系数；c 为常数；u 为误差项。利用 Stata 软件分别拟合各年份数据。

各年份表达式如下：

1929 年：$\ln y = 8.0053 + 0.4739\ln x - 0.1492\ (\ln x)^2$

1975 年：$\ln y = 12.4486 + 0.7573\ln x - 0.1819\ (\ln x)^2$

1990 年：$\ln y = 8.9207 + 0.2699\ln x - 0.1155\ (\ln x)^2$

2010 年：$\ln y = 9.2889 + 0.2284\ln x - 0.1226\ (\ln x)^2$

2013 年：$\ln y = 9.3678 + 0.1648\ln x - 0.1129\ (\ln x)^2$

从表 48.2 中可以看出，采用二次项函数后，函数均表现出稳定的非线性关系，且均通过了显著性检验。“位序-规模”的对数回归中二次项在统计上显著，不仅 F 值与 R^2 更大，且实际拟合效果均更好，二次项模型要优于线性模型。这与已有文献的研究结论较为一致（Black and Henderson，2003）。聚落的位序与规模之间存在正向影响，但位序的二次项对规模产生负向影响，即存在着驱动力与耗散力的竞争，并且二次项的

耗散力大于单次项的驱动力，总体上实现了聚落规模随排序的降低而增加。这可能是由不同聚落之间的竞争和替代作用造成的。

表 48.2　不同年份的二次回归模型

年份	模型参数	Coef	a	b	样本数	F 值	R^2	Adj R^2
1929	系数	8.0053***	0.4739***	−0.1492***	218	1037.17	0.9061	0.9052
	Std. Err.	0.1252	0.0696	0.0094				
	t	63.93	6.81	−15.77				
1975	系数	12.4486***	0.7543***	−0.1819***	288	313.38	0.6874	0.6852
	Std. Err.	0.2767	0.1437	0.0183				
	t	45.00	5.25	−9.94				
1990	系数	8.9207***	0.2699***	−0.1155***	297	885.20	0.8576	0.8566
	Std. Err.	0.1535	0.0792	0.0100				
	t	58.11	3.41	−11.53				
2010	系数	9.2889***	0.2284***	−0.1226***	295	990.00	0.8715	0.8706
	Std. Err.	0.1659	0.0857	0.0109				
	t	56.00	2.67	−11.29				
2013	系数	9.3678***	0.1648***	−0.1129*	290	891.72	0.8614	0.8604
	Std. Err.	0.1695	0.0879	0.0112				
	t	55.26	1.87	−10.10				

* 表示检验在 10%的水平上显著，** 表示检验在 5%的水平上显著，*** 表示检验在 1%的水平上显著。

48.3.2　分形维数偏大但降速加快

聚落等级具有明显的分形特征（刘继生和陈彦光，2003）。理论上，聚落规模分布的分形维数和齐夫维数的乘积等于 1，但如果是 OLS 估计所得，两者的乘积应等于判定系数（R^2）（谈明洪和范存会，2004），即聚落位序-规模的分形维数表达式为

$$D = R^2/q \tag{48.4}$$

式中，q 为齐夫指数；R^2 为 OLS 回归估计的判定系数。

从表 48.3 中可以看出，因分形维数与齐夫指数的换算关系，其表现出与齐夫指数相反的趋势。如果去除聚落面积所表示聚落规模的 1975 年，以人口数量反映的聚落规模的分形维数在 1929～2010 年有降低的趋势。这与近代以来西方工业化国家的城市位序-规模的长时段趋势相一致（Roehner，1991），但分维值相对偏大。1929～1990 年的分形维数共降低 0.0602，降低率仅为 0.9868‰/年，而 2010 年比 1990 年降低 0.1367，降低率达 13.67‰/年。2010 年前，聚落的分形维数降低加快，规模越大的聚落其规模增加越快，中小聚落发展较慢，从而整体体系等级差异增加，聚落规模分布趋于集中。2013 年的分形维数有轻微的增加，与改革开放后短时期内中国城市位序-规模的分维值随时间增加的结论相一致（谈明洪和吕昌河，2003）。从理论上讲，分形维数方向的改

变可能意味着聚落体系时空演变的相变（刘继生和陈彦光，2003）。产生这种情况的原因可能是城市规模（主要以人口为指标）有门槛值，而县域聚落属于自然村落，其人口受外界干预较少且规模过小。只有当乡村聚落人口增长到一定程度，才能表现出与城市聚落一样的分形规律。

表 48.3　不同年份的分形维数

项目	1929 年	1975 年	1990 年	2010 年	2013 年
分形维数 $D=R^2/q$	1.3283	0.8950	1.2681	1.1314	1.1508

48.3.3　基尼系数较小但增加明显

基尼系数常用来衡量一个国家或区域的居民收入差距的指标。同样，一个国家或区域的聚落因为历史基础、区位优势、经济社会发展水平等条件的影响，聚落之间也必然产生分化，可以用基尼系数衡量聚落规模的集散程度（王颖等，2011）。基尼系数（G）的简化表达式为

$$G=1-\frac{1}{n}\left(2\sum_{i=1}^{n-1}W_i+1\right) \tag{48.5}$$

式中，W_i 为第 1 组累计到第 i 组的人口（或面积）规模占全部人口（或面积）的百分比；G 为 0～1。当所有的聚落人口规模都一样大时，$G=0$，这时聚落体系中聚落规模达到最大的分散程度；当聚落规模集中于一个聚落时，$G=1$。一般来讲，基尼系数越小，聚落规模分布越分散；越接近 1，聚落规模差异越大。一般认为基尼系数在 0.6 以上表示城市规模分布极不平衡（王颖等，2011）。

从表 48.4 中可以看出：①基尼系数相对较小。至 2013 年，基尼系数仅 0.4585，相对于有的研究认为城市的基尼系数在 0.5～0.6 之间（王颖等，2011），巩义聚落规模的基尼系数相对较小。②基尼系数值逐渐增加。随着时间的推移，巩义聚落规模的基尼系数增加的趋势较为明显，拉大了聚落人口规模的差距，说明聚落分化明显，较大的聚落数量增长和大的聚落规模在进一步增大。③基尼系数的增长率加速。1929～1990 年仅增加了 0.0511，增长率为 0.84‰/年；1990～2010 年增加了 0.0649，增长率达 6.49‰/年，后者是前者增长率的 7.73 倍。反映了 20 世纪 90 年代后，农区城镇化的加速发展。

表 48.4　不同年份的基尼系数

系数	1929 年	1975 年	1990 年	2010 年	2013 年
基尼系数	0.3385	0.3449	0.3896	0.4545	0.4585

48.4　聚落的空间格局演变与机制分析

聚落演变主要受自然环境、区位和社会经济等因素的影响，其中，自然环境限制了

聚落的基本格局与演变方向。依据高程（DEM）可按<200m、200～500m、>500m 划分为山区、丘陵、平原 3 类地形（图 48.8）。通过 ArcGIS10.0 把村庄进行配比，按人口（人）和面积（m^2）划分等级（图 48.9～图 48.13）。其中，人口以<2000、2000～4000、4000～6000、6000～8000、>8000 分别划分为Ⅴ级、Ⅳ级、Ⅲ级、Ⅱ级、Ⅰ级 5 个等级（其中，1929 年最大值为回郭镇，其人口达 5460 人，没有 6000～8000、>8000 两个等级）。1975 年聚落面积（m^2）以<150000m^2、150000～30000m^2、300000～450000m^2、450000～600000m^2、>600000m^2 也分别划分为Ⅴ级、Ⅳ级、Ⅲ级、Ⅱ级、Ⅰ级 5 个等级。对该空间数据可做如下分析。

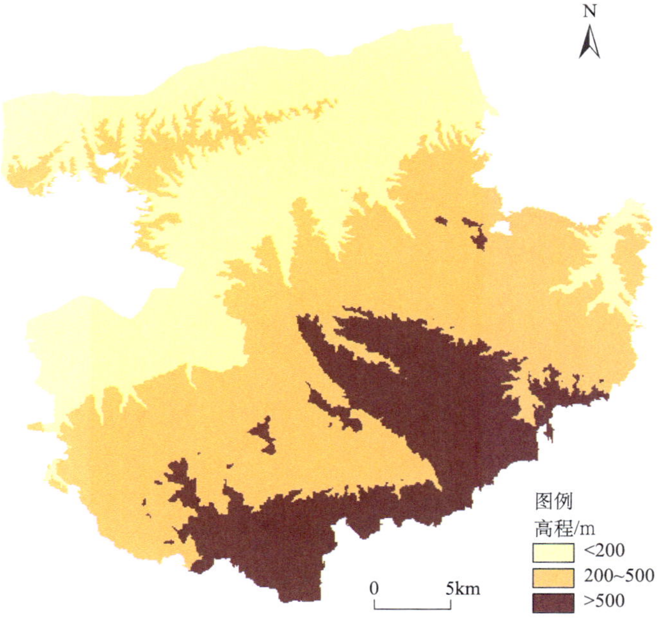

图 48.8 巩义市的 DEM

48.4.1 沿河线状格局变化

在农业社会，区域中心聚落往往位于主要支流与干流的交汇处（陆玉麒，2002）。巩义古县城（公元 386～1964 年）位于站街镇老城村，离西泗河与洛河交界处不足 2.5km。近 1500 年一直是全县的政治、经济、文化的中心。除县城之外，沿岸依赖优越的农业条件发展了许多大聚落。20 世纪 20 年代，全县人口排名前 10 的聚落 9 个位于洛河河谷平原地带；丘陵区西南、东南各有 8 个Ⅳ级聚落；山区仅有 9 个Ⅴ级聚落。随着乡村工业化的推进，聚落功能变化，工业与农业分离并向城镇集中，聚落增加了工业生产职能，加剧了聚落之间的分化。矿产开发在丘陵区兴起新的中心聚落、高等级聚落，如米河、小关、涉村等脱颖而出，而平原区的洛口镇、芝田镇、康店、南河渡等则

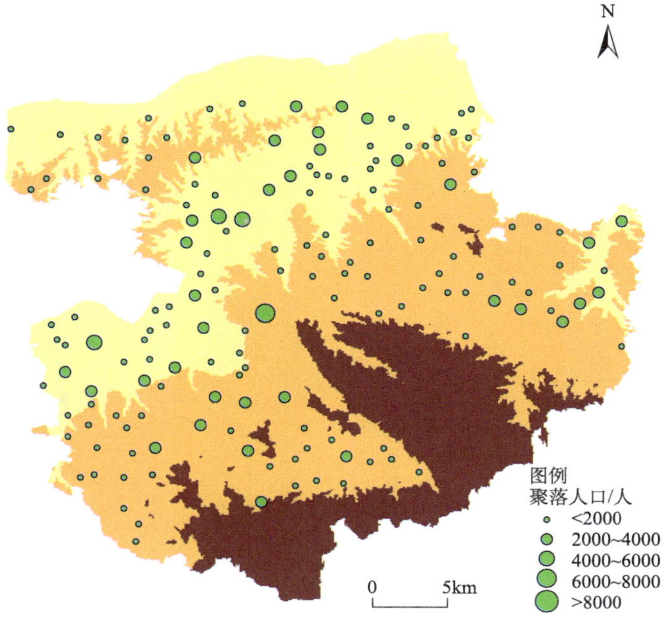

图 48.9　1929 年聚落等级

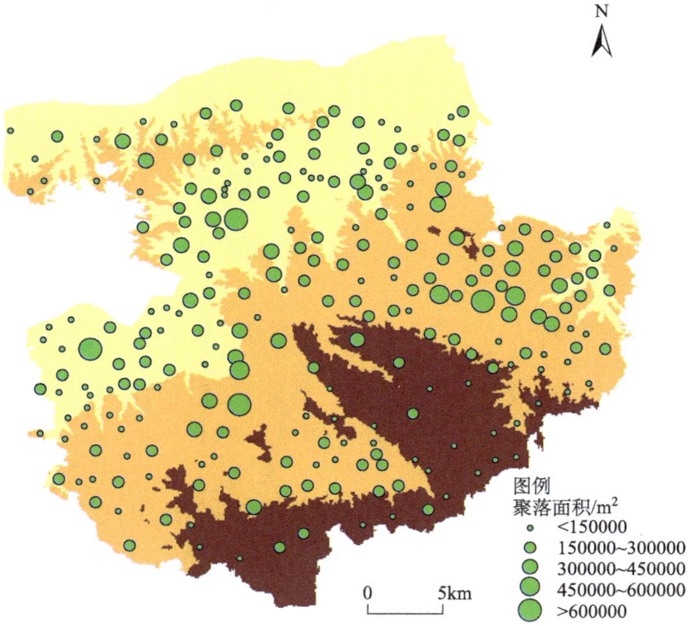

图 48.10　1975 年聚落等级

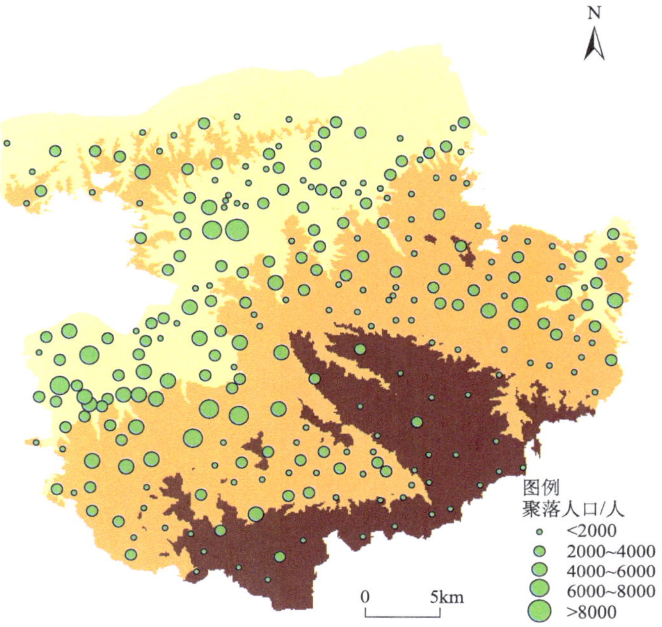

图 48.11　1990 年聚落等级

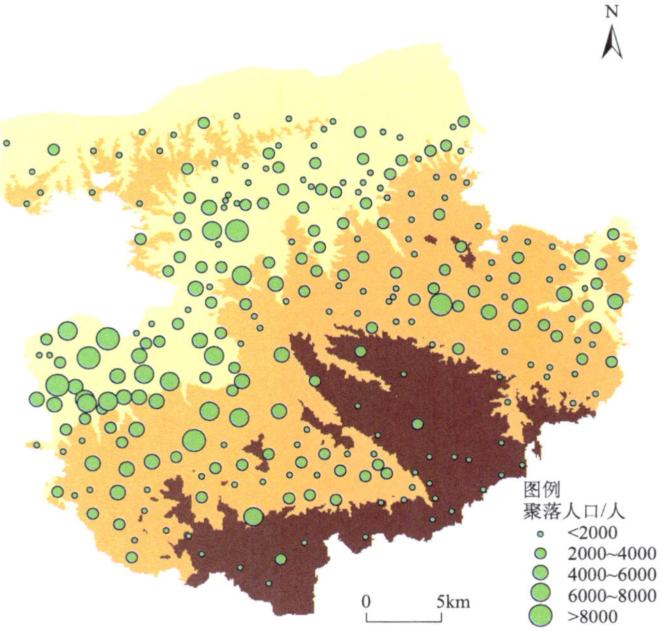

图 48.12　2010 年聚落等级

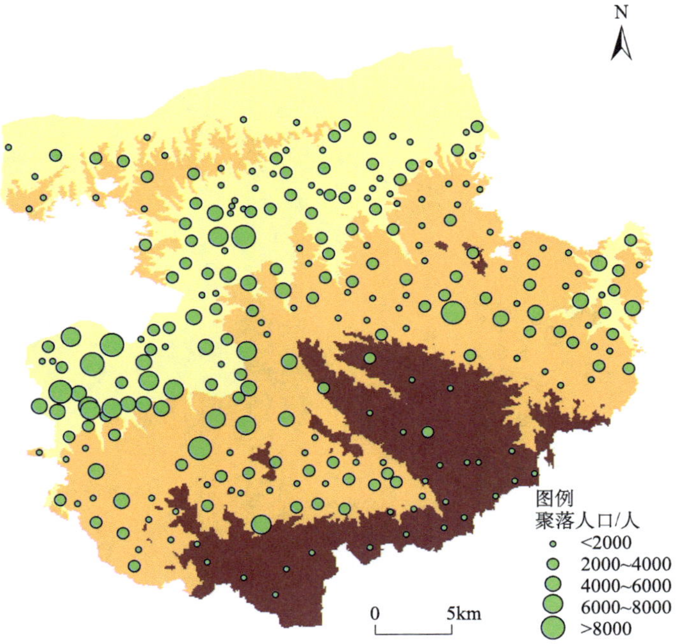

图 48.13　2013 年聚落等级

相对衰落。至 1975 年，丘陵区已各有Ⅰ级、Ⅱ级聚落，Ⅲ级聚落从 1 个跃增到 13 个；山区聚落仍停留在低等级别（表 48.5、图 48.1、图 48.9～图 48.13）。1990 年以来，海拔较高的山区一些村落加速消亡（安乾等，2014），聚落人口在平原与丘陵地区更加集中（李小建，2009；李君和陈长瑶，2010）。随着扶贫开发、生态移民、工程移民等，山区小聚落大都迁离（许家伟和乔家君，2009），更加剧了在平原、丘陵集聚的趋势，平原、丘陵的Ⅰ级聚落分别达 4 个和 3 个，而山区缺失Ⅲ级以上的高等级聚落。几千年农业社会形成的"沿河线状"的空间格局发生了重大改变。

表 48.5　不同地形的等级分布

地形	等级	1929 年	1975 年	1990 年	2010 年	2013 年
平原	Ⅰ级	0	2	1	4	4
	Ⅱ级	0	1	3	9	8
	Ⅲ级	3	12	13	16	15
	Ⅳ级	20	49	57	43	48
	Ⅴ级	54	42	35	42	37

续表

地形	等级	1929 年	1975 年	1990 年	2010 年	2013 年
丘陵	Ⅰ级	0	2	0	2	3
	Ⅱ级	0	2	3	3	3
	Ⅲ级	1	13	12	11	8
	Ⅳ级	14	54	45	49	46
	Ⅴ级	68	54	76	72	69
山区	Ⅰ级	0	0	0	0	0
	Ⅱ级	0	0	0	0	0
	Ⅲ级	0	1	0	0	0
	Ⅳ级	0	8	5	4	3
	Ⅴ级	9	19	28	26	27
总计	—	169	259	278	281	270

注：因空间配准原因，聚落数量与统计数据存在差别，但缺少的样本基本上均为小聚落，对分析结果影响不大。

48.4.2　网络等级结构形成

矿产资源开发、现代交通发展、经济联系加强和交流空间扩大，形成了大量的采矿点、乡村集镇、农副产品加工中心、工业中心和镇级行政中心。随着人口的增加，巩义的聚落数量不断增加，1990 年达 297 个，61 年增加了 79 个（表 48.6）。聚落人口平均规模从 1929 年的 1426 人/个，提升至 2013 年的 2854 人/个。最大聚落人口，从 1929 年的 5460 人跃升至 2013 年的 122603 人，增幅达 22.5 倍。从人口规模上看，1990 年之前没有Ⅰ级聚落，城镇化进程缓慢。随着中国城镇化的快速推进，2010 年Ⅰ级聚落猛然增加到 5 个，Ⅱ级聚落也增加到 12 个。2013 年，Ⅰ级聚落对低等级聚落均产生了巨大的“虹吸”作用，甚至Ⅱ级与Ⅲ级聚落也分别下降了 2 个和 1 个，产生了人口越过中等聚落直接向高等聚落聚集的现象，预示着聚落规模-位序变动方式的改变。在此过程中，聚落等级从 3 个等级成长为 5 个等级。聚落等级结构从 1929 年的“1∶6∶29”演变到 2013 年的“1∶2∶5∶20∶29”，考虑到自然村的大量存在、市城区周边小聚落和山区小聚落的归并等因素，前者近似于行政原则形成 $k=7$ 的“1∶6∶42”，而后者与市场原则形成 $k=3$ 的“1∶2∶6∶18∶54”类似。体现了相对隔绝的地区聚落分布符合行政原则，而开放经济中更趋于市场原则的中心地等级结构（克里斯泰勒，1998）。单户聚落成长为村落，进而分化出集、镇、城等，大聚落的形成与发展，使空间结构出现显著的不平衡，最终形成了“县城—镇—中心村—行政村—自然村”等级结构鲜明的网络结构。在此系统中，市政府所在城区是区域核心，河流及交通线形成轴线，各镇区构成网络系统，其他聚落组成外围空间，形成 5 级聚落规模等级。

表 48.6　不同年份的等级分布

等级	1929 年	1975 年	1990 年	2010 年	2013 年
Ⅰ级	0	4	1	5	5
Ⅱ级	0	2	6	12	10
Ⅲ级	6	28	25	27	26
Ⅳ级	40	119	113	100	103
Ⅴ级	172	134	151	150	144
总数	218	287	296	294	288

48.4.3　核心聚落转移替代

行政中心一般是在区域起核心作用的聚落，行政中心的变换可导致聚落地位的更替，出现老行政核心聚落的相对衰落与新行政中心的迅猛扩张（魏后凯，2014）。在研究期内，县城（县治）出现了 3 次替代：①从老城到站街镇。进入近现代社会以后，水运地位下降，而铁路、公路等地位明显上升，成为交通联系的主要方式。同时，由于黄河大堤逐步抬高，水患的影响已经严重影响了老城作为县城的地位。1927 年县城从老城迁往站街镇。②从站街镇到孝义镇。由于地形影响，站街镇无足够的扩展空间，1946 年 10 月，站街城区面积仅有约 0.5km^2，且地处县域东北部，交通不便，不利于县域的治理（河南省巩县志编纂委员会，1989）。孝义镇位置靠近中部，建有兵工厂等现代企业（1937 年仅兵工厂就有工人 4452 人，职员 210 人，合计 4662 人，此外，还有几千名学徒工、小工、临时工，如果加上驻厂的警卫人员，员工总人数在 1.2 万人左右（河南省巩县志编纂委员会，1989），1964 年县政府迁入孝义镇，形成巩义新的中心镇。③从孝义镇到新城。城镇化的快速推进，巩义市城区的扩张加快，产城融合的推进加速，2012 年城区常住人口已达 11.6 万人，《巩义新城规划》中新城区位居老城区以东，巩义市四大班子及 21 个行政单位已经入驻办公。与此同时，其他核心聚落也完成了转换。20 世纪 40 年代，随着向南公路开通，涉村逐渐取代芝田成为南山区的商品集散地；小关为东山区的平坦地带，且交通方便，集市渐兴，形成东站镇、孝义镇、回郭镇、米河镇、小关、涉村六大商业中心。随着工业化和城镇化的推进，丘陵区相继设立了竹林镇、涉村镇、小关镇、大峪沟镇、北山口镇等，而平原区的城镇，如鲁庄镇、康店镇等，还有原来兴盛的运河城镇，如河洛镇、南河渡镇逐渐丧失优势，甚至在新的行政区划调整中撤销或合并，如河洛镇与南河渡镇合并成为河洛镇。因此，核心聚落随着社会经济等因素的变化而逐渐出现转移替代。

48.5　结论与讨论

城镇化是一个自然历史过程，是中国社会经济发展必然遇到的重要过程。研究探索城镇化问题，应放在人类发展的大格局、经济社会发展的大趋势中去思考。中国几千年前的独特的聚落发展模式受到新型城镇化的挑战。因此，政府主导下和规划指导下的聚落空间重构是一个十分重要的科学和实践问题。为此，可以在人口经济发展变化的大势下，通过增量调整和存量优化，重构聚落的规模格局。本章以具有长时段居住历史的河南省巩义市 1929～2013 年近百年的村庄数据，使用齐夫指数、分形维数与基尼系数，分别测度了近百年县域聚落规模-位序的演变，试图为县域城镇化的规划和实施提供具有操作性的参考。

相对于城市，本章发现巩义市聚落具有如下特征：①齐夫指数偏小但增长较快。县域较低位次的中小聚落较多，大聚落发育不突出，具有农村聚落特征，但聚落规模越大，规模增加的速度越快。②分形维数偏大但降速加快。规模越大的聚落其规模增加越快，聚落规模分布趋于集中。县域聚落规模过小，只有当聚落人口增加到一定程度，才能与城市表现出一样的分形规律。③基尼系数较小但增加明显。县域聚落基尼系数相对较小但增加显著，且增长率在 20 世纪 90 年代后加速。同时，聚落位序-规模具有“翘尾”现象，二次项模型拟合效果优于线性模型，且二次项的耗散力大于单次项的驱动力。在空间演变上表现出如下特征：①沿河线状格局变化。核心聚落由“沿河平原线状”格局逐渐向“平原-丘陵片状”格局转变，山区聚落仍旧停留在低等状况。②网络等级结构形成。高等级聚落数量增加且规模增大引起聚落等级增加，聚落空间结构由行政原则向市场原则转变，最终形成 5 级聚落等级结构。③核心聚落转移替代。县城的迁移带来聚落位序-规模变化，工业化与城镇化加速了丘陵区聚落的兴起，以及平原聚落和沿河聚落的相对衰落，从而聚落等级之间产生转移替代。

进一步分析，聚落空间格局现在和将来与过去聚落演化历史有一定的承继性，但还必须考虑其他因素的影响。例如，工业化和农业现代化引起经济结构和就业结构的急剧变化，一定在人们的居住方式、居住区位中反映出来。伴随着人口的乡城迁移，一些农村聚落必然出现消亡。这种数量的减少和规模的变化在某些情况下会超出历史演进趋势，具有突变特征。尽管如此，考虑长时期的历史演进规律，可对未来的聚落格局提供有益借鉴。长时期的聚落格局是人地关系长期互相作用的结果。还需要注意的是，县域聚落等级规模结构并不是处在一个封闭的地域单元，而是镶嵌在一个开放的空间结构中。对于巩义而言，更广阔的区域影响着该县域聚落及其空间结构演变的方向。毫无疑问，几千年来形成的郑、汴、洛“点-轴结构”对其产生了持久而深刻的影响。

相对于之前以国家、区域、城市群和城市规模-位序的宏观大尺度研究，本章以微观尺度的村庄做了尝试与努力，但也有以下不足需要进一步的探究：①利用城市理论对县域聚落进行分析的合理性。采用的齐夫指数、分形维数、基尼系数均为城市理论，研究结论均与城市研究有一定的差异，其间的深层原因需要深入挖掘。②指标选取的两难性。人口分析中很难把镇区和自然村的人口剥离出来，而面积分析中聚落的边界很难清晰界定，通过进一步的对比研究为城镇化实施提供更为精准的建议。

致谢：感谢巩义市国土资源局马振杰局长、地籍科万明勇科长，统计局周占龙局长、综合科邹君科长的大力支持。

参考文献

安乾，连倩倩，李小建. 2014. 河南巩义市村落终结的类型与机制分析. 经济地理，34（12）：125～132

陈彦光，刘继生. 1999. 城市规模分布的分形和分维. 人文地理，14（2）：43～48
方创琳. 2013. 中国城市发展格局优化的科学基础与框架体系. 经济地理，33（12）：1～9
海贝贝，李小建，许家伟. 2013. 巩义市农村居民点景观特征演变及驱动力分析. 地理研究，32（12）：2257～2269
河南省巩县志编纂委员会. 1989. 民国二十六年巩县志. 郑州：中州古籍出版社
李君，陈长瑶. 2010. 村域“居住场势”非均衡态势下的山区农户移民搬迁研究——基于河南省巩义市温堂村 69 户搬迁农户的实证分析. 经济地理，30（7）：1164～1169
李强，陈宇琳，刘精明. 2012. 中国城镇化“推进模式”研究. 中国社会科学，（7）：82～100
李小建. 2009. 农户地理论. 北京：科学出版社
李小建. 2014. 全面理解新型城镇化内涵. 人民日报，12-18
李小建，罗庆. 2014. 新型城镇化中的协调思想分析. 中国人口·资源与环境，24（2）：47～53
刘继生，陈彦光. 2003. 河南省城镇体系空间结构的多分形特征及其与水系分布的关系探讨. 地理科学，23（6）：713～720
刘彦随，刘玉，翟荣新. 2009. 中国农村空心化的地理学研究与整治实践. 地理学报，64（10）：1193～1202
刘彦随，杨忍. 2012. 中国县域城镇化的空间特征与形成机理. 地理学报，67（8）：1011～1020
陆大道. 1998. 区域发展及其空间结构. 北京：科学出版社. 137～141
陆玉麒. 2002. 区域双核结构模式的形成机理. 地理学报，57（1）：85～95
沈体雁，劳昕. 2012. 国外城市规模分布研究进展及理论前瞻——基于齐夫定律的分析. 世界经济文汇，（5）：95～111
施坚雅. 1998. 中国农村的市场和社会结构. 史建云，徐秀丽译. 北京：中国社会科学出版社
谈明洪，范存会. 2004. Zipf 维数和城市规模分布的分维值的关系探讨. 地理研究，23（2）：243～248
谈明洪，吕昌河. 2003. 以建成区面积表征的中国城市规模分布. 地理学报，58（2）：285～293
王法辉. 1989. 我国城市规模分布的统计模式研究. 城市问题，（1）：14～20
王颖，张婧，李诚固，等. 2011. 东北地区城市规模分布演变及其空间特征. 经济地理，31（1）：55～59
魏后凯. 2014. 中国城镇化进程中两极化倾向与规模格局重构. 中国工业经济，（3）：18～30
沃尔特·克里斯泰勒. 1998. 德国南部的中心地原理. 常正文，王兴中，等译. 北京：商务印书馆
新华社. 2014. 国家新型城镇化规划（2014～2020 年）. 3-17. http：//news. xinhuanet. com/city/2014-03/17/ c _ 126276532. htm
许家伟，乔家君. 2009. 山地丘陵区农户迁居模式研究——以巩义市为例. 乡镇经济，25（10）：26～29
郑衡泌. 2010. 城市郊区城镇化的历史继承性——以宁波鄞州区为例. 经济地理，30（5）：761～765
Berry B J L，Kozaryn A O. 2012. The city size distribution debate：Resolution for US urban regions and megalopolitan areas. Cities，29（S1）：17～23
Black D，Henderson V. 2003. Urban evolution in USA. Journal of Economic Geography，3（4）：343～372
Elvin E，Skinner G. 1974. The Chinese City between Two Worlds. Stanford：Stanford University Press. 331～358
Giesen K，Suedekum J. 2011. Zipf's law for cities in the regions and the country. Journal of Economics Geography，11（4）：667～686
Giesen K，Zimmermann A，Suedekum J. 2010. The size distribution across all cities-double Pareto Lognormal strikes. Journal of Urban Economics，68（2）：129～137
Guerin-Pace F. 1995. Rank-Size distribution and the process of urban growth. Urban Studies，32（3）：

551～562

Li S J, Sui Daniel. 2013. Pareto's law and sample size: A case study of China's urban system 1984-2008. GeoJournal, 78 (4): 615～626

Long H L, Liu Y S, Wu X Q, et al. 2009. Spatio-temporal dynamic patterns of farmland and rural settlements in Su-Xi-Chang region: Implications for building a new countryside in coastal China. Land Use Policy, 26 (2): 322～333

Roehner B M. 1991. The long term trend toward increased dispersion in the distribution of city sizes. Environment and Planning A, 23 (12): 1725～1740

Rosen K T, Resnick M. 1980. The size distribution of cities: An examination of the Pareto Law and primacy. Journal of Urban Economics, 8 (2): 165～186

Rozenfeld H D, Rybski D, Gabaix X, et al. 2011. The area and population of cities: New insights from a different perspective on cities. The American Economic Review, 101 (5): 2205～2225

Soo K T. 2014. Zipf, Gibrat andgeography: Evidence from China, India and Brazil. Papers in Regional Science, 93 (1): 159～181

Soo K. 2005. Zipf's law for cities: A cross-country investigation. Regional Science and Urban Economics, 35 (3): 239～263

UN-Habitat. 2008. State of the World's Cities (2008-2009): Harmonious Cities. London: Sterling VA

Val G R. 2010. The evolution of US city size distribution from a long-term perspective (1900-2000). Journal of Regional Science, 50 (5): 952～972

Ye X Y, Xie Y C. 2012. Re-examination of Zipf's law and urban dynamic in China: A regional approach. Annals of Regional Science, 49 (1): 135～156

Zipf G K. 1949. Human Behavior and the Principle of Least Effort. Cambridge: Addison-Wesley